Microeconomics

The Roundtable Series in Behavioral Economics

The Roundtable Series in Behavioral Economics aims to advance research in the new interdisciplinary field of behavioral economics. Behavioral economics uses facts, models, and methods from neighboring sciences to establish descriptively accurate findings about human cognitive ability and social interaction and to explore the implications of these findings for economic behavior. The most fertile neighboring science in recent decades has been psychology, but sociology, anthropology, biology, and other fields can usefully influence economics as well. The Roundtable Series publishes books in economics that are deeply rooted in empirical findings or methods from one or more neighboring sciences and advance economics on its own terms — generating theoretical insights, making more accurate predictions of field phenomena, and suggesting better policy.

Colin Camerer and Ernst Fehr, editors

Behavioral Game Theory: Experiments in Strategic Interaction by Colin F. Camerer

Microeconomics: Behavior, Institutions, and Evolution by Samuel Bowles

Advances in Behavioral Economics, edited by Colin F. Camerer, George Loewenstein, and Matthew Rabin

The Behavioral Economics Roundtable

Henry Aaron
George Akerlof
Linda Babcock
Colin Camerer
Peter Diamond
Jon Elster
Ernst Fehr
Daniel Kahneman
David Laibson

George Loewenstein
Sendhil Mullainathan
Matthew Rabin
Thomas Schelling
Eldar Shafir
Robert Shiller
Cass Sunstein
Richard Thaler
Richard Zeckhauser

Microeconomics

BEHAVIOR, INSTITUTIONS, AND EVOLUTION

Samuel Bowles

RUSSELL SAGE FOUNDATION
NEW YORK
PRINCETON UNIVERSITY PRESS
PRINCETON AND OXFORD

Published by Princeton University Press, 41 William Street, Princeton, New Jersey 08540
In the United Kingdom: Princeton University Press, 3 Market Place, Woodstock,
Oxfordshire OX20 1SY
And the Russell Sage Foundation, 112 East 64th Street, New York, New York 10021
All Rights Reserved

Library of Congress Cataloging-in-Publication Data

Bowles, Samuel.
Microeconomics : behavior, institutions, and evolution / Samuel Bowles.
p. cm. — (The roundtable series in behavioral economics)
Includes bibliographical references and index.
ISBN 0-691-09163-3 (alk. paper)
1. Microeconomics.   2. Institutional economics.   3. Evolutionary economics.
I. Title.   II. Series.
HB172.B67 2003
338.5—dc21   2003049841

British Library Cataloging-in-Publication Data is available

This book has been composed in Sabon

Printed on acid-free paper. ∞

www.pupress.princeton.edu

www.russellsage.org

Printed in the United States of America

10 9 8 7 6 5 4 3 2 1

List of Credits

Quotation from "Mending Wall" by Robert Frost used with permission of Henry Holt
    and Company.
Quotation from "16 tons" by Merle Travis used with permission of Warner-Chappell
    Music, a division of Warner Brothers.
Map of Italy in the fifteenth century (Figure 13.1) adapted from *Atlas of Medieval Europe*
    by Donald Matthew, used with permission of Andromeda, Oxford, Ltd.
Chapter 13 makes substantial use of work co-authored with Jung-Kyoo Choi and Astrid
    Hopfensitz that appeared in the *Journal of Theoretical Biology* (2003) 23:2, pp. 135–
    47, and is used here with permission from Elsevier.

For Libby and for Herb

Contents

Preface

Microeconomics grew out of two courses for doctoral candidates at the University of Massachusetts that I have taught over the past decade, one addressed to new developments in micro-economic theory, and the other a seminar in institutional, behavioral, and evolutionary economics. These courses develop economic models to address real world problems using a series of mathematical problem-solving exercises. The book is intended for readers not only interested in a synthesis of contemporary social science reasoning applied to problems of economic institutions and behavior but also wanting to learn the basic modeling skills necessary to participate — as a user or a producer — in further development of the field.

The book is intended for use in graduate-level microeconomics courses, as well as courses in institutional and evolutionary economics and formal modeling courses in sociology, anthropology, and political science. It could also be used in advanced undergraduate courses in these subjects. General readers may find the book a useful introduction to the emerging paradigm of evolutionary social science. Little previous exposure to economics is presumed. The mathematical techniques are limited to what is generally covered in a two-semester calculus sequence.

The book originated long ago when over a period of years I taught the advanced microeconomic theory course to doctoral candidates at Harvard University. While the content of the course reflected the then-unquestioned neoclassical model, seeds of doubt were nurtured in long discussions with my co-teachers, Wassily Leontief, Tibor Scitovsky, and David Kendrick, as well as from reflection on our students' often puzzled reactions to the material. The difference between the text published based on that course (Bowles, Kendrick, and Dixon 1980) and this book measures the distance traveled by economic theory in the intervening decades.

But the two books share a common emphasis on the importance of acquiring basic modeling skills through exposure to intellectually challenging yet mathematically tractable problem-solving exercises. The extensive problem sets at the end of this book offer practice in developing these skills as well as examples of applications of the theory to important real world problems. In the body of the text I have italicized frequently used terms where they are first introduced (and defined) in the text (the definitions can be located by consulting the index). To reduce footnote clutter, I have gathered extensive suggestions for readings on related subjects at the end of the book. The epigraphs that open each chapter serve to remind you that the problems addressed in these pages have been around for a while and probably will not be fully resolved anytime soon, and that they extend far beyond economics. (If you suspect the authors of the epigraphs are among those with whom I conduct imaginary conversations, you would not be far wrong, though I would not want to invite them all to dinner on the same evening!)

I draw on recent developments in evolutionary economics, game theory, the theory of economic institutions, behavioral and experimental economics, and other contributions to microeconomics. While the tools of analysis are from economics (with some borrowing from biology), the subject matter is nondisciplinary, augmenting the usual economic subject matter with concerns of culture, power, asymmetric social relationships, social networks, and norms. I also make considerable reference to empirical studies, beginning each chapter with an empirical puzzle that an adequate theory should be able to address. I do this both because economic theory benefits from the challenge of illuminating real world problems, and to ground the assumptions of the models in what is known about actual human behaviors and institutions.

While the exercise of power in the economy plays an important role in the models I develop, the need to limit the length of the book has precluded more than passing attention to governments and other centralized allocation processes, and political decision making.

Many of the ideas presented here were developed jointly with Herbert Gintis (especially those in chapters 8, 9, 10, and 14). His text in game theory (Gintis 2000) constitutes a valuable complement to this book. Important contributions to these pages have also come from my graduate students at the University of Massachusetts, whose suggestions and criticisms account for many improvements in the text. Some of the material in chapters 11, 12, and 13 draws on my collaboration with Jung-Kyoo Choi, Astrid Hopfensitz, and Yong-Jin Park. I have also benefitted from the comments of the doctoral candidates I have taught at the University of Siena. My teaching assistants over the years — especially Katie Baird, Jung-Kyoo Choi, Minsik Choi, Alper Duman, Christina Fong, James Heintz, Mehrene Larudee, Edward McPhail, Yong-Jin Park, Dori Posel, and Eric Verhoogen — are also responsible for numerous improvements.

Comments on the entire manuscript by Kaushik Basu, Greg Dow, Karla Hoff, Suresh Naidu, Ugo Pagano, Peter Skott, and Michael Wallerstein have made the book much better. I am especially grateful to Jung-Kyoo Choi and Elisabeth Wood who read multiple versions of the manuscript, correcting many errors and suggesting important improvements. I have also benefitted from the contributions of Robert Boyd, Steven Burks, Jeffrey Carpenter, Henry Farber, Ernst Fehr, Duncan

Foley, Gerald Friedman, Herbert Gintis, Carol Heim, Jack Hirshleifer, James Jaspers, Arjun Jayadev, Donald Katzner, Richard Lewontin, Mehrene Larudee, Paul Malherbe, John Miller, Karl Ove Moene, Melissa Osborne, Peter Richerson, Ariel Rubinstein, Cosma Shalizi, D. Eric Smith, Eric Alden Smith, Kenneth Sokoloff, Jorgen Weibull, Peyton Young, and Junfu Zhang.

I would also like to thank the MacArthur Foundation for financial support as well as the University of Siena (and especially the Certosa di Pontignano), the Santa Fe Institute, and the University of Massachusetts for providing ideal research environments. I am indebted to my very competent research assistants Bridget Longridge and (especially) Bae Smith, to Margaret Alexander and Timothy Taylor of the Santa Fe Institute Library, and to Lolly Brown, Marcus Daniels, Kevin Drennan, Brent Jones, Seth McMillan, and Carolyn Resnicke of the Santa Fe Institute. Finally I want to thank Peter Dougherty, Tim Sullivan, and Brigitte Pelner of Princeton University Press for bringing this work to fruition.

Additional materials related to this book can be found at http://www.santafe.edu/~bowles/.

I dedicate this book to my dear friend Herbert Gintis and to my beloved wife Elisabeth Wood. Collaborating with Herb over three decades has enriched my thinking on every aspect of microeconomics. He is a virtual co-author. Libby's unwavering enthusiasm for the project and her trenchant criticisms of its content are reflected in every page.

Santa Fe, New Mexico
August 2003

Microeconomics

Economics and the Wealth of Nations and People

> [Economics is the study of] human behavior as a relationship between given ends and scarce means.
>
> — Lionel Robbins, *An Essay on the Nature and Significance of Economics* (1935)

> An economic transaction is a solved political problem. . . . Economics has gained the title Queen of the Social Sciences by choosing solved political problems as its domain.
>
> — Abba Lerner, "The Economics and Politics of Consumer Sovereignty" (1972)

TO ITS FOUNDERS, the subject of political economy was the wealth of nations and people.

In the fourteenth century, Ibn Battuta, one of the leading geographers and explorers of his age, traveled widely in Asia, Africa, the Middle East, Russia, and Spain. In 1347, he visited the land we now call Bangladesh. "This is a country . . . abounding in rice," he wrote. He described traveling along its waterways, passing "between villages and orchards, just as if we were going through a bazaar."[1] Six centuries later, a third of the people of Bangladesh are undernourished and the country is among the world's poorest.

At the time of Ibn Battuta's visit to Bangladesh, Europe was reeling under the impact of the bubonic plague, which took the lives of a quarter or more in many cities. Manual workers in London, probably among the better off anywhere on the continent, consumed fewer than 2000 calories per day.[2] The shortage of labor following the plague somewhat boosted real wages through the middle of the next century, but over the next four centuries, real wages of laborers did not rise in

---

The first epigraph comes from Robbins (1935:16), the second from Lerner (1972: 259).

[1] His account is published in Ibn Battuta (1929:267, 271). A second source (Yule 1886:457) quotes him as observing, "I have seen no region of the earth in which provisions are so plentiful," but this may be a mistranslation due to Yule or to the French source on which he relied.

[2] This account follows Allen (2001). The wage series below can be found at http://www.econ.ox.ac.uk/members/robert.allen/wagesprices.htm.

any European city for which records exist; in most, wages fell by substantial amounts—in Northern Italy to half their earlier level. Over the past two centuries, however, real wages rose dramatically, first in England, where they increased *ten-fold*, and somewhat later but by even greater amounts in other European cities.

What accounts for these dramatic reversals of fortune? The most plausible answer, very briefly, runs as follows. The emergence and diffusion of a novel set of institutions that came to be called *capitalism* brought about a vast expansion in the productivity of human labor. This led to higher wages when workers' bargaining power was eventually augmented by the expansion of workers' political rights and by the drying up of the pool of new recruits from agriculture, household production, and other parts of the economy that were not organized according to these new institutions. This happened in Europe and not in Bangladesh.

What *did* happen in Bangladesh, as in much of the Mughal Empire and what became British India, was a growing entrenchment of the power and property rights of powerful landlords. Their influence was already substantial before the British, but during the Bengal Presidency it was greatly strengthened by the Permanent Settlement of 1793. This act of the colonial rulers conferred de facto governmental powers on the landlords by giving them the right to collect taxes (and to keep a substantial fraction for themselves). The fact that British taxation and land tenure policy was not uniform throughout the Raj provides a natural experiment to test the importance of these institutions for subsequent patterns of backwardness or development. Banerjee and Iyer (2002) compared the post-Independence economic performance and social indicators of districts of modern-day India in which landlords had been empowered by the colonial land tenure and taxation systems with other districts in which the landlords had been bypassed in favor of the village community or direct taxation of the individual cultivator. They found that the landlord-controlled districts had significantly lower rates of agricultural productivity growth stemming from lower rates of investment and lesser use of modern inputs. The landlord-controlled districts also lagged significantly in educational and health improvements.[3] These findings suggest a remarkable persistence of the effects of an institutional innovation that occurred a century or more earlier.

---

[3] The details of the causal connection between landlord control and these subsequent results remain to be explored. Because colonial practices changed over time in response to exogenous events (such as the revolt by Indian soldiers in 1857) and over space in response to the idiosyncrasies of local administrators, Banerjee and Iyer were able to identify independent sources of variation in the land tenure and taxation policies not due to pre-existing conditions.

The effects of institutions on economic performance is further affirmed by a dramatic turn in land tenure in the Indian state of West Bengal.[4] Following its election in 1977, the Left Front government of the state implemented a reform under which sharecroppers who registered with the Department of Land Revenue were guaranteed permanent and inheritable tenure in the plots they cultivated as long as they paid the landlord a quarter of the crop. Prior to the reform, the modal landlord's crop share had been one half, and landlord's had routinely used the threat of eviction to enhance their bargaining power with the sharecroppers. The cultivators' increased crop-share significantly increased the incentives to work the land productively. The security of tenure had two possibly offsetting effects: it enhanced the cultivators' incentive to invest in the land, while restricting the ability of the landlord to elicit high levels of output by threat of eviction. A further indirect effect may have also been at work. The increased economic security of the sharecroppers led to their more active participation in local politics; partly as a result, the local councils—the *panchayats*—became more effective advocates of the interests of the less well-off in the acquisition of agricultural inputs, credit, and schooling.

The effects of the reform have been estimated from a comparison of agricultural productivity between West Bengal and neighboring Bangladesh (a similar region in which no such reforms were implemented) and by exploiting the fact that the implementation of the reform (measured by the fraction of sharecroppers registering for its benefits) varied considerably within West Bengal. The resulting estimates are imprecise, and it remains difficult to determine which causal mechanisms were at work, but the effects of the reform appear to have been very substantial: rice yields per hectare on sharecropped land were increased by about fifty percent. Having lagged behind most Indian states prior to the reform, agricultural productivity growth in West Bengal has been among the most rapid since the reform.

The enduring importance of institutions is likewise suggested by the work of Sokoloff and Engerman (2000) concerning an analogous New World reversal of fortune. They estimate that in 1700 Mexico's per capita income was about that of the British colonies that were to become the United States, while Cuba and Barbados were at least half again richer. At the close of the eighteenth century Cuba had slightly higher per capita incomes than the United States, and Haiti was probably the richest society in the world. At the opening of the twenty-first century, however, the per capita income of Mexico was less than a third of the United States', and Haiti's was lower yet. In a series of papers, Sokoloff

---

[4] This account is based on Banerjee, Gertler, and Ghatak (2002) and Bardhan (1984).

and Engerman provide the following explanation.[5] In the parts of the New World in which sugar and other plantation crops could be grown (Cuba and Haiti) or in which minerals and indigenous labor were abundant (Mexico), economic elites relied on bonded labor or slaves, and consolidated their power and material privileges by means of highly exclusive institutions. These restricted access by the less well-off to schooling, public lands, patent protection, entrepreneurial opportunities, and political participation. As a result, over the ensuing centuries, even after the demise of slavery and other forms of coerced labor, opportunities for saving, innovation, and investment were monopolized by the well-to-do. Literacy remained low, and land holding highly concentrated. As the source of wealth shifted from natural resource extraction of manufacturing and services, these highly unequal economies stagnated while the far more inclusive economies of the United States and Canada grew rapidly. The ways their less exclusive institutions contributed to the success of these North American economies remains somewhat unclear, but a plausible hypothesis is that broader access to land, entrepreneurial opportunities, and human capital stimulated growth.

The source of the institutional divergence among the colonies of the New World appears to be their initial factor endowments, more than the distinct cultures or colonial policies of the European states that conquered them. British Belize and Guyana went the way of Spanish Honduras and Colombia; Barbados and Jamaica went the way of Cuba and Haiti. The Puritans who settled Providence Island off the coast of Nicaragua forsook their political ideals and became slave owners. Slaves on the island outnumbered the Puritans when it was overrun by the Spanish in 1641. According to its leading historian, "[T]he puritan settlement . . . with its economy fueled by privateering and slavery looked much like any other West Indian colony" (Kupperman 1993, p. 2). At the time of its demise, Providence Island was attracting migrants from the more famous Puritan colony far to the north; two boatloads of hapless Pilgrims arrived from Massachusetts just after the Spanish takeover.

A final example is provided by the precipitous collapse of Communist Party rule in the Soviet Union and its Eastern European allies around 1990 and the transition of the new states to market-based economies. Figure P.1, presenting the levels of gross domestic product (GDP) per capita relative to the year 1990 for fourteen of these nations, reveals dramatic differences in their trajectories. After a decade of transition,

---

[5] See also Engerman, Sokoloff, and Mariscal (2002) and Acemoglu, Johnson, and Robinson (2002).

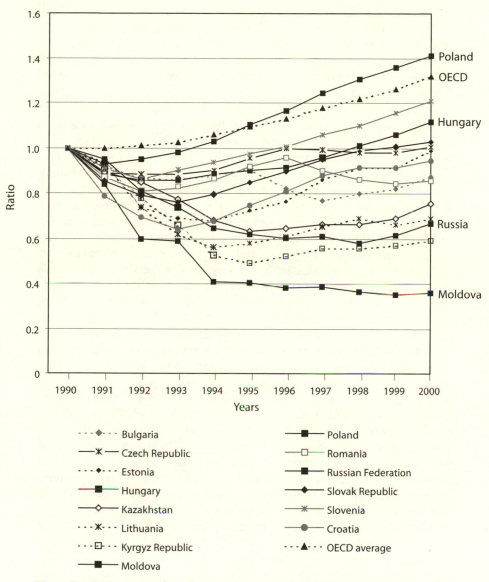

Figure P.1 Divergence of ex-Communist economies' real GDP per capita (relative to 1990). Source: World Bank (Statistical Information Management Analysis data base).

Poland's per capita income stood at 40 percent above the initial level, while Russia's had declined by a third and Moldavia's had fallen to less than 40 percent of the initial level. Over the same period China's per capita income more than doubled (not shown). Among these fourteen economies, only Poland out-performed the (unweighted) average of the OECD economies.

While the success of China's gradual reforms has been the subject of extensive study, the differences among the countries undertaking a rapid transition are poorly understood. A possible explanation is that, starting from quite similar institutions, small differences in the content or timing of reform packages or chance events resulted in large and cumulative differences in performance, because some countries (e.g., Hungary and Poland) were able to capture the synergistic effects of institutional complementarities while others were not (Hoff and Stiglitz 2002). Other explanations stress the substantial institutional differences among the countries or their differing levels of trust or other social norms. What is not controversial is that divergences in performance of this magnitude, emerging in less than a decade, suggest both the importance of economic institutions and the pervasive influence of positive feedback effects, whereby both success and failure are cumulative.

I have deliberately chosen cases that dramatize the central role of institutions. Other comparisons would suggest different, or at least less clear-cut conclusions. Over the period 1950–1990, for example, countries with democratic and authoritarian regimes appear to have differed surprisingly little in their overall economic performance (controlling for other influences) with major differences appearing only in their demographic record, with slower population growth in democracies (Przeworski, Alvarez, Cheibub, and Limongi 2000). Nonetheless, the examples above — the divergence of living standards in Europe from many parts of the world, the reversal in New World fortunes, and the heterogeneous consequences of economic liberalization in the once-Communist nations — are of immense importance in their own right and, as subsequent examples show, are hardly atypical.

What can modern economics say about the wealth and poverty of nations and people? No less important, what can it *do*?

CONTRARY to its conservative reputation, economics has always been about changing the way the world works. The earliest economists — the Mercantilists and the Physiocrats — were advisors to the absolute rulers of early modern Europe; today's macroeconomic managers, economic development advisors, and architects of the transition from Communism to market-based societies, continue this tradition of real world engagement. Economists have never been strangers to policy making and constitution building. The hope that economics might assist in alleviating poverty and securing the conditions under which free people might flourish is at once its most inspiring calling and its greatest challenge.

Like many, I was drawn to economics by this hope. Having been a schoolboy in India and a secondary school teacher in Nigeria before turning to economics, I naturally came to the field expecting that it would address the enduring problem of global poverty and inequality. At age eleven I had noticed how very average I was among my classmates at the Delhi Public School—in sports, in school work, in just about everything. A question has haunted me since: how does it come about that Indians are so much poorer than Americans given that as people we are so similar in our capacities? And so I entered graduate school hoping that economics might explain, for example, why workers in the United States produce almost as much in a month as those in India produce in a year, and why the Indian population is correspondingly poor (Hall and Jones 1999). We now know that the conventional economic explanations fail: by any reasonable accounting, the differences in the capital-labor ratio and in the level of schooling of the U.S. and Indian workforces explain much less than half of the difference in productivity. It seems likely that much of the gap results from causes more difficult to measure and, until recently, less studied by economists: differences in historical experience, institutions, and conventional behaviors. These are the subject matter of this book.

Alfred Marshall's (1842–1924) *Principles* was the first great text in neoclassical economics. It opens with these lines:

> Now at last we are setting ourselves seriously to inquire whether it is necessary that there should be any so called "lower classes" at all: that is whether there need be large numbers of people doomed from their birth to hard work in order to provide for others the requisites of a refined and cultured life, while they themselves are prevented by their poverty and toil from having any share or part in that life. . . . [T]he answer depends in a great measure upon facts and inferences, which are within the province of economics; and this is it which gives to economic studies their chief and their highest interest. (Marshall 1930:3–4)

Marshall wrote this in 1890. I suspect he would be disappointed by the progress economics made towards these lofty aims in the century that followed.

THE NEOCLASSICAL PARADIGM that Marshall helped found was ill-suited to the task he set. Its defining assumptions precluded analysis of many key aspects of economic progress and stagnation, among them the exercise of power, the influence of experience and economic conditions on people's preferences and beliefs, out-of-equilibrium dynamics, and the process of institutional persistence and change.

Drawing on the contributions of many — economists and others — this book presents a theory of how individual behaviors and economic institutions interact to produce aggregate outcomes, and how both individuals and institutions change over time. It is based on assumptions that are quite different from those that define the neoclassical paradigm. In what follows, I use the term *Walrasian paradigm* (for Leon Walras [1834–1910], another of the founders of neoclassical economics) in preference to the more open-ended term "neoclassical." By *Walrasian* I mean that approach to economics that assumes that individuals choose actions based on the far-sighted evaluation of their consequences based on preferences that are self-regarding and exogenously determined, that social interactions take the exclusive form of contractual exchanges, and that increasing returns to scale can be ignored in most applications. With some refinement, these assumptions account for the distinctive analytical successes and normative orientation of the Walrasian approach. The term *paradigm* refers to the core subject matter taught to students.

The approach developed here retains many of the fundamental tenets of the Walrasian paradigm and of the classical school that it superceded. Among these are a familiar triplet of ideas: that when individuals act they are trying to accomplish something; that intentional action is constrained by the effects of competition; and that the aggregate outcomes of large numbers of individuals interacting in this manner are typically unintended. These tenets have provided the foundation for the development of economics since its inception, and account for its many analytical insights. Other aspects of the Walrasian paradigm, however, are replaced.

The Walrasian approach represents economic behavior as the solution to a constrained optimization problem faced by a fully informed individual in a virtually institution-free environment. Robbins' celebrated definition of the subject (in the epigraph) reflects this equation of economics with constrained optimization. The passage of time is represented simply by a discount rate; people do not learn or acquire new preferences over time; institutions do not evolve. The actions of others are represented by nothing more complicated than a given vector of market-clearing prices, while proximity is captured by a cost of transportation. Property rights and other economic institutions are represented simply by a budget constraint. An economic actor in this model is roughly Robinson Crusoe, with prices standing in for nature. The economist's Crusoes inhabit a world in which goods are scarce, but whatever institutions are necessary to coordinate their activities in an optimal manner are freely available. The "supply" of optimal institutions can thus be ignored for the same reason that Adam Smith used to explain why economists need not theorize about the value of water: they are free goods.

This description of the Walrasian paradigm is a caricature, of course, but a recognizable one, of the economics taught in leading doctoral programs as recently as the early 1980s. Since then a combination of new analytical tools—especially game theory and information economics—and the increasingly evident empirical inadequacies of the Walrasian model have combined to alter the way economics is taught and practiced. Economic agents no longer interact simply with nature or some other parametric environment, but also with each other, and strategically. Their interactions are no longer fully described by the prices of the goods they exchange because some aspects of their transactions are not expressed in enforceable contracts.

Nonetheless, in practice, even as some of the standard Walrasian assumptions are dropped, common tenets of the older paradigm are evident in many of the new approaches. Robert Solow expressed these as "equilibrium, greed, and rationality," meaning that when economists "explain" something—say, unemployment—they mean that it can be represented as a unique stationary outcome in a model of interactions among self-interested individuals with advanced cognitive capacities and predispositions. Other ways of "explaining" unemployment may be entertained, but this is the default option. Solow's concern about the adequacy of the trinity of core tenets is increasingly supported by both empirical and conceptual advances.

The approach I present here is based on the more modest, but perhaps more enduring, classical tenets of intentional action, competition, and unintended consequences. Just as the Walrasian paradigm assumes a particular kind of social interaction as the standard case—caricatured as Robinson Crusoe above—the approach here is designed to illuminate a generic situation based on the three empirically observed characteristics of structures of social interaction, individual behaviors, and technologies, introduced below. Here I simply outline the salient facts of these generic interactions and point to some important implications. I take up the task of modeling these interactions (and providing some relevant empirical evidence) in the subsequent chapters.

Non-contractual social interactions. When individuals interact, it is the exception, not the rule, that everything passing between them is regulated by a complete and readily enforced contract. Instead, noncontractual social interactions are ubiquitous in neighborhoods, firms, families, environmental commons, political projects, and markets. While many of these noncontractual social interactions take place in nonmarket settings, they are also important in determining economic outcomes in highly competitive markets. Thus, in the pages that follow, I treat the grocery market with complete contracting — a staple of introductory economics textbooks — as a special case. The generic case is illustrated by labor markets and credit markets, where the promise to work hard or to repay the loan is unenforceable, or local environmental commons problems, where individual resource exploitation imposes noncontractible spillovers on others. A characteristic of markets with incomplete contracts is that one or both participants in a simple dyadic transaction typically receive rents, that is, payments above their next best alternative. In labor and credit markets, some workers and borrowers are unable to transact the quantities they prefer at the going terms of exchange; that is, they are quantity constrained, and the resulting markets do not clear in equilibrium, exhibiting excess supply (e.g., of labor) or excess demand (for loans).

If many aspects of economic interactions are not governed solely by contracts, how *are* they governed? The answer is that noncontractual aspects of interactions are governed by a combination of norms and power. An employment contract does not specify any particular level of effort, but the employee's work ethic or fear of job termination or peer pressure from workmates may accomplish what contractual enforcement cannot.

The idea that power is exercised in competitive market transactions will strike some readers as a commonplace; but to others it will appear a contradiction in terms. To neoclassical economists (like Abba Lerner, in the epigraph), "[A] transaction is a solved political problem." It is "solved" by the device of complete contracts, so that everything of interest to all parties to a transaction can be enforced by the courts. With all the terms of a transaction contractually specified, nothing is left for the exercise of power to be *about*. For the same reason, norms are redundant: if the employee's contract were to specify a given amount of work for a given amount of pay and if work effort were readily verifiable, then the employer would care little about the work ethic of the employees. Relaxing the complete contracting assumption thus not only explains why many markets do not clear, it also reveals an important economic role for both power and norms, bringing the theory closer to the way observers and participants view real world exchanges.

Adaptive and other-regarding behaviors. Recent behavioral experiments by economists (confirming and extending earlier work by other social scientists) as well as observation in natural settings suggests a reconsideration of both the "rationality" and "greed" tenets in Solow's trinity. Individuals intentionally pursue their objectives, but they do this more often by drawing on a limited repertoire of behavioral responses

acquired by past experience than by engaging in the cognitively demanding forward-looking optimizing processes assumed alike by the
Walrasian approach and by much of classical game theory. In many
situations, emotions such as shame, disgust, or envy combine to produce a behavioral response. Moreover, while self-interest is a powerful
motive, other-regarding motives are also important. In experiments and
in real life, people frequently are willing to reduce their own material
well-being not only to improve that of others but also to penalize others
who have harmed them or others, or violated an ethical norm. These
so-called *social preferences* help explain why people often cooperate toward common ends even when defection would yield higher material
rewards, why incentive schemes based on self-interest sometimes backfire, and why firms do not sell jobs.

Thus models whose *dramatis personae* are simply identical individuals conforming to the self interest axioms of *Homo economicus* are
often unilluminating. For many questions, adequate models must take
account of the fact, confirmed in experiments and in natural settings,
that people are both *heterogeneous* — some more self-interested, others
more civic minded, for example — and *versatile* — actions adapting to
situations rather than reflecting a single, all-purpose behavioral predisposition. As a result of both behavioral heterogeneity and versatility,
small differences in institutions can make large differences in outcomes,
some situations inducing selfish individuals to act cooperatively and
others inducing selfish behaviors by those predisposed to cooperate.

Economists have commonly regarded behaviors that violate the stringent canons of formal rationality as idiosyncratic, unstable, or irrational, in short, not exhibiting the regularities that would allow scientific analysis. But the fact that experimental subjects consistently exhibit
such "irrationalities" as intransitivity, loss aversion, inconsistency in
temporal discounting, and the overvaluation of low probability events,
suggests these behaviors are not only common but also susceptible to
analysis.

People acquire their behavioral responses in part by copying the behaviors of those who, in similar situations, they perceive as successful
by some standard or by acting to maximize one's gains given one's beliefs about how others will act. But other influences are also at work,
including conformism and other types of frequency-dependent learning
unrelated to the payoffs associated with behaviors. As a result, predictions of behavior based on forward-looking maximization of payoffs
may be quite misleading. Moreover, behavioral responses acquired by
individuals in one environment are unlikely to be acquired by the same
individuals were they to be functioning in an entirely different environment. In this sense, not only individual beliefs (about the consequences

of their actions) but also individual preferences (their evaluations of the outcomes) are endogenous. The "given ends" invoked by Robbins is a useful simplification in many analytical tasks but is an arbitrary and misleading restriction in others.

Generalized increasing returns. Economic and other social interactions often lead to patterns of what Gunnar Myrdal (1956) termed "cumulative causation," or what are now called "positive feedbacks." *Positive feedbacks* include economies of scale in production, but the term refers more broadly to any situation in which the payoff to taking an action is increasing in the number of people taking the same action. More generic illustrations include, for instance, the fact that the payoff to learning a particular language depends on the number of speakers or that the payoff to engaging in a collective action depends on the number of participants. To distinguish this large class of positive feedback cases from the subset based on increasing returns to scale in production, I will use the term *generalized increasing returns* rather than increasing returns to scale. Institutional synergies may generate generalized increasing returns. For example, private ownership of property, competitive markets, and the rule of law often implement highly efficient solutions to allocational problems, but only if all three components are present and almost all members of the society adhere to these principles. Generalized increasing returns due to these institutional complementarities appears to be a source of divergence in the growth trajectories of the New World and ex-Communist economies mentioned above. Generalizing increasing returns may help to account for the increase in inequality among the peoples of the world over the past century and a half, despite the catching up of Japan, China, and other East Asian nations.[6]

These positive feedbacks create economic environments in which small chance events have durable consequences over very long time frames, and in which initial conditions may have persistent so-called "lock-in" effects. The "poverty traps" faced by peoples and nations as well as the "virtuous circles" of affluence enjoyed by others exhibit the effects of these influences. In the presence of generalized increasing returns, typically there exist more than one stationary outcome with the property that small deviations from that outcome are self-correcting. These multiple stable equilibria may be displaced by what appear in our models as exogenous shocks, mutations, or idiosyncratic play, but that in the real world take the form of wars, climatic changes, strikes, or other events not included in the model under examination.

A result may be infrequent but dramatic periods of change in institutions, behaviors, technologies, and the like as a population moves from

---

[6] See Bourguignon and Morrison (2002) and the works cited there.

the neighborhood of one equilibrium to another, often followed by long periods of stability. Biologists use the term *punctuated equilibria* to refer to this alternating pattern of stasis and rapid change (Eldredge and Gould 1972). The collapse of Communism is an example. Another is the demise of foot binding of young women in China. This painful and disabling practice endured for a millennium, resisting attempts to end it over the centuries, yet it disappeared in the course of just a decade and a half in the early part the last century (Mackie 1996). The existence of multiple equilibria may also explain why seemingly similar populations may come to have quite different norms, tastes, and customs, often resulting in the widely observed pattern of *local homogeneity and global heterogeneity*, distinctive national cuisines and food tastes providing an example.

There is no reason and little evidence to suggest that the institutions and behaviors that result from processes in which generalized increasing returns are at work are in any sense optimal. Following the fall of Communism in the Soviet Union and Eastern Europe, for example, many economists confidently predicted that once state property was abolished, a workable configuration of capitalist institutions would spontaneously emerge. But in Russia and many of the other transitional economies, a decade of lawlessness and kleptocracy implemented a massive concentration of wealth under institutions providing few incentives for enhanced productivity or investment. The disappointing economic results of the end of Communist rule in these countries underlines the fallacy of the conventional view that good institutions are free in a world of material scarcity.

In the pages that follow, institutions, like goods, are taken to be scarce. The three basic assumptions outlined above — the noncontractual nature of social interactions, adaptive and other-regarding behaviors, and generalized increasing returns — define the generic case, my default option. The three are related. Relaxing the complete contracting assumption without modifying the behavioral assumptions of Walrasian economics is untenable, for the importance of other-regarding preferences, as we will see, is considerably enhanced when contractual incompleteness is taken into account. Similarly, the process by which preferences evolve exhibits strong generalized increasing returns. The reason is that norms generally take the form of conventions, adherence to which is in one's interest only as long as most others do the same. So relaxing the conventional behavioral assumptions raises doubts about nonincreasing returns. Finally, if generalized increasing returns are common, many different outcomes may be equilibria. Of these, the states most likely to be observed will depend critically on institutions governing the relevant dynamics, including such things as the exercise of power, collective action, and other forms of noncontractual social interaction. What is called *equilibrium selection* operates almost entirely through processes absent in the Walrasian model.

WHILE MOST of what follows is the result of recent research, virtually all of the models and ideas presented there were anticipated by writers half a century ago or more, sometimes much more. The importance of adaptive agents (with realistic cognitive capacities and predispositions) whose behaviors were based on local information was central to the work of Friedrich Hayek (1945) and Herbert Simon (1955). Simon's pioneering work on the incomplete nature of the employment contract (Simon 1951) and the role of authority in the functioning of firms formalizes the earlier work of Ronald Coase (1937) and long before Coase, Marx (1967). The basic concepts of game theory, bargaining, and other nonmarket social interactions were introduced in the early writings of John Nash (1950a), John von Neumann and Oskar Morgenstern (1944), Thomas Schelling (1960), and Duncan Luce and Howard Raiffa (1957). Nash even suggested the basic ideas of evolutionary game theory in his doctoral dissertation (Nash 1950b). Nash's famous solution to the bargaining problem was first proposed much earlier by F. Zeuthen (1930), in a work introduced glowingly by Joseph Schumpeter. Endogenous preferences were central to the work of James Duesenberry (1949) and Harvey Leibenstein (1950), both drawing on the much earlier work of Thorsten Veblen (1934 [1899]) and developing themes initially raised by Smith (1937) and Marx. The famous paradox of Maurice Allais (1953) pointed to problems with the expected utility hypothesis that have only recently attracted serious attention. The way that positive feedbacks support multiple equilibria was the key idea in Gunnar Myrdal's 1955 Cairo lectures (mentioned above). The application of biological reasoning to economics, now prominent in evolutionary game theory, was introduced a half-century ago by Armen Alchian (1950) and Gary Becker (1962).

The fact that most of the key ideas presented in the pages that follow were anticipated during the 1950s or before but ignored in subsequent decades poses an intriguing question. Why did the Walrasian paradigm become virtually synonymous with economics in the third quarter of the twentieth century only to be displaced at the century's end by a set of ideas most of which had been articulated by well-placed academics just prior to the rise to prominence of the Walrasian paradigm? Herbert Gintis and I (Bowles and Gintis 2000) have attempted to answer the question, but to address it here would be a diversion.

RELAXING the canonical Walrasian assumptions to take account of non-contractual social interactions, adaptive other-regarding behaviors, and generalized increasing returns will require a method more empirically grounded and less deductive than the usual Walrasian approach. Making little reference to the specifics of time, or place, or indeed any empirical facts, the Walrasian paradigm deduced a few rather strong predictions concerning the outcomes likely to be observed in the economy. The expansion of the domain of economics to include the family, the organization of production, and political activity such as the voluntary provision of public goods, lobbying, and voting, produced valuable insights unattainable using the conventional methods of sociology and political science. But research in these areas, as well as the return to prominence of the classical economists' concern with long-term economic growth and distribution, have cast doubt on the generality of the standard assumptions. Responding to the malaise now felt among economists, the American Economic Association's *Journal of Economic Perspectives* devotes a regular column to "anomalies," which they define as follows:

> Economics can be distinguished from other social sciences by the belief that most (all?) behavior can be explained by assuming that rational agents with stable well defined preferences interact in markets that (eventually) clear. An empirical result qualifies as an anomaly if it is difficult to "rationalize" or if implausible assumptions are necessary to explain it within the paradigm. (Thaler 2001)

Readers responded avidly to the invitation to write in with their favorite examples.

In place of deduction from a few (once) uncontroversial behavioral and institutional axioms, economics has increasingly (if unknowingly for the most part) moved toward an approach that combines the mathematical advances of the last century with three of the methods of the classical economists. From Adam Smith to John Stuart Mill and Karl Marx (and excepting David Ricardo), the classical economists were *nondisciplinary* (the disciplines had not been invented), *concerned about the empirical details* of the social problems of their day, and *modest about the degree of generality to which their theories aspired*.

First, the study of the economy must draw upon the insights of all of the behavioral sciences, including ecology and biology. The Walrasian assumptions provided a rationale for a rigid division of labor among the disciplines. Its defining assumptions allowed Walrasian economists to disavow an interest in other-regarding behaviors, norms, the exercise of power, or history as some other discipline's concern and in any case not pertinent to the workings of the (Walrasian) economy. While the traffic across the disciplinary boundaries has in the last half-century consisted primarily in the export of economic methods to the other behavioral sciences, there is much to be imported if the role of power, norms, emotions, and adaptive behaviors in the economy are to be understood. Core economic phenomena such as the workings of competition, incentives, and contracts cannot be understood without the insights of the other behavioral sciences.

Second, relaxation of the Walrasian assumptions confronts us with an embarrassment of riches. In the absence of some empirical restrictions or theoretical refinements, the price of generality will be vacuousness. This was the conclusion of Hugo Sonnenschein (1973b:405) concerning Walrasian theory of market demand: "The moral . . . is simply this: if you put very little in, you get very little out." But the same applies to any post-Walrasian paradigm. Few empirical predictions will be forthcoming if individuals may be self-interested or not depending on the person and the situation, if some interactions are governed by contracts, others by handshakes, and others by brute force, and if there exist multiple stable equilibria.

The need for empirical grounding of assumptions is nowhere clearer than in the analysis of individual behavior, where the process of enriching the conventional assumptions about cognition and preferences can easily descend into ad hoc explanation unless disciplined by reference to facts about what real people do. It is not enough to know that self-interest is not the only motive; we need to know which other motives are important under what conditions. These restrictions are most likely to come from one of the sources that undermined the Walrasian paradigm, namely, the great advances in empirical social science stemming from new techniques in econometrics, the improvement in computational capabilities and data availability, experimental techniques, and continuing progress in quantitative history.

Theory, too, can provide useful restrictions on the set of plausible assumptions and outcomes. The modeling of genetic and cultural evolution, for example, can help restrict the range of plausible behavioral assumptions by distinguishing between those emotions, cognitive capacities, and other influences on behaviors whose emergence and diffusion can plausibly be accounted for over the relevant periods of human history, and those that cannot. Similarly, while generalized increasing returns may support a large number of equilibria, some of these equilibria are extremely inaccessible under any plausible dynamic process. By contrast, other equilibria may be both accessible and robust. In this case, specification of an explicit dynamic process — for example, an account of how individuals adapt their behaviors in light of their recent experiences and the experiences of those whom they observe — may allow the elimination of what may be termed *evolutionarily irrelevant equilibria*. Making explicit the dynamics governing a system gives us an account of its out-of-equilibrium behavior and thus not only helps in the process of equilibrium selection but also in studying the response to shocks and other problems for which the standard comparative static method is ill-suited.

Third, the quest for ever more general theories will continue to engage students of the economy, and there is still much to be learned by studying such topics as markets in general. But for the foreseeable future it seems likely that insights will come from models that take account of the specific institutional and other aspects of particular types of economic interaction. For the classical economists it was evident that labor markets differ in fundamental ways from credit markets, which in turn differ from shirt markets or foreign exchange markets, and so on. Models may be more specific with respect to time and place, as a way of capturing the importance of time-varying institutions or different cultures. If the exciting novelties of the Walrasian era were highly abstract theorems of surprising generality, the excitement in the coming years may come from compelling answers to such questions as are raised by the empirical puzzles concerning the wealth of nations and people, with which I began.

It would be salutary for economists to focus more on answering such questions and less on demonstrating the use of our increasingly sophisticated tools. But it seems that a more problem-driven and less tool-driven approach will require yet more sophisticated tools. The mathematical demands of the theoretical framework I am proposing will be greater, not less, than that of the Walrasian paradigm. The reason is that models that represent noncontractual social exchanges among individuals who are both heterogeneous and versatile in their behaviors and who interact in the presence of generalized increasing returns do not allow the standard simplifications such as price-taking behavior and convex production sets that made Walrasian models tractable. As has long been recognized in physics and biology, many important problems do not yield simple closed form solutions, or indeed any solutions at all that are susceptible to simple interpretation. In these cases — some of which you will encounter in chapters 11 through 13 — computer simulations of the relevant social interactions will prove insightful as a complement (not a substitute) for more traditional analytical methods. Simulations have been extensively used in developing the ideas on which this book draws. Simulations do not yield theorems or propositions that are generally true; rather, like experiments, they yield a wealth of data that may point to unambiguous conclusions but often do not.

THOUGH MOTIVATED by an interest in the impact of economic institutions on human well-being, I have adopted an evolutionary rather than a social engineering approach. Like the idea of "selfish genes" seeking to maximize their replication or an auctioneer presiding over a general equilibrium exchange process, the omniscient and omnipotent social engineer seeking to maximize social welfare is a fiction whose usefulness depends on keeping in mind its fictive character. Social outcomes — even those involving states and other powerful bodies — are the combined result of actions taken by large numbers of people acting singly. Such devices as fictive auctioneers, social engineers, or anthropomorphic genes cannot substitute for an understanding of how real individuals behave and the ways that distinct institutions generate population-level dynamics that aggregate these behaviors to produce social outcomes. The evolutionary character of the analysis will become evident in the way that individual behaviors are modeled, the kinds of population-level dynamics studied, the ways that behaviors and institutions co-evolve, and the absence of any grand blueprints for human betterment. The evolutionary approach is modest about what interventions can accomplish, but it does not restrict the economist to purely contemplative pursuits. I take up questions of good governance and policy in the concluding chapter.

The first part of the book introduces a variety of models applied to what I have just called the generic social interaction, namely, noncontractual social interactions among adaptive agents in the presence of generalized increasing returns. I begin with two chapters on institutions and the evolution of structures of social interactions before turning to preferences and beliefs. The unconventional ordering of these topics — most microeconomics texts start with preferences — reflects the importance of institutions as influences on the norms, tastes, and understandings that individuals bring to the situations in which they act. I then investigate allocational inefficiencies that occur in noncontractual interactions, and the problem of dividing the gains to cooperation that arises when these inefficiencies can be overcome. The middle part of the book concerns the institutions of capitalism, and especially markets, lending institutions, and firms. I give particular attention to the way that the incomplete nature of most contracts gives rise both to a well-defined political structure of the economy and to an important role for social preferences. The last part concerns the process of cultural and institutional change; I emphasize the role of technical change, collective action, and intergroup conflict as constituent parts of the process by which the rules governing social interactions and individual behaviors coevolve. Here I address the evolution of familiar institutions such as private property and customary rules of division, as well as the puzzling evolutionary success of other-regarding individual behaviors. The concluding chapter compares three structures governing economic interactions — markets, states, and communities — and explores ways that they might serve as complementary approaches to handling problems of allocation and distribution.

In 1848, John Stuart Mill (1965) published *Principles of Political Economy*, the first great textbook in microeconomics; it was the staple of instruction in the English-speaking world until displaced by Marshall's *Principles* a half-century later. Mill's readers may have been reassured to read, "Happily, there is nothing in the laws of Value which remains for the present writer or any future writer to clear up; the theory of the subject is complete" (p. 420). When I studied economics in the 1960s during the heyday of the Walrasian paradigm, a similar complacency reigned. This book conveys no such reassurance. Our understanding of microeconomics is fundamentally in flux. Little is settled. Nothing is complete.

PART I

Coordination and Conflict: Generic Social Interactions

CHAPTER ONE

Social Interactions and Institutional Design

> Two neighbors may agree to drain a meadow, which they possess in
> common; because 'tis easy for them to know each others mind; and each
> must perceive, that the immediate consequence of his failing in his part,
> is the abandoning of the whole project. But 'tis very difficult and indeed
> impossible, that a thousand persons shou'd agree in any such action; it
> being difficult for them to concert so complicated a design, and still
> more difficult for them to execute it; while each seeks a pretext to free
> himself of the trouble and expense, and wou'd lay the whole burden on
> others.
> —David Hume, *A Treatise of Human Nature, Volume II* (1739)

> This is how men could imperceptibly acquire some crude idea of mutual
> commitments and the advantages to be had in fulfilling them. . . . Were
> it a matter of catching a deer, everyone was quite aware that he must
> faithfully keep to his post in order to achieve this purpose; but if a hare
> happened to pass within reach of one of them, no doubt he would have
> pursued it without giving it a second thought, and that, having obtained
> his prey he cared very little about causing his companions to miss theirs.
> —Jean-Jacques Rousseau, *Discourse on the Origin
> and Foundations of Inequality among Men* (1755)

GETTING THE RULES RIGHT

Like the overnight train that left me in an empty field some distance
from the settlement, the process of economic development has for the
most part bypassed the two hundred or so families that make up the
village of Palanpur. They have remained poor, even by Indian standards:
less than a third of the adults are literate, and most have endured the
loss of a child to malnutrition or to illnesses that are long forgotten in
other parts of the world. But for the occasional wristwatch, bicycle, or
irrigation pump, Palanpur appears to be a timeless backwater, untouched
by India's cutting edge software industry and booming agricultural
regions.

Seeking to understand why, I approached a sharecropper and his three

The first epigraph is from Hume (1964:304), and the second from Rousseau (1987:62).

daughters weeding a small plot.[1] The conversation eventually turned to the fact that Palanpur farmers sow their winter crops several weeks after the date at which yields would be maximized. The farmers do not doubt that earlier planting would give them larger harvests, but no one, the farmer explained, is willing to be the first to plant, as the seeds on any lone plot would be quickly eaten by birds. I asked if a large group of farmers, perhaps relatives, had ever agreed to sow earlier, all planting on the same day to minimize the losses. "If we knew how to do that," he said, looking up from his hoe at me, "we would not be poor."

Planting on the right day, like successfully draining the meadow in Hume's example or preventing the unraveling of Rousseau's stag hunt, is a solution to a problem called a *social dilemma* or *coordination problem*. Thomas Hobbes and the other founders of European political philosophy, as well as the great classical economists from Adam Smith to John Stuart Mill, sought to discover the institutions that by addressing problems like these would be most conducive to human well-being. For them an over-arching question was: how can social interactions be structured so that people are free to choose their own actions while avoiding outcomes that none would have chosen? I call this the *classical constitutional conundrum.*

We now would say: they were interested in getting the rules right. A contemporary restatement of the conundrum would define "outcomes" as equilibria of a game specified by the structure of social interactions along with an account of how, given this institutional environment, individuals might come to act in such away that a particular outcome (perhaps one of many stable equilibria) might occur and persist over long periods. "Avoiding outcomes that none would have chosen" would be refined as the pursuit of a *Pareto-efficient* outcome, namely one for which no other feasible outcome would be preferred by at least one, and not less preferred by any.

I will make extensive use of the notion of Pareto efficiency, so a comment on its shortcomings is in order. As a basis for choice among allocations, the Pareto standard is at once too weak and too strong. It is too strong because in any practical application, large numbers of people will be involved, and it is almost always the case that a change in policy or institutions inflicts costs on some participants, even in the long run. This being the case, the Pareto standard has a strong status quo bias. The Pareto standard is too weak because it abstracts from other desiderata of an allocation. The most important of these is the principle that the distribution of benefits entailed by an allocation should be fair.

---

[1] Lanjouw and Stern (1998) provide a detailed account of the economy and social structure of Palanpur.

Thus, the idea that good rules support Pareto-efficient equilibria hardly exhausts constitutional desiderata, but, subject to these two caveats, it is certainly among them. Unfortunately, including Pareto efficiency as a desideratum does not provide much guidance in making policy choices. There may be many reasons to prefer a Pareto-inefficient outcome over a Pareto-efficient one; all that is precluded is a preference for a particular outcome when some other feasible outcome is Pareto superior to that outcome. But few practical choices take this form: most policy alternatives cannot be Pareto ranked in this way.

The constitutional conundrum has broad contemporary relevance, including environmental protection on a global scale, the determination of work effort among members of a production team, the production and distribution of information, and the formation of the neighborhoods in which people live. The fact that since the emergence of capitalism, the aggregate effect of millions of individuals, each acting independently in pursuit of their own objectives, has been a long-term improvement in the material living conditions of most of those participating suggests that tolerably good solutions can be found to problems much more challenging than the Palanpur farmers' planting date, Hume's meadow, and Rousseau's stag hunt. How it comes about that large numbers of strangers with little or no concern for one another's well-being routinely act in mutually beneficial ways is one of the great puzzles of human society, and one that I will try to illuminate. But there is also unmistakable evidence of failures to solve modern day coordination problems: systematic overuse of some resources (the natural environment) and underutilization of others (human productive capacities), for example, and the enduring poverty of the people of Palanpur and villages like it around the world.

The reason why uncoordinated activities of individuals pursuing their own ends often produce outcomes that all would seek to avoid is that each person's actions affect the well-being of others and these effects are often not included in whatever optimizing process or rule of thumb results in the decisions made by self-interested actors. These unaccounted-for effects on others are sometimes called *externalities* or *spillovers*. Economists once treated these external effects as exceptional, the standard example being the one farmer's bees transporting pollen among a neighboring farmer's apple trees. But as the above examples suggest, they are ubiquitous in a modern economy.

The classical constitutional conundrum may be posed in this manner: what rules governing interactions among people would simultaneously facilitate the pursuit of their own ends, while inducing each to take adequate account of the effects of their actions on others? The first clause ("pursuit of their own ends") simply recognizes that any solution to coordination problems will be substantially decentralized, and none that seek to simply override individual intentions is either workable or desirable. The key challenge is in the second clause: where a person's actions unavoidably affect the well-being of others, how can these effects be made sufficiently salient to influence the actor's behavior in appropriate ways?

If the "others" are our kin, or our neighbors, or friends, our concern for their well-being or our desire to avoid social sanction might induce us to take account of the effects of our actions on them. Reflecting this fact, an important response to the constitutional conundrum — one that long predates the classical economists — is that concern for the well-being of others should extend to all of those with whom one interacts, thus internalizing the effects of one's actions on others. With the increasing scope of markets over the last half-millennium, however, individuals have come to interact not with a few dozen, but with hundreds and indirectly with millions of strangers. And so, with the maturation of capitalism and growing influence of economic reasoning, the burden of good governance shifted from the task of cultivating civic virtue to the challenge of designing institutions that work tolerably well in its absence.

Modern day *implementation theory*, the *theory of mechanism design*, and *optimal contract theory* embody this tradition, asking what forms of contracts, property rights, or other social rules might achieve some desired aggregate social objective when that objective is shared by none of the participants. A prominent example is the Fundamental Theorem of Welfare Economics, which identifies the conditions under which well-defined property rights and competitive markets support Pareto-efficient competitive equilibria. The theorem thus provides a formalization of Adam Smith's argument that under the right institutional conditions, individuals pursuing their self-interest will be "led by an invisible hand" to implement socially desirable outcomes.

The problem of draining Hume's meadow or preventing Rousseau's stag hunt from unraveling are interesting precisely because — like almost all social interactions — they are situations for which the rather stringent axioms of the Fundamental Theorem do not apply. How difficult it might be to sustain the cooperation necessary for a socially beneficial outcome in these cases depends on the underlying structure of the interaction, namely, the beliefs and preferences of the individuals, the cause-and-effect relationships governing the translation of actions into outcomes, whether the interaction is episodic or ongoing, the number of people involved, and so on. The difficulty of solving the problem also depends on the information structure of the interaction — who knows what, when, and whether the information can be used to enforce contracts or governmental regulations.

All of these influences on the likely success or failure of the drainage, the hunt, or any other common project depend on the particular institutions governing the interactions among the participants. Markets, families, governments, communities, and other institutions relevant to an interaction influence the constraints and incentives as well as the information, norms, and other evaluative concerns of the participants in the interaction. An adequate analysis of coordination problems and their possible attenuation must illuminate how these institutions work. For this task the minimal representation of institutions in the Walrasian paradigm is substantially inferior to the more elaborate modeling of institutions made possible by game theory.

My main objective in this chapter is both to introduce some basic ideas of game theory and to use these ideas to provide a taxonomy of social interactions and their outcomes. I postpone until chapter 3 an in-depth consideration of individuals and their preferences. Of course, most institutions are not designed — or at least they do not function according to any blueprint — but I will delay treatment of institutions as *evolved* rather than *designed* until chapter 2. Questions of the stability of equilibria (or why we should be concerned with equilibria at all) will also be skirted in this chapter, as they are best handled once we have an explicit model of how things change in out-of-equilibrium situations, introduced in chapter 2. I begin with an example that illustrates the formal structure of the challenges raised by Hume and Rousseau.

COORDINATION AND CONFLICT: AN EXAMPLE

Garrett Hardin (1968) famously described a group of herders overgrazing a pasture and driving it to ruin, coining the term *tragedy of the commons* and giving social science one of the most evocative metaphors since Smith's invisible hand. Indeed, Hardin called his tragedy a "rebuttal to the invisible hand." These two metaphors are powerful because they capture two essential but sharply contrasting social situations. When guided by an invisible hand, social interactions reconcile individual choice and socially desirable outcomes. By contrast, the *dramatis personae* of the commons tragedy pursue their private objectives to disastrous consequences for themselves and others.

Hardin chose the bucolic setting for his tragedy for concreteness only; the underlying problem applies to a wide class of situations in which individuals typically cannot or do not take account of the effects of their actions on the well-being of others. These include traffic congestion, payment of taxes and other contributions to common projects, the preservation of group reputations, team work, and many more.

An example will illuminate the structure of the problem, raising a large number of issues to be addressed in greater analytical detail in subsequent chapters. Consider two fishers, Jay and Eye, who share access to a lake and catch fish there which they consume. Fish are plentiful enough so that additional fishing always yields more fish to each of the two, but the more fish one catches, the fewer the other catches in an hour of fishing. Each of them decides how much time to spend fishing, selecting the amount that maximizes their own well-being. Suppose that this optimization process, when carried out separately and without any binding agreement between the two, leads each to fish eight hours a day and that the net benefits (no pun intended) of this activity are just sufficient to match the next best alternative for each (perhaps working for wages in the nearby town). Define the benefits flowing from this so-called *fallback option* (or reservation position) as $\underline{u} > 0$ for both fishers. They each know that if they both fished less, they could each be better off, their smaller catch being more than offset by their greater leisure. Assume that they study the matter and determine how they would fare if they both limited their hours to six (we'll assume that this is the only alternative to eight hours), or if one fished eight and the other six. They normalize their payoffs so that they assign a number 1 to the outcome of both fishing less, and zero to the one who fishes less while the other continues fishing more. Table 1.1 shows the relevant payoffs (according to convention, the row player's payoffs are listed first).

The tragedy of the fishers is a *prisoners' dilemma*. This is a situation in which for each individual there is an action that, if taken, yields higher payoffs than any of the other available actions independently of what the other does (the other actions are said to be *dominated*). But when all individuals act to maximize their payoffs by taking this action the outcome is worse for both than some other outcome they could have achieved by acting differently. Thus fishing for six hours is dominated because $\alpha > 0$ and $\underline{u} > 0$, and it is Pareto superior to eight hours because $\underline{u} < 1$.

It might seem a simple matter to determine that they should just agree that each will fish six instead of eight hours, but this is far from the

TABLE 1.1
Tragedy of the Fishers: A Prisoners' Dilemma

Jay	Eye	
	Fish 6 hours	*Fish 8 hours*
Fish 6 hours	1, 1	0, $1 + \alpha$
Fish 8 hours	$1 + \alpha$, 0	$\underline{u}, \underline{u}$

case, for two reasons. The first is that they may have no way of enforcing an agreement, or even knowing if the agreement has been violated. While each may know how many hours the other has fished on a clear day, on a foggy day it may be impossible to know, and in any case each one's knowledge of how much the other fished may be insufficient to enforce an agreement judicially. This is the problem of *asymmetric* or *unverifiable* information, the former describing a situation in which what someone knows another does not, and the latter that in which what someone knows cannot be used in court.

The second problem arises because the six-hours-a-day arrangement is an agreement *both* to fish less *and* implicitly to divide the benefits of fishing less in a particular way, namely, equally. But the fishers of course realize that they need not agree on six hours each. They could instead agree that Eye will fish eight hours and Jay four hours, or vice versa. The fishers have two problems, not one. The first, concerning *allocation*, is to determine how much fishing to do in total, namely, how to restrict the total hours of fishing, and the second, concerning *distribution*, is how to divide the benefits to fishing less, should they agree to do so.

Figure 1.1 illustrates the fishers' opportunities and predicament. In figure 1.1, as before, six and eight hours of fishing are the only alternative actions on a given day, but now Eye and Jay may adopt strategies whereby they fish eight hours one day and six the next, as well as other combinations over a period of time. Further, I assume that any allocation must be agreed to by both fishers.

The payoffs {1, 1} are feasible and implementable by the six hour rule, but more complex agreements can implement any point within the set *abcd*. For example, point *d* can be implemented simply by Eye agreeing to fish six hours every day, and Jay's fishing eight. While Eye would surely not agree to this (Eye does worse under this arrangement than if each fishes 8 hours), Jay might offer to fish six hours a fraction of the time equal to $\underline{u} + \varepsilon$ (ε is a small positive number) and eight the rest, while requiring Eye to fish six hours all the time, threatening to fish eight hours all the time if Eye refused. Eye might well accept, for Eye would then expect a net gain of one during $(\underline{u} + \varepsilon)$ of the time and $\underline{u}$ the rest, the alternative being to get $\bar{u}$ all of the time, which would occur if Jay carried out the threat. Jay would then gain net benefits of one when they jointly fished six hours, which would happen $(\underline{u} + \varepsilon)$ of the time, and $(1 + \alpha)$ the rest of the time when Jay fished eight hours and Eye only six. Jay's proposed contract is indicated by point *f* in figure 1.1. All the points along *cfd* can be achieved by a contract of the form above: Jay works six hours for a fraction of the time, β and eight hours the rest, while Eye works six hours all the time, giving the utilities $u_i = \beta$ and $u_j = \beta + (1 - \beta)(1 + \alpha)$. Of course Eye would reject contracts along *fd*.

If Jay is able to precommit to such an offer, Jay is the *first mover* and

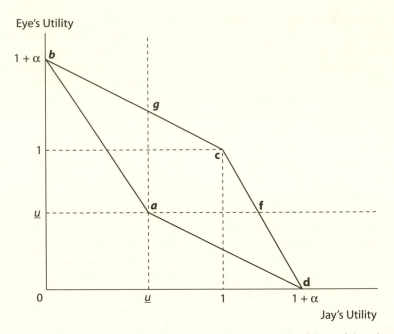

Figure 1.1 The tragedy of the fishers. Note at **c** both the fishers fish 6 hours while at **a** they both fish 8 hours.

has the *first mover advantage*. Of course, Eye might have made the identical offer to Jay. In this case the order of play (including who gets to be the first mover) makes a difference. A moment's reflection will confirm that there is not just one but rather an infinite number of agreements that are at once mutually beneficial (compared to the eight-hour rule) and efficient. An efficient agreement is one for which there exists no alternative that benefits at least one of the fishers without making the other worse off. These so called *Pareto-improving* (over the dominant strategy equilibrium outcome) and *Pareto-efficient* agreements are all the points along *fcg* in the figure (called the *Pareto frontier*.)

The fishers might have quickly agreed on the joint limitation to six hours if that were the only alternative to both fishing eight hours. But they might fail to agree once the range of possible agreements is enlarged; they may find that more options may be worse than fewer. This is because the indeterminate nature of the division of the benefits of fishing less raises the question of fairness and thus brings to bear considerations not captured in the game as described thus far. Eye, for example, might reject the disadvantageous "take-it-or-leave it" offer by Jay. But the same outcome might have been acceptable had it been arrived at in an impartial manner (by flipping a coin, for example), or had the benefits to fishing less been donated to a good cause rather than captured by Jay. If Eye and Jay cannot agree on a division, it may be that no agreement to restrict fishing is possible. But a third party, the government, might impose a seven hour limit on both fishers and then let them bargain to some more refined agreement if they are able. Or the fishers might come to adhere to an environmental norm inducing each independently to restrict his catch. The norm would imply a new payoff matrix in which the concern about environmental damage or the imposition of costs on the other fisher were taken into account.

It is just this type of indeterminacy that economic and other institutions address, answering such questions as who is positioned to make a take-it-or-leave-it offer, what other actions are available to the relevant parties, what information asymmetries or lack of verifiability bear on the problem (and, as a result, what agreements are enforceable by third parties), and what norms may affect the outcome of the conflict.

Real fishers, of course, are not acting out a tragic script, as Hardin supposed; nor are they prisoners of the dilemma they face. They are often resourceful in seeking solutions to the problem of overfishing. Turkish fishermen, for example, allocate fishing spots by lot and then rotate them. Information sharing among fishers discourages cheating, while governmental regulations supplement local social-network-based enforcement (Ostrom 1990).The extant rules regulating access to fishing are a small selection — from a much larger set of rules once tried — that have succeeded at least well enough to allow the communities using them to persist and not abandon their rules in favor of some other. As we will see, the persistence of rules does not require that they be efficient, only that they be reproduced over time. Nonetheless, we might expect a community of fishers who have hit on the ways of sustaining joint limitation to six hours to do better in competition with groups that overfish, and to be copied by other groups. We will return to the example of the fishers in chapter four to explore the analytics of how taxes, asymmetric power relations among actors, social norms, and other aspects of social interactions affect outcomes.

How might game theory illuminate the tragedy of the fishers and similar problems?

GAMES

Games are a way of modeling *strategic interactions*, that is, situations in which the consequences of individuals' actions depend on the actions taken by others, and this mutual interdependence is recognized by those involved. A *game* is a complete identification of the players, a list for each player of every course of action available to him (including actions contingent on the actions taken by others, or on chance events) — known as the *strategy set* — the payoffs associated with each *strategy profile* (combination of strategies), as well the order of play and who knows what, when. Players may be individuals or organizations such as firms, trade unions, political parties, or national states. In biological applications, subindividual entities such as cells or genes are also players.

Even this brief introduction reveals two great virtues of game theory as a contribution to the study of economic institutions and behavior (I will consider the drawbacks presently). First, few social interactions can be reduced to the interaction of an agent with a *given* environment (as is accomplished by the price-taking axiom and the other unrealistic assumptions of the Walrasian model). Most interactions have a strategic component, and game theory is designed to analyze the manner in which individual action is influenced by the fact that this interdependence is commonly recognized by one or more parties to an interaction. Second, the complete specification of a game requires detailed attention to the institutional environment in which the interaction takes place; outcomes often hinge on these details (for example, who takes the first move) in ways that would not be revealed in frameworks that suppress rather than highlight institutional detail. Game theory does not provide substantive insights any more than mathematics or any other language does. But it often provides a clear way of expressing insights originating elsewhere and for understanding the role of particular assumptions in a line of reasoning.

The "tragedy of the fishers" example above is a game, presented in what is called its *normal* (or strategic) *form*. This means that the time sequence of the actions taken by each player is not explicitly represented, the assumption being made that each player moves without knowing the move of the others. The *extensive form* of a game makes explicit the order of moves, and who knows what at each stage in the game. Moves made earlier in time need not be known by those making later moves, of course. An example of a game in extensive form is the representation of the experimental ultimatum game as a game tree in chapter 3. The extensive form conveys more information about the interaction in the sense that many extensive-form games may be represented by the same normal form game. When, as is common, the normal-form representation is used, this is because the additional information in the extensive form is thought to be irrelevant to how the game will be played.[2] As you will see in chapter 3, experimental subjects'

---

[2] Who moves first may affect behavior even if the second mover does not know what

behaviors appear to be quite sensitive to details that at first glance would not seem to affect the structure of the game (the name given to the game, for example, or the labeling of the players). Thus it is not a good idea to reduce an extensive form game to its normal form unless there is good reason to think that the temporal order of play will have no effect on the behaviors of the players.

The *outcome* of a game is a set of actions taken by the players (and the associated payoffs). Game outcomes cannot be deduced from game structures alone but require, in addition, a plausible *solution concept*, that is, a specification of how those involved might play. The relationship between games and their outcomes is far from settled, with sharply contrasting approaches. *Classical game theory* stresses sometimes quite demanding forward-looking cognitive evaluations by the players. By contrast, *evolutionary game theory* stresses rule-of-thumb behaviors that are updated by a backward-looking learning process, that is, in light of one's own or others' recent experience.

Two solution concepts are widely used in classical game theory: *dominance* and *Nash equilibrium*. Dominance purports to say what will *not* happen (and in some cases, by a process of elimination, is illuminating about what *will* happen). Dominance gives strong predictions of outcomes in such games as the prisoners' dilemma in which every player will choose some particular strategy irrespective of what the others do. (Games solvable by dominance are degenerate strategic interactions in that the action taken by each does not depend on the actions taken by others.) The idea behind the Nash equilibrium is that there may be one or more outcomes that no individual has any incentive to alter his strategy given the strategies adopted by all the others.

Both dominance and the Nash equilibrium are based on the notion of a *best response* strategy. A strategy may be an unconditional action (such as drive on the right), but it may also be a prescription for acting contingent on the prior actions of others or chance. "Fish six hours a day no matter what" is a strategy, as is "Fish today as many hours as the other fished yesterday" (called tit for tat). A firm's wage offer and promotion ladder contingent on worker performance is a strategy, as is an employee's choice of an effort level; a bank's interest rate, system of monitoring its clients, and method of handling their defaults is also a strategy; and so on. Thus a *strategy is a description of an action or actions to take under every situation that may be encountered in the game*. In addition to the *pure strategies* that make up the strategy set, an individual may adopt a *mixed strategy*, namely, a probability distri-

---

the first mover did. Examples are provided in Camerer and Weber (2003) and Rapoport (1997).

bution over some or all of the pure strategies in the set. For example, one could let a coin flip determine if one fished six or eight hours.[3]

Let there be n players indexed by $i = 1 \ldots n$, and a strategy set for each is called S_i. Suppose the jth player selects a particular strategy $s \in S_j$. Let s_{-j} represent the strategies adopted by all other players (chosen from their strategy sets S_{-j}) and $\pi_j(s, s_{-j})$ the payoff to j under the strategy profile (s, s_{-j}). The payoff is j's evaluation of the outcome produced by the strategy profile (s, s_{-j}). Strategy s is j's *best response* to the strategies adopted by the others if no strategy available to j would result in higher payoffs for j. That is,

$$\pi_j(s, s_{-j}) \geq \pi_j(s', s_{-j}) \ \forall \ s' \in S_j, s' \neq s$$

which may be read: j's payoff to playing s against the given strategy profile of all others (s_{-j}) is not less than the payoff to playing any other strategy s' in j's strategy set against s_{-j}. A *strict best response* is a strategy for which the strict inequality holds for all s', while a *weak best response* is one for which the above expression holds as an inequality for at least one alternative strategy s'. A *weakly dominant strategy* is one for which no strategy yields a higher payoff regardless of the strategy choice of the others and that for some strategy profile yields higher payoffs. So s is weakly dominant if

$$\pi_j(s, s_{-j}) \geq \pi_j(s', s_{-j}) \ \forall \ s' \in S_j \text{ and } \forall \ s_{-j} \in S_{-j}$$

with the strict inequality holding for at least one strategy profile. A strategy is strictly dominant if no strategy weakly dominates it, that is, when the above inequality is strict in all cases. I reserve the terms "best response" and "dominance" (without the weak or strict modifier) for the stronger concept. If there exists a dominant strategy for each player, then the strategy profile in which all players adopts their dominant strategy is termed a *dominant strategy equilibrium*. Overfishing in the tragedy of the fishers is an example. Surprisingly, it may not always make sense to play a dominant strategy, but to see why, I will need to introduce another important solution concept — risk dominance — which I will do presently.

A *Nash equilibrium* is a strategy profile in which all players' strategies are best responses to the other strategies in the profile; if all of the best responses making up this strategy profile are unique (they include no weak best responses), then the Nash equilibrium is said to be strict. Because players have no reason to change their behaviors (the equilib-

---

[3] While mixed strategies sometimes provide a handy modeling device (e.g., the monitoring and working example in chapter 8), for technical reasons they have been given much more attention by game theorists than is justified by any resulting illumination of human behavior.

rium is a mutual best response), it is said to be stationary, it is this characteristic that justifies calling it an equilibrium. This interpretation is based on the assumption that individuals will not *jointly* agree to alter their strategies. Responding to John Von Neumann's objection that people are not really all *that* uncooperative, John Nash (to whom we owe this and other contributions to game theory) once called it "the American way."

Finally, *iterated dominance* is a procedure by which a player may eliminate from consideration any of the *other* players' strategies that are strictly dominated (i.e., would not be advantageous to adopt in any strategy profile). Truncating the other players' strategy sets in this manner changes the structure of the game such that the game truncated by iterated dominance may have a Nash or dominant strategy equilibrium even though the complete game did not.

The Structure of Social Interactions

People interact in an endless variety of ways, but there are generic classes of interaction. Some game theoretic terminology will provide an insightful classification. The first distinction — between cooperative and noncooperative games — refers to the institutional structure governing the interaction. The second — between common interest and conflict games — refers to the extent to which the game's payoffs exhibit conflict or common interest among the players.

Cooperative and noncooperative games. Imagine an interaction for which it is the case that everything that both is affected by the actions of the players and is of concern to any of the players is subject to binding (meaning costlessly enforceable) agreement. This is termed a *cooperative* interaction (or a *cooperative game*; I use the terms game and interaction interchangeably, when appropriate). The term does not refer to the feelings of the parties about each other but simply to the institutional arrangements governing their interactions. As we will see, cooperative games may be highly conflictual: for example, the purchase of a house generally pits the interests of the buyer against the seller, but if a deal is struck, it is generally enforceable and its terms cover all of the aspects of the transfer that are of interest to the parties.

More commonly, however, something about the interaction is not subject to binding agreement. Such situations are modeled as *noncooperative games*. In some cases, part of an interaction may be addressed cooperatively, as when an employer and an employee bargain over a wage and working hours. Other aspects of the same interaction may be noncooperative because of the impossibility of writing or enforcing the relevant contracts. Examples include how hard the worker works or whether the employer will invest the resulting profits in this plant or elsewhere. As is the case with cooperative interactions, the parties to noncooperative interactions may have sharply conflicting interests, or share broadly common objectives; the term "noncooperative" refers simply to the fact that their interaction is not fully covered by a binding agreement. By the same token, many aspects of loving relationships among friends and family are noncooperative interactions, for example, the promise to do one's best to get a friend a job may be completely sincere, but it is not a binding agreement.

Common interest and conflict. Some interactions have the character of traffic patterns: traffic jams are a generally poor outcome, and managing to avoid them would benefit everyone. In other interactions, like settling on a price of a good to be exchanged or the division of a pie, more for one means less for the other. Many of the differences among scholars and policy makers grappling with questions of institutional design can be traced to whether they believe that the ills of society are the result of common interest problems like traffic jams or of conflicting interest problems like the division of a fixed pie. In one case, institutions may be represented as problem solvers and in the second as claim enforcers. But most institutions do both. Thus, it may be impossible to analyze the problem-solving and distributional aspects of institutions in isolation. It will be useful to have some language to differentiate between these classes of problems; to do this I will refer to the *common interest* and *conflict* aspects of an interaction, starting with pure cases.

A game in which the payoffs to only one of the strategy profiles is Pareto optimal and the payoffs associated with all strategy profiles can be Pareto ranked can be described as a *pure common interest game.*[4] What this means is that one outcome is better than all other outcomes for a least one participant and not worse for any participant, and there is a second best outcome that, while Pareto inferior to the first best outcome, is Pareto superior to all the rest, and so on. Thus, there is no outcome that any player would strictly prefer over an outcome preferred by any other player. As a result, conflict among the players is entirely absent.

Here is an example. A firm consists of an employer and an employee:

---

[4] The term "common interest game" has been used to refer to a payoff structure such that all players prefer a given outcome to any other (for example Aumann and Sorin 1989 and Vega-Redondo 1996); the definition here is stronger (hence the "pure") as it requires not only that a mutually preferred outcome exist but that all outcomes be Pareto rankable. Outcomes can be Pareto-ranked if the preference orderings of the outcomes — most to least preferred — of all the participants are such that if an individual prefers outcome A to outcome B, no individual prefers B to A.

TABLE 1.2
Pure Common Interest Payoffs:
The Firm Survival Game

	Invest	*Do not*
Work	1, 1	p_2, p_2
Do not	p_1, p_1	0, 0

Note: the employer is the column player the worker is the row player: and $1 > p_1 > p_2 > 0$.

If the firm succeeds, both get 1; if it fails, both get 0. The probability of success depends on actions taken (noncooperatively) by the two: the employer may invest in the firm or not, and the employee may work hard or not. If the employer invests and the worker works hard, the firm will surely succeed. In the opposite case the firm fails with certainty (table 1.2). If the employer invests and the worker does not work the firm succeeds with probability p_1, and in the opposite case the firm succeeds with probability $p_2 < p_1$. Suppose that both players choose the action that maximizes their expected payoffs, namely, the weighted sum of the payoffs occurring for each strategy chosen by the other(s), weighted by likelihood the player assigns to each of these events. It is easy to confirm that pure common interest games have a dominant strategy equilibrium, namely, the single Pareto-optimal outcome. (This is a game in which expected payoffs depend on a probabilistic out-come—the firm's success—which is influenced by the strategy profile adopted by the players. A realization of a stochastic process is some-times referred to as *nature's move*.)

An interaction is termed a *pure conflict* game if all possible outcomes are Pareto optimal. An example is any zero sum game (meaning that for every strategy profile, the sum of the payoffs sum to zero). Pure conflict is illustrated by the set of strict Nash equilibria in the Division Game originally suggested by Schelling (1960). A dollar is to be divided be-tween two individuals according to the following rules: without prior communication each player submits a claim of any amount, and if the claims sum to one or less the claims are met; otherwise, each gets zero. A portion of the payoff matrix for this game is as shown in table 1.3 (assuming that claims must be made in units of pennies). The off-diago-nal strategy pairs are clearly not strict Nash equilibria (e.g. the lower right pair is a mutual weak best response and hence a nonstrict Nash equilibrium, as a claim of zero is also a best response to a claim of 100). The bold strategy pairs are the strict Nash equilibria of the game (there are 101 of them). Notice that each is Pareto optimal, so the outcomes

TABLE 1.3
The Division Game

Claims	0	1	. . .	99	100
0	0,0	0,1		0,99	0,100
1	1,0	1,1		**1,99**	0,0
.					
.					
.					
99	99,0	**99,1**		0,0	0,0
100	**100,0**	0,0		0,0	0,0

making up the set of strict Nash equilibria of the Division Game describe a pure conflict interaction. The fact that all outcomes of pure conflict games are efficient in the Pareto sense does not mean that the rules defining the game are efficient; there may be other rules (that is, other ways of regulating the interaction given its underlying structure) that would yield outcomes that are Pareto superior to those defined by the pure conflict game. We will return to this.

Figure 1.2 depicts the payoffs in a generic two-person game in which each player has two strategies; hence, there are four strategy profiles and associated payoffs labeled **a** through **d**. For the pure conflict game, the payoffs are arrayed in a "northwest-to-southeast" direction (because each is a Pareto optimum, no outcome can lie to the "northeast" of any other), while in the pure common interest case they lie along a "southwest-to-northeast" axis, indicating that they can be Pareto ranked. The Firm Survival Game is an example of the class of pure common interest games in that the payoffs to the players are identical for each strategy profile (they share a "common fate") so the outcomes in figure 1.2 would be arrayed along a 45° ray from the origin. Similarly, a zero sum game is a strong form of a pure conflict game in which the payoffs would be arrayed along a line with a slope of -1.

Most social interactions are such that both common interest and conflict aspects are present. Driving on the right- or the left-hand side of the road is a matter of indifference to most people as long as others do the same. By contrast, while there are mutual gains to all people's speaking the same language, people are far from indifferent about *which* language they speak; thousands have died in wars on the subject. One of the reasons why the prisoners' dilemma has attracted so much attention is that it combines both common interest and conflict aspects.

Figure 1.1 (the tragedy of the fishers) illustrates both the conflict (northwest-to-southeast) and common interest (southwest-to-northeast)

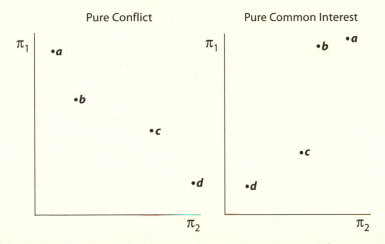

Figure 1.2 Pure conflict and pure common interest games. Note: the points **a, b, c,** and **d** indicate the payoffs to two players for each of four possible strategy profiles.

dimensions of the payoffs. A natural measure of the extent of the common interest as opposed to the conflict aspect of the payoff structure is available in *symmetric games* such as the tragedy of the fishers. (A symmetric game is one in which the payoff matrix for one player is the transpose of the payoff matrix of the other.) This measure, η, is given by the size of the improvement over the dominant strategy equilibrium made possible by cooperation $(1 - u)$, relative to the difference in payoffs when the two adopt different strategies, $1 + \alpha$:

$$\eta = \frac{1 - u}{1 + \alpha}.$$

For values of u and α such that the payoffs describe a prisoners' dilemma $\eta \in (0,\overline{1})$ with values approaching zero indicating virtually pure conflict, and approaching unity virtually pure common interest.

The cooperative–non-cooperative and conflict–common interest distinctions give us the typology of interactions presented in figure 1.3 with some examples for illustration. For example, the repayment of loans (analyzed in chapter 9) is a conflictual noncooperative interaction because repayment benefits the lender at a cost to the borrower, but the borrower's promise to do so is not enforceable (if the borrower has no funds). The evolution of individual property rights during the period of human history before the existence of states may have been at least initially a noncooperative common-interest interaction. By contrast, modern property rights are determined through cooperative interactions taking the form of enforceable restrictions on use and the like.

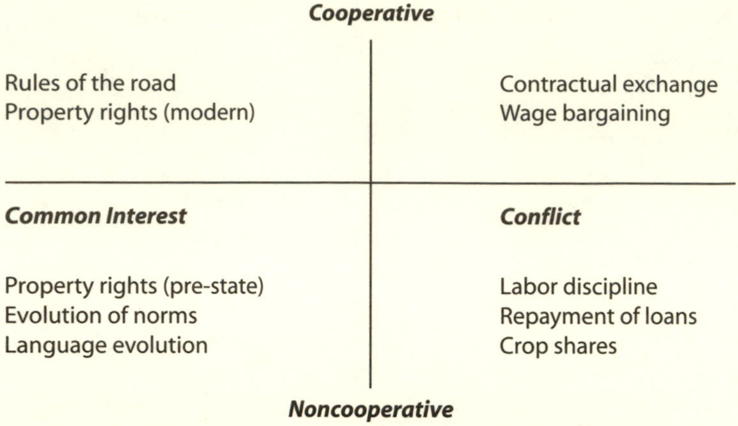

Cooperative

| Rules of the road
Property rights (modern) | Contractual exchange
Wage bargaining |

Common Interest | *Conflict*

| Property rights (pre-state)
Evolution of norms
Language evolution | Labor discipline
Repayment of loans
Crop shares |

Noncooperative

Figure 1.3 Aspects of social interactions. Note: it is not difficult to think of some property rights which should be placed on the conflict side of the graph; likewise some aspects of language evolution evolved by coercive imposition (that is, cooperatively) rather than non-cooperatively.

Another important aspect of social interactions is their temporal structure. An interaction may be repeated over many periods with the same players, possibly for a known number of periods or with a known probability of termination following each period. These are *repeated games*; nonrepeated games are often called *one-shot games*. Finally, many interactions resemble exchanges in which there is a single buyer and single seller; but in addition to these *dyadic*, or two-person, games there are many interactions involving large numbers, generically referred to as *n-person games*. Symmetric two person games with just two strategies are called *2 × 2 games*.

COORDINATION FAILURES

We now return to the constitutional conundrum, initially expressed as the challenge of ensuring that the pursuit of individual interests does not lead to "outcomes that none would have chosen." These undesirable outcomes are *coordination failures*, which are said to occur when the noncooperative interaction of two or more people leads to a result which is not Pareto optimal.[5] I refer to *coordination problems* as those situations in which coordination failures occur with significant likeli-

[5] This is an inclusive definition of the term coordination failure, which is sometimes restricted to situations in which a Pareto-inferior equilibrium obtains when another (Pareto-superior) equilibrium exists. My definition includes cases in which no equilibrium exists.

TABLE 1.4
The Invisible Hand Game

	Corn	Tomatoes
Corn	2, 4	4, 3
Tomatoes	5, 5	3, 2

hood. Familiar market failures such as those resulting from environmental externalities are a type of coordination failure, but the broader concept includes all types of noncooperative interaction, not simply those taking place in market interactions. Arms races and traffic jams are thus examples of coordination failures. An important class of coordination failures — state failures — arise when the equilibrium actions of governmental officials result in a Pareto-inferior outcome. I use the broader term *coordination failure* (rather than market failures) to draw attention to the fact that *all* institutional structures share with markets the tendency to implement Pareto-inefficient outcomes.

Coordination failures may arise in out-of-equilibrium situations, but analytical attention has focused on equilibrium outcomes in which coordination failures arise in two cases. In the first, one or more Pareto-inferior outcomes may be Nash equilibria; in the second, there does not exist any Pareto-optimal outcome that *is* a Nash equilibrium. As a benchmark, consider a 2 × 2 game in which there exists a single Nash equilibrium and it is Pareto optimal, as in table 1.4. I call it the Invisible Hand Game because the self-interested actions of both actors yield an outcome that maximizes the well-being of each. (Namely, if Row grows tomatoes and Column grows corn, they each receive five, which is the best that either could do.) In this case, each not only pursues self-interested objectives but benefits from the fact that the other does as well. Row's choice of a strategy will depend on what he believes Column will do. Imagine that Rational Row notices that for Column, growing tomatoes is dominated, and therefore (using iterated-dominance reasoning) decides to grow tomatoes. But suppose that instead of pursuing his self-interest, Crazy Column flips a coin and as a result of the toss, grows tomatoes too. The example underlines that even if there is a unique Nash equilibrium, we still need to understand how players arrive at it, a topic to which we will return in chapter 2.

By contrast, in the Prisoners' Dilemma Game we have seen that a dominant strategy equilibrium exists and is Pareto inferior. A coordination failure results because the harm inflicted on the other by one's defection is not reflected in the payoffs of the defector, so neither prisoner takes adequate account of their actions' effects on the other.

Coordination failures arise for the same reason in the *Assurance Game*. But the game structure differs in an important way from the prisoners' dilemma: the Assurance Game payoff matrix is such that there exist more than one equilibrium, one or more of which may be Pareto inferior. (Games with this structure are sometimes called coordination games, but I will not use this term so as to avoid confusion with the terms "coordination failure" and "coordination problem" introduced above.) Thus, while a Pareto-optimal strategy profile may be the outcome of the game, it need not be. Examples include learning a language or a word processing system (its value depends on how many others have learned it), participating in a collective action such as a strike or a cartel (the expected benefits depend on the numbers participating), and the determination of employment in an entire economy (if all employers hire, the wages paid will support a level of aggregate demand justifying a high level of employment.) Other examples include the adoption of common standards (systems of weights and measures, academic credentials, computer operating systems, VHS as opposed to Betamax video technology), firms training skilled labor (if workers may move among firms, the private returns for a given firm offering training depend on the number of other firms engaging in training), and group reputations (if your trading community is known to be opportunistic, it may be a best response for you to behave opportunistically).

As these examples suggest, in Assurance Games, coordination failures occur because of generalized increasing returns or what is sometimes called *strategic complementarity*: individual payoffs are increasing in the number of people taking the same action. If I adopt the same word processing program as my colleagues, I confer benefits on them, but these benefits are not included in my decision process. (Compare this with the Invisible Hand Game above in which specialization is advantageous, so one persons' growing corn renders the other's payoff to growing corn lower.)

Because strategic complementarities may give rise to multiple equilibria, outcomes may be *path-dependent* in the sense that without knowing the recent history of a population it is impossible to say which equilibrium will obtain. In this case quite different outcomes are possible for two populations with identical preferences, technologies, and resources but with different histories. To see this, return to the farmers of Palanpur, whose crop yields would be higher if they all were to plant earlier in the year. But if a single farmer were to plant early, the seeds would be taken by the birds that would flock to his plot. Suppose there are just two farmers who interact noncooperatively for a single period with the payoffs in table 1.5. I'll assume that planting late gives a higher return if the other farmer planted early than if both plant late. The first

TABLE 1.5
Planting in Palanpur:
An Assurance Game

	Early	Late
Early	4, 4	0, 3
Late	3, 0	2, 2

planter gets all the predators, but if planting is simultaneous, predators are "shared" equally. While the mutual early planting equilibrium is clearly the only Pareto optimum, mutual late planting is also an equilibrium.

The payoff matrix describes a poverty trap: identical individuals in identical settings may experience either an adequate living standard or deprivation, depending only on their histories. The planting in Palanpur problem is a special kind of assurance game in which there exist two or more *symmetrical pure strategy equilibria* (meaning that all players adopt the same pure strategy). These equilibria are called *conventions*, namely, mutual best response outcomes that are sustained by the fact that virtually all players believe that virtually all other players will best respond. (We return to the historical contingency of outcomes in chapter 2 where the analytical tools of population level dynamics are introduced.)

The games thus far introduced (plus a common children's game) allow an illustration of the sources of coordination failures listed in table 1.6. In the children's game, common around the world (English speakers call it "Rock Paper Scissors" and for others it is "Earwig Human Elephant") there is no Nash equilibrium in pure strategies.[6] Thus, no Pareto optimum is a Nash equilibrium, but because the game is zero sum (payoffs to each strategy profile sum to zero) all outcomes are Pareto optima. Because Pareto inferior outcomes cannot result, Rock Paper Scissors is not a coordination problem, even though there is no reasonable way to play the game (which is why it is fun to play).

The representation of different structures of social interaction as games has allowed a taxonomy of how coordination problems may arise. It also suggests a strategy for addressing the constitutional conun-

---

[6] Here is a variant of the game: on the count of three you and your partner each put forward either a flat palm (paper), a fist (rock), or two fingers in a V (scissors), with the rule that rock beats ("smashes") scissors, scissors beats ("cuts") paper, and paper beats ("covers") rock, the winner and loser gaining and losing a point each respectively. (A tie produces no score, but can result in mutual hilarity occasioned by rock fights, scissor wars, and paper coverups.) How the earwig beats the human is still a mystery to me; but then try explaining why paper beats rock. See Sato, Akiyama, and Farmer (2002).

TABLE 1.6
Sources of Coordination Failures

	P-inferior Nash exists	*No P-inferior Nash*
No P-optimum is Nash	Prisoners' dilemma	
A P-optimum is Nash	Assurance Game	Invisible hand

drum: if the likely outcome of the an interaction is Pareto inferior to some other feasible outcome, introduce policies or property rights that will change the game structure to make the second outcome more likely. An example follows.

The key difference between prisoners' dilemmas and Assurance Games is that in the former the undesirable outcome is the only Nash equilibrium, so the only way that any of the other outcomes can be supported is by a permanent intervention to change the payoffs or the rules of the game. In the assurance game, by contrast, a desirable outcome (mutual early planting, for example) is an equilibrium, so the challenge to governance is limited to the less challenging *how to get there* problem rather than also having to solve the more demanding *how to stay there* problem. In debates on the appropriate type (and duration) of government interventions in the economy, key differences among economists and others concern whether one believes that the underlying problem resembles a Prisoners' Dilemma Game or an Assurance Game. Interventions may be called for in both cases, but Assurance Game problems may sometimes be reasonably well addressed by one-time rather than permanent interventions. It is partly for this reason that a common approach to averting coordination failures is to devise policies or constitutions that transform the payoff matrix so as to convert a prisoners' dilemma into an Assurance Game by making the mutual cooperate outcome a Nash equilibrium. An interaction that is a prisoners' dilemma if played as a one-shot game, may be an Assurance Game with mutual cooperate a Nash equilibrium if played as a repeated game, as we will see in chapter 7.

But while a Pareto-optimal Nash equilibrium exists in an Assurance Game, that fact alone is not sufficient to guarantee a mutually beneficial solution; unsolved coordination failures arising from Assurance Game–like interactions are ubiquitous. An important reason is that one's decision about how to play depends on one's beliefs about how others will play, and the way that people cope with this indeterminancy may result in sub-optimal outcomes. The problem is illustrated in figure 1.4, in which the expected payoffs of planting late and early (π_l and π_e, respectively) are just linear functions of the payoffs in the Planting in Palanpur

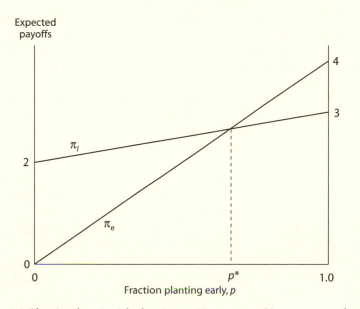

Figure 1.4 Planting late is risk dominant. Note: $p^* = \frac{2}{3}$ so $\pi_l > \pi_e$ for $p = \frac{1}{2}$. The intercepts of the vertical axes are the payoffs in the payoff matrix on p.

matrix above. Suppose you are the Row farmer in Palanpur and have no information on the likely play of the Column farmer, attributing equal likelihood to Column's two strategies. You will choose late planting because your expected payoffs are then $2\frac{1}{2}$ (that is, $\frac{1}{2}(3) + \frac{1}{2}(2)$), while the expected payoff to early planting is 2. Even if the mutual early planting equilibrium were somehow to be attained, if you thought that the other might switch strategies by whim or by mistake, it might be difficult to sustain the early planting convention. To see why, imagine that the zeros in the figure were instead −100, namely, the payoff associated with the destruction of one's crop and as a result being without food.

As the underlying idea here will recur in the pages that follow, a few definitions (restricted to 2×2 games) will help. Call a convention in which both play strategy k, a k-equilibrium. The other is strategy k'. Define the *risk factor* of a k-equilibrium as the smallest probability p such that if one player believes that the other player is going to play k with probability greater than p (and k' with a probability less than $(1 - p)$) then k is the strict best response for the individual to make. The equilibrium with the lowest risk factor is the *risk dominant equilibrium*.

In the example above, the risk factor of the late planting equilibrium is ⅓, which is less than the risk factor of the early planting equilibrium (⅔). Late planting is termed Row's *risk dominant strategy*, namely, the strategy that maximizes the expected payoffs of a player who attributes equal probabilities to the strategies open to the other player. Because this is true for the column player as well, mutual late planting is the *risk dominant equilibrium*. Figure 1.4 illustrates these concepts. The fraction planting early is p, while π_l and π_e are the expected payoffs to planting late and early, respectively, conditional on one's belief about p. The early planting equilibrium is termed the *payoff dominant equilibrium*: An equilibrium is payoff dominant if it there is no other equilibrium which strictly Pareto dominates it. In our example, early planting is payoff dominant because the payoffs in this equilibrium exceed the payoffs for both players in the late planting equilibrium.

Notice that the farmers are assumed to maximize expected payoffs, which implies that they are risk neutral, so the fact that the risk dominant but Pareto-inferior equilibrium may obtain does not presume risk aversion on the part of the farmers. (Risk neutrality and risk aversion are discussed in chapters 3 and 9.) Note also that the coordination failure does not arise in this case due to a conflict of interest between the farmers, as it did in the prisoners' dilemma faced by the fishers. Each of the fishers prefers that he fish more and the other fish less. But both farmers prefer mutual early planting over any other outcome. Their failure to coordinate on the mutually desired outcome is the result of uncertainty about the actions to be taken by the others and not due to a conflict of interest. The prediction that the risk-dominant equilibrium will be favored over the payoff-dominant equilibrium is strongly supported by the actual play of experimental subjects in games capturing the logic of the planting in Palanpur problem (Van Huyck, Battalio, and Beil 1990). We will see (in chapter 12) that risk dominant equilibria may persist over long periods even when a payoff dominant equilibrium exists.

Thus even if a policy intervention succeeded in converting a Prisoners' Dilemma Game to an Assurance Game, the desired Pareto-optimal outcome may not result. A more ambitious objective is to convert the underlying social interaction from a prisoners' dilemma to an Invisible Hand Game. To see how this might work, consider a generic prisoners' dilemma with the payoffs a, b, c, and d in table 1.7. (Ignore the payoffs in bold type for the moment.) The interaction is a prisoners' dilemma if $a > b > c > d$ and $a + d < 2b$, the second requirement expressing the fact that the expected payoff of both Row and Column is greater if they cooperate than if one were to defect and the other cooperate, with the assignment of the two roles being decided by chance. Suppose Row and Column decided to embrace "cooperate" as the norm and to adopt a liability rule according to which anyone violating the

TABLE 1.7
Implementing a Desired Outcome by Transforming Property Rights

Row	Column	
	Cooperate	Defect
Cooperate	b, b	d, a
	b, b	**$d + (b - d), a - (b - d)$**
Defect	a, d	c, c
	$a - (b - d), d + (b - d)$	c, c

Transformed payoffs are in bold.

norm must compensate those whose payoffs are reduced as a result of the violation, with compensation sufficient to exactly offset the losses (we will postpone the important question of the enforcement of the new property rights). Thus if Row defects on Column, Row initially gets a as before but then must compensate Column for the costs his defection has inflicted, that is, compensation sufficient to give Column a payoff of b (which would have occurred had the norm not been violated). If they both defect, they both gain c but then must compensate the other by a transfer of $b - c$. The transformed payoff matrix for Row's payoffs is thus given by the bold entries in the figure below.

Did the improved property rights succeed? Because $a - b + d < b$ by the definition of a prisoners' dilemma, cooperate is a best response to cooperate and mutual cooperation is a Nash equilibrium. Cooperate is also a best response to defect (because $b > c$), so cooperate is the dominant strategy and mutual cooperation is the dominant strategy equilibrium. Thus a redefinition of property rights (to take account of liability for damages) implements a social optimum by inducing each to take account of the effect of his actions on the other. The property rights redefinition transformed the game from a mixed conflict and common interest game to a pure common interest game. However, as we will see in subsequent chapters, most coordination failures do not allow such simple solutions. The reason is that the identification of the defection and the assessment of the relevant damages requires information that either is not available to the relevant parties or is not useable in a court of law or any other feasible body charged with enforcement of the relevant rights.

GAMES AND INSTITUTIONS

Do games illuminate institutions? *Institutions* (as I use the term) are *the laws, informal rules, and conventions that give a durable structure to social interactions among the members of a population.* Conformity to the behaviors prescribed by institutions may be secured by a combination of centrally deployed coercion (laws), social sanction (informal rules), and mutual expectations (conventions) that make conformity a best response for virtually all members of the relevant group. Institutions influence who meets whom, to do what tasks, with what possible courses of action, and with what consequences of actions jointly taken. It is clear from this definition that an institution may be formally represented as a game. The labor market institutions explored in chapters 8 and 10 are modeled in this way: the relevant institutions define what the employer may do (vary the wage as first mover, terminate the job) and may not do (physically punish the employee), and similarly for the worker (vary the level of work effort) with the payoffs to the two depending on the strategy profile. These labor market and firm-level institutions are modeled as games. Institutional innovations such as minimum wages or regulations governing terminations may be considered as ways of altering the strategy sets, payoffs, information structure, and players such that the equilibrium of the game may be displaced.

But to understand why institutions might change, it will sometimes be insightful to represent an institution not as a game but rather as the equilibrium of an underlying game. Because institutions are persistent rather than ephemeral it is natural to represent them as stable equilibria of an underlying game in which the strategy set encompasses a wide range of possible actions (whip the shirking worker, refuse to hand over the goods produced to the employer) that are not observed in the institutional set up described above but could be part of some other equilibrium strategy profile. Thus, to continue the employer-employee example, the expectation that the employer and not the employee will have possession of the goods produced is a mutual best response, that is, an *outcome* of some game (or, more likely, games), presumably one in which the players include not only employers and employees, but also police and judicial officials and many others. When a particular set of mutual best responses is virtually universal in a population over an extended period of time, it constitutes one or more institutions.

In chapters 2 and 11 through 13, I will model property rights, crop shares, rules governing resource sharing, and the like as equilibria, and study the manner in which these equilibria may evolve in response to chance events, collective action by those affected, and exogenously induced changes in the structure of the relevant underlying games. In chapter 2, I model the process of racial segregation of a residential neighborhood to illustrate how an institution (segregated residences) can be understood as the equilibrium of a game.

There is no inconsistency and little risk of confusion in representing

TABLE 1.8
Rousseau's Stag Hunt

	Hunt stag	Hunt hare
Hunt stag	½ Stag	0
Hunt hare	1 hare	1 hare

Note: the entries are Row's outcomes; payoffs can be calculated using the fact that one-third of a stag is worth one hare.

institutions both as games and also as equilibria of an underlying game. Which is appropriate will depend on the analytical problem at hand. If we are interested in understanding why the poor are credit constrained (chapter 9), modeling the lender-borrower relationship as a game will be adequate (and asking about the origins of limited liability and the other underlying property rights is a distraction). On the other hand, if we want to know why limited liability exists, we would model this aspect of property rights as the outcome of an underlying game. Similarly, if we wanted to know why primogeniture is less common in Africa than in Asia, we would need to model rules of inheritance as conventions, that is, as equilibria of Assurance Games.

The term "institution" is sometimes also used to refer to such individual entities as a particular firm, a trade union, or a central bank; but to avoid confusion I will call these entities *organizations*. One may also treat organizations as if they were individual players in a game; this may be insightful as long as one has reason to think that the entity does indeed act as a unit; treating the firm as a single person may make more sense than applying the same logic to "the working class."

Rousseau's stag hunt illustrates the relationship between games and institutions. Suppose you observe a group of hunters, who hunt for hare, though there are stag in the forests around them. You wonder why they do not hunt stag, and consult the Stag Hunt Game (table 1.8) seeking an explanation. Assume there are two hunters, who decide, independently and without knowledge of the other's choices, either to hunt for stag (capturing one and consuming it equally if they both hunt stag, and otherwise capturing—and hence consuming—nothing) or to hunt for hare (bagging one hare and consuming it, independently of what the other does). For the moment, we assume that the hunters do not expect to meet again. Finally, each hunter values a third of a stag as much as one hare. The hunting technology (not the payoffs) is summarized in table 1.8. The game captures important aspects of the relevant institutions, for example, that they do not decide jointly what to hunt (or to be more precise, they have no means of binding themselves to abide by any decision they might make), that if both participate in the stag hunt, the kill will be shared equally, and that even if one hunts hare, rendering the other's stag hunting fruitless, one may consume the hare without sharing. This exemplifies using a game to describe an institution, along with the relevant technologically given cause and effect relationships.

By itself, however, the game is not very illuminating. Given the payoffs, both mutual hare hunting and a joint stag hunt are conventions (it is an Assurance Game), so without knowing anything about the beliefs of the hunters about the likely actions of the other we would not be able to predict whether the hare or the stag would be in jeopardy. Imagine, now, that the interaction is ongoing, and that in the previous period both hunted hare (for whatever reason); one of the hunters considers hunting stag this period instead. For this to be in the interest of the hunter (considering only this period's payoffs), she would have to expect that the other would do the same, attaching a likelihood of at least two-thirds to this occurrence. In making this assessment she would need to know something of the history of this group of hunters, and in particular, past outcomes of the game, possibly including complex outcomes such as joint stag hunting on weekends or solitary hare hunting on weekdays. If the undecided hunter has no such clues to go on and therefore attaches equal likelihood to the other hunter's two actions, she will hunt hare, for it is transparent that while mutual stag hunting is the payoff dominant equilibrium, hare hunting is risk dominant. Thus mutual expectations (whether arising from historical experience or from any other source) are as much a part of explaining why it is hare rather than stag that they hunt as is the assumption that they have no way of subjecting one another to binding agreements.

Notice, also, that some aspects of the game taken as exogenously given in the above account may be explained as the result of other institutions, that is, as the equilibria of underlying games. The practice of allowing the hare hunter to consume his catch even if the other has nothing, or dividing the stag equally may (as we will see) be modeled as outcomes of an underlying game in which these particular property rights are an equilibrium and in which other property rights (share the hare, for example, or, the stag goes to the one whose arrow felled it) could have obtained.

While game theory illuminates many important aspects of institutions and economic behavior, there are serious gaps in our current knowledge. First, while much of the use of game theory in the social sciences concern 2×2 games of the type introduced here, the relevant numbers involved in many social interactions are much greater and the strategy sets far more complicated. The analysis of n-person games or games with large strategy sets lacks the simplicity, tractability, and transparency of the above games. The 2×2 games introduced thus far are best considered metaphors for much more complex problems, often pointing to important aspects of interactions but falling far short of an adequate analysis. Steps towards realism need not come at too high price in tractability, however. Two-person interactions are often embedded in interactions of much larger populations, as in the population level analysis of the Hawk Dove Game presented in chapter 2, the exchange games in chapter 7, and the conventions studied in chapters 11 through 13. And it is often possible to model a complex set of interactions as a series of separable two-person or larger interactions. When we turn to the analysis of the firm, for example, it will be analyzed using a two-person interaction between employer and employee, a separate two-person interaction between the firm and a lending institution, and a large-n interaction on competitive goods markets.

But many of the decentralized solutions to coordination problems based on such things as game repetition and reputation (presented in chapter 7) have far wider applicability to two-person (or very small n) interactions than to the large-n interactions that characterize many of the coordination problems of interest. The exaggerated emphasis on two-person games (due in part to their pedagogical value) that are amenable to solution in a repeated game framework may have contributed to the view that coordination failures are exceptional rather than generic aspects of social interactions.[7]

The fact that game theory has made less progress with noncooperative n-person interactions than with either cooperative or two-person games is hardly a criticism of the approach, for it arises because game theory addresses intrinsically complex aspects of human interaction that are abstracted from in other approaches. What makes the analysis of interactions among many individuals intractable is the assumption that they act strategically rather than taking the others' actions as given. Where one can abstract from strategic action—as in competitive markets for goods governed by complete contracts and in which only equilibrium trades take place, namely, the paradigmatic Walrasian case— much of the analysis is reduced to a single individual interacting with a

---

[7] Pedagogy, not realism, must also explain why so much attention has been given to symmetric games. The games that real people play are *asymmetric* in the sense that players often come with (or acquire) labels that assign to them different strategy sets and payoffs: men and women, insiders and outsiders, employers and employees, typically interact asymmetrically. Asymmetrical games are common in game theoretic models of labor markets, credit markets, and other situations in which institutions allocate individuals to distinct structural positions (borrower, lender) with different strategy sets. These models appear in chapter 2 and in chapters 5 through 10.

given set of prices, technological blueprints, and constraints. But, as we will see, there are many important interactions — labor markets, credit markets, markets for information and for goods of variable quality — for which this particular way to achieve tractability is not insightful.

Second, the main solution concepts of classical game theory — dominance (direct, iterated, and risk) and Nash equilibrium — are intended to supply the standard of reasonable ways that the game would be played. But they are not entirely adequate as a guide to what will happen. Other than the prisoners' dilemma, few games have dominant strategy (or iterated dominance) equilibria, and many (pure strategy) games do not even have Nash equilibria. Iterated dominance may not be robust as a solution concept because it is a reasonable way to play only if the other players have the same understanding of the game and its payoffs, are using the same solution concept, and are not prone to make errors (the common knowledge and common rationality assumptions.)

The Nash concept is more robust: if we are concerned with the explanation of durable (as opposed to ephemeral) phenomena, it is natural to look at outcomes for which it is true that no one with the ability to alter the outcome through his actions alone has an interest in doing so. Thus, we can say that a Nash equilibrium is an outcome at which there are no endogenous sources of change (this is an adequate definition of any *equilibrium*). By confining our attention to stable Nash equilibria the concept is made considerably more useful. But as a guide to outcomes, even under the assumptions of common rationality and common knowledge, the stable Nash equilibrium is incomplete in two ways. First, we need to know how reasonable play would lead to a Nash equilibrium and why it might be stable. This requires attention to what the players do in out-of-equilibrium situations. In some cases, there is little reason to think that reasonable play would lead to the Nash equilibrium. If you doubt this, try to explain why one would expect players in the Rock Paper Scissors Game to play the mixed-strategy Nash equilibrium for that game (that is, play each with probability ⅓, the only Nash equilibrium). Second, many games have many Nash equilibria, so the Nash concept alone cannot predict outcomes; information about initial conditions plus an analysis of out-of-equilibrium behavior are required to understand which of many Nash equilibria will obtain. Thus, historical contingency and dynamics (including learning) are necessary complements to the Nash concept.

The problem of indeterminacy arising from the multiplicity of equilibria has been addressed in different ways by classical game theory and evolutionary game theory. Classical game theory has sought to narrow the set of possible outcomes through restrictions on the behaviors of the players based on ever stronger notions of rationality. These additional restrictions, called *refinements*, preclude equilibria involving strategies which include *noncredible threats* (i.e., those that would not be best responses ex post should they fail to be effective), or are not robust to small deviations from best-response play ("trembles") or payoffs, or that are supported by beliefs that fail to make appropriate use of all the available information (e.g., that do not make use of backward induction or iterated dominance).

By contrast, evolutionary and behavioral game theory addresses the above limitations by relaxing the common knowledge and common rationality assumptions and by using empirically (mostly experimentally) grounded assumptions about how real people interact. Evolutionary game theory, for example, typically assumes that individuals have limited information about the consequences of their actions, and that they update their beliefs by trial-and-error methods using local knowledge based on their own and others recent past experience. In contrast to the highly intelligent and forward-looking players in classical game theory, the subjects of evolutionary game theory are "intellectually challenged" and backward looking. Because there is little evidence that individuals are capable of (or predisposed to) conducting the quite demanding cognitive operations routinely assumed by classical game theory, I will proceed (in chapters 2 and 3) to develop a set of assumptions more in line with empirical knowledge. A second reason for rejecting the classical approach is that it is a mistake to think that indeterminacy among equilibria can be settled by game theory itself, without reference to the particular history of the players. Embracing rather than seeking to skirt the fact that social outcomes will be influenced by the recent past — that history matters — attests to a necessary insufficiency of theory, not its weakness.

A third concern about game theory as the foundation of the analysis of economic institutions and behavior is its narrow scope. Society is not well-modeled as a single game, or one with an unchanging structure. An approach to games that would be adequate to understanding society would have to take account of the following characteristics. Games are *overlapping*: people regularly participate in many distinct types of social interaction ranging from firms, to markets, to families, to citizen-state relationships, neighborhood associations, sports teams, and so on. Credit markets are often linked to labor and land markets, for example, and loan agreements that would be infeasible in a credit market taken in isolation may be possible when the borrower is also the employee of the lender, or the renter of his land, and in both cases subject to eviction should default occur. The overlapping character of games is also important because the structure of one game teaches the players lessons and imparts direction to cultural evolution, affecting not only how they play the game in subsequent periods but how they play the other games they are involved in. Citizens endowed with well-defined individual liberties and democratic rights in their relationship to their government may, for example, seek to invoke these in the workplace. Games, in other words, are *constitutive* of the players' preferences. Furthermore, not only the players evolve; the rules do as well. The games are thus *recursive* in the sense that among the outcomes of some games are changes in the rules of this or other games. In the pages that follow, I will introduce *overlapping* and *asymmetric* games in the analysis of firms, credit markets, employment relationships, and class structure. *Constitutive* and *recursive* games will be used to analyze the coevolution of preferences and institutions.

CONCLUSION

Why, then, do the farmers of Palanpur remain poor, planting late and bearing the costs of the other coordination failures that appear to limit their economic opportunities? Why do meadows go undrained and stags roam the forest unmolested? The long term persistence of Pareto-inferior outcomes is a puzzle of immense intellectual challenge and practical importance.

A number of possible impediments to solving coordination problems have been mentioned thus far (I will return to them in subsequent chapters). Coordination failures that are readily avoided among two individuals may pose insurmountable obstacles if a hundred or a thousand individuals are interacting, as Hume pointed out in his comment on the difficulty of securing the drainage of the meadow. The underlying interaction may be such that the dominant strategy is noncooperation (as in the prisoners' dilemma). Because of nonverifiable information or for other reasons, there may be no way of transforming the relevant game to remove this obstacle. The changes in the rules of the game necessary to avert a particular coordination failure may be resisted due to the open endedness of institutions and the losses some players might as result fear due to the effect of institutional changes on some *other* game. Even if a payoff dominant equilibrium exists, it may not obtain because some other equilibrium is risk dominant and there is no way of coordinating expectations. If, as is often the case, an acceptable division of the gains from cooperation cannot be assured, those involved may prefer noncooperation to cooperation. Finally, where the degree of common interest is small (as opposed to conflict), the gains to mutual cooperation may be insufficient to justify the risk or the cost of securing conditions to implement cooperation.

It was once widely thought that governmental intervention could readily attenuate the most serious coordination failures. But few would now share Hume's optimism, expressed in the sentence immediately following the passage quoted in the epigraph: "Political society [meaning a government] easily remedies . . . these inconveniences" (Hume 1967: 304). "There are persons," Hume wrote, "whom we call . . . our governors and rulers, who have no interest in any act of injustice . . . and have an immediate interest . . . in the upholding of society" (pp. 302–3). Among the reasons for our modern skepticism that "political society easily remedies these inconveniences" is the realization that institutions and policies are not simply instruments ready to be deployed by Hume's well-meaning public servants. Rather, they are the products of evolution as well as design and are themselves subject to the same kinds of coordination failures introduced above.

So far I have identified a number of Pareto-inferior outcomes as Nash equilibria. Understanding the underlying coordination failures, the impediments to their solution, and how they might be overcome requires an understanding of why individuals take the actions that implement and sustain inefficient Nash equilibria over long periods. To answer these questions we need to understand how both individual behaviors and social institutions evolve over time. In chapter 2 we introduce the tools of evolutionary modeling to address these issues.

CHAPTER TWO

Spontaneous Order: The Self-organization of Economic Life

> Such were the Blessings of that State;
> Their Crimes conspir'd to make them Great;
> Thus every Part was full of Vice;
> Yet the whole Mass, a Paradise; . . .
> The worst of all the Multitude
> Did Something for the Common Good
> > — Bernard Mandeville *The Fable of the Bees, or Private Vices,*
> > *Publick Benefits* (1705)

> I observe, that it will be for my interest to leave another in the possession of his goods, provided he act in the same manner with regard to me. . . . And this may properly be call'd a convention. . . . [T]he stability of possession . . . arises gradually, and acquires force by a slow progression, and by our repeated experience of the inconveniences of transgressing it. . . . In like manner are languages gradually establish'd by human conventions without any promise. In like manner do gold and silver become the common measures of exchange.
> > — David Hume, *A Treatise of Human Nature, Volume II* (1739)

IN MILWAUKEE, LOS Angeles, and Cincinnati, over half of white residents, when asked, said they would "prefer" to live in a neighborhood in which 20 percent or more of their coresidents were African American (with one in five preferring equal numbers of each; Clark 1991). Few live in integrated neighborhoods; their preferences were elicited in litigation concerning housing segregation in these and other cities. (Most African Americans preferred fifty-fifty neighborhoods.) The respondents may have misrepresented their preferences, of course; but those sincerely seeking integrated neighborhoods would have been disappointed. The housing market in these cities produced few mixed white–African American neighborhoods even though these were apparently in substantial demand. In Los Angeles, for example, virtually all whites (more than 90 percent) live in neighborhoods with fewer than 10 percent

The first epigraph comes from Mandeville (1924) reprinted on page 24 of the sixth edition (1732). The second comes from Hume (1964:263).

black residents, while 70 percent of blacks live in neighborhoods with fewer than 20 percent whites (Mare and Bruch 2001). Why is the aggregate result so seemingly at odds with the distribution of preferences? Imagine your surprise had I reported that one in five wanted a backyard swimming pool and were prepared to pay the going cost of it, yet few had pools? Why does the ability to pay get you a pool but not an integrated neighborhood?

One of the great challenges in the social sciences is to understand how aggregate outcomes are often different from anyone's intent, sometimes better (as Bernard Mandeville in the epigraph above and Adam Smith, in the epigraph to chapter 6 suggest) but sometimes worse, as an American family seeking a multi-racial neighborhood might suspect. Economists specialize in unintended consequences and, since Bernard Mandeville and David Hume, have studied the way the actions of many individuals acting on their own produce aggregate outcomes that nobody intended. The many sophisticated models of this process are one of the distinctive contributions of economics. More important than the models is the insight that no obvious relationship links the motives of the people engaging in an interaction and the normative properties of the aggregate outcomes occurring as a result of their interactions. For example, what are called "invisible hand arguments" show how the alchemy of good institutions can transform base motives into valued outcomes, so that, as in Mandeville' s *Fable*, "the worst of all the multitude did something for the common good."

This brings us back to the classical economists problem of "getting the rules right." Of course, even the "right" institutions are for the most part not designed at constitutional conventions. Rather, particular property rights and other forms of economic governance owe their existence and their mode of operation to the path-dependent consequences of often uncoordinated and accident-prone actions of a multiplicity of actors over a long period. Examples include the emergence and persistence of customary division rules and other aspects of property rights (such as fifty-fifty crop shares and "finders keepers"), norms supporting market exchanges, and the conventional use of pronouns expressing deference or solidarity.

In this chapter, I will ask: *in large populations, how do persistent structures of interaction evolve in the absence of deliberate design?* This is but a modern statement of the age-old question of institutional evolution: what accounts for the emergence, diffusion, and disappearance of social rules? The classical economists were no less interested in how we got the rules we have than in getting the rules right. A prominent modern exponent of the evolutionary tradition initiated by Hume and Smith is Frederick Hayek, whose approach sometimes is termed "the theory of spontaneous order" or "the self-organization of society." By contrast to the constitutional design approach, which posits a benevolent social planner or other actors seeking to implement socially optimal aggregate results, in evolutionary models none of the actors has preferences defined over aggregate outcomes.

The two traditions—constitutional and evolutionary—deploy different analytical techniques and distinct metaphors. The "institutions by design" tradition represents social rules as analogous to devices originating in the human imagination, evaluated by their problem-solving capacity and implemented if they meet a test of efficacy. Classical cooperative and noncooperative game theory are now the standard analytical techniques of this approach, not only by economists but also by philosophers such as Robert Nozick, John Rawls, and David Gauthier as well. By contrast, the spontaneous order tradition sees institutions as analogous to languages: the evolution of social rules, like the acquisition of an accent, is the product of countless interactions, the aggregate consequences of which are often unintended. Institutions thus evolve by trial and error, taking place, as Marx once put it, behind the backs of the participants. The title of Richard Dawkins' best-selling book likens evolutionary processes to a *Blind Watchmaker*. But the evocative metaphors of Dawkins or Marx do not tell us what the process is, only what it is not. Evolutionary game theory is a way of illuminating this process and is the favored analytical technique of this approach.

I begin with an overview of the basic structure of evolutionary reasoning. I follow that with an example—residential segregation—designed to illustrate some of the tools of evolutionary modeling. I then present a formal model of the process of differential replication—the replicator dynamic model. The concepts of evolutionary stability introduced in the next part along with the replicator dynamic provide a behavioral foundation for the Nash equilibrium. To illustrate how these analytical tools can be used to study economic institutions, I then use an extension of the Hawk Dove Game to model the evolution of property rights. I conclude with a critical evaluation of the evolutionary approach.

Evolutionary Social Science

We study individual behavior primarily to understand aggregate results. Our concern is not why this particular person is without a job but with the rate of unemployment, not how scrupulous a given person is in paying taxes but the distribution of tax compliance in the population. Understanding an individual's preferences and beliefs, and the way institutions structure the constraints he faces, allows the prediction of individual behavior. But to explain aggregate outcomes we cannot simply sum the predicted individual behaviors, because the actions taken by each typically affect the constraints, beliefs, or preferences of the others. Taking account of these feedback effects can be done with population-level models that link individual actions to outcomes for the population as whole.

By far the most fully developed population-level approach in the social sciences is the model of general competitive market equilibrium, perfected in the middle of the last century by Kenneth Arrow, Gerard Debreu, Tjalling Koopmans, and others. Under rather restrictive assumptions, it aggregates the individual actions of producers and consumers to an economy-wide vector of prices, outputs, and the allocation of resources to alternative uses. The general equilibrium model provides the setting for the Fundamental Theorem of Welfare Economics mentioned in chapter 1 and explored more fully in chapter 6. Simplified versions of this model have attracted wide application not only in economics but also in the social sciences generally, where analogies to competitive economic equilibrium are found in electoral competition, the marriage market, and the like. I have mentioned the model's shortcomings in the prologue and will return to them briefly in the pages to follow, especially chapters 6 through 10.

Other than the Walrasian general equilibrium model, the only fully developed class of population-level models are those depicting evolutionary dynamics of biological systems under the combined influences of chance, inheritance, and natural selection. The similarity between the two approaches is striking: both model systems of competition in which practices or designs with higher payoffs proliferate. Nor is this surprising: Charles Darwin (1809–1882) got the idea of natural selection in 1838 while reading the classical economist Thomas Malthus (1766–1834). The close association of the two approaches predates even this; the first explicit treatment of an evolutionary dynamic in a biological model that I am aware of (a predator-prey model of the type made famous by Alfred Lotka [1880–1949] and Vito Volterra [1860–1940]) was published just ten years after the *Wealth of Nations*, by Joseph Townsend (1971) in his *A Dissertation on the Poor Laws by a Well Wisher to Mankind*.

But the biological models differ in important ways from the economic. While biologists employ equilibrium concepts in ways similar to economists, they have given much more attention to the explicit modeling of the dynamic processes governing the distribution of traits in a population. This task is facilitated by the fact that they have a model of the process of heritable innovation based on mutation and recombination. By contrast, economics has no generally accepted theory of innovation despite widespread recognition of its importance. Application of the biological model to human evolution has produced insights but misses the important fact that humans produce novelty intentionally and often through collective action and not simply by chance. (I address this problem in chapter 12.) A related difference is that while optimization is a behavioral postulate in the economic approach, it is necessarily an *as if* shortcut in biological modeling, where the work of optimization is done by the process of competition and selection rather than through the conscious choice of strategies by individual members of a species. If the economic models make excessive demands on individual cognitive capacities, the biological models applied to humans make far too few.

In recent years, anthropologists, biologists, economists, and others have adapted models from biology to the study of human populations in which traits may be transmitted by learning as well as genetically. One strand of this literature has developed models of cultural evolution by modifying the biological models to take account of distinctive human capacities, notably our ability to learn from our own experiences and from one another and to update our strategies in light of the information we process. A second strand, evolutionary game theory, has modified classical game theory to take account of our limited cognitive capacities by positing agents who update their behaviors using imperfectly observed local information. Thus, the two strands—the theory of cultural evolution and evolutionary game theory—have amended very different starting points—models of natural selection and classical game theory, respectively—in the first case, augmenting the assumed level of human cognitive prowess, and diminishing it in the second.

Both evolutionary game theory and models of cultural evolution describe the interactions of *adaptive agents*, eschewing both the zero-intelligence agents of the standard biological models and the highly cognitive agents of classical game theory. Adaptive agents adopt behaviors in a manner similar to the way people come to have a particular accent or to speak a particular language. Forward-looking payoff-based calculation is not entirely absent (those aspiring to upward mobility may adopt upper-class accents), but conscious optimizing is not the whole story. The answer to "why do you talk like that?" is generally "because I was born where people talk like that" not "because I considered all the ways of speaking and decided that my utility would be maximized by speaking this way."

Thus individuals are the bearers of behavioral rules. Analytical attention is focused on the success or failure of these behavioral rules themselves as they either diffuse and become pervasive in a population or fail to do so and are confined to minor ecological niches or are eliminated. The *dramatis personae* of the social dynamic thus are not individuals but behavioral rules: how *they* fare is the key; what individuals *do* is important for how this contributes to the success or failure of behavioral rules.

Other distinctive characteristics of the evolutionary approach include the modeling of *chance, differential replication, out of equilibrium dynamics*, and *population structure*.

First, *chance* plays a central role in evolutionary dynamics, even when the stochastic events are small or infrequent. Chance events may take the form of heritable novelty (as with *mutations*). Chance may also be introduced as *behavioral innovations*, which (like mutations) are not best responses. Unlike mutations, behavioral innovations are not transmitted genetically. Rather, they may be passed on to the next generation and copied by others by cultural transmission, that is, through the learning processes of adaptive agents. What is called *matching noise* is another way that chance affects evolutionary dynamics. When small numbers of individuals in a heterogeneous population are randomly paired to interact, the realized distribution of types with whom one is paired over a given period may diverge significantly from the expected distribution. The difference between the realized distribution and the expected distribution reflects *matching noise* and may have substantial effects.

Nobody doubts that chance events make a difference: exogenous shifts in tastes or technologies will displace the price and quantity equilibrium in the standard comparative static model of a market equilibrium. How, then, are evolutionary models different? First, mutations, behavioral innovations, and matching noise are distinct because these sources of stochastic events are endogenous to evolutionary models. Second, in the presence of generalized increasing returns, small chance events often have large and persistent effects due to positive feedbacks, rather than being counteracted by negative feedbacks.

It might be thought that chance events would introduce noise in evolutionary models, affecting nothing more than the pace of change or the second order question of whether we should expect to observe exact equilibrium states in the real world or only states in the neighborhood of equilibria. But this is far from true: taking account of chance often affects the direction (not just the pace) of evolutionary change, and, perhaps surprisingly, far from muddying the analytical waters, introducing noise in evolutionary models often allows us to say more rather than less about the likely outcome. (Examples appear below, and in chapters 5 and 12.)

Neither chance nor intentional innovation is sufficient to understand the evolution of human institutions and behaviors. It is these sources of novelty in combination with the second characteristic of the evolution-

ary approach—*differential replication* (sometimes called *selection*)—
that gives direction to evolutionary processes. A key idea here is that
the institutional and behavioral characteristics of individuals and societies that we commonly observe are those that have been copied and
diffused—in short, replicated—while competing rules, beliefs, and preferences have suffered extinction (or have been replicated only in marginal niches).

As the models introduced shortly will show, differential replication
takes many forms, broadly grouped under the headings genetic and cultural. The population distribution of behaviors that are influenced by
genes may change because of the proliferation of some genotypes at the
expense of others. The distribution of genotypes changes over time due
to random events (drift) and natural selection. In models of this process,
payoffs measure the reproductive success of the associated phenotypes,
that is, fitness. It is simplifying, and sometimes not misleading, to ignore
the details of genetic inheritance and of the relationship between genotype and phenotype and to treat a behavior as if it was the phenotypic expression of a single gene and to study the determinants of the
reproductive success of that gene. (This is done in studying the dynamics of the hawk-dove game below.) The mapping from genes to behaviors is for the most part unknown and certainly contains few if any
of the simple gene-behavior correspondences assumed by this method.

Cultural traits refer to behaviors that are learned rather than transmitted genetically from parents. Learning from parents is sometimes
termed *vertical cultural transmission*, while learning from teachers and
others of one's parents generation is called *oblique transmission*, and
learning from members of one's age group is called *horizontal transmission*. The analogue to differential fitness in models of cultural evolution
is the rate at which people give up one behavior in favor of another.
This differential copying process, like genetic inheritance, is poorly understood, but it involves a tendency to adopt a given behavior for one
or more of the following reasons: because it is common in one's locality
(*conformism, exposure*), because in one's own past experience it yielded
higher payoffs than other behaviors (*reinforcement learning*), or because the behavior maximizes expected payoffs given the individual's
beliefs about the distribution of others' behaviors in the population
(*best-response updating*). Because it is simple, plausible, and versatile, I
model cultural transmission with best-response updating, sometimes
combined with conformist learning.

The processes of genetic and cultural evolution are strongly influenced by social structure—assortative mating, patterns of residence and
migration, and the like. Because these and many other aspects of social
structure are based on learned behaviors, the distribution of culturally

transmitted traits in a population can influence genetic evolution. This, and the converse process — genetic distributions influencing cultural evolution — are termed *gene-culture evolutionary processes* (I model an example of this in chapter 13). While mutually determining, there is a major difference in the pace of cultural and genetic change. Changes in gene distribution occur with the passing of generations and in response to rare chance events, while cultural learning may take the form of epidemic diffusion of behaviors, as occurred with the proliferation of the general use of familiar pronouns in many European languages during the course of a single decade, the 1960s.

Whether cultural or genetic, the process of differential replication is commonly modeled using *replicator equations* describing a *replicator dynamic*, introduced below. The replicator dynamic provides an alternative to comparative static analysis and other approaches in which time is not explicitly modeled. It gives us a complete account of out-of-equilibrium movements in population frequencies based both on empirically plausible assumptions about individual cognitive capacities and behaviors and on a representation of the details of social interactions (who meets whom, to do what, with what payoffs, with what information, and the like). Thus, taking *explicit account of out-of-equilibrium dynamics* is a third characteristic of evolutionary approaches.

Two advantages follow from explicit dynamic analysis. First, one discovers what I call *evolutionarily irrelevant equilibria*. Explicit dynamics illuminate the relationship between the solution concepts of the previous chapter — Nash equilibrium and dominance — and the more complete and robust notion of evolutionary stability. We will see (here, in chapter 6, and especially in chapter 12) that under plausible models of differential replication, some Nash equilibria may turn out to be virtually irrelevant to how real societies work, once we take evolutionary processes into account.

A second advantage of explicitly modeling dynamical processes is that there exist nonequilibrium states of substantial importance in the functioning of real-world economies. Because this claim challenges a basic tenet of conventional thinking in economics, let me illustrate it with an empirical example. Many markets exhibit a remarkable long-term coexistence of what one would think of as winners and losers, contrary to what one would expect if economies were approximately in equilibrium. Among firms producing the same products and selling to the same customers in the highly competitive metal-forming industry in the United States in the early 1990s, for example, the most successful firms (as measured by labor productivity) were well over three times as productive as the least, with the 75th percentile about twice the 25th percentile (Luria 1996). In Indonesia's electronics industry — a part of the highly competitive global market — data from the late 1990s show that the firms at the 75th percentile were *eight* times as productive as those in the 25th percentile (Hallward-Driemeier, Iorossi, and Sokoloff 2001). Of course, the Indonesian case is extreme, some of these differences are just statistical noise, and the high-performance firms will expand and the low-performance firms will tend to exit the industry. But the selection process is apparently sufficiently weak, even in these very competitive industries, to cast doubt on the usefulness of the assumption that all firms are operating on the production possibility frontier. The instantaneous implementation of equilibria is of course even less likely to be observed in environments in which entry and exit is more restricted, or in which the actors in question are not specialists in making money but individuals simply going about life.

Abstracting from disequilibrium states on grounds that they are ephemeral is generally a poor guide on practical matters. Continuing the above example, a significant contributor to the end of the post–World War II golden age of rapid productivity growth in the U.S economy was a reduction in the rate at which low productivity firms were being weeded out (Bowles, Gordon, and Weisskopf 1983). The rapid rate of productivity growth in the Swedish economy during the third quarter of the past century was in part due to the shift in labor and other resources from low- to high-productivity firms induced by a deliberate policy of wage equalization and the consequent failure of low-performing firms (Hibbs 2000).

Though insightful on these and other policy issues, the analysis of out-of-equilibrium dynamics is considerably more demanding than the conventional comparative static approach. But long term average behavior of the variables of interest can often be studied analytically or simulated, often yielding quite strong results. Examples are provided in chapters 11 through 13.

A fourth characteristic idea in evolutionary modeling is that *populations are structured hierarchically, and differential replication can take place at more than one level*. Individuals interact with individuals, but individuals also constitute groups (e.g., families, firms) and other higher order entities (e.g., nations, ethnic groups), and these multi-individual groups also interact. Individuals in turn are a grouping of interacting cells. The process of differential replication is typically taking place at many levels simultaneously: within individuals, among individuals, among groups, and so on. For example, within a firm, different behaviors (working hard or being laid back, for example) are being copied or abandoned by individuals, while among firms the organizational structures of the more profitable enterprises are being copied while the least prof-

TABLE 2.1
Some processes underlying the evolution of behaviors

| Replicator | Level of Selection | |
	Individual	Group of Individuals
Learned behaviors	Social learning (conformism, reinforcement learning, best response)	Emulation of other groups' conventions, cultural assimilation of unsuccessful groups
Genes	Differential reproductive success, drift	Biological extinction of unsuccessful groups, reduced fitness of subjugated populations

itable firms are failing. Thus, what is replicated (or not) may be traits of individuals such as their preferences or beliefs; but the institutions and other group-level characteristics of firms, ethnic communities, or nations are also subject to differential replication. An adequate theory must illuminate the process by which group structure emerges in a population of individuals, how the boundaries among the resulting higher-level entities are maintained, and how they pass out of existence. The simultaneous working of differential replication at more than one level, called *multi-level selection* (or group selection), produces what is termed a coevolutionary process governing the dynamic trajectories of both individual and group level characteristics. (An example—the coevolution of individual preferences and group structures—is provided in chapter 13.)

Table 2.1 summarizes the varieties of the processes introduced above, distinguishing between the *replicators* (the traits being copied) and the levels of selection (the units among which the implicit competition for success in replication takes place). A replicator is something that is copied; genes and jokes are replicators, as are individual preferences and beliefs, and group-level conventions and other institutions.

Explaining behaviors and institution by reference to differential replication may seem an obvious tautology. True, differential replication is an accounting system invaluable as a check on the logic of a complex argument. But it is also an analytical framework offering insights that are unlikely to emerge from other perspectives. Of course, making good this claim will require an account of the replication process itself, whether it be the profit-based regulation of the survival or demise of firms with differing organizational structures, the differential biological fitness or cultural emulation of individuals with differing behavioral patterns, the diffusion or demise of society-level institutions through the process of intergroup conflict, or some other selection process.

An example will illuminate some of the distinctive features of the evolutionary approach.

RESIDENTIAL SEGREGATION: AN EVOLUTIONARY PROCESS

How might an evolutionary social scientist explain the coexistence of preferences for multi-racial neighborhoods with the observation that few neighborhoods are integrated? Here is an example, one that illustrates some characteristic outcomes of evolutionary modeling: *multiple equilibria* and the *historical contingency* of outcomes, the pattern of *local homogeneity and global heterogeneity* and the long term *persistence of Pareto-inferior outcomes*. Consider a single neighborhood (one of many) in which all housing units are equally desirable to all members of the population. Individuals' preferences for living in this neighborhood depend solely on the racial composition of the neighborhood. In this neighborhood and in the surrounding population, "greens" prefer to live in a mixed neighborhood in which they outnumber the "blues" by a small fraction, and "blues" correspondingly do not prefer segregation but would rather not be outnumbered by the "greens." I will express these preferences by the price, p_g and p_b, that greens and blues, respectively, would be willing to pay for a house in the neighborhood, each depending on the fraction of homes in the neighborhood occupied by greens, $f \in [0,1]$. The following equations are a way to express the preferences described above (see figure 2.1):

$$p_b(f) = \tfrac{1}{2}(f + \delta) - \tfrac{1}{2}(f + \delta)^2 + p$$
$$p_g(f) = \tfrac{1}{2}(f - \delta) - \tfrac{1}{2}(f - \delta)^2 + p \tag{2.1}$$

with $\delta \in (0, \tfrac{1}{2})$ where p is a positive constant reflecting the intrinsic value of the identical homes. Differentiating both functions with respect to f and setting the result equal to zero, we see that the ideal neighborhood for greens (that which maximizes p_g) is composed of $\tfrac{1}{2} + \delta$ greens, while blues prefer a neighborhood with $\tfrac{1}{2} - \delta$ greens. As the difference between the optimal neighborhoods (that for which they would pay the highest price of a home) of the greens and the blues is 2δ, I will refer to δ as the extent of discriminatory tastes of the two types (δ could differ between the two groups, or one group might not care about the racial composition at all, of course). I will normalize the size of the neighborhood to unity so I can refer indifferently to the fraction of greens and the number of greens.

Suppose that during each time period some fraction α of both the greens and the blues in this neighborhood consider selling their house to a member of the surrounding population. Prospective buyers from outside the neighborhood visit the neighborhood in proportion to the current composition of the neighborhood. The fraction of prospective buyers who are green is thus f. Prospective buyers and sellers are randomly matched; imagine that the house-hunting visitors just knock on the door of a randomly selected house. Thus, in any period the expected number of greens seeking to sell their house who are contacted by a house-hunting blue is $\alpha f(1 - f)$. Each prospective seller meets just one buyer per period, either making a sale or not, the probability of making the sale depending on the difference between the buyer's valuation of the home and the seller's valuation if the former exceeds the latter, both given by eq. (2.1). Thus, if a blue considering selling meets a green and if f is such that $p_g > p_b$ then the probability that a sale will take place is $\beta(p_g - p_b)$ where β is a positive constant relating the price difference to the probability of a sale.

We are interested in the evolution over time of the distribution of types in the neighborhood. Assuming the neighborhood is large enough so that we can take the expected values to be a close approximation of realized values, and using a prime (′) to indicate "next period" we can write f' as a function of f to take account of the fact that in any period some of the greens may sell to a blue while some of the blues may sell to a green. Thus

$$f' = f - \alpha f(1 - f)\rho_b\beta(p_b - p_g) + \alpha(1 - f)f\rho_g\beta (p_g - p_b) \quad (2.2)$$

where $\rho_b = 1$ if $p_b > p_g$ and is zero otherwise, and $\rho_g = 1$ if $p_g \geq p_b$ and is zero otherwise. (Obviously, $\rho_b + \rho_g = 1$.) The equation may be read as follows: the expected fraction green next period is the fraction green this period minus any greens who sold to a blue (the second term on the right hand side), plus any blues who sold to a green (the third term). The second term on the right hand side, for example, is the loss of greens through sales to blues; αf is the number of greens seeking to sell, of these $(1 - f)$ will be matched with a blue, and if the blue's price exceeds the greens' price, the sale will take place with probability $\beta(p_b - p_g)$. The third term may be interpreted analogously, in the case that green prices exceed blue prices, in this case blues selling to greens. Using $p_b + p_g = 1$, we can rearrange the equation as follows:

$$\Delta f = f' - f = \alpha f(1 - f)\beta(p_g - p_b) \quad (2.3)$$

from which it is clear that $\Delta f = 0$ if $p_g = p_b$ (no sales take place among those prospective buyers and sellers of different types who do meet because buyers do not value the homes more than sellers). Note

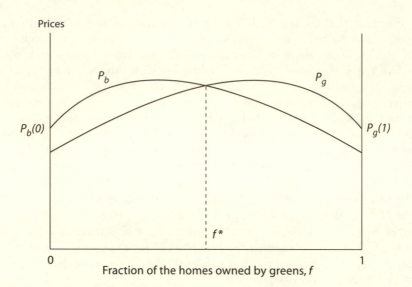

Figure 2.1. Spontaneous segregation in a residential community. The two functions give the maximum value a blue and a green is willing to pay for a home as a function of f, the fraction of the community that is green. Note that both greens and blues prefer an integrated neighborhood to living with their own kind in a completely segregated community.

that $\Delta f = 0$ also if $f = 0$ or $f = 1$ (the neighborhood is visited only by prospective buyers of the same type as the homogeneous population already there). Equation (2.3) is called a "replicator dynamic equation." With some further rearranging it can be rewritten in the sometimes more convenient form $\Delta f = \alpha f \beta (p_g - \underline{p})$ where $\underline{p}$ is the average price or $\underline{p} = f p_g + (1 - f) p_b$.

A stationary value of f is a stable equilibrium if an exogenous change in f produces (by the dynamic described in eq. 2.3) a Δf of the opposite sign, that is, if $d\Delta f/df < 0$. If this inequality holds, a change in f is self-correcting. Figure 2.1 illustrates this model. Inspection of the figure (or a little calculation) confirms that a half-blue–half-green composition of the neighborhood is an equilibrium ($\Delta f = 0$, because $p_g = p_b$), but it is not stable (because $d\Delta f/df > 0$) so a small chance displacement of the fraction from the fifty-fifty distribution will not be self-correcting but rather will cumulate, leading to a completely segregated neighborhood. Notice, too, that for $\delta < \frac{1}{4}$ both greens and blues would prefer the integrated neighborhood to the segregated outcome, even if the segregation resulted in only "their" types living in the neighborhood. (The above can be confirmed by checking that $p_b(\frac{1}{2}) = p_g(\frac{1}{2}) > p_g(1) = p_b(0)$.)

Thus, the segregated stable equilibria that we expect to be the only durable outcomes of this interaction are *Pareto inferior* to a set of integrated neighborhood compositions that are unsustainable as stable equilibria in this model. Remarkably, this result holds even if δ is arbitrarily small; complete segregation results even if the two groups have virtually identical tastes and the optimal neighborhood for both is very close to fifty-fifty. Finally, confirming that complete segregation (of either type) is a stable equilibrium is easy. Thus, neighborhoods will be *locally homogeneous* while otherwise identical neighborhoods will be composed entirely of the other group, exhibiting *global heterogeneity*. Which composition a neighborhood will exhibit will be *historically contingent*: if, in the recent past, f was less than f^*, we would expect to find $f = 0$, for example.

The coordination failure arising in this case comes about because when a household decides to live in a community, its choice affects the well-being of residents in the community to which it moves as well as the one it left. The composition of a community is thus both the "commodity" that the family is choosing and the unintended product of the choices of all families. There is no reason why the resulting outcome will be efficient, whether sorting is based on preferences for racial composition, as here, for highly educated neighbors (Benabou 1993), or for neighbors who are homeowners (Hoff and Sen 2002), or for other reasons.

I have modeled the process of market equilibration by explicitly tracking the results of social interactions (who meets whom, and what do they do). Individuals made use of only local knowledge: they did not seek out the very best deal, they simply made a transaction with positive probability as long as it was mutually beneficial and not otherwise. The racial composition of the neighborhood was determined by a replication process that determined the occupation of residences by members of one or another group. The dynamics of neighborhood composition was derived by studying which residences replicated their ownership pattern and which ones switched. In chapter 6 I will contrast this social interaction approach to modeling markets with the Walrasian model.

Modeling the Evolution of Behavior

Like the racial composition of the neighborhood, the distributions of individual behavioral rules or institutional characteristics of groups in a population and their evolution over time depends on which traits are copied and which are abandoned. "Traits" are any characteristic of an individual or group that may be adapted by others, abandoned, or retained. If the children of Catholics are likely to retain their parents' religion and the children of Protestants are not, the fraction of Catholics in the population will rise (assuming that all families have the same number of children and that these are the only two types in the population). If firms recognizing a trade union among its employees fail at a higher rate than nonunion firms, and if new firms tend to copy the more profitable firms, union density will fall.

Differential replication may result from people or organizations deliberately seeking to acquire traits, rules, and so on that have proven successful to others. Differential replication, however, may also take place through less instrumental means: the process of copying may be described by a *conformist transmission process* according to which the replication of traits is frequency dependent, the more prevalent traits in a population being favored.[1] And though sometimes called "spontaneous," the process of differential replication may work through the coercive exercise of power by nations, classes, or organizations, as when those who lose wars are constrained to adopt the culture, schooling, and constitutions of winners.

The details of the transmission process are important, and I will take up these and other more complicated cases in subsequent chapters when I model how economic and other institutions shape the evolution of preferences. Here I model an important, if overly simple case in which successful behaviors are copied. This is the process of *payoff monotonic updating*, namely, the class of transmission mechanisms with the property that behaviors with above-average payoffs are adopted by others and thus increase their share of the population. I also assume that individuals are *randomly paired* to interact.

Let there be one of two mutually exclusive traits (x and y) present in each member of a large population.[2] The traits may be adherence to differing behavioral rules, food tastes, or any durable aspect of behavior that affects payoffs. Thus x might be "price goods at their marginal cost," "work hard," "have an additional child," "reciprocate gifts," or "eat a healthy breakfast each day." The trait y represents an alternative rule in each case. The model is readily extended to populations with more than two traits. I model the evolution of *cultural traits*, namely, those that are acquired through learning (from parents, others in the previous generation, peers, etc.) rather than through genetic inheritance.

[1] Some reasons for thinking conformist transmission to be important are offered in Boyd and Richerson (1985) and Bowles (2001). A model of conformist updating is presented in chapter 11.

[2] The mathematics of dynamical systems analysis underlying the models presented here is clearly reviewed in Weibull (1995) and presented more fully in Hirsch and Smale (1974).

Thus, the model below represents behavioral updating as a process of switching from one trait to another rather than the differential production of offspring. (But the model below is readily adapted to the case of genetic transmission of traits, as I will show in the Hawk Dove example below.) I ask how many copies of each trait are made at the end of each period. (An individual who leaves no copies in the next period has switched to another trait; one who leaves two copies has retained his trait and been copied by another.) Notice that the individuals live forever and are simply bearers of the traits; it is the traits themselves that will be more or less successful in generating copies. I normalize the size of the population to unity.

The structure of the transmission process is this: individuals implement the strategy dictated by their trait in a game that assigns payoffs to each depending on their and others' behaviors. Following this, the traits are replicated with the traits whose bearers gained higher payoffs making relatively more copies and thus generating a new population frequency of the traits. Suppose members of the population are randomly paired to interact in a symmetrical two-person game, the payoffs of which are denoted $\pi(i, j)$, the payoff to playing trait i against a j-playing partner. For any population frequency of the x trait, $p \in [0,1]$, the expected payoffs are thus

$$
\begin{aligned}
b_x(p) &= p\pi(x, x) + (1 - p)\pi(x, y) \\
b_y(p) &= p\pi(y, x) + (1 - p)\pi(y, y)
\end{aligned}
\tag{2.4}
$$

Read the first equation: "With probability p an x-person is paired with another x-person gaining payoff $\pi(x, x)$, and with probability $(1 - p)$ is paired with a y-person gaining payoff $\pi(x, y)$."

At the beginning of each period, some fraction of the population, $\omega \in (0, 1]$, may update their trait upon exposure to a "cultural model" (a competitor, a teacher, a coworker, or a neighbor, for example). The remainder of the population does not update irrespective of their experiences. The fact that not all members of the population are in updating mode captures the fact that we typically adopt behaviors — often during adolescence — and then retain them over a period of time. Of course, the updating concerning some traits may be very frequent — preferred manner of dress, for example — while we update other traits only very occasionally — religion, for example. How quickly we update, like the other aspects of the learning process being modeled, is not given but itself responds to evolutionary pressures, but we simplify here by abstracting from the endogenous nature of the updating process itself.

If the cultural model and the individual have the same trait, it is retained by the individual; this will happen with probabilities p and $(1 - p)$ for the x's and y's, respectively (both the model and the individual produce a single replica — themselves — in the next period). But if the individual and the model have different traits, then the individual retains or replaces the trait on the basis of the payoffs enjoyed by the two in the previous period. The payoffs experienced by the cultural model and the individual depend on the particular pairing experienced by the two and hence vary with the population frequency of each trait. Of course, the individual could sample from the payoff experiences of a larger group rather than simply comparing his own payoffs with the model's, but this would make little difference at this point. If the individual switches, then the model has made two replicas, and the individual none. (In chapter 11, I use this model to study the emergence and spread of individual property rights.)

Consider a cultural model (a y-person) and an individual x-person, who experienced payoffs B_y and B_x, respectively, the previous period (these will not generally be equal to b_y and b_x, respectively, due to matching noise). A small difference in payoffs need not induce a switch or even be noticed, so we say that with probability $\beta(B_y - B_x)$ the x-person will switch if $B_x < B_y$. If $B_x \geq B_y$, the individual does not switch. The coefficient β is a positive constant reflecting the greater effect on switching of relatively large payoff differences, scaled so that the probability of switching varies over the unit interval. Letting $\rho_{y>x} = 1$ if the payoff of the y-person exceeds that of the x-person and zero otherwise, and taking expected values (the population is large), we can write the expected population frequency with trait x in time $t + 1$, denoted by p', as

$$p' = p - \omega p(1 - p)\rho_{y>x}\beta(b_y - b_x) \\ + \omega p(1 - p)(1 - \rho_{y>x})\beta(b_x - b_y) \qquad (2.5)$$

This expression may be read as follows: in any period there are p x-persons, and a fraction of these, ω, will be eligible for updating, each of these ωp x-persons will be paired with a y-model with probability $(1 - p)$, and with probability $\rho_{y>x}\beta(b_y - b_x)$ the information they acquire about payoffs will lead them to switch. Offsetting the x's lost in this manner, some of the y-individuals will encounter x-models and by an analogous process will convert to x-persons. Rearranging, we can rewrite eq. (2.5) as

$$\Delta p = p' - p = \omega p(1 - p)\beta(b_x - b_y) \qquad (2.6)$$

From eq. (2.6) it can be seen that the direction and pace of updating depends on the value of p in two ways. First, $p(1 - p)$, the variance of the trait, measures the number of x-persons who will be paired with a y-person, extreme values of p making this very unlikely. Second (writing it so as to make explicit the functional dependence of the b's on p) the expression $\omega\beta\{b_x(p) - b_y(p)\}$ captures the effect of p on payoffs and thereby on updating. Notice that larger values of ω and β—a larger fraction in updating mode, and individual switching more responsive to payoff differences—accelerate the dynamic when $b_x \neq b_y$. Writing $\underline{b} = pb_x + (1 - p)b_y$ as the population average payoff, eq. (2.6) is more compactly expressed as

$$\Delta p = \omega p \beta(b_x - \underline{b}), \qquad (2.6')$$

which is the general form (applicable to any number of traits) of the discrete-time *replicator dynamic*, a way of modeling dynamical systems formalized by Taylor and Jonker (1978) with wide applicability in population biology and the evolutionary social sciences.[3]

As eq. (2.6) makes clear, there are two necessary components in this analysis of evolutionary change: *variance* and *differential replication*. Variance, represented by the term $p(1 - p)$, is essential because the more nearly homogeneous a population is, the slower will be the evolutionary process. Notice that $p(1 - p)$ reaches a maximum for $p = \frac{1}{2}$, so an evenly divided population will maximize the rate of change in p, holding other influences constant. Differential replication—sometimes termed *selection*—is represented by the term $\omega\beta\{b_x(p) - b_y(p)\}$. The pressure of differential replication (or selective pressure) will be weak if a small fraction of the population is in updating mode, if payoff differences are small, or if the response to payoff differences is small. Eq. (2.6) or (2.6') gives a complete description of the relevant one-dimensional dynamical system. As there are just two traits, the *state space* in this application, namely, all possible outcomes, is simply all of the values that p may take over the unit interval. For this reason the resulting dynamical system is termed "one-dimensional." *Notice that eq. (2.6) is identical to the expression describing the dynamics of the segregated residential housing market, eq. (2.3).*

For every value of p the replicator equation gives the mapping $\Delta p = \gamma(p)$, where the function γ, termed a *vector field*, defines for each state in the state space the direction and velocity of change at the state. We are generally interested in knowing the states p^* such that $\gamma(p^*) = 0$, called *stationary states* (also called rest points or a critical points of the dynamic), and the stability properties of these states, determined

---

[3] I have expressed the replicator equation in discrete rather than continuous time because many of the problems to be addressed in the pages that follow are characterized by natural units of time (such as a generation), giving the discrete time version a more transparent interpretation. The continuous and discrete time dynamics differ somewhat, though not in ways that are important for what follows (Weibull 1995).

by $\gamma(p^* + \varepsilon)$, where ε is an arbitrarily small perturbation of p. From eq. (2.6′) it is clear that $\Delta p = 0$ if

$$b_x(p) - b_y(p) = 0 \qquad (2.7)$$

or if p is either 0 or 1 (because when $p = 1$, $b_x = \underline{b}$). For $p \in (0,1)$ Δp takes the sign of $b_x - b_y$, expressing the fact that updating is payoff-monotonic.

Given the one dimensionality of this dynamical system, the stability properties of its stationary states are easy to describe: an equilibrium is asymptotically stable (self-correcting) if the derivative of eq. (2.6′) with respect to p is negative (that is $d\Delta p/dp < 0$) requiring that:

$$\frac{db_y}{dp} - \frac{db_x}{dp} = \pi(y, x) - \pi(y, y) - \pi(x, x) + \pi(x, y) > 0. \qquad (2.8)$$

This says, as one would expect, that should the population frequency of x's increase for some exogenous reason, the expected payoff difference between the y's and the x's will increase (so the increase in x will be negated by the fact that it creates a situation differentially favoring the y's.) *Asymptotic stability* of a stationary state, p^*, means that all sufficiently small perturbations in the population composition will result in changes leading back to p^*. *Lyapunov stability* requires only that all small perturbations in p will not result in further movements *away* from p^*. (Lyapunov stability is sometimes termed *neutral stability*.) I will use the term "stability" (without adjective) to refer to the stronger, asymptotic (self-correcting) concept. Asymptotic stability obviously implies Lyapunov stability. The distinction between the two stability concepts becomes important when individual behaviors are subject to (even arbitrarily small amounts of) stochastic influences such as mutation, or idiosyncratic (non–best response) play. An illustration is provided in chapter 11. Eq. (2.8) expresses the intuition that asymptotically stable equilibria must be characterized by negative feedbacks: increases in the frequency of x's reducing the relative advantage of the x's.[4] Where eq. (2.8) fails to obtain (and is strictly less than zero), the equilibrium is unstable due to positive feedbacks: a chance increase in p will benefit the x's more than the y's and thereby displace p away from p^*.

The process of updating can then be explored in two ways. First, if an interior equilibrium is stable, we can study the way that exogenous influences might displace the equilibrium by exploring how p^* is affected

----

[4] There is a technical difficulty that I do not address. In the discrete time dynamic treated here it is possible that the updating process moves p in the direction of p^* when it is perturbed, but that overshooting takes place. I assume that the time period is short enough (and hence ω is small enough) to preclude this.

by changes in the underlying game and updating process. This would be done by differentiating the equilibrium condition (2.7) with respect to exogenous determinants of the replicator equation, including not only whatever technological and other data determine the structure of payoffs and other aspects of the game but also such institutionally determined aspects of the transmission process as the pairing rule for the game or for meeting cultural models, the frequency of given actors meeting, and the possible presence of influences on updating other than payoffs, such as conformism. I will use this approach to study the effect of economic institutions on the evolution of preferences in chapters 3, 7, and 11.

Second, if a unique interior unstable equilibrium exists, we will have two stable equilibria with a homogeneous population of either all x or all y (as in the case of the segregated housing market). In this case we may want to study the path-dependent process by which we may end up at one or the other. To do this we would look at the *basin of attraction* of each stable stationary state, defined as the set of initial states for which the unperturbed dynamical system moves toward that equilibrium. In the one-dimensional system studied here, should the unique interior stationary state p^* be unstable, then the basin (or interval) of attraction of $p = 0$ is the range of values of p over which $\Delta p = \gamma(p) < 0$ and hence the population will gravitate towards $p = 0$. Thus the interior (unstable) equilibrium p^* divides the unit interval into the two basins of attraction, with $\Delta p > 0$ for $p > p^*$ and $\Delta p < 0$ for $p < p^*$. In the housing segregation model the basin of attraction of the all blue equilibrium is given for values of $f < f^*$.

As we will see, many of the simplifications used in deriving the model can be relaxed. But there is a crucial assumption in the above reasoning that is at once essential, hard to do without, and quite limiting. I took expected values as a reasonable approximation of actual payoffs, but the size of many of the populations we study—the residents in the neighborhood studied in the previous section, or the employees of a firm—is far too small to justify this assumption. Thus, for example, if p is the frequency of x-persons and pairing is random, the expected number of x's paired with an x was given as p^2 but by chance the value could be as large as p (assuming an even number of x's) or as few as zero, and both will happen quite frequently in small groups. This problem of matching noise and other small-n influences on the evolutionary dynamic may seem a quibble, but it is not. In chapters 12 and 13 you will see that the small size of groups combined with chance makes a big difference not only in the pace but also in the direction of evolutionary dynamics.

A second limitation of the replicator dynamic is that the equations defining the system do not depend on time, that is, the system is *autono-*

mous or *time homogeneous*. Thus, the system abstracts from histori-cally varying influences on the equations, such as the state of knowl-edge, technology, institutional facts taken as given, or the weather. Of course, if we understood the dynamics of these time-varying influences, we could include them as state variables in the dynamical system. Whether the time-homogeneous nature of the replicator dynamic is a problem or not depends on the question at hand; for many problems, abstracting from, say, climate change is reasonable and for some it is not. The interpretation of the emergence of individual property rights in chapter 11 is a case in which variations in weather make a significant difference. If the selection processes described by the replicator dynamic are slow relative to the changes in the underlying technologies and other exogenous data defining the underlying game, the dynamical system may never reach the neighborhood of the stationary values of p (as these will be continually displaced by exogenous changes.)

A third problem with the replicator dynamic is suggested by its name: it cannot be used to study innovation. To study genuine novelty (as opposed to differential replication of existing traits), I need to introduce the complementary concept of an evolutionarily stable strategy.

Evolutionary Stability and Societal Outcomes

Under what conditions can a population be "invaded" by a new trait? Concrete examples of such an invasion include the rapid spread of the practice of having small rather than large families in many countries over the past century. Or think of late feudal European society, "in-vaded" by a small number of Italian and other merchants using entirely new business practices such as double-entry bookkeeping and the com-munity responsibility system of contractual enforcement (Greif 2002, Padgett 2002). The invaders prospered and eventually transformed the feudal order. Other examples include corrupt business practices invad-ing a community of honest traders, or the deferential forms of address of a linguistic community being invaded by familiar pronouns.

While the replicator dynamic is a convenient analytical tool, a trait absent from a population in period t cannot be copied in period $t + 1$. Recall that the stationarity condition for p is satisfied at $p = 1$ and $p = 0$, irrespective of the payoffs that might accrue to the absent strat-egy, were it present. These values of p are always stationary in the repli-cator dynamic but may not be Nash equilibria and may not be asymp-totically stable: small perturbations around $p = 0$ and $p = 1$ may not be self-correcting. It is not difficult to extend replicator dynamic models to take account of both innovations and chance; we will return to these stochastic evolutionary models in the closing chapters. Here, rather than explicitly incorporating chance into the replicator equation, we will introduce a handy shortcut for getting innovation into the picture, the notion of evolutionary stability.

Not surprisingly, biologists pioneered the modeling of innovation. Their interest in whether a small number of mutants could proliferate in a large population motivated the key concept of an *evolutionarily stable strategy*. The basic idea is that a population all playing an evolutionary stable strategy will repel an invasion of individuals playing some other strategy. Consider a large (strictly, infinite) population in which individuals are randomly paired to interact (along the lines of the model immediately above.) Suppose, as above, that we are considering two behavioral traits, x and y. Trait y is evolutionarily stable against x if there exists some positive fraction of the population, $p^\sim$, such that if the fraction of the population playing x is less than $p^\sim$, then the incumbent strategy (y) will produce more replicas than x and hence will eliminate the entrant. I will introduce a case shortly in which you will see that the "*invasion barrier*" $p^\sim \in (0, 1)$ is an unstable interior equilibrium and it defines the boundary of the basin of attraction of $p = 0$ and $p = 1$ mentioned above.

To see what evolutionary stability entails, we want to know what will happen in a large population composed entirely of y's if a small number of x's are introduced. Using eq. (2.6′), this means evaluating Δp at $p = \varepsilon$ where ε is arbitrarily small. We know that Δp will have the sign of

$$b_x(\varepsilon) - b_y(\varepsilon) =$$
$$\{\varepsilon\pi(x, x) + (1 - \varepsilon)\pi(x, y)\} - \{\varepsilon\pi(y, x) - (1 - \varepsilon)\pi(y, y)\}$$

A behavioral trait y is an *evolutionarily stable strategy* (ESS) with respect to some other strategy x if and only if $b_x(\varepsilon) - b_y(\varepsilon) < 0$, which for arbitrarily small ε is the case when

$$\pi(y, y) > \pi(x, y) \qquad (2.9)$$

or when

$$\pi(y, y) = \pi(x, y) \qquad \text{and} \qquad \pi(y, x) > \pi(x, x).$$

Thus, an ESS is a best response to *itself* (at least weakly, and if it is a weak best response to itself then the other strategy is not a best response to *it*self). As small perturbations of p around an ESS are (by the above reasoning) self-correcting, we know that every ESS is a symmetric Nash equilibrium that is asymptotically stable in the replicator dynamic. Where the mutant may be a weak best response to itself (that is, the last inequality in eq. (2.9) is not strict, but instead $\pi(y,x) \geq \pi(x,x)$)

then y may be *neutrally stable*: the invader may not be eliminated, but it will not proliferate as a result of payoff monotonic updating, either.[5] Of course, such a *neutrally stable state* (NSS) can be invaded through a process of drift (that is, further exogenously generated innovations) and this has important implications in some applications (see, e.g., chapter 11). The NSS and the ESS are thus increasingly stringent evolutionary refinements of Nash equilibria. Every ESS is an NSS and every NSS is a Nash equilibrium; but of course the converse is not true.

The converse of evolutionary stability is the capacity to invade, which Axelrod and Hamilton (1981) termed *initial viability*.[6] If x is initially viable against y then y is not an ESS. Notice that y's status as an ESS with respect to x says nothing about its status with respect to some other trait k or two mutants k and x occurring simultaneously.

We often want to know if a mixed population (that is, one for which $p \in (0, 1)$) is invadeable by a rare mutant. We can do this by noting that a population, all of which adopts the same mixed strategy, is for this reason homogeneous in strategies even though it is behaviorally heterogeneous in the sense that at any given moment different individuals take different actions. Representing the polymorphic population as one in which all individuals adopt a mixed strategy (playing x and y with probability p^* and $(1 - p^*)$ respectively), we can refer to this mixed strategy as an *interior* (or *mixed*) ESS with respect to some other strategy k if, should a small number of k's be introduced, they would be eliminated. For p^* to be an ESS, it must be stationary and asymptotically stable in the replicator dynamic; were this not the case, the expected payoffs to the strategies making up the mixed population (called the *support* of the mixed strategy) would be unequal in the neighborhood of p^*, so the payoff to one of these strategies in the support would exceed the payoff to the mixed strategy and a mutant bearing this pure strategy could invade.

Just as the replicator model is uninformative about dynamics on the "edges" of a population (that is, for $p = 0$ or $p = 1$), the concepts of initial viability and evolutionary stability are unilluminating about the dynamic governing p when it is interior. It is generally useful to combine the two approaches, asking of the stationary extreme values of p whether it is an ESS, that is, asymptotically stable.

The Hawk Dove Game illustrates these concepts. As everyone knows, Hawks are hawkish, and Doves are peace loving. The game is commonly applied to culturally or genetically transmitted human behavioral traits such as aggression and sharing, but it was initially developed to

---

[5] Thus every NSS is Lyapunov stable.
[6] In biological usage, "viable" means capable of living and developing normally.

TABLE 2.2
Hawk Dove Game (row player's payoffs)

	Hawk	Dove
Hawk	$a = (v-c)/2$	$b = v$
Dove	$c = 0$	$d = v/2$

Note: fitness (number of offspring produced)
is equal to ϕ plus the game payoffs.

study contests among other animals. Here is the game. Doves, when they meet, share a prize, while when Hawks meet, they fight over the prize, inflicting costs on one another; and when a Hawk meets a Dove, the Hawk takes the prize. A similar account maintaining the feathered metaphor but actually applying to automobiles, makes it a "chicken" game in which the "hang tough" drivers never swerve, so when they meet, they crash, but when they meet a "chicken" (one who swerves), they garner (presumably psychological) benefits, while the swerver is humiliated. The prize to be divided is v, the cost of losing a fight is c, and the probability of a Hawk winning a contest against another Hawk (they are identical) is ½. Doves divide the prize equally and without cost. Thus, the payoff matrix is as shown in table 2.2, from which it is readily seen that as long as $c > v$ neither H nor D is an ESS. (A handy way to search for ESS's in large matrices of row payoffs is to ask: is the entry in the main diagonal the largest entry in the column? If it is, that column represents an ESS.)

Members of this population are randomly paired, so letting $b_h(p)$ and $b_d(p)$ be the expected payoff to being a Hawk and a Dove, respectively, in a population in which the fraction of hawks is p, the expected payoffs illustrated in figure 2.2 are:

$$b_h(p) = pa + (1 - p)b$$
$$b_d(p) = pc + (1 - p)d \tag{2.10}$$

To illustrate the use of the replicator equation in a fitness-based evolutionary process, assume that at the end of a period, each member of the population produces a number of exact replicas (excluding mutations) equal to φ plus the payoff to the game, so the payoffs are in units of offspring surviving to reproductive age, that is, *fitness* (φ is called the "baseline fitness"). The assumption that a single member (rather than a pair) produces offspring simplifies the modeling; this *clonal* or *asexual* reproductive assumption is a simple (and often useful) alternative to the more realistic modeling of replicator processes based on sexual re-

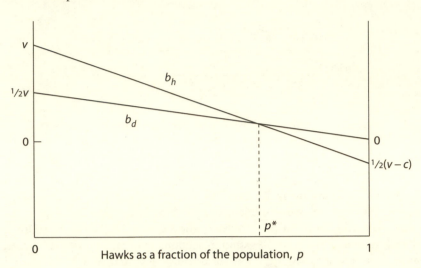

Figure 2.2 Frequency-dependent payoffs in the Hawk Dove Game. The number of replicas is equal to the payoffs plus a constant.

production. Normalizing the total population to unity, we can write next year's population frequency of hawks, p' as

$$p' = \frac{p(b_h + \varphi)}{pb_h + (1-p)b_d + \varphi} \qquad (2.11)$$

Read the numerator to say, "There were p Hawks in the population this year and each of them made $b_h + \varphi$ offspring, giving us $p(b_h + \varphi)$ Hawks next year." The denominator gives us the total number of Hawks and Doves combined, next year. Given the normalization of population size to unity, the total replicas made is also equal to the average or $\bar{b}$.

We are interested in Δp, so subtracting p from both sides of eq. (2.11) we have

$$\Delta p \equiv p' - p = \frac{p(b_h + \varphi)}{\underline{b}} - \frac{p\{p(b_h + \varphi) + (1-p)(b_d + \varphi)\}}{\underline{b}} \qquad (2.12)$$

which, with a little rearranging, and using the values in the payoff matrix to express $(b_h - b_d)$ as $\frac{1}{2}(v - pc)$, gives us

$$\underline{b}\Delta p = p(1 - p)(b_h - b_d) = p(1 - p)\frac{1}{2}(v - pc), \qquad (2.12')$$

which is exactly the replicator dynamic equation already derived (by different routes) for the model of residential segregation and the general case of cultural trait updating presented in previous sections.

Stationary interior values of p are those for which $b_h(p) = b_d(p)$, so using eq. (2.10) and solving for p^*, the stationary frequency of Hawks in the population, we have

$$p^* = \frac{b-d}{b+c-a-d} = \frac{v}{c} \qquad (2.13)$$

from which it can be seen that the equilibrium fraction of Hawks is increasing in the prize and decreasing in the cost of fights, as one would expect. (You can check that $p^* = v/c$ is stationary by substituting this value into eq. (2.12′).) The equal payoff condition defining stationarity of p makes it clear that p^* is a Nash equilibrium: if the fraction of Hawks is p^*, then both strategies are weak best responses.

Is the equilibrium above stable? We see that

$$\frac{d(b_h - b_d)}{dp} = \frac{d\{^1/_2(v - pc)\}}{dp} = -^1/_2 c < 0 \qquad (2.14)$$

so an increase in the prevalence of Hawks will disadvantage Hawks relatively speaking (thereby inducing a reduction in Hawk frequency next period). The stability condition (2.14) requires that the Hawks' expected payoff function in figure 2.2 is "steeper" (the absolute value of its slope is larger) than that for Doves, expressing the negative feedbacks referred to above. Both $p = 0$ and $p = 1$ are also stationary in the replicator dynamic (the latter because $b_h(1) = \underline{b}(1)$). However, neither is a Nash equilibrium as can be seen from the fact that $b_h(0) > b_d(0)$ and $b_h(1) < b_d(1)$. This is just a reminder that if there is only one strategy to replicate, a population frequency governed by a replicator dynamic will remain unchanged. But such a population may be invadeable by a mutant.

The existence and stability properties of an interior equilibrium are related to the ESS concept in the following way (for the general case in which the strategy set is (x, y) and p is the fraction of the population who are x-types: if neither strategy is an ESS there will be an asymptotically stable interior equilibrium. Likewise, if both strategies are ESSs there will be an unstable interior equilibrium while both $p = 0$ and $p = 1$ are asymptotically stable (as you can confirm is the case in the Assurance Game introduced below). In this case, the unstable interior equilibrium is the invasion barrier $(p^\sim)$ that is part of the definition of the ESS. These correspondences are summarized for a population game with two strategies, x and y, in table 2.3.

Does the analysis of evolutionary stability support predictions about outcomes? If neither x nor y are ESSs, if innovation is not precluded and if the updating process is governed by the replicator dynamic, we get a clear prediction: population frequencies at or near p^* should be

TABLE 2.3
ESS and the existence and stability of interior equilibrium

	y *is an ESS*	y *is not an ESS*
x *is an ESS*	$p^* \in (0, 1)$ unstable	$p^* = 1$ stable
x *is not an ESS*	$p^* = 0$ stable	$p^* \in (0, 1)$ stable

Note: p^* is a fraction of the population that are x-types that is stationary in the replicator dynamic.

commonly observed. If this is the case, returning to the examples, we would expect to find the coexistence of large and small families, corrupt and honest business practices, and the like. We get clear predictions in two other cases as well: if one strategy is an ESS and the other is not, then we would expect to find a population composed entirely of the ESS. This is because under the stated conditions any practice that can invade will continue to gain adherents until it is universal.

What of the case in which both x and y are evolutionary stable strategies? As we have seen in chapter 1, this is a case in which history will matter, but can we say more than that? Suppose the members of a large population are paired randomly to play the symmetric Assurance Game whose payoffs appear in table 2.4 — for example, a variant of the Palanpur planting problem in chapter 1 with cooperating and defecting representing planting early and late, respectively, and with the payoff as indicated. As it is an Assurance Game, both CC and DD are mutual best responses, so the payoffs must be such that $c < a$ and $b < d$, and (continuing the Palanpur example), we will further assume that $a > d$. Then letting $p \in [0,1]$ be the fraction of defectors in the population, we can write expected payoffs as a function of p, and equating the expected payoffs to Cooperate and Defect we find the stationary value of p,

$$p^* = \frac{c - a}{b - a + c - d}$$

TABLE 2.4
Assurance Game (row payoffs)

	Cooperate	*Defect*
Cooperate	$\pi(C, C) = a$	$\pi(C, D) = b$
Defect	$\pi(D, C) = c$	$\pi(D, D) = d$

Note: $\pi(D, C) < \pi(C, C) > \pi(D, D) > \pi(C, D)$

Writing b_c and b_d as the expected payoffs to Cooperate and Defect, the denominator is just the effect of variations in p on the difference between the payoffs to Cooperate and the payoffs to Defect or

$$\frac{d(b_c - b_d)}{dp} = \pi(C, D) - \pi(C, C) + \pi(D, C) - \pi(D, D) = b - a + c - d < 0.$$

What this means is that if $\varepsilon > 0$, then $b_c(p^* + \varepsilon) < b_d(p^* + \varepsilon)$ so defectors are relatively advantaged, and a small increase in the frequency of defectors will cause further increases in p. Similar reasoning shows that $p = 0$ and $p = 1$ are ESSs (and hence are symmetric Nash equilibria that are stable in the replicator dynamic).

"History matters" in this situation because, barring exogenous events, a population for which $p < p^*$ in the recent past, will move towards $p = 0$. But to see that we can sometimes say more, suppose we were to observe a large number of islands on which isolated groups of individuals play this same single-shot Assurance Game over a long period of time. We are told that at some prior point, their strategies had all been determined randomly, after which they updated according to the above replicator dynamic. If the unstable interior equilibrium p^* is less than $\frac{1}{2}$, then we would be right to predict that most of the groups would be composed entirely of defectors. If strategies were initially randomly chosen, then the expected value of the initial population frequency would be $\frac{1}{2}$, and therefore it would be true that for most groups $p > p^*$, which implies that $\Delta p > 0$. As a result, most groups would have evolved to uniform defection. Notice that this may occur even if (as in the Palanpur example) mutual cooperation is payoff dominant: where the mutual defect equilibrium is risk dominant we know (from the definition of risk dominance) that $p^* < \frac{1}{2}$ so the basin of attraction of the all defect equilibrium will be the larger of the two. The outcome with the larger basin of attraction occurs with higher probability simply because chance events are more likely to place the population in larger rather than smaller basins of attraction.

The Assurance Game with stochastically determined initial conditions illustrates two important if somewhat counterintuitive results. First, adding stochastic variation to a model may allow stronger predictions than would be attainable in a model without chance. Predicting that all Defect in the above example as the likely outcome is more informative than saying that "history matters." In this case, chance provides what is called an *equilibrium selection* device, that is, a way of identifying a particular equilibrium as more the likely outcome of a game when there is more than one equilibrium. Second, even asymptotically stable Nash equilibria may be virtually irrelevant to predicting societal outcomes; in this case, chance selects against the payoff-dominant equilibrium.

Cases of this type are the subject of stochastic evolutionary game theory. In chapter 12, I will apply the idea that chance sometimes is a strong equilibrium selection device to explain why some institutions are more common than others, and to investigate the process of institutional innovation. What determines the size of the basin of attraction of an equilibrium and what stochastic or other processes might propel a population from one basin of attraction to another thus emerge as key questions. But a simpler example of the relationship between games and institutional evolution will be more useful here.

THE EVOLUTION OF PROPERTY RIGHTS

The Hawk Dove Game may shed some light on the constitutional issues raised in chapter 1. Is the population equilibrium $p^* = v/c$ a desirable outcome? Clearly not. The average payoff is maximized for $p = 0$, that is, when there are no Hawks at all. Thus the equilibrium in this population is Pareto inferior to any $p < p^*$ (notice in figure 2.2 the payoff to both Hawks and Doves is declining in the fraction of Hawks, so *both* are better off the fewer Hawks there are). The Hawk Dove equilibrium is a biological analogue to a market failure: the stationary distribution of genetically determined behavioral types in the population generated by natural selection based on differential fitness fails to maximize average fitness. At p^*, both Hawks and Doves are best responding; neither could increase fitness by switching type (were this possible). But average fitness is maximized at $p = 0$. This is hardly surprising given that the reproductive success of each type — its fitness — fails to take into account the effect each exerts on the fitness of the others.

Given the Hobbesian nightmare of grabbing and fighting that the Hawk Dove equilibrium describes, it is not surprising that the game has been used to explore the possibility of a spontaneous emergence of conventions concerning ownership and division of valued resources. The possibilities include banning Hawks, labeling Hawks and giving Doves the option to refuse any interaction with a Hawk, adopting a pairing rule that makes like-with-like pairings more common (and thereby ensuring that the costs of Hawkery will be more fully borne by Hawks, thus internalizing the external dis-economies they generate), flipping a coin when Hawks meet rather than fighting to determine who gets V, and so on.

The constitutional and evolutionary issues can now be joined: how can the structure of social interactions — who is paired with whom, to

TABLE 2.5
Hawk Dove Bourgeois Game (row player's payoffs)

	Hawk	Dove	Bourgeois
Hawk	$(v-c)/2$	v	$v/2 + (v-c)/4$
Dove	0	$v/2$	$v/4$
Bourgeois	$(v-c)/4$	$v/2 + v/4$	$v/2$

play which games—be arranged to yield desirable outcomes in populations of autonomous actors like those described above? And under what conditions are these institutional remedies likely to be evolutionarily successful (that is, to be capable of proliferating when rare)? For the game above this means: what changes in the structure of social interactions could reduce p^*, the equilibrium fraction of Hawks, or even eliminate Hawks entirely?

The waste that characterizes the Hawk-Dove equilibrium results from Hawks fighting, not from their exploitation of Doves (the latter may seem unjust, but it is carried out without waste). So a solution is to find a way to reduce the number of contested interactions. One way, proposed by one of the originators of the game, the biologist John Maynard Smith (1974), is to suppose that the prize is a site, such as a spider's web or a foraging territory, that is occupied or possessed at any moment by one of the two in the pair, and then to introduce a strategy that is conditioned on one's ownership status. The strategy Maynard Smith suggested is "if owner play Hawk, if intruder play Dove," which he labeled "Bourgeois" (see table 2.5).

Assume that possession is never in question and that in any interaction the members of the pair have an equal probability of being an owner. For example, when a Bourgeois meets a Hawk, half of the time Bourgeois is not the possessor and so acts like a Dove, avoiding a fight, while the other half of the time Bourgeois, as owner, fights (which the Hawk of course also does) and with probability ½ wins, yielding an expected payoff of $(v - c)/4$. Then the expanded strategy set and expected payoff matrix looks like the figure (the bold entries simply reproduce the payoffs of the standard game). It can be seen at once that Bourgeois is an ESS (compare the diagonal payoff with the other entries in the Bourgeois column). Thus a Bourgeois population could not be invaded by either Hawks or Doves. Male Hamadryas baboons and a number of other animals appear to behave according to a Bourgeois strategy, respecting the possession of females or food by other even smaller members of the same species (Sigg and Falett 1985).

The possibility that property rights *could* have emerged this way does not preclude the emergence of other and possibly competing rules of division and ownership. Notice that while Bourgeois defends what is his, an equivalent strategy that I'll call "Robin Hood" would be: "if intruder, act like a Hawk; if possessor, act like a Dove." (You may think this fanciful, but Maynard Smith (1974) reports that at least one animal—a spider with the improbable name *Oecibus civitas*—does just this, leading to a spider's version of musical chairs.) Without further elaboration, the evolutionary properties of Bourgeois and Robin Hood are identical because both reduce the frequency of fights in exactly the same way (if you doubt this, write down the relevant payoff matrix). The key to the success of Bourgeois and Robin Hood is that they both make use of additional information—who is the possessor—to create an asymmetry among the players (because only one of the pair can be a possessor) that allocates contested claims without fighting (assuming that multiple Robin Hood intruders do not arrive simultaneously). Any other asymmetry, as long as it is not easily mistaken, would have done as well. But it is harder to come up with workable asymmetries than you might think; try using "if taller than the other, play Hawk." What happens between players of about the same height?

But even more so than with superiority in height, possession may be ambiguous. Among the male Hamadryas, for example, fights occur frequently when there is ambiguity of possession. Let us consider the case in which some fraction of the time $\mu \in [0, 1]$ intruding Bourgeois players mistakenly believe they are possessors, or in any case act that way, playing Hawk, while in the role of possessor they always play Hawk as before. Can this strategy, which I'll call Contested Bourgeois, be an ESS? To answer this, we need to consider the expected payoffs to this strategy, when played against itself to determine if Contested Bourgeois can be a mutual best response (and hence an ESS). Using $B(\mu)$ to refer to the Contested Bourgeois strategy, we have

$$\pi(B(\mu), B(\mu)) = \tfrac{1}{2}[(1 - \mu)v + \mu\tfrac{1}{2}(v - c)] + \tfrac{1}{2}\mu\tfrac{1}{2}(v - c)$$
$$= \tfrac{1}{2}(v - \mu c).$$

The first term on the right-hand side expresses the fact that with probability one-half the individual is a possessor, playing Hawk, facing an intruder who as a contested Bourgeois "correctly" plays Dove $(1 - \mu)$ of the time, granting V to the possessor, but μ of the time "mistakenly" plays Hawk, leading to the conflict payoff $(v - c)/2$. The second term on the left repeats this mistaken conflict payoff for the cases in which the individual is an intruder. As expected, the payoff is declining in the degree of property rights contestation, μ, and reproduces the Hawk-to-Hawk payoff when $\mu = 1$, and the mutual uncontested Bourgeois payoff when $\mu = 0$.

Could an invading Hawk proliferate in a homogeneous population of Contested Bourgeois individuals? Its expected payoffs against Contested Bourgeois are

$$\pi(H, B(\mu)) = \tfrac{1}{2}(v - \mu c) + \tfrac{1}{4}(1 - \mu)(v - c)$$

As this expression is clearly less than $\pi(B(\mu), B(\mu))$ for $\mu < 1$, the Hawk invasion will fail.

But the expected payoff to a mutant Dove in a Contested Bourgeois world is $(1 - \mu)v/4$, which, for some values of $\mu < 1$ exceeds $(v - \mu c)/2$ so that Dove is a best response to Contested Bourgeois. Thus Contested Bourgeois need not be an ESS. If contestation over property rights is sufficiently likely, the Dove mutants will proliferate. A Dove invasion of a Contested Bourgeois population may seem surprising. But it follows directly from the fact that if because property rights are ill-defined or for some other reason contested, the Contested Bourgeois strategy does not fully eliminate costly conflicts. By contrast, Dove does accomplish this, even if possession is ambiguous, for the simple reason that Dove behavior is not conditioned on possession. Thus, where conflicts are costly, equal sharing rules may be evolutionarily successful, even if they are vulnerable to occasional exploitation by those not observing the rule.

The Contested Bourgeois's "mistakes" are an example of nonbest response play (sometimes called idiosyncratic). Like the treatment of risk dominance in chapter 1 and chance in the Assurance Game above, the analysis of Contested Bourgeois strategy suggests that chance (in the form of idiosyncratic play) may add more than just noise to an evolutionary dynamic. But thus far idiosyncratic play, like mutation, has been simply odd rather than purposeful. As we will see, sometimes actions modeled as "mistakes" are done for a reason (though possibly one not captured by the model). The importance of nonbest response play is developed further in modeling the process of collective action and institutional change (chapter 12) and in the coevolution of preferences and institutions (chapter 13).

Conclusion: Accidental Institutions?

I conclude with two questions: are evolutionary models illuminating about real historical processes? And, if institutions *did* evolve spontaneously, how good a job of coordinating human activity would they do?

The above model shows that private property rights *could have* evolved spontaneously, that is, without definition and enforcement by states or other third parties. But *did* they? That question is far from settled.

Not only property but other economic institutions as well — money and markets, for example — are said to have evolved this way, as a matter of historical fact. Hayek (1945:528) wrote: "The price system is just one of those formations which man has learned to use . . . after he stumbled upon it without understanding it." Robert Sugden (1989:86) seeks to explain how "rules regulating human action can evolve without conscious human design and can maintain themselves without there being any formal machinery for enforcing them." He terms this "spontaneous order" and goes on to suggest "that the institution of property itself may ultimately be a form of spontaneous order." By contrast, Marx (1967:742), described the eclipse of common property in favor of individual property as "the forcible creation of a class of outlawed proletarians, the bloody discipline that turned them into wage-laborers, [and] the disgraceful action of the State which employed the police to accelerate the accumulation of capital," and concludes (1967:760): "If money 'comes into the world with a congenital blood stain on one cheek,' capital comes dripping from head to foot, from every pore, with blood and dirt." One would not describe this process as spontaneous.

Of course nobody supposes that a single model as simple as the Hawk Dove Bourgeois game provides an adequate framework for understanding something as complex and historically contingent as the process by which property rights have been modified over the years. Models do not explain history, but they may tell us where to look. Seriously assessing the explanatory adequacy of any such model (or models) would require careful study of the type that has been devoted to the transformation from feudal to modern property rights (Aston and Philpin 1985), the end of slavery (Genovese 1965, Fogel and Engerman 1974), or the modification of property rights in the course of the colonialism or industrial revolution (Horwitz 1977, Sokoloff and Engerman 2000), or the modernization of simple societies (Ensminger 1996). Differences in the thrust of Hayek's and Sugden's thinking on the one hand and Marx's on the other concern not the idea of evolutionary modeling per se but what the basic ingredients of an adequate evolutionary model must be. For example, from the above quotation it is clear that in a model of Marxian inspiration there would be a substantial role for coordinated collective action and intergroup conflict, while the other authors might give less importance to these aspects of historical processes. Evolutionary modeling will have done the study of institutional change a great service if it can provide a framework for integrating the aggregate effects of large numbers of individuals each acting singly and seeking their own ends while occasionally acting jointly with others for whom institutional change is a project, not an accident. I will return to these questions in chapter 11 (where the model I develop will be in the spontaneous order tradition) and chapter 12 (where the model will represent a Darwin-Marx hybrid).

My second concluding question is: how good is the "blind watch-maker"? If the rules governing social actions spontaneously evolved rather than having been designed, might they nonetheless be efficient? The striking claim of invisible hand theories is that they may be. A celebrated result in biology, Fisher's fundamental theorem, asserts that under appropriate conditions natural selection generates increasing average fitness levels (Fisher 1930, Price 1972). Analogous reasoning is common in the social sciences: Douglass North (1981) summarized this view as follows, "Competition in the face of ubiquitous scarcity dictates that the more efficient institutions will survive and the inefficient ones perish."[7] Just as fitness maximization suggests certain features of species design in distinct ecologies, the axiomatic status of efficient outcomes in some economic models supports strong propositions about the types of institutions one would expect to find in particular environments (Williamson 1985, Ouchi 1980). Similarly, a core idea in Marx's historical materialism (expressed in the epigraph to chapter 11) is that the advance of technology may make status quo institutions anachronistic. When this happens they are replaced by institutions better able to coordinate economic activity given what he called the new "forces of production." In Marx's view, institutions eventually adapt to the problem-solving needs dictated by the advance of technology.

But analytical models supporting claims of this type are rarely offered and difficult to develop. The best known invisible hand results do not apply: the assumptions of Fisher's fundamental theorem are no less restrictive than those of the economic theorem of the same name. Both exclude empirically important types of interactions: in the case of Fisher's theorem, epistatic (nonadditive) and other frequency-dependent fitness effects of genes and, for the economists' theorem, interpersonal effects not subject to complete contracting (externalities). Interactions with frequency-dependent individual payoffs, like those considered in this and the previous chapter, violate these assumptions. Recall that the average fitness of a hawk dove population is maximized not at the equilibrium frequency of hawks, v/c, but at zero. This average fitness maximum, Dawkins (1989b:200) pointed out, might be implemented by "a conspiracy of doves" but it would not come about through the spontaneous evolutionary processes described in this chapter.

Neither the economists' nor the biologists' fundamental theorem ap-

[7] See Jensen and Meckling (1979). North, whose work has done much to dispel this view, commented: "But the fact that growth has been more exceptional than stagnation or decline suggests that 'efficient' property rights are unusual in history" (North 1981:6).

plies in cases in which the interactions are of the type described in these simple, and seemingly common settings. The key idea here is simply that individual optimization — either intentional or implicit as is the case with natural selection based on fitness differences — does not generally produce globally optimal results, even if the individuals are far sighted and the selection process operates over a very long time horizon.[8] The idea that competitive selection of group-level institutions (for example, the conventions studied in chapter 1) might yield optimal results raises problems even more severe than those confronting invisible hand arguments applied to individual traits or to the provision of individual goods. There are four reasons why this is true.

First, institutions exhibit analogues to both external economies (spillovers) and generalized increasing returns: the feasibility and effectiveness of an institution typically depends both on the fraction of a population governed by it and on the set of coexisting institutions. Some institutions may be complementary, each enhancing the functioning of the other, while some institutions may reduce the effectiveness of other institutions leading to what is termed institutional crowding out. (We shall return to these questions — with examples — in the concluding chapter.) These are institutional analogues to positive and negative spillovers among individuals, and they make it highly unlikely that any process of competitive selection among group-level institutions would hit upon the most effective combination. Because the behaviors prescribed by an institution are mutual best responses and because of institutional complementarities, there typically exist multiple stable configurations of institutions. Some of these may be very inefficient and yet persist over long periods. Examples are amply documented in the anthropological and historical literature. The Fore people in New Guinea persisted in a form of cannibalism fatal to themselves. Hungry Tasmanians and Icelanders were surrounded for centuries by oceans teeming with fish that they did not bother to catch.[9] (The Tasmanians had been a fishing people but for unknown reasons gave it up 4000 years ago.)

Second, even where there exist evolutionary processes selecting among group level institutions, these will generally fail to implement efficient solutions. A group's military prowess (rather than any plausible measure of efficiency) may account for success in intergroup conflict (chapter 13). A payoff-dominant convention (e.g., planting early in Palanpur)

---

[8] The most that can be said is that *strictly dominated* strategies will be eliminated under plausible evolutionary dynamics — this is because dominated strategies are never a best response, independently of what others do, so the problem of noncontractual social interactions does not arise. Remarkably, even this weak statement is not true in discrete time dynamics (Weibull 1995).

[9] Durham (1991), Edgerton (1992), Eggertsson (1966), Henrich (2002).

may be bypassed by a within-group evolutionary dynamic because the other equilibrium is risk dominant and therefore has a larger basin of attraction (chapter 12).

Third, the range of institutional or behavioral variation among which selection is taking place may be highly restricted. As Ugo Pagano (2001) has pointed out, the creation of novel institutions is akin to the emergence of new species; it requires the confluence of a large number of improbable variations in the status quo. But ever since Darwin grappled with the problem in *The Origin of Species*, the production of novel designs through random variation has remained a puzzle. Biologists recognize "unoccupied ecological niches" that persist over very long periods, capable of supporting organisms that occupy similar niches elsewhere but lacking mutations and other chance events that would have brought them into existence (Maynard Smith 1998:289). Similarly, common human behavioral traits, such as punishing those who violate norms, could not have appeared fully developed as the result of either a single mutation or a behavioral innovation by a single individual (a shared norm is also needed, a solitary punisher would run fitness reducing risks, and so on). There are a great many varieties of human behavior and institutions that have not yet been tried.

Finally, the rates of change induced by real world selection processes — whether the operate on genetically or culturally transmitted characteristics — may be slow relative to the pace of changes induced by other sources, such as chance events, or exogenous changes in knowledge, or the number and types of competing individuals, organizations, or technologies.

These four points may be expressed more visually. Selection processes implement a kind of hill climbing, but the hilltop need not bear any close relationship to normative criteria such as efficiency. There may be many hilltops, so a population may never explore much of the topography and may climb the wrong hill; the rate of ascent may be overwhelmed by shifts in the underlying topography so no hilltop is ever reached. Hayek was a leading proponent of invisible hand arguments, and advanced a prudential argument against tinkering with the products of evolutionary selection processes. But he was nonetheless circumspect about any claims to optimality for what evolution produces: "I do not claim that the results of [evolutionary processes] are necessarily 'good' any more than I claim that other things that have long survived such as cockroaches have moral value" (Hayek 1988:27).

While showing that existing invisible hand arguments are misleading when applied to institutions and behavioral traits, the above reasoning does not preclude other models by which evolutionary processes might be shown to implement efficient solutions, at least in some approximate or second-best sense. And even if we were to conclude that the blind watchmaker is not a very good craftsman, this would not diminish the importance of evolutionary approaches. We will return to these questions when we consider the efficiency properties of the process of institutional change in chapters 11 through 13, introducing two modeling approaches — stochastic evolutionary game theory and evolutionary dynamics based on multi-level selection. Both approaches give analytical expression of surprisingly strong versions of invisible hand arguments. A conspiracy of doves will also make an appearance.

CHAPTER THREE

Preferences and Behavior

> Political writers have established it as a maxim, that in contriving any
> system of government . . . every man ought to be supposed to be a
> *knave* and to have no other end, in all his actions, than his private
> interest. By this interest we must govern him, and, by means of it, make
> him, notwithstanding his insatiable avarice and ambition, cooperate to
> public good.
>
> —David Hume, *Essays: Moral, Political and Literary* (1742)

> Let us return again to the state of nature and consider men as if . . .
> sprung out of the earth, and suddenly, like mushrooms, come to full
> maturity without any kind of engagement to each other.
>
> —Thomas Hobbes *De Cive* (1651)

GROWING CORN IS BIG business in Illinois. Using highly capital-intensive
technologies and computer-generated business plans, some farmers cul-
tivate a thousand or more acres, much of it on plots rented from multiple owners. In the mid-1990s, over half of the contracts between
farmers and owners were sharecropping agreements, and over four-
fifths of these contracts stipulated a fifty-fifty division of the crop between the two parties. In the southern part of the state where the soil is
on average less fertile, there are counties where contracts giving the
tenant two-thirds of the crop are common. In these counties there are
few contracts of fifty-fifty or any division other than two-thirds, despite
considerable variation in land quality within these counties.

Rice cultivation in West Bengal in the mid-1970s seems light years
away from Illinois. Poor illiterate farmers in villages isolated by impass-
able roads much of the year, and lacking electronic communication,
eked out a bare living on plots that average just two acres. We have
already seen (in the Prologue) that they shared one similarity with Illinois's farmers, however: the division between sharecroppers and owners
was fifty-fifty in over two-thirds of the contracts. (Ibn Battuta, whose
visit to Bengal was also mentioned in the prologue, had noted—and
deplored—exactly the same division of the crop six centuries before.)
Other contracts were observed, but none of them constituted more than

The first epigraph is from Hume (1964:117–18), the second from Hobbes (1949:100).

8 percent of the total.[1] An even more striking example is from the U.S. South following the Civil War, where sharecropping contracts divided the harvest equally between the landlord and tenant irrespective of the quality of the land or whether the tenant was a freeborn white or a newly freed slave: "This form of tenancy was established everywhere in the South. It flourished with all possible combinations of soil quality and labor conditions"(Ransom and Sutch 1977:91, 215).

The puzzle of fifty-fifty sharecropping is the following: an equal split of the crop means that tenants on fertile land will have higher payoffs to their effort and other inputs than those on poor land. But if tenants are willing to work for the lower returns on the less good land, why should the owners of good land concede half of the crop to *their* tenants? The conventional economic theory of sharecropping predicts that the owner will capture the returns to land quality through variations in the crop share (Stiglitz 1974). But Burke and Young (2000) show that the Illinois sharecropping contracts allow the tenants on good land to capture a third of the differential return attributable to land quality, effectively transferring millions of dollars from owners to farmers.

A plausible interpretation of these facts is that farmers and owners around the world have hit on fifty-fifty as a seemingly fair division, and that attempts by owners to capture all of the returns to high quality land through the use of variable shares would be defeated by the tenants' retaliation. If true, this interpretation suggests that a predisposition to fairness, as well as the desire to punish those who violate local norms, may be motives as powerful as profit maximization and the pursuit of individual gain.

John Stuart Mill (1965[1848]) noted the striking global pattern of equal division in sharecropping, as well as local conformity to alternative shares in which fifty-fifty is not observed. Mill's explanation? "The custom of the country is the universal rule" (149). Custom may well be the proximate cause, but this explanation begs the question: why fifty-fifty as opposed to fifty-two–forty-eight? Why did the Bengalis and the Americans come up with the same number? We know from the analysis of the division game in chapter 1 that *any* exhaustive division of the crop is a Pareto-efficient Nash equilibrium: why this particular one? Even more puzzling: why does it persist when there appear to be huge profits to be made by offering lower shares on higher quality land? And when the shares do change, as we have seen happened in West Bengal in the 1980s and 1990s, why do they all change at once, reflecting the pattern of local homogeneity and punctuated equilibrium we encountered in chapter 2?

---

[1] Young and Burke (2001), Burke and Young (2000) and Bardhan (1984).

If motives such as fairness and retribution or simply adherence to convention override material self-interest in the highly competitive environment of Illinois agriculture it may be wise to reconsider the behavioral assumptions of economics, which conventionally has taken self-interest — summarized by the term *Homo economicus* — as its foundation. The need for a second look at *Homo economicus* is clear when considering problems of distribution such as sharecropping and other bargaining situations in which concerns with equity are likely to be salient. But the problem is much more general, and the canonical model of behavior seems to frequently fail even when fairness issues are absent.

Consider the following case (Gneezy and Rustichini 2000). Parents everywhere are sometimes late in picking up their children at day-care centers. In Haifa, at six randomly chosen centers, a fine was imposed for lateness (in a control group of centers, no fine was imposed). The expectation was that punctuality would improve. But parents responded to the fine by even greater tardiness: the fraction picking up their kids late more than doubled. Even more striking was the fact that when after sixteen weeks the fine was revoked, their enhanced tardiness persisted, showing no tendency to return to the status quo ante. Over the entire twenty weeks of the experiment, there were no changes in the degree of lateness at the day-care centers in the control group.

The authors of the study reason that the fine was a contextual cue, unintentionally providing information about the appropriate behavior. The effect was to convert lateness from the violation of an *obligation* that the parents were at some pains to respect, to a commodity with a price that many were willing to pay. They titled their study "A Fine is a Price" and concluded that imposing a fine labeled the interaction as a market-like situation, one in which parents were more than willing to buy lateness. Revoking the fine did not restore the initial framing of punctuality as an obligation, it just lowered the price of lateness to zero. The fact that monetary incentives for punctuality induced even greater tardiness is both counter to the predictions of the standard economic model and of general relevance to the problem of designing effective contracts and economic policies. In Hume's terms, the Haifa day-care centers designed a constitution for knaves, and they seemingly produced knaves rather than improved behaviors.

The weaknesses of the conventional model suggested by the puzzle of the fifty-fifty crop share and the fact that fining the Haifa parents backfired are evident in arenas of more conventional economic interest, such as labor markets, team production, tax compliance, the protection of local environmental commons, and other forms of public goods provision. Included is the importance of fairness motives in wage setting and other exchanges (Bewley 1995, Blinder and Choi 1990). Equally puzzling in the standard paradigm is the fact that individuals bother to vote given that the likelihood that their vote is decisive is vanishingly small, as well as their significant support, when they do vote, for tax-supported income transfers to the poor even among those sufficiently rich and upwardly mobile to be very unlikely ever to benefit directly from them (Fong 2001, Gilens 1999). Finally, studies at Continental Airlines, Nucor Steel, and other companies have found that group incentives are effective even where the gains are shared among such a large number that the individual payoff to one's own effort is negligible (Hansen 1997, Knez and Simester 2001).

Seeking a more adequate behavioral foundation for economics and the other social sciences, in this chapter I draw upon recent research to present a reformulation of the standard approach, one that retains a central role for individuals' preferences, beliefs, and constraints in explaining what people do, while emending the conventional model in three ways.

First, many behaviors are best explained by what are termed *social preferences*: in choosing to act, individuals commonly take account not only of the consequences of their actions for themselves but for others as well. Moreover they often care not only about consequences but also about the intentions of other actors. An important example of social preferences are *reciprocity* motives, according to which people are generous toward those who have behaved well (toward them or others) while punishing those who have not behaved well. Reciprocity motives induce people to act this way even in situations (such as one-shot interactions) in which generosity and punishing behaviors are personally costly and bear no expectation of subsequent or indirect reward. (These cases are examples of what I term *strong reciprocity*, to distinguish this behavior from reciprocation with the expectation of future reward, sometimes termed *reciprocal altruism*.) Other social preferences to be considered are *inequality aversion*, *envy* (or spite), and *altruism*.

By contrast, the conventional assumption is that individual behavior is entirely explained by what is loosely termed self-interest, by which I mean *self-regarding preferences defined over outcomes*. According to this view, our concerns extend neither to the outcomes experienced by others nor the processes generating the outcomes. F. Y. Edgeworth, a founder of the neoclassical paradigm, expressed this view in his *Mathematical Psychics* (Edgeworth 1881:104): "The first principle of economics is that every agent is actuated only by self-interest." Self-interest is not presumed by rationality (one could have transitive and complete altruistic or masochistic preferences), but it is commonly treated as axiomatic in economics (and sometimes confused with rationality). Thus, while self-interest is not formally implied by the conventional approach, it is generally assumed in practice. The assumption acquires considerable predictive power in strategic situations when it takes the form of what I term the *self-interest axiom*, namely, individual self-interest coupled with the belief that others are also motivated by self-interest.

Second, individuals are *rule-following adaptive agents*. By this I mean that we economize on our limited cognitive resources by acting according to evolved rules of thumb. The term "boundedly rational" is sometimes used to describe the cognitive limits of real human actors, but I do not use it as it suggests irrationality. It is not the boundedness of our rationality that I would like to stress but rather our limited capacity and predisposition to engage in extraordinarily complex and costly cognitive exercises. Among these evolved behavioral rules are ethical prescriptions governing actions toward others, namely, *social norms*, conformity to which is both valued by the actor (i.e., the norm is internalized) and supported by social sanction. This approach contrasts with the conventional view in which behavior is the result of often quite demanding individual cognitive processes addressing both evaluative and causal issues (is this state desirable? how can I bring it about?). This conventional *individual cognition-centered* view excludes behavior based on such things as visceral reactions (like disgust, fear, or weakness of will), habit, or evolved rules of thumb, and it presumes (against a considerable body of evidence) that individuals are both able and predisposed to make quite advanced inferences about what others will do and about the way the world works.

Third, behaviors are context dependent, in three senses. Situational cues are used to determine the behaviors appropriate in any given setting. Moreover, we evaluate outcomes from a particular point of view, namely, our current state or the state experienced by a member of our reference group. Finally, social institutions influence who we meet, to do what, and with what rewards; as a result, our motivations are shaped through the process of cultural or genetic transmission introduced in chapter 2. Thus, our *preferences are situationally specific and endogenous*. If one's experiences result in durable changes in preferences, they are said to be endogenous, which will happen if experiences affect either social learning or (over the very long run) genetic inheritance. This may be compared with situation- or state-dependent preferences that are time invariant (over time, one behaves the same way in the same situation). Because endogenous preferences involve learning or genetic changes, behavior in the same situation changes over time.

This approach contrasts with the conventional view that preferences do not depend on one's current state and are either unchanging or change solely under the influence of influences exogenous to the problem under investigation. George Stigler and Gary Becker (1977) expressed this view in their essay *De Gustibus Non Est Disputandum*: "One does not argue about tastes for the same reason that one does not argue about the Rocky Mountains—both are there, and will be there next year, too, and are the same to all men" (76). They were repeating, in less poetic terms, Hobbes' point about mushrooms.

Nobody takes the conventional assumptions literally, of course. Edgeworth observed that the self-interest assumption is literally true only in limiting situations ("contract and war"), and Hume, in the sentence immediately following this chapter's first epigraph, mused that it is "strange that a maxim should be true in politics which is false in fact." Hobbes invoked a deliberately fanciful analogy to abstract from the social formation of preferences as part of a thought experiment, not as a description of real people.

While recognizing that the standard assumptions are often violated empirically, most economists have shared Becker and Stigler's endorsement of the simple canonical model of exogenous and self-regarding preferences. The broad acceptance of its tenets—not as empirical truths but as close enough approximations to be useful analytical shortcuts—is explained in part by their substantial contribution to both intellectual discipline and clarity. The standard assumptions provide a common intellectual framework resistant to ad hoc explanation on the basis of empirically unobserved individual differences or changes in tastes over time. Abandoning the standard model opens the door to explanations of behaviors on the basis of vague concepts like "psychic income" or "animal spirits."

For a new behavioral foundation to be a contribution to social science rather than an invitation to ad hoc explanation, we need more empirical information about preferences and how we come to have them as well as more adequate models of behavior under less restrictive preference assumptions. The extraordinary production of empirical findings by experimental and behavioral economists and other social scientists in recent years has made such a reformulation not only possible but overdue. Here and in later chapters, I make extensive use of experimental results. The reason is that this relatively new method in economics has for the first time allowed the testing in controlled settings of well-formulated hypotheses concerning the behavioral assumptions of economics.

In the next section I introduce what I call a behavioral interpretation of preferences and rational action, followed by a review of a number of empirical anomalies in the conventional treatment of preferences. I then turn to recent research on social preferences, introducing both experimental results and two new utility functions. I postpone until chapters 7, 11, and 13 the formal modeling of how preferences evolve, why people often adhere to ethical norms, and why other-regarding motives such as generosity and fairness are common.

PREFERENCES, REASONS, AND BEHAVIORS

When individuals act, they are generally trying to *do* something, however wisely or otherwise. An implication is that individuals' purposes and their understandings about how to carry them out, along with the constraints and incentives posed by societal rules and individual capacities, are key ingredients in accounting for individual actions. What people do in any situation therefore depends on their preferences and their beliefs.

Beliefs are an individual's understandings of the relationship between an action and an outcome. In many cases beliefs enter trivially in choice situations and so are not explicitly addressed: we routinely assume for example that people know the payoff consequences of their actions in simple games. In other situations — particularly in strategic interactions without dominant strategies — beliefs may become all important: the effect of my attending a meeting may depend on who else is there and so my decision to attend or not will depend on my expectation of who else will attend, which in turn will depend on *their* beliefs about whether others will attend, and so on. In other situations the structure of the interaction may be ambiguous and understood differently by different players. In these situations, how we come to have the beliefs we do and how we update our beliefs in light of our experience assumes central importance.

Preferences are reasons for behavior, that is, attributes of individuals — other than beliefs and capacities — that account for the actions they take in a given situation.[2] Preferences thus include a heterogeneous melange: tastes (food likes and dislikes, for example), habits, emotions (such as shame or anger) and other visceral reactions (such as fear), the manner in which individuals construe situations (or, more narrowly, the way they frame a decision), commitments (like promises), socially enforced norms, psychological propensities (for aggression, extroversion, and the like), and one's affective relationships with others. To say that persons act on their preferences means only that knowledge of the preferences would be helpful in providing a convincing account of the actions (though not necessarily the account that would be given by the actor, for as is well known, individuals are sometimes unable or unwilling to provide such an account).[3]

This "reasons for behavior" interpretation of preferences may be con-

[2] A more precise term for this conception of preferences might be the cumbersome expression suggested by Nowell-Smith (1954): "pro and con attitudes."

[3] See Nisbett and Wilson (1977). Shafir, Simonson, and Tversky (2000) provide an interpretation of what they call "reason-based choice" similar to that in Nowell-Smith and here.

trasted with two conventional approaches. The first postulates that individuals seek to maximize their utility, equating utility to well-being, pleasure, or happiness, in the tradition of Jeremy Bentham and the early nineteenth-century utilitarians. In the more recent revealed preference approach, by contrast, a preference ordering is nothing more than a complete *description* of consistent behavior, and any connection to a hedonistic calculus is gratuitous. Neither approach is entirely adequate.

If our objective is to explain behavior, the revealed preference approach is vacuous because it is silent on the question of motives and reasons: while these are hardly sufficient to an explanation, they are rarely uninformative. The revealed preference view once attracted adherents impressed by the now-antiquated methodological fiat that subjective states are not knowable, so a scientific approach must focus on observable behaviors. By contrast, the utilitarian approach is substantive; the subjective states central to this view—pleasure, pain, satisfaction, anxiety, and other hedonic experiences—are now an active field of scientific study and measurement. But treating behavior as synonymous with the pursuit of well-being is misleading: the reasons for our actions also include addictions, weakness of will, myopia, and other well-documented dysfunctional aspects of human behavior. The fact that the same term—utility—is conventionally used both as an explanation of behavior and as a standard for evaluating social outcomes has forced economists to take an unduly limited view of both behavior and social evaluation.

To review thus far, along with the set of feasible actions and the associated outcomes, beliefs and preferences provide an account of individual action. Recall that I have defined institutions as the population-level laws, informal rules, and conventions that give a durable structure to social interactions. In game theoretic terms, an institution is a game (which, as we have seen in chapter 1, may also be the outcome of an underlying game), preferences are the evaluation of the payoffs, and beliefs are the players' understandings of the expected payoff consequences of each strategy in their strategy set (i.e., their understanding of the game and its payoff structure plus the likelihood of others' actions).

As preferences, beliefs, and institutions are easily confounded, consider a concrete case. The common practice in many countries of driving on the right-hand side of the road is an institution; it is a convention, that is, an equilibrium of an Assurance Game, and the convention is supported by laws. In these countries it is a best response to drive on the right, and it is also illegal to do otherwise. People do not *prefer* driving on the right, per se, they prefer avoiding crashes and fines, and were everyone else to drive on the left without breaking the law, they would drive on the left as well. The belief that others will drive on the right sustains the institution of driving on the right, which in turn sustains the belief. Beliefs and preferences are facts about individuals that sustain this particular equilibrium, while institutions — represented in this case by the driving-on-the-right equilibrium — are facts about groups of people.

A version of the beliefs and preferences framework, which I will term "conventional," has provided the behavioral foundation for economics and is increasingly applied throughout the social sciences. An individual's behavior is modeled using a utility function: $U = U(x, y, z)$. The arguments of $U - x$, y, and z — describe a *state* that may be a simple list of goods consumed or more complex formulations like a cold beer on a hot evening three days from now in the company of friends in an Islamic society that prohibits the consumption of alcohol. The utility function is taken to be a numerical representation such that higher values of U are chosen (said to be preferred) over lower values, the state (x, y, z) being chosen over (x', y, z) if $U(x, y, z) > U(x', y, z)$.

The utility function is *complete*, meaning that every state can be ordered by a relationship of either preference or indifference with respect to every other state. The ordering is also *transitive*, meaning that the orderings it gives do not include inconsistent orderings such as (x, y, z) preferred to (x', y, z), which is preferred to (x'', y, z), but (x'', y, z) is preferred to (x, y, z). Finally the utility function is (usually implicitly) assumed to be *time invariant* over the relevant period: when, say, prices change exogenously, the individual responds to the new prices and not also to coincident changes in the utility function. When individuals act according to a complete and transitive utility function they are said to be *rational*.[4] Other ways of acting — inconsistency of choice induced by whim or incompleteness of preferences over unimaginably horrible outcomes, for example — are not thereby deemed *irrational*, of course, they are simply forms of action not covered by this model perhaps better deemed *non*rational.

The conventional model is routinely extended to cover risk and uncertainty. *Risk* is said to exist if a consequence of an action in the individual's choice set is a set of possible outcomes each occurring with a *known* probability. By contrast, if one or more of the actions open to the individual may cause more than one outcome, the probabilities of which are *unknown*, *uncertainty* exists. Both are ubiquitous aspects of choice. Deciding whether to rent a cottage at the beach knowing that with probability p it will rain is an example of risk. In these cases the

---

[4] Other rationality restrictions are sometimes imposed. For example, the weak axiom of revealed preference requires that if (x, y, z) is preferred to (x', y, z) then (x, y, z, a) will be preferred to (x', y, z, a).

individual is assumed to maximize *expected utility*. The expected utility of an action is the utility associated with each possible consequence of the action multiplied by the probability of its occurrence: U(beach cottage) = (1 − p)U(beach cottage in the sun) + pU(beach cottage in the rain).

The maximization of expected utility requires more than the simple ordering of each possible state (that suffices to determine behavior under certainty) as it uses information about how much better one state is than another. In a pioneering work on game theory, John von Neumann and Oskar Morgenstern (Neumann and Morgenstern 1944), showed that an expected utility maximizing individual's choices are invariant for additive or linear transformations of the utility function. (What this means is that if an individual's behavior is described by the utility function u then her behavior is also described by any function of the form $v = \alpha + \beta u$ where $\beta > 0$.) What are termed *von Neumann-Morgenstern utilities* embody this restriction. They have already made two unannounced appearances in chapter 1: in the treatment of risk dominance, and when I normalized the payoffs associated with the fallback positions in the conflict of interest games. Von Neumann-Morgenstern utilities exhibit cardinality over the states *for a given individual* but not *between* individuals; they indicate how much better the beach in the sun is compared to the beach in the rain *for you*, but not how much better either is *for you* than *for me*. All of the payoffs subsequently used here are Von Neumann-Morgenstern utilities unless specified otherwise.

In the case of uncertainty, the known probability weights are replaced by the individual's subjective estimates of the unknown probabilities. It is generally assumed that individuals modify their estimates on the basis of recent experience by a process termed *Bayesian updating*; Reverend Thomas Bayes (1702–1761) was an early writer on probability theory. The Bayesian approach to rational action assumes that individual decision making under uncertainty is based on expected utility maximization based on subjective probabilities updated in this manner. (The Bayesian approach obviously presumes von Neumann-Morgenstern utilities.) The difference between risk and uncertainty in practice is often blurred except in limiting cases, where truly known probabilities are involved such as allocation mechanisms that are randomized by a coin toss.

An important application of these ideas is the concept of *risk aversion*, measured by the degree of concavity of a utility function U(W), where W is the wealth of the individual. The intuition is that if the marginal utility of wealth is sharply declining in wealth, as will be the case for a "very concave" utility function, then one would value $75,000 with certainty a lot more than an even chance of $50,000 or

$100,000. Thus, an individual whose utility is concave in wealth will be averse to a lottery over two prizes if she could have, instead, a certain prize equal to the expected value of the lottery. For this reason, a measure of the degree of risk aversion is $-U''/U'$, called the Arrow-Pratt measure.[5] An individual is *risk neutral* if utility is linear in wealth or $U'' = 0$; $U'' > 0$ implies *risk seeking*.

A second essential extension is to choices over states at different dates. This is accomplished by discounting future states at a constant *discount factor* δ, which is an inverse measure of the degree to which we discount future events due to myopia, the unlikelihood of surviving to some future date, and other reasons.[6] For a person who values future states the same as current states, $\delta = 1$ while for more present oriented individuals, $\delta < 1$. According to the *discounted utility* approach, δ is defined such that an individual is indifferent between adding x to her consumption y at time t and adding some other increment, x', n periods later, at $t + n$ if

$$U(y + x)\delta^t + U(y)\delta^{t+n} = U(y)\delta^t + U(y + x')\,\delta^{t+n} \quad (3.1)$$

Thus, extended to cover risk and intertemporal choice, the conventional model captures the important intentional aspect of human behavior and combines broad applicability with formal tractability. At first glace it appears to impose few substantive restrictions on the analysis of behavior other than the exclusion of the perhaps unimportant cases of incompleteness and inconsistency just mentioned. But this is not correct: the above formulation is a substantive theory of behavior, and embodies strong claims about what kinds of things people take account of and how they do this. This model does not fare well in light of recent empirical research about behavior.

Situation-Dependent Preferences

One of the best documented falsifications of the conventional model arises because preferences (and hence behaviors) are *situation dependent* in the following sense. Suppose ω_i is a vector representing a state i (e.g., one described by (x,y,z) above), an element of the set of possible states Ω, and $U_i(\omega_j)$ is the utility associated with state $\omega_j \in \Omega$ *for an individual currently experiencing state ω_i*. Let $U_i(\omega)$ represent this individual's preference ranking of all the possible states when that individual is in state i. Then preferences are situation dependent if the rankings

---

[5] See Mas-Colell, Whinston, and Green (1995) for further elaboration.
[6] The discount factor $\delta = 1/(1 + r)$ where r is the rate of time preference.

by the same individual in a different state, given by $U_k(\omega)$ differ from those given by $U_i(\omega)$ for some i and k. Situation dependence is also called state dependence, but I use the former in recognition of the substantial literature in psychology on the importance of situations as influences on behavior.

An important example of situation dependence, termed *loss aversion*, arises because people value losses (negatively) more highly than equivalent gains. The size of the loss aversion coefficient is surprisingly large: estimates from both experiments and natural settings find that the disutility of a small loss is between two and two-and-a-half times the utility of a small gain. The utility function is thus sharply kinked at the status quo (and the kink moves when the status quo changes). Closely associated is the *endowment effect*: the minimal price that would induce an individual to sell something she now possesses is substantially higher than the maximum price she would be willing to pay to acquire the same good. (Loss aversion and the endowment effect are examples of a broader class of situation-dependent effects, namely *status quo bias*.)

Loss aversion and endowment effects have been extensively documented in experiments by economists and psychologists, and they provide plausible explanations of important anomalies in everyday economics. For example, the fact that U.S. stock returns have consistently exceeded bond returns by a wide margin is an outstanding puzzle in economics. It was once thought to be a result of risk aversion among investors, but a simple calculation (Mehra and Prescott 1988) shows that the level of risk aversion necessary to explain the difference is implausibly large. For risk aversion to account for the stock return puzzle, investors would be indifferent between an even chance of $50,000 and $100,000 and a sure thing of $51,209. A more compelling account (Benartzi and Thaler 1995) holds that investors are not averse to the variability of returns per se (after all, most are quite rich), but they react strongly to the prospect of losses, and stock returns over a year are negative much more often than bond returns.

The loss aversion interpretation of the stock return puzzle makes it clear that a precise formulation of loss aversion and other aspects of situation-dependence requires explicit treatment of the time dimension; if investors had a five-year time horizon, they would experience few negative returns, so the loss aversion explanation implies a particular time horizon, evidently a rather short one. An individual who experiences a loss will eventually treat the new situation as the status quo. We know, for example, that people who anticipated that a severe physical handicap would be unbearable often become quite satisfied with life after living with the handicap for a matter of years. A well-documented situational determinant of preferences is simple exposure (Zajonc 1968). People come to value more the things (for example, foods) they've been exposed to longer. Rats are no different: those brought up on Mozart prefer his music to Schoenberg (Cross, Halcomb, and Matter 1967). Sometimes preferences adjust to situations virtually instantaneously — students in endowment-effect experiments bonded with the coffee mugs given them in a matter of minutes! — but the lags are considerably greater in many cases.

Situation dependence — in the form of loss aversion, endowment effects, and long-term endogeneity of preferences — by no means exhausts the empirical shortcomings of the conventional model. Like the assumption of situation independence, the conventional treatment of intertemporal choice is strikingly counterintuitive and strongly contradicted by behavioral evidence.[7] Suppose you were indifferent between one meal at your favorite restaurant now and two such meals a year from now. Then according to eq. (3.1) you would also be indifferent between one meal (call it x) twenty years from now and two meals (that's x') twenty-one years from now. To see this, notice that this indifference relationship can be equivalently expressed (divide both sides of (3.1) by δ^t) as

$$U(y + x) - U(y) = \{U(y + x') - U(y)\}\delta^n.$$

Thus the difference in your utility made by the delay of the two meals does not depend on when it happens in real time, but only on the amount of time elapsed between the time of the first (one-meal) and the second (two-meal) event. This so called *stationarity property* of the discounted utility model is a temporal analogue to state independence: *how one evaluates states is assumed not to depend on where one is evaluating them from.* This is not only counterintuitive; it is contradicted by extensive experimental and other evidence (interestingly, for other animals as well as humans). For most people, as the example suggests, the delay of a year is a lot more salient if it occurs sooner rather than later, suggesting what is called a *hyperbolic discount function*, according to which a state in year t is discounted not at the rate δ^t but instead at the rate

$$\delta(t) = (1 + \alpha t)^{-\beta/\alpha} \qquad \text{with} \qquad \alpha, \beta > 0 \qquad (3.2)$$

which for large values of α indicates that the value of future states is rapidly declining in the near future, after which the decline is sharply attenuated (so that, for example, you might be quite impatient about waiting a year for your favorite meal but only somewhat less impatient in evaluating the long-term consequences of global warming).[8] Hyperbolic discounters will exhibit preference reversal behavior: of two prizes

---

[7] This paragraph draws on Loewenstein and Prelec (2000).

[8] The departure from constant discounting is governed by α; you may confirm that as α goes to zero eq. (3.2) reproduces the standard exponential discount function $\delta(t) = e^{-\beta t}$.

A and *B* of differing amounts and occurring at different future dates, one may prefer *A* over *B* at the present but with the passage of time prefer *B* over *A*. A hyperbolic discounter might, for example, take the one meal now over the two meals a year from now but also choose the two meals twenty-one years from now over the one meal twenty years from now. But if this is the case, after the passage of nineteen years, the hyperbolic discounter would choose the one meal sooner over the two meals later, thus reversing his choice. A number of studies (surveyed in Angeletos, Laibson, Repetto, Tobacman, and Weinberg 2001) suggest that the hypberbolic discounting approach provides better predictions than the conventional approach of individual savings behavior, accounting for the empirically-observed significant increases in consumption from predictable increases in income, and the sharp reduction in consumption upon retirement.

As in the case of intertemporal choice, well-established empirical regularities are anomalous from the standpoint of the conventional expected utility analysis of choice in the presence of risk. Recall that this framework requires that individuals evaluate the actions they may take according to the linear sum of the probability of each possible consequence occurring, multiplied by the utilities associated with each consequence. Thus, events occurring with arbitrarily small probability should be treated virtually indistinguishably from events that will certainly not occur. But it is well established that people do not evaluate lotteries over risky events this way: an event that will happen with certainty is regarded as quite different than something that will happen with probability $(1 - \varepsilon)$, no matter how small ε is. Conversely, knowing that one is not HIV positive is hardly the same thing as knowing that one may be HIV positive, but with an arbitrarily small probability ε. Paul Samuelson (1963) called this the "epsilon ain't zero" problem.

A second problem arises: if risk aversion (as measured by the concavity of the utility function in wealth) is used to explain why people turn down bets over stakes in the 0 to $1,000 range, then it cannot possibly explain why virtually *any* bets are accepted over large stakes. An economist who had observed an individual reject the opportunity to flip a coin to either win $1010 or lose $1000 would invoke risk aversion as the explanation. But Matthew Rabin (2001) pointed out that the level of risk aversion necessary to explain this choice would also imply that the same individual would turn down a coin flip for either an $80,000 loss or a $349,400 gain. The problem is that for small stakes, a concave utility function is approximately linear, and the amount of concavity necessary to explain why small stakes bets are sometimes rejected implies that most bets over large stakes — even very lucrative ones in expected value terms — would never be accepted.

The idea that sharply diminishing marginal utility of wealth arising from a concave utility function would disincline an individual from risk taking over large stakes is surely correct. But the two problems above suggests that concavity alone cannot explain behavior in the face of risk. The first is familiar: the conventional approach abstracts from loss aversion. The second is deeper: even if the utility function were continuously differentiable (not kinked at the status quo state, as would be the case if loss aversion were present), its concavity fails to capture the reasons people have for wishing to avoid risk and the emotions they experience in the face of risk. Among these are anxiety and fear when they do not know what will happen or the possibility of regret (or shame) at having taken a chance which ex post did not pay off. The model correspondingly fails to understand the reasons why people of very limited wealth engage in risky activities such as gambling: it is unlikely that their utility functions are *convex* in wealth, and if they are, it then begs the question of why the same individuals also purchase insurance. A more plausible explanation of gambling, and of driving too fast, too, is that some people enjoy taking particular *kinds* of risks.

Situation-dependent utilities, as well as the specific shortcomings of the expected utility maximization approach to risk and the discounted utility approach to intertemporal choice, suggest that a more empirically grounded view of the reasons for behavior is called for. Daniel Kahneman, Amos Tversky, Richard Thaler, and their coauthors have suggested a series of reformulations called *prospect theory* (the key papers are presented in Kahneman and Tversky 2000). Its main contribution is to take account of four aspects of choice not well handled in the conventional paradigm. The first is the problem (mentioned above) that people do not evaluate risky decisions according to the expected utility hypothesis: they overweigh the importance of unlikely events. The second is to take account of *framing*, namely, the fact that equivalent outcomes are treated differently depending on the manner in which either the outcomes or the decision setting are described. One of the reasons for situation-dependent behavior is that situations often frame choices in a particular manner. (Examples will be given in the next section.) Third, Kahneman and others, returning to an aspect of classic utilitarianism, have reintroduced substantive measures such as actually experienced hedonic utility.

Fourth, prospect theory has developed a conceptual framework for dealing with the situation-dependence of behaviors. This fundamental reformulation is that if the utility function is to explain actual behavior, its arguments should be *changes in states* or *events* rather than states. Thus, the value individuals place on states depends on the relationship of the state to the status quo (or possibly some other reference state,

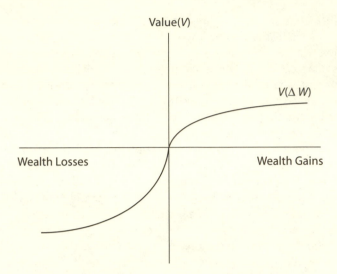

Figure 3.1 A situation-dependent value function. ΔW is the change in wealth. Note: the 'kink' at $\Delta W = 0$ indicates loss aversion.

such as an aspiration level or the states enjoyed by peers). Experimental and other empirical studies suggest that the resulting so-called value function has the three characteristics illustrated in figure 3.1, namely, that value is defined on changes in wealth rather than levels, that the value function is "kinked" at the status quo with a loss aversion coefficient of about two or a bit more (the function immediately to the left of the status quo is twice as steep as to the right), and that the marginal value of changes is diminishing with larger deviations from the status quo having ever smaller marginal effects on the individual's valuation of the event so that the value function is convex in losses and concave in gains (called the *reflection effect*).

A shortcoming of this literature to date, as the loss aversion interpretation of the stock premium puzzle revealed, is that situation dependence is an incomplete representation of preferences unless it is joined with an account of how preferences dynamically adjust to new situations, which is to say, how preferences evolve. The experiments and other data introduced here show that situations induce preferences; but they tell us little about the process by which people adjust to a new situation, whether it be stock market losses, the lost of sight, the promotion into a managerial position, or the transformation of a simple hunter-gatherer society to a modern market-based economy. I will return to the evolution of preferences under the influence of changing economic situations in chapter 11.

The shortcomings and reformulation considered in this section have addressed the formal core of the conventional theory of rational action. The recent accumulation of empirical anomalies concerning the substantive aspect of the theory, namely, the axiom of self-interested behavior, has also motivated reformulations based on the concept of social preferences.

SOCIAL PREFERENCES

In one-shot prisoners' dilemma experiments, the rate of cooperation is commonly between 40 and 60 percent, despite mutual defection being the dominant strategy equilibrium (Fehr and Fischbacher 2001b). Many subjects prefer the mutual cooperation outcome over the higher material payoff they would get by defecting on a cooperator. When they defect, it is because they hate being taken advantage of; many defect to avoid risking this, not because it is the payoff maximizing strategy independently of the other's actions. These results suggest that people care about others, and they care about why things happen independently of the outcome. *Social preferences* are these *other-regarding* and *process-regarding* reasons for behavior.

Here is an example of *process-regarding preference*: you may accept with equanimity a bad outcome determined by a coin flip, while angrily refusing the outcome were it imposed by someone whose intention was to harm you. A process-regarding preference is defined as an evaluation based on the reasons why a state occurred rather than any intrinsic characteristic of the state. Other examples include a desire to help the less well off only if their poverty is the result of bad luck rather than laziness, keeping promises, and a predisposition to share things acquired by chance but not those acquired by one's effort. *The key aspect of process-regarding preferences is that the evaluation of a state is conditional on how it came about.* Behaviors are process sensitive for two reasons: the processes that determine an outcome often reveal important information about the intentions of others (e.g. the deserving poor), and they often provide cues concerning socially appropriate behaviors.

Other-regarding preferences include spite, altruism, and caring about the relationship among the outcomes for oneself and others. What Hobbes called the desire for "eminence" or a preference for "fair" outcomes are examples, as is Thorsten Veblen's "pecuniary emulation" exemplified by a desire to "keep up with the Joneses" (Veblen 1934 [1899]). *The key aspect of other-regarding preferences is that one's evaluation of a state depends on how it is experienced by others.* In analyzing preferences defined over the experiences of others (as well as one-

TABLE 3.1
A taxonomy of behaviors: costs and benefits to self
and others

	Cost to self	Benefit to Self
Benefit to other	Altruism	Mutualism
Cost to other	Spite	Selfish

self), it will be helpful to consider the following taxonomy (see table 3.1) of the distribution of benefits and costs when two people interact.

The left-hand column lists behaviors that are specifically precluded by the self-interest axiom. A behavior is *altruistic* if it confers a benefit on another while inflicting a cost on oneself (this standard biological definition is restricted to benefits and costs and does not concern intentions). Inflicting a cost on another at a cost to oneself (the lower left) may be motivated by spite, envy, inequality aversion (if the other is richer), or the desire to punish those who have done harm to you or to others or who have violated social norms. The right-hand column is familiar territory for economists. Because in the conventional model market exchange is undertaken for self-interested reasons, it must confer benefits on both parties and hence is an example of what biologists call *mutualism* (when it occurs between members of different species). Other examples include seemingly generous behaviors that increase an individual's payoffs over the long term due to repeated or indirect interactions. Following Robert Trivers (1971) these behaviors are sometimes called "reciprocal altruism," a misnomer given that the reciprocal altruist benefits from the behaviors in question. The Dalai Lama's terminology is more accurate: "The stupid way to be selfish is . . . seeking happiness for ourselves alone. . . . The intelligent way to be selfish is to work for the welfare of others" (Dalai Lama 1994:154). I restrict the term self-interested to the behaviors in the right column to avoid the tautological use of the term to mean any act that is voluntarily undertaken. The altruist may give with pleasure, but clarity is not served by calling this self-interest.

Everyday observation of others as well as introspection suggests that other-regarding and process-regarding preferences are important. I will shortly introduce experimental evidence that confirms these impressions. But I want to stress that the main evidence for social preferences comes not from experiments but from real world economic and other behaviors that are inexplicable in terms of self-interest (without resort to extensive ad hoc reasoning). Some of these behaviors were referred to in the introduction of this chapter. Others include volunteering for dangerous military and other tasks, tax compliance far in excess of that which would maximize expected incomes (in some countries), participating in various forms of collective action, and conforming to norms and laws in cases in which one's transgression would not be detected. Humans are unique among animals in the degree to which we cooperate among large numbers of non-kin; some of this cooperation is surely the result of institutions that make cooperative behavior a best response for people with self-regarding preferences (making cooperation a form of mutualism), but nobody seriously thinks that *all* of it can be explained this way.

There is an extensive literature on altruism, social comparison and other aspects of social preferences. I will illustrate the importance of social preferences by reference to *strong reciprocity*, not to be confused with the self-interested behaviors described by Trivers's "reciprocal altruism" and related concepts such as "indirect reciprocity" (conferring benefits on those who have benefitted others and receiving benefits in return as a result). By contrast to these "intelligent ways of being selfish," strong reciprocity motives may induce behaviors that are altruistic in the biologists' sense, conferring benefits to others in one's group at a cost to oneself. But reciprocity differs from altruistic behavior, which is not conditioned on the type or actions of the other.

The commonly observed rejection of substantial positive offers in the experimental Ultimatum Games is an example of reciprocity motives. Experimental protocols differ, but the general structure of the Ultimatum Game is simple. Subjects are anonymously paired for a single interaction. One is the "responder," and the other the "proposer." The proposer is provisionally awarded an amount ("the pie," "the pot," or some other culinary metaphor) known to the responder to be divided between proposer and responder. The proposer offers a certain portion of the pie to the responder. If the responder accepts, the responder gets the proposed portion and the proposer keeps the rest. If the responder rejects the offer, both get nothing. Figure 3.2 presents a version of the game in extensive form, with A's payoffs first. In this version the proposer simply chooses between two offers: divide the pie equally (5,5) or keep 8 and offer the respondent 2.

In this situation, the self-interest axiom predicts that an individual's actions are best responses defined over the outcomes of the game based on beliefs that other players also conform to the self-interest axiom. The self-interested proposer A will (by backward induction) determine that the responder B will accept the offer of 2 (because A believes that B is also self-interested) and so will propose the 8,2 split, which B will accept. In games in which an offer lower than 2 is possible, the self-interest axiom predicts that the proposer will offer either zero or the smallest

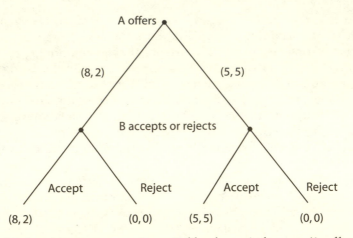

Figure 3.2 An ultimatum game. Note: Unlike the typical game, A's offer is restricted to just (5, 5) or (8, 2).

possible amount (in most games, the proposer can choose all values in whatever unit the pie is denominated from zero to the entire pie).

This game has been played anonymously for real money in hundreds of experiments with university student subjects in all parts of the world. The prediction of the self-interest axiom invariably fails. Modal offers are typically half of the pie, mean offers generally exceed 40 percent of the pie, and offers of a quarter or less are rejected with probabilities ranging from 40 to 60 percent. In experiments conducted in the United States, Slovakia, Japan, Israel, Slovenia, Germany, Russia, Indonesia, and many other countries, the vast majority of proposers offer between 40 and 50 percent of the pie (Fehr and Gaechter 2000b).

These results are interpreted by many as evidence for reciprocity motives on the part of the responder, who is willing to pay a price (forgoing a positive payoff) to punish the proposer for making an offer deemed unfair. The behavior of proposers is more complicated. Whether the large number of even splits (and other seemingly fair or near-fair offers) is explained by adherence to fairness norms or altruism by the proposer or to self-interestedness informed by a belief that the responder may reject an unfair offer cannot be easily determined. Substantial offers violate the self-interest axiom in *either* case, but the proposer does not exhibit reciprocity for the simple reason that as first mover he has no information about B on which to condition his behaviors. The evidence for reciprocity motives thus comes from the responders' behaviors, not the proposers'. Other interpretations—the respondents may be seeking to implement an egalitarian outcome rather than to punish the proposer, for example—have been suggested, but as we will see presently, the evidence for reciprocity motives is quite compelling.

Results challenging the fundamental behavioral model in economics were bound to be subjected to critical scrutiny. Some wondered if the results were due to the relatively low stakes in the game. But subsequent experiments conducted among university students in Indonesia for a "pie" equal to three months average expenditures reproduced the same results (Cameron 1998). Experiments with U.S. students with a pie of $100 to $400 did not alter the results (Hoffman, McCabe, and Smith 1996, Fehr and Fischbacher 2001b). Behavior consistent with social preferences has been common in other high-stakes game — for example, a gift exchange game in Russia with earnings two- to three-times the monthly income of the subject (Fehr and Fischbacher 2001b). It appears that the violations of the predictions of the standard model are not the result of the stakes being too small to focus the attention or elicit the true motives of the experimental subjects. Others suggested that subjects' may have misunderstood the game, but later experiments in which subjects played the game many times with different partners lent no credence to this concern (Fehr and Fischbacher 2003). A final skeptical suggestion was that the subjects may not have adapted their behavior to the nonrepeated nature of the interaction, perhaps following rules of thumb derived from more common repeated interactions. But experimental subjects readily distinguish between repeated and nonrepeated interactions (adapting their behaviors accordingly). And in any case, use of a rule of thumb consistent with the observed play contradicts the standard model, however it came about. While debate concerning the interpretation of the games continues, there is a consensus that other-regarding motives are involved.

That other-regarding motives are important is not the only lesson. Suppose the ultimatum game in figure 3.2 were to be played with slight modifications in the protocol. In the experiment called Γ_1, the designation of proposer (occupied by A in the figure) is determined, as it is in most experiments, by a coin flip: if the coin says that A is the proposer, the game is as in figure 3.2. In Γ_2 the proposer is selected as in Γ_1 but a second coin is then flipped determining which action A will take. A then makes the indicated offer and finally B rejects or accepts. Introspection, as well as experimental results, suggest that the two games are fundamentally different in the behaviors they will evoke from B, even though B is choosing among the identical payoffs in both. In games like Γ_2, low offers are accepted that in Γ_1 would be rejected. A plausible explanation of the difference concerns reciprocity. In Γ_2 reciprocity motives will not come into play because B knows that, should the coin flip dictate the 8,2 proposal, A did not *intend* to make an unfair offer but was merely

TABLE 3.2
Varieties of ultimatum game play

Game	Results	Interpretation	Source
Γ_1 Standard	Modal offer ½, offers < 20% rejected	Reciprocity by respondent	Cited in text
Γ_2 Randomized offers	Few rejections of low offers	Proposer not responsible	Blount (1995)
Γ_3 Roles chosen by quiz	Many low offers, few rejections	Proposer "deserving"	Hoffman, McCabe, Shachat, and Smith (1994)
Γ_4 "Exchange Game"	Many low offers, few rejections	Situational framing	Hoffman, McCabe, Shachat, and Smith (1994)
Γ_5 No "fair" offers possible	Low offers not rejected	Proposer's intentions matter.	Falk, Fehr, and Fischbacher (2003)
Γ_6 Punishment by third party	C punishes A's low offer to B	Generalized fairness norms	Fehr and Fischbacher (2001a)
Γ_7 Standard: Au/ Gnau	Offers > ½ common and are rejected	Endogenous and situation-dependent prefs	Henrich, Bowles, Boyd, Camerer, Fehr, Gintis, and McElreath (2001)
Γ_8 Standard: Machiguenga	Many low offers, very few rejections	Endogenous and situation-dependent prefs	Henrich (2000)

constrained to do so by the rules of the game. The comparison illustrates process-regarding preferences: in both cases B got a bad offer, but in the second case the process determining the bad deal made it clear that it did not come about as a result of A's bad intentions. Had rejections of low offers in Γ_1 been motived by inequality aversion rather than reciprocity motives, for example, Γ_2 would have been played the same way.

Now consider Γ_3, in which the proposer position is designated not by a random draw but on the basis of a current events quiz taken prior to the play of the game, with A, the higher scorer, becoming the proposer, to whom B responds. Experimental subjects play Γ_3 differently than the standard Γ_1: proposers are more likely to keep a substantial fraction of the pie to themselves, and quite unequal proposals are frequently accepted. Now alter the game again, this time simply by naming Γ_4, "The Exchange Game" rather than "Divide $10." What the game is *called* should have not effect on behavior in the conventional framework, but it does: proposers offered less and lower offers were accepted. These and other experiments are summarized in table 3.2.

It is not difficult to think of reasons why people play Γ_3 differently from Γ_1: responders may feel that the proposers' low offers should not be punished as they reflect the proposers' greater deservingness (having earned the role of proposer by their test score). But what of Γ_4, "The Exchange Game"? It seems likely that the experimental subjects took the name of the game as a situational cue and as a result acted on the more self-regarding motivations in their behavioral repertoires. But however one understands the differences, they cannot be accounted for by the structure of the game's payoffs, for these remain unchanged by the differing processes of role designation, framing, and selection of actions. Another variant of the game (Γ_5) reaffirms the impressions that rejections are motivated by the desire to punish unfairness on the part of the proposer, not simply by the desire to avoid accepting an uneven split: retain the 8,2 offer of the standard game, but restrict the proposer to 10, 0 (an even more "unfair" offer) as the only alternative to 8,2. Rejections of the 8,2 offer were less than a quarter as frequent in Γ_5 than in Γ_1.

An important role for ethical values is suggested by Γ_6, which involves three people and is not strictly an Ultimatum Game. A assigns some part of the pie to B (who simply receives the offer and has no other role); then C, who has observed the pie size and the offer, may choose to reduce A's payoff by allocating some of C's endowment (like the pie provided by the experimenter) for this purpose. Allocations by A of half or more of the pie to B are never punished; but when A gives B less than half, C is willing to pay to punish A. In this case C acts very much like the responder in the standard Ultimatum Game but is responding to a seemingly unfair offer not to himself but to another (anonymous) person. Fehr and Fischbacher found than punishment by such third parties as C is only slightly less strong than punishment by the recipient of a low offer in the standard ultimatum game setup.

I report also two experiments in which the subject pool is not—as is usually the case—composed of university students but instead were members of fifteen small-scale societies with little contact with markets, governments, or modern institutions. My colleagues and I (a team of 17 anthropologists and economists) designed the experiments to explore whether the results reported above are common in societies with quite different cultures and social institutions (Henrich, Bowles, Boyd, Camerer, Fehr, Gintis, and McElreath 2004). The fifteen societies included hunter-gathers, herders, and farmers. Among the Au and Gnau people in Papua New Guinea, offers of more than half of the pie were common, and high and low offers were rejected with equal frequency. This seemingly odd result is not surprising in light of the practice of competitive gift giving as a means of establishing status and subordinacy in these and many other New Guinea societies. By contrast, among the Machiguenga in Amazonian Peru, almost three-quarters of the offers were a quarter of the pie or less and there was just a single rejection, a pattern strikingly different from the experiments conducted thus far. However, even among the Machiguenga, the mean offer was 27 percent, suggesting that offers exceeded the expected payoff maximizing offer.

Analysis of the experiments in the fifteen simple societies we studied led us to the following conclusions: behaviors are highly variable across groups, not a single group approximated the behaviors implied by the self-interest axiom, and between group differences in behavior seem to reflect differences in the kinds of social interaction experienced in everyday life. The evidence for economic conditions affecting behavioral norms is quite compelling. For example, the Aché in Paraguay share equally among all group members some kinds of food (meat and honey) acquired through hunting and gathering. Most Aché proposers contributed half of the pie or more. Similarly, among the Lamalera whale hunters of Indonesia, who hunt in large crews and divide their catch according to strict sharing rules, the average proposal was 58 percent of the pie. Moreover the Indonesian whale hunters played the game very differently from the Indonesian university students mentioned above.

The Ultimatum Game is one of many in which experimental subjects have behaved in ways that are strongly at variance with the predictions of the self-interest axiom. Colin Camerer and Ernst Fehr (2004) survey seven games in which experiments have suggested the salience of social preferences. One of these, the Public Goods Game, is both important as an analogy to many real world economic problems, and instructive about human behavior. It is sometimes called an *n*-person prisoners' dilemma because it has the same incentive structure: if players conform to the self-interest axiom, contributing nothing to the public good (analogous to defection) is the dominant strategy equilibrium, but universal contribution maximizes total payoffs. Here is the game: n players are each given an "endowment" y and then simultaneously select an amount $c_i \in [0,y]$ to contribute to the public good. Each player's payoffs are $\pi_i = y - c_i + m\Sigma_j c_j$ for $j = 1 \ldots n$. This describes a Public Goods Game if $m < 1 < mn$. The first of these inequalities implies that the individual's best response is to contribute nothing, and the second implies that total payoffs (summing over the group) are maximized if everyone contributes his entire endowment. Variants of the Public Goods Game have been used to model individual extraction from a common pool environmental resource; applications include contribution to joint projects such as payment of taxes and participating in strikes.

The prediction of the self-interest axiom ($c_i = 0 \ \forall \ i$) is consistently contradicted in experiments (surveyed by Ledyard 1995). In one-shot games contributions average about half of the endowment, while in multi-period games contributions begin around half and then decline, so that a majority of players contribute nothing in the final round of a ten-round game. This decline in contribution was initially thought to confirm the conventional model, the idea being that once the subjects had figured out the game, they contributed nothing. But an experiment in which a second ten-round public goods game was unexpectedly begun at the end of the first ten-round game suggests that this is not the case: in the second game players again began with contributions of about half. Many have interpreted the decline in contributions as a reflection of the disappointment of expectations that others would contribute more, along with the desire to punish low contributors (or at least not to be taken advantage of) in a situation in which this could only be done by reducing one's own contributions.

Strong support for this latter view is provided by an ingenious experiment designed by Fehr and Gaechter (2002): it has the same public goods structure as above except that after individuals contributed, their contributions were made known (by an identifying number only, not by name, of course) to all group members, who then had the opportunity to punish others in the group, imposing a cost (payoff reduction) on both the punisher and the punished.[9] In one experiment with this game, Fehr and Gachter adopted what is called the perfect strangers treatment: after each round of the ten-round experiment the groups were reshuffled so that players knew that no player would ever encounter any other player more than once. Thus, the motivation for punishment could not be self-interest. If low contributors respond to punishment by contributing more in subsequent rounds, they raise the payoffs of others but not of the punisher (due to the perfect strangers treatment). Thus punishment is no less a public good than the initial contribution. This is transparently the case on the last round of the game, when the last action taken by any player is the decision to engage in costly punishment of fellow group members: those who punish under these condi-

[9] An earlier experiment of this type with similar results is Ostrom, Gardner, and Walker (1994).

tions must value punishment per se rather than any anticipated consequence of punishment for their game payoffs based on the modification of the behaviors of others.

In Fehr and Gaechter's Public Goods Game with punishment, contributions started at about half the endowment (as in the standard game) but then *rose* rather than fell over the course of the game. My coauthors and I (reported in Bowles and Gintis 2002b) implemented a similar game in which we confirmed what one would expect: punishment is directed at low contributors, and they respond strongly to punishment. Those who thought they could cheat on the last round by reducing their contributions paid dearly for their mistake. We also found something quite unexpected. When those contributing *above* the mean were punished (as they occasionally were), they sharply *reduced* their contributions. Even more striking is the fact that the positive response to punishment by the low contributors was not a best response defined over the game payoffs. Taking account of the observed relationship between the expected amount of punishment and one's offer, zero contribution remained the best response, but nonetheless those punished responded by contributing more.

A reasonable interpretation of these experiments is that, as in the Ultimatum Game, people are willing to pay to punish those who violate social norms even when there is no expectation of future or indirect payoff. In other words the subjects were acting in accordance with reciprocity motives. But something else seems to be at work. The fact that punishment induced more contribution by the shirkers (contrary to the payoff-maximizing choice, even when the likely punishment is taken into account) suggests that social sanction by peers may mobilize feelings of shame in situations in which the punishment carries some legitimacy (in the eyes of the person punished). In two similar experiments — one in the laboratory and one in the field among farmers in Zimbabwe — "punishment" merely conveyed displeasure and did not reduce the payoffs of the one punished. But the fact that those punished contributed more in subsequent periods shows the strong effects of social sanction, consistent with the "shame" interpretation (Barr 2001, Masclet, Noussair, Tucker, and Villeval 2003). In chapter 4 I provide a model of how social preferences such as shame and reciprocity may support cooperation in public goods interactions.

The Public Goods Game provides a nice example of situation-dependent behaviors and framing. Jean Ensminger conducted public goods experiments with the Orma, a herding people in Kenya, as part of the multi-cultural experimental project mentioned above. When the Orma need some public good — a new primary school or the repair of a road, for example — members of the community are asked for a voluntary contribution to the project, the amounts increasing in the amount of wealth (cattle) of the family. This system of voluntary public goods provision is called *harambee*. When Ensminger explained the Public Goods Game to her subjects, they promptly dubbed it the "*Harambee* Game," and their contributions were strongly predicted by their (real world) wealth, just as would have been the case in a real *harambee*. When the Orma subjects played the Ultimatum Game, they did not analogize it to the *harambee* (or apparently to any other aspect of their everyday life) and wealth did not predict any aspect of their experimental play.

Do people behave in natural settings the way they do in experiments? The relationship between experimental play and real world behaviors is complex, and I do not want to claim an overly close correspondence between the two. Contrary to the (misguided, in my view) hopes of some experimenters, experimental games do not tap abstract motives uncontaminated by situations. In this, experimental play is much like any other behaviors and the experiment is just another situation.[10] The game situation, the instructions of the experimenter, and the like are a very strong frame and we cannot expect them to be without effect. Experiments do not reveal the essence of a universal human nature. Rather, they simply show that common behaviors in generic social interactions are readily explained by social preferences, thus suggesting that the many real world examples of seeming violations of the self-interest axiom are not the result of the peculiarities of the particular real world examples.

An Empirically Based Social Preference Function

In response to the violations of the self-interest axiom in a number of experiments, economists have attempted to reformulate a utility function capable of explaining the above behaviors in a parsimonious manner. Is there a utility function that is at once simple enough to be tractable and sufficiently robust to explain not just one of the experimental anomalies but all of them? There now exist a number of utility functions that are capable of explaining a wide range of experimental behaviors (Falk and Fischbacher 1998, Fehr and Schmidt 1999, Bolton and Ockenfels 1999, Rabin 1993, Charness and Rabin 1999, Levine

[10] Loewenstein (1999) provides a skeptical but balanced assessment. Behaviors in games have been shown to predict real world behaviors in a few cases: those who trusted in a trust experiment by Glaeser, Laibson, Scheinkman, and Soutter (2000), for example, exhibited more trust in a number of real world situations. By contrast, answers to standard survey questions on trust were completely uncorrelated with any measured behaviors (experimental or non-experimental).

1998). The basic ingredients of the proposed utility functions are self-interest, altruism, spite, fair-mindedness, and reciprocity. The functions differ in the way that these components are combined, and the types of behaviors the authors wish to stress.

Here is a utility function (proposed by Fehr and Schmidt) that takes account of both self-interest and what they term "inequality aversion." A fair (i.e., inequality averse) utility function of person i (interacting with just one other person, j) is given by

$$U_i = \pi_i - \delta_i \max(\pi_j - \pi_i, 0) - \alpha_i \max(\pi_i - \pi_j, 0) \qquad (3.3)$$

where π_j and π_i are the material payoffs to the two individuals, and $\delta_i \geq \alpha_i$ and $\alpha_i \in [0,1]$. This utility function expresses individual i's valuation of her own payoff as well as her aversion to differences in payoff, with disadvantageous differences $(\pi_j - \pi_i > 0)$ being more heavily weighted (δ_i) than advantageous differences (α_i). The upper bound on α precludes what might be termed "self-punishing" levels of aversity to advantageous inequality: an individual with $\alpha = 1$ cares only about the other's payoffs (if they fall short of his own). By contrast, a person (i) very averse to disadvantageous inequality might prefer $\pi_j = \pi_i = 0$ to $\pi_i = 1$ and $\pi_j = 2$, so δ may exceed 1.

To see the implications of fair-mindedness for both sharing and punishing behaviors, suppose the two are to divide one unit $(\pi_i + \pi_j = 1)$ and that $\alpha_i > \frac{1}{2}$. In this case $dU_i/d\pi_i < 0$ for all divisions such that $\pi_i - \pi_j > 0$. Thus individual i's preferred share would be to divide the unit equally (so if the share initially favored i over j, i would prefer to transfer some of the payoff to j). Similarly, if $\delta_i \geq \frac{1}{2}$ and payoffs were divided so that j was to receive 0.6 and i 0.4, i would be willing to pay 0.1 to reduce the payoffs of j by 0.3 so that both received 0.3. Even more striking, in this case, i would refuse an offer of less than 0.25 if by doing so both would receive nothing (as in the Ultimatum Game).

Fair-mindedness may explain another experimental anomaly mentioned at the outset: a substantial number of experimental subjects in one-shot prisoners' dilemma games cooperate (despite defecting being the dominant strategy in the game payoffs). A fairminded row player (one with the above Fehr-Schmidt utility function) facing the standard prisoners' dilemma material payoffs $a > b > c > d$ would cooperate if he knew the column player would cooperate as long as the disutility he experienced from advantageous inequality is sufficiently large, or $\alpha > (a - b)/(a - d)$ (see table 3.3).

If this inequality obtains (which it may because the right-hand side is necessarily less than unity), then the resulting game is no longer a prisoners' dilemma but rather an Assurance Game, so there exists some critical value $p^* \in (0,1)$ such that if Row believes that Column will

TABLE 3.3
Standard Prisoners' Dilemma and Fair-minded
Utility Payoffs for Row

	Cooperate	*Defect*
Cooperate	b	d
	b	**$d - \delta(a - d)$**
Defect	a	c
	$a - \alpha(a - d)$	**c**

Note: utility payoffs for fairminded row player are in bold.

defect with probability less than p^*, then his best response is to cooperate. You can also readily show that $dp^*/d\alpha > 0$ while $dp^*/d\delta < 0$, so if this interaction took place among randomly paired fairminded players in an evolutionary setting of the type modeled in the previous chapter, increasing the disutility of advantageous inequality enlarges the basin of attraction of the mutual cooperate equilibrium while increasing the disutility of disadvantageous inequality does the opposite.

In an experiment designed to estimate the parameters of a function like eq. (3.3) Loewenstein, Thompson, and Bazerman (1989) created a variety of scenarios that had in common that an amount had to be divided, but the situations differed in the personal relationship among the participants (negative, neutral, or positive) and in the nature of the interaction (business, other). They found that disadvantageous inequality was strongly disliked, irrespective of the nature of either the personal relationship or the transaction. By contrast, advantageous inequality was disliked by 58 percent of the subjects in the nonbusiness transaction but was preferred by most in the business transaction, being disliked by only 27 percent. The nature of the personal relationship mattered, too: in the positive personal or neutral relationship setting, 53 percent disliked advantageous inequality, while in the negative relationship setting only 36 percent did. This experiment provides direct evidence on inequality aversion and is also consistent with the view that behaviors are commonly conditioned on one's belief about the other person (positive or negative) and are situationally specific (business or not).

Fairminded preferences are defined over outcomes, but reciprocal preferences depend as well on one's belief about the intention or type of the individual one is dealing with. Following ideas initially laid out by Rabin (1993) and Levine (1998), the following function incorporates self-interest, altruism, and reciprocity. An individual's utility depends on his own material payoff and that of other individuals $j = 1 \ldots n$ according to

$$U_i = \pi_i + \Sigma_j \beta_{ij} \pi_j \qquad \text{for } i \neq j \tag{3.4}$$

where β_{ij}, the weight of j's material payoff in i's preferences, is

$$\beta_{ij} = \frac{a_i + \lambda_i a_j}{1 + \lambda_i} \; \forall \, j \neq i \tag{3.5}$$

and $a_i \in [-1,1]$ and $\lambda_i \geq 0$. The parameter a_i is i's level of unconditional good will or ill will (altruism or spite) toward others, and $a_j \in [-1,1]$ is i's belief about j's good will, while λ_i indicates the extent to which i conditions his evaluations of others' payoffs on (beliefs about) the other's type. If $a_i = 0$ and $\lambda_i > 0$, then individual i is a nonaltruistic reciprocator (exhibits neither good will nor spite unconditionally but conditions her behavior on the goodness or spitefulness of others).

If $\lambda_i = 0$ and $a_i \neq 0$, then i exhibits unconditional altruism or spite, depending on the sign of a_i. The denominator is augmented by λ_i so that $\beta_{ij} \leq 1$, thereby restricting one's valuation of the others' payoffs to being no greater than one's own. Note that $d\beta_{ij}/d\lambda_i$ has the sign of $(a_j - a_i)$, which means that the level of reciprocity affects the extent to which others' payoffs enters into one's own evaluation, increasing it if the other is kinder than oneself, and conversely. If $a_j = a_i$ then $\beta_{ij} = a_i$ for any level of reciprocity.

Like the inequality-averse function, this reciprocity-based utility function can be used to explain generous and punishing behaviors. The analysis is considerably more complicated, however. In most social interactions we have some prior beliefs about the others' types based on knowledge of their prior behavior, cues based on other facts about them (including their status as an "insider" or an "outsider" in the current interaction), and the situation itself. Thus one's beliefs about the others' types and hence one's valuation of their benefits plausibly depends on their past actions, which depend on their beliefs on one's own type, and so on. If one is a reciprocator and believes that others are altruistic, one may engage in conditional generosity. But if the generosity is not reciprocated, one may update one's beliefs about the others' types and engage in punishment or at least withdrawal of generosity, as was witnessed in the public goods experiments. Thus, behaviors may be both path dependent and situationally specific: a situation that induces beliefs that others are altruistic may support high and sustainable levels of generosity, while the same individuals interacting in another situation may engage in mutually costly spiteful punishment. The path-dependent and situationally specific nature of behaviors may explain why subjects' play is so affected by changes in experimental protocols that would be irrelevant were the conventional model correct. It also might illuminate why such large differences in behaviors are found in our cross-cultural study.

CONCLUSION

The inequality-averse and reciprocity-based functions just presented are important steps toward the construction of a more adequate conception of behavior. But the process is ongoing and far from completion. The evidence that inequality aversion and reciprocity motives are common does not suggest that people are irrational. Indeed, strong experimental evidence indicates that when individuals give to others (e.g., in a Dictator Game) their behavior conforms to the transitivity assumptions and other requirements of rational choice (Andreoni and Miller 2002). Moreover, people respond to the price of giving, giving more when it costs them less to benefit the other. The importance of other-regarding motives thus does not challenge the assumption of rationality but rather suggests that the arguments of the utility function should be expanded to account for individuals' concerns for others.

The experimental and other evidence also suggests an adequate formulation should take account of the behavioral heterogeneity of most human groups. Using data from a wide range of experiments, Ernst Fehr and Simon Gaechter estimate that between 40 and 66 percent of subjects exhibit reciprocal choices. The same studies suggest that between 20 and 30 percent of the subjects exhibit conventional self-regarding outcome-oriented preferences (Fehr and Gaechter 2000b, Camerer 2003). Loewenstein, Thompson, and Bazerman (1989) distinguished among the following types in their experiments:

> *Saints* consistently prefer equality, and they do not like to receive higher payoffs than the other party even when they are in a negative relationship with the opponent . . . *loyalists* do not like to receive higher payoffs in neutral or positive relationships, but seek advantageous inequality when in negative relationships . . . *Ruthless competitors* consistently prefer to come out ahead of the other party regardless of the type of relationships. (p. 433)

Of their subjects, 22 percent were saints, 39 percent were loyalists, and 29 percent were ruthless competitors (the rest could not be classified).

Thus, the objective of a reformulation of the behavioral foundations of economics should not be some new *Homo sociologicus* to replace *Homo economicus*, but a framework capable of taking account of heterogeneity. This task is essential because heterogeneity makes a difference in outcomes, but it is challenging because the effects are not adequately captured by a process of simple averaging. The outcome of interaction among a population that is composed of equal numbers of saints and ruthless competitors will not generally be the average of the outcomes of two populations with just one type, because small differences in the distribution of types in a population can have large effects on how *everyone* behaves.

Moreover, seemingly small differences in institutions can make large differences in outcomes. Imagine a one-shot Prisoners' Dilemma Game played between a self-interested player (for whom Defect is the dominant strategy in the simultaneous moves game) and a reciprocator (who prefers to Cooperate if the other cooperates and to Defect otherwise) (Fehr and Fischbacher 2001b). Suppose the players' types are known to each. If the game is played simultaneously, the reciprocator, knowing that the other will Defect, will do the same. The outcome will be mutual defection. If the self-interested player moves first, however, she will know that the reciprocator will match whatever action she takes, narrowing the possible outcomes to {Cooperate, Cooperate} or {Defect, Defect}. The self-interested player will therefore cooperate and mutual cooperation will be sustained as the outcome. Recall, as another example, that in the Public Goods-With-Punishment Game, those with reciprocal preferences not only acted generously themselves, but they apparently also induced the selfish types to act *as if* they were generous. But had there been too few reciprocators, all players (reciprocators and self-interested types alike) would have converged to zero contribution.

In addition to heterogeneity across individuals, versatility of individuals must also be accounted for. In the Ultimatum Game, proposers often offer amounts that maximize their expected payoffs, given the observed relationship between offers and rejections: they behave self-interestedly *but expected responders not to.* Moreover, *the same individuals* when in the role of responder typically reject substantial offers if they appear to be unfair, thus confirming the expectations of the proposer and violating the self-interest axiom.

Finally, as we have noted earlier (and will discuss in chapter 11), preferences are to some extent learned rather than exogenously given: durable changes in an individual's reasons for behavior often take place as a result of one's experience. This means that populations that experience different structures of social interaction over prolonged periods are likely to exhibit differing behaviors, not simply because the constraints and incentives entailed by these institutions are different but also because the structure of social interaction affects the evolution of both behavioral repertoires, the ways in which situations cue behaviors, and the way outcomes are evaluated. (Because the functioning of institutions depends on the preferences of the individuals involved, it will also be the case that institutions are endogenous with respect to preferences; I model the resulting process, called the *coevolution of preferences and institutions*, in chapters 11 through 13.)

Progress in the direction of a more adequate behavioral foundation for economics must take account of these three aspects of people: namely, their *heterogeneity, versatility*, and *plasticity*.

New theories must also address two challenges. The first concerns the normative status of preferences. If preferences are to explain behaviors, they cannot unassisted also do the work of evaluating outcomes. The reason is that some common reasons for behavior—weakness of will, spite, and addiction come to mind—often induce behaviors the outcomes of which few would condone.

The second challenge arises because the experimental and other evidence indicating the importance of social preferences poses a difficult evolutionary puzzle. If many of us are fairminded and reciprocal, then we must have acquired these preferences somehow, and it would be a good check on the plausibility of social preference theories and the empirical evidence on which they are based to see if a reasonable account of the evolutionary success of these preferences can be provided. Generosity toward one's genetic relatives is readily explained. The evolutionary puzzle concerns nonselfish behaviors toward non-kin (meaning behaviors bearing individual costs with no benefit, or the lefthand column in table 3.1, above.) Among non-kin, selfish preferences would seem to be favored by any payoff-monotonic evolutionary processes, whether genetic or cultural. Thus, the fairmindedness that induces people to transfer resources to the less well off, and the reciprocity motives that impel us to incur the costs of punishing those who violate group norms, on this account, are doomed to extinction by long term evolutionary processes. If social preferences are common, this conventional evolutionary account must be incorrect.

In later chapters I return to this question and provide a series of models explaining the evolutionary success of social preferences. In particular I will explore the contribution to the evolutionary success of nonselfish traits made by characteristic structures of human social interaction, namely, social segmentation, repeated interactions, and reputation building (in chapter 7) and the enforcement of group-level norms and intergroup conflict (in chapters 11 and 13). In many cases the evolutionary success of what appear to be unselfish traits is explained by the fact that when an accounting of long-term and indirect effects is done, the behaviors are payoff-maximizing, often representing forms of mutualism. But I will also introduce plausible models accounting for the evolutionary success of behaviors that benefit other members of ones's group at a cost to oneself.

Like the theory of social preferences, prospect theory also raises evolutionary puzzles. Hyperbolic discounters act in time-inconsistent ways; their average payoffs over a long period would be increased if they conformed to the dictates of the discounted utility model. Similarly, those who overweigh low probability events will earn lower expected payoffs than competitors who do the proper expected utility maximization. This does not mean that those using time-inconsistent discounting and violating the expected utility axioms are doomed, but given that either genetic or cultural evolution tends to favor those with higher payoffs, it does pose a puzzle. Similarly, loss-averse individuals forgo opportunities for substantial expected gains in risky situations. Their loss aversion thus disadvantages them in competition with others whose utility function is not kinked at the status quo. These evolutionary conundrums raised by prospect theory have received less attention than the puzzle of social preferences. I will not address them further, except to note that the initial evidence for hyperbolic discounting came from pigeons and rats, so this is not a uniquely human behavior.[11]

In chapter 4 I generalize the kinds of coordination problems introduced in chapter 1 as 2×2 games, and analyze the impressive variety of institutions, norms, and other ways people have developed to avoid or attenuate coordination failures. Social preferences, we will see, play a central role in this process.

[11] Hyperbolic discounting in humans and other animals is described in Ainslie (1975), Green and Myerson (1996), and Richards, Mitchell, de Wit, and Seiden (1997).

CHAPTER FOUR

Coordination Failures and Institutional Responses

In such a condition, [in the state of nature] . . . there is no place for
Industry; because the fruit thereof is uncertain, and consequently no
Culture of the Earth . . . And therefore every thing is his that getteth it
and keepeth it by force: which is neither Propiety nor Community; but
Uncertainty.

— Thomas Hobbes, *Leviathan* (1651)

Right now, my only incentive is to go out and kill as many fish as I can
. . . any fish I leave is just going to be picked by the next guy.

— John Sorlien, Rhode Island lobersterman

JOHN SORLIEN, the lobsterman, would not strike you as the kind of
Homo economicus you might find in a textbook or in Hobbes' state of
nature. He is actually an environmentalist of sorts, and as president
of the Rhode Island Lobsterman's Association he is up against a serious
problem of incentives, not a shortcoming of human nature. When he
started lobstering at age twenty-two, he set his traps right outside the
harbor at Point Judith, within a few miles of beach, and made a good
living. But the inshore fisheries have long since been depleted, and now
his traps lie seventy miles offshore. He and his fellow lobstermen are
struggling to make ends meet (Tierny 2000).

Across the world in Port Lincoln, on Australia's south coast, Daryl
Spencer, who dropped out of school when he was fifteen years old and
eventually drifted into lobstering, has fared notably better. During the
1960s the Australian government assigned licenses — one per trap — to
fishermen working at the time, and from that time on, any newcomer
seeking to fish off of Port Lincoln had to purchase licenses. Spencer
bought his first licenses for the present-day equivalent of about a thousand U.S. dollars each. His licenses are now worth well over a million
U.S. dollars (considerably more than his boat). More than giving
Spencer a comfortable nest egg, the policy has limited the Australian
loberstermen's work: Spencer has sixty traps, the maximum allowed;
Sorlien pulls eight hundred traps and makes a lot less money.

Point Judith and Port Lincoln represent extremes along a continuum

The first epigraph is from Hobbes (1983: 186, 296), the second from Tierny (2000: 38).

of failure and success in solving coordination problems. One wonders of course why the Point Judith fishermen do not simply emulate the Australians, especially since one of Solien's friends and a fellow Point Judith lobsterman visited Port Lincoln, returning with tales of millionaire fishermen living in mansions. But getting the rules right is a lot more difficult than the Port Lincoln story may suggest, and good rules often do not travel well. One of the common impediments to successful coordination in social dilemmas is that the rules that solve the problem also implement a division of the gains to cooperation. Had the young Daryl Spencer not agreed one day to help out a lobsterman friend by filling in as a deck hand, someone else would now be a millionaire, and Spencer might still be painting houses and complaining about the high price of lobsters.

Conflicts over the distribution of the gains to cooperation have sunk many otherwise viable agreements to limit the depletion of fishing stocks. A confederation of tribes of northwest Native American salmon fishers seeking to limit their catch decided to allocate shares of a given maximum catch to each tribe.[1] In the course of months of debate and bargaining, the following principles of division were advanced, with each proposal more or less transparently benefitting one or another tribe or class of individual: shares allocated in proportion to a tribe's number of members; shares proportionate to the number of fishermen in a tribe; individual shares based on each fisher's investment; one tribe, one share; shares to each tribe based on their aggregate investment in hatcheries and protection of the habitat; shares to each tribe based on the tribe's expenditure on lobbying efforts vis a vis the U.S. federal government; and, finally, shares to each tribe in proportion to the relative quantities of fish taken at the time of the initial treaty. Neither unrestricted competition nor marketable permits to catch specified amounts was proposed. The variety of proposals and their disparate effects on the distribution of income among the tribes suggest how challenging it may be to agree on a rule for sharing the gains to cooperation.

Coordination problems are ubiquitous — depleting a fishing stock is little different in the formal structure of its incentives than clogging the freeways or the Internet, arms races, free-riding on work mates, conspicuous consumption, fiscal competition among nation states, or leaving it to somebody else to tell the neighbors to turn down the volume on their TV. The ubiquity of these so-called commons problems explains the resonance of Hardin's famous tragedy, introduced in chapter 1, and the impressive amount of human ingenuity that has been invested in finding ways to avoid or mitigate their costly consequences.

[1] Described in Singleton (2004).

TABLE 4.1
A taxonomy of goods

	Rival	*Non-rival*
Excludable	Private goods	Spite goods
Non-excludable	Common property	Public goods

Hardin's tragedy has a particular setting—a common property resource problem—but the underlying structure exhibits a problem common to all coordination problems, which we saw in chapter 1, arise when one individual's actions confer benefits or costs on others that are not subject to contracts rewarding the actor for the benefits and penalizing him for the liabilities. As a result, these "external" effects are not taken account of when the individual chooses an action. *Common property resources* (also called *common pool resources*) are defined by two characteristics: it is difficult to exclude users (*nonexcludability*), and the use of the resource by one diminishes the benefits available to other users (*rivalness*). Shirts exhibit rivalness (my wearing this shirt precludes your wearing it), while information typically is nonrival (the fact that I know what time it is does not preclude your benefitting from the same information.) These two characteristics give the taxonomy in table 4.1.

Examples of common property resources and their associated coordination problems include congestion in transportation and communications networks, overuse of open access forests, fisheries, and water resources, and even status symbols and the social-climbing rat races they engender. An important example of common property goods inspired by Thorsten Veblen's concept of conspicuous consumption are termed *positional goods*, examples of which include power and prestige: rivalness exists because the value of the good depends on its distribution—one person's power is enhanced by someone else's lack of power. Similarly, conspicuous consumption of luxury goods is valuable precisely because it is not emulated by everyone.

Goods that are nonrival but for which users may readily be excluded (the opposite of common property resources) might be called "spite goods" because exclusion may not be welfare enhancing under these conditions. Examples include collecting a toll on a little used highway or charging admission to an uncrowded museum. Common property resources share the defining characteristic of difficulty of exclusion with public goods, and characteristic of rivalness with private goods. By contrast, public goods are both nonexcludable and nonrival, differing in both these respects from private goods. The incentive structure of public goods and common pool resource problems is the following.

A group of n members have a common project to which each may contribute effort and from which they all may benefit. Letting $e_j \geq 0$ be the effort devoted to the project by the jth member, the utility function of member j (identical for all members) is

$$u_j = be_j + c\gamma - \delta(e_j) \qquad (4.1)$$

with $\gamma = \gamma(\Sigma e_k)$ for $k = 1 \ldots n$, where the disutility of contributing, $\delta()$, is increasing and convex in its argument and the total supply of the public good, γ, is increasing in the sum of contributions of the members, so $\gamma' > 0$. The project is producing a public good if $c > 0$. (It is a public "bad" if $c < 0$, and the terms below apply in this case, too, but for ease of presentation I will assume $c > 0$.) The good is nonexcludable because $be_j + c\gamma > 0$ may occur when $e_j = 0$ (i.e., when member j is free riding on the contributions of others). The good is nonrival because the benefit enjoyed by j conditional on the level of the public good produced, namely, c, is independent of the numbers participating. If $c > 0$ and $b = 0$, we have a *pure public good*; if $c > 0$ and $b > 0$, the project is producing an *impure public good*. (Of course, if $c = 0$ and $b > 0$, it is a pure private good.)

Public goods are underprovided (and public bads overprovided) because $c \neq 0$, so individuals acting noncooperatively do not take account of the benefits their effort confers on others, namely, $c\gamma'$. To see this, assume $b = 0$ (a pure public good) and, ignoring subscripts (because the members' utility functions are identical), the sum of their sum of utilities, ω, is

$$\omega = n(c\gamma - \delta(e)) \qquad (4.2)$$

Setting e to maximize ω requires $cn\gamma' = \delta'$, thereby equating the marginal benefit of effort devoted to the public good to the marginal disutility of effort. Each individual, selecting e to maximize utility (eq. 4.1) noncooperatively, will, however, set $c\gamma' = \delta'$, and will thereby contribute suboptimally (this is a maximum only if $c\gamma'' < \delta''$, namely, that the disutility of effort is increasing in effort at a greater rate that the marginal product of effort).

By contrast to the public good case, a common pool resource problem has the following form. Assume $\gamma = \gamma(\Sigma e_k)$ is increasing and then decreasing in its argument. And let the individual benefit from the project (which was $be_j + c\gamma$ in the public goods case) be $s_j(e_j)\gamma$, where $\Sigma s_j = 1$ for $j = 1 \ldots n$, with $s_j()$ increasing in its argument and identical for all agents. The jth member's utility for this common pool resource case is thus

$$u_j = s_j(e_j)\gamma - \delta(e_j) \qquad (4.3)$$

Thus, member j gets a share of the good, s_j, determined by his level of effort, and the shares are exhaustive, so the good is rival. The good is nonexcludable because any member is free to devote effort to the project. Again making use of the fact that identical members will contribute the same amount, e, total utility in this case is

$$\omega = \gamma(ne) - n\delta(e) \tag{4.4}$$

Because the common pool resource is a rival good, the social optimum (found by setting e to maximize ω) requires (for positive e) that $\gamma' = \delta'$, which, as one would expect, requires that the marginal benefit equals the marginal disutility of effort. But the individual noncooperative optimization (varying e_j to maximize u_j in eq. 4.3) gives the first order condition for each member

$$s_j'\gamma + \gamma's_j = \delta'_j$$

The terms on the left are the marginal benefit of increased contribution; they capture the effect of greater effort on one's individual share of the resource plus the effect of additional effort on the value of the resource times the individual's share. If $\gamma' < 0$, as would be the case if the resource were a fishery or other environmental resource of the type described above, total utility would be maximized by setting $e = 0$ for each member. But unless the individual's share of the degradation of the resource, $\gamma's_j$, is large, noncooperative determination of effort levels will result in overexploitation. This is because $s_j'\gamma + \gamma's_j$ will be positive (even with $\gamma' < 0$), leading to a positive level of effort being expended.

When the actions open to individuals are limited to a set of distinct strategies, both public and common property goods problems take the form of n-person Prisoners' Dilemma Games with a Pareto-inferior dominant strategy equilibrium, introduced in chapter 1. In this chapter I will analyze a more general case in which actors may vary their strategies continuously in two generic models of a coordination problem. I call it generic because it encompasses the underlying reason for coordination failures—incomplete contracts—and yet includes the "invisible hand" interaction as a limiting case. Virtually all interesting common property or public goods problems involve large numbers of people, but the underlying structure of incentives and possible resolutions of the problem are more transparently introduced in the two-person example (returning to the fishers), with which I will begin in the next section. I then present an n-person version of the same model, illustrating it with the problem of team production. I show how social preferences such as shame, guilt, and reciprocity may allow coordination of the actions of large numbers of people in their mutual interest. I close with a taxonomy of coordination problems based on the nature of the underlying noncontractual effects.

The Tragedy of the Fishers Revisited

The setting. We return to the two fishers, now called Upper and Lower for ease of notation, who fish in the same lake, using their labor and their nets. They consume their catch and do not engage in any kind of exchange, nor do they make any agreements about how to pursue their economic activities. Yet the activities of each affect the well-being of the other: the more Upper fishes, the harder it is for Lower to catch fish, and conversely. To be specific (using lower case letters for Lower, upper case for Upper):

$$y = \alpha(1 - \beta E)e$$
$$Y = \alpha(1 - \beta e)E \qquad (4.5)$$

where y, Y = the amount of fish caught by Lower, Upper over some given period; α = a positive constant which varies with the size of the nets of each; β = a positive constant measuring the (adverse) effect of Upper's fishing on Lower's catch and conversely; and e, E = the amount of time (fraction of a twenty-four-hour day) that Lower, Upper each spend fishing.[2] Of course, we would generally expect α and β to differ for the two fishers (one may have larger nets, and for this reason may have a larger impact on the fishing success of the other than conversely), but for simplicity they are equal. Each derives well-being from eating fish and experiences a loss of well being with additional effort, according to the utility functions:

$$u = y - e^2$$
$$U = Y - E^2 \qquad (4.6)$$

Best Responses and Nash Equilibria. Best responses are no longer a single strategy conditional on a given action by others (as in chapter 1, where the strategy sets were discrete) but are now *best response functions*, indicating for every action that may be taken by the other what is the best response, namely, that which maximizes the actor's utility for that level of the other's action. The best response function is derived by maximizing the utility of each agent conditional on the actions taken by others.

The fact that *we* derive the best response function this way does not imply that individuals consciously solve this (sometimes quite complicated) optimizing problem every time *they* take an action. The general point here, relevant to the rest of the book, is that the use of optimizing

---

[2] The average and marginal productivity of a fisher does not vary with the amount of fishing he does but is reduced by the fishing of the other (recall that in any practical setting, the other is the total fishing effort of a large number of others). Assuming that output is linear in the effort of each, but declining in the effort of the sum of the others' effort, is a reasonable approximation for large n.

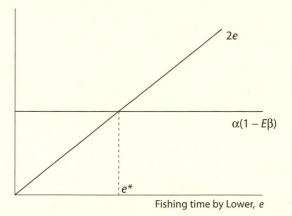

Figure 4.1 Lower's choice of e equates the marginal disutility of labor to the marginal benefit of fishing time given Upper's action, $\underline{E}$.

models as analytical tools does not require that the models be accurate descriptions of way that individuals arrive at decisions, as long as the individuals act *as if* they were solving such problems. In many, perhaps most, cases a reasonable assumption about humans is that we act like the adaptive agents modeled in chapters 2 and 3; that is, we occasionally observe what others like us are doing and tend to copy those who seem to be doing better. We may consciously decide on a behavioral rule of thumb designed to work well on the average and then abide by it unless it produces unsatisfactory results. Adapting one's behaviors in this way will lead the fishers to act *as if* they were maximizing, at least on the average and in the long run.

The optimum problem that yields Lower's best response function, then, is to vary e so as to maximize

$$u = \alpha(1 - \beta E)e - e^2.$$

Differentiating u with respect to e and setting the result equal to zero to find the optimal level of effort gives us the first order condition

$$u_e = \alpha(1 - \beta E) - 2e = 0,$$

which clearly requires Lower to equate the marginal (utility) productivity of her labor (the first term) with the marginal disutility of her effort (the second term), as is illustrated in figure 4.1.

This first order condition gives us a simple closed form best response function:

$$e = \frac{\alpha(1 - \beta E)}{2} \qquad (4.7)$$

The best-response function for Upper is derived in the same way.

There is another way to represent the best response function that will be illuminating for what follows. Using the utility functions above we can write Lower's utility function as a function of her and Upper's effort levels:

$$v = v(e, E)$$
$$V = V(e, E)$$

Presented in (e,E) space, as in figure 4.2, these functions describe familiar indifference loci (only Lower's are presented), and by setting

$$dv = v_e de + v_E dE = 0$$

we see that

$$\frac{dE}{de} = -\frac{v_e}{v_E}$$

Thus, we know that the slopes of the indifference loci (for Lower) are $-v_e/v_E$, and analogously for Upper. The thought experiment that gives the best response function is to hold constant some level of Upper's fishing time and ask how much fishing Lower would do under these circumstances. In figure 4.2 this is represented by treating the horizontal dotted line at $\underline{E}$ (an arbitrarily selected level of Upper's effort) as a constraint, and letting Lower maximize her utility, finding the point of tangency between her highest feasible indifference locus and the constraint. The slope of the constraint is zero, so the optimum requires that the slope of Lower's indifference locus be zero as well, and this requires that $v_e = 0$, as we saw above.

I write Lower's best response function as $e^* = e^*(E)$, the asterisk indicating a solution to an optimum problem. The representation of $e^*(E)$ in figure 4.2 is the locus of points for which $v_e = 0$ and at which Lower would therefore have no incentive to change what she did. We know that the Nash equilibrium must be a mutual best response. The Nash equilibrium value of e can thus be calculated by substituting Upper's best response function into Lower's best response function and solving for e, as is illustrated in figure 4.3. Because of the (assumed) symmetry of the problem, we have, for both Lower and Upper:

$$e^N = \frac{\alpha}{2 + \alpha\beta} = E^N \qquad (4.8)$$

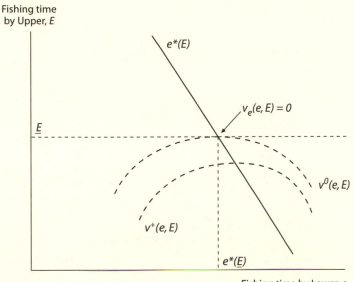

Figure 4.2 Lower's best response function, $e^*(E)$.

What do these values tell us? Without knowing the institutional structure of the interaction between the fishers we have no way of saying what their levels of fishing will be: these Nash equilibrium values might be irrelevant if one of the fishers is the first mover, for example. But it might be an unlikely outcome for an even simpler reason: this Nash equilibrium might be unstable.

Disequilibrium Dynamics and Stability. Stability requires that small perturbations of the equilibrium values be self-correcting. To see if this is true we need to know something about the out-of-equilibrium behavior of the fishers: what do they do when they are not at a Nash equilibrium? It is sometimes illuminating to think of the figure as a topographical map with $e^* = e^*(E)$ describing a ridge. Lower's optimizing process is a hill-climbing algorithm: for $e \neq e^*$ Lower's first order conditions are not satisfied, and for $e < e^*$ we can see from figure 4.1 that $\alpha(1 - \beta E) > 2e$, or the marginal benefit of fishing exceeds the marginal (disutility) cost of fishing, so Lower will choose to fish more.

The out-of-equilibrium dynamics of the system are modeled as follows: consistent with the idea that people have limited cognitive capacities, we assume that the fishers use a rule of thumb: at the end of this period, change one's behavior in the direction of what would have been optimal given what the other individual did this period. This is short-sighted in both directions: it looks backward only one period (using only this period's information to determine what to do next period),

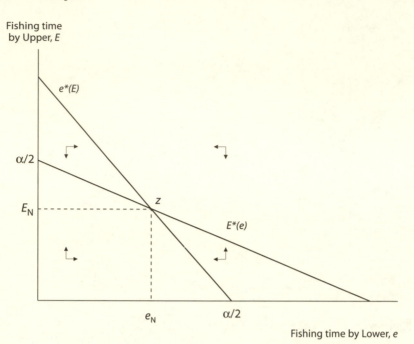

Figure 4.3 Out-of-equilibrium dynamics and a stable Nash equilibrium. Note: the arrows indicate the response to disequilibrium of the two fishers (horizontal movement for Lower, vertical for Upper.) The point z is the Nash equilibrium

and it does not look forward at all (assuming that the other's action will not change between this period and next). It amounts to the following rule: next period, move in the direction of the action that would have been optimal this period. Letting e' and E' be the fishers action next period, this rule of thumb gives us

$$\Delta e \equiv e' - e = \gamma(e^* - e)$$
$$\Delta E \equiv E' - E = \Gamma(E^* - E)$$

where γ and Γ are both positive fractions $\in$ (0,1] reflecting the speed of adjustment (how much of the gap between desired and actual level of fishing this period is closed by the choice of next period's level of fishing). Of course the speed of adjustment might differ between the two fishers (Lower might be a creature of habit with γ close to zero, and Upper a lightening responder like *Homo economicus* with $\Gamma = 1$). The dynamics of the system expressed by these equations say that each moves towards her or his best response function, as indicated by the arrows in figure 4.3.

But perhaps surprisingly, the fact that each fisher moves towards his or her best response function is not sufficient to insure stability of the

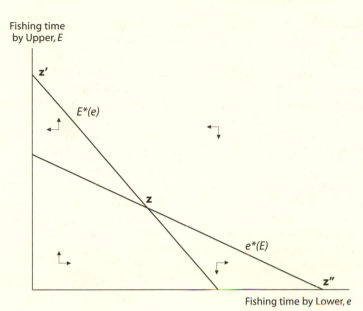

Figure 4.4 An unstable Nash equilibrium (z). Note there are also two stable Nash equilibria (z′ and z″)

Nash equilibrium outcome defined by their intersection. To see why this is so, suppose that the best response functions were such that if Upper fished one more hour, Lower would fish two fewer hours ($de^*/dE = -2$), and conversely; and imagine that the two are currently fishing at the Nash equilibrium values. Figure 4.4 gives the out-of-equilibrium dynamics: the Nash equilibrium is a saddle, and a perturbation of the Nash values is not self-correcting.

Whether a Nash equilibrium is asymptotically stable depends on the relative slopes of the two best response functions. Consider first a stable case, figure 4.3. For the Nash values to be stable, it must be that neither fisher is overly responsive to the other; that is, in figure 4.3, the $E^*(e)$ function should be "flatter" than the $e^*(E)$ function. Using the best response function's derived above this requires that

$$\frac{\alpha\beta}{2} < \frac{2}{\alpha\beta} \tag{4.9}$$

requiring that $\alpha\beta < 2$, which implies that the effect of variations in Upper's fishing on Lower, de^*/dE, be smaller in absolute value than 1. The expression is more complex where α and β differ for the two fishers, but the underlying intuition is the same: stability requires that actors do not over react.

Stability may be considered a necessary but not sufficient condition for a Nash equilibrium to be a good prediction of actual behavior. One reason why this is true is familiar: as we saw in chapter 2, there may be many stable Nash equilibria, as in figure 4.4. The second reason is less transparent: realistic rules for how individuals adapt their behavior to recent experience may fail to move players to the Nash equilibrium, even if it is unique and stable. In very complicated interactions, individuals may fail to "learn" how to play the Nash equilibrium. But even in a seemingly simple game — for instance, Rock, Paper Scissors — neither real people nor computer simulated agents generally play the Nash equilibrium strategies even after hundreds of rounds of the game (Sato, Akiyame and Farmer 2002). Rock Paper Scissors has a single mixed-strategy Nash equilibrium (play each randomly with probability one-third), but few players do this. Games with a single pure strategy Nash equilibria are much easier to play, even if their structure is much more complicated than Rock Paper Scissors.

Pareto-Inferior Outcomes. Is the Nash equilibrium Pareto optimal? We know that this would require a tangency of the two fishers indifference loci, or

$$\frac{v_e}{v_E} = \frac{V_e}{V_E}$$

This equation defines the *efficient contract locus*, namely, the locus of all Pareto-efficient pairs of fishing times by the two. We know that from any allocation at which both are fishing and the indifference loci are not tangent — that is, at which they intersect — there exists a different allocation that would make both better off. But the Nash equilibrium is a point on both best response functions, defined respectively by $v_e = 0$ and $V_E = 0$. At the Nash equilibrium, the two indifference loci cannot be tangent; in fact, they are perpendicular. So the Nash equilibrium is not Pareto optimal in this case. Two points on the efficient contract locus, p and ω, are indicated in figure 4.5.

To see why the Nash equilibrium is Pareto inferior, imagine that the two fishers could agree each to fish an arbitrarily small amount less. How would this affect their well-being? We know that $V_e < 0$ and $v_E < 0$ (because each's fishing gets in the way of the other, as indicated by β in their production functions). So for $de < 0$ and $dE < 0$, representing their hypothetical agreement to fish a little less, we need to evaluate the change in the utility of each:

$$
\begin{aligned}
dv &= de v_e + dE v_E \\
dV &= de V_e + dE V_E
\end{aligned}
\tag{4.10}
$$

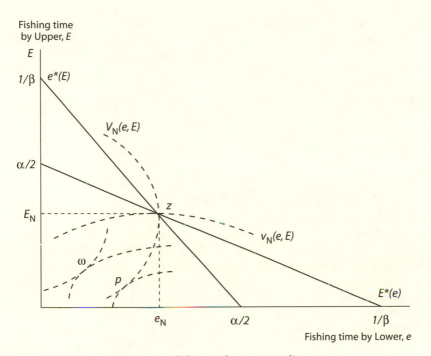

Figure 4.5 Nash equilibrium: stability and nonoptimality

Note that $v_e = 0$ and $V_E = 0$ because these equalities define the fishers' best response functions and the Nash is a mutual best response. Thus, both expressions above are positive: the utility of each would be enhanced by an agreement to fish a little less. Notice the basic logic here: each one would like the other to fish less, and (this is the important part) *because they have set their own fishing at its optimum level, they do not care about (infinitesimally small) reductions in their own fishing.* The lens created by the two indifference loci in figure 4.5 contains the Pareto improvements over the Nash equilibrium, z.

If a deal can be enforced, there's a deal to be made. But how might such an agreement be arrived at, and how might it be enforced?

Averting the Fishers' Tragedy

The tragedy of the fishers illustrates the generic source of coordination failures: given their preferences, the property rights relevant to the case, and other aspects of the incentives that shaped their decisions, the negative impact of their fishing on each other (v_E and V_e, respectively) was not part of in the optimizing process of each. Indeed, under the presumed rules of the game—a non-repeated, non-cooperative interaction—and preferences—self-regarding—it is hard to see how they could have averted the tragedy. But, like the south Australia loberstermen, some real fishers manage their common resource very well. When individuals cooperate to sustain a commons it is generally because they have managed to convert the commons tragedy into a different game or they do not have entirely self-regarding preferences, or both. This is where institutions come in.

Hardin (1968) believed that "freedom in the commons means ruin to all" (p. 1244), and as a result he advocated—"mutual coercion mutually agreed upon" (p. 1247). His Hobbesian pessimism overlooked the many noncoercive ways that local communities have averted the tragedy (Ostrom, Burger, Field, Norgaard, and Policansky 1999). Approaches include better definition and fewer impediments to the exchange of property rights, mutual monitoring, adherence to collectively beneficial social norms, and many more. Three basic approaches to commons regulation may be identified: *privatization* of the commons, *regulation* of the commons by a *government* or other *outside party*, and *regulation through local interactions* among the fishers themselves. These three approaches are sometimes referred to as markets, states, and communities, respectively (Ostrom 1990, Ouchi 1980, Taylor 1997, Bowles and Gintis 2002b). The ability of each of the above approaches to avert or attenuate the tragedy depends on the ways in which each approach exploits the available information relevant to the problem and affects its use by the relevant parties, as well as on the distinctive capabilities of the relevant institutions—states, markets, and communities—to affect behaviors. While most approaches observed in practice (those mentioned above, for example) will pragmatically combine elements of all three, I will introduce them singly to clarify their properties.

The models below will greatly oversimplify the actual institutions by which local communities address these and other coordination failures. The diversity and complexity of the institutions actually involved is stunning. For example, Ostrom (1999) and her colleagues' field research uncovered twenty-seven different local rules for excluding others from access to common property resources. These were based on such things as residency, age, caste, clan, skill level, continued use of the resource, use of a particular technology, and so on. As these exclusion rules were often used in combination, the number of institutionalized boundary definitions greatly exceeds twenty-seven. The rules governing the access to the resource for those not excluded were equally diverse (as the competing allocation rules proposed by the northwest coast fishers mentioned in the introduction suggests). The observed rules governing membership, allocation, and other aspects of commons governance in combination generate literally thousands of hypothetical commons governance institutions. Many hundreds are observed in practice.

Privatization. Suppose one of the fishers, Lower, say, owned the lake and as owner could exclude Upper or could regulate the amount that Upper fished. In this case, Lower will maximize her utility by varying both e and E. Assume that Upper's options are such that his utility is zero in the next best alternative. An obvious constraint on Lower's optimization problem is the requirement that if Upper is to do any fishing at all, Upper must receive at least as much as his next best alternative. This restriction is termed Upper's *participation constraint* (if it is violated, Upper will not participate; if it is satisfied even weakly (as an equality) we assume that Upper participates). I will consider below why it is not optimal for Lower to exclude Upper from fishing entirely.

Two types of interaction among the fishers might take place under privatization. Lower might issue a permit allowing Upper to continue to fish independently but to catch not more than a given number of fish, requiring Upper to pay for the permit a sum that does not violate the participation constraint. Alternately, Lower might offer Upper an employment contract under which Upper would fish under Lower's direction and the fish caught by Upper would be Lower's property, Upper's compensation being a wage (paid in the fish caught by the two of them) sufficient to offset the disutility of Upper's labor (and thus to satisfy the participation constraint).

In the permit case, Lower determines both optimal levels of fishing effort ($e\tilde{}$ and $E\tilde{}$) and then issues Upper a permit to fish at level $E\tilde{}$ in return for Upper paying a permit price of F. To take account of the participation constraint, we express Lower's offer to Upper as the solution of a standard constrained maximization problem, namely, to vary e and E to maximize

$$\omega = \alpha(1 - \beta E)e - e^2 + F \qquad \text{subject to} \quad \alpha(1 - \beta e)E - E^2 \geq F$$

We know that satisfying Upper's participation constraint will be costly to Lower (the two are not satiated, nor do they love work so much that providing for the other is costless), so the constraint will be satisfied as an equality. We can use this expression to eliminate F from the above expression. Thus Lower should select e and E to maximize

$$\omega = \alpha(1 - \beta E)e - e^2 + \alpha(1 - \beta e)E - E^2$$

Note that this is just the joint surplus (total catch minus the total disutility of labor). The solution to this problem ($e\tilde{}$ and $E\tilde{}$) is Lower's allocation plan, which is implemented along with a distribution plan that requires Upper to pay a fee of $F\tilde{} = \alpha(1 - \beta e\tilde{})E\tilde{} - E^{-2}$ for permission to fish $E\tilde{}$ hours. Because the participation constraint is satisfied as an equality, the solution will be Pareto efficient (it is one of the points on the efficient contract locus).

Lower's allocation plan is determined by setting e and E according to the first order conditions:

$$\omega_e = \alpha(1 - \beta E) - 2e - \alpha\beta E = 0$$
$$\omega_E = \alpha(1 - \beta e) - 2E - \alpha\beta e = 0$$

Note how these differ from the first order conditions defining the individual best responses in the noncooperative interaction above: they are identical except for the last term, which captures the effect of Lower's fishing on Upper's well being (in the first equation) and conversely (in the second). Solving for the level of fishing of each, we have:

$$e^\sim = \frac{\alpha}{2 + 2\alpha\beta} = E^\sim \qquad (4.11)$$

which is obviously less than the Nash equilibrium level ($\alpha/(2 + \alpha\beta)$, from eq. (4.8)) for the noncooperative interaction modeled in the previous section. Notice that as β goes to zero, eliminating the overfishing interdependence, the Nash equilibrium becomes the joint surplus maximizing solution, as one would expect. The joint surplus maximizing allocation is indicated by point ω in figure 4.5.

The optimal allocation plan is based on the assumption that the participation constraint had to be met. But why would it not be optimal for Lower to simply select $E = 0$ and have exclusive access to the lake? The reason (in this case) is that the marginal cost of compensating Upper's fishing effort goes to zero as E goes to zero, so some positive level of E will be optimal. (Alternative reasonable specifications of the model would have Lower exclude Upper from fishing—for example, if Upper had a very advantageous next-best alternative, making it expensive for Lower to satisfy his participation constraint.)

Instead of issuing a permit, Lower might have employed Upper. This case differs because Lower now owns the fish that Upper catches but must devote some of this fish to paying a wage W to Upper sufficient to satisfy Upper's participation constraint. Knowing that the participation constraint is satisfied as an equality allows us to use the fact that the wage paid must just offset Uppers disutility of effort or $W = E^2$. Lower now must choose e and E to maximize the expression

$$\alpha(1 - \beta E)e - e^2 + \alpha(1 - \beta e)E - W,$$

which (substituting in the value of W given by the participation constraint) is identical to the problem solved in the permit case. The basic structures of the permit and the employment cases are thus indistinguishable: because in both cases Upper will gain only an amount equal to the disutility of labor, Lower chooses e and E to maximize the joint surplus, recompenses Upper for the disutility of Upper's labor, and keeps the rest.

Privatization produces Pareto-efficient outcomes because the decision maker optimizes subject to the other's binding participation constraint. The utility gained by the other is simply given by his next best alternative, so the question of distribution between the two is settled in advance. As a result, the owner — as residual claimant on the joint surplus — maximizes her utility by choosing an allocation which maximizes the total utility of the two. The key here is that the owner is powerful enough to determine the distribution of gains independently of the allocation of fishing times and so has no incentive to adopt any but the most efficient allocation. In chapter 5 I will show that this is not generally the case and that when the independence of distribution and allocation fails, private allocations tend to be inefficient.

External Regulation. It is often impossible for a single party to own an entire common property resource (imagine establishing property rights in fish in the open ocean). And for many such common property resources, were a single ownership unit to exit, it could easily be sufficiently large to preclude effective competition on the relevant markets, thereby inducing familiar market failures associated with the exercise of market power. In this case a government or some other external party may be able to improve on the Nash equilibrium of the noncooperative game described above.

As with privatization, two alternatives suggest themselves. First, the planner (the government), knowing all the relevant information, could select e and E to maximize total surplus. The planner might then implement this outcome by *direct regulation*, simply issuing a fishing permit allowing each fisher to fish a given number of hours. Thus point ω in figure 4.5 is the planner's optimal allocation. Assuming the planner had no reason to favor one fisher over the other from the standpoint of distribution, ω would be both the allocation and the distributional plan. Notice the same point represents the allocational outcome (but not the distributional outcome) for the privatization case.

Rather than implementing the optimal allocational plan by fiat, however, the planner might desire to let the fishers each decide how much to fish but to alter the incentives facing them in such a way as to avert the coordination failure that occurs without government intervention. This is the approach to welfare economics pioneered by early twentieth century economists Alfred Marshall and A. C. Pigou (1877–1959); the modern form of this approach is implementation theory, mentioned in chapter 1. According to this approach, the planner proposes a *tax* on fishing designed to eliminate the discrepancy between the social and private marginal costs and benefits of fishing. Assume that the proceeds will be given back to the fishers as a lump sum, and that they ignore this lump sum in their calculations (as they would were there two thousand rather than just two fishers, as in a more realistic case.) The problem is thus for the planner to select a tax that will maximize the sum of the fishers utilities when the fishers choose how much to fish, given the tax.

What is the optimal tax? The problem can be posed this way: find the tax that would transform the objective functions of the two fishers so that their individual best response functions would be identical to those implied by the first order conditions of the joint surplus maximum problem, namely,

$$e = \frac{\alpha(1 - 2\beta E)}{2}$$

$$E = \frac{\alpha(1 - 2\beta e)}{2}.$$

Working backward from the desired first order conditions to the implied individual payoffs and hence the tax rate, we see that the transformed utility function u^τ would have to have the form (for Lower)

$$u^\tau = \alpha(1 - \beta E)e - e^2 - \tau e$$

and that if Lower's first order condition is to mimic that implied by joint surplus maximization, namely,

$$\frac{du^\tau}{de} = \alpha(1 - \beta E) - 2e - \alpha\beta E = 0$$

the tax rate per hour of Lower's fishing time must be $\tau = \alpha\beta E$. Check this by substituting the tax rate into Lower's maximum problem and differentiating with respect to e. The result should reproduce the first order conditions for the joint surplus maximum problem. Lower's tax obligation depends on Upper's fishing time because the effect of Lower's fishing on Upper's well-being depends on how much Upper fishes.

I assume that as the government is able to compel obedience to its regulations, the planner can implement his desired plan whether in the form of the direct regulation or the tax incentive. But how can the planner acquire the necessary information? Notice that to set the appropriate tax or determine the optimal levels of e and E, the planner used information on both the preferences and the fishing technology of both fishers. To see that getting this information might be an insurmountable task, suppose the fishers were many, each with a distinct technology unobservable by the planner, given by α_i for the ith fisher. Now assume as the ith fisher, you know the above optimal tax will be implemented, and the planner asks you to reveal your α_i. What is your answer? And assuming that the fishers know one anothers' technologies, if the planner asks you about the α's of the other fishers, what is your answer? A plausible answer is that you might report to the planner the values of the various αs that maximized your utility but would be inaccurate. (You would overstate yours and understate theirs.)

Local Interactions. Maybe the fishers themselves could arrive at a solution, making use of the fact that they know things that the planner does not. If there were truly just two fishers on this lake, then their relationship would almost certainly be ongoing, and the repetition of the interaction would allow each to use the threat of retaliation to enforce a more nearly optimal outcome. In dyadic relationships (for example of buyer and seller), repeated interactions works well to maintain cooperation; in chapter 7, I introduce game repetition as a way of sustaining norms that underpin the process of exchange in most real world markets. But in the many-person settings appropriate for most public goods and common property resource problems, cooperation is much more difficult to sustain in this manner. It will be easier to explain why this is so once repeated games are introduced, so I postpone this.

There are two types of local interactions approaches: those based on *asymmetries* among the fishers, and those that are not and that may require some rough equality or at least solidarity among them.

Among the former are those based on the disproportionate wealth or power of one of the fishers. Suppose that Lower had the ability to select her level of fishing and commit to it in such a way that Upper understood that nothing Upper could do would alter Lower's fishing activity. Upper of course could then select his level of fishing given what Lower had done. Then Lower is the *first mover* or Stackelberg leader. (Heinrich von Stackelberg [1905–1946] used this model to represent price setting among duopolists.) How would Lower decide how much to fish? The first mover will begin by determining what the second mover will do in response to each of the first mover's actions, and then select the action that maximizes her own utility given the second mover's best response function. This is a simple but important change in the assumed behavior of the fishers: Lower now recognizes and takes advantage of the fact that by choosing various levels of fishing she can affect the level chosen by Upper. Lower's behavior is thus *strategic* (it takes account of the effect of her actions on the actions of the other).

Notice that in this case Lower' optimization was constrained not by a given level of Upper's *utility* (as when the participation constraint is binding), but by Upper's *behavior* as given by the his best response function. As a result, the solution will not be Pareto optimal. Lower's first-mover advantage allows her to better her position by comparison to the Nash equilibrium, in this case at the expense of Upper, whose outcome as second mover is worse than the Nash equilibrium. The deterioration of Upper's position as a result of his being second mover is not a general result: perhaps surprisingly, the second mover may be better-off or worse-off by comparison to the Nash equilibrium of the simultaneous moves game. (An example of the second mover doing better as "Stackelberg follower" than in the Nash equilibrium will be offered presently.)

If Lower had even more power, she could make Upper a *take-it or leave-it offer*, specifying not only how much *she* would fish, but how much Upper is to fish, too, along with the threat that should Upper not accept the offer, Lower would simply fish at the level of the Nash equilibrium of the simultaneous-moves game. This situation simply reproduces the ownership case but with the participation constraint now being that Upper must do at least as well as at the Nash outcome. The outcome is obviously Pareto efficient.

Like the privatization and state solutions above, the local interactions-based solutions relying on asymmetries among the fishers may encounter serious information problems due to the fact that the underlying information is private, and the fishers may find it advantageous to hide or distort the information they make available. This will be particularly the case when the information is required by an outsider (as in the state solutions) or is provided from one of the fishers to the other in which the resulting outcomes are highly unequal (and therefore likely to foster social distance or lack of common norms such as reciprocity).

An approach based on more symmetrical relations among the fishers would be a *bargained outcome enforced by mutual monitoring*. The two fishers might share their information and decide to fish at the joint surplus-maximizing optimum (each fishing the same amount and enjoying equal utility as a result), using mutual monitoring to detect noncompliance, and threatening to return to fishing at the noncooperative level (the Nash outcome of the simultaneous moves game) should the other violate the agreement. Thus they might define the noncooperative outcome as their *fallback position* (or threat point) with the efficient contract locus of the initial problem representing and the fallback position defining the *bargaining set*, namely, the set of all outcomes that are Pareto superior to the fallback. We will develop the analytical tools for studying this case in chapters 5 and 7.

Notice that the bargaining *cum* mutual monitoring solution relies on three important facts about many small group interactions: (1) participants are likely to have good information about the others' preferences, technologies, and actions, (2) they agreed on what both considered a fair division rule (in this case fifty-fifty), and (3) they may discipline each other at limited cost due to their proximity and shared norms. These three characteristics of small groups often give them capabilities in solving coordination problems that are unavailable to purely state- or market-based approaches. The Public Goods Game experiments described in chapter 3 make it clear that people are willing to punish fellow group members whose behaviors violate norms, even when inflicting the punishment is costly and in situations when there can be no material benefit stemming from the fact that those punished generally modify their behavior (for example, on the last round of a game). I will return to mutual monitoring (among members of a production team) in the next section.

A second approach is to take account of the fact that frequent social interaction among the fishers gives them not only information about one another but also a concern about the others' well-being. We know from experiments with Prisoners' Dilemma and Public Goods Games (Frey and Bohnet 1996, Sally 1995, and Kollock 1992) that solving or attenuating these and related coordination failures is facilitated by social identification and communication among the participants—even when no binding agreements can be made—and is impeded by social distance. Thus, the preferences and beliefs relevant to the problem may depend on the institutional approach to solving the problem: states, markets, and communities (hierarchical or egalitarian), each evoking differing preferences.

To see how a concern for the other might help solve the underlying coordination problem, imagine that the utility of each was as defined above plus some weight $a \in [0,1]$ placed on the utility of the other, so that Lower's utility would now be

$$u = \alpha(1 - \beta E)e - e^2 + aU$$

and analogously for Upper. Then the first order conditions defining the individual best responses would be

$$\alpha(1 - \beta E) - 2e - a\alpha\beta E = 0$$
$$\alpha(1 - \beta e) - 2E - a\alpha\beta e = 0$$

which shows that each would then take account of a fraction, a, of the disutility that their fishing impose on the other. A concern for the well-being of the other might thus substitute for the tax approach to attenuating the coordination failure.

What level of concern for the other would implement the social optimum? For the above first order conditions to mimic those of the joint surplus maximization problem, each fisher would have to be fully as other-regarding as self-regarding (namely, $a = 1$). This may suggest why most successful communities (even the most utopian, such as the contemporary Amish or Hutterites) do not rely entirely on good will, but supplement it with mutual monitoring and punishment for transgression of norms.

A common feature of the above approaches to averting the tragedy is that whoever is making the the allocation (e,E), it is determined by taking account of the costs inflicted on one by the fishing of the other. In the altruism case this is obvious, and only a bit less so when the planner jointly maximizes the utilities of the two. But it is also true in the more surprising case of privatization and the powerful first mover making a take-it-or-leave-it offer. Because, in these two cases, the participation constraint is binding, and the owner or first mover takes account of the well-being of the less fortunate fisher in a manner no different than this fisher would himself. These two cases highlight a major difference. While all of the approaches (except incomplete altruism and Stackelberg leadership) implement a Pareto-optimal allocation, they differ substantially in the distribution of well-being in the resulting outcome.

I will now introduce another important example, team production, to illustrate an n-person interaction and to see how clever contracts or social preferences can sometimes surmount coordination problems.

Team Production

In modern economies a ubiquitous example of a common pool resource problem arises from the team nature of production; groups of producers — often employees of a given firm, sometimes numbering in the hundreds — contribute to production and share in the resulting output. The team might also be a group of professionals sharing a practice (common among doctors and lawyers) or a cooperative firm owned by its workers.

Suppose members of a team of n members jointly produce a good, the level of output depending on an action (call it "work effort") taken by each of the n members, $a_i \in [0,1]$, according to the production function

$$q = g\mathbf{a} - k \qquad (4.12)$$

where $\mathbf{a} = \Sigma a_i$, summed over the n team members and g and k are positive constants (known to the team members). As team members are identical, I will drop the subscripts, except where they are necessary to avoid ambiguity. There are evidently no inputs other than the actions of the team members (maybe this is a dance company that performs in public places). The identical utility functions of each of the producers are $u = u(y, a)$, where y is the income of the worker and u is decreasing and convex in a and increasing and concave in y. Team members' reservation utility is z.

The members of the team seek to devise a method of allocating the income produced by the team among its members, recognizing that members may seek to free ride on the efforts of their teammates. To provide an efficiency benchmark, the team members engage in a thought experiment, dusting off the ever-useful Robinson Crusoe, who as a social isolate does not have to worry about coordination failures. They know that if production could be carried out by a single producer who also owned the resulting output, the producer-owner would select a level of effort to maximize utility, giving the first order conditions

$$u_y g + u_a = 0 \qquad (4.13)$$

or $g = -u_a/u_y$, equating the marginal productivity of the action to the marginal rate of substitution between effort and goods in the producer's utility function. The team members then seek to implement the allocation (the level of the a's) implied by this first order condition for each member. They first consider disbanding the team so that each may work alone as Robinson did. But there is a reason why the team exists: I assume that due to the fixed costs k, the level of effort implementing the above first order condition, a^*, is such that $u(ga^* - k, a^*) < z$. The Crusoe solution is not feasible due to the high level of fixed costs.

Of course, if the members could credibly agree on the actions each would take, then they could easily implement Crusoe's effort level as a cooperative solution. But it is commonly the case that while output is readily measured, the actions taken by the individuals are either not fully observable or, more generally, the information concerning the actions taken by each is not sufficient to enforce contracts written in a (that is, it is not verifiable).

Suppose the team meets to devise a solution that will take the form of a contract expressed in terms of the information that *is* verifiable. They reason as follows: the team offers its members a contract, and each individual member of the team then best responds. Notice the similarity to the hypothetical social planner's problem in the fishers' tragedy. Devising the right contract thus requires that for any contract proposed at the meeting, the group will first determine the members' best responses, then aggregate these responses to get total output that would result under this contract and the resultant incomes of the members. The members' best response functions are thus a constraint — called the *incentive compatibility constraint* — on the team's optimizing problem. Of course, the contract must give the team members a level of utility not less than

their fallback position, thereby satisfying their *participation constraint.*
The team as a whole has the role of first mover (and is also the principal
in a single-principal multi-agent problem of the type analyzed at length
in chapter 8).

Suppose the members consider a proposal that shares net income
equally, offering each member a per period income of

$$y = \frac{q - x}{n}$$

where $x \geq 0$ is whatever amount of income the team decides to allocate
to common projects, and is selected to satisfy the team members participation constraint or

$$u\left(\frac{q^* - x}{n}, a^*\right) \geq z$$

The asterisks indicate the equilibrium levels of team member effort and
resulting output under the contract. How would this work? A given
member's optimizing problem is to vary a_i to maximize

$$u_i = \left\{\frac{g(a_1 + \ldots + a_n) - x)}{n} - a_i\right\}$$

(Here I have retained the subscript i for the member in question, as it is
essential to remember that while the members are — for analytical convenience — assumed to be identical, each acts independently and takes
the actions of the others as exogenous when making her own decision.)
Setting $du_i/da_i = 0$, we have the first order condition:

$$\frac{u_y g}{n} + u_a = 0$$

or

$$\frac{g}{n} = -\frac{u_a}{u_y}$$

requiring that the marginal rate of substitution be equated to the marginal product of the action *divided by the team size.* Comparing this to
Robinson Crusoe's first order conditions (eq. 4.13), we see that the incentives the proposed contract is providing to the team members are
diluted by team size. This example of free riding is called the *1/n problem* in team production.

Undeterred, the team continues looking for the right contract. Some-one comes up with the clever idea of paying *each* member the *entire* output minus a constant, that is, offer each member of the team $y = q^* - v$ where v is a constant chosen so that $q^* - n(q^* - v) = x$ (thus, as before, x remains for common projects once all members are paid) and, as before, the asterisks indicate the values resulting when team members have best responded to the contract. It is easy to see that team members, independently maximizing their utility, will choose the action according to Crusoe's first order condition, namely, $u_y g + u_a = 0$, thereby mimicking Robinson Crusoe and surmounting the $1/n$ problem. This contract implements the efficient outcome because it induces each member to take account of her entire (marginal) contribution to pro-duction (rather than just one nth of it). Arrangements like this, which implement Pareto-optimal allocations, are termed *optimal contracts*.

Pleased with his clever idea, the inventor of the optimal contract is sure that his teammates will endorse it. But they do not. To see why, introduce some real world risk to the problem. Let output now be

$$q = \{ga - k\}(1 + \varepsilon)$$

where ε is a stochastic influence on production (with zero mean and variance σ known to the team members). Were ε observable (and veri-fiable) then the previous contract written in terms of expected rather than realized output could be implemented as long as the firm could borrow when necessary to allow the required payments of $ga - k - v$ to each member. But if ε is nonverifiable, then the contract would neces-sarily be written in terms of actual output. Suppose the optimal contract ensured that team members received an *expected* income sufficient to satisfy their participation constraint. Given the stochastic nature of out-put, however, for teams of any significant size each member's *realized* income in any period could be a large multiple of that figure *of either sign*. This is because each member is residual claimant on the entire team's *realized* output, and shocks to total output would realistically dwarf any individual's reservation position. A contract under which a team member would be required in some periods to pay the team a substantial amount is not likely to be attractive for any but risk-neutral members or those with virtually unlimited access to credit. As a result, for all but very wealthy team members or very profitable teams, no contract of this type could satisfy the participation constraint.

The members try another approach: peer monitoring. While the ac-tions taken by each are not verifiable, each member has some informa-tion about what his or her teammates are doing and could use this information to implement an agreed-upon level of effort, through the use of informal sanctions such as social disapproval or perhaps even fines imposed by the members on those who contribute less than the stipulated amount. It might seem at first glance that if it is costly (either materially or psychologically) to the members to sanction one another, they would refrain from doing so, for while the costs are borne by the individual punisher, the benefits of greater compliance with the agreed upon effort norm are shared equally by the members as a whole. Thus, punishing norm violators would seem to confront the same $1/n$ problem that induces free riding in members' choice of an effort level. But both Ultimatum and Public Goods Games experiments surveyed in chapter 3 show that people are willing to punish those who they consider to have violated a norm.

A review of the social preference functions introduced there confirms that either fairness-based or reciprocity-based utility functions readily motivate this kind of costly punishment of norm violators. The norm violator imposes disadvantageous inequality on the norm followers who, if fairminded, may wish to reduce the violator's payoffs even if it reduces their own payoffs, too. Moreover, the violation of the norm is an indication of lack of deservingness on the part of the violator, and reciprocity motives would imply that team members could enhance their utility by punishing the miscreant (quite apart from any anticipated behavior modification by the shirker). Moreover, emotions of shame may be evoked by punishment of fellow group members, as the experiments in chapter 3 suggest. An example will clarify how this might work to attenuate the coordination problem arising in team production. The example will also show how social preferences can be used in the analysis of social interactions.

Suppose members of the team have the following motivations. They are *self-interested* and thus care about their own material payoffs.[3] They are unconditionally *altruistic* or *spiteful* and thus place some weight, positive or negative (or zero), on the payoffs of others players independent of their beliefs about the others' types or past behavior. They are *reciprocators* and thus the value they place on the payoff of others (positively or negatively) depends on their beliefs about the others' type. They have norms about how much they should contribute; if they violate the norm they experience *guilt*. Finally, they experience *shame* if they violate their own norms and are publically sanctioned for this behavior. These motives (excepting spite) may induce team members to take more adequate account of the effects of their actions on fellow team members. The altruism and reciprocity of the members may lead them to value the payoffs of team members and thus to contribute more on their behalf. Reciprocity motives may induce a member to punish

[3] The model that follows is presented in more detail in Bowles and Gintis (2002a).

those contributing little to the team's output. Shame may enhance the effects of being punished by others. Finally, guilt may induce a high level of contribution.

Consider a team with two members, i and j. As before, the output of the team varies linearly with the contributions of the members, each member receiving an amount $\varphi < 1$ times the sum of the contributions. Each may allocate a fraction $a_k \in [0, 1]$ for $k = i, j$ of one unit to the team and the remainder $(1 - a_k)$ to a private project. After each has made an allocation, the contributions of each to the project are made known to the other, and i may impose a penalty μ_{ij} on j, while j may impose μ_{ji} on i, at a cost $c(\mu)$, which is $c\mu^2/2$. Abstracting from the cost of one's own punishing of others for the moment, the material payoff to member i is thus

$$\pi_i = 1 - a_i + \varphi(a_i + a_j) - \mu_{ji} \qquad (4.14)$$

Each member suffers a guilt cost $\gamma(a^* - a)^2$ if his contribution deviates from his contribution norm (a^*). It may seem odd that the member experiences guilt in contributing too much, but contributing less than $1 - a^*$ to the private project may violate a norm (the private project may be care of one's own children, for example). Below, I assume that members contribute less than their norm, but this is just a simplification to facilitate interpretation of the results. As in the reciprocity-based utility function in chapter 3, the weight β ("benevolence") placed by the member on the other member's payoffs depends on both unconditional altruism (or spite) and reciprocity. Member i's benevolence towards j is

$$\beta_{ij} = \alpha_i + \lambda_i(a_j - a_i^*) \qquad (4.15)$$

where $\alpha_i \in [-1, +1]$ is i's unconditional spite or altruism, and λ_i his degree of reciprocity $\in [0, 1]$. The level of reciprocal motivation therefore depends on the extent to which j has deviated from i's contribution norm: if j has contributed to their joint project more than i's norm, and $\lambda_i > 0$, then i experiences good will toward j and positively values his payoffs. But if j and contributed less than a_i^* then i may experience malevolence toward j ($\beta_{ij} < 0$) and enhance his utility by paying to reduce j's payoffs. (To reduce notational and computational clutter, I have eliminated the λ_i in the denominator of the expression in chapter 3.) I do not include in i's valuation of j's payoffs, the costs to j of punishing i, because it seems implausible that i will increase his contribution because he cares about j and realizes that j will have to bear the costs of punishing him if he (i) contributes too little.

Finally, to reflect the fact that shame is a social emotion evoked by the contempt of ones associates as expressed by their willingness to incur costs to punish a behavior, shame is measured as

$$s_i = \sigma_i(a_i^* - a_i)\mu_{ji} \qquad (4.16)$$

Thus σ is a measure of one's susceptibility to shame. Punishment by others thus inflicts both material costs and subjective costs, the total being $\mu_{ji}(1 + \sigma_i(a_i^* - a_i))$. If both members have the same contribution norm and abstracting from spite, it will not occur that a member who has exceeded his own norm will nonetheless be punished. To avoid this complication in the numerical case I consider below, I assume $a_i^* = a_j^*$, and α_i and α_j are both nonnegative.

Combining the above terms we have the utility of the ith individual

$$u_i = \pi_i + \beta_{ij}\pi_j - \gamma_i(a_i^* - a_i)^2 - \sigma_i(a_i^* - a_i)\mu_{ji} - \frac{c\mu_{ij}^2}{2}. \qquad (4.17)$$

Utility is thus the sum of the individual's own material payoffs (including the cost of being punished) plus the valuation of the others material payoffs minus the subjective valuation of guilt and shame, minus the cost of punishing j. An analogous function describes j's utility (change or reverse the subscripts). Note that i makes two choices; first choose a_i, then in light of what j has contributed, decide what if any punishment to direct at j.

If j is contributing an amount such that $\beta_{ij} = \alpha_i + \lambda_i (a_j - a_i^*) < 0$, member i will choose to punish j. The utility-maximizing level of punishment, found by differentiating u_i with respect to μ_{ij} and setting the result equal to zero, is given by $c\mu_{ij} = -\beta_{ij}$, namely, choose the level of punishment that equates the marginal cost of punishment (the left-hand side) to the marginal benefit of punishment, namely, the negative of the valuation placed on the payoff of the other (as long as $\beta_{ij} < 0$, and choose zero punishment otherwise). Where punishment is positive, it is clearly increasing in λ and decreasing in α, as one would expect.

We assume that i knows that the punishment by j, if positive, will be $\mu_{ji} = -\beta_{ji}/c$, and substituting this value into i's utility function, i will choose the level of contribution to satisfy

$$-1 + \varphi(1 + \beta_{ij}) + \frac{\lambda_j}{c} + 2\gamma_i(a_i^* - a_i) + \sigma_i\left\{-\frac{\beta_{ji}}{c} + (a_i^* - a_i)\frac{\lambda_j}{c}\right\} = 0. \qquad (4.18)$$

This condition requires that a_i be chosen so as to equate the marginal cost and benefits of contributing. The term $-1 + \varphi(1 + \beta_{ij})$ gives the marginal cost of contributing and the marginal increment both to one's own material payoffs, and to the other as well, the latter valued by i's benevolence towards j, while λ_j/c is the marginal reduction in punishment occasioned by contributing more. The next term is marginal reduction in guilt, and the last term is the reduction in shame occasioned

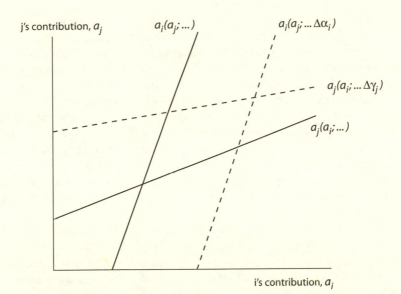

Figure 4.6 Equilibrium contributions to the team project, with social preferences. The dashed lines show the effects of increased altruism by i and increased guilt by j.

both by more closely approximating one's norm and by invoking less punishment. Recalling that $\beta_{ij} = \alpha_i + \lambda_i(a_j - a_i^*)$, for $\lambda_i > 0$ total differentiation of the first order condition reveals that $da_i/da_j > 0$, so i's contribution increases with j's contribution. It is also true that for $a_i^* > a_i$, $da_i/d\gamma_i > 0$ and $da_i/d\sigma_i > 0$, so an increase in guilt motives and the susceptibility to shame raise i's contribution. Member j's utility maximization yields the analogous first order condition.

One can rearrange the first order condition (4.18) to give a closed form expression for a_i as a function of a_j and the parameters introduced above. This is member i's best response function. (It is cumbersome, and unnecessary, as the comparative statics are readily inferred from the first order condition.) The best response functions given by i's and j's first order conditions are shown in figure 4.6. The dashed lines in the figure illustrate the comparative static effects: an upward shift in j's best response function induced by an increase in susceptibility to guilt, $\Delta\gamma_j$, and a rightward shift in i's best response function induced by an increase in i's level of altruism. The model is readily generalized to a team of n members.

Were social motives absent, neither member would contribute (because the marginal material benefit is less than the marginal cost of contributing, as long as $\varphi < 1$). But significant levels of reciprocity will induce members to punish their low-contributing mates, and this alone, or in combination with shame, may support high levels of contribution. Even in the absence of punishment, altruism or guilt can also support high levels of contribution. As the interaction is somewhat complex, it is a good idea to check that a plausible Nash equilibrium exists. Assume i and j are identical non-altruistic reciprocators, and dropping subscripts, suppose $\varphi = 0.6$, $\alpha = 0.0$, $a^* = 0.5$, $\lambda = 0.3$, $\gamma = 0.6$, $\sigma = 0.6$, and $c = 0.75$. Then $a^N = 0.5$; that is, members implement the common contribution norms, and as a result, they experience no shame or guilt and do not punish one another. As a result, both gain 0.1 in material benefits net of their contribution from the project (that is, $0.6(0.5 + 0.5) - 0.5$).

Recall that lacking social preferences they would not have contributed at all, so the fact that *in equilibrium* they do not experience shame, guilt, or benevolence toward the other does not imply that these motives are unimportant. As confirmation, consider the same two individuals in a disequilibrium state, at which j is contributing 0.4 and i is contributing only 0.1. By shirking, i captures 0.2 in net material benefits from the project (that is, $0.6(0.1 + 0.4) - 0.1$). But j would experience strong malevolence toward i ($\beta_{ji} < 0$) and as a result would punish i heavily, inflicting 0.16 in material costs and inducing additional subjective costs of 0.04 in shame on i. These, along with i's subjective costs of guilt (0.10), would reduce i's utility to -0.1. In this situation, i's best response is an increase in contribution. There is no reason why social preferences will not be experienced in equilibrium (though it seems unlikely that high levels of shame, guilt, and *mutual* punishment would be persistent). To see how this might arise, suppose the two members held different contribution norms, with $a_j^* > a_i^*$. Both might adhere to their own norms when in equilibrium and hence not experience guilt or shame. But at these equilibrium values, the fact that i was a shirker according to j's norms might induce j to punish i, and this punishment would be part of the incentives accounting for i meeting his own norm.

The following attributes of the model are noteworthy. First, altruism and reciprocity may be mutually offsetting, because a reciprocal member, if sufficiently altruistic, will not punish a shirking teammate, but may harbor no (net) benevolence toward the shirker either. The result will be low levels of contribution by both. Second, a person who contributes little, due to a low contribution norm, a^*, will also be less responsive to punishment. This can be seen from the effect of punishment on utility, namely, $-1 - \sigma_i (a_i^* - a_j)$. Third, when one or more members have reciprocal preferences, the interaction will exhibit positive feedbacks, with the actions of one of the team inducing changes in the actions of the others. Figure 4.6 describes a unique stable Nash equilibrium in the presence of these feedbacks. But it is not difficult to conceive of interactions with multiple stable equilibria, some with high contributions and some with low, separated by unstable equilibria — tipping points defining the boundary of the basins of attraction of the stable equilibria.

A Taxonomy of Coordination Problems

The underlying structure of both the fishers and the team production problems can be simply expressed in a symmetric game framework. A population engages in an activity, each individual taking some action, $a \in [0,1]$, with the resulting reduced-form utility function of one of the identical members $u = u(a; p, \alpha)$ where p is a vector of any relevant prices assumed to be common across all members of the population and α is a vector of the actions taken by the other individuals. The price vector and α are to the right of the semicolon indicating that they are taken to be exogenous by each individual when each varies a to maximize u. Thus we are considering interactions in which there are many agents, and each agent's effect on the economic environment (p) and others' actions (α) is negligible. The function is a reduced form because the detailed description of the states that it evaluates — the amount of effort, leisure, goods of various types, on which a has an effect — are suppressed to focus on the interaction among the members of the population. The activity is joint because $u_\alpha \neq 0$: what the others do, directly affects the individual's well-being. The outcome of a noncooperative interaction among these individuals is likely to be Pareto inefficient, because the direct effects on one's actions on the others utility (that is, u_α) are not accounted for in the individuals' optimization.

One solution to the problem would be to transform it from a noncooperative to a cooperative game, perhaps by letting a state determine the values of a for each individual. The reasons why this solution may be infeasible or undesirable have already been mentioned. Within the noncooperative game framework, there are three generic ways to avert the coordination failures that may arise in joint activities. None are practical ways of averting the problem entirely, but understanding their logic will help clarify some of the relevant institutional options.

The first idealized solution is to alter the institutional setup so that individual utility is maximized subject to a binding participation constraint for each of the others. The allocation resulting from this maximum problem must be a Pareto optimum (by definition). To see this, suppose an allocation is such that the chooser's own indifference locus is *not* tangent to the indifference locus representing the participation constraint of one of the others. This allocation cannot be a solution to the stated constrained optimizing problem, for in that case the chooser could do better by adopting a different allocation. The privatization solution to the fishers' problem, by establishing residual claimancy on the lake's *entire* output and control of its use by a single individual, while constraining the owner to satisfy the other's participation constraint as an equality, made a single person the owner of all of the consequences of his actions, a kind of fictive Robinson Crusoe. I'll call this the *binding participation constraint solution*.

A second way of averting a coordination failure is to alter the underlying interaction so that the actions of others affect each individual only through the price vector, so $u_\alpha = 0$. The Pigouvian taxes in the fishers example approximated this result by imposing a price (in the form of a tax) on one's own fishing equal to the costs that it imposed on others. In this case the utility function becomes $u = u(a; p(\alpha))$, and the individual takes the price vector as an exogenous constraint on the optimizing process. The resulting allocation will be such that for every individual the common price vector is tangent to their indifference locus (the arguments of which are the various proximate determinants of their utility, such as work effort, goods, and the like mentioned above). But this of course means that the indifference loci of all members of the population have a common slope (all marginal rates of substitution are equal among all pairs of goods), thus implementing a Pareto optimum. This is the *complete contracting solution*.

A third way of averting the coordination failure is the simplest: it may be possible to structured the interaction so that social preferences can substitute for complete contracts. In the fishers case we saw that complete altruism by all individuals (each caring about the others as much as about themselves) would implement a social optimum. While this utopian approach has little practical relevance, it is sometimes the case that the peer monitoring and sanctioning by a minority of group members who are motivated by other-regarding preferences can induce other individuals to act *as if* they cared about the others. The public goods game with punishment introduced in chapter 3 is an example. This is the *social preferences solution*.

While sharing a common structure and a common set of possible institutional responses, coordination problems also differ in two important ways: the sign of the direct effect of the others' actions on one's utility (positive or negative externalities) and the sign of the effect of others' actions on one's own actions (determining whether strategies are complements or substitutes). These two distinctions will be clarified by a two-person example in which we abstract from the price effects represented by the p vector, above. Consider two symmetric individuals (Lower and Upper, again) with identical utility functions:

$$u = f(a, A)$$
$$U = f(A, a)$$

where a and A are the actions taken by the two individuals, and the f function is concave in its first argument. (Symmetry allows us to use the same function $f()$ for the two individuals, but with the arguments reversed.) The coordination problem arises because of the direct effect of the action of each on the utility of the other: that is, f_2, the derivative of f with respect to the second argument, is not zero. Suppose these two functions take the following form:

$$u = \alpha + \beta a + \gamma A + \delta aA + \lambda a^2$$
$$U = \alpha + \beta A + \gamma a + \delta aA + \lambda A^2 \qquad (4.19)$$

where $\lambda < 0$ to reflect the fact that taking the action is subjectively costly to the individual. The best response functions of these two individuals (varying a and A to maximize u and U respectively) are

$$a^* = -\frac{\beta + \delta A}{2\lambda}$$

$$A^* = -\frac{\beta + \delta a}{2\lambda} \qquad (4.20)$$

The first distinction mentioned above concerns the effects of other's actions on the *level* of individual's utility, that is,

$$u_A = \gamma + \delta a$$
$$U_a = \gamma + \delta A$$

These effects may be positive, as in the team production example, or negative, as in the case of the fishers. These are called *positive and negative external effects*, respectively.

The second distinction concerns the effect of the others' action on the *marginal utility* of one's own action:

$$u_{aA} = \delta = U_{Aa}$$

If $\delta < 0$, the actions are *strategic substitutes*. As can be seen from eq. (4.20), this means that the individual will best respond to a change in the other's action by changing his action in the opposite direction. The tragedy of the fishers is an example. If $\delta > 0$, by contrast, the individual will best respond by changing his action in the same direction as the other. These are called *strategic complements*. In the public goods prob-

TABLE 4.2
A taxonomy of coordination problems

	Externalities	
Strategies	Negative: $u_A < 0$	Positive: $u_A > 0$
Substitutes: $u_{aA} < 0$	Tragedy of the fishers	Team production
Complements: $u_{aA} > 0$	Conspicuous consumption	Fiscal competition

lem presented in the introduction of this chapter, the effort levels of the group members are strategic complements if $\gamma' > 0$ and $\gamma'' > 0$. The reason is that if the total output of the public good is increasing and convex in the total effort provided, then the marginal benefit of member i's effort is increasing in the level of effort of member j, so $de_i^*/de_j > 0$. As this example shows, strategic complementarity generates positive feedbacks. By contrast, the effort levels are strategic substitutes if $\gamma'' < 0$.

Examples of the four cases implied by these two distinctions — positive and negative externalities, and strategic substitutes and complements — are given in the table 4.2.

It may seem puzzling that a negative externality may induce a strategic complementarity. But think of the phenomenon of conspicuous consumption, first analyzed by Thorsten Veblen (1934 [1899]) over a century ago. The other's luxury consumption not only makes the individual feel less well-off ($u_A < 0$, $U_a < 0$), but it induces her to consume more to attenuate her status anxiety (because $u_{aA} > 0$, $U_{aA} > 0$). The result may be a kind of a consumption arms race.[4] Other examples include literal arms races: one country's increased arms reduce the security of the other, and may raise the marginal utility of that country's armaments, thereby inducing a positive response. Biology provides many examples of such arms races, with competition for mates leading to such otherwise dysfunctional features as peacocks' elaborate tails. Another example of negative externalities and complementary strategies are corrupt practices: one's corrupt activities reduces others' well-being but may increase the marginal benefit to them of also engaging in corrupt practices. In these cases the effect of the others' action on the level of one's utility is of opposite sign than the effect on the marginal returns to ones own action.

Positive externalities with strategic substitutes is the converse case. Consider team production with an equal sharing contract as above, but assume (more realistically than above) that each individual's marginal

[4] See Schor (1998), Frank (1997), and Bowles and Park (2001).

utility of goods is declining in the amount of goods consumed. In this case, the externality is positive (I benefit from your action, as we both get $1/n$ of the result). But my diminishing marginal utility of goods induces me to reduce my effort when you increase yours (your and my effort are strategic substitutes).

A final example illustrating positive externalities and complementary strategies is fiscal competition among nations or jurisdictions within nations. Consider two nations in both of which the government (considered as an individual) seeks to maximize a weighted sum of employment and the level of government expenditure that is financed by a linear tax on profits at the rate a and A. Because firms relocate among nations in response to after-tax profit rate differentials, the level of employment in one of the countries is determined by its own tax rate and the other country's tax rates. Employment declines in the own-country tax rate and increases in the other country' tax rates: thus the external effect is positive. If it is also true that the negative responsive of employment to the own-country tax rate is greater, the lower is other countries' tax rates, then the two countries' tax rates are strategic complements. (Working problem 12 will clarify this case.)

For a two-country world (Upper and Lower) the two best response functions are as shown in figure 4.7, with their intersection, labeled **N**, the Nash equilibrium, and the level of utility of each nation given by the indifference loci, labeled U_N and u_N. Preferred indifference loci for Upper are those above U_N (because Upper benefits when Lower's tax rate is higher), and Lower's preferred indifference loci are to the right of u_N. It can be seen at once that there exists a Pareto-improving lens of mutually beneficial higher tax rates defined by the tax rates above U_N and to the right of u_N. The proof that this lens exists is identical to the proof that the Nash equilibrium in the fishers case is Pareto inefficient. But here, Pareto improvements require increases in the actions taken by the two agents rather than reductions as was the case with the fishers. The reason is that the externality is positive, so the countries' actions (taxes) are sub-optimal at the Nash equilibrium. Notice two things about this case.

First, were Lower to be in a position to act as first mover, it would of course benefit. But Upper would also be better off as a result. To see this, recall that in selecting its tax rate, Lower would not, as in the Nash case, take Upper's tax rate as exogenous but would take account of the impact of its choice of a tax rate on Upper's best response. Thus country Lower would vary a to maximize $u(a, A)$ subject to $A = A(a)$. This optimum problem gives us the Stackelberg equilibrium (with Lower the leader) labeled S. Notice that S is within the lens of Pareto improvements over the Nash equilibrium. It is not surprising that Lower has

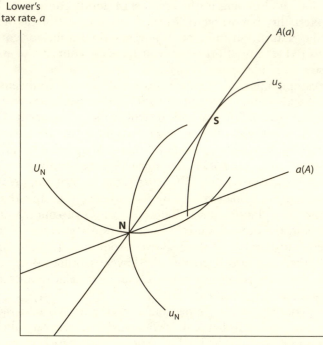

Figure 4.7 Fiscal competition: Nash and Stackelberg equilibria. Note: Lower is the Stackelberg leader.

benefitted by being first mover; but it is a bit counterintuitive that the Stackelberg follower is better off than in the symmetric Nash equilibrium. The reason is that in the presence of strategic complementarity, the leader's action induces the follower to take a similar action; we know that at the Nash equilibrium both countries are adopting suboptimal levels of taxation. Thus there exists a common increase in the action that will benefit both players. In this case, the self-interested exercise of power by one player is mutually beneficial. (You may wish to return to the example of the fishers and be sure you understand why the exercise of first-mover advantage by one fisher did not benefit the other: the difference arises because in the fishers' activities were strategic substitutes.) Of course there is no reason in the model why Upper could not have been the Stackelberg leader (the game is symmetric). In cases like this, the outcome is indeterminate and the model needs to be supplemented by information about military, geopolitical, or other asymmetries among the nations that may influence their power to make the binding commitments required of a first mover.

The fact that the first-mover advantage may benefit the second mover (by comparison to the Nash equilibrium of a simultaneous moves game) is a reminder that the exercise of power has both allocative and distributive effects. In this case, making the first move and the ability to commit to it is not just redistributive, it is also productive: power is used to get a larger slice of the pie, but its exercise also enlarges the pie. Thus, even when power is exercised in a self-interested way, it may be mutually beneficial. The idea is not new. Thomas Hobbes (1968 [1651]) used it three-and-a-half centuries ago to justify allocating executive powers to a sovereign ruler, for reasons explained in the epigraph. In chapter 10, I will return to the productive as well as distributive use of power in economic relationships.

The second important feature of this case is that there is no guarantee that the Nash equilibrium will be either stable or unique. Assume as in the case of the fishers, that players' out of equilibrium behavior moves them towards their best response function. Thus for Lower, $\Delta a = \beta\{a^*(A) - a\}$, with $\beta > 0$, and analogously for Upper. Given this dynamic, figure 4.7 illustrates a stable Nash equilibrium. But the fact that the best response functions have slopes of the same sign could have produced additional intersections (that is, multiple Nash equilibria). In this case, we could Pareto rank the stable Nash equilibria (U and u are increasing along the best response functions, and both are upward sloping).

An interesting line of inquiry — one inspired by invisible hand reasoning with respect to institutions discussed in chapter 2 — would be to ask if we have any reason to expect that a system modeled in this way, if perturbed by stochastic influences, would spend most of its time in a state near the Pareto-superior high tax equilibrium. The problem is similar to the cases of multiple equilibria with discrete rather than continuous strategies already encountered in assurance games (e.g., planting in Palanpur in chapter 1). Without knowing the recent history of the interactions and the details of how the players change their strategies when out of equilibrium, one cannot say much about the likely state of the system. But it seems likely that risk-dominant equilibria would be more persistent than payoff dominant equilibria, should both exist. We will return to this question in the closing chapters.

Conclusion

Any solution to a coordination problem implements not only an allocative outcome — how much fishing each will do, the tax rates of the various countries, and so on — but a distributive outcome as well, the level of well-being for each of the players implied by the allocative outcome and whatever redistributive measures are part of the solution (such as the purchase of the fishing permit in the privatization case). The distribution of the benefits of cooperation, should cooperation occur, depends on the particular transformation of the game which makes cooperation possible. An implication is that conflicts may arise about how best to address the coordination problems that people face: some participants may prefer a less efficient solution to the allocational problem because it supports a distribution of the benefits of cooperation that favors them.

As a result (and for other reasons as well), differences among the players — in wealth, skills, political rights, group identity, information — will influence both the nature of the coordination problem and the types of solution that may be implemented. In his classic treatment of collective action problems, Mancur Olson (1965) reasoned that small, highly unequal groups would most readily solve these problems. It is easy to see, for example, that if there were decreasing marginal returns to the aggregate level of fishing and one of the fishers had a much larger net than the others and so could be assured of catching most of the fish, then his best response would approximate the allocation of a single owner of the lake. In this case inequality in wealth among the fishers would attenuate the coordination failure. Similarly, if one among the nations were much larger than the others, and powerful enough to commit to a given tax rate, it could, as first mover, implement a Pareto improvement over the Nash equilibrium in the simultaneous moves game.

But inequality may also be an impediment to cooperation. Had the production team members modeled above been of different ethnic groups, or of vastly differing wealth, the altruism and reciprocity among them might have been insufficient to induce high levels of effort. Increased social distance among members might have undermined the effectiveness of mutual monitoring and sanctioning by peers. The reason is that sanctioning may be ineffective in heterogenous populations due to the less powerful shaming effect of social disapproval by someone not of one's own group. Moreover, members might have had less demanding norms of contribution if the beneficiaries of the public goods were heterogeneous, including those considered by some members as "outsiders" as well as "insiders." Thus, the results of a recent study of participation in church, local service, and political groups, as well as other community organizations providing local public goods in the U.S. by Alesina and Ferrara (2000), are not altogether surprising. They found that participation in these groups was substantially higher where income is more equally distributed, even when a host of other possible influence are controlled.

Thus the feasibility of an efficient allocation may depend on the distribution of wealth and power and on the extent and kinds of non-economic heterogeneity in a group. Moreover, even in homogeneous groups there is little reason to expect that observed solutions will be efficient, given the fact that the the the actors typically pursue distributional objectives, with the efficiency properties of the allocational outcome a by-product rather than an objective. Only in those rare cases where allocational and distributional outcomes are independent (as modeled in the privatization case, above) will this problem not arise.

Field studies confirm the inseparability of distributional and allocational aspects of the governance of common property resources.[5] A study of water management in forty-eight villages in the South Indian state of Tamil Nadu found lower levels of cooperation in villages with high levels of inequality in landholding. Moreover, lower levels of compliance were observed where the rules governing water supply were perceived to be crafted by the village elite. A similar study of fifty-four farmer-maintained irrigation systems in the Mexican state of Guanajuato found that inequality in landholding was associated with lower levels of cooperative effort in the maintenance of the field canals. In other cases inequalities based on traditional hierarchies have made a positive contribution. Another study of Mexican water management, for example, found that increased mobility of rural residents undermined the patron-client relationships that had been the foundation of a highly unequal but environmentally sustainable system of resource management (Garcia-Barrios and Garcia-Barrios 1990). And in the port of Kayar, on the Petite Côte of Senegal, a cooperative effort to limit the catch (to support higher prices, not to protect fishing stocks) owed its success in part to the leadership of the wealthy local traditional elite of elders. Heterogeneity within groups of commons users affects outcomes in other ways. The fishing agreement in Kayar, for example, was threatened by conflicts between locals and outsiders using differing technologies, and other attempts to limit fishing failed due to the indebtedness of fishers to fish sellers (who opposed the limits) and because the wives of many of the fishermen were fish sellers.

A field experiment among commons users in rural Colombia suggests that inequality may impede cooperation by obstructing communication. Juan Camilo Cardenas implemented common pool resource experiments among villagers who rely for their living on the exploitation of a nearby forest. In Cardenas' game, the subjects choose to withdraw a number of tokens from a common pool, and after all subjects had taken

---

[5] Studies surveyed below are collected in Baland, Bowles, and Bardhan (2004). See particularly the essays by Gaspart and Platteau, Cardenas, and Bardhan and Dayton-Johnson, on which the following account is based.

their turn, the tokens remaining in the pool were multiplied by the experimenter and then distributed to the players, the tokens then being exchanged for money. This is similar to the Public Goods Game experiment in chapter 3 except that subjects decide how much to withdraw rather than how much to contribute. For an initial set of rounds of the game, no communication was allowed. But in the final rounds of the game, subjects were invited to converse for a few minutes before making their decisions. Cardenas expected that communication would reduce the level of withdrawals from the common pool (as has been the case in similar experiments), even though it does not alter the material incentives of the game.

Communication was indeed effective among groups of subjects with relatively similar wealth levels (measured by land, livestock, and equipment ownership); their levels of cooperation increased dramatically in the communication rounds of the experiment. But this was not true of the groups in which there were substantial differences in wealth among the subjects. In one group, one of the wealthiest subjects tried in vain to persuade his mates to restrict their withdrawals, thus maximizing their total earnings. "I did not believe Don Pedro," one of the less well-off women in his group later explained. "I never look him in the face." She was right: Pedro (not his real name) had withdrawn the maximal amount.

We turn in chapter 5 to the distribution of the gains to cooperation and how distributional conflicts may preclude solutions which would otherwise be feasible.

CHAPTER FIVE

Dividing the Gains to Cooperation:
Bargaining and Rent Seeking

> [T]he efforts of men are utilized in two different ways: they are directed to the production or transformation of economic goods, or else to the appropriation of goods produced by others.
> — Vilfredo Pareto, *Manual of Political Economy* (1905)

> . . . The balance between these modes of economic activity—the one leading to greater aggregate wealth and the other to conflict over who gets the wealth—provides the main story line of human history. . . . Karl Marx, though a flop as an economist, did appreciate the importance of the dark side, the conflict option.
> — Jack Hirshleifer, (1994) Presidential Address,
> Western Economic Association

> [I]t is lamentable to think how a great proportion of all efforts and talents in the world are employed in merely neutralizing one another. It is the proper end of government to reduce this wretched waste to the smallest possible amount, by taking such measures as shall cause the energies now spent by mankind in injuring one another, or in protecting themselves against injury, to be turned to the legitimate employment of the human faculties . . .
> — J.S. Mill, *Principles of Political Economy* (1848)

IN RESPONSE TO judicial harassment, indebtedness, and poverty, the *plebs* of the Roman Republic sought economic and legal relief by a time-honored strategy; secession. In 494 B.C., they left Rome en masse and threatened to settle permanently outside its walls and to draw up their own constitution. The worried Roman patricians, wrote Livy, wondered, "What would happen, if in the present situation, there were a threat of foreign invasion" (Livy 1960 [27 B.C.]:141). The plebs were bargaining, of course, and they repeated the ploy on three other occasions over the next two centuries. Their effective use of what we now call their *outside option* got them their own magistrates (the famous

---

The first epigraph is from Pareto (1971:341), the second from Hirshleifer (1994:2), the third from Mill (1965:979).

tribuni) and a measure of self-government including the passage of their own laws, called *plebiscita*, from which the word plebiscite is derived (Jones 1968:55–56).

A major production bottleneck in the late nineteenth-century California food-canning industry was the highly skilled work of putting tops on the cans, or "capping" as it was called. The few difficult-to-replace cappers exacted substantial rents from their employers because of their indispensable role in production and the perishable nature of the goods at harvest time.[1] The invention of a contraption called Cox's capper changed this, but the firms that avidly purchased the device did not initially use it to cap cans, as it was not cost effective at the going wages. Rather, it was deployed as a part of the firms' bargaining strategy and simply held in abeyance should the (human) cappers' demands become excessive. Writing twenty-six years after he invented the machine, James Cox recalled the canning owners' strategic need for the mechanical capper: "The helplessness of the canner [vis-à-vis the human cappers] made him a willing advocate of every mechanical means, and made possible the working out, through frequent failures and heavy losses, the perfected mechanical means now in use" (Phillips and Brown 1986:134). Sometimes firms invest in technologies whose primary aim is to improve their bargaining position: the installation of on-board computers, called trip recorders, in company-owned trucks, described in chapter 8, is another example.

When people collaborate in a productive activity—a firm, a marriage, a group of fishers seeking to restrict overexploitation of their resource, a landlord and a sharecropper—they typically produce a joint surplus, a level of benefits net of costs such that each may be better-off engaging in the joint activity than if they did not. When this is the case, the participants receive a share of the entity's joint surplus, or what Aoki (1984) termed *organizational rents*. The joint surplus is just the difference between the benefits (net of direct costs) each gains from the joint activity and the benefits each would receive in their next best alternative.

For concreteness, return to the two fishers of the previous chapter, now seeking to determine how they will resolve their conflict of interest over the distribution of the joint surplus that would result should they cooperate to restrict their catch.[2] The change in focus from allocation to distribution is paralleled by a change in assumptions about institutions. The allocational outcomes studied in chapter 4 were determined nonco-

---

[1] I describe similar examples in Bowles (1989). The canning case is from Phillips and Brown (1986).

[2] Virtually all useful bargaining theory refers to the two-person case, so I set aside *n*-person bargaining situations.

operatively — we assumed the fishers could not jointly agree to and implement a given number of hours of fishing each. By contrast, here we assume that if the fishers agree on an allocation and its implied distribution of the joint surplus, the institutional environment is such that it can be implemented.

As before, using lowercase letters to refer to the first (or "Lower") and upper case for the second ("Upper"), e and E are respectively the fishing effort of Lower and Upper. We write their (von Neumann-Morgenstern) utility functions compactly as $v = v(e, E)$ and $V = V(e, E)$, with $v_e > 0$, $v_E < 0$, $V_e < 0$, and $V_E > 0$ over the economically relevant range of and E. When the fishers acted noncooperatively (in chapter 4), the resulting Nash equilibrium levels of exploitation of the lake of e^N and E^N were shown to be Pareto inefficient in that each fisher would be better-off if both fished less. In chapter 4, I considered a number of ways the fishers might seek to improve on this outcome, including establishing private ownership of the lake and implementing a tax on fishing. We found that these and the other improvements in the governance of the fishers' interactions enhanced the utility of one or both and could (under idealized conditions) implement a Pareto-optimal allocation. This is an outcome on the efficient contract locus defined by

$$\frac{v_e}{v_E} = \frac{V_e}{V_E},$$

meaning that the indifference loci of the two are tangent, as is shown in figure 4.5.

We can also represent the same efficient contracts locus in (v, V) space as in figure 5.1. The Nash equilibrium of the noncooperative game yields utilities $v^N(e^N, E^N) = z$ and $V^N(e^N, E^N) = Z$. The efficient contract locus can be expressed as the implicit function $\gamma(V(E, e), v(e, E)) = 0$. Points above and to the right of the efficient contract locus are infeasible. (You may want to check that you understand figure 5.1 by locating the points p and ω from figure 4.5 on this figure.) Figure 5.1 represents the bargaining problem first defined by John Nash: a set of bargainers (in this case, just two) with conflicting interests may either fail to agree, in which case they receive their reservation positions given by point z in the figure, or reach an agreement yielding outcomes giving the utility pairs in the (convex) *bargaining set* given by **zab**. The *bargaining frontier* are the utilities associated with is the locus of agreements satisfying (5.1) such that $v \geq z$ and $V \geq Z$, that is, points on the efficient contract locus that are in the bargaining set.

Suppose the fishers may agree on any technically feasible outcome (e, E) and that any outcome agreed to can be implemented without cost.

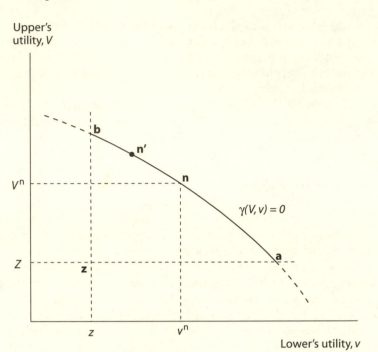

Figure 5.1 The bargaining set and the bargaining frontier. The fallback position is the Nash equilibrium of the noncooperative game indicated by point z while the Nash bargain is indicated by **n**. The bargaining frontier is **ab** and the bargaining set is **zab**.

What will be the outcome of the bargaining? We can restrict the range of possible bargains to the bargaining set (settlements outside it are either infeasible, violate the participation constraint, or both). But other than that, if there is a single lesson of both bargaining theory and the behavioral economics of bargaining, it is that the outcome depends on the institutions governing the bargaining process, with seemingly minor differences in the structure of interaction sometimes yielding major differences in distributional outcomes. These institutional differences are captured — if only very approximately — in the two approaches presented below.

But first I will explain why bargaining problems are so common in modern economies.

THE BARGAINING PROBLEM

As the Roman patricians discovered, each participant in a joint project must receive benefits at least as great as in his next best alternative (otherwise he would refuse to participate). This *participation constraint* restricts the range of possible distributions of benefits among those collaborating. If the participation constraints of all participants are satisfied as an equality, then the question of distribution is settled; each participant gets a payoff equivalent to the next best alternative. But when there is a joint surplus, the participation constraint need not be binding (satisfied as an equality) for any of the participants; it must fail to bind in the case of at least one (from the definition of a joint surplus). Thus as the example of the fishers shows, those participating in joint activities implement not only allocational outcomes — namely, what, when, where, and how to produce — but also distributional outcomes — who gets what, when.

There may exist a single participant who is able to claim virtually the whole of the joint surplus by credibly making to the other participants take-it-or-leave-it offers that are only barely superior to their next best alternatives. But where this is not the case, people engaged in a common project yielding a joint surplus face what is called a *bargaining problem*: they must determine how the organizational rents are distributed. The term *bargaining power* conventionally refers to the relative share of the joint surplus gained by a participant in a bargaining problem. When the sharecropping tenants in West Bengal increased their shares from half to three-quarters during the late 1970s and early 1980s (Prologue), we call this this an increase in their bargaining power. (In chapter 10, I point to some of the ambiguities and problems with the term, but retain it for now.[3]) Because the joint surplus is net of the participants' next best alternatives, bargaining power bears no obvious relationship to a participant's total income: the sharecropper may be in dire poverty and the landlord extremely rich, but if they share equally in the joint surplus, their bargaining power is said to be equal.

A long tradition in economics dating back to John Stuart Mill and Vilfredo Pareto has distinguished between allocational issues that are the subject matter of economics, and the bargaining problem and other issues of distribution that are the proper concerns of other disciplines. Robbins's famous definition of economics equates its subject matter to the study of allocational problems. By contrast, who gets what, when,

---

[3] Briefly, as the West Bengal case illustrates, the conventional usage is tautological: bargaining power does not *explain* what share of the joint surplus participants get, it simply *is* what they get. The usage is unsatisfactory in other respects as well: in principal agent models, introduced subsequently, it is generally in the interest of the principal to assign a share of the joint surplus to the agent. The reasons have nothing to do with bargaining as it is commonly understood, but rather with incentives. As we will see in chapter 10, in many of these situations, the principal, not the agent, exercises power even when the agent receives all of the joint surplus.

how, is the influential definition of the subject matter of political science given by Lasswell and Kaplan (1950).[4]

Others have acknowledged that distribution is central to economics, but they have addressed it independently of allocation. This would make sense if allocational outcomes had no effect on distributional outcomes, and conversely. This might occur, for example, if an unquestioned norm postulated that the joint surplus of a firm should be distributed equally. In this case all participating would favor the allocation that maximized the joint surplus. As a result of the question of distribution being settled, there would be no conflict of interest over questions of allocation. The Lamalera whale hunters encountered in chapter 3 provide an example: they cooperate in the hunt without conflict about how best to catch the whale because the division of the catch is settled in advance and does not depend on how the whale was hunted.

Another reason sometimes proposed for separating the bargaining problem from the allocational problem sees bargaining as a consequence of disequilibrium or lack of competition. According to this interpretation, except in the short run, the competitive process will eliminate all organizational rents so that in equilibrium all participants are indifferent between their current transaction and their next best alternatives. In this case, the distribution of benefits within the collaborating group is entirely determined by the members' participation constraints. The bargaining problem vanishes.

The two key ideas underpinning the separation of distribution and allocation may thus be summarized as follows: competition eliminates organizational rents, and causal effects among distribution and allocation are absent. These assumptions are useful simplifications in the analysis of a class of problems in which it is reasonable to posit two additional assumptions. First, all aspects of individual interactions are governed by complete and costlessly enforceable contracts. Second, only competitive equilibrium transactions take place. However, it is now widely recognized that these assumptions define a rather special case.[5] I adopt three less restrictive assumptions.

First, organizational rents are a ubiquitous feature of all systems of production, and certainly of modern competitive capitalist economies. For example, firms operating in competitive product and labor markets generate substantial rents, some of which are distributed to employees in the form of pay and working conditions superior to the employees'

---

[4] They added that "distribution depends on myth and violence (on faith and brigandage) as well as bargaining" (Lasswell and Kaplan 1950:291).

[5] Aoki (2001), Milgrom and Roberts (1990b), Hart (1995), and Williamson (1985) are examples with particular relevance to what follows.

next best alternatives. As we will see in some detail in later chapters, these and other organizational rents arise when utility-maximizing private individuals are unable to write complete and costlessly enforceable contracts. That is, rents arise in private competitive interactions because of the scarcity of optimal institutions. Organization rents do not owe their existence to government interventions (though their levels and distribution are certainly affected by public policies).[6] Nor are they simply reflections of the out-of-equilibrium and noncompetitive aspects of real economies (though both disequilibrium and noncompetitive transactions do influence organizational rents).

Second, advancing one's distributional claims is a resource-using activity; thus, individuals will seek to implement allocations that favor their claims on organizational rents. The employers who purchased Cox's capper, and the trucking companies that install on-board computers, are doing just this. Anticipating conflict over the distribution of the joint surplus, collaborators in a joint project allocate their time and other resources between organizational rent-seeking activities and productive activities. The allocation of resources to advance distributional claims is not confined to organizational rent seeking, of course, and includes theft, political activities aimed at creating and capturing rents, the use of force among nations, and many other examples that I will not address.

Third, conflicts over the distribution of organizational rents may contribute to inefficiency in three ways. The most obvious example is *bargaining breakdowns leading to foregone mutually beneficial opportunities*. If a group of potential participants in a project cannot agree on how organizational rents are to be distributed, they may delay its implementation or abandon the project, forgoing entirely the joint surplus rather than agreeing to a lesser share. The pleb's departure from Rome is an example; mutually beneficial interactions between patricians and plebs were foregone during the period of secession. Other examples of bargaining breakdowns are strikes and lockouts and failures to conclude a transaction even when there exist terms that would confer benefits on both seller and buyer. Another example is the rejection of substantial offers in ultimatum game experiments because they are deemed unfair.

Even where these breakdowns are avoided, distributional conflicts may contribute to inefficiency in a second way, by providing incentives

---

[6] Buchanan, Tollison, and Tullock (1980) and other contributors to the literature on rent seeking trace persistent rents to government activities, and distinguish between the "good" results of rent dissipation through competition in the economy and the "bad" results of rent seeking arising through government interventions.

for *diversion of resources from productive use to unproductive rent seeking activities*. (The terms "productive" and "unproductive" have no normative connotation. A scarce input that appears as an argument in a firm's production function is a productive resource; when it is used for some other purpose, a productive resource is being devoted to an unproductive activity.) Substantial amounts of resources may be devoted directly to organizational rent seeking—lawyers and labor relations experts exemplify this in trade unions' bargaining with employers. As we will see, resources devoted to competitive rent seeking may (under reasonable conditions) entirely eliminate the joint surplus. A third source of inefficiency is *distortion in the allocation of productive resources*. The bargaining power of those contributing to the joint surplus will be affected by the technologies in use (think of Cox's capper), the location of production, and other aspects of the allocation of inputs. As a result, participants will each seek to implement allocations that maximize their own returns rather than the joint surplus.

My conclusion is that organizational rent seeking is common and that it has important effects on how resources are used in the process of production. Thus, understanding bargaining is as important for understanding resource allocation—the canonical core of economics—as it is in analyzing distributional outcomes. While the economics of bargaining has benefitted from advances in game theory and experimental economics, there is as yet no empirically supported and widely endorsed theory of bargaining. To some extent, this unsatisfactory state simply reflects the fact that scholars studying bargaining have not all been studying the same problem.

Some have sought—through the empirical study of labor relations or through controlled laboratory experiments, for example—to understand how people behave in bargaining situations and how institutions governing the bargaining typically lead to distinct outcomes.[7] A second approach has been to determine theoretically what outcomes would occur if individuals were characterized by a high level of cognitive capacity and particular motivations—the canonical self-regarding and outcome-based preferences. Finally, some have sought to determine what bargaining outcome would be socially desirable, that is, an outcome that meets a normative criterion such as fairness or efficiency. Of course, the insights from behavioral studies of bargaining may shed little light on what kinds of bargains a very brainy *Homo economicus* might strike (were he to exist), and conversely. And neither of these approaches has any obvious relevance for the third approach, normative bargaining theory.

---

[7] Roth (1995) and Card (1990), for example.

In this chapter, I will review the two main contributions to the second and third approaches — the process-based alternating offers model due to Rubinstein (1982) and others, and Nash's normative bargaining model (Nash 1950a) — and point out a number of important lacunae in our current understanding of bargaining.[8] I then introduce an evolutionary model of bargaining designed to address some of the shortcomings of the existing models. In the penultimate section, I show how organizational rent seeking may lead to inefficient allocations. In the conclusion I review evidence on the extent of inefficient bargaining and suggest some reasons why bargaining inefficiencies are so common.

BARGAINING POWER AND DISTRIBUTIONAL OUTCOMES: THE NASH MODEL

John Nash developed his bargaining model to determine what outcomes (if any) would meet a set of conditions that may best be described as principles that would guide an impartial arbitrator committed to the proposition that interpersonal comparison of utility is meaningless (*utilities are ordinal*). These conditions are as follows: first, the outcome should be *Pareto optimal* (that is, on the bargaining frontier). Second, the outcome should be *symmetrical* in the sense that if the game-defining interaction is symmetrical, then the bargained payoffs should be equal. Third, the outcome should be *invariant to linear transformations of the utility functions* of the parties. A fourth condition — termed the *independence of irrelevant alternatives* — requires that if the bargaining set shrinks (so that the new set contains no outcomes not in the old set) but the previous Nash outcome remains feasible and the reservation position remains unchanged, then the bargaining outcome should remain unchanged. Similarly, if the bargaining set should expand, then the new Nash outcome must be either the ex-ante Nash outcome or some outcome that was not in the first bargaining set.

While the first two of Nash's conditions are uncontroversial, it is not difficult to think of situations in which we would regard the decision taken by a Nash-informed arbitrator as unfair. The most obvious problem is that by precluding interpersonal utility comparisons, the arbitration scheme cannot take account of the relative need of the two parties. One might think that the fairness of a bargain should be judged by the final states that result, so that whether a surplus should be split fifty-fifty or some other way would depend on how wealthy the two parties

---

[8] Important contributions to the alternating offers model include Shaked and Sutton (1984) and Stahl (1971).

are, independently of this particular bargain. Effectively, Nash sets aside any consideration of the fairness of the fallback positions (and the possible need for a fair bargain to compensate for unfair next best alternatives). Note, also, that it follows from the fourth condition that an improvement in one (but not the other) of the bargainers' opportunities — for example a large increase in the maximum amount that she *could* gain — may have no effect on the bargained outcome. This aspect of Nash's bargaining solution strikes many as unfair, and it is addressed in the alternative solution proposed by Kalai and Smorodinsky (1975). But as Nash's model has been used primarily to study how bargains *are* struck, not how they *should be*, we will set aside the normative origins (and possible shortcomings) of this approach and present it simply as an account of the bargaining process.

The unique bargain that meets Nash's four conditions is that which maximizes the product of the gains in utility over the fallback position (or simply the product of the shares of the joint surplus going to the two bargainers if these are expressed in the appropriate utility units). Suppose Lower and Upper are dividing a prize normalized to unity, x is Lower's share, and each have concave von Neumann-Morgenstern utility functions $v(x)$ and $V(1-x)$. Their fallback positions are zero. Then the so called *Nash product* ω is

$$\omega = v(x)V(1-x).$$

The value of x that maximizes this expression must satisfy the first order condition

$$\frac{v'(x)}{v(x)} = \frac{V'(1-x)}{V(1-x)} \tag{5.1}$$

and this division, x^*, constitutes the *Nash solution* to the bargaining problem. Equation 5.1 makes it clear that if Lower and Upper have identical utility functions (or one is a linear transformation of the other) they will split the prize evenly. It is also the case (as will become clear if you work problem 13) that if they have different utility functions, the bargainer whose marginal utility of the prize diminishes most rapidly will receive the smaller share. Recognizing this fact, it is sometimes said that the more risk averse bargainer (the one with the more concave utility function) will receive less. But behavior in the face of risk is not an explanation of *why* the one with the more concave utility function is disadvantaged because the determination of x^* is unrelated to risk in the Nash bargaining framework, which is entirely deterministic.

Applications of this approach generally introduce the bargainers' fallback positions, z and Z explicitly. It is conventional to define the fallback position as the utility they get if their interaction ends. But many interactions endure "for better or for worse": think of couples, neighbors, and jobs. It is insightful in these cases to represent the alternatives as interacting either cooperatively (agreeing) or noncooperatively (failing to agree), rather than the more standard interpretation, namely interacting cooperatively or not at all.[9] The term "outside option" is applied to the conventional interpretation of z and Z (termination of the relationship) while z and Z are the "inside option" when defined as the payoff to an ongoing noncooperative interaction. Because in the latter case the fallback position is given by the *Nash equilibrium* of a noncooperative interaction, and Pareto improvements over this outcome may be secured by a bargained agreement, the outcomes in the bargaining set may be termed the gains to cooperation over noncooperation. The *Nash solution* is one way of determining how these gains will be shared.[10]

It is also common in applications to take account of differences in the bargainers' capacities and situations, leading to differing bargaining power. This requires dropping Nash's symmetry assumption, to model what is termed the *generalized Nash bargain*. Introducing the fallback positions z and Z explicitly, this is the allocation $(x, 1 - x)$ that maximizes the *generalized Nash product* $\omega(\alpha)$ where

$$\omega(\alpha) = (v(x)) - z)^{\alpha}(V(1 - x) - Z)^{1 - \alpha}$$

The exponent $\alpha \in [0,1]$ (which is ½ in the case of symmetry) is sometimes termed the *bargaining power of Lower*. The allocation that maximizes this expression (for $\alpha \in (0,1)$) is that which distributes utilities to Lower and Upper to satisfy the first order condition:

$$\frac{\alpha v'}{(v - z)} = \frac{(1 - \alpha)V'}{(V - Z)}.$$

A simplification will make this result a bit more transparent. Let the bargainers' utilities be linear in the prize according to $v = x$ and $V = (1 - x)$. This amounts to assuming that the bargainers are dividing

[9] Applications of this bargaining structure to relationships between members of a couple are in Lundberg and Pollak (1993) and to employer employee relationships in chapter 8 below.

[10] If the fallback position yields no joint surplus (i.e., the noncooperative interaction gives both parties their next best alternative), then the gains to cooperation are identical to the sum of the organizational rents (or the joint surplus). However, as we will see in chapters 8 and 9, the payoffs in the noncooperative outcome may exceed the next best alternative for one or more of the parties. The organizational rents constituting a joint surplus need not arise through cooperation and their distribution need not be determined by bargaining. For example, they may arise as incentive devices in noncooperative interactions and be distributed unilaterally by a principal as in a standard principal agent problem (chapters 7–10).

a prize worth one util. Thus the joint surplus is $1 - (z + Z)$. Simplifying the above first order condition in this manner and solving for x^*, we get Lower's utility resulting from the Nash bargain. I denote this v^n, with the lower-case n superscript indicating the Nash bargaining solution (not the noncooperative Nash equilibrium denoted by N). Thus we have

$$v^n = z + \alpha(1 - (z + Z)) = (1 - \alpha)z + \alpha(1 - Z) \qquad (5.2)$$

Lower's utility is equal to her fallback position (z), plus a share α of the joint surplus. The second expression makes it clear that if Lower had all the bargaining power, ($\alpha = 1$), she would get $1 - Z$ (namely, her fallback plus all the joint surplus), and with no bargaining power would get z.

The Nash solution accounts for bargaining outcomes in a way that both is simple and corresponds to many common intuitions. For example, it implies that one's fallback position will influence the outcome and that a fifty-fifty split is a likely outcome among people who are not different in any relevant ways. Given the importance of norms of fairness in actual bargaining situations, the Nash approach also has the advantage of being explicitly normative. The fact that Nash may have failed to capture many people's intuitive ideas of what makes a fair outcome is a separate point.

The drawbacks are there by design: Nash wanted to characterize a *good* bargaining outcome; he did not intend the model to illuminate real world bargaining processes. As a result, Nash bargaining never fails; nobody ever receives the fallback payoff (unless they have zero bargaining power). This unrealistic implication is deliberate: Nash's axioms require that the outcome is on the Pareto frontier. Equally important, bargaining power is simply assumed (with the symmetry assumption, $\alpha = 1 - \alpha = \frac{1}{2}$) and the process of bargaining — with its threats, offers, and counteroffers — is absent.

ENDOGENOUS BARGAINING POWER IN THE ALTERNATING OFFERS MODEL

The alternating offers model, as its name suggests, addresses the problem of bargaining power by explicitly modeling the bargaining process, effectively inverting Nash's approach.[11] Nash had asked what outcome

---

[11] This is sometimes termed the noncooperative approach to bargaining, in contradistinction to Nash's cooperative approach. But in view of the fact that in the alternating offers model — like the Nash model — the parties can costlessly implement whatever terms they agree on, the distinction diverts attention from the real differences in approach.

is consistent with a set of social welfare axioms expressing a concept of *collective rationality*, without considering why individual bargainers might arrive at this outcome. By contrast, the alternating offers model describes the process of bargaining as a sequence of offers and counteroffers governed by an explicit set of rules and asks what outcome is consistent with the axioms of *individual rationality*. It makes no normative judgement about the outcome. The approach captures two key features of real world bargaining. First, the process of bargaining is time consuming and delay is costly due to the bargainer's impatience, risk of breakdown, opportunities forgone, or for other reasons. Second, the party for whom these costs are least has greater bargaining power and secures a larger share. Bargaining power thus derives from the capacity to benefit by inflicting costs on the other.

If the Nash model corresponds to a case in which the two fishers had simply hired an arbitrator to hand down a solution to their bargaining problem, in the alternating offers framework Upper and Lower determine the outcome themselves, within the constraints set by the rules of the bargaining process. These rules determine that the party designated "first mover" makes an offer to the other that, if accepted, ends the interaction. If the offer is rejected, each bargainer receives reservation payoffs z and Z during that period. Consistent with our interpretation of the fallback as the payoffs to noncooperative play, this means that following the rejection of any offer (and hence in every period prior to an agreement) the bargainers interact noncooperatively and receive z and Z (imagine a work team and an employer continuing production without a contract while the negotiation is taking place). If the first mover's offer was rejected, a given amount of time, Δ, passes and then the second mover makes a counteroffer. The process goes on over an infinite time horizon until an offer is accepted. Along with these rules, the discount factors measuring Upper's and Lower's patience will be important determinants of the outcome: we express these as δ_u and δ_l.[12]

Remarkably, this game has a unique equilibrium outcome. I will not provide a proof—for this see Osborne and Rubinstein (1990)—but rather explain how it is determined. We assume, as before, that the the bargainers are dividing a one-util prize so $v + V = 1$, and we simplify even further setting the reservation positions $z = Z = 0$. Suppose that Lower is the first mover and that there is some amount $v^\sim$ that is the

---

These are the attention to individual optimizing behaviors in the alternating offers model and to collective rationality in the Nash approach.

[12] The *discount factor* is $1/(1 + \rho)$, where ρ is the rate-of-time preference (sometimes called the rate-of-time discount). Thus, a discount factor of unity indicates infinite patience, that is, a rate-of-time preference of zero.

maximum that Lower can receive in any round of the game when in the role of offerer. Of course, we do not know what this amount is (yet) and neither does Lower. But it will be the same in every period in which it is Lower's turn to offer, as the game is assumed to be stationary (time invariant), so that if we get to round t (a round in which Lower is to make an offer), the game is no different in any way from the situation that confronted lower at $t - 2$, $t - 4$, and so on.

Let the first round of the game be $t = 0$ and suppose that the bargainers engage in backward induction, thinking ahead to the situation that would confront them if they got to $t = 1$, namely, Upper's turn to make an offer. At that point Upper would know that if he were to offer Lower an amount $\delta_l \tilde{v}$, it would be accepted. The reason is that given Lower's rate of time preference, Lower is indifferent to getting $\delta_l \tilde{v}$ in $t = 1$ or getting $\tilde{v}$ in $t = 2$ when Lower is the offerer. If this offer were made and accepted, Upper would keep an amount $(1 - \delta_l \tilde{v})$. This being the case, in $t = 0$ Lower would know that offering $\delta_u(1 - \delta_l \tilde{v})$ would induce Upper to accept, while Upper would reject a smaller offer (knowing that Lower would be prepared to accept an offer of $\delta_l \tilde{v}$ one period later). In other words, Lower knows that $1 - \delta_u(1 - \delta_l \tilde{v})$ is the most she can get in period 0. But we already know that the most Lower can get when in a position to make an offer is $\tilde{v}$, so equating these two expressions we have

$$\tilde{v} = 1 - \delta_u(1 - \delta_l \tilde{v})$$

and solving for $\tilde{v}$,

$$\tilde{v} = \frac{1 - \delta_u}{1 - \delta_l \delta_u} \tag{5.3}$$

Lower will reason that if this is the most she can get whenever she is making an offer, she should make this offer at the start and avoid postponing the payoffs until a subsequent round. So Lower will make this offer, Upper will accept, and the bargain will be concluded.

If we drop the assumption that fallback positions are both zero we have a more general case, and one which will allow a comparison between the alternating offers bargain and the Nash bargain. Reintroducing Z and z gives Lower's share as

$$\tilde{v} = \frac{(1 - Z)(1 - \delta_u)}{1 - \delta_l \delta_u} + \frac{z \delta_u(1 - \delta_l)}{1 - \delta_l \delta_u}$$

This will be more transparent if we express $(1 - \delta_u)/(1 - \delta_l \delta_u) \equiv \beta$, with $(1 - \beta) \equiv \delta_u(1 - \delta_l)/(1 - \delta_l \delta_u)$. Then the above outcome can be written

$$v^\sim = \beta(1 - Z) + (1 - \beta)z = z + \beta(1 - z - Z), \qquad (5.4)$$

which reproduces eq. (5.3) above when $z = Z = 0$, as we would expect.[13] Eq. (5.4) shows that Lower receives her fallback z plus a share β of the joint surplus, $(1 - z - Z)$.

The model identifies four determinants of the outcome: the bargainers' *discount factors, other costs of delay* (which vary inversely with the fallback utilities), which bargainer has the *first move,* and the period of *time elapsing between offers.* Notice that had Lower been infinitely patient ($\delta_l = 1$), she would have gained the entire surplus irrespective of Upper's discount factor, unless he too were infinitely patient. In this case, the equilibrium bargain is undefined for the transparent reason that infinite patience eliminates the key element of the bargaining process, namely, the costly passage of time.

To get some idea of the magnitudes involved, assume that $z = Z = 0$ and imagine that Upper is poor, has limited access to credit, and regularly borrows against his credit card, paying a real interest rate of 15 percent, while Lower is very wealthy and can borrow and lend unlimited amounts at the real prime rate of interest, say, 4 percent. If these figures indicate the annual rates of time preference of the two, and if Δ is one year, then the discount factors are $\delta_l = 0.96$ and $\delta_u = 0.87$ and (using eq. (5.3)), $v^\sim = 0.76$, so Lower gets three times a much as Upper.

How much of Upper's disadvantage stemmed from being second mover, and how much from Upper's greater impatience? It turns out that the first-mover advantage does not matter much. Here is why. If the two had the same rate of time preference with discount factor δ, we can use eq. (5.3) to show that Lower would have received

$$v^\sim = \frac{1-\delta}{1-\delta^2} = \frac{(1-\delta)}{(1-\delta)(1+\delta)} = \frac{1}{1+\delta}.$$

This means that if Upper had the same rate-of-time preference as Lower (4 percent), Lower's share would have been reduced from 0.76 to 0.51;

---

[13] This result is easily derived. If at $t = 2$, Lower can secure an agreement for $v^\sim$ in perpetuity, to avoid a rejection Upper will have to make her an offer with a present value of at least $z + \delta_l v^\sim/(1 - \delta_l)$ in $t = 1$. Note: Lower will settle for less than $v^\sim$ if offered in $t = 1$ because to get $v^\sim$ she has to wait a period, and the reservation utility z does not offset the waiting costs. So the best Upper can do then is offer her a share $1 - V^+ = z(1 - \delta_l) + \delta_l v^\sim$, retaining V^+ (in perpetuity if the offer is accepted). But if Upper can get V^+ in $t = 1$, Lower will have to offer him at least an equivalent amount in $t = 0$ to secure an agreement. So reasoning as above, the most Lower can get is $1 - Z(1 - \delta_u) - \delta_u V^+$. We know that the best Lower can get in any period in which she makes an offer is also $v^\sim$ itself, so $v^\sim = 1 - Z(1 - \delta_u) - \delta_u V^+$. Substituting $V^+ = 1 - z(1 - \delta_l) - \delta_l v^\sim$ into this expression and solving for $v^\sim$ gives eq. (5.4).

virtually all of Lower's larger share is due to Lower's greater patience, not to her first-mover advantage. Even if both had Upper's higher rate-of-time preference, Lower's share would still have been close to ½ (namely 0.53). Evidently, only if bargainers are extremely impatient is the first-mover advantage of significance, even when the time elapsed between offers (which in this case is assumed to be a year) is quite large. As Δ, the time between periods, goes to zero, the first-mover advantage disappears entirely, as one would expect. Perhaps surprisingly, the substantial impact of differential rates of time preference remains even as Δ goes to zero; we will return to this anomaly.

How is the equilibrium bargain, $v^\sim$, in the alternating offer game related to the Nash bargain, v^n? A transparent comparison is possible if we assume identical fallback positions $Z = z$, take the limit as Δ goes to zero, and denote the rates of time preference (not the discount rates) by ρ. Then we have:

$$v^\sim = \frac{z\rho_l}{\rho_u + \rho_l} + \frac{(1-z)\rho_u}{\rho_u + \rho_l}$$

which, using $\beta^\circ = \rho_u/(\rho_u + \rho_l)$ as a measure of Upper's rate of time preference relative to Lower's, can be written as

$$v^\sim = (1 - \beta^\circ)z + \beta^\circ(1 - z) \tag{5.5}$$

Comparing eqs. (5.5) and (5.2) shows that the parameter of the generalized Nash model measuring Lower's bargaining power (α) is identical to the relative size of the rates-of-time preference expressed by β° (with Lower's share being favored by a higher time preference rate for Upper).[14] Where the two have the same rate-of-time preference (and Δ goes to zero), the limit result is identical to the Nash bargain under the assumption of symmetry (first-mover advantage in the alternating offers case having vanished by our assumption of arbitrarily short bargaining periods).

The transparency of this comparison relies on the assumption that the fallback position in both cases is not the payoff to ending the interaction, but is rather the payoff associated with an ongoing noncooperative interaction with the same partner. What matters in the alternating offers model is the cost of waiting another period (which varies inversely with z), called the bargainer's *inside option*. The payoff associated with some *other* interaction that the bargainer might undertake if the current one entirely broke down is irrelevant in the alternating offers model (unless

---

[14] The magnitude of the first-mover advantage is indicated by $\beta - \beta^\circ$, where the rates of time preference are equal, $\beta = 1/(1 + \delta)$ and $\beta^\circ = \frac{1}{2}$. First-mover advantage vanishes as the time elapsed between offers is reduced because as Δ goes to zero, δ goes to unity.

it exceeds the equilibrium offer, in which case the latter will be rejected and the relationship will end). By contrast, a conventional interpretation of the Nash bargain defines z as the payoff if interacting with the next best alternative *partner* (the *outside option*), not as the payoff to interacting with the same partner but without an agreement.

The alternating offers approach does not preclude taking account of outside options. Recall that the outcome of the noncooperative interaction was the *inside* option in the above example; but this noncooperative outcome generally depends on outside options. For example, in the labor discipline model of the employment relationship developed in chapter 8, the Nash equilibrium of the noncooperative game between employee and employer depends on the employee's access, should his employment be terminated, to unemployment insurance, and to an alternative job. In this case, the outside option is the employee's fallback position for the process determining the noncooperative equilibrium wage. The employer and employees might seek to improve their transaction by "bargaining up" from this noncooperative equilibrium, the terms of which would constitute the inside option for their bargaining process. (A model of bargaining nested in a noncooperative model of employer-employee interaction is presented in chapter 8.)

Shortcomings and Evolutionary Extensions

Is the alternating offers model, then, an adequate basis for studying real world bargains? Its strength is that by going inside the black box of the bargaining process, the alternating offers model requires the detailed specification of the institutions governing bargaining. It also provides an account—in terms of relative time preferences and (to a lesser extent) first-mover advantage—of the bargaining power parameter assumed to be exogenous in the Nash model. But the approach also has shortcomings.

First, as eq. (5.5) makes clear, what matters in determining the outcome is the *relative* cost of waiting (which is why the infinitely patient partner gets the whole surplus, even if the other is very patient—but not infinitely so). The total cost of waiting (or the amount of waiting) can be vanishingly small without diminishing the importance of differences in time preference in determining the bargainers' shares. As Kreps (1990b:562) points out, even if offers and counteroffers are returned every few seconds, the effects of differences in the bargainers' rates-of-time preference are undiminished. Moreover, among bargaining partners with the same rate of time preference, the bargainer who can reply to an offer in two seconds will take three-quarters of the surplus if she is paired with a slowpoke who takes six seconds to reply. Where bargaining is not time consuming or costly in other ways, it is surprising that the relative costs of bargaining (even if trivial) will determine the result. Thus, the way that bargaining outcome is determined by the relative costs of waiting is implausible for many applications.

Second, as in the Nash approach, bargaining never breaks down and outcomes are always Pareto efficient. Both models thus fail to capture some salient facts of real world bargaining (reviewed shortly).

A third concern is that not all bargaining situations allow the role of outside options to be introduced into the alternating offers framework in the manner above. Yet we find it strongly counterintuitive to think that in these cases outside offers make no difference. To see why, suppose A and B are partners in a project and they each has outside options normalized to zero. Their alternating offers bargain gives B some amount v_b that is close to one-half of the joint surplus. Now suppose that B's outside option improves so that the payoff to terminating the project is no longer zero, but $v_b - \varepsilon$, where ε is a small positive number. No other aspect of the bargaining environment is changed. This change in the outside option has no effect on the equilibrium of the alternating offers bargaining game, but it transforms the situation from one in which A and B are splitting the joint surplus about equally to one in which A receives virtually all of it.

Finally, the individuals assumed by the alternating offers approach are only barely recognizable as human actors. There is considerable experimental evidence that people (mostly college students) do not engage in the cognitively demanding backward induction on which the model is based (Crawford 2002, Binmore et al. 2002).[15] Moreover, in both the alternating offers model and in the Nash approach (as a model of how actual bargainers act), it is assumed that the bargainers know the utility functions of their counterparts. This is not only untrue, it is confounded by the fact that in bargaining situations people typically go to great lengths to falsify their preferences. (In a bargaining situation during the Cold War, President Richard Nixon is said to have considered trying to

---

[15] There is something paradoxical about a model of bargaining as a process in which no bargaining ever takes place (because the first offer is always accepted if the bargainers are acting according to the assumptions of the model). There may be a good reason why experimental subjects do not generally do much backward induction in situations like this: to do it, they would have reason inconsistently, namely, that they are hypothetically at time $t = 1$ or $t = 2$ *and* that both bargainers are acting on the same backward induction. But if this behavioral assumption *were* true, one would never get to $t = 1$, so if they actually *were* at $t = 1$ they would have to reconsider their behavioral assumptions, in which case they would not act as the model posits.

convince his Russian counterparts that he was irrationally committed to a particular U.S. position.)

The fact that the cognitive assumptions of the models just reviewed are unrealistic may not be a decisive shortcoming, however. What is critical is not that people *think* like that but rather that they *act* like that. It seems likely that real individuals in bargaining situations eschew complex backward induction and iterated dominance thinking, and instead adopt customary rules of thumb that have served them well or have been seen to be successful when used by others. Of course, to say that a share is customary is not to explain it. But it does say something about *how to* explain it, namely, by modeling the evolution of distributional norms and customs under plausible assumptions about cognitive capacities and learning. It may well be that the behavioral rules that emerge from this process of learning by adaptive agents support outcomes that are approximated by the alternating offers model or the Nash approach, or both. Let us see if this is true.

Suppose there is a norm dictating that a fractional share, x, of a pie normalized to one is to be allocated to a player called Row, the remainder $(1 - x)$ going to another called Column. Their (concave, von Neumann-Morgenstern) utility functions are $u(x)$ and $v(1 - x)$, respectively. Their interaction differs from the population games modeled thus far in which individuals were paired randomly with other members of the population. The population now includes subpopulations — Rows and Columns — and the matching is done across the population segments, Rows being randomly paired with Columns. Rows do not interact with Rows, nor do Columns interact with Columns. Rows, for example, might be employers, and Columns, employees. Or they might be buyers and sellers. Row and Column do not have recourse to Nash's impartial arbitrator, nor are they inclined to do the backward induction required of Rubinstein's bargainers. They have limited memories and even more limited foresight, basing their actions entirely on the recent past behavior of those with whom they interact, and occasionally trying to improve on their current bargain. We will see that under some conditions, the Nash bargaining solution emerges as the likely outcome of this interaction.

Rows and Columns number n_R and n_C, respectively, and are randomly paired to play the division game introduced in chapter 1. If the shares claimed by the two sum to one or less, they receive their claims, with associated utility $u(x)$ and $v(1 - x)$, both functions being increasing and concave. Otherwise, they get zero, the utility of which is normalized to zero for both. Assume for the moment that $n_R = n_C$.

Individuals know the distribution of play in the previous period and best respond to this distribution with probability $(1 - \varepsilon)$, where ε is a small positive fraction measuring the rate of nonbest response (or idiosyncratic) play. With probability ε they "probe" to see if they can get a better deal by increasing their claim, the Rows claiming $x + \Delta$ and the Columns claiming $1 - x + \Delta$, where Δ is a discrete change in claim. Assume that $\Delta = 0.1$, so a probe is an attempt to increase their claim by this amount. As long as ε is small, the norm will be sustained over long periods, as both Rows and Columns best respond to the past distributions in which virtually everyone is adhering to the norm. But occasionally the chance occurrence of a large fraction of nonbest responding probers in one subpopulation, say the Rows, will induce the best responding Columns to claim less. Knowing this, in the next period all of the best responding Rows will demand more, and (unless additional chance idiosyncratic play interferes) a new norm will have been established by a kind of "tipping" process.

Because this process works by the bunching of chance events, it is clear that norms will evolve, and over a sufficiently long period all norms over the interval 0.1 to 0.9 will be observed with positive probability. (I assume that no individual ever makes a claim of zero, as such a claim could not occur as a chance probe, nor could it be a strict best response.) But some norms will be more robust than others, persisting over long periods and recurring quickly when displaced.[16] What can we say about these persistent norms?

Define λ as the probability of moving from norm x to $x + \Delta$ in a given period as the result of a "tipping" event as described above, with μ the probability of moving from x to $x - \Delta$. The norm will tend to increase if $\lambda > \mu$, and conversely. These probabilities will depend on the minimum number of nonbest responses required to induce best responding players to adopt a lesser claim. Consider Row's best response, given that last period a fraction κ of Columns claimed not the norm of $(1 - x)$ but instead $(1 - x + \Delta)$. Row knows that reducing his claim to $x - \Delta$ will guarantee this lesser payoff, while persisting with the norm risks getting nothing with probabily κ. Row's best response is to adhere to the norm if

$$(1 - \kappa)u(x) \geq u(x - \Delta) \qquad (5.6)$$

---

[16] What follows is a variant of the evolutionary model of bargaining due to Young (1993), the main difference being that in my formulation, differing subpopulation size has the same effect as differing amounts of information (sample size) in Young's model (large sample size or small population size confers an advantage).

and to claim the lesser amount otherwise. (I assume that the norm is not abandoned unless it is a strict best response to do so.) Expressing eq. (5.6) as an equality and solving for κ gives us the critical value of κ, namely,

$$\kappa^* = \frac{u(x) - u(x - \Delta)}{u(x)}$$

such that if in the previous period $\kappa > \kappa^*$, the best response of the Rows in this period is to reduce their claim. Similar reasoning shows that if ρ is the fraction of idiosyncratic responses among the Rows, the best response for the Columns is adhering to the norm if

$$v(1 - x)(1 - \rho) \geq v(1 - x - \Delta)$$

and to claim the lesser amount otherwise. The critical value of ρ is thus

$$\rho^* = \frac{v(1 - x) - v(1 - x - \Delta)}{v(1 - x)}$$

An example will clarify how a norm changes. Suppose the current norm is $x = 0.2$, and $\Delta = 0.1$, so when Rows "probe" they demand 0.3 and when Columns probe they demand 0.9. Having observed some fraction of "probers" on the other side the previous period, what is the expected payoff to conceding (π') and to conforming to the norm (π^*) for the Row player? Suppose $u = x$ and $v = (1 - x)$. Then:

$$\pi^{*R} = (1 - \kappa)x \qquad \text{and} \qquad \pi'^{R} = x - \Delta.$$

The minimum fraction of Columns who probed last year that is sufficient to induce the Rows to concede, κ^*, is the value of κ that equates these two expected payoffs, or $\kappa^* = \Delta/x$, which for this numerical example gives $\kappa^* = \frac{1}{2}$. Reasoning in a similar manner for the Columns, the minimum fraction of probing Rows last period sufficient to induce the Columns to concede is the value of ρ that equates

$$\pi^{*C} = (1 - \rho)(1 - x) = 1 - x - \Delta = \pi'^{C}$$

giving $\rho^* = \Delta/(1 - x)$, or, for our numerical example, $\rho^* = \frac{1}{8}$. The result is that because $\rho^* < \kappa^*$, it takes fewer probing Rows to induce the Columns to concede than vice versa, so if the rates of probing and group sizes are equal, the norm is more likely to tip "up" to 0.3, than down to 0.1.

Note that the critical values ρ^* and κ^* are just the utility difference between the norm-determined payoff and the lesser claim, divided by the utility of the norm-determined payoff. Writing these two critical values as a function of the norm, the concavity of the utility functions insures that $\rho^*(x)$ is increasing in x, while $\kappa^*(x)$ is decreasing in x. The probability of a transition from one norm to the other varies inversely with the critical number of nonbest responses required to dislodge it. Thus to summarize so far, $\lambda = \lambda(\rho^*(x))$ and $\mu = \mu(\kappa^*(x))$ with $\rho' > 0$, $\kappa' < 0$, $\lambda' < 0$, and $\mu' < 0$. We thus define a stationary norm as one for which

$$\lambda(\rho^*(x)) = \mu(\kappa^*(x)) \tag{5.7}$$

Because we have assumed that group size and the error rates are identical across subpopulations, eq. (5.7) requires simply that $\rho^*(x) = \kappa^*(x)$ or

$$\frac{v(1-x) - v(1-x-\Delta)}{v(1-x)} = \frac{u(x) - u(x-\Delta)}{u(x)} \tag{5.8}$$

If Δ is small, this can be approximated by

$$\frac{\Delta v'(1-x)}{v(1-x)} = \frac{\Delta u'(x)}{u(x)}.$$

Note that, eliminating Δ from eq. (5.8), we have an expression similar to eq. (5.1), namely, the condition defining the Nash solution to the axiomatic bargaining problem. Does this similarity suggest that under some conditions, the evolutionary model approximately replicates the axiomatic Nash solution? It does. Equation 5.8 is the first order condition giving the maximum of

$$\eta = \Delta \ln v(1 - x) + \Delta \ln u(x) = \Delta v(1 - x)u(x)$$

Recalling that the no-contract utility is zero, η is just Δ times the "Nash product" of utility gains over one's fallback; the x that maximizes this expression gives the Nash solution to the bargaining problem. Thus, a plausible evolutionary process among individuals with limited knowledge and cognitive capacity yields this common bargaining solution as its most likely outcome. The solid lines in figure 5.2 illustrate a case in which the Rows and Columns are equally numerous and equally aggressive, the stationary norm x^* thus approximating the Nash outcome.

But this is a rather contrived result, stemming from the assumptions adopted. If subpopulation sizes differ, or if one group is more aggressive than the other, probing more frequently, we get a result that differs from the standard Nash outcome in ways that shed some light on the determinants of bargaining power. To see this, first note that for critical values, κ^* and ρ^*, that exceed the error rate, the probability that nonbest responses exceed the critical values will vary positively with the rate of nonbest response play and inversely with the size of the group. The first

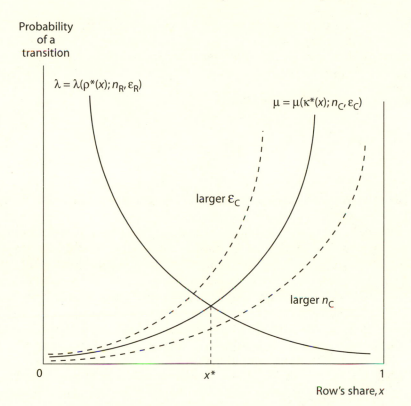

Probability
of a
transition

$\lambda = \lambda(\rho^*(x); n_R, \varepsilon_R)$

$\mu = \mu(\kappa^*(x); n_C, \varepsilon_C)$

larger ε_C

larger n_C

0 x^* 1

Row's share, x

Figure 5.2 Evolutionary determination of bargaining outcomes. The probabilities of a transition to a larger or smaller share for Row are λ and μ, respectively, and x^* is approximately the Nash solution when $n_C = n_R$ and $\varepsilon_C = \varepsilon_R$.
The dashed lines show the effects of Column players being more aggressive
(larger ε_C) and more numerous (larger n_C).

is obvious; the second results from the fact that in very small groups the
realized fraction of nonbest responses will frequently assume substantial
values, while this will happen only very rarely with large groups. Thus,
subscripting the error rate for the two groups, we have

$$\lambda = \lambda(\rho^*(x); n_R, \varepsilon_R)$$

and

$$\mu = \mu(\kappa^*(x); n_C, \varepsilon_C)$$

with both functions decreasing in their first and second argument and
increasing in the third. The dashed lines in fig. 5.2 show the effect of an
increment in Column error rate, shifting upwards its μ function and
enhancing its share, and an increase in the size of the Column popula-

tion (shifting μ downwards and decreasing its share). Equating λ and μ and differentiating totally with respect first to Rows' group size and the norm, and then with respect to the error rate and the norm, and setting the results to zero, we have

$$\frac{dx^*}{d\varepsilon_R} > 0$$

and

$$\frac{dx^*}{dn_R} < 0.$$

We may conclude that the smaller and more aggressive a group is, the larger its share in the stationary norm.

Remarkably, the Nash solution was proposed by Frederik Zeuthen (1930) with an application to employer-employee bargaining. Unlike Nash, who derived his result from postulates of collective rationality, Zeuthen's solution to what he called the problem of "economic warfare" was psychologically motivated. Zeuthen's key idea is that in a bargaining situation, the party whose loss from a concession is least is more likely to concede. Zeuthen's concession rule replicates eq. (5.6), with x being some demand Row has made against Column, with $x - \Delta$ a demand that Column would surely accept, and $1 - \kappa$ being Row's belief concerning the probability that Column will concede. Thus $(1 - \kappa)$ is Row's estimate of the likelihood that *not* making a concession will result in a successful transaction under the favorable (no concession) terms, that is, the likelihood that the Column player with whom Row is paired will adhere to the norm, rather than seeking to do better than the norm by probing.

A limitation of the evolutionary approach is that the "probing" for a better deal is uncorrelated across individuals, while in many bargaining situations the Rows and the Columns participate in some organization—a business association or a trade union, for example—and their efforts to better their share of the prize are collective rather than individual. In chapter 12, I return to this problem, by embedding a model of collective action in an evolutionary dynamic.

ORGANIZATIONAL RENT SEEKING AND THE INEFFICIENCY OF BARGAINING

Three sources of inefficiency in bargaining were identified in the introduction: *bargaining breakdowns leading to foregone mutually beneficial opportunities*, the *diversion of resources from productive use to un-*

productive rent-seeking activities, and the *distortion in the allocation of resources engaged in productive activities* undertaken to enhance individual shares. The distinction between the second and third source is not always easy to make, as the case of Cox's capper suggests. Did expenditure on this device constitute a diversion of resources from productive uses to unproductive rent seeking? Or was it a distortion in the allocation of productive resources? The security guard at the workplace who deters employee theft is clearly the former, but what of the work supervisor who both monitors employees' effort levels and engages in production problem solving? Expenditures whose sole purpose is to enforce a contract or to enhance bargaining power are sometimes called "transactions costs" as distinct from "production costs." But the distinction lacks precision, as the above examples suggest. The vagueness of the term is especially evident once one recognizes that the production technologies in use — Cox's capper or labor saving harvesting equipment — will reflect current or past conflicts over the division of the joint surplus. This is the reason why I generally avoid the term. Even if transactions costs cannot easily be disentangled from production costs, however, the distinction is sometimes clear enough to be illuminating.

Consider the case of bargaining inefficiencies arising from the distortion in the allocation of productive resources. Suppose each of two contributors to a joint project can allocate their efforts to two different activities, both of which contribute to the pair's joint surplus and both of which also may affect the individual's fallback position. To be concrete, the two may be engaged in joint production, and the choice of activities might be the development either of a general skill or of a skill specific to this particular production process and of no value except in this particular transaction. Both skills contribute to surplus production, but only the former enhances the fallback position of the individual (general skills improve one's next best transaction, while specific skills do not).

We can model the resulting inefficiency as follows. Suppose each individual (Lower and Upper, again) contributes one unit of effort to production, dividing it between the first activity and the second, with e and E the amounts devoted to the second (transaction specific) activity by Lower and Upper, respectively. Having chosen e and E, then produce the joint surplus $Q = Q(e, E)$ with $Q_e(0, E)$ and $Q_E(e, 0)$ both positive and $Q_e(1, E)$ and $Q_E(e, 1)$ both negative so that there exists some interior allocation, e^*, E^* both $\in (0, 1)$, which maximizes Q and for which $Q_e = Q_E = 0$. To capture the fact that investing in the first activity (the general skill) enhances the fallback position of each, we write the individual fallback positions as $z(e)$ and $Z(E)$, with z' and Z' both negative: thus, investing in the specific skill lowers each player's payoff should the relationship end. Suppose they cannot bargain over the allocation of e and E (they cannot observe or infer the choices made by the other). Instead they choose e and E noncooperatively and then divide the resulting output according to the Nash bargain (with α the exogenously given bargaining power of Lower). Thus, using eq. (5.2), Lower receives

$$y = z(e) + \alpha\{Q(e, E) - z(e) - Z(E)\}$$

Lower will select e to maximize y, giving the first order condition

$$z_e + \alpha(Q_e - z_e) = 0$$

or

$$\alpha Q_e + (1 - \alpha)z_e = 0$$

The result is that Lower does not implement the joint surplus maximizing allocation (namely, e^* for which $Q_e = 0$) unless Lower has all the bargaining power ($\alpha = 1$) and hence is the residual claimant on the entire joint surplus. But $\alpha = 1$ will not result in an optimal allocation on Upper's part. If $\alpha = 1$ then Upper's first order condition, namely $((1 - \alpha)Q_E + \alpha Z_E = 0)$, would require ignoring the impact of E on Q entirely, leading Upper to set $E = 0$, which is obviously suboptimal.

This particular problem of bargaining inefficiency will thus arise whenever e and E are not subject to contract. The example illustrates what are called *transaction specific investments*, namely, the value of the activity in the project—the "transaction"—is not the same as its value in the fallback position. But the underlying problem is more general: *bargaining inefficiency arises whenever some aspect of the allocation of productive resources both affects the bargaining outcome and is not subject to contract.*

Turning to the diversion of productive resources to unproductive rent-seeking activities, consider a case where one of two employees will be given a promotion worth v. Both understand that the employer will choose between the two based on his estimate of the employee's diligence and dedication to the firm, indicated by the number of hours worked during the period prior to the promotion. Let c be the cost to each employee of working an additional hour. At the beginning of the period each begins work and continues working until one of them stops and the other is promoted. How many hours will they work?

There is no symmetric pure strategy equilibrium, as the best response to the other working t hours is to work either $t + \varepsilon$ (and win) or 0 (and avoid any costs). The steelworkers, whose long conflict with their employer in Ravenswood, West Virginia resembles this model, expressed the $t + \varepsilon$ logic on a banner "How long will we fight? One day longer than the company!"[17] However, a mixed strategy (at the end of each hour, drop out with probability p) may be an equilibrium. For the mixed strategy with p the probability of dropping out to be a symmetric equilibrium it must be that an agent playing against a p-player does no better by dropping out than by staying in, and hence has p itself as the (weak) best response to a p-player.[18] The return to dropping out is 0 and the expected return to staying in against a p-player is

$$p(v - c) - (1 - p)c$$

Setting this expression equal to zero implies that the equilibrium mixed strategy is $p^* = c/v$. If each player quits with probability p^*, the probability that the game ends after each round is $1 - (1 - p^*)^2 = 2p^* - p^{*2}$ and the expected duration of the game, t^*, is just the inverse of this probability. If we define periods to be sufficiently short (so p^* is small, or what is equivalent, we can ignore the possibility of simultaneous quitting), then the expected duration is approximated by $1/2p^*$. Then, using $p^* = c/v$, we see that $t^* = v/2c$. If the game lasts t^* hours, the cost to the two is $2ct^*$, which (using $t^* = v/2c$) is equal to v. Thus, the total costs devoted to capturing the prize exactly equal the prize itself. Of course, the winner ends up with a net gain of $v/2$ while the loser bears total costs of $v/2$.

This is known as a *war of attrition*, a distant cousin of the Hawk Dove Game introduced in chapter 2. It can be applied to a broad class of competitive rent-seeking behaviors leading to an escalation of unproductive expenditures. Examples include influencing governmental decisions or allocations within firms, firm strategies when competing for market shares, cramming for examinations on which only the relative grade counts, arms races, and acquiring redundant educational credentials.[19] The underlying structure is that individuals undertake an unproductive investment attempting to get a prize in a tournament-like setting. Depending on the relationship between the individual investment and the probability of winning the prize, total costs expended may exceed, equal, or fall short of the prize.

[17] Juravich and Bronfenbrenner (1999). Seeking to prove them wrong, the company offered college scholarships to the children and grandchildren of workers willing to replace the locked-out workers (Milbank and Rigdon 1991).

[18] This is because for a mixed strategy to be a Nash equilibrium, it must be that all of the pure strategies in its support (making it up) have the same expected payoff. Were this not the case, the pure strategy with the highest expected payoff would be the best response, rather than the mixed strategy itself.

[19] There may be valuable byproducts of these "unproductive" rent seeking expenditures — those attempting to influence government officials may do so by providing valuable information to the public, for example — but these productive aspects of the expenditure are not required to induce the wasteful rent-seeking.

The model above shows why it is rational for the individuals competing for the prize to invest, but it does not explain why those awarding the prize should adopt such a wasteful contest as the basis for the award. Could they not profit simply by promising to award a prize of $v/2$ to the best candidate, while expending some of their savings devising ways to make this choice? They could do this if better ways of making the choice could be devised. But this is often impossible. Suppose an employer wishes to hire a diligent worker to do manual tasks. He hits on the ingenious idea of hiring those who remained in school the longest. Although the job makes no intellectual demands on the employee, the idea makes sense because the cost of continuing in school will be lower for the more diligent, while those who don't persevere drop out. Schooling might then be taken by the employer as a difficult-to-fake signal of a trait, diligence, which is unobservable to the employer. Using this signal as the basis for hiring may be the best the employer can do. The result will be a war of attrition-like escalation of educational credentials. Whether one regards the unproductive expenditures of rent seeking (the extra hours of work, the redundant schooling) as wasteful then depends on one's assessment of alternative means of making such choices.

Using costly signaling to communicate an unobserved underlying trait is common to many animals—bullfrogs loudly croak and male red deer roar to announce their strength and suitability as a mate, devoting substantial amounts of energy to their advertising bill (Gintis, Smith, and Bowles 2002). It is surprising that in so many areas of human competition we can do no better in allocating prizes.

Conflicts of Interest and Bargaining Breakdowns

A common bargaining problem is the division game presented above and in chapter 1 in which two individuals make claims on a given amount, with both getting nothing if their claims sum to more than the prize. Recall that all divisions that exhaust the prize are mutual best responses; the bargaining problem is then simply to determine which of these Nash equilibria will occur. Bargaining is thus sometimes represented as a selection device among Pareto-efficient Nash equilibria. The task of bargaining theory is simply explaining why we should expect one outcome on the bargaining frontier as opposed to another.

By contrast, I have given greater prominence to aspects of the bargaining problem leading to Pareto inefficient outcomes *inside* the bargaining frontier. The Norwegian economist Leif Johansen reflected on the tendency of bargaining to assume an ever larger role in society,

eclipsing both market- and state-determined allocations in the Scandinavian nations and throughout the advanced economies. He reached a
similar conclusion: "Bargaining has an inherent tendency to eliminate
the potential gain which is the object of bargaining" (Johansen 1979:
520).

Are bargaining inefficiencies empirically important? There is some evidence that they are. David Card (1990) reports that from 10 to 15
percent of contract negotiations involving large numbers of workers in
the private sectors of Canada and the United States result in work stop-
pages. Salop and White (1988:43) report high rates of breakdown in
legal disputes associated with anti-trust litigation in the United States
while Salop and White (1988) and Kennan and Wilson (1993) note that
dispute rates often underestimate the extent of costs, observing that, as
one would expect in a war of attrition, legal fees paid by all parties
frequently surpass the amounts awarded to the successful party.

As these studies suggest, most evidence about bargaining inefficiencies
is based on two kinds of data, concerning breakdowns and the allocation of resources to directly share-enhancing ends. But there is some
evidence of misallocation of surplus producing resources as well. A
number of studies indicate that allocations of resources within households are systematically distorted to enhance the share of the male head
of household. Udry, Hoddinott, Alderman, and Haddad (1995) estimated production functions for agricultural plots cultivated by men and
by women in Burkina Faso and found that the value of household output could be increased by 10 to 15 percent by reallocating resources
from the male- to the female-tilled plots. As the cultivators control the
incomes generated by their plots, this efficiency-enhancing reallocation
would have the effect of raising women's access to income relative to
men's. This is presumably one of the reasons it does not occur. Posel
(2001) studied rural migrants in South Africa and found that household
income could be substantially increased if more women and fewer men
migrated. In both cases it seems likely that the reduction in the family's
joint surplus reflected share-enhancing efforts by the males, who exercised greater claim on the income from their own plots (in Burkina
Faso) or from their own wages (in South Africa) and hence distorted
within-family resource allocation in this direction. Of course, had the
males in the families studied by Udry and colleagues and Posel had
sufficient bargaining power to dictate the distributional shares *irrespective of the pattern of resource allocation*, they would have been better
off simply maximizing the joint surplus and then implementing their
favored distribution. These studies reaffirm an important principle: *bargaining inefficiencies arise when the ability to press distributional claims
is influenced by the allocation of resources.*

TABLE 5.1
Conflict of Interest

	U	D
L	a: 1, 0	b: v, γ
R	c: σ, τ	d: 0, 1

The letter referes to the strategy profile, shown in figure 5.3, followed by person 1 (row) and person 2 (column) payoffs.

One may expect, then, that where conflicts of interest are particularly great, bargaining efficiency is more likely to be compromised. But like "bargaining power," the term "conflict of interest" is vague. Can we say *how much* conflict of interest there is in a game? The definition of pure conflict games in chapter 1 captures the important idea that in conflictual situations, one's gain requires the others' loss. A measure of *the degree of conflict of interest* should express the same idea. We can develop such a measure, based on Axelrod (1970) as extended by Wood (2004), using the two-person conflict of interest game in table 5.1 and figure 5.3 as an example. First, we assign utility levels to the outcomes such that the worst outcome for each (that is, outcome **a** for person 2 and outcome **d** for person 1) has a payoff of zero, while the best outcome for each has a payoff of 1. There are two pure strategies, L and R for 1 and U and D for 2; let the payoffs be as indicated, where σ, τ, γ, and v are all positive constants between zero and one. If we call the difference between the most one can get and the least one can get *the stakes of the game*, this normalization reduces the stakes for the two players to a unit square, as indicated in figure 5.3, where the points **a** through **d** are the payoffs to the strategy profiles indicated in the payoff matrix above. Points **c** and **b** indicate that $\sigma + \tau \geq 1$ and $\gamma + v \leq 1$.

The intuition I would like to draw on is that if an outcome such as **c'** in figure 5.3 were possible (instead of **c**), we would say that the game exhibited less conflict of interest, for the best that either could do (at the expense of the other) is not much better than what they could both get jointly. First, consider the case in which linear combinations of any outcome determined by the use of pure strategies are possible. For example, the outcomes along the line **ac** in figure 5.3 will occur if 2 plays U while 1 randomizes her choice between L and R, varying the probability of selecting L from unity (the pure strategy which gives point **a**) to zero (the pure strategy giving point **c**).

It is obvious that all points below and to the left of **acd** are feasible (those on the boundary can be implemented as described above, and

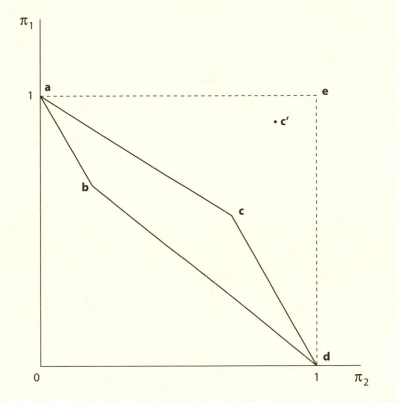

Figure 5.3 The degree of conflict of interest. Conflict of interest is measured by the fraction of the normalized stakes of the game (the unit square) which is infeasible (acde). Points **a, b, c, d** refer to the strategy profiles in table 5.1.

those in the interior of the set can be implemented in the same way, with some of the potential payoffs simply being thrown away). Outcomes in the set **acde** are not feasible, however. A convenient measure of the degree of conflict of interest, φ, is simply the size of this infeasible set of outcomes relative to the stakes of the game (which by the normalization of payoffs is unity):

$$\varphi = 1 - \max\left\{\frac{\tau + \sigma}{2}, \frac{\upsilon + \gamma}{2}\right\}$$

or (given that we have assumed $\alpha + \beta \geq 1$)

$$\varphi = 1 - \frac{\tau + \sigma}{2}$$

Had the payoff structure been such that $\tau + \sigma < 1$, the boundary of the bargaining set would be given by combinations of outcomes **a** and **d**, dividing the unit square in half, and giving $\varphi = \frac{1}{2}$ as the maximum degree of conflict of interest.

This lower bound on φ, however, only makes sense if linear combinations of outcomes based on pure strategies are possible. But this may not be the case: sometimes the stakes of the game are defined in such a way that they are indivisible (meaning that enjoying a part of the benefit, or enjoying it part of the time, is impossible). Examples include two ethnic groups at war over what shall be the national religion or language, or a couple in conflict over whether to have children or not. To take the latter case, and assuming that the best outcome for one is to have children and for the other the best outcome is to remain childless, it does not make much sense to say that because each can attain an expected utility of one-half just by deciding the issue by a coin toss that the degree of conflict is $\varphi = \frac{1}{2}$. In cases such as this, the bargaining set need not be convex, and φ may vary over the entire unit interval.

Further evidence of bargaining inefficiency comes from experiments. We have already encountered experimental evidence that disagreement on the distribution of rents can induce bargaining breakdowns that deny both parties any share of the surplus. An example is the common rejection of even substantial but seemingly unfair offers in the ultimatum games described in chapter 3. An early (and neglected) set of experiments casts light on sources of bargaining breakdowns. Rapoport and Chammah (1965) asked seventy randomly matched (unacquainted) pairs of University of Michigan students to play one of seven variants of a prisoners' dilemma three hundred times in succession. Though the players were not allowed to communicate directly, they seemingly attempted to induce cooperative responses in their partners, and some succeeded quite well.[20] The payoff matrices of the seven games exhibited a wide range of structures: some were close to pure coordination games with little conflict, while others were close to pure conflict games; that is the games varied greatly in the measure η of the coordination as opposed to conflict aspect of the game as defined in chapter 2. Similarly, they exhibited different degrees of conflict of interest φ.

I wondered if the players' behavior in the game was correlated with degree of conflict of interest in the game or the extent to which the

[20] The subjects engaged in a repeated game with a known number of rounds in which the dominant strategy on the last round is to defect, but knowing that one's opponent would defect on the last round, the dominant strategy on the next to the last round is also to defect, and so on, leading to the prediction that defection should be complete on all rounds. Not surprisingly, the subjects did not undertake this complicated backward induction (or if they did, they assumed their partner would not) and as a result did better.

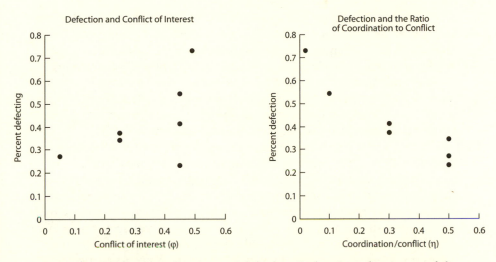

Figure 5.4 Conflict, coordination and defection. Each point refers to one of the seven experimental games implemented by Rapoport and Chammah (1965). Conflict of interest, φ, and the extent to which the payoffs approximate a pure coordination (as opposed to pure conflict) game, η, are calculated from the payoff structure of each game. The calculations also use data from Axelrod (1970).

game approximated a pure coordination game. To find out, I calculated the measures of φ and η for each of the seven games, and then investigated whether the frequency of defection was statistically associated with these measures of conflict. The results, in figure 5.4, show a strong inverse relationship between η and the frequency of defection (the simple correlation is −0.95). Where there is much to gain by cooperating and little to gain by defecting, the subjects found ways of cooperating. The degree of conflict, φ, is less closely associated with defections (though the correlation is still substantial: 0.55). These results suggest that the payoff structure facing individuals—and especially the gains to cooperation relative to the gains and costs possible through unilateral action—affect the likelihood of bargaining breakdowns.

CONCLUSION

Economists increasingly reject the view that a firm, a family, a government or any other group can be treated as an individual, and have turned to modeling these entities as strategically interacting individuals. Because these interactions do not take the form of competitive exchange governed by complete contracts, organizational rents arise in these entities, and their distribution is subject to bargaining. Thus with the demise of the unitary actor model of families, firms and other groups, the analysis of bargaining has assumed a more important role in economics. An adequate theory of bargaining should explain how a joint surplus is divided and how bargaining outcomes evolve over time. Neither the Nash nor the alternating offers models are entirely adequate from this perspective. Improvements in our understanding of bargaining will incorporate three aspects absent from the standard models.

The first is that bargaining behavior is influenced by the bargainers' fairness concerns and other distributional norms. In many cases, so settled are the bargained outcomes that the longstanding term for the institution — *mezzadria, metayage,* or *ardhika* (in Italian, French, and ancient Sanskrit) for sharecropping, for example — actually names the share (one-half in each case).[21] Many bargaining breakdowns — strikes in the real world and rejections of substantial offers in ultimatum games, for example — are difficult to explain without reference to participants' reactions to situations that they consider to be unjust. Empirically observed bargaining cannot be understood by models that exclude fairness, reciprocity, and other social preferences of the bargainers.

The second is that we need to *explain* bargaining power rather than assume it. This requires "going behind" the proximate determinants of bargaining outcomes. The preferences, beliefs, and institutions that influence bargaining power evolve under many influences, among them are the bargained outcomes themselves. Recall that until the late 1970s, the customary share of the tenant rice farmer in West Bengal had for centuries been one-half of the crop, and these arrangements had encountered little effective opposition over the years. But any attempt, today, to revoke the now-customary higher share (three-quarters) would be seen as a gross violation of a norm, that would be energetically (and probably effectively) resisted. We may say, then, that bargaining outcomes, norms of distribution, and bargaining power coevolve. Bargained outcomes are thus likely to be path dependent, and there may be many outcomes capable of persisting over long periods. Bargaining theory may increasingly study these persistent long-term outcomes in evolutionary bargaining frameworks rather than seeking to identify a unique equilibrium outcome.

The third is that bargainers typically have very incomplete information about the preferences and other aspects of their opponents. Models

[21] Sharecropping is not the only example of this. Traditional in-kind loans in the village of Palanpur (which you encountered in chapter 1), are called *deorh* from the Hindi *der*, meaning one-and-a-half, referring to the fact that wheat borrowed at any time prior to the harvest is repayable at 50 percent interest at harvest time (Lanjouw and Stern 1998).

based on more realistic information assumptions, like that in the evolutionary extensions section above, address this issue.

Economists dissatisfied with the efficient bargaining prediction of the standard models sometimes explain bargaining breakdowns by information asymmetries among the bargainers. For example, if employers and workers had the same information, they would both predict the same distribution of likely costs and outcomes of a strike. In light of this common information, they would settle in advance, thus avoiding the costs. But if information is not common, workers may engage in a costly strike to communicate their solidarity and resolve to the employer, or they may unwittingly demand an amount violating the employer's participation constraint.

There is undoubtedly some truth to this view, as is attested to by the fact that parties are sometimes surprised when a mutually beneficial deal does not go through. But at least in the experimental situations mentioned, asymmetric information does not provide an adequate explanation of bargaining breakdowns. In the ultimatum games, for example, proposers frequently make offers quite close to the expected payoff-maximizing amounts (that is, the amounts that maximize payoffs in light of the observed rejection behavior of the respondents). These proposers may be disappointed at a rejection but apparently are not surprised. It is difficult to see what additional information the respondents might need to induce them not to reject what appear to be unfair offers. Indeed, rejection rates are *lower* when respondents do not know the size of the pie the proposer is dividing. The most likely reason why information asymmetries lead to fewer bargaining breakdowns in this case is that if the pie is not known, it is difficult for the responder to form a clear concept of what a fair offer would be, so rejections for violations of fairness are fewer. Thus a source of bargaining breakdowns that may be more important than asymmetric information occurs when bargainers have different views about what a fair outcome might be. Fairness norms may have evolved because they allowed groups which used them to exploit economies of scale and cooperation which would otherwise have been precluded by breakdowns and other inefficiencies associated with bargaining. I return to this idea in chapter 11.

A major contributor to bargaining failures that has not been formally modeled is the fact that getting to the bargaining frontier may require new institutions or precedents, that with some probability will later be deployed to the disadvantage of one the bargainers. If this is the case, one or both of the parties may prefer the fallback position to taking a chance on a lottery whose possible payoffs include not only a movement to the bargaining frontier but also an outcome worse than their current reservation position. Many examples come to mind. In the face of increasing competition, a moderation of wage demands by workers may be in the interest of both employers and employees But its successful implementation may require that the firm make its accounts public, a move that, while supporting a Pareto improvement in this case, may prove disadvantageous to the firm in other arenas. Early business opposition to Keynesian economics in the United States apparently did not stem so much from a failure to recognize the benefits that businesses could reap from a reduction in macroeconomic cyclical volatility, as from concern that a more interventionist state might also undertake other policies of a less business-friendly nature. The retarded development of representative political institutions and fiscal reform during the century before the French revolution provides another case. Jean-Laureut Rosenthal (1998:101) writes,

> Despite the clear connection between fiscal institutions and economic growth, the evolution of these institutions [was] constrained by the ruler's concern over the impact of fiscal reform on his . . . autonomy in other areas like foreign policy. France . . . had a "representative" institution that could have raised the efficiency of the fiscal system, yet the Crown chose not to exercise it for a century and a half. The Crown thus was willing to forego increases in fiscal efficiency and increases in economic activity in order to preserve its autonomy.

The Crown's reluctance to summon the Estates General was not misplaced, as the events of 1789, following its first meeting since 1614, amply testified. This appears to be another case in which unresolved conflicts over the distribution of the joint surplus, along with the open-ended nature of institutions that might resolve bargaining breakdowns, contribute to the likelihood of suboptimal bargaining outcomes.

PART II

Competition and Cooperation: The Institutions of Capitalism

CHAPTER SIX

Utopian Capitalism: Decentralized Coordination

> It is not from the benevolence of the butcher, the brewer, or the baker that we expect our dinner, but from their regard to their own interest.
> — Adam Smith, *Wealth of Nations* (1776)

> [H]e intends only his own gain, and he is in this, as in many other cases, led by an invisible hand to promote an end which was no part of his intention. Nor is it always worse for the society that it was not part of it. By pursuing his own interest he frequently promotes that of the society more effectually than when he really intends to promote it.
> — Adam Smith, *Wealth of Nations* (1776)

> Good fences make good neighbors.
> — Robert Frost, "Mending Wall" (1915)

MY NEIGHBORS in the small town of Leverett, Massachusetts, were surprised when the town's zoning board approved a twice-rejected petition for a waiver of environmental regulations, thereby allowing construction of one or more houses at the top of Long Hill, overlooking the town center. The new owner of the hill had promised to take the Town to court should the third petition be rejected. Town officials, explaining their reversal, pointed out that the Town had no funds to hire a lawyer. They invited any citizens who objected to the waiver to take legal action privately. The craggy wooded hill and adjacent pond had been private land longer than anyone could remember, but for generations it had been open to all for picnicking and hiking, and there was strong sentiment that the land should be preserved as a public recreation area. A group of citizens formed with this objective, but after a year of costly legal skirmishing it appeared likely that the owner of the hilltop would eventually be able to clear the necessary legal hurdles and prevail in court.

The citizens group then proposed purchasing Long Hill, reasoning that if the hill were more valuable to the members of the town as a recreation area than to the owner as a home site, a deal could be made. They faced formidable obstacles in raising the substantial sum that this

---

The first epigraph is from Smith (1937:2), the second from Smith (1937:423), and the third from Frost (1915:11–13).

would require. Contributing to "The Hill" (as the donations came to be called) posed a classic public goods problem: no individual contribution could be large enough to significantly affect the likelihood of success, while enjoyment of the hill, should the purchase go through, could not be made conditional on one's contribution. Thus, if individual preferences were self-regarding, the project would fail.

What actually happened was a second surprise: after a year of fund raising—including sales of home-baked goods and other traditional New England forms of public contribution—a substantial fraction of the town's families contributed sufficient funds to buy the hill. Long Hill was purchased by the citizen's group and given to the Town; it is now a public recreation area.

A long tradition in economics, dating back to the writings of Alfred Marshall and A. C. Pigou (1877–1959) at the beginning of the twentieth century, has identified situations such as homebuilding on Long Hill as market failures. Zoning and other forms of public regulation have been advocated as the appropriate governmental response. A familiar example is the implementation of an optimal allocation of fishing effort by means of "green taxes" (chapter 4). Robert Sugden (1986:3) describes this approach in somewhat unflattering terms:

> [L]ike the U.S. Cavalry in a good Western, the government stands ready to rush to the rescue whenever the market "fails" and the economist's job is to advise it on when and how to do so. Private individuals, in contrast, are credited with little or no ability to solve collective problems among themselves.

The citizens of Leverett had done exactly what Sugden laments that economists fail to consider: through a voluntary exchange, they had privately solved a collective action problem and rectified a market failure. In reality they solved *two* collective action problems. The first concerned how the hill would be used, and its solution involved the transfer of property rights from the owner to the citizens' group and then to the Town. The second problem was who would pay for the buyout, and its solution involved an appeal to other-regarding preferences as a motivation for voluntary contributions to a public good. Like the fishers in the examples of chapters 1 and 4, they had solved both the allocational problem (the hill should be open for public recreation) and the distributional problem (the citizens of the town should contribute voluntarily to the necessary purchase of the land). The dozen or so citizens most involved in the process collectively spent literally thousands of hours making this happen, mostly in meetings. (Other activities included (illegally) planting a row of trees across the owner's newly constructed (also illegal) driveway to the hilltop and inviting the entire town to a pancake breakfast at the top of the hill when it was still privately owned.)

In this chapter, I consider two important *general decentralized allocation mechanisms*, competitive markets and private bargaining over property rights, through an investigation of two important theoretical results, the Fundamental Theorem of Welfare Economics and the Coase theorem. (Coase's "theorem" does not warrant an upper case T because there is no theorem.) A decentralized allocation mechanism has two characteristics. First, a decentralized allocation mechanism is *privacy preserving* in that individual actions are based on individual preferences, beliefs, and constraints alone.[1] In the fishing case studied in chapter 4, both the overfishing allocation and the social optimum that resulted under the environmental taxes are privacy preserving. The planner's determination of fishing levels by fiat, in contrast, is not privacy preserving, though it results in the same allocation as the environmental taxes. Second a decentralized allocation is *polyarchal*; it results from the interplay of the actions of many individuals, and no individual's preferences over aggregate outcomes are decisive. An institution may be privacy preserving without being polyarchal: some models of market socialism, for example, relied on competitive markets to implement an allocation determined *ex ante* by planners. Examples of decentralized allocation mechanisms include the model of residential segregation in chapter 2, the tragedy of the fishers in chapter 4, and the exchange of well-defined property rights studied in this chapter.

We will be particularly concerned with the question: when do decentralized allocation mechanisms implement a Pareto optimum? As we will see, the conditions under which this occurs are quite stringent. Unlike the generic class of interactions studied in the previous chapters, which are of broad application in real economies, the models introduced in this chapter may be considered a quite abstract limiting case. While they are unlikely to be of direct empirical relevance, they are of interest for four reasons. First, the Fundamental Theorem and the Coase theorem express important tendencies at work in competitive processes, and the insights gained from them will be essential in considering less restrictive cases. Second, it is difficult to make sense of many recent developments in economics (including those presented here) without understanding these staples of microeconomic theory. In particular, the Fundamental Theorem (along with its underlying assumptions and apparent policy implications) has been an animus stimulating the develop-

---

[1] Strictly speaking, virtually all institutions are privacy preserving in that there remains room for individuals to best respond even if the choice set is highly restricted.

ment of a post-Walrasian paradigm in economics. Third, the Fundamental Theorem and the Coase theorem are sometimes treated in economics not as illuminating limit cases but rather as the standard general case and the starting point for the analysis of actual capitalist economies. Understanding the theorems well enough to see why this is mistaken is important.

Finally, attempts to clarify the conditions under which Adam Smith's radical claims for the invisible hand *might be* true have occupied some of the best minds in economics over two centuries. What they found out is of some interest for that reason alone. Kenneth Arrow and Frank Hahn (1971:vi–vii) put it this way:

> There is by now a long and . . . imposing line of economists from Adam Smith to the present who have sought to show that a decentralized economy motivated by self interest and guided by price signals would be compatible with a coherent disposition of economic resources that could be regarded in a well-defined sense as superior to a large class of possible alternative dispositions. . . . It is important to understand how surprising this claim must be to anyone not exposed to the tradition. . . . That [this claim] has permeated the economic thinking of a large number of people who are in no way economists is itself sufficient grounds for investigating it seriously. It is important to know not only whether it *is* true but whether it *could be* true. (original emphasis)

One thing is clear: the main contributors to this literature, among them Arrow and Coase, do not share the view, still held by some economists, that the assumptions of their theorems are approximated in real economies. Thus, the results presented below are best seen as a model of utopian capitalism, which like utopian socialism, illuminates ideal aspects of a system unrealizable in practice. Even this idealized model of capitalism is an odd utopia, however, for, as we will see, it abstracts from problems of distributive justice.

Decentralized Allocation and The Fundamental Theorem

Suppose two individuals, me (in lower-case letters) and you (upper case) are to determine the allocation of two goods, a single unit of each is available, you getting X and Y and me getting x and y (with $x + X = 1$ and $y + Y = 1$; i.e., we will allocate all the goods). Our utility functions reflect the fact that we are self-interested:

$$u = u(x, y)$$
$$U = U(X, Y)$$

where both functions are increasing and concave in both arguments. One way to arrange the allocation is to say that I can allocate the goods however I want as long as you receive some given level of utility, call it $\underline{U}$. Supposing I know your utility function, and substituting $1 - x$ for $\overline{X}$ and $1 - y$ for Y in your utility function, I would solve the problem: choose x and y to maximize $u = u(x,y)$ subject to $U(1 - x, 1 - y) \geq \underline{U}$. The result of this optimization process must lead me to allocate the two goods so that

$$\frac{u_x}{u_y} = \frac{U_x}{U_y}$$

which is to say, our two marginal rates of substitution in consumption are equal, or equivalently that our indifference loci are tangent. Allocations satisfying this condition are points on the *efficient contract locus*.[2]

Working backward, then, we can see that the optimum problem I solved ensured that the allocation would be a Pareto optimum. What does this have to do with coordination failures? Everything. Coordination failures, as we have seen, occur in noncooperative interactions when people do not take appropriate account of the effects of their actions on the well-being of others. Taking "appropriate account" of the effects of one's actions on others means evaluating one's own actions in terms of the others' marginal rates of substitution, as the above first-order condition indicates. Thus, if interacting individuals optimize subject to a constraint on the level of utility of those with whom they interact, their maximization process will take appropriate account of the effects of their actions on others. In chapter 4, I termed this the "binding participation constraint solution" to coordination problems ($U \geq \underline{U}$ would be the participation constraint in this case).

Of course, nobody does this kind of constrained optimization explicitly. To see why, suppose a benevolent social planner sought to implement a Pareto-optimal allocation. He would be thwarted by the difficulty of knowing the utility functions of the participants. Ideally, however, competitive markets achieve the same result without anyone needing to know the utility functions of anyone else.

To see how a decentralized price system can achieve this result, consider the simple case above, as described in the so-called Edgeworth box

---

[2] This condition (along with the associated second order conditions for a maximum) defines the efficient contract locus for allocations such that $x \in (0, 1)$ and $y \in (0, 1)$. A more complete statement of the problem would take explicit account of the fact that allocations may not be negative. For values of x and y such that either participant is allocated all or none of either of the goods ("corner solutions"), the above tangency condition is replaced by an appropriate inequality.

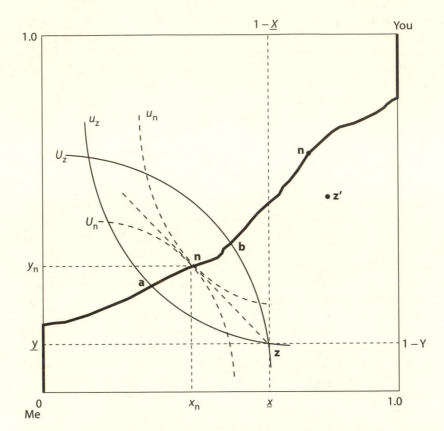

Figure 6.1 Competitive equilibrium (**n**) with initial endowments **z**. The efficient contract locus (including the noninterior allocations for which the Pareto optimality conditions are expressed as inequalities) is in bold.

in figure 6.1, where the unit square represents the (normalized) availability of the two goods and each point in the square represents a feasible allocation (that is, one that just exhausts the supply of both goods). The indifference loci for me are convex to the lower left origin while the indifference loci for you are convex to the upper right origin. Thus, each point in the square is associated with a given level of utility for the two participants, indicated for each by the indifference locus on which that point occurs.

Assume we each have a positive *initial endowment* $(\underline{x}, \underline{y})$ and $(\underline{X}, \underline{Y})$ of the goods. The term endowment is intended to suggest an exogenous distribution of wealth, the determination of which is outside the model. Suppose an initial interior endowment is represented in figure 6.1 by point **z**, namely, an allocation such that $u_x/u_y < U_x/U_y$ so the above condition for a Pareto-optimal allocation is violated (your relative valuation of good x over good y exceeds mine). As a result, I might wish to exchange some of my x for some of your Y, and you would conversely wish to trade some of your Y for some of my x, so a trade may be possible. But at what price? Any trade resulting in an allocation in the lens formed by the two indifference loci, U_z and u_z, is both feasible and represents a Pareto improvement over the initial endowments. It seems plausible to limit trades to this lens, but to say more about the likely price and resulting allocation we need to specify the institutions governing our interaction.

If you know my utility function and have the power to make a take-it-or-leave-it offer (specifying the amounts of both goods to be exchanged) you will find the allocation that maximizes U subject to $u \geq u_z$, namely, point **a** on the efficient contract locus in figure 6.1, and then offer me the trade that implements that allocation. If I know your utility function and can set the price at which we will exchange but not the amounts to be exchanged, I will first determine your best response to every price ratio I might offer (called your *offer curve*, not shown) and then maximize my utility subject to this constraint. In this second case, because I am taking your best-response function as the constraint on my optimization rather than a given level of utility (as was done in deriving the efficient contract locus and in the take-it-or-leave-it case), the resulting allocation will not be on the efficient contract locus. Neither of these two cases gives a complete account of the exchange process, for we would first need to know which of us was first mover and the offers to which we could credibly commit. Moreover, the examples unrealistically assume that both utility functions are common knowledge.

Alternately, we might interact symmetrically (with neither having first mover advantage) and, without knowledge of each other's utility functions, simply agree to any exchange that raised our utility. As a result we might engage in a series of trades, always implementing Pareto improvements. In this case the process would continue until we reached some point on the efficient contract locus (on the segment **ab**); but without knowing more about the details of our exchange process, we cannot say where. Other trading processes could be given, but enough has been said to underline the point that other than confining the outcome to the Pareto-improving lens of allocations, one cannot say much about the outcomes of the exchange process unless the institutions governing it are specified.

The Walrasian exchange process is one such institutional specification. The Walrasian exchange process is "competitive" (sometimes "purely competitive") in that producers and consumers face the same prices (*the law of the single price*) and treat them as given (*parametric prices*). In addition to being competitive in this sense, the Walrasian exchange process precludes exchanges at any but the equilibrium prices (*no disequilibrium trading*). The more common definition of competitive exchange — large numbers of noncolluding buyers and sellers with insignificant entry and exit costs — neither requires nor entails the law of the single price, parametric prices, or no disequilibrium trading. To capture the logic of the Walrasian assumptions, imagine a third party — called the Auctioneer — whose job it is to suggest price ratios at which we might trade and to ensure that no trading takes place until prices are found such that markets clear. The Auctioneer simply announces various prices, and for each price we indicate how much of one good we are willing to exchange for the other. This hypothetical process continues until a market-clearing price is hit upon (that is, a price is found such that that my desired purchases of your Y are exactly offset by your desired sales of Y, and similarly for the other good). Under reasonable assumptions, there is at least one price ratio that will accomplish this, and when it is found, market-clearing trades take place and the resulting allocation — called the competitive equilibrium — will be Pareto efficient.

The reason for this last important result is that in competitive equilibrium, each actor optimizes with respect to a given set of relative prices. By equating one's own marginal rate of substitution to the price ratio, given that the other is doing the same thing, one unwittingly equates one's marginal rate of substitution to the other's marginal rate of substitution. In other words,

$$\frac{u_x}{u_y} = \frac{p_x}{p_y} = \frac{U_x}{U_y}$$

We can introduce production of the two goods, with c_x, c_y, C_x, *and* C_y the marginal costs of producing the two goods for the two individuals. Because profit maximization under competitive conditions requires that prices equal marginal costs, we now have

$$\frac{u_x}{u_y} = \frac{U_x}{U_y} = \frac{p_x}{p_y} = \frac{c_x}{c_y} = \frac{C_x}{C_y}$$

Thus, because both individuals are optimizing with respect to the same price vector, they equate their own marginal rate of substitution in consumption as well as their marginal rate of transformation in production (the ratio of marginal costs) to the other individual's marginal rates of substitution and transformation, thereby implementing a Pareto optimum.

This process thus achieves a truly remarkable result: without either party knowing anything about the other's preferences, prices implement a Pareto-optimal allocation. If you are unimpressed, imagine that our example concerned a hundred individuals, not just two, and consider the problem faced by a benevolent planner charged with efficiently allocating the goods among the individuals. Our benevolent planner would have to know (which means to devise ways of finding out) the utility functions of each of the members of the population.

The result is expressed formally in the First Fundamental Theorem of Welfare Economics, proved independently by Arrow and Debreu (1954), which shows that *if the exchange of goods or services is subject to complete contracts (called the market completeness assumption), all equilibria supported by competitive exchange (namely the above process) are Pareto optimal.* Thus, the set of allocations that are competitive equilibria are also Pareto optima. In the above example, market completeness obtained because the utility of each actor depended on the actions of the other only through the goods acquired in exchange; thus, nonmarket (or noncontractual) interactions were absent. As can be seen from figure 6.1, the first Fundamental Theorem says nothing about the distribution of well-being: competitive equilibria may implement desperation for some and affluence for others; all it precludes are outcomes in which mutual gains remain unexploited.

The Second Welfare Theorem addresses matters of distribution. Suppose an additional requirement (*the convexity assumption*) is met, namely, that individuals' indifference maps and firms' production possibility sets are convex, ruling out increasing returns.[3] Then the Second Fundamental Theorem shows that *given the convexity and market completeness assumptions, any Pareto-optimal allocation can be supported as a competitive equilibrium for some assignment of initial endowments.* To see its importance, suppose that the citizens of an economy wish to redistribute income to the less well-off and select a particular Pareto-optimal allocation as their preferred outcome; the second theorem says that this outcome can be implemented by some reassignment of property rights (changing the assignment of initial endowments) followed by a Walrasian exchange process. Thus, under the assumptions of the second theorem, wealth redistribution *cum* exchange represents a mechanism capable of implementing *any* feasible Pareto optimum.

Figure 6.2 illustrates the second theorem, representing the same information as in figure 6.1, but with the goods-allocation space of figure 6.1 transformed into utility space (points **a**, **b**, **z**, **z'**, **n**, and **n'** represent the same allocations in the two figures). Suppose that the members of a society decide that the distribution of utility at **n** (the competitive equi-

---

[3] Where this assumption is violated, it may be the case that no competitive equilibrium exists.

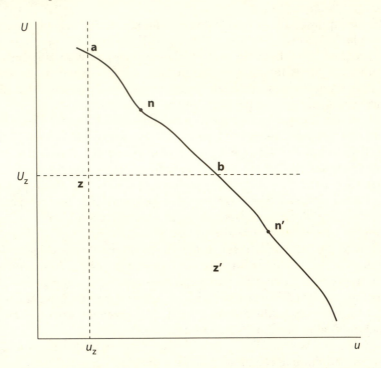

Figure 6.2 Competitive exchange supports an outcome on the utility possibility frontier (efficient contract locus).

librium resulting from the initial endowment **z**) is unethical and that the outcome **n′** would be preferable. Then the theorem shows that a redistribution of initial endowments (say from **z** to **z′**) followed by Walrasian exchange will implement the preferred allocation. The second theorem seems to suggest a way of implementing fair outcomes by combining governmental interventions (the redistribution of endowments) with market exchange. But, as we will see, this is not quite true.

The result of the first theorem that (under appropriate assumptions) competitive equilibrium is efficient has been widely discussed, and we shall return to it. A more subtle implication is that the two theorems taken together appear to leave little room for ethical concerns about the operation of a competitive market system except for the distribution of well-being; and this is determined not by markets per se but rather by the distribution of initial endowments. In other words, at equilibrium prices, the distribution of wealth is the same at point **z** (endowments) and point **n** (competitive allocation); this is true because the equilibrium price vector is an iso-wealth locus, and it passes through both points. Kenneth Arrow (1971:6) pointed out that under the conditions specified

by the theorems: "Any complaints about [the market system's] operation can be reduced to complaints about the distribution of income . . .
[but] the price system itself determines the distribution of income only
in the sense of preserving the status quo." John Roemer's treatment of
the Marxian theory of exploitation was based on the same correspondence between initial wealth and eventual access to consumption: "If
the exploitation of the worker seems unfair, it is because one thinks the
initial distribution of capital stock, which gives rise to it is unfair"
(Roemer, 1988:54).

Arrow's and Roemer's observations had been anticipated by the U.S.
Supreme Court in its *Coppage v. State of Kansas* (1915:17) decision:

> [W]herever the right of private property exists, there must and will be in-
> equalities of fortune; . . . it is impossible to uphold the freedom of contract
> and the right of private property without at the same time recognizing as
> legitimate these inequalities of fortune that are the necessary result of the
> exercise of those rights.

Some, like the philosopher David Gauthier (1986:93), have drawn more
expansive conclusions:

> The operation of a market cannot in itself raise any evaluative issues. Market
> outcomes are fair if, but of course only if, they result from fair initial distribu-
> tions. . . . [T]he presumption of free activity ensures that no one is subject to
> any form of compulsion, or to any type of limitation not already affecting her
> actions as a solitary individual. . . . [Thus] morality has no application to
> market interaction under the conditions of perfect competition.

General Competitive Equilibrium

At first glance, the Fundamental Theorem appears to be a striking vin-
dication of Adam Smith's conjecture that the competitive exchange of
claims on property would lead as if by "an invisible hand to promote an
end which was not part of" the participants' intentions. But few economists take the First Fundamental Theorem as an exoneration of any real
world market institutions. Fewer still take the second theorem as a prescription for wealth redistribution to implement a distributionally fair
Pareto optimum. Amartya Sen (1985:11) wrote that the second theorem
"belongs to the revolutionists' handbook."

There are four reasons for the limited applicability of the Fundamental Theorem. The first three concern the shortcomings of the underlying
model rather than the theorem itself. First, the Walrasian exchange process is not really about capitalism, or any other market system. Franklin

Fisher (1972:1) commented that it "describes nobody's actual behavior in most markets." Nor does it capture even the idealized logic of a system of decentralized allocation among agents with limited information. The Walrasian exchange process is highly centralized, requiring the assistance of the omniscient and omnipotent Auctioneer to preclude out-of-equilibrium trading. Perhaps surprisingly, markets play no role in this model, nor is the model consistent with any plausible process of equilibration. The reason is that buyers and sellers do not set prices (they are "price takers"). Arrow and Hahn (1971:325) drew attention to this lacuna: "If we did not stipulate . . . an auctioneer, we would have to describe how it comes about that at any moment of time two goods exchange on the same terms wherever such an exchange takes place and how these terms come to change under market pressure." The Auctioneer thus obviates the need for a theory of market dynamics.

As an empirical matter, of course, everybody knows that the Auctioneer is an invention, but economics textbooks generally presume that little is lost in abstracting from how traders actually interact, set prices, and the like. While not unreasonable, this view is a radical renunciation of the of the Walrasian project, which sought to derive propositions about aggregate economic behavior solely from individual actions in a privacy preserving and polyarchic — that is, decentralized — institutional setting. The staple classroom account with which instructors fill the resulting gap in logic is entirely plausible: excess demand (i.e., demand exceeding supply at a given price) leads to price increases that in turn eliminate excess demand. But students who have learned that actors are price takers may wonder who changes the price.

The students' confusion points to a serious shortcoming. Suppose we wanted to model the workings of an abstract market economy. What is it that we need a theory *of*? One might start with basic facts: individuals are heterogeneous in preferences and endowments, they trade voluntarily and hence will refuse exchanges that make them worse off, trade is perpetual, and prices (and quantities) are quite persistent over long periods. The traders know their own preferences but not those of (most) others. Add to this a decentralization requirement: allocations must be privacy preserving and polyarchal. Thus there must be no coordinating mechanism (trades take place if they are mutually beneficial and not if not, and that's about all one can say). What does an adequate account of this require?

The question brings us to a second problem. We need a theory of how the process of trading transforms an arbitrary initial endowment (z in figure 6.1) into an allocation and a vector of prices that are stationary (in the absence of exogenous shocks). This requires a property called *quasi-global stability*, namely, that from an arbitrary initial state, the economy converges to some equilibrium.[4] But even this rather weak requirement is not fulfilled. The reason is instructive. In the Walrasian general equilibrium model, global stability (quasi or not) depends on the shape of the excess demand functions of the goods making up the economy. Hugo Sonnenschein (1973a and b) showed that the usual assumptions about consumer preferences and behavior impose virtually no restrictions on the excess demand functions. Because of their essentially arbitrary nature, systems of excess demand functions can be constructed with arbitrary second partial derivatives. But these determine the stability properties of the system. Thus, under the usual assumptions of the behavior of consumers even quasi-global stability cannot be assured.[5] Sonnenshein's negative result has proven resilient: subsequent work has shown that there do not exist even remotely plausible additional restrictions on preferences or endowments sufficient to provide significant additional restrictions on the shape of the excess demand functions. Thus, the Auctioneer is a necessary fiction. It is not an innocuous shorthand way of expressing a coherent but more complicated account of how out of equilibrium behavior leads prices converge to their equilibrium values.

The virtually unrestricted dynamics of the Walrasian general equilibrium system challenge a common interpretation of the Second Fundamental Theorem, namely, that redistribution followed by market exchange can implement any Pareto optimum. But without an account of how out-of-equilibrium behaviors of the market participants move the system to a competitive equilibrium, the Walrasian model does not show this. All that Arrow and Hahn claim for it is that "in a certain sense any desired efficient allocation can be achieved by redistribution of initial assets followed by the achievement of an equilibrium" (Arrow and Hahn 1971:95). They are careful not to suggest that the equilibrium can be achieved without the assistance of a fictive Auctioneer or some other social engineer. They illustrate the second theorem with an example of "an omniscient state" that "computes a price vector . . . satisfying the hypotheses of the theorem."

---

[4] One might want to restrict these to a limited number of discrete equilibria. Global stability — without the quasi — requires that the economy converge to a unique equilibrium. I will postpone the problem of multiple equilibria for a moment.

[5] Scarf (1960) had earlier provided a series of examples of plausible trading processes that failed to exhibit global stability. Sonnenschein's 1973 papers were extended by Mantel (1974), Debreu (1974), and Kirman and Koch (1986). The open endedness of the dynamics of the Walrasian general equilibrium model are surveyed in Mas-Colell, Whinston, and Green (1995) who candidly remark: "[E]conomists are good . . . at recognizing a state of equilibrium but are poor at predicting precisely how an economy in disequilibrium will evolve" (p. 620).

Third, the Walrasian general equilibrium model is incomplete. It would be a stunning achievement if the model allowed us to say that, given a set of preferences, endowments, and technologies, the process of competitive exchange would result in a given allocation and price vector. We would then have a parsimonious list of the determinants of the the state of the economy under given institutions and initial conditions. But this is not what the Walrasian general equilibrium model does. Except under extremely limiting assumptions, it cannot be shown that the competitive equilibrium is unique.[6] Thus, even setting aside the above dynamic problem of why prices would converge to their equilibrium values, knowledge of initial endowments, preferences, and technologies is insufficient to determine a unique stationary outcome. In a system with many equilibria, the determination of outcomes requires information from outside of the Walrasian model, namely, an explicit analysis of out-of-equilibrium dynamics as well as knowledge of the recent history of the system.

Fourth, it is widely recognized by leading contributors to this literature that the market completeness assumption is generally false. Market incompleteness was once considered an exceptional phenomenon, concerning things like lighthouses (public goods) or one farmer's bees pollinating the neighbor's apple trees (an external economy). But market incompleteness is no longer considered exotic or bucolic. The Prisoners' Dilemma, Assurance, and Hawk-Dove Games introduced in chapter 1 all illustrate coordination failures that arise because not everything "exchanged" in social interactions is covered by complete contracts. Examples go considerably beyond the obvious examples of environmental spillovers. As we will see, many interactions central to the functioning of any modern economy — the employment of labor, the lending of money and the production and distribution of information, for example — exhibit market failures. The reason is that where — as in these examples — the market completeness assumption fails, individual optimization is not generally constrained by the other's indifference loci or by relative prices that are tangent to them. As a result, the critical equality of marginal rates of substitution does not obtain. (I will return to this in the next four chapters.)

Violations of the assumptions of the Fundamental Theorem need not be pervasive to sharply limit their relevance to real world issues of pol-

---

[6] For example, uniqueness can be shown if production sets are convex and there are no price effects on individual wealth (the goods making up individual wealth are held in the same proportion by all; the wealthy simply have proportionally more of everything), or if commodities are gross substitutes (requiring a price increase of one good to result in increases in demand for *all* other goods). On the latter, see Katzner (2003). Economies with many goods clearly do not conform to these assumptions even approximately.

icy and institutional design. In a competitive economy of the type represented by the fundamental welfare theorems, let there be n marginal conditions (marginal rates of substitution equal marginal rates of transformation, as above) defining a Pareto optimum. Suppose some violation of the assumptions (for example, the existence of monopoly in one sector leading to price's exceeding marginal cost) prevents just one of the marginal conditions from obtaining. What has come to be called the *general theorem of the second best*, advanced by Lipsey and Lancaster (1956–1957) shows that in this case, the second-best welfare optimum (taking the violation as given) may require that one or more of the *other* $n - 1$ marginal conditions also be violated. Thus, a single violation of the relevant efficiency conditions means that fulfilling the remaining marginal conditions may result in an allocation that is Pareto inferior to an allocation implementable by more extensive violations of the efficiency conditions. The intuition behind this result is that the allocational distortions caused by the violation of one of the efficiency conditions can generally be attenuated by countering distortions induced by other violations. An example: if a producer generates environmental external diseconomies (and therefore produces more than the Pareto-optimum level of output), this distortion can be countered if the producer is a monopoly (and thus chooses an output at which price exceeds marginal cost, thereby restricting output). A competition policy that induced this producer to choose the competitive output level such that $p = mc$ could be welfare reducing rather than welfare enhancing.

How decisive are these four limitations of the Walrasian general equilibrium model and its most famous theorem? The nonuniqueness of equilibria in the model has important implications for both economic policy and analysis. For example, the policies appropriate for displacing a unique equilibrium to improve social well-being differ markedly from those capable of displacing an economy from one equilibrium to a superior equilibrium. A one-time intervention (even a small one) may accomplish the latter, while the former may require ongoing interventions. Equally important, the ubiquitous nature of contractual incompleteness has stimulated the development of an alternative to the Walrasian approach that gives fundamentally different empirical predictions (the lack of market clearing, for example) and normative results (Pareto-inefficient equilibria, for example). Joseph Stiglitz (1987) has gone as far as suggesting the "abrogation of the law of supply and demand."

Stiglitz is right about the Walrasian model; but much of conventional economic reasoning about markets remains valuable. The lack of an adequate theory of market equilibration is certainly a glaring lacuna, but it may be possible to repair this. For example, Stephen Smale (1976) introduced an element of market realism by abandoning the Auctioneer and allowing transactions take place at nonequilibrium prices. In his model, starting from an initial endowment, individuals participate in a series of exchanges consistent only with the requirements that the transaction increase the satisfaction of the parties to the exchange and that no such exchanges remain unexploited. Convergence to an equilibrium price vector and Pareto-efficient allocation occur in this model.

Duncan Foley (1994) adapted a statistical mechanics model from physics to refine Smale's results, identifying some utility-enhancing series of exchanges as more likely than others. Foley's description of his model economy is an exemplary expression of an abstract non-Walrasian market system:

> [A]gents enter the market knowing only the transactions they view as improving their condition given their endowments, preferences, technology, and expectations; [they] encounter other agents; and make mutually advantageous transactions in a disorderly and random fashion. (p. 322)

The equilibrium allocation in Foley's model is approximately Pareto optimal. From a methodological standpoint, the interesting twist in Foley's work is that the stationarity of the price vector is achieved in the presence of ongoing trade. It is stationary not because all individuals have satisfied their first order conditions for profit- or utility-maximization, but instead because the exchange activities of very large numbers of traders approximately cancel out. Thus, the individuals making up the system are in motion, but one of its aggregate properties (the price vector) is stationary. Foley writes:

> Walrasian theory seeks to predict the actual market outcome for every individual agent, while the statistical approach seeks only to characterize the equilibrium distributions of agents over outcomes, without predicting the fate of specific agents. (p. 343)

Foley's concept of equilibrium, borrowed from physics, is thus at odds with the usual economic concept that requires that aggregate stationarity be built up from stationarity of all of the lower-level units making up the aggregate. This may be considered an advantage of his approach, for it allows trade to take place at stationary prices, something we commonly observe in real economies.

The work of Foley and Smale underlines the point that quasi-global stability can be shown under plausible assumptions in a model of competitive exchange. Sonnenschein's result thus was more a negative finding about the Walrasian approach, not about the idea of general competitive equilibrium. It was taken as a bombshell only because of the hegemonic status of the Walrasian paradigm at the time. The widespread sense that the abstract economic theory of multimarket competitive interactions of large numbers of agents had reached a dead end is thus quite misplaced. Indeed, Foley's and Smale's work shows that a model of how large numbers of agents with limited information interact in a decentralized manner to produce aggregate outcomes can retain many features of the conventional economic reasoning about markets. These include prices adjusting in plausible ways to excess demand, convergence to an equilibrium, and (approximate) Pareto optimality of the allocation when impediments to trade and nonmarket interactions are absent.

There are, however, two important implications of explicitly modeling the process of trade and allowing trades at disequilibrium prices. First, it is not possible to associate a particular initial endowment (z in figure 6.1) with any particular equilibrium outcome (n). Individuals starting with endowments z may, through a series of trades, end up at (or very near) any point along the efficient contract locus between a and b (including these points). Smale comments: "The exact equilibrium depends on factors such as which agents first encounter each other" (p. 212). Second, identical agents with identical endowments end up with unequal bundles of final consumption. The distribution of the surplus achieved through trading at disequilibrium prices will typically favor one of the traders (the one selling goods at above equilibrium prices or buying at below equilibrium prices). The result of a series of such trades will be quite unequal (the resulting equilibrium being close to a or b) with high probability. This occurs even if the traders have identical preferences. By contrast in the Walrasian case, in equilibrium, identical traders enjoy identical consumption bundles.

As a result, when out-of-equilibrium trading occurs, the equilibrium price vector (tangent to the traders' indifference loci at some point on the contract curve) does not generally pass through the initial endowment point. This feature of the out-of-equilibrium trading models may seem unimportant, and as a matter of the descriptive adequacy it certainly is. But in models for which there does not exist a single mapping from the endowment point to the competitive outcome, Gauthier's claim that "the operation of a market cannot in itself raise any evaluative issues" is no longer true, nor is Arrow's observation that markets merely preserve the status quo. Whether the inequalities emerging in the trading process among identical individuals are of significant magnitude remains an open question.

The Coase Theorem

The canonical approach to coordination failures in welfare economics is that the government should impose taxes or subsidies calibrated to implement a social optimum. This is done by transforming each individual's objective function, and hence their first order conditions, so that each—operating under the additional incentives provided by the tax or subsidy—will act *as if* he is taking account of the effects of his actions on others. Compelling arguments for "green taxes" and subsidization of schooling are routinely made on these grounds, invoking reasoning originating with Alfred Marshall and A. C. Pigou early in the past century.

Ronald Coase (1960) challenged this view. He reconsidered Pigou's case of a railroad whose engines' sparks ignite fires in the farmlands through which they pass, causing damage. Pigou had asserted, conventionally, that on efficiency grounds the railroad should be liable for the damage, as the anticipation of the liability would induce it to take account of the effect of its actions on others. (The example may now sound quaint: the British law covering cases such as this, and endorsing the Pigouvian position, was established exactly a century before Coase wrote.) Coase responded that "if the railroad could make a bargain with everyone having property adjoining the railway line and there were no costs involved in making such bargains, it would not matter whether the railway was liable for damages caused by fires or not" (p. 31). This surprising conclusion is motivated by the observation that if the costs of the fires exceeded the cost of preventing the sparks (say, by redesigning the engines), then those harmed could simply pay the railroad a sufficiently large sum to induce them to agree to prevent the sparks.

Coase's proviso—costless bargaining—is important, and unlike many who have invoked Coase against governmental regulation, Coase himself stressed it:

> [I]f market transactions were costless all that matters (questions of equity aside) is that the rights of the various parties should be well defined and the results of legal actions easy to forecast. But . . . the situation is quite different when market transactions are so costly as to make it difficult to change the arrangement of rights established by the law." (p. 19)

Roughly: good fences make good neighbors.

What came to be called the Coase theorem thus achieves a seemingly dramatic extension of the Fundamental Theorem of Welfare Economics: *even where markets are incomplete and hence nonmarket interactions occur, efficient allocations will be made as long as those affected are able to bargain efficiently over the rights governing the actions giving rise to the nonmarket interactions.* Because there is some controversy about what the theorem means, it may be useful to consult its author. In his Nobel lecture, Coase (1992) wrote:

> What I showed . . . was that in a regime of zero transactions costs, an assumption of standard economic theory, negotiations between the parties would lead to those arrangements being made which would maximize wealth, and this irrespective of the initial assignment of rights. (p. 717)

Here is how it works (when it works). A and B are two neighbors; B is a night-owl who plays the Grateful Dead late into the night, while A worships the rising sun and hence wants to go to sleep early.[7] A curfew is proposed specifying the time of night, x, after which no music is to be played. If A could determine the curfew she would set $x = a$, while B would select $x = b$, with $b > a$. The Coase theorem says that it doesn't matter for efficiency which of the two determines the curfew or even if some third party determines it as long as the two can efficiently bargain to rearrange the relevant property rights, meaning in this case the curfew itself. Bargaining is efficient if the outcome is on the bargaining frontier (and hence is Pareto efficient.) Suppose the bargaining takes the form of a payment from B to A of an amount y in return for A agreeing to a later curfew than whatever is initially announced ($y < 0$ is a payment from A to B for an earlier curfew).

Let the utility functions of A and B, respectively, be,

$$u = y - \alpha(a - x)^2$$
$$v = -y - \beta(b - x)^2 \qquad (6.1)$$

where α and β are positive constants indicating the importance of the curfew time relative to income in the well-being of each. For simplicity, let $\alpha + \beta = 1$. It is important for what follows that the two utility functions are comparable and exhibit a constant marginal utility of income.

Suppose you are the mayor of the town and, knowing the above functions, you wish to set x to maximize total social utility, $W = u + v$. Differentiating W with respect to x and setting the result equal to zero we have

$$x^* = \alpha a + \beta b \qquad (6.2)$$

This social optimum is just a weighted sum of the two preferred curfew times. I'll call this the *socially efficient outcome* and relate it later to the class of Pareto-efficient outcomes. If $\alpha = \beta$, the socially optimal curfew is midway between the two preferred times. This is as one would expect because each experiences rising marginal disutility as the curfew time diverges from their preferred times, and the sum of the disutility is minimized by equating the marginal disutilities. This entails choosing the midpoint if the two have identical utility functions. Figure 6.3 illustrates this: the area under the two functions is total social disutility, which is minimized by setting $x = x^*$, e.g. if $x = x^+ > x^*$, the marginal benefit to A of an earlier curfew (y^+) exceeds its marginal cost to B (y^-).

Would private bargaining achieve the same result? Consider what would appear to be the worst case, no curfew at all, which means that

---

[7] This example is inspired by Farrell (1987).

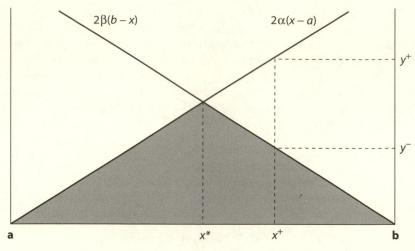

$2\beta(b-x)$ $2\alpha(x-a)$

y^+

y^-

a x^* x^+ b

Hour of the curfew, x

Figure 6.3 The social optimum **curfew**. The horizontal axis is the time of the curfew, ranging from early (**a**) to late (**b**). The area under the two marginal disutility loci is the sum of disutilities; it is minimized by a curfew set at x* the social optimum.

in the absence of any bargaining between the two, B will impose Jerry Garcia on A until b o'clock every night. To see if a bargain might be struck, consider the interaction between the two as illustrated in figure 6.4. The time of the curfew is on the horizontal axis and the payment from B to A is measured vertically. The loci $\underline{u}$ and $\underline{v}$ are combinations of curfew times and payments that, for each, are as good as their preferred curfew time with no payments; preferred and inferior combinations are indicated by the other indifference loci.

The above social optimum occurs midway between **a** and **b** at a point on the horizontal axis at which the two indifference loci are tangent, that is, where

$$2\alpha(x - a) = 2\beta(b - x) \qquad (6.3)$$

Because the marginal utility of income is constant for both, the indifference loci are simply vertical displacements of one another (notice that y does not appear in the above expression for the slopes of the indifference loci). Thus, other tangencies are found along a vertical line through x^*, giving the efficient contract locus, labeled *ecl*. Efficient outcomes will set the curfew at x^* but will differ in the payments among the neighbors.

Suppose that B were to play music until b o'clock. Then B would get

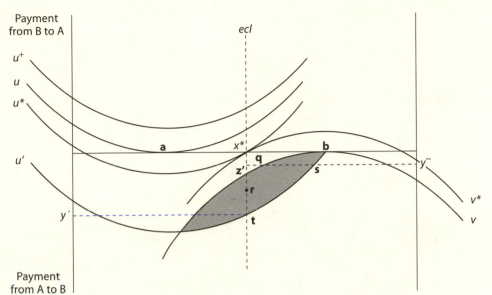

Figure 6.4 Optimal Cosean bargaining. Note x^* is the social optimum irrespective of the initial allocation of rights. The horizontal axis is the time of the curfew, with **a** and **b** indicating A's and B's optima. A's indifference loci are ordered $u^+ > \underline{u} > u^* > u'$ while for B, $v^* < \underline{v}$.

utility v while A would get u'; both would prefer any point in the lens formed by the indifference loci for these levels of utility. The lens must exist because at **b**, $dv/dx = 0$ (*b* is *B*'s preferred curfew time) while $du/dx < 0$ (it is after *A*'s bedtime), so there will exist some $dx < 0$ and some payment from *A* to *B* that will make both better-off. This lens in (y, x) space gives us the bargaining set **bz't** in (u, v) space (figure 6.5).

We do not know what bargain the two will strike. We know from chapter 5 that this will depend on the institutions and norms governing the bargaining process. We assume that any outcome must be agreed to and hence cannot be worse for either party than the curfew of *b* with no payments between the two. If *B* can make a take-it-or-leave-it offer to *A*, for example, the outcome will be **t** (*A* pays *B* the amount y', and the curfew is set at x^*), with *A* gaining a utility greater than u' by an arbitrarily small amount. If the outcome is determined by an arbitrator subscribing to the Nash bargaining axioms, they will end up at a point such as **r**. If they engage in alternating offers bargaining and if *B* is either first mover or has a lower rate of time preference, the outcome will be somewhere between **t** and **r**. And so on.

What we *do* know is that—here is the Coasian proviso—*if the insti-*

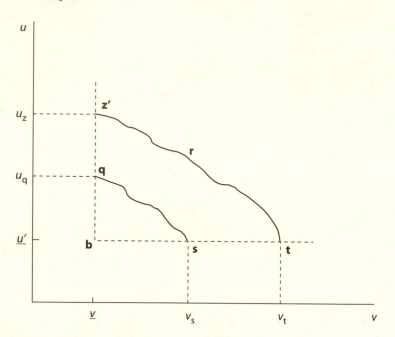

Figure 6.5. The bargaining set is truncated by A's limited wealth.

tutions and norms governing the bargaining process allow efficient bargains, the outcome will be Pareto efficient, that is, somewhere along the Pareto frontier of the bargaining set (or, equivalently, along the efficient contract locus within the Pareto-improving lens). The range of outcomes consistent with efficient Coasian bargaining differ from the standpoint of distribution, but all are Pareto efficient. So Coase is right: who holds the property rights does not matter ("questions of equity aside").

Of course it may be the case that A is not wealthy and does not have (and cannot borrow) the funds necessary to compensate B. Assume, for concreteness, that A has access to only y^-, thus truncating the Pareto-improving feasible lens in figure 6.4 to **bqs** and the bargaining set to **bqs** in figure 6.5. The bargained outcome, constrained by A's lack of wealth, will not be socially efficient. Of course, had the initial allocation of entitlements been such that x were quite close to x^*, then Coasian bargaining would have achieved the socially efficient result, despite A's wealth constraint.

But problems arise in the general case even where borrowing is unlimited. A special—and certainly false—assumption concerning the utility functions in eq. (6.1) is that the marginal utility of income is independent of the level of income. Rewrite the utility functions in eq. (6.1) as

$$u = u(\underline{y} + y) - \alpha(a - x)^2$$
$$v = v(\underline{Y} - y) - \beta(b - x)^2 \qquad (6.1')$$

where $\underline{Y}$ and $\underline{y}$ are the incomes of B and A from sources other than this bargain, and the functions u and v are increasing and strictly concave in their arguments. The expression equating the slopes of the indifference loci and hence defining the efficient contract locus is now

$$\frac{2\alpha(x - a)}{u'} = \frac{2\beta(b - x)}{v'} \qquad (6.3')$$

If we assume that $\underline{Y} = \underline{y}$ and that the two functions $u()$ and $v()$ are identical, the indifference loci are still tangent at x^* (which under these assumptions is still the social optimum), but the efficient contract locus is no longer vertical. The reason is that the marginal subjective cost of making a transfer to the other party is rising in the size of the transfer, while the marginal subjective benefit to the recipient is declining in the amount, thus making the transfer process less attractive to both parties. Figure 6.6 illustrates the new efficient contract locus.

Now return to the case in which B holds the de facto property right. Efficient bargaining will, as before, yield an outcome on the efficient contract locus, so the result will be Pareto efficient. But it will not be socially efficient, as the only distribution of property rights that will achieve x^* is the imposition of that curfew ($x = x^*$) by fiat (following which no bargaining will occur). In this case, the initial distribution of property rights *does* matter for social efficiency but not for Pareto efficiency (as long as the Coasian proviso holds). The difference arises because unlike Pareto efficiency, *social* efficiency introduces the "questions of equity" that Coase set aside; here, equity enters implicitly through the explicit (equal) weighting of the utilities of the two. If initial conditions are highly unequal (for example, $x = b$), social efficiency may be impossible to implement without making B worse off. In this case, the socially efficient outcome will not occur through private bargaining.

TWO-AND-A-HALF CHEERS FOR THE COASE THEOREM

Coase's contribution proved controversial because it appeared to radically enlarge the class of situations in which decentralized allocation mechanisms would implement efficient solutions, thereby limiting the appropriate scope of state intervention. Thus Buchanan and Tullock (1962:47–48) wrote:

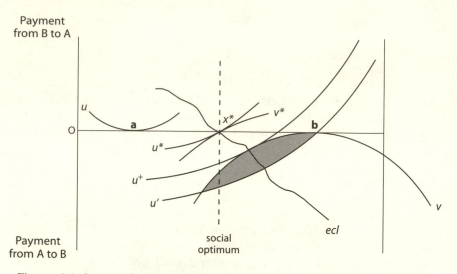

Payment
from B to A

Payment
from A to B

Figure 6.6 Coasean bargaining with diminishing marginal utility of income. Note: efficient bargaining will implement a point on the efficient contract locus, but this will not be socially efficient unless the initial allocation of rights is x^*.

> If the costs of organizing decisions should be zero, all externalities would be eliminated by voluntary private behavior regardless of the initial structure of property rights. There would, in this case, be no rational basis for state or collective action beyond the initial minimum delineation of the power of individual disposition over resources.

Among the more surprising claims said to be based on Coase's reasoning is the assertion that the assignment of property rights is efficient in actual economies, and that transitions from one economic *system* to another could be seen as the outcome of efficiency-enhancing Coasian bargaining. Harold Demsetz (1966:348) reasoned:

> [I]t might be thought that a firm which uses slave labor will not recognize all the costs of its activities, since it can have its slave labor by paying subsistence wages only. This will not be true if negotiations are permitted, for the slaves can offer to the firm a payment for their freedom based on the expected return to them of being free men. The cost of slavery can thus be internalized in the calculations of the firm. The transition from serf to free man in feudal Europe is an example of this process.

When the Coase theorem is presented sufficiently precisely to be correct, however, all it says is that if there are no impediments to efficient bargaining then outcomes will be efficient. This seems disappointingly similar to the Fundamental Theorem itself, accomplishing little by way of relaxing the stringent assumptions required by the theorem. As Farrell (1987) pointed out, the information conditions under which the Coase theorem holds — no impediments to efficient bargaining — are exactly those that would also allow complete contracting. So where the Coase theorem works, the Fundamental Theorem also holds, so the Coase theorem is unnecessary. Where the Fundamental Theorem fails (due to contractual incompleteness), the zero bargaining costs assumed by the Coase theorem are also unlikely to obtain.

Some have concluded on this basis that when the Coase theorem is needed, it fails, and is therefore of little relevance. But this interpretation misunderstands Coase's contribution. What he pointed out is that from an inefficient initial endowment (like the allocation z in figure 6.1), market exchange of the Walrasian type is *not the only way* to get to a point on the efficient contract locus or at least closer to it (in the Pareto sense). His result is therefore very much in the spirit of the later contributions of Smale and Foley, mentioned above. While the Fundamental Theorem did not seem to have any policy implications, Coase's contribution is to have shown that more precisely defined and easily tradeable property rights, and more efficient bargaining environments, could make a substantial contribution to attenuating coordination failures in second-best situations in which the assumptions of both theorems do not hold.

The theorem may be read not so much as a case against the Pigouvian tradition of tax-and-subsidy welfare economics but rather as a specification of the conditions under which private rearrangements of property rights may attenuate coordination failures where neither markets nor states succeed. Interpreted this way, it makes two valuable contributions. First, by indicating what is required — efficient bargaining — the Coase theorem makes clear just how improbable it is that private decentralized allocations will be Pareto efficient. In this respect, it may resemble the Fundamental Theorem: it neither advocates nor opposes decentralized solutions; rather it clarifies what is required for the results to be Pareto efficient.

Second, the theorem correctly points to the removal of impediments to efficient private bargaining over the rearrangement of initial property rights as a way of addressing coordination failures. As part of a variegated policy package, this approach may be complementary (not antithetical) to centrist solutions such as rearrangement of property rights by fiat or the Pigou-Marshall tax subsidy approach. The conclusion that creating better defined property rights will improve allocative efficiency (as it will remove impediments to efficient bargaining), however, is not always true. This is because (as we will see in chapter 14), more clearly defined or easily transferable property rights may undermine *other*

230 • Chapter 6

methods for attenuating coordination problems. This is an extension of the reasoning of the second-best theorem that will be more transparent after modeling precisely the process of informal contractual enforcement by communities and other small groups.

Finally, the theorem underlines the value of distinguishing between efficiency arguments and distributive justice arguments concerning policies for coping with market failures. Many current advocates of the Pigouvian position—for instance, that polluters should pay for the harm they do—are less than clear about whether the reason is allocative, distributive, or both. This point ranks just half a cheer, however, because the more common inference from the theorem concerning distribution and allocation—that distribution of property rights does not matter for allocational efficiency—is in general wrong, the reason being that impediments to efficient bargaining are common (chapter 5), credit constraints limit the resources individuals may deploy in Coasean bargaining (chapter 9), and the distribution of wealth influences both the bargaining impediments and the credit constraints.

Conclusion

Given that coordination failures—in greater or lesser degree—are endemic to most noncooperative interactions, one may wonder why the Fundamental Theorem and the Coase theorem have attracted such attention. No doubt some of the interest in the theorems stems from the misreading that holds that they demonstrate the desirability of limiting government's role in the economy to the definition and enforcement of property rights. But the question of the optimality of competitive equilibrium outcomes now plays virtually no role in scholarly discussions of economic policy and institutions. Attention has been refocused on the more relevant question of choices among feasible institutions and policies supporting second-best outcomes, a topic to which I return in the closing chapter.

In this practical task the lessons of the Fundamental Theorem and the Coase theorem remain important. Under the right conditions, individuals acting autonomously in pursuit of their own interests may implement socially desirable outcomes. Enhancing the capacity of private actions to accomplish these social ends is an important aim of policy and constitution making.

Reasons of distributive justice are sometimes advanced against this invisible hand perspective. Redistribution to the poor may be accomplished by overriding the prices arising from private transactions, that is, by imposing nonequilibrium prices favoring the poor when they trade with higher income individuals (as when the poor exchange labor for wage goods). But as the Second Welfare Theorem suggests, there is another way to redistribute material well-being—through the reallocation of assets or the opportunity to acquire assets. If fair-minded governments are to choose between policies to alter the prices at which goods exchange and interventions to redistribute initial assets, the latter may sometimes be preferred on efficiency grounds. This is especially the case where the paucity of assets among the poor is explained by missing markets and incomplete contracts in the relevant transactions concerning credit, schooling, insurance, information, and the like.

The enduring interest of the Fundamental Theorem and the Coase theorem, however, does not stem from their contribution to illuminating these and other practical matters. Rather it is due to the light they shed on the surprising ways that allocation mechanisms such as market competition and bargaining can sustain an economic order, that is, an ongoing regular structure of interaction. Adam Smith's most radical idea was not that laissez faire would support an optimal order (he made no such claim), but rather that the exchange of property titles on a competitive market constitutes a kind of economic constitution, namely, a rule that translates individual preferences into aggregate social outcomes. That a coherent economic order could be based on entirely self-interested actors, each making use of only local information, is a remarkable claim. The fact that Walrasian general equilibrium theory has not adequately modeled a decentralized process of competition does not detract from its central contribution to clarifying the conditions under which Smith's invisible hand reasoning might be at least approximately correct. Moreover, non-Walrasian general equilibrium theory of the kind pioneered by Smale and Foley does provide a model of privacy-preserving and polyarchal resource allocation that yields approximately Pareto-optimal outcomes under the same market completeness assumption invoked by the Fundamental Theorem. Coase's contribution was to point out that, starting from an arbitrary endowment, bargaining among self-interested agents using only local information can produce Pareto-efficient outcomes without the assistance of the fictive Auctioneer. In a sense, then, Smale's and Foley's formal demonstration of this is very much in the Coasean spirit.

Both Smith and Coase sought to delineate more clearly the appropriate role of governments in economic affairs, not to deny the importance of a role for governments. I'll let Coase (1960:717) have the last word about his theorem.

Of course it does not imply, when transactions costs are positive, that government actions . . . could not produce a better result than relying on negotiations between individuals in the market. Whether this would be so could be discovered not by studying imaginary governments but what real governments actually do. My conclusion: let us study the world of positive transactions costs.

As someone who devoted many an evening over a period of years to the restoration of Long Hill for public enjoyment, I agree with Coase. This is the world to which we now turn.

CHAPTER SEVEN

Exchange: Contracts, Norms, and Power

[W]here *[there]* is no trust, there can be no contract.
— Thomas Hobbes, *De Cive* (1651)

"The game seems to be going on rather better now," she said. "Tis so," said the Duchess: "and the moral of it is — 'Oh, 'tis love, 'tis love, that makes the world go round.'" "Somebody said," whispered Alice, "that it's done by everyone minding their own business."
— Lewis Carroll, *Alice's Adventures in Wonderland* (1865)

In an economic theory which assumes that transaction costs are non-existent, markets have no function to perform and it seems perfectly reasonable to develop the theory of exchange by an elaborate analysis of individuals exchanging nuts for apples in the edge of the forest or some similar fanciful example . . .
— Ronald Coase, *The Firm, The Market, and the Law* (1988)

IBN BATTUTA, the fourteenth-century Arab geographer, reported that along the Volga River long distance trade took the following form:

Each traveler . . . leaves the goods he has brought . . . and they retire to their camping ground. Next day they go back to . . . their goods and find opposite them skins of sable, miniver, and ermine. If the merchant is satisfied with the exchange he takes them, but if not he leaves them. The inhabitants then add more skins, but sometimes they take away their goods and leave the merchant's. This is their method of commerce. Those who go there do not know whom they are trading with or whether they be jinn or men, for they never see anyone. (Battuta 1929:151)

Herodotus (1998) describes similar exchanges between the Carthaginians and the people of Libya in the fifth century B.C. After having left their goods, Herodotus reports, the Carthaginians withdraw and the Libyans "put some gold on the ground for the goods, and then pull back away from the goods. At that point the Carthaginians . . . have a look, and if they think there is enough gold to pay for the cargo they take it and leave." Herodotus describes how the process continues until

The first epigraph is from Hobbes (1949:101), the second from Caroll (1982:104), the third from Coase (1988:7–8).

an acceptable price is hit upon, remarking with surprise that "neither side cheats the other . . . [the Carthaginians] do not touch the gold until it is equal in value to the cargo, and the natives do not touch the goods until the Carthaginians have taken the gold" (pp. 300–301). Alvise da Ca da Mosto, a fifteen century Venetian working for the Portugese crown, reported a similar practice in Mali, regarding it as "an ancient custom which seems strange and hard to believe" (Giri 1983:23).

But is the so called *silent trade* really so odd?[1] Transfers of goods among strangers can be dangerous, ranging from gifts at one extreme, through mutually advantageous exchanges, to what might be called plunder at the other. The potential gains from trade are often greater the more distant geographically or socially are the parties to the exchange: the salt brought by the Tuaregs from the Atlas Mountains across the Sahara to the Kingdom of Ghana was not available locally, and the gold and tropical nuts the Tuaregs gained in silent trade with the Ghanaians was not available in North Africa. The silent trade provided a bargaining environment (apparently an alternating offers game with exit options, from Ibn Battuta's description) capable of exploiting gains from trade in cases in which both the potential gains and the danger were substantial. The fact that the parties to a silent trade did not meet helped reduce the chances of outbreaks of violence among the often heavily armed traders. But it does not explain what surprised Herodotus, namely, why the Carthaginians did not take the gold and run.

The silent trade is one of the great many ways that people have devised to underwrite the exchange process. Among these is the late medieval European "community responsibility system" whereby traders of one community disciplined their own members who cheated outsiders, thereby enhancing their reputation and trading opportunities (Greif 2001). Also included are the ancient protected "ports of trade" that provided security for traders in the no-man's-land between hostile empires and states. But most of the devices facilitating exchange are anything but exotic. Lisa Bernstein writes about the contemporary diamond industry.

> [D]isputes are resolved not through the courts and not by the application of legal rules announced and enforced by the state . . . [but rather by] an elaborate, internal set of rules complete with distinctive institutions and sanctions. (Bernstein 1992:115)

---

[1] Some of the purported evidence concerning the silent trade is unreliable, but it is certain that the practice was quite widespread in Africa and southeastern Asia, and examples are found in Europe and other parts of Asia. Informative skeptical accounts are Price (1980) and de Moraes Farias (1979).

A strong preference for exchanging within one's group—whether it be linguistic, racial, or neighborhood—while shunning outsiders as well as dealing only with people of known reputations are common trading practices. The benefits of these in-group trading practices in facilitating exchange must outweigh the costs of foregone gains from trade with excluded exchange partners and foregone economies of scale. Examples include communities with heightened insider/outsider distinctions, such as the Pennsylvania Amish and many ethnic business networks. Similar practices, including ostracism of those violating norms, are common among stock option traders on the floor of a major U.S. securities exchange, where small "crowds" of traders congregate at unique locations to trade a particular underlying stock (or small set of stocks) in a manner more reminiscent of an outdoor farmers' market than the anonymous interactions of textbook markets (Baker 1984).

Among these exchange-promoting devices are complete contracts enforceable by third parties (the courts) at zero cost to the exchanging parties. But many, perhaps most, of our important exchanges we engage in are not covered by complete contracts. Money is lent in return for an unenforceable promise to repay. Owners of firms would like to constrain managers to maximize the present value of future returns to the owners, but managerial contracts fall far short of this. Other employees work under contracts that do not even bother to mention that the worker should work hard and well. The contracts signed by residential tenants may include clauses requiring that they maintain the value of the property, but aside from gross neglect, the liability for not doing so is unenforceable. Insurance contracts prescribe (but typically cannot enforce) prudent behavior on the insured. Families devote a sizeable fraction of their budgets to purchasing educational and health services, the quality of which is rarely specified in a contract (and would be unenforceable if it were). Parents care for their children with the hope—but no contractual insurance—of reciprocation in their later years. Within the household, couples often implement a quite specialized division of labor and extensive exchange without contractual provisions.

Not only about the marriage contract, but of the vast majority of exchanges as well, it appears that Emile Durkheim was right when he observed "Not everything in the contract is contractual . . . . the contract is not sufficient in itself but is possible only thanks to a regulation of the contact, which is social in origin" (Durkheim 1967 [1902]:189, 193). This insight is an essential component of the theory of social exchange later developed by Peter Blau (1964). The key idea is that one party offers a payment, while the other incurs "diffuse future obligations, not precisely specified ones, and the nature of the return cannot be bargained about but must be left to the discretion of the one who makes it" (p. 93).

These are all cases of exchanges with *incomplete contracts*, that is, exchanges in which some aspect of the transaction is not specified in a contract that is enforceable at no cost to the exchanging parties. (The loan contract, for example, gives a complete specification of the terms of repayment, but these terms are not enforceable ex post, while the labor contract does not specify all of the activities the employer would like the employee to do.)

There are many reasons why contractual incompleteness is the rule rather than the exception. First, third-party enforcement of contracts requires information that is available to both parties *and* is recognized in courts of law. Second, contracts are generally executed after a passage of time, and a complete contract must thus specify outcomes for every possible future state. A complete specification of these future states cannot generally be made, and in any case it is not ordinarily cost-effective to specify what to do in each state, even if they can be anticipated. Third, many of the services or goods involved in the exchange process are inherently difficult to measure or to describe precisely enough to be written into a contract. Fourth, for some transactions there is no judicial apparatus capable of enforcing contracts; many international transactions are of this type. A final, surprising reason, which I will explore in the penultimate section of this chapter, is that even where the nature of the goods or services to be exchanged would permit a more complete contract, a less complete contract may be favored for motivational reasons.

As the final reason suggests, the degree of contractual incompleteness is not exogenous and may respond to the levels of trust and reciprocity exhibited by the relevant population of traders. For example, whether a good's quality is readily determined and contractually specified is in many respects a choice, not a given. The black rooster on the wine label assures the buyer that it really is made from grapes grown in the Chianti region of Italy; the Chiquita sticker on each banana places the reputation of the company's quality control department on the line. Such entities as Sugar Number 11, Corn Number 2 Yellow, or Light LA Sweet (that's oil) are not the gifts of pristine nature. They are created by a process of standardization, one that deliberately sought to eliminate difficult to monitor differences in quality.

An example is the mid-nineteenth century transformation of mid-Western U.S. grain (Cronon 1991). Once a heterogeneous amalgam with countless differences in sizes, strains, and qualities differing from sack to sack, grain was transformed into a small number of homogeneous commodities. Newly created grades of white winter, red winter, and spring wheat came to be of such uniform quality that ownership of grain no longer pertained to any sack or particular lot of grain but simply to a specified amount. Grain had become an abstract commodity, and readily enforceable contracts could be written simply for an amount of the commodity rather than for any specific entity, like a kilowatt hour of electricity. Remarkably, the standardization of grain was accomplished by an entirely private body, the Chicago Board of Trade, memberships in which would themselves become marketable commodities before the nineteenth century ended.

But unlike Red Winter Wheat #2 and membership in the Chicago Board of Trade, much of what is transacted in a modern economy is not subject to complete contracting. Three important consequences of the incomplete nature of most contracts will be explored in this chapter. First, long-term trading relationships are common even when markets are highly competitive. As a result, the numbers involved in an interaction are typically much smaller than those trading in the relevant markets. Second, in part because exchanges are durable and personal rather than ephemeral and anonymous, the motives relevant to the exchange process go beyond self-interest to include trust and a concern for fairness. And third, one or more parties to an exchange may be able to advance their interests by exercising authority over others. The fact that power can be exercised in competitive equilibrium, and that its exercise may be profitable, may seem surprising, as all parties to an exchange are free to terminate the transaction.

I will begin with a symmetrical bilateral transaction (like the silent trade) and illustrate how norms facilitating exchange might proliferate in a population. These models will show why a handshake is sometimes indeed a handshake, and may explain the trusting behaviors that surprised Herodotus and that underpin most modern transactions. Thus, norms of trust or fairness may attenuate the allocative inefficiencies arising from the incompleteness of contracts. But they seldom eliminate the problem altogether. For this reason, in the third section, using a standard principal agent model, I will consider how in asymmetric interactions—buyer/seller or borrower/lender, for example—the exercise of power may address the problem of incomplete contracts in the absence of other-regarding preferences The key result is that when contracts are incomplete, repeated interactions may allow the exercise of power (by principals over agents) in ways that facilitate exchanges and reduce the resulting allocative inefficiencies. The fourth section explores the ways that other-regarding preferences and the contractual structure of exchanges interact, each affecting the evolution of the other. The conclusion is that markets function through the interacting effects of contracts, norms, and the exercise of power.

A word of caution is in order. Models of the ways the parties to a transaction cope with the incompleteness of contracts sometimes presuppose that individuals are able and predisposed to access large quantities of information and to process the information in quite complicated ways. But the limited nature of information and information-processing capacity is commonly the reason for the contractual incompleteness that the transactors face. It is obviously inconsistent to base a theory of contractual incompleteness on informational and cognitive limits and then proceed to model the process of exchange under incomplete contracts as if individuals' information and cognitive capacities were virtually unlimited. For this reason, it is useful to check that individuals with empirically realistic cognitive and behavioral traits might act in the ways posited in the models. I do this in the next section by modeling market behavior governed by a very simple learning rule: copy those who are doing well.

Market Norms

Consider a population composed of a large number of people who interact in pairs to engage in an exchange in which they may either behave opportunistically (e.g., steal one another's goods) or exchange goods at a given price. Call these strategies "defect" and "cooperate" with payoffs describing a prisoners' dilemma, as indicated in table 7.1, with the familiar payoffs $a > b > c > d$, and $a + d < 2b$. This is a game of incomplete property rights, as each may take actions inflicting costs on the other without liability. As was seen in chapter 1, complete property rights would specify that a party stealing the goods of a cooperating exchange partner should pay the damages, $b - d$, in which case the payoff structure would no longer describe a prisoners' dilemma.

Given the incomplete property rights, however, we know that DD is the dominant strategy equilibrium of this game. The problem, then, is to understand why we so often observe mutual cooperation in exchanges that appear to have this structure. Moreover, in contrast to the predictions of this game (universal defection), populations are typically heterogeneous, some playing C, and others playing D at a given time. The explanation must be that the prisoners' dilemma payoff matrix *seems* to describe the relevant information but does not. We will see that introducing the idea of market norms, and adding a few important details about the institutions governing how people interact, will indeed explain why cooperation is not all that rare in situations like this.

Recall that social norms are ethical prescriptions governing actions

TABLE 7.1
The One-Shot Exchange Game Payoffs

	C	D
C	b, b	d, a
D	a, d	c, c

toward others. It is easy to see that a norm—say, of honesty or hard work—could provide the basis for mutually beneficial transactions even where complete contracting is impossible. If the employee's work ethic precludes his or her shirking on the job, the fact that the employee's effort level cannot be specified in a contract would not deter the employer from engaging the worker. If the seller is compelled by a norm of honesty to tell the buyer exactly the quality of the product being transacted, the fact that quality cannot be determined contractually will not impede the trade.

What is not so easy to see is why these norms might be common, given that violating the norm may offer opportunities for individual gain. If individual behaviors are consciously or unintentionally adopted in response to the expected payoffs associated with the behaviors, the existence of these and other ethical norms that underpin market transactions is something of a puzzle.

The early twentieth-century journalist H. L. Mencken provided an explanation, one anticipating the thinking of many contemporary game theorists and biologists: a "conscience is the inner voice which warns that somebody may be looking" (Mencken 1949:617). Mencken's jaded assessment is only half right, however, because people often incur costs to uphold a norm even when no one is looking. In these cases, the norm has been internalized; adhering to it is an objective of the individual, the pursuit of which may justify incurring lower material payoffs. The puzzle is to understand why people come to have these norms. A plausible answer (explored in chapters 11 and 13) is that systems of socialization favor the internalization of the social norms that are prevalent in a group, and that groups that internalize those norms that facilitate mutually beneficial exchanges are likely to propagate their norms in a larger population. This may occur through emulation, emigration, conquest, or survival in the face of ecological and other crises. In this case, those who adopt the norms may be less materially successful than their fellow group members who eschew the norms; the proliferation of the norms is due to the success of the groups in which the norm-adherence is common. This process is called *group selection*.

But there is another way that norms such as honesty and hard work may proliferate: those adhering to these norms may on average reap higher material payoffs than their fellow group members who eschew the norms. If the process of cultural transmission favors those with higher payoffs (as in the models introduced in chapter 2), these norms will be copied and proliferate. In this case, the proximate reason for the honest or hard-working behaviors is the value the individual places on the norm itself, not the anticipation of gain. The higher payoff explains why the individual came to embrace the norm.

It may seem odd to suggest that superior material payoffs explain the success of ethical prescriptions that lead individuals to forego opportunities for material gain. But the theory (and empirical study) of cognitive dissonance provides some reasons to expect the norms of the successful will be copied. Dissonance arises when one's values preclude actions that would otherwise be rewarding. One of the ways of coping with dissonance is to modify one's behavioral rules to be consistent with the perceived imperatives of achieving other ends. Because material success is widely sought, dissonance reduction will favor copying the norms of the successful. But there are other reasons, structural rather than psychological, why the norms of the successful may be favored in the replication process. Those who are successful may obtain positions — as governmental leaders, media figures, and teachers, for example — in which they have privileged access to the population as cultural models and thus may be copied disproportionately for reasons associated with their location in the social structure rather than because of their success per se. Others deemed equally successful (for example, equally rich) but less well-placed culturally would be less emulated. The process of cultural transmission is strongly influenced by the structure of social interactions, with the tendency to copy the successful being a likely consequence of the way that many — but far from all — societies are organized.

Because the norms that we live by are general prescriptions and typically are acquired before adulthood, they exercise a persistent influence on behaviors in a variety of settings. John Stuart Mill (1998 [1861]:71) commented that people "go out upon the sea of life with their minds made up on the common questions of right and wrong." As a consequence, living by norms acquired by a process of copying the materially successful is not the same thing as maximizing material success. Our norms often lead us to work hard and be honest even when someone is *not* looking.

Suppose that an individual adhering to a norm will adopt a particular strategy in the above game, and will continue doing so until an opportunity for updating occurs, at which point the individual will switch norms if the expected payoff to some other norm is higher. Using the replicator dynamic model developed in chapter 2, I will use three models to show how cooperative behaviors—acting so as to avoid the mutual defect option in the above game—might become common. These models will show that market institutions allowing for repeated interactions, nonrandom pairing of exchange partners, and reputations may support norms that sustain high levels of cooperation and hence facilitate reaping the gains from trade. These models describe different ways that the structure of social interactions may induce individuals to take account of the consequences of their actions: (1) due to repeated rounds of the interaction with a given exchange partner, (2) through being paired with like-minded people, and (3) through benefits enjoyed in future play of a single-shot game with other partners.

Model 1: Repetition and Retaliation. One-shot interactions describe some economic exchanges—buying and selling in spot markets, some casual day labor markets, for example—but not others—such as the long term employment or credit relationships described in chapters 8 and 9. Some interactions endure over generations, as in small communities where the children of sharecroppers and landlords renew the relationships of their parents and grandparents, or in very stable residential neighborhoods. Often relationships are not only ongoing but overlapping, with employers providing not only a job but also credit or insurance. If the interaction is to be repeated with substantial probability, cooperation may be supported by the threat of retaliation against defectors—the threat being more effective the more likely the repetition. If repetition is sufficiently likely and if the time elapsing between repetitions is sufficiently brief (or the relevant rates of time preference sufficiently low), the prisoners' dilemma is transformed into an Assurance Game with two equilibria: mutual defect (as before) and mutual cooperate.

Repetition changes the interaction in two ways. It allows more complicated strategies, ones that take account of one's partner's prior actions, and it requires that payoffs be accounted for as expected gains over the entire interaction. Players might now want to adopt the so-called nice tit-for-tat strategy: cooperate on the first round and on all subsequent rounds do what your partner did on the previous round. To keep things simple let us confine the choice of strategies to just nice tit-for-tat (T) and unconditional defect (D).[2]

Suppose that individuals are randomly paired to play, and after each

---

[2] The strategy set is immense once repetition is introduced. Assuming (as I do) that the players have just a one-period memory eliminates a large number of strategies (e.g., defect if the other defected on the two previous rounds but not otherwise). But nice tit-for-tat and unconditional defect do not exhaust the available strategies even with just a single period memory: unconditional cooperate and nasty tit-for-tat (defect on the first round and then do what the other did in previous round thereafter) are both possible, for example.

TABLE 7.2
Payoffs for the Iterated Exchange Game

	Tit for Tat	Defect
Tit for tat	b/ρ	$d + (1-\rho)c/\rho$
	b/ρ	$a + (1-\rho)c/\rho$
Defect	$a + (1-\rho)c/\rho$	c/ρ
	$d + (1-\rho)c/\rho$	c/ρ

round of play the above interaction is terminated with probability ρ and that repetitions occur over a sufficiently brief period to justify ignoring the players' rates of time preference (an assumption of no consequence in what follows). When two tit-for-tatters meet, for example, they will both cooperate on the first round, and then continue to do so until the interaction is terminated (i.e., for an expected total duration of $1/\rho$ rounds) giving expected benefits of b/ρ.[3] When a tit-for-tatter meets a defector, the former will get d on the first round, and then both will defect until the game terminates. The expected number of rounds after the first round is the probability that there will be a second round $(1 - \rho)$ times the expected number of rounds at the beginning of any period, namely, $1/\rho$. The resulting expected payoffs are thus $d + c(1 - \rho)/\rho$. The payoff matrix for the iterated game appears in table 7.2.

Let the fraction of the population adopting tit-for-tat be τ (the remainder adopting unconditional defect), and $\pi^T(\tau)$ and $\pi^D(\tau)$ the expected payoff to a tit-for-tat player or a defect player, respectively, in a population τ of whom are tit-for-tatters. Then we have

$$\pi^T(\tau) = \tau\frac{b}{\rho} + (1-\tau)\left\{d + \frac{(1-\rho)c}{\rho}\right\}$$

$$\pi^D(\tau) = \tau\left\{a + \frac{(1-\rho)c}{\rho}\right\} + (1-\tau)\frac{c}{\rho}$$

(7.1)

which, when equated to determine the equilibrium population fraction τ^*, yields

$$\tau^* = \frac{c - d}{2c - a - d + (b - c)/\rho}$$

(7.2)

Eqs. 7.1 and 7.2 are shown in figure 7.1.

For payoffs and termination probability such that

---

[3] The expected number of rounds is:
$1 + (1 - \rho) + (1 - \rho)^2 + \ldots = 1/\{1 - (1 - \rho)\} = 1/\rho$.

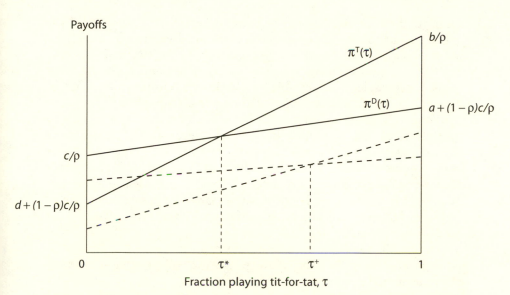

Figure 7.1 The retaliation effect. τ is the fraction playing tit for tat; $\tau \in (\tau^*, 1]$ is the basin of attraction of the cooperative equilibrium. Note that an increase in the probability of termination (dashed lines) reduces the expected cost of future retaliation for a defector and diminishes the basin of attraction of the cooperative $\tau = 1$ equilibrium, by shifting the unstable equilibrium from τ^* to τ^+

$$\frac{b-c}{a-c} > \rho \tag{7.3}$$

and for $c - d > 0$ it will be the case that $\tau^* \in (0,1)$ giving an interior equilibrium. (If eq. (7.3) were an equality, τ^* would be unity. Condition (7.3) also insures that the denominator of eq. (7.2) is positive.) The second condition ($c - d > 0$) must be true because the one-shot payoffs describe a prisoners' dilemma. The condition (7.3) will be true when the gains from mutual cooperation ($b - c$) relative to the gains from a single period defection ($a - c$) are great relative to the termination probability.

But τ^* is unstable, small deviations from τ^* not resulting in a convergence back to τ^*. This is because

$$\frac{d(\pi^D(\tau) - \pi^T(\tau))}{d\tau} < 0 \tag{7.4}$$

violating the stability condition: an increase in τ reduces the expected payoff to D relative to T. But as the payoffs were equal at τ^*, this means that the expected payoff to D must therefore be inferior to T for $\tau > \tau^*$, which by the dynamic process described in chapter 2 will lead to an increase in τ rather than a return to τ^*. As a result there are three equilibrium population frequencies, namely 0, τ^*, and 1, the first and third being stable. The unstable equilibrium τ^* defines the boundary between the basin of attraction of the two stable equilibria.

It is readily confirmed that condition (7.3) implies that the payoff to nice tit-for-tat in a population with no defectors exceeds the payoff to defect in that population or $b/\rho > a + (1 - \rho)c/\rho$, making tit-for-tat a best response to itself. Recall that tit-for-tat is an evolutionarily stable strategy against unconditional defect if there exists some positive frequency of D in this population, μ, such that if the population share of Defect is below μ, the process of differential replication of traits will lead to its elimination and thus invasion by a group of defectors comprising less than μ of the population will fail. Where (7.3) holds tit-for-tat is an evolutionarily stable strategy, and the critical value of μ in the above definition is $1 - \tau^*$.

Two results follow. First, the interaction will have an equilibrium of universal cooperation if the probability of termination is sufficiently low (universal defect also remains an equilibrium). This follows directly from condition (7.3). Second, an increase in the probability of termination will increase τ^*, diminishing the size of the basin of attraction of the cooperative equilibrium. This is because (from eq. (7.2)),

$$\frac{d\tau^*}{d\rho} = \frac{(b-c)\tau^{*2}}{\rho^2(c-d)} \tag{7.5}$$

which must be positive if the initial payoffs are a prisoners' dilemma and if $\tau^* > 0$.

Model 2: Segmentation. The mutual defect equilibrium in the simple one-shot exchange game described at the outset was based on the assumption that members of a population are randomly paired to interact. But nonrandom pairing is a frequent characteristic of many interaction structures. Examples include members of a population residing in villages who engage in frequent exchanges with coresidents and occasionally exchange goods at a single market serving the entire population. The probability of being paired with a cooperator will then depend on one's own type as long as the frequency of cooperators differs across villages. Ethnic groups may differ in the frequency of cooperators, and members of all groups may interact more frequently with "insiders" than with "outsiders." Cooperators may seek to avoid defectors and use a noisy signal of an individual's type to select partners. Where pairing is nonrandom, the likelihood of meeting one's own type (one adopting the same strategy) is typically greater than its share of the population—called positive assortation. When this occurs, cooperation may be evolutionarily stable even in one-shot interactions.

Assume that individuals in the larger population are either defectors or cooperators in a single-period prisoners' dilemma, and as before they periodically update their type in response to the relative success of the two strategies. The communities into which the traders are segmented are more homogeneous with respect to type than is the larger population, likes tending to cluster with likes. The clustering of likes with likes attenuates the problem of opportunism when contracts are incomplete because cooperating in a prisoners' dilemma confers advantages on those with whom one interacts, while defecting inflicts costs. Thus, because positive assortation pairs likes with likes, it raises the payoffs to cooperators and lowers the payoffs to deflectors. The segmentation thus has the effect of internalizing the noncontractible benefits of both cooperation and defection. The defector does not bear the cost of his own defection, but some *other* defector does, and this reduces the likelihood that cooperators will switch to defection when they update. A similar argument holds for the benefits that cooperators confer: with segmentation, these benefits are internalized within the group of cooperators. Segmentation thus supports a greater frequency of pro-social traits in a population. Of course, it will be in the interest of defectors to seek to disrupt systems that result in positive assortation, by avoiding detection, by trading preferentially in communities with above average frequencies of cooperators, and the like.

Suppose people live in villages that are homogeneous by type and a fraction s of their interactions takes place in their village, the rest occurring in the city where the types were mixed. Define the degree of segmentation as follows: if the fraction of the population who are cooperators is α, the probability that a cooperator will be paired with a fellow cooperator is no longer α but $s + (1 - s)\alpha$, where s is the *degree of segmentation* of the population.[4] Correspondingly, the probability of a defector meeting a fellow defector is now $s + (1 - s)(1 - \alpha)$. If $s = 1$ likes are paired with likes whatever the population composition, and if $s = 0$ pairing is random, homogeneous sub-groups are not necessary for segmentation to occur; the "village" and "city" example is just particularly transparent case. We take the pairing rule implied by the degree of segmentation as an exogenously given characteristic of the clustering of types supported by residence patters, ethnic boundaries, or any other structural characteristic giving rise to nonrandom matching.

---

[4] The degree of segmentation is thus similar to the degree of relatedness in genetic models.

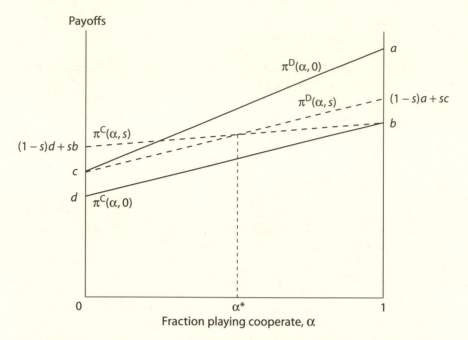

Figure 7.2 Increased segmentation increases the frequency of cooperators. The payoffs shown allow a stable interior equilibrium. But in the absence of segmentation (the solid lines), universal defection results. With segmentation, the fraction cooperating is α^*.

Let $\pi^C(\alpha, s)$ and $\pi^D(\alpha, s)$ be the expected payoffs to cooperators and defectors, respectively, in a population, α of whom are cooperators, the members of which are paired nonrandomly according to the degree of segmentation s. Then we have,

$$\pi^C(\alpha, s) = sb + (1 - s)\{\alpha b + (1 - \alpha)d\} \qquad (7.6)$$

$$\pi^D(\alpha, s) = sc + (1 - s)\{\alpha a + (1 - \alpha)c\} \qquad (7.7)$$

The equilibrium level of cooperation in this population is given by the value of α equating the two above expected payoffs, or

$$\alpha^* = \frac{s(d - b) + c - d}{(1 - s)(b - d - a + c)} \qquad (7.8)$$

Depending on the payoff matrix, this equilibrium may be stable or unstable; in the latter case, α^* marks the boundary between the basin of attraction of stable equilibria at $\alpha = 1$ and $\alpha = 0$. Figure 7.2 illustrates the case where α^* is a stable interior equilibrium. The condition for stability in the replication dynamic requires that the denominator of the

TABLE 7.3
Payoffs for the Inspect Variant of the
Exchange Game

	Inspect	Defect
Inspect	$b - δ, b - δ$	$c - δ, c$
Defect	$c, c - δ$	c, c

above expression for $α^*$ be negative, requiring for $α > 0$, that the numerator also be negative. The intuition behind this result is transparent from the figure: the slope of the expected payoff function for Defect, namely, $(1 - s)(a - c)$ must exceed that of Cooperate, $(1 - s)(b - d)$. Stability thus obtains when the reward from unilateral defection on a co-operator $(a - b)$ is larger than the penalty of cooperating against a defector $(c - d)$.

Four results follow. First, there exists some value of $s < 1$ such that universal cooperation is an equilibrium. It is simply the value of s for which $α^* = 1$ or $(a - b)/(a - c)$, which is less than 1 because the prisoners' dilemma payoffs are such that $b > c$. Second, there exists some value of $s < 1$, such that for s greater than this value, some level of cooperation may be sustained as an equilibrium. This is the value of s for which $α^* = 0$ or $(c - d)/(b - d)$, which is less than 1 because $c < b$. Third, if $α^*$ is stable, an increase in segmentation will increase the frequency of cooperation in the population. This is because $dα^*/ds$ has the sign of $(c - b)(b - d - a + c)$, which is positive for a stable equilibrium. Fourth, if $α^*$ is unstable, an increase in segmentation will enlarge the basin of attraction of the universal cooperation equilibrium (the reasons are as above).

Model 3: Reputation. Some interactions are anonymous, but in most cases we know something about who we are dealing with, and in many cases this makes a difference. When this is the case, establishing a reputation for being conditionally cooperative will often be an equilibrium strategy. Suppose that one can determine whether a partner is a conditional cooperator by paying an "inspection cost" $δ > 0$. A conditional cooperator is one who inspects and responds to a cooperative partner by cooperating and to a defector by defecting; call these Inspectors. The only other type is unconditional Defect (table 7.3).

Let $α \in [0,1]$ be the frequency of Inspectors in the population. As long as there is a cost of inspection, there will be a universal defect equilibrium in which $α = 0$. And if $b - c > δ$, there will be another equilibrium $α = 1$, with only Inspectors present. If both strategies are present in equilibrium, they must have the same expected payoffs or $π^I(α) = π^T(α)$. These payoffs are:

TABLE 7.4
How within-group payoff-based updating may support cooperation

Model	Effect favoring cooperation	Necessary structure of interaction	Examples
Retaliation	Withdrawal of later coopera-tion	Frequent or long lasting interac-tions (ρ low)	Taylor (1987), Fudenberg and Maskin (1986)
Reputation	Cooperative repu-tations are re-warded	Low cost of infor-mation about others (δ low)	Kreps (1990a), Shapiro (1983), Nowak and Sig-mund (1998)
Segmentation	Advantageous pairing for co-operators.	Nonrandom pair-ing of agents (s high)	Hamilton (1975), Axelrod and Hamilton (1981), Grafen (1979)

$$\pi^I(\alpha) = \alpha(b - \delta) + (1 - \alpha)(c - \delta)$$
$$\pi^D(\alpha) = c \qquad\qquad (7.9)$$

and equating these yields

$$\alpha^* = \frac{\delta}{b - c} \qquad\qquad (7.10)$$

But at this equilibrium, $d\{\pi^I(\alpha) - \pi^D(\alpha)\}/d\alpha > 0$, so α^* is unstable, and represents the boundary between the basin of attraction of the two equilibria $\alpha = 1$ and $\alpha = 0$. Because $d\alpha^*/d\delta > 0$, an increase in the cost of determining one's partner's type will shrink the basin of attrac-tion of the all Inspect equilibrium. Thus, a low cost of knowing the type of those with whom one interacts may make possible a population equi-librium in which it pays to establish a reputation for conditional cooperation.

In the models above, cooperation is sustained between self-regarding traders whose behaviors evolve according to a payoff-monotonic updat-ing process. "It's done," as Alice said, "by everyone minding their own business." The models have shown how structures of interaction that allow retaliation, segmentation, and reputation might favor the evolu-tion of *seemingly* other-regarding behaviors by converting cooperation from an individually costly behavior to one that confers benefits not only on others but also on the actor as well (making cooperation a mutualistic behavior in the terms of chapter 3). Table 7.4 summarizes these models.

The norms that allow mutually advantageous market exchanges are not the vestigial remnants of a pre-market social order, nor are they mere expressions of some innate predisposition to cooperate or some other unexplained *deus ex machina*. Market norms are sustained by the structure of market and other social interactions in which the traders routinely engage. Bronislaw Malinowski (1926:40), writing about exchange patterns among the Trobriand Islanders, concluded:

> The real reason why all . . . economic obligations are normally kept, and kept very scrupulously, is that failure to comply places a man in an intolerable position. . . . The honourable citizen is bound to carry out his duties, though his submission is not due to any instinct or intuitive impulse or mysterious "group sentiment", but to the detailed and elaborate working of a system, in which every act has its own place and must be performed without fail. . . . [E]very [one] is well aware of its existence and in each concrete case he can foresee the consequences.

The same could be said of modern day securities markets, the diamond business, or the internal workings of most modern firms.

ASYMMETRIC INFORMATION AND PRINCIPAL AGENT RELATIONSHIPS

The exchange process above was modeled as a symmetrical game, but it is often the case that parties to an exchange *know* different things and can *do* different things. What people know and what actions they can take are often determined by their structural location in the exchange process. An employee, for example, will certainly know how hard she worked during the past hour, or if she worked at all, while her employer may not know this. The employer, by contrast, may be able to further his objectives by committing himself to a take-it-or-leave-it wage offer, while the employee may not be able to benefit from making a take-it-or-leave-it offer to provide some amount of labor services at a given wage.

These asymmetries arise because the employer has *first-mover advantage* and the employee has *private information* (i.e., knows something of potential benefit that the other does not). The first is *a strategic asymmetry*: the employer's action set includes potentially advantageous actions not open to the employee — in this case, precommitment. The second is an example of *asymmetric information*. Unsurprisingly, the employer will use the strategic asymmetry to attempt to overcome the problems of labor discipline arising from the information asymmetries.

When a party to an interaction has information not known to others, we say that information is *asymmetric* (otherwise, information is symmetric). Information is *uncertain* if relevant information is revealed ("nature moves") after at least one party to the interaction has chosen his action (otherwise information is certain). *Incomplete* information occurs when some information relevant at the outset of the interaction is not revealed to at least one party. It is sometimes suggested that asymmetric information is the source of contractual incompleteness. But this is not quite right. What counts for the feasibility of a complete and third-party-enforceable contract is not only whether the relevant information is *known*, but also whether information is *verifiable*, that is admissible in a court of law or some other body that is capable of enforcing its terms.

The problem of enforceability of contracts depends on institutions in other ways as well. The ability of a lender to enforce a debt contract against a borrower may be greatly influenced by whether the society in question imprisons those unable to pay their debts. The Monte dei Paschi di Siena, probably the oldest bank in the world (founded in 1472), for a century or so possessed the right to execute deadbeat borrowers, and no doubt benefitted from this addition to its strategy set (unless, of course, the deadbeats had studied game theory and understood that carrying out the threat might not be the most effective way for the bank to collect).

Transactions between lenders and borrowers, or employers and employees, are members of a large class of exchanges that can be modeled as principal agent relationships. These are called *agency problems*; they arise when either the actions or attributes of the agent (or an agent's project) are relevant to the net benefits enjoyed by the principal but are not known to the principal or are not verifiable. (The lender and the employer are the principal; the borrower and the employee, the agent.) The problem of *hidden attributes* is sometimes called *adverse selection* (e.g., those who know they are ill will purchase more health insurance than those who know they are well). The *hidden actions* problem is called *moral hazard*, the term originating in the insurance industry and expressing the concern that the insured might undertake more risks than they would in the absence of insurance.

The canonical form of a moral hazard problem is the following: when one party, the principal (P) benefits from an action (a) which is taken by another party (A), the agent, which is costly for A to perform and not subject to costlessly enforceable contracting, we call P the principal and A the agent. A key implication of this definition is that P is the *residual claimant* on some noncontractible consequence of A's actions, meaning that what A does affects P's well-being after all of P's contractual obligations have been fulfilled. The outcome influenced by the agents' action, q, is observable:

$$q = \alpha(a) + \mu, \qquad\qquad (7.11)$$

where μ is an unobserved stochastic influence on q with mean zero. But a is not observable by P or is observable at a sufficiently high cost to make contracting for a infeasible. Were it not for the fact that μ is unobservable, the principal could infer a by observing q and knowing the function $\alpha()$ and μ. P's objective function is $\pi(q(a), \ldots)$; A's is $u(a, \ldots)$, with $\pi_q q'$ and u_a of opposite sign (so that there is a conflict of interest between P and A over the level of a.). Two characteristics of an interaction are necessary and sufficient for a principal agent problem to arise: there must exist a *conflict of interest* over some aspect of the exchange that is *not subject to costlessly enforceable contracting*.

A second common form of principal agent problem arises when the agent A^i is one of a team of n agents engaged by the (single) P, as in the work team case studied in chapter 4. In the above case, (given by eq. 7.11), the stochastic influence on q makes it impossible for P to determine A's action; in the second case, the team nature of the agents' activity make it impossible to infer any given agent's action, even if output is known and is a deterministic function of the agents' actions.

When the claims arising from an exchange cannot be enforced by a third party (the courts), one or both parties to the exchange will adopt strategies to secure advantage in the transaction. Bowles and Gintis (1993) call this *endogenous enforcement* because the parties to the exchange themselves engage in contractual enforcement activities rather than leaving this task to outsiders to the exchange who are specialized in enforcement activities (again, the courts). Endogenous enforcement may be pursued by transferring some control over the noncontractible actions from the agent to the principal (as when a banker becomes a member of the board of directors of a firm to which the bank lends), or by requiring up-front fees, bonds, or collateral, or by giving the agent a share of the resulting revenues of the project, all of which reduce the degree of conflict of interest between principal and agent. Another common endogenous enforcement strategy is for P to offer A a transaction more valuable than A's next best alternative and then to monitor A's actions, promising to renew the contract with A conditional on the level of a revealed by the monitoring, and to terminate the relationship otherwise. This is termed a *contingent renewal* enforcement strategy; it is effective because A receives an *enforcement rent* equal to the difference between A's valuation of this transaction and his or her next best alternative. A is willing to take account of P's objectives concerning the level of a, knowing that failure to do so will result (with some probability) in the loss of the rent (that is, renewal of the contract is contingent on the agent's performance).

TABLE 7.5
Examples of principal agent relattionships

Good or service	Noncontractible aspect	Endogenous enforcement	Principal/agent
Labor services	Labor effort, care	Contingent renewal	Employer/employee
Managerial services	Effort, maximizing owners' profits	Profit sharing, contingent renewal	Owner/manager
Debt	Level of risk taken	Collateral, shared control	Lender/borrower
Sovereign debt	Probability of default	Trade sanctions, other interventions	Lending government/borrowing government
Goods	Product quality	Contingent renewal by buyer	Buyer/seller
Public policy	Choice and implementation	Contingent renewal, referendum	Citizen/government official
Residential tenancy	Care of residence, local amenities	Security deposit, contingent renewal	Landlord/tenant
Agricultural tenancy	Labor effort and quality, care of land	Shared residual claimancy	Landlord/sharecropper
Equipment rental	Care of the equipment	Deposit, ownership share in equipment	Owner/renter

Table 7.5 lists some of the major principal agent relationships. Note that these include some of the most important markets in a modern capitalist economy: labor, credit, and management. Contingent renewal models also apply to nonmarket relationships as the public policy example in the figure indicates. Other applications not pursued here are to "patron client relationships" (Fafchamps 1992, Platteau 1995) and relationships between men and women in couples. The client and the woman provide difficult-to-monitor services (e.g., loyalty in political conflicts and quality of care of children, respectively) in return for well-defined quantities (patronage jobs, a share of the wage).

Some of the principal agent problems in table 7.5 arise because one of the parties is not sufficiently wealthy. For example, were the sharecropper wealthy enough, she would surely purchase the land she works rather than working under a share contract. In other cases, the wealth of the parties to the exchange has a major influence on the nature of the underlying incentive problem. A loan applicant who has invested substantial amounts of her own wealth in the project will be believed by the lender when she affirms her belief that if funded the project will succeed. Because most people have a quite limited level of wealth, the property rights they hold—whether they own land or rent it, for example—and therefore whether they are the residual claimant on the consequences of their noncontractible actions, will depend on how the credit market works. Credit markets are thus both a main example of principal agent relationships and a key to understanding the institutions governing *other* problems of incomplete contracting. We return to the credit market in chapter 9.

While the details will differ from one principal agent problem to another, sometimes in essential ways, the underlying structure of the problem is illuminated by a simple model of a problem arising because the quality of a good is not subject to contract. I give a cursory overview of the model here to preview the important implications of contractual incompleteness; similar models will be developed more fully in chapters 8 and 9. Do problem 17 if you are curious about how the model works.

Consider the supplier of a good of variable quality. The supplier's per period utility depends solely on the price paid by the demander of the good (only one of which, at most, will be supplied), and the quality of the good supplied ($q \in [0, 1]$). Thus we can express the supplier's utility as $u = u(p, q)$. Providing quality requires effort and hence is onerous so u is increasing and concave in its first argument and decreasing and convex in its second. The demander of the good buys such goods from n identical suppliers, transforms them somehow (perhaps by putting labels on them), and then sells them to consumers. The quality of the good is not subject to a costlessly enforceable contract. Perhaps the good, like a bottle of wine or a complicated piece of custom software, must be used before its quality can be determined. For simplicity I assume that its quality is known to the buyer following its purchase, but this information is not verifiable and so quality cannot be specified in the contract. The identical suppliers all provide the same quality q, so let revenue resulting from the sale of the product to the consumers be just $r(qn)$, which is increasing and concave in its argument. Faced with contractual incompleteness, the buyer offers the supplier a contingent renewal contract as follows: the buyer announces a price p with a promise to continue the transaction in subsequent periods unless the buyer finds the quality of the goods provided to be inadequate, in which case the transaction will be terminated, the latter occurring with probability $t(q)$ where $t' < 0$ (providing more quality diminishes the likelihood of termination).

The buyer will first determine the supplier's best-response functions (they are identical) expressing quality supplied as a function of price offered. The supplier will vary q to maximize present value of expected utility v, where v depends on the termination function $t(q)$, the supplier's fallback position (also a present value) should the transaction be terminated z, and the price offered by the supplier p or $v = v(q; p, z)$. Setting $v_q = 0$ gives the supplier's best-response function $q(p)$. (This function is derived in chapter 8 for a similar problem; see equations 8.2 to 8.5.) The resulting best response function can be written

$$u_q = t'(v - z) \tag{7.12}$$

requiring that the supplier equates the marginal cost of providing quality (the left-hand side of eq. (7.12)) to the marginal benefit of providing quality (the right-hand side). In other words, choose q so that the marginal disutility of providing greater quality is equal to the reduction in the likelihood of termination occasioned by providing greater quality (t') multiplied by the net advantage of the transaction over the fallback position ($v - z$).

The buyer will therefore know that (over the economically relevant values of the variables) $q'(p) > 0$. The reason is that the higher the price offered, the more valuable is the transaction to the supplier and the greater quality he will supply to avoid termination of the transaction. The best-response function $q(p)$, show in figure 7.3, is also termed the *incentive compatibility constraint* facing the buyer. Note that if the buyer offered a price such that the supplier's participation constraint were satisfied as an equality, or $v(q(p); p, z) = z$, the right hand side of eq. (7.12) would be zero, and hence the supplier would incur no positive marginal disutility to supply quality because there would be no cost of termination. As a result the supplier would simply set $q = 0$. I assume this is not profit maximizing for the buyer.

The buyer's profit is revenue minus the cost of acquiring the goods; so he varies p, and n, the number of suppliers to contract with, to maximize $\pi = r(nq(p)) - pn$. Setting the partial derivatives π_n and π_p equal to zero gives the buyer's first order conditions:

$$qr' = p \tag{7.13}$$
$$\frac{q}{p} = q'$$

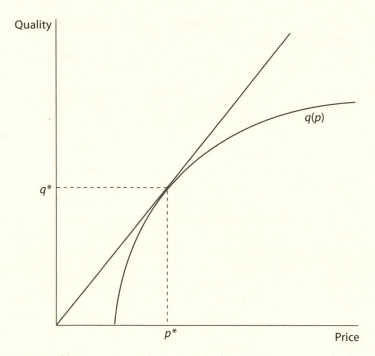

Figure 7.3 Equilibrium price and quality. The buyer maximizes profits by select-ing a price such that $q' = \dfrac{q}{p}$.

These conditions direct the buyer to set n (the number of units bought) so that the marginal revenue equals the price and to set the price so that the marginal effect of the price on quality (q') is equal to the average quality per dollar of expenditure (q/p). The resulting profit maximum is illustrated in figure 7.3, from which it is clear that q' is the slope of the best response function (the marginal effect of price on quality) and q/p is the average quality/price ratio given by the ray from the origin.

Because $v\,(q^*; p^*, z) > z$, suppliers identical to the one modeled here but not engaged in any transaction (and receiving the fallback z) would prefer to be transacting with the buyer. They might seek to disrupt the above transaction by offering a lower price and promising higher qual-ity. But recalling that all agents are identical, the supplier would recog-nize the promise to behave in a way different from the best-response function as false and reject the offer. In the competitive equilibrium, the supplier thus receives a rent above his or her next best alternative.

Seven characteristics about the equilibrium just described are remark-able. They are not specific to this example but occur quite generally in contingent renewal models of principal agent relationships. All will be further developed in subsequent chapters.

A Pareto-Inefficient Equilibrium. Because the buyer's optimizing problem took the supplier's best-response function (incentive compatibility constraint) as a constraint, rather than the supplier's participation constraint (namely, $v \geq z$) and because the two differ, the competitive equilibrium q^*, p^*, cannot be a Pareto optimum. This is because at the equilibrium $v_q = 0 = \pi_p$. The supplier and the buyer have set these derivatives equal to zero in solving their respective maximum problems. As a result, in equilibrium, they are indifferent to sufficiently small variation in quality and price, respectively. But in equilibrium it is also true that $\pi_q > 0$ and $v_p > 0$, that is, the buyer benefits from higher quality and the seller benefits from a higher price. This being the case, there exists some increase in both p and q which would make both seller and buyer better off. A related case is addressed in the next chapter.

Equilibrium Rents. The supplier receives a rent above his or her next best alternative ($v > z$). This occurs despite the fact that agents without a transaction are free to attempt to underbid those who are transacting. The difference $v - z$ is called a "rent" because it is the amount by which the supplier's value of the job exceeds his next best alternative. This *enforcement rent* coupled with the threat of termination induces the supplier to offer a higher level of quality.

Equilibrium without Market Clearing. The existence of the supplier's enforcement rent implies that markets do not clear in equilibrium, for a necessary condition of the latter is that all traders be indifferent between their current transaction and their next best alternative. The buyers are on the *short side* of the market (the side on which the desired number of transactions is least), while the suppliers are on the *long side* of the market. In equilibrium, some of the suppliers would prefer to transact at the equilibrium price but fail to make a transaction (they are *quantity constrained*).

Durable Dyadic Transactions. The buyer and seller will interact over many periods, even though there are many identical buyers and sellers; competitive equilibrium will be characterized by a series of durable bilateral trading islands rather than a sea of anonymous traders engaged in one-shot interactions in spot markets.

Price Making. The buyer is a *price maker*, not a price taker, as in the standard competitive model with complete contracts. The reason why the buyer does not treat the price as parametric is the contractual incompleteness concerning the quality of the good. Price making does not derive from any noncompetitive aspect of the assumed market structure.

Endogenous Claim Enforcement through the Exercise of Power. The buyer maximizes profits by threatening to sanction the supplier by terminating the transaction and withdrawing the enforcement rent. Because of this threatened sanction, the supplier acts in the buyer's interests in ways that would not have occurred in the absence of the threat. Thus, the buyer benefits from the ability to exercise power over the supplier. When one or more parties to an exchange uses actual or threatened sanctions to press claims we have a case of *endogenous enforcement.*

Endogenous Preferences. The buyer has an interest in the psychological makeup of the supplier, namely, the disutility of effort, the subjective valuation of the transaction and the fallback, and the like. Moreover, the buyer has a means for bringing about changes in the supplier's preferences. The reason is that the buyer has offered and secured an ongoing relationship with the supplier on terms which give the buyer authority. Thus, the buyer also has an opportunity to affect the psychological evolution of the supplier by structuring their interactions in ways to reduce the supplier's disutility of effort, if these can be found. What differentiates this from the complete contracting case is not that the buyer cares about the supplier's preferences. Rather, it is that the buyer interacts over an extended period with the same supplier and thus both cares about and has the opportunity to affect *this particular* supplier's preferences. By contrast, the spot market associated with complete contracting would present the buyer with a public goods problem. All buyers would have an interest in affecting the preferences of all suppliers, reducing the disutility of effort, as this will reduce the supply price of quality. But absent some form of collective action (compulsory socialization for a work ethic for all suppliers, for example), each would not invest in transforming suppliers' preferences because the returns to the investment would be shared by all buyers and could not be appropriated by the investor.

CONTRACTS AND BEHAVIOR IN MARKETS

Thus, where contracts are complete, there is little economic reason to be concerned about one's exchange partner's psychological makeup or moral commitments. Moreover, there is no way that these personal traits could be affected, if one were concerned. By contrast, the above principal agent model, the earlier models of retaliation, segmentation, and reputation, and the team production with social preferences model in chapter 4, all suggest a different view — that where contracts are incomplete, the trading networks, firms, and other institutions that have evolved to cope with the resulting incentive problems will favor interactions that are personal, strategic, durable and in which both norms and the exercise of power play important roles.

The result is a correspondence between the degree of contractual incompleteness and market structure. This is illustrated by the contrasting structures of the rice and raw rubber trade in Thailand. Ammar Siamwalla (1978) noted the impersonal structure of the wholesale rice market — in which the quality of the product is readily assayed by the buyer. He contrasts this with the personalized exchange based on trust in the raw rubber market — in which quality is impossible to determine at the point of purchase. Similarly, in Palanpur, India, wheat and rice as well as seeds and fertilizer are standardized, easily measured commodities, and thus are subject to relatively complete contracting. They are bought and sold in region-wide markets in which transactions are governed by little more than the going price and the budget constraints of the participants. By contrast, exchanges concerning labor, credit, the use of land, and the services of farm assets such as bullocks take place almost entirely within the village, and often within the same caste. Palanpur sharecroppers express strong preferences for contracting with "honest" or "straightforward" landlords who reciprocate this attitude; sharecropping contracts were disproportionately within castes. Moneylenders in the village rarely extend loans to those or not known to them or not living in Palanpur.[5] Leaving behind the fanciful world of "individuals exchanging nuts for apples in the edge of the forest," about which Coase complained, the exchange process is no longer anonymous and ephemeral.

An interesting implication is that traders in markets with incomplete contracts will exhibit different behaviors than those in complete contracting markets. The reason is that the types of contracts in use influence the structure of economic interactions, and these, in turn, affect the equilibrium distribution of behaviors. This is one of the lessons of the models surveyed in table 7.4. Recall that the conditions for retaliation, segmentation, and reputation to support high equilibrium levels of cooperation are repeated interactions, pairing conditioned on type, and low-cost information about the types of others. These are likely to be found in frequently repeated, multifaceted, face-to-face situations like stable residential neighborhoods, firms with limited labor turnover, and similar groupings sometimes referred to as communities (Bowles and Gintis 2002b, Ostrom 1990) or clans (Ouchi 1980). This reasoning may help resolve a puzzle thrown up by recent experimental research.

In experimental markets for goods covered by complete contracting, subjects quickly attain the competitive equilibrium prices and market

[5] See Lanjouw and Stern (1998), especially 84–85 and 486–8.

clearing predicted by the model of self-regarding outcome-based prefer-ences. Smith and Williams (1992:121) observed that "experimental market research has provided an empirical foundation for tenets of eco-nomic theory that were already well established . . . under most condi-tions markets are extremely efficient in facilitating the movement of goods." Vernon Smith, whose pioneering work launched the field in the 1970s, concluded that experimental economics had provided strong support for the conventional Walrasian model. Social scientists familiar with experimental research by psychologists found this claim surprising, however, for as we have seen in chapter 3, considerable evidence was accumulating that cast doubt on the behavioral assumptions of the stan-dard model. If the psychologists were right about the empirical short-comings of the conventional assumptions about individual behavior, why did the experimental markets studied by Smith and his colleagues at the University of Arizona confirm the economists' expectations about the aggregate outcomes of market interactions?

The puzzle deepened in the 1990s with new market experiments by Smith and others in which the standard equilibrium predictions failed to obtain. In a series of experiments simulating markets with goods of variable quality and labor markets, Ernst Fehr and his coauthors at the University of Zurich found that experimental subjects often received rents above their next best alternative, and these rents were not com-peted away even in highly competitive environments. Those offering rents to their trading partners generally did better than those not offer-ing rents.

What accounts for the success of the Walrasian paradigm in predict-ing the outcomes of the early experiments in Arizona and its failure to predict the results obtained in Zurich? It was quickly determined that the answer was not that the Swiss differ from the Americans; nor could the result be due to differences in the degree of competition in the ex-perimental markets. (Fehr and his group often induced intense competi-tion among one or the other side of the market by letting the buyers outnumber the sellers, or vice versa.) When the Zurich subjects engaged in complete contracting market experiments, they replicated the Ari-zona results. Instead, the difference in the behaviors of the Arizona and Zurich subjects is explained by the fact that Smith's initial experiments assumed complete contracts while Fehr's were based on contractual incompleteness.

Fehr and his coauthors (surveyed in Fehr and Gaechter 2000b) found that contractual incompleteness induces reciprocal behaviors among subjects and that this has durable effects on competitive equilibrium. An example of the importance of contractual incompleteness is an experi-mental labor market in which effort is selected by the "worker" after a wage offer is made by the "firm." The equilibrium predicted by a model of self-regarding preferences in a one-time interaction (namely, offer the lowest wage, provide the lowest effort level) does not occur. Rather, "firms" offer wages higher than necessary and "workers" reciprocate by working harder than the minimum. This does not occur when the experiment is altered so that effort is not subject to the "worker's" choice (effectively completing the contract by eliminating its noncontractual element). Relatedly, Peter Kollock (1992:341) investigated "the structural origins of trust in a system of exchange, rather than treating trust as an individual personality variable" with similar results. Using an experimental design based on the exchange of goods of variable quality, Kollock found that trust in and commitment to trading partners as well as a concern for one's own and others' reputations emerges when product quality is variable and noncontractible but not when quality is contractible.

Brown, Falk, and Fehr (2002) designed a market experiment to explore the effects of contractual incompleteness on the pattern of trading. As in the above model, the good exchanged varied in quality, with higher quality more costly to provide. In the complete contracting condition the level of quality promised by the supplier was enforced by the experimenter, while in the incomplete contracting condition the supplier could provide any level of quality (irrespective of any promise or agreement with the buyer). Buyers and sellers knew the identification numbers of those with whom they were interacting, so they could use information they had acquired in previous rounds as a guide to whom they would like to interact with, the prices and quality to offer, and the like. Buyers had the opportunity to make a private offer (rather than broadcasting a public offer) to the same seller in the next period, thus attempting to initiate an ongoing dyadic relationship with the seller.

Very different patterns of trading emerged under the complete and incomplete contracting conditions. In the first, 90 percent of the trading relationships lasted less than three periods (and most of them were single shot). By contrast, only 40 percent of the relationships were this brief under the incomplete contracting condition, and most traders formed trusting relationships with their partners. Buyers in the incomplete contracting condition offered prices considerably in excess the supplier's cost of providing quality (just as in the principal agent model of the previous section). When buyers were disappointed by the quality supplied, they terminated the relationship, thereby withdrawing the implied rent from the supplier. Other differences are summarized in table 7.6 The differences were particularly pronounced in later rounds of the game, suggesting that the traders learned from their experiences, and updated their behaviors accordingly.

TABLE 7.6
Contractual incompleteness and market social structure: experimental evidence

Structure of interactions	Complete contracts	Incomplete contracts
Duration	One shot	Contingent renewal
Offers	Public	Private
Price determination	Haggling, offers rejected	Price setting by short sider
Traders' relationship	Anonymous	Trust, retaliation for cheating
Market networks	Many weak links	Bilateral trading islands

Source: Brown, Falk, and Fehr (2002)

These experimental results suggest that trust or reciprocity may depend on the form of the contract, contractual incompleteness sometimes supporting trusting and reciprocal behaviors. The converse is also true: lower levels of trust and reciprocity would plausibly lead those designing contracts and the relevant enforcement environments to be willing to pay more for more complete contracts. Avner Greif (1994) analyzed the divergent cultural and institutional trajectories of the Genovese and North African Maghrebi traders in the late medieval period from this perspective. The individualism of the Genovese traders precluded the collectivist contractual enforcement techniques of the Maghrebi traders, but it also provided an impetus for the development and perfection by the Genovese of the ultimately more successful state and other third-party enforcement of contractual of claims.

The underlying process jointly determines the distribution of contracts and the distribution of behavioral norms in the population, a dynamic sometimes termed the *coevolution of institutions and preferences*. To study this process, consider a population of buyer and sellers who are paired randomly for a single interaction.[6] They trade a good whose quality (high (H) or low (L)) is determined by the seller and is costly for the buyer to determine ex ante. The buyer may offer one of two contracts. If the complete (C) contract is offered, the seller receives a fixed compensation just sufficient to offset the costs of providing low quality. These are C-type buyers. According to the incomplete (I) contract, the buyer pays the cost of producing low quality, plus half of the net profits resulting from the transaction. These are I-type buyers. Sellers are also of two types. R-type sellers interpret the I-contract as a sign of trust on the part of the buyer, and reciprocate by providing high quality, incurring an additional cost of δ_H. When offered a C-contract,

---

[6] Peter Skott suggested this model.

TABLE 7.7
Payoffs among reciprocal and self interested sellers exchanging a variable
quality good with buyers offering complete and incomplete contracts

Buyer ↓	Seller → Reciprocator (R)	Selfish(S)
Incomplete contract (I)	$\pi^H/2$, $\pi^H/2 - \delta$	$\pi^L/2$, $\pi^L/2$
Complete contract (C)	π^L, $-\delta$	π^L, 0

however R-type sellers feel mistrusted, experiencing a subjective cost
δ_H, and they retaliate, provide low quality. S-type sellers are completely
self-regarding and provide low quality irrespective of the contract. The
buyer's profits (net of compensating the seller sufficient to offset the cost
of low quality) are π^H and π^L for high and low quality respectively. To
reduce notational clutter, let $\delta_H = \delta_L = \delta$, and to make the problem
interesting, I further assume that $\pi^H > 2\pi^L$ and $\pi^H - \pi^L > 2\delta$. The
payoffs (buyers first, sellers second) appear in table 7.7.

Writing the fraction of the sellers who are reciprocators as ω, the
expected payoffs to buyers offering the I- and C-contracts are:

$$v^I = \omega \frac{\pi^H}{2} + (1-\omega)\frac{\pi^L}{2}$$
$$v^C = \omega\pi^L + (1-\omega)\pi^L = \pi^L \tag{7.14}$$

Similarly, writing the fraction of the buyers offering incomplete contracts as φ, the expected payoffs to the R- and S-sellers are

$$v^R = \varphi\left(\frac{\pi^H}{2} - \delta\right) + (1-\varphi)(-\delta)$$
$$v^S = \varphi\frac{\pi^L}{2} + (1-\varphi)0 = \frac{\varphi\pi^L}{2} \tag{7.15}$$

The expected payoffs given by eq. (7.14) and (7.15) appear in figure
7.4, with ω^* and φ^* giving the frequencies of I-type buyers and R-type
sellers that equate the expected payoffs.

What kinds of contracts and behaviors would we expect to observe in
this population? One's intuition is that likely outcomes would include a
high frequency of both incomplete contracts and reciprocating sellers or
the opposite: a predominance of both complete contracts and self-interested sellers. These correct intuitions are readily formalized. The dynamical system we want to study concerns the state space defined by all
possible combinations of contractual and behavioral strategies or

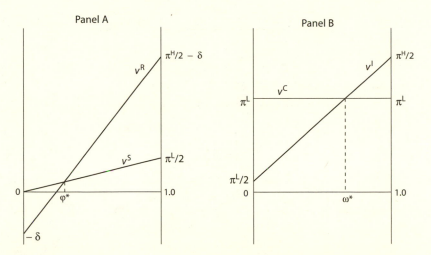

Figure 7.4 Payoffs to reciprocal and self interested behaviors (left panel) and incomplete and complete contracts. φ is the fraction of buyers offering incomplete contracts, ω is the fraction of suppliers who are reciprocators.

$\varphi \in [0,1]$ and $\omega \in [0,1]$. We wish to explore the movement of both φ and ω over time. Suppose that both suppliers and buyers periodically update their strategies by switching to strategies with higher payoffs according to the familiar replicator dynamic equations

$$\frac{d\varphi}{dt} = \varphi(1-\varphi)(v^{I} - v^{C})$$

$$\frac{d\omega}{dt} = \omega(1-\omega)(v^{R} - v^{S})$$

(7.16)

The stationary values of φ and ω in this dynamic are $d\varphi/dt = 0$ for $\varphi = 0$, $\varphi = 1$, and $\omega = \omega^{*} = \pi^{L}/(\pi^{H} - \pi^{L})$, and $d\omega/dt = 0$ for $\omega = 0, \omega = 1$, and $\varphi = \varphi^{*} = 2\delta/(\pi^{H} - \pi^{L})$. The resulting dynamical system is illustrated in figure 7.5, with the arrows indicating the out-of-equilibrium adjustment given by eq. (7.16). The point $(\varphi^{*}, \omega^{*})$ is stationary, but it is a saddle, as will be confirmed by reference to figure 7.4 and eq. (7.16): small movements away from φ^{*} or ω^{*} are not self-correcting. For randomly chosen initial states the population will move to $(\varphi^{*}, \omega^{*})$ with zero probability. The asymptotically stable states are $(\varphi = 0, \omega = 0)$ and $(\varphi = 1, \omega = 1)$, confirming the above intuition. Which occurs is determined by the initial state.

Notice that in the state with universal reciprocity and incomplete contracting, the incomplete contracts are offered as a best response to the presence of reciprocators in the population. Complete contracts are technically feasible, but as long as the fraction of reciprocators exceeds

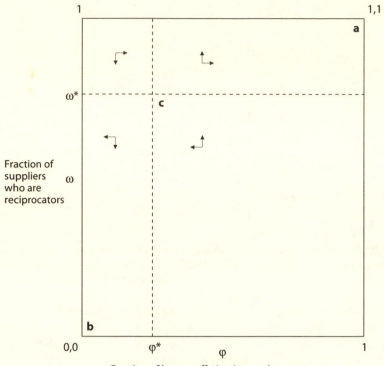

Figure 7.5 The coevolution of contracts and behaviors. The arrows indicate the directions of change implied by the assumed dynamic. States **a**, **b**, and **c** are stationary; **c** is a saddle.

ω^*, complete contracts are less profitable. The degree of contractual completeness is thus influenced by technology (the cost of monitoring a complete contract, for example, often depends on the nature of the good or service exchanged), but the extent of contractual completeness will also be influenced by the distribution of behavioral norms.

CONCLUSION

There are thus both analytical and empirical reasons for believing that the unconventional social preferences introduced in chapter 3 assume special importance in nonmarket interactions and in market exchanges governed by incomplete contracts. Kenneth Arrow (1971:22) wrote, "In the absence of trust . . . opportunities for mutually beneficial cooperation would have to be foregone . . . norms of social behavior, including ethical and moral codes, (may be) . . . reactions of society to compensate for market failures." Of course, norms rarely provide perfect substitutes for complete contracts, so market failures arising from contractual incompleteness are common. The vastly different ways that people have attempted to cope with the resulting incentive problems and bargaining failures, and the ways that these attempts have interacted and been shaped by chance events, account for some of the institutional diversity that one discovers when real exchanges are investigated.

The models introduced here suggest four conclusions. First, where contracts are incomplete, exchange is often facilitated when traders discriminate in favor of "insiders" and engage in other parochial practices, when long term commitment to a trading partner are common, where exchange is personalized, and the like. In the Walrasian paradigm, these exchange-supporting interaction structures are termed "market imperfections" and are opposed as impediments to "flexibility." Second, just as norms concerning exchange evolve under the influence of the existing distribution of contracts and other aspects of the institutional environment, the institutions governing the exchange process evolve in response to the distribution of norms in the population. A result of this coevolutionary process is that an equilibrium must account jointly for the stationarity of both the institutional environment and the norms and other aspects of the preferences of the relevant actors. The fact that there may be many such equilibria, some of them unstable, has important implications for the problem of governance and policy making that I will discuss in the final chapter. Third, where exogenous (third party) enforcement of contractual claims is absent, exchange is often facilitated by the exercise of power by one of the parties to a transaction. This fact suggests that exchange is, in many cases, a political process, thereby questioning the conventional view that politics is absent when people voluntarily exchange on competitive markets. Fourth, the exercise of power in the exchange process, along with the effect of market structures on the evolution of norms, suggests that politics and culture cannot be excluded from economic theory. The reason is not simply that the economy is embedded in a larger social system but also that understanding the workings of the economy itself require attention to its cultural and political aspects.

Whether the models presented here and in chapters 8 and 9 capture the essential aspects of real world exchanges with incomplete contracts remains a matter of debate. For this reason, I will provide empirical evidence where it bears on the adequacy of the models to come. But the importance of contractual incompleteness is not in question. Herbert Simon (1951) pioneered the study of exchanges with incomplete contracting. Forty years later, he imagined "a mythical visitor from Mars" approaching earth in a spaceship

> equipped with a telescope that reveals social structures. The firms reveal themselves, say, as solid green areas. . . . Market transactions show as red lines connecting the firms forming a network in the spaces between them. . . . No matter whether our visitor approached the United States or the Soviet Union, or urban China or the European Community, the greater part of the space below it would be within the green areas, for almost all of the inhabitants would be employees, hence inside the firm boundaries. Organizations would be the dominant feature of the landscape. A message sent back home, describing the scene would speak of "large green areas interconnected by red lines." It would not likely speak of "a network of red lines connecting green spots." (Simon 1991:27)

The most important organizations governing exchanges in modern economies are firms, the directors of which combine other peoples' labor and other peoples' money (neither subject to complete contracting) to produce and market goods and services. Labor and credit markets are typical of the many important exchanges that do not take the canonical form in which well-defined commodities are traded, like the nuts and apples in Coase's fanciful example. Instead, what is exchanged are more complex bundles of obligations and claims concerning who should do what under what conditions. Coase (1992:717) put it this way: "[W]hat are traded on the market are not, as is often supposed by economists, physical entities, but the rights to perform certain actions." In chapters 8 and 9 we study how firms, labor markets, and credit markets structure the rights to perform actions concerning other people's labor and other people's money.

CHAPTER EIGHT

Employment, Unemployment, and Wages

> Assuming equilibrium, we may even go so far as to abstract from
> entrepreneurs and simply consider the productive services as being, in a
> certain sense, exchanged directly for one another.
> — Leon Walras, *Elements of Pure Economics* (1874)

> It is plain that commodities cannot go to market and make exchanges of
> their own account. We must therefore have recourse to their . . . owners
> . . . who must . . . not appropriate the commodity of the other, and part
> with his own, except by means of mutual consent.
> — Karl Marx, *Capital, I* (1867)

ON THE MORNING OF January 5, 1914, a virtually unknown mechanic
turned automobile producer named Henry Ford shocked his colleagues
and competitors by announcing that he would pay his workforce a minimum of five dollars for an eight-hour day, at once shortening the work
day and more than doubling the hourly rate of pay for the vast majority
of his employees.[1] Ford was not responding to insufficient labor supply:
a reporter arriving that morning for the press conference at which the
announcement would be made noticed a line of several hundred workers seeking employment. In the weeks following the announcement, the
queue outside the gates swelled to over twelve thousand, almost as many
as were working inside. Remarkably, profits rose, supported by a more
than a twofold increase in output per hour of production labor. Ford
was to become a household word around the world, and *Fordism* a
peculiarly American approach to labor relations.

For the lucky employees who had been in the right place at the right
time, the basic facts of work life inside the plant changed beyond recognition. The previous year Ford's labor force had averaged 13,623. During the course of that year 50,448 employees had walked out the door,
most had quit; 8,490 had been fired. The year following the announcement, employment had grown by a third, but the number quitting had
fallen to a tenth of its earlier level, and only twenty-seven employees
had been discharged. Changes of this magnitude clearly cannot be ex-

---

The first epigraph is from Walras (1954:225), the second from Marx (1967:84).
[1] This account is based on Raff (1988).

plained by cyclical variations in supply and demand in the local labor market. It seems unlikely that Ford doubled the wage to attract better workers or to retain those in whom the company had invested expensive training; a Ford superintendent boasted that "two days is . . . ample time to make a first-class core molder of a man who has never seen a core-molding bench in his life." Exactly why Ford did it remains a mystery. More important, the success of his gamble is a puzzle, for it is inconsistent with the Walrasian view that profit maximization entails paying one's employees a wage equal to their supply price (their next best alternative).

In the neoclassical framework, productive services do not literally exchange directly for each other as Walras suggested in the *Elements*. But his whimsy is not far from the truth: a firm is simply a feasible production set given by available technologies, that is presided over by a manager. The manager selects the mix of inputs and outputs that maximizes the owners' wealth, buying inputs and selling outputs on markets with exogenously given prices. It is easy to see why Ford's five-dollar day would not make sense in this model.

There are three basic ingredients of a more adequate model. The first is the insight of Ronald Coase (1992: 717), mentioned at the close of chapter 7, that "what are traded on the market are not, as is often supposed by economists, physical entities, but the rights to perform certain actions." The second is Marx's commonplace that exchange requires the owners of the productive services to interact face to face. The third is Henry Ford's discovery that employees may reciprocate good pay with hard work.

Marx was the first to stress the fact that the employment contract did not concern such things as the amount or quality of work done; rather, it specified the hours during which the employee agreed to submit to the authority of the employer. According to Marx (1973:275), the employee's actual supply of effort to the production process was not secured by contract but was rather an "appropriation of labor by capital" that "only by misuse could . . . have been called any kind of exchange at all." Anticipating Ford (not to mention late twentieth-century developments in economic theory), Marx (1967:544) pointed out that an increase in the wage might reduce the cost of labor. Like Marx, Coase stressed the central role of authority in the firm's contractual relations: "[n]ote the character of the contract into which a factor enters that is employed within a firm. . . . [T]he factor . . . for certain remuneration agrees to obey the directions of the entrepreneur." Indeed, Coase (1937:387, 389) *defined* the firm by its political structure:

> If a workman moves from department Y to department X, he does not go because of a change in prices but because he is ordered to do so . . . the distinguishing mark of the firm is the suppression of the price mechanism.

Coase sought to understand why firms exist at all, and what determines the extent of what he called (borrowing Dennis Robertson's phrase) these "islands of conscious power in this ocean of unconscious cooperation."

Herbert Simon (1951) provided the first model of the firm along these lines. He represented the employment contract as an exchange in which the employees transfer authority over their work tasks to the employer in return for a wage. Simon stressed the advantage to the employer of this arrangement given the unavoidable uncertainty about the tasks that would be required over the course of the contract, and therefore the high cost of agreeing to a complete contractual specification of the activities to be performed. I will term the approach pioneered by these disparate authors the Marx-Coase-Simon model of employment relationships. A characteristic of the employer-employee interaction in this approach is that social preferences — especially motives of reciprocity and fairness — play an important part in determining outcomes.

The Employment Relationship

The model of the labor market and the employment relationship to follow is a variant of what may be termed the *effort regulation* or *labor discipline model* based on *contingent renewal*. (I explain later why I find the common term "efficiency wage model" misleading.)

The Problem. Work effort cannot be contracted for because information concerning an employee's effort is known to the employer at best very imperfectly and is not verifiable (not admissible in court). Even if the information were verifiable, a contract to pay an employee according to a very noisy signal of effort would expose the worker to a subjectively costly level of risk. Yet work effort is an argument in the production function of the employer. The problem could be avoided if the person doing the work, like Robinson Crusoe, were also the residual claimant on the resulting output, as would be the case were it feasible to implement optimal contracts for team production of the type modeled in chapter 4. But for reasons explained there, such a contract would also expose the employee to an unacceptable level of risk. Individual level production would also make the worker a residual claimant on her efforts, but economies of scale generally make team production a necessity. (To capture these economies of scale assume that engaging in production at any level requires one unit of capital, and that this requirement makes individual production unprofitable.)

Let $e \in [0, 1]$ be effort per hour of work (it could be simply the fraction of the hour in which the worker is "working" as opposed to "not working"). Per period output is

$$y = y(he) + \varepsilon \qquad \text{with } y' > 0 \text{ and } y'' < 0 \qquad (8.1)$$

where h is the number of worker "hours" hired (assumed to be a single "hour" per worker, so that h is also the number of identical workers hired), and ε is a mean zero disturbance term. Output is contractible, but the input levels of particular workers cannot be inferred from the output levels both because of the team nature of production and the stochastic term in the production function.

The following summarizes the employer-employee interaction. The principal (the employer) knows the agent's (worker's) best-effort response, $e(w, m; z)$, given each wage rate w and level of monitoring m, with an exogenously determined worker's fallback position z (arguments of a function to the right of the semicolon are exogenous). At the beginning of a period, the employer selects (so as to maximize profits) and announces: a termination probability $t(e, m) \in [0, 1]$ with $t_e < 0$ and $t_m > 0$ over the economically relevant ranges; a wage rate, w; and a level of monitoring per hour of labor hired m. Both the wage and the monitoring inputs are measured in the same units as per period output. Following the employer's announcement of her effort-incentive strategy, and hence knowing the above, the worker selects e so as to maximize his present value of lifetime utility. At the end of the period, the worker is paid and experiences the utility he incurs as a result of his effort and pay, and his employment is renewed or terminated, the latter occurring with probability $t(e, m)$. If the worker's job is terminated, he obtains a present value of lifetime utility of z and is replaced by an identical worker from the unemployment pool. If the worker retains the job, the same interaction takes place the next period; thus, the interaction is stationary (or time invariant).

The termination schedule $t(e, m)$ is crucial to the working of the model. A simplified termination schedule could be based on the idea that during any period there is a probability, $\eta(m)$, that the employer will "see" the worker in which case the employer will know with certainty if the worker is working or not. Suppose that in the absence of monitoring, the employer will not see the worker, so $\eta(0) = 0$, and that $\eta' > 0$. This would give a termination schedule $t = \eta(m)(1 - e)$, from which it can be seen that $t(0, \eta(m)) = \eta(m)$ and $t(e, \eta(0)) = 0$. What is essential to the model is that for positive levels of monitoring, increased effort reduces the probability of termination: $t_e = -\eta(m)$. Similarly, increased monitoring increases the marginal effect of working harder on avoiding termination: $t_{em} = -\eta'(m)$

The Worker's Best Response. The worker's per period utility function is

$$u = u(w, e) \qquad (8.2)$$

with $u_w \geq 0$ and $u_e \leq 0$ over the economically relevant ranges. This does not mean that employees would prefer to offer no effort all, but rather that any outcome for which $u_e > 0$ cannot be an equilibrium allocation, for in this case the employee could unilaterally implement a higher effort level, thereby raising both the employer's profits and his own utility. The worker varies e to maximize the present value of expected utility over an infinite horizon, given a rate of time preference of i:

$$v = \frac{u(w,e) + (1 - t(e))v + t(e)z}{1 + i} \tag{8.3a}$$

or using the stationarity assumption and rearranging

$$v = \frac{u(w,e) - iz}{i + t(e)} + z \tag{8.3b}$$

where the first term on the right-hand side of the rearranged expression is the *enforcement rent* introduced in the previous chapter; in this case it is also termed an *employment rent*. So we have: *present value of the job = employment rent + fallback position.* Given this objective, the worker selects e so as to set

$$v_e = 0 \tag{8.4}$$

which requires:

$$u_e = t_e(v - z) \tag{8.5}$$

Thus, the worker will choose the level of effort that equates the marginal cost of effort to the marginal benefit of effort. Starting from a low level of e, the worker should increase effort until the marginal disutility of effort just offsets the marginal gain in the present value of utility occasioned by the associated reduction in the termination probability. The above first order conditions (8.4 or 8.5) define the worker's best response function as shown in figure 8.1.

An example may clarify the best response function. Consider an individual for whom the wage is a "good" and work is a "bad" whose disutility depends not only on the level of effort but also on how fairly it is rewarded. Suppose the employee's utility function is

$$u = w - \frac{aw^f/w}{1 - e}$$

where a is a positive constant and w^f is an exogenous wage norm called the "fair wage." The disutility of effort represented by the second term is rising in effort (at an increasing rate). Note that it is also declining in

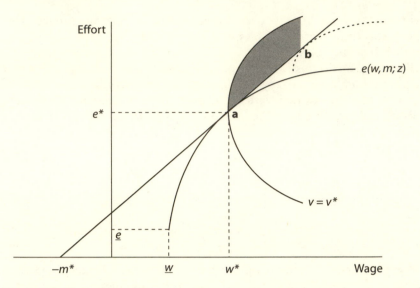

Figure 8.1 The employee's best response function and the employer's optimal offer. Point **a**, namely, a wage offer of w^* and an effort response of e^*, jointly fulfills the first order conditions of the employee's and employer's optimum problems. The optimal level of monitoring is m^*, the determination of which is not shown here (see figure 8.3). Point **b** is one of the Pareto optima making up the efficient contract locus (not shown.) The shaded area are outcomes that are Pareto superior to **a**. The slope of the line **ab** is $e^*/(w^* + m^*)$.

the wage relative to the fair wage, indicating that hard work that is fairly rewarded is less onerous than less effort at a wage considered to be unfair. The underlying motivation may reflect a variant of the reciprocal preference function introduced in chapter 3: the employee may take the wage offer as an indication of the employer's type and experience less disutility of effort in working hard for a generous or fair boss.

Suppose the employer can costlessly observe the worker, but the information is not verifiable, so as before e is noncontractible, monitoring is absent, and the termination function is simply $t = 1 - e$. The above utility function means that for a finite wage the disutility of effort becomes infinite as e approaches 1 so the employee will not choose $e = 1$ and as a result we know that $t > 0$. Assume that the employee's fallback position is normalized to zero and the rate of time preference is also zero (this simplification gives a closed form expression for the best response function but is obviously unrealistic). Then rewriting 8.3b we have

$$v = \frac{u(w,e)}{t(e)} = \frac{w - (aw^f/w)(1-e)^{-1}}{1-e}$$

and because $t_e = -1$ we can write eq. (8.5) for this case as

$$-\frac{aw^f/w}{(1-e)^2} = -\frac{w - (aw^f/w)(1-e)^{-1}}{1-e}$$

This best response function can be written as an explicit expression for the employee's effort (simply by rearranging terms) as

$$e = 1 - \frac{2aw^f}{w^2} \tag{8.6}$$

As one would expect, the level of effort is increasing and concave in the wage and decreasing in the level of the fair wage. You may find it instructive to derive the same best esponse function assuming conventional preferences (without the fairness motive) by simply eliminating the (w^f/w) term from the utility function. A comparison of the two best response functions shows the importance of social preferences.

Before going on, four comments are in order. First, we need to confirm that the threat of firing embodied in the ex ante announcement of the $t(e, m)$ function is credible (i.e., will be in the interest of the employer to carry out ex post — once a shirking worker has been detected). Why would the employer fire one worker only to hire another identical one? Assuming that employees observe one another's effort levels, and that any termination is common knowledge, then should acts of shirking not be punished by firing, the employees would cease to believe the announced $t(e, m)$. Thus, the firing of shirking workers is required to sustain the belief that the announced termination function is actually in force.[2] Second, in a more complete treatment the $t(e, m)$ schedule (not just m) would be designed by the employer (whether a worker is terminated might depend, for example, on the cost of recruiting and training a replacement), but doing so complicates the model without adding much illumination.

Third, the infinite horizon optimization problem is simply a way of deriving a best response function describing the employee's behavior; it need not describe the employee's thought process. The employee may be following a work norm (dictating a given level of effort) that evolves by

[2] The assumption that the game is common knowledge and is stationary means that the workers would believe that $t(e, m)$ is in force in any case. However, modeling a dynamic process by which workers learn the de facto termination function as a result of the observed terminations would add substantial complication and little insight.

the process of payoff-based updating described in chapters 2 and 7. Eq. 8.5 (the best response function) gives the work norm that maximizes payoffs and hence will tend to be adopted.

Fourth, one may ask, How does the employer know the employees' best response functions? Just as the employee may hit upon a best response function through trial and error methods (with payoff-based updating), the employer can arrive at an estimate of the best response functions by varying the labor discipline strategy and observing the effects on aggregate output. Of course there are many circumstances under which this learning process would be inefficient or biased, but I will assume that the employer arrives at an accurate estimate. (Remember: knowing the best response function is not the same thing as being able to write a contract in e, because e is nonverifiable.)

Profit Maximizing. The employer, who faces a competitive market for the output in which the given price is 1, varies m, w, and h to maximize expected profits (she is risk neutral).

$$\pi = y(he(w, m; z)) - (w + m)h \qquad (8.7)$$

The first order conditions for a maximum are,

$$\pi_h = y'e - (w + m) = 0 \qquad (8.7a)$$

$$\pi_w = y'he_w - h = 0 \qquad (8.7b)$$

$$\pi_m = y'he_m - h = 0 \qquad (8.7c)$$

from which we can see that a profit maximum requires that,

$$e_w = \frac{e}{w + m} = e_m \qquad (8.8a)$$

$$y' = \frac{w + m}{e} \qquad (8.8b)$$

The former requires that the average level of effort per dollar of expenditure on labor be equal to the marginal impact of variations in both wages and monitoring expenditures. This is the so-called Solow condition (after Robert Solow, who first derived it) extended to include monitoring inputs. The other first order condition is analogous to the familiar condition for a profit maximum that the wage equal the marginal product of labor. With effort endogenous, this condition requires that the marginal productivity of *effort* be equal to the cost of a unit of *effort* (including the cost of monitoring). Expressed equivalently as $y'e^* = w^* + m^*$, the first order conditions require that the marginal productivity of labor time (evaluated at the levels determined by the

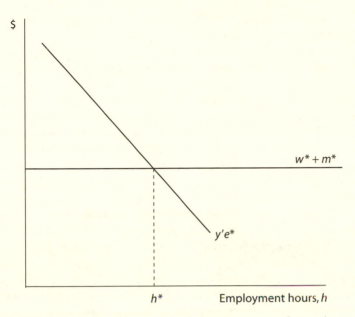

Figure 8.2 The firm's optimal hiring level. Note: w^*, m^*, h^*, and e^* are the solution to the first order conditions in the text.

Solow condition) equal the hourly cost of an hour of labor, as is shown in figure 8.2.

Because h does not appear in the worker's best response function, the profit-maximizing process can be described sequentially: the employer first solves the labor discipline problem, selecting m and w to satisfy eq. (8.8a). Then, substituting e^* and w^* from eq. (8.8a) into eq. (8.8b), she determines how many hours of labor to hire. Finally substituting e^*, w^*, m^*, and h^* into eq. (8.7) she determines if this production plan is sufficiently profitable to undertake, given the alternative uses the capital required.

To illustrate the equilibrium contract, return to the above example. Recall that $m = 0$. Using the best response function (8.6), the wage will be set to satisfy eq. (8.8a) or

$$\frac{e}{w} = \frac{1 - 2aw^f/w^2}{w} = \frac{4aw^f}{w^3} = e_w$$

giving the optimal wage w^* as

$$w^* = (6aw^f)^{1/2}$$

If $a = 1$ and $w^f = 6$ then it is optimal for the employer to offer the fair wage. The employee's optimal-effort response to the employer's optimal wage offer is found by substituting this value of w^* into eq. (8.6), giving $e^* = \frac{2}{3}$. If $w^f = 24$, however, the profit maximizing wage is half the fair wage. For fair wages less than 6, it is optimal for the employer to exceed the fair wage norm.

Choice of Technology. Now consider a more general production function with a nonlabor input, $y(k, E)$, where k is the per period input of the nonlabor input, $E = he$ is the total input of effort, and as before the function is increasing and concave in its arguments. Suppose that variations in k are associated with differing spatial or other arrangements of the production process affecting the ease of monitoring the work process. For example, highly capital-intensive processes such as the assembly lines that Henry Ford pioneered may be "machine paced," greatly simplifying the identification of low-effort workers. To reflect this fact, the termination function is now $t = t(e, m, k)$, an example might be $t = \eta(m, k)(1 - e)$ where $\eta(m, k)$ is the probability that a nonworking employee will be detected. As before $\eta()$ is increasing in m. If η is increasing in k (as the assembly line example suggests), then $t_{ek} < 0$; because the more k-intensive technology facilitates the monitoring process, it augments the (negative) effect of effort on the probability of termination. In this case we might say that the k-intensive production process is more "transparent" from the standpoint of the monitor and that a less k-intensive process is more "opaque." Opposite cases also exist. The important point is not the sign of t_{ek} but the fact that the choice of technology will generally affect the ease of monitoring one way or the other, namely $t_{ek} \neq 0$.

What will be the effect of variations in k on the employee's best-response function? Using the new termination function and differentiating eq. (8.5) totally with respect to k and e we find that

$$\frac{de}{dk} = \frac{t_{ek}}{u_{ee} - t_{ee}}$$

which, using the second order condition for the employee's maximum problem, shows that de/dk takes the sign of $-t_{ek}$. Thus, if k-intensive technologies are more transparent, increases in k shift upwards the best response function (by increasing the employee's marginal benefit to increased effort). The choice of the level of the k input which maximizes profits will reflect this effect. Letting ρ be the per period rental price of a unit of k, and differentiating the profit function (using the augmented production function) partially with respect to k, we now have an additional first order condition:

$$\pi_k = y_k + e_k h y_E - \rho = 0 \tag{8.7d}$$

The choice of the k-input will thus equate the rental price of the k-input not to its marginal productivity but to its marginal productivity *plus* its effect on the supply of effort times the marginal productivity of effort. The presence of this "labor discipline effect" on the choice of technology means that it will not generally be the case that

$$\frac{y_k}{y_E} = \frac{\rho}{\mu}$$

where $\mu = (w + m)/e$ is the cost of a unit of effort. As a result, the marginal rate of substitution in production (the slope of a production isoquant) will not be equal to the factor price ratio in competitive equilibrium. The reason is that inputs are valued not only for their contribution to production but also for their effects on the labor discipline environment. (Monitoring is a pure case of such an input, for it does not appear in the production function at all.) For the remainder of the chapter, I ignore the nonlabor input, k, for simplicity of presentation.

CHARACTERISTICS OF THE EQUILIBRIUM TRANSACTION

The values of e, h, w, and m satisfying eqs. (8.5) and (8.8) constitute the equilibrium transaction, namely, a mutual best response by the employer and employee. Note five things about the equilibrium.

First, workers generally face quantity constraints. In general, the participation constraint does not bind, that is, $v^* > z$. This implies that the labor market does not clear: identical workers receiving z would prefer to be employed receiving v but are unable to make a transaction. Those workers unable to make a transaction are *quantity constrained*, unable to purchase or sell as much as they want at the going terms of exchange.

Second, the resulting exchange (e^*, w^*) is *Pareto inefficient*. This must be the case because at these values the first order conditions of the employer and the employee require that

$$v_e = 0 \qquad \text{but } \pi_e > 0$$

and $\tag{8.9}$

$$v_w > 0 \qquad \text{but } \pi_w = 0;$$

and thus there exists some (sufficiently small) values $(\Delta e, \Delta w)$ such that

$$v(e^* + \Delta e, w^* + \Delta w) > v(e^*, w^*)$$

and

$$\pi(e^* + \Delta e, w^* + \Delta w, \ldots) > \pi(e^*, w^*)$$

Thus, there exists a small increase in effort accompanied by a small increase in the wage that would be Pareto improving. Because the employer has selected not only w but m as well to maximize profits, an analogous demonstration shows that a small decrease in monitoring and a small increase in effort is Pareto improving.[3]

Third, *nonproductive labor* and other nonproductive inputs will be hired in competitive equilibrium. An example of purely nonproductive inputs are those used in monitoring workers. Their inputs do not appear in the production function but are hired by a profit-maximizing firm because they contribute to the firm's objectives in other ways. We know that purely nonproductive inputs will be hired because for $m = 0$, $t_e = 0$ (without monitoring, working harder does not alter the probability of termination) so $e(w, 0; z) = \underline{e}$ (the fallback effort level is chosen). If we assume that $e = \underline{e}$ does not maximize profits, it follows that $m^* > 0$.

Fourth, the competitive equilibrium is *technically inefficient*: there exists an alternative allocation in which the same output is produced with less of one input and not more of any (this defines technical inefficiency). Suppose that the employer were required (by an omnipotent Being) to raise the wage by Δw and instructed to lower the level of monitoring by an amount Δm, just sufficient to restore effort to the equilibrium level, so,

$$e(w^*, m^*; z) = e(w^* + \Delta w, m^* - \Delta m; z) \qquad (8.10)$$

If the Being also stipulates that hours of employment remain as before, output will be unchanged. But one of the inputs, monitoring, has been reduced: the resources represented by Δm are now freed up for productive use. So the competitive equilibrium (e^*, w^*, m^*, h^*) is technically inefficient in the standard sense defined above. The case is illustrated in figure 8.3.

The reasons for the inefficiency are instructive. Enforcement strategies typically combine both monitoring (which has a social opportunity cost as it represents resources with alternative uses, e.g., the labor of the monitor, or the resources required to produce the surveillance equipment) and an enforcement rent, in this case $v - z$ (which is a pure transfer and hence entails no social opportunity cost). Thus, because both monitoring and the wage are costly to the employer, while only

---

[3] The labor discipline approach is sometimes termed the "efficiency wage" model because Leibenstein (1957) and other early contributors to this literature suggested that to take account of the effects of nutrition, variable effort and the like, labor should be measured in "efficiency units" rather than hours. The usage stuck, but is a misnomer, because (in contrast to the Walrasian model) the equilibria described by the model are both technically inefficient (see below) and Pareto inefficient.

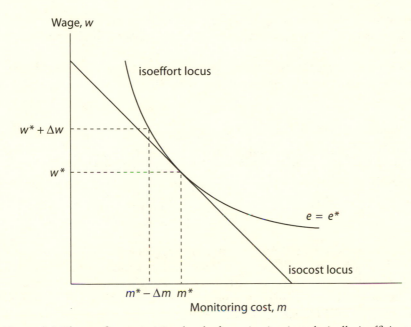

Figure 8.3 The profit maximizing level of monitoring is technically inefficient.

monitoring is socially costly, we have a standard case in which the private marginal costs are different from social marginal costs and a market failure results, as expected. From a social efficiency standpoint, then, competitively determined labor discipline strategies generally overuse monitoring and underuse enforcement rents. More carrot and less stick would affect a technical efficiency improvement. Notice that if more capital intensive technologies are associated with more transparent production processes (as in the above example), the same demonstration holds for capital goods: technical efficiency improvements could be made (over the competitive equilibrium transaction) by raising wages and reducing the capital input.

Fifth, the equilibrium transaction will also be characterized by *Pareto suboptimal workplace amenities* such as flexible work hours, a respectful and safe work environment, and the like. In the standard Walrasian model the employer is constrained by the workers' labor supply decision (participation constraint), and for this reason the employer is induced to provide workplace amenities as a way of lowering the cost of labor: a more worker-friendly job will attract prospective employees at lower wages. Because the participation constraint is the worker's own utility in the next best alternative, the employer will maximize profits by evaluating the importance of workplace amenities (relative to other arguments of the worker's utility function) exactly as the worker does. Does this result hold when effort is noncontractible? We will see that it does not.

Suppose the employee's utility function is expanded to include a measure of work amenities provided (per hour of work), α

$$u = (w, \alpha, e)$$

with $u_\alpha > 0$ over the relevant range, and that one unit of amenities costs p per hour of labor hired for the employer to provide. Then we have a new present value $v(e, w, \alpha, z)$, of the job and a new best response function $e(w, m, \alpha, z)$ and an additional first order condition for the employer

$$\pi_\alpha = y'he_\alpha - hp = 0 \qquad (8.7e)$$

This condition requires that the marginal revenue product of amenities (the first term) must be equal to the marginal (and average) cost of providing amenities. It is clear that the employer will take some account of the workers' preferences for amenities because $e_\alpha > 0$; having a more pleasant job will induce the worker to provide more effort (the value of the job to the worker now being greater).

Will the employer will take *sufficient* account of the employee's preferences? The answer is no. Workplace amenities are no different from wages in this model; they are valued by the worker and costly for the employer to provide. We have already seen that the profit-maximizing employer's offer, (w^*, e^*) will be Pareto inferior to some other combination of e and w characterized by small increases in both. The same reasoning applies to working conditions: because at the competitive equilibrium $(e^*, w^*, \alpha^*, m^*)$

$$\pi_\alpha = 0 \qquad \text{and} \quad v_\alpha > 0 \qquad (8.11)$$

$$v_e = 0 \qquad \text{and} \quad \pi_e > 0 \qquad (8.12)$$

so a small improvement in workplace amenities accompanied by a small increase in effort would be Pareto improving.

What accounts for the difference between the Walrasian and post-Walrasian treatments in this case? In the former, the participation constraint is binding, so the firm's iso-profit locus is tangent to the workers' indifference locus in equilibrium, resulting in Pareto-optimal job design. In the latter case, the participation constraint does not bind and the firm is constrained by the employee's best response function instead. As the best response function does not coincide with the participation constraint, the latter equilibrium is not Pareto optimal.

THE LABOR MARKET IN GENERAL EQUILIBRIUM

The employment relationship at a single firm is of course embedded in a market system with many of such firms and other actors. To study this, suppose there is a very large number of identical firms employing labor as above and that the relevant markets are perfectly competitive in the sense that there are no barriers to entry or exit. If firm profits (net revenues minus the opportunity cost of capital) are positive then firms enter, while negative profits induce firms to exit. Thus, the equilibrium number of firms is determined by the above first-order conditions and the *zero profit condition*:

$$\pi = y(he(w, m, z)) - (w + m)h - \delta = 0 \qquad (8.13)$$

where δ is the given per-period cost of fixed inputs (the unit of capital) and h, e, m, w satisfy the first order conditions above. Notice that z, (the only variable in eq. (8.13) other than δ that is not determined by the above first order conditions), is now represented as being endogenous. How is z determined?

The Worker's Fallback Position. For some values of $\underline{e}$ and $\underline{w}$, $v(\underline{e}, \underline{w}) = z$, so the worker is indifferent between his job — meaning providing effort $\underline{e}$ and receiving $\underline{w}$ — and the next best alternative, namely z. The worker's participation constraint is satisfied as an equality. We can see from eq. (8.5) that in this case $u_e = 0$ must obtain (the level of effort chosen when the employment rent is zero is that for which the disutility of labor is zero). Thus the utility of the transaction $(\underline{e}, \underline{w})$ is the per period equivalent of z, or $u(\underline{e}, \underline{w}) = iz$. The work level $\underline{e}$ is thus the amount of work per hour that the worker would choose to perform in the absence of any incentive strategy by the employer.

But what is z? As labor is assumed to be identical, the worker's expected wage in alternative employment must be the same as in the current employment, so the cost of being terminated is the reduction in well-being experienced during a spell for unemployment. A terminated worker will spend the next period unemployed, receiving an unemployment benefit (or other earnings-replacing transfer) equal to b while doing no work (and presumably engaging in job search). The unemployed thus experience the per-period utility $u(b, 0)$ which may reflect the utility of leisure, the social stigma of being out of work, and the like. At the end of each period there is a probability λ that the unemployed worker will find work and thus exit the unemployment pool; so the expected duration of unemployment is $1/\lambda$. Thus,

$$z = \frac{u(b,0) + \lambda v + (1-\lambda)z}{1+i}$$

$$= \frac{u(b,0) + \lambda v}{i + \lambda}$$

This is the fallback position defined in the same way as the present value of the job. We see that $dz/d\lambda > 0$ if $v - z > 0$, requiring $iv - u(b, 0) > 0$. This means that an increase in the probability of exiting the unemployment pool improves the fallback position of the worker, as long as the per-period benefits of having a job (iv) exceed the per-period benefits of not having one ($u(b, 0)$).

Comparative Statics. Recall that $(w + m)/e = \mu$ is the *cost of a unit effort*. Because an increase in the employee's fallback position shifts his best response function to the right, it can readily be shown that $d\mu/dz > 0$, meaning that the unit cost of effort varies with z, as one would expect. Because of this, profits also vary inversely with z, that is, $d\pi/dz < 0$.

In general competitive equilibrium the worker's fallback (z) must be such that the profit- and utility-maximizing levels of e, m, h, and w chosen by firms and workers satisfy the zero profit condition. It is the entry and exit of firms induced by positive or negative profits and the resulting aggregate employment effects that yield this equilibrium level of z. Here is the process. With n firms producing, each employing h as defined by the first order conditions (8.7), total employment H is defined by $nh \equiv H$, where I normalize labor supply to unity, so H is the aggregate employment *rate*. The likelihood of exiting the unemployment pool varies with the level of employment, so

$$\lambda = \lambda(H, \ldots) \qquad \text{with } \lambda' > 0$$

from which we know from ($dz/d\lambda > 0$) that

$$z = z(H, \ldots) \qquad \text{with } z' > 0$$

so the worker's fallback position improves when the employment rate increases, as expected. Now suppose that the number of firms is such that $\pi > 0$, inducing the entry of additional firms. The resulting additional employment raises H, which raises z, which in turn raises the unit cost of effort. Firm entry continues until eq. (8.13) is satisfied, thus determining the equilibrium aggregate employment level H as well as $z(H)$.[4]

BARGAINED PARETO IMPROVEMENTS

If Pareto improvements over the competitive equilibrium (the points in the shaded lens in figure 8.1) are technically feasible, why are they not realized? Why do the worker and the employer not agree upon a slightly higher level of both the wage and effort? Or a work amenity like flexible work hours and more effort? The answer is that such an agreement is not enforceable. The wage and hours are contractible, but the effort level is not. Such agreements are technically feasible but behaviorally unfeasible given the information structure of the problem and the institutions defining the interaction. Thus, the fact that e^*, w^*, m^*, h^* is Pareto inefficient does not tell us if the inefficiency could be eliminated or attenuated under feasible alternative contractual or other institutional arrangements. If the worker were the sole employee, then ownership of the firm's assets might be transferred to the worker who, as a self-employed producer and residual claimant on the income stream resulting from his efforts, could dispense with the need for monitoring. As we will see in chapter 9, the worker-owner's benefits from an optimal effort choice in the absence of monitoring might be sufficient to pay the former employer a fixed return on the assets sufficient to compensate her for the loss of the assets. But even if the absence of scale economies permitted this Robinson Crusoe solution, it might be infeasible if the employee were risk averse or credit constrained, as we will see in chapter 9. In these cases, the worker might prefer to continue work under the contracts described above rather than be a worker-owner, even if he were *given* the asset.

Consider another possible institutional remedy. Suppose the work team is organized as a trade union and can bargain with the employer. Because the members of the work team are identical, the union simply implements the unanimous decisions of its members. Moreover, suppose the members' information on one another's work actions allows them to use peer monitoring to implement a common level of work effort. This means the transaction is no longer restricted by the individual workers' best response functions. Equilibrium outcomes may thus in-

---

[4] The equilibrium will exist as long as positive profits are possible when $H = 0$ and profits are negative if labor demand equals labor supply, a sufficient condition for which is that $z(1) > y(h) - \delta$. Because $\pi(H)$ is monotonic, the equilibrium is unique.

clude $\{w, e\}$ pairs above the best response function if an agreement between the union and the employer can be secured. Assume the rest of the interaction as described above is unaffected. In particular, the employer's termination function remains in force and the employer determines the level of employment in the usual way, that is, by equating the marginal revenue product of effort to its effective cost. Of course, the union could bargain over the types of monitoring, the termination function, and the level of employment, but introducing these complications would not illuminate the main point in what follows.

Recognizing the possibility of a Pareto improvement over the competitive equilibrium $\{w^*, e^*\}$, the employer and worker promise to offer respectively $\{w^+ > w^*\}$ and $\{e^+ > e^*\}$ where $\{w^+, e^+\}$ is a Pareto improvement over $\{w^*, e^*\}$, the noncooperative Nash equilibrium described above. Any $\{w^+, e^+\}$ pair in the Pareto-improving lens in figure 8.1 could be the proposed transaction above. The two parties are thus engaged in a bargaining interaction in which the bargaining set is the entire lens of Pareto improvements and the bargaining frontier is the efficient contract locus. The fallback position in this bargaining problem is not that the employer and work team refuse to transact at all, but rather that they transact at the Pareto-inferior noncooperative level $\{w^*, e^*\}$. The bargaining problem, with per period payoffs is illustrated in figure 8.4.

If a binding agreement could be made to implement the two offers w^+ and e^+ then we would expect an outcome like $\{w^+, e^+\}$ to be quite common, at least where employees are able to engage in peer monitoring and to bargain collectively with their employers. The $\{w^+, e^+\}$ deal may be impossible to write into a binding agreement, however. For example, the employer cannot detect violations of the agreed upon effort levels by observing the aggregate level of output if there are other unobserved influences on output, which is generally the case.

If no binding contract can be made to enforce their agreement, the employer and union might be able to implement the Pareto-superior outcome by adopting strategies of conditional cooperation (nice tit-for-tat): each implements its part of the Pareto-improving transaction $\{w^+, e^+\}$ as long as the other does but defects to the Pareto inferior $\{w^*, e^*\}$ if the other defects. While these strategies sound abstract, variants of them are often observed. It is not uncommon for unions to threaten to "work to rule" — that is, to undertake only the tasks that are explicitly required contractually, while employers often condition higher wage payments on changes in work rules implementing higher effort levels.

Suppose that the action set of each is restricted to just $\{e^*, e^+\}$ for the

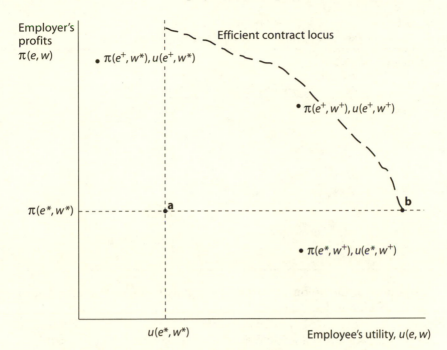

Figure 8.4 The employer's and union's bargaining problem: per period payoffs. Note: the bargaining set is the area bounded by the payoffs in the noncooperative interaction and the efficient contract locus. If the strategies available were unconditional w^+ and w^* for the employer and e^+ and e^* for the employee, the game is a prisoners' dilemma. Point **a** is the equilibrium of the noncooperative game (indicated by point **a** in figure 8.1) while point **b** is a point on the efficient contract locus (indicated by point **b** in figure 8.1).

union and $\{w^*, w^+\}$ for the employer and their strategy sets are to play the noncooperative equilibrium values unconditionally, or the conditional cooperation (nice tit for tat) strategies described above. There could be many other strategies but these truncated strategy sets are sufficient to make the point. Using the notation above, the present values of expected payoffs for the two bargainers are given in table 8.1. Consider the expected payoff to the union adopting unconditional e^* if the firm has offered conditional w^+. In the first period each worker receives the per-period utility of receiving high pay for little work $u(e^*, w^+)$ and then with probability $t(e^*)$ is fired, receiving the fallback asset z as a result, and with probability $(1 - t(e^*))$ retained, but thereafter receives the payoffs at the noncooperative equilibrium (because the firm defects

TABLE 8.1
Present value of expected payoffs in the repeated bargaining game

Employer →		
Union ↓	*Conditional w$^+$*	*Unconditional w**
Conditional e$^+$	$v^+ = \dfrac{u(e^+,\, w^+) - iz}{i + t(e^+)} + z$ $\pi^+ = \dfrac{\pi(w^+,\, e^+)}{i}$	$\dfrac{u(e^+,\, w^*) + (1 - t(e^+))v^* + t(e^+)z}{1+i},$ $\dfrac{\pi(e^+,\, w^*) + \pi^*}{1+i}$
Unconditional e*	$\dfrac{u(e^*,\, w^+) + (1 - t(e^*))v^* + t(e^*)z}{1+i}$ $\dfrac{\pi(e^*,\, w^+) + \pi^*}{1+i}$	$v^* = v(e^*,\, w^*,\, z),$ $\pi^* = \dfrac{\pi(w^*,\, e^*)}{i}$

in response to the union's e^*). The other payoffs may be interpreted in similar fashion (table 8.1).

We know that $v^+ > v^*$, so for sufficiently low i it can readily be shown that conditional e^+ may be the best response to conditional w^+. The one period gain for the employee made possible by the high pay for little work outcome $\{e^*, w^+\}$ is more than offset by the difference between v^+ and v^* (as well as the greater likelihood that the e^*-playing union member will be terminated at the end of the first period and thus receive z.) Similarly, for sufficiently low i, conditional w^+ will be the best response to conditional e^+. Thus, the $\{w^+, e^+\}$ outcome is implementable under some conditions. Of course if the single-period gain to defection is great enough, or the likelihood of retaining the job small enough, or the level of time discounting great enough, the cooperative outcome is not implementable as a Nash equilibrium.

This structure — bargaining up from a noncooperative interaction to a Pareto-superior cooperative outcome — captures important empirical facts about work relations. One often finds cooperative and noncooperative (and often highly conflictual) workplaces not only in the same industry but even in different production units of the same firm.[5] Typically, large firms with unionized labor forces are more likely to implement the cooperative solution. The markets for jobs in these firms are sometimes referred to as the *primary labor market*, characterized by long-term employment, well-defined promotion ladders, infrequent firing

---

[5] The same model has broad applicability to other types of collaborations such as marriages (Lundberg and Pollak 1993), in which cooperative and noncooperative outcomes are also observed.

for cause, and a sharing of the gains to cooperation between workers and owners. Other sectors of the economy (often characterized by insecure employment, short job ladders, and low wages) implement the noncooperative outcome and make up the *secondary labor market*. These differences are illustrated in the above bargaining example by $t(e^+) < t(e^*)$ and the shared gains to cooperation $\pi^+ > \pi^*$ and $v^+ > v^*$. Notice that according to this interpretation, a pure form of the labor discipline model applies to the secondary labor market, while a hybrid model — bargaining up from the inefficient outcomes of the noncooperative outcome — better describes the primary labor market.[6]

How might the structure of an economy affect the viability of the cooperative outcome? Notice that the termination probability has the same effect on the viability of the cooperative outcome as does the rate of time preference. If termination is likely (t is large) the cooperative outcome will be difficult to sustain as an equilibrium. Consider a more realistic termination function in which the probability of job loss is the sum of the probability of termination for cause, $t(e)$, and the probability τ of termination for other reasons (demand fluctuations or relocation of the firm, for example). Modifying the payoff table to take account of not-for-cause terminations would require adding a τ to $t(e)$ wherever the latter appears in table 8.1. It then becomes clear that high levels of not-for-cause terminations make it more difficult to sustain the cooperative outcome. Thus, bargaining-based Pareto improvements in the effort-wage transaction are more likely to be sustained where two institutions coexist: labor unions with the capacity to bargain with employees and to implement peer monitoring on the one hand, and macroeconomic policies that moderate the volatility of aggregate demand fluctuations on the other. This is an example of what is termed *institutional complementarity*, a situation in which the beneficial effects of one institution are enhanced by the presence of the other. (I will return to institutional complementarities in the final chapter.) Where institutional complementarities are strong we would expect to see either the coexistence of both effective collective bargaining and effective macroeconomic stabilization or the absence of both.

Why Don't Firms Sell Jobs?

But there may be a simpler way to achieve not simply a Pareto *improvement* over the noncooperative outcome but also to implement a Par-

[6] An alternative interpretation offered by Bulow and Summers (1986) holds that the high wages of the primary labor market are explained by the fact the "efficiency wage" model applies there but not in the secondary labor market that is characterized by market clearing at low wages. Their interpretation seems doubtful, however, given high levels of involuntary unemployment among demographic groups typically seeking work in the secondary labor market.

eto-*efficient* outcome. The key result in the above demonstration of Pareto inefficiency is that the participation constraint of the worker does not bind, and for this reason the worker receives what I have termed an enforcement rent. But why should this be? Has the employer overlooked an opportunity to increase profits? Could not a firm, noticing that the worker receives a substantial increase in the present value of expected lifetime utility when the job is secured, simply charge a fee for granting the job (Carmichael 1985)? If the firm exploited this opportunity, the worker might then pay the firm an up-front fee of $v^* - z^*$ and thus, having paid the job fee, would be just indifferent to taking the job but, importantly, would *not* be indifferent to losing it. Consider how this would work.

The job fee to be considered is a one-time nonreturnable transfer required by the employer as a condition of employment (this is sometimes misleadingly called a bond.) Assume that the worker's total wealth is $v + \kappa$ where as before v is the value of the job and κ is "other wealth." As the worker finances the job fee from κ, the fee simply reduces worker wealth. I assume this has no marginal effects on the worker's behavior. For this reason the worker's best response function $e(w)$ is unaffected. I will assume that the employer is effectively constrained (by due process or reputation considerations) from opportunistically adopting a firing function to take advantage of the fee by augmenting the level of new hires. The cost to the worker of reducing other wealth by a dollar is equivalent to the reduction of a dollar of v-wealth. Because h is the number of workers hired, it is also the number of job fees collected. To simplify exposition, I have abstracted from monitoring entirely (e is known to the employer but this information is nonverifiable).

The employer varies h, w, and B to maximize

$$\pi = y(he(w)) - hw + iBh \qquad (8.14)$$

subject to

$$v(e(w), w - iB) \geq z$$

where i is the rate of return, B is the size of the fee, and $v(.)$ is the ex ante present value of the job with fee B. The term $w - iB$ is the net wage, taking account of the opportunity cost to the employee of foregoing returns iB on the employee's wealth.

The associated Lagrangean optimization problem is given by

$$r = y(he(w)) - hw + iBh + \gamma\{v(e(w), w - iB) - z\}$$

with the first order conditions:

$$r_w = y'he' - h + \gamma(v_w + v_e e') = 0 \qquad (8.15a)$$

$$r_h = y'e - w + iB = 0 \qquad (8.15b)$$

$$r_B = ih - i\gamma v_w = 0 \qquad\qquad (8.15c)$$

$$r_\gamma = v - z = 0 \qquad\qquad (8.15d)$$

From (8.15b) we may determine the employment level as that which equates the marginal product of effort y' with the cost of an hour of labor $(w - iB)$ per unit of effort done per hour, or the cost of a unit of effort, or

$$y' = \frac{w - iB}{e} \qquad\qquad (8.16)$$

From the Lagrangian expression, γ is readily interpreted as the shadow price of the participation constraint and, from (8.15c) this is,

$$\gamma = -\frac{dr}{dz} = \frac{h}{v_w} \qquad\qquad (8.17)$$

Eq. (8.17) gives the effect on profits of a change in the worker's fall-back, namely, the increase in wages necessary to satisfy the worker's participation constraint $(1/v_w)$ times the level of employment. We can also see that for positive employment levels and nonsatiation $(v_w > 0)$ $\gamma > 0$, so the participation constraint is binding.

Eliminating h from (8.15a) and substituting in the above value of γ we have,

$$y'e' - 1 = -1 - \frac{e'v_e}{v_w}$$

which upon rearranging gives

$$y' = -\frac{v_e}{v_w} \qquad\qquad (8.18)$$

Combining eqs. (8.16) and (8.18) we have

$$\frac{w - iB}{e} = -\frac{v_e}{v_w} \qquad\qquad (8.19)$$

which requires that the cost of a unit of effort to the firm (the left side of 8.19) be equal to the (negative of the) marginal rate of substitution between wages and effort in the worker's iso-present-value locus (the right side).

The problem and its solution may be interpreted as follows. In figure 8.5, let the horizontal axis represent both the wage received by the worker, w, and the wage cost incurred by the employer, $w - iB$. The

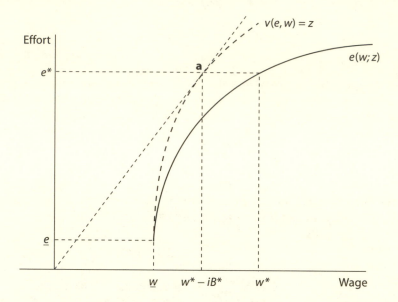

Figure 8.5 Optimal job fees clear the labor market and implement a Pareto optimum. The employer identifies point **a** as the solution that maximizes e/w, the effort elicited from the employee per unit of cost. To implement this outcome the employer offers the wage of w^* (to which the employee responds with e^*) with a fee of B^*.

employer identifies the iso-v locus for which $v = z$ (because she knows that the participation constraint will be binding). Along this locus there is some point (**a**) that maximizes the slope of a ray from the origin or $e/(w - iB)$ thus satisfying eq. (8.19). This point, being off the worker's best response function, is of course not directly obtainable: offering the wage $w^* - iB^*$ would not induce the worker to supply e^* of effort. The wage rate is then determined as that sufficient to induce the worker to supply e^*. And the level of the fee is that which implements point **a**, satisfying the participation constraint as an equality. With w, B, and e all determined, h^* is determined, by eq. (8.15b). The employer then checks to see if at the equilibrium it would be more profitable to hire no labor and/or if the worker is satiated. If neither is the case the assumption that the participation constraint is binding is sustained and the profit maximum has been correctly identified.

The equilibrium with the optimal job fees is strikingly different from the previous case. First, as the participation constraint binds, the worker is indifferent to taking the job or not. The labor market thus clears; there are no workers involuntarily unemployed. This result underlines an important limitation of labor market clearing as a policy

objective: if jobs are made sufficiently unattractive there may be no excess demand. Second, while ex ante (before taking the job) rents are
zero, ex post rents are actually larger than in the no fee case (for a given
z, the optimal wage is higher, as it is set not only to induce effort but
also to enhance the value of the fee that may be extracted from the
prospective worker). Third, the wealth of the worker is reduced and the
profits of the employer increased. In general equilibrium the effect
would be to increase the number of firms and the level of employment
(until z rose sufficiently to restore the zero profit condition).

This model seems to predict that job fees would be common (and
substantial) and that as a result involuntary unemployment would be
rare. But few firms charge workers an up-front job fee, and while surro-
gates for job fees, such as an initial low-wage probation period exist,
they are rarely of a magnitude remotely close to that which would make
the worker indifferent to taking the job.[7]

Does this mean that employers are simply not taking advantage of a
profitable opportunity? Like finding a $500 bill on the street, this is not
unheard of, but it seems unlikely. Why then does it not happen? To say
that prospective employees do not have much money to pay a job fee is
not a compelling answer, as the worker's limited wealth merely restricts
the sums that could be extracted, but does not refute the logic of the
argument, which would still predict optimal fees and hence clearing labor markets. A more convincing explanation is that the employee's positive motivations towards the employer are important in inducing high
quality work and high effort levels, and these positive motivations are
eroded by the employer driving the hardest possible bargain. Two types
of evidence support this interpretation.

First is that employers are reluctant to cut wages during periods of
high unemployment, apparently for reasons of employee morale and
motivation. Truman Bewley (1999) sought to understand the reluctance
of employers to take advantage of the employees' declining reservation
position during recessions by cutting wages. His extensive interviews
showed that employers fear the effect of wage cuts on employee morale.
The reason why employers refrain from cutting wages during a recession may apply with equal or greater force to the fact that most do not
charge fees for jobs, even if the rents associated with the jobs are
substantial.

Second, as we saw in the previous chapter, subjects in experimental

[7] In the United States, jobs that offer high rents typically offer them for beginning as
well as tenured workers, casting doubt on the interpretation of lower initial wages as
implicit job fees. Implicit job fees may take nonmonetary forms, as when an employer
secures political support from a prospective worker or extracts sexual favors.

labor markets typically exhibit strongly reciprocal preferences, providing high levels of effort in response to "employer" offers which are seen to be generous (Fehr, Kirchsteiger, and Riedl 1998). Where job fees were among the possible employer strategies that were tried, they were abandoned by experimental subjects because profits fell as a result of the negative response of the "employees."

A further reason why job fees are uncommon may be that prospective employees do not trust that reputation effects or due process would be sufficient to deter employers from firing workers without cause to increase the number of fees collected.

The fact that job fees are uncommon is sometimes taken as an indication that the labor discipline model above is of little empirical relevance, but the evidence above suggests that when extended to include the types of social preferences described in chapter 3, the model *is* consistent with the fact that job fees are rare. The most plausible interpretation is that a wage offer yielding an ex post job rent may be taken by the employee as either a sign of employer generosity (if it is unaccompanied by a job fee) or simply as a profit-maximizing strategy (if it is combined with a job fee). Thus, charging a job fee affects the beliefs of the employee about the intentions (or type) of the employer and the employee responds accordingly. This interpretation points to the importance of considerations of fairness and morale in wage setting, and motivates the designation of employment as a kind of gift exchange (Akerlof 1982).

Labor Discipline and Incentives: Evidence

As there are many plausible labor market models that have amended the conventional Walrasain assumptions, I should explain why I have focused on a particular class of models. The main reason is that the labor discipline model based on contingent renewal is consistent with a number of uncontroversial facts about the working of the economy (while the conventional model is not).

First is the existence of substantial employment rents in most jobs. One cannot capture the income-related aspects of these rents by comparing the income levels of those with and without jobs, as these groups differ with respect to many traits other than employment status. The most theoretically appropriate measure is a typical employee's loss of benefits and earnings occasioned by an exogenously induced spell of unemployment as would take place due to a plant closing. Henry Farber (2003:2), surveying the considerable literature on the subject, concluded that "displaced workers suffer substantial periods of unemployment and that earnings on jobs held after displacement are substantially lower than pre-displacement earnings." This summary remained true even during the period of strong labor demand of the 1990s. In the United States, the cost of job loss (an estimate of the present value $(v - z)$ using a rate of time preference of 10 percent) may be between half and one-and-a-half of annual earnings, depending on pretermination job tenure.[8]

In subjective terms, the rents may be considerably larger due to the social stigma and other discomforts associated with being without work. A number of studies have documented the loss in subjective well-being (measured by a series of survey questions) associated with a job loss or being without work. One study (Winkelmann and Winkelmann 1998), using a panel data set allowing comparisons of the same individual in different employment states, found that the subjective effect of joblessness per se was much larger than the subjective cost of the associated income loss.[9] There may be jobs in which employees are indifferent to continuing in employment or having their employment terminated, as the Walrasian model predicts, but the evidence is overwhelming that most employees have a strong preference to remain employed.

Second, real wages tend to vary with the level of employment (Bowles 1991, Blanchflower and Oswald 1994), as the effort regulation model predicts. (In the conventional Walrasian model, for a given capital stock, additional employment must *lower* the marginal product of labor and hence the wage.)

Third, employers devote substantial personnel and other resources to monitoring their employees' effort levels, expenses that would be inconsistent with profit maximization were effort levels either invariant or subject to a costlessly enforceable contract.

Fourth, labor effort appears to be quite variable and is rarely subject to contract. While group-based pay is a common practice, pay by the individual piece is extremely rare outside of the clothing and footwear industry (Petersen 1992). Moreover when a pay system for auto glass installers in the United States shifted from hourly wages to piece rates, output per worker rose by one-fifth (Lazear 1996). Similarly, British Columbia tree planters randomly assigned to piece rate compensation outperformed other planters randomly assigned to a fixed wage by 20

[8] This approximation is based on calculations using Farber's estimates. See also Burda and Mertens (2001).

[9] Blanchflower and Oswald (1994) estimated the additional income needed to compensate for being without work as $60,000, but as this is based on a comparison of those with and without jobs, conditional on a large number of demographic and other measures, it may overstate the subjective cost of job loss (joblessness may be but one of many reasons the unemployed are unhappy and congenitally unhappy people may be more likely to be jobless.)

percent (Shearer 2001). These large responses to improved incentives suggest that employees exercise substantial control over their work effort. Even larger effects of effort incentives on productivity were found in a study of farmers who worked under a variety of contracts. Laffont and Matoussi (1995) found that productivity of Tunisians working as hired labor was half as great as when working under full residual claimancy (family labor). Moreover, individuals were 50 percent more productive when they worked under fixed-rent contracts (and hence were full residual claimants on the results of their effort) than when they worked under the diluted effort incentives of share cropping. An unusual longitudinal study of the Philippines, found:

> [W]orkers evidently supply more effort under a piece-rate payment scheme or in own-farm work compared to time-wage employment as reflected in the fact that they deplete their body mass by approximately 10% more, net of calorie consumption, when working under a piece-rate scheme than on their own plots. . . . [T]he same worker consumes 23% (16%) percent more calories per day when employed under a piece rate payment scheme (own-farm employment) than when employed for time wages. (Foster and Rosenzweig 1994:214)

A study in the United Kingdom using observations of individual employees' work activities found that work effort responded strongly to macroeconomic conditions, as one would expect from the effort regulation model, higher unemployment levels inducing higher intensity of work (Schor 1988). A time series study in the United States found that labor productivity varied strongly with the size of employment rents, conditional on movements in the capital labor ratio, the level of capacity utilization, and other variables standard in productivity econometrics (Bowles, Gordon, and Weisskopf 1983). Other evidence suggests that these labor discipline effects are stronger in the secondary labor market than in the unionized primary market, and stronger in countries with weaker labor unions.

The infrequency of firings for cause is not evidence against the labor discipline models, for an effective discipline strategy might result in no firings whatsoever (as in Shapiro and Stiglitz 1984). Moreover even if termination for cause is not explicitly part of the employer's labor discipline strategy — as in the primary labor markets of many European economies — employer assessments of worker effort are widely used in selection for promotion or layoffs, effectively reproducing the effects of termination for cause as an incentive for hard work.

Some of these facts may be explained by rent sharing, transaction specific assets, and other models of the employment relationship introduced in chapter 10. I suspect that an adequate understanding of labor markets and the employment relationship may require hybrid approaches including other non-Walrasian models not developed here. Many of the facts presented below are consistent with more than one of these models.

Conclusion

The stimulus for much of the new theoretical work on labor markets came from dissatisfaction with the microeconomic aspects of macroeconomic models of aggregate employment and unemployment. Macroeconomists were prominent among the early innovators. Models based on incomplete contracting for effort or other aspects of the labor exchange explained how a competitive equilibrium could exhibit involuntary unemployment, thereby narrowing the hiatus between standard theory and empirical observation.

In the process, the standard theories of the labor market and the firm were substantially transformed. Robert Solow (1990) summarizes the direction of change in the title of his book *The Labor Market as a Social Institution*, and Arthur Okun (1981) captured the key new role of trust and other social preferences in his term "the invisible handshake." The importance of reciprocity motives and other social preferences in explaining why firms do not sell jobs underlines the futility of simply introducing incomplete contracting into an otherwise unaltered Walrasian framework. Experiments summarized in the penultimate section of the previous chapter suggest that contractual incompleteness enlarges the role of social preferences in determining equilibrium outcomes.

Three implications of the new theories have received less notice. The first was already mentioned in the discussion of the firm's choice of capital inputs when labor effort is not subject to contract. If the difficulty of monitoring labor effort differs across technologies, the choice of technology will be influenced by the nature of the labor discipline problem. Thus, such aspects of the labor discipline environment as prevailing norms, whether terminated workers have access to unemployment insurance, and other influences on the worker's effort choice, will affect the profitability of alternative technologies. This view contrasts with the standard model in which the choice of technology responds to factor scarcities as indicated by factor prices. It also raises doubts that institutions — the conventional firm, for example — can be explained by the requirements of exogenously given technologies. A more plausible view is that technologies and institutions coevolve, each influencing the development of the other.

Here is an example. When U.S. trucking companies installed on-board computers during the 1980s, they vastly improved their ability to monitor the actions of the drivers (Baker and Hubbard 2000). Trip recorders provided the company with verifiable information on the speed, idle time, and other details of the operation of the truck about which there was a conflict of interest between the driver and the company. For example, the cost of operating the trucks (paid by the company) was increasing and convex in the speed of the truck; drivers preferred to drive faster than the cost-minimizing speed and to take longer breaks. Drivers who owned their trucks were residual claimants on their revenues minus these and other costs, and hence of course internalized the costs of fuel and depreciation, realizing significant savings as a result. For this reason, before the introduction of trip recorders, owner-operators successfully competed with company fleets on those runs for which the conflicts of interest between drivers and companies were particularly strong.

Using the trip recorders, companies were able to write contracts based on the speed at which the truck was driven and to provide drivers other incentives to act in the companies' interests. Unlike other on-board computers (electronic vehicle managements systems, or EVMSs), the trip recorders provided no improvement in coordination between truckers and dispatchers, as the information was available to the company only on the completion of the trip. The sole function of the trip recorders was to improve the contractibility of aspects of drivers behaviors in which there was a conflicting interest between the drivers and the companies. By improving the companies' contractual opportunities, the trip recorders had two effects. First, they brought about a significant decline in the market share of owner-operators. Second, drivers in trucks with recorders drove slower. In contrast, the capacity of the EVMSs to improve coordination between drivers and dispatchers lowered costs but had no special effects on the distribution of contracts or ownership in the industry.

In this case, a technology was chosen because it enlarged the set of feasible contracts in a way that enhanced profits. If technologies are endogenous in this sense, it becomes difficult to give a precise definition to the term *transactions costs*. In the model developed above, it is clear that monitoring costs are transaction costs. However, equation (8.7d) shows that the firm's willingness to pay to use the k-input is explained by the contribution this input makes both to production and to labor discipline. Are the costs of using the k-good transaction costs? If so, what fraction of the cost of the k input should be allocated to transaction costs as opposed to costs of production? The costs of the trip recorders installed on trucks were almost purely transactions costs. But what of the EVMSs that like the trip recorders allowed contracts with stronger incentives for drivers and also greatly improved coordination? The same ambiguity arises with respect to the wage. We saw that a wage increase accompanied by a decrease in monitoring could sustain the same level of labor effort. It would seem odd to call the reduction in monitoring a decrease in transaction costs given that the total cost of hiring labor has risen. Are wages, then, also transaction costs? These ambiguities about the meaning of the term seem inescapable and explain why I make little use of the transaction cost framework here.

A second implication of the new labor market models is that because the employment relationship persists over many years, the workplace is a cultural environment in which employees' preferences and beliefs evolve. In this, workplaces are no different from schools or neighborhoods, for they influence who meets whom, to do what, and with what rewards associated with what behaviors. An empirical example will suggest the importance of these effects. Over a period of three decades, Melvin Kohn and his collaborators have studied the relationship between one's position in the authority structure of one's workplace—giving as opposed to taking orders—and the individual's valuation of self-direction and independence in their children, as well as one's own intellectual flexibility and personal self-directedness. They concluded that "the experience of occupational self-direction has a profound effect on people's values, orientation, and cognitive functioning."[10] His collaborative study of Japan, the United States, and Poland (Kohn, Naoi, Schoenbach, Schooler, and Slomczynski 1990) yielded cross-culturally consistent findings: people who exercise self-direction on the job also value self-direction more in other realms of their life (including child-rearing and leisure activities) and are less likely to exhibit fatalism, distrust, and self-deprecation. Kohn and his co-authors (1983:142) reason that "social structure affects individual psychological functioning mainly by affecting the conditions of people's own lives." Kohn concludes, "The simple explanation that accounts for virtually all that is known about the effects of job on personality . . . is that the processes are direct: learning from the job and extending those lessons to off-the-job realities" (Kohn 1990: 59).

As the personality dimensions mentioned by Kohn are part of individuals' preferences explaining how they raise their children, what kind of

---

[10] See Kohn (1969), Kohn, Naoi, Schoenbach, Schooler, and Slomczynski (1990), Kohn and Schooler (1983), and Kohn (1990). The quote is from p. 967 of the co-authored 1990 work. The studies take account of the possibility that personality is affecting job structure rather than vice versa.

leisure activities they engage in, and the like, this is strong evidence that preferences are endogenous with respect to workplace organization.

A third, related, implication is that norms of wage fairness, work ethic, and other social preferences are not exogenous but rather evolve under the influence of current wages, work effort, and working conditions as well as influences outside the workplace. A substantial discrepancy between the wage norm and the equilibrium wage, for example, may result in the erosion of the norm or successful collective action by employees to improve their situation.

We do not know what Henry Ford had in mind when he announced the five-dollar day. The fact that output per worker hour more than doubled following the increase suggests that workers' effort rose substantially. (Ford increased the level of supervision along with the wage, so the likelihood that slack work would be tolerated undoubtedly fell.) Whether the workers' increased effort was a response to the carrot of Ford's seeming generosity (reducing the disutility of effort, for example, on the left-hand side of eq. (8.5)) or to the stick of closer supervision and increased employment rents (increasing the right hand side of eq. (8.5)), we cannot say.[11]

---

[11] Raff (1988) thinks the increase in supervisory input is inconsistent with the labor discipline model, but he appears to assume (implausibly) that supervision and the wage are substitutes rather than complements in the labor discipline strategy, counter to the reasoning presented here.

CHAPTER NINE

Credit Markets, Wealth Constraints, and Allocative Inefficiency

> The English are still imbued with that doctrine, which is at least debatable, that great properties are necessary for the improvement of agriculture, and they seem still convinced that extreme inequality of wealth is the natural order of things.
> — Alexis de Tocqueville, *Journeys to England and Ireland* (1833–1835)

> You load sixteen tons, and what do you get?
> Another day older and deeper in debt.
> Saint Peter don't call me 'cause I can't go,
> I owe my soul to the company store.
> — Merle Travis, *"Sixteen Tons"* (1947)

> [Lending money] is profitable for those who enforce their authority with the stick.
> — Harpal, a money lender in Palanpur

IN THE U.S. South prior to the Emancipation Act (1863) it was said that cotton was king. But it was not until after the Civil War that cotton truly ascended to the throne among crops: in the quarter of a century following the demise of slavery, the production of cotton relative to corn (the main food crop) increased by 50 percent.[1] This intensification of the cotton monoculture was puzzling to observers at the time as it coincided with a slight *downward* trend in the price of cotton relative to corn. Moreover, there were no changes in the technical conditions of production that would have offset the adverse price movement; in fact, the growth of corn yields appears to have outpaced cotton yields during this period. Nor can the shift from corn to cotton be explained by changes in factor supplies: the Cotton South experienced a serious labor shortage following the war, which should have led some farmers to abandon cotton in favor of corn, a much less labor-intensive crop.

What then explains the growing dominance of cotton? To answer this

---

The first epigraph is from Tocqueville (1958:72), the third from Lanjouw and Stern (1998:552).

[1] This account is based on Ransom and Sutch (1977).

we need to investigate the structure of local credit markets. To finance the crop cycle, most farmers — poor sharecroppers and rental tenants, for the most part, many of them former slaves — purchased food (including corn) and other necessities on credit during the growing season. Because there typically was a single merchant in each locality, the food and other prices at which the farmers accumulated their debt were inflated by the monopoly power of the merchant-lender. The loans were repaid when the crop was sold at the end of the season. Most farmers were too poor to post collateral, so the merchant-lenders secured their loans by means of a claim (a lien) on the farmers' future crop in case of default. This *crop lien* system, according to its most prominent students, Roger Ransom and Richard Sutch, favored cotton:

> In the view of the merchant, cotton afforded greater security for such loans than food crops. Cotton was a cash crop that could readily be sold in a well-organized market; it was not perishable; it was easily stored. . . . For these reasons the merchant frequently stipulated that a certain quantity of cotton be planted. . . . It was the universal complaint of the farmers that the rural merchants predicated his willingness to negotiate credit on the condition that sufficient cotton to serve as collateral had been planted. (Ransom and Sutch 1977:160)

The crop lien system that came to prominence in the post-Emancipation South was an ingenious solution to the problem of providing credit to asset-poor borrowers. It substituted the farmer's unenforceable promise to repay the loan in the future by an action observable by the lender *before* the granting of credit, that is, with the sharecropper's having *already* planted cotton on which the merchant had first claim.

Taking account of the relative resource costs and prices of the two crops, Ransom and Sutch estimate that the cotton farmer purchasing corn on credit could have increased his income by 29 percent by shifting resources from cotton to corn. But this was precluded by fact that because the farmer had little wealth, he needed credit, and for the same reason, credit was conditioned on planting cotton. The result, according to Ransom and Sutch was that

> The southern tenant was neither owner of his land nor manager of his business. . . . [H]is independent decision making was limited to the mundane and menial aspects of farming. The larger decisions concerning land use, investments in the farm's productivity, the choice of technology, and the scale of production were all made for him. (p. 170)

The peculiarities of credit markets also help to explain a contemporary puzzle. Residential tenancy incurs inefficiencies typical of the principal agent relationships studied in chapters 7 and 8, yet over a third of

U.S. families rent rather than own their home (Savage 1995). A residential tenant's maintenance of the property and civic actions to enhance the quality of the neighborhood environment contribute to the value of the owner's property but cannot be specified in an enforceable contract. Thus tenants have incentives to supply too little maintenance and to participate too little in enhancing local amenities. Owner-occupied residences avoid the resulting incentive problems because the person taking the maintenance or civic amenities actions and the residual claimant on the benefits of these actions are the same individual, namely, the owner.

As an empirical matter, home ownership induces better care of the residence and also higher levels of participation in local government activities (Glaeser and DiPasquale 1999, Verba, Schlozman, and Brady 1995). Why, then, is renting rather than owning one's residence so common, especially among those with low incomes?[2] The answer is that renters do not have access to mortgage credit: in 1993, only 13 percent of renting families could secure a loan to buy even a low-priced home (one at the tenth percentile of homes ranked by price in the family's neighborhood; Savage 1995). The remaining 87 percent of renters had too few assets net of outstanding debt and too little income to secure a conventional mortgage.

Lack of wealth may preclude the poor from acquiring the assets that would allow more efficient solutions to incentive problems, as in the above cases of agrarian and residential tenancy. But in many cases even if the poor were to be given ownership of the relevant assets, they might elect not to hold them. A final example shows this. The redistribution of land to small holders in Chile during the early 1970s was intended to benefit the poor, in part by placing residual claimancy in the hands of the farmer and thereby providing incentives for both investment and greater effort, leading to higher levels of productivity.[3] The land transfers coincided with a boom in the market for exported fruit. But few of the land reform beneficiaries had the capital to finance the long gestation period for tree crops, and credit was generally not available to small holders. As a result, few shifted from food to fruit production. At the same time, the value of their land rose dramatically as a result of the fruit boom. Unable to take advantage of the favorable price of fruit, by the early 1990s 57 percent of the original 48,000 beneficiaries had sold their land. The transfer of wealth to the poor had been accomplished,

---

[2] In 1990, in the ten largest U.S. urban areas, among families with children and with annual incomes less than $15,000, 82 percent did not own their homes, while over 85 percent of families with children with incomes over $50,000 are home owners (U.S. Census). Overall, 64 percent of American families were owner-occupiers in 1993 (Savage 1995).

[3] This account is based on Carter, Barham, and Mesbah (1996) and Jarvis (1989).

but the realignment of incentives intended by the land reform had failed due to the credit constraints facing poor farmers (and most likely to their risk aversion in the face of highly variable fruit prices as well).

All three examples contrast sharply with a world of complete and costlessly enforceable contracts. In the Walrasian setting, wealth conveys quantitative advantages — it determines the location of one's budget constraint — but all participants in the economy face the same contractual opportunities (and hence the same prices) irrespective of their holdings. The poor are constrained to buy less than the rich, but they transact on the same terms. By contrast, where contracts in financial markets are incomplete or unenforceable, individuals lacking wealth are either precluded from engaging in a class of contracts that are available to the wealthy or enter these contracts on unfavorable terms. Thus, wealth differences have qualitative effects, excluding some and empowering others.

The most obvious reason why wealth influences contractual form is that only those with sufficient wealth can undertake projects on their own account. Those with sufficient wealth to do this can assign to themselves full rights of both residual claimancy and control over the relevant assets. They thereby eliminate costly incentive problems. A second reason is that wealth ownership attenuates the incentive problems arising from contractual incompleteness in principal agent relationships. Wealthier agents generally have access to superior contracts because the wealth of the agent allows contracts that more closely align the objectives of principal and agent. This is the case, for example, when the borrower has sufficient wealth to post collateral or put her own equity in a project. The agent who provides collateral or equity to her project experiences enhanced incentives to supply effort, to adopt risk levels preferred by the principal, to reveal information to the principal, and to act in other ways that advance the principal's interests but that cannot be secured in a contract.

Those lacking wealth, for example, may acquire education and other forms of human capital on less favorable terms than the rich and as a result may forego investments in learning whose private and social returns exceed their costs. Similarly, as we have seen, in residential housing markets, those with sufficient wealth are more often owners and therefore residual claimants on the actions they take to improve the property and the neighborhood, while the asset-poor are more likely to be renters. Thus, differences in wealth are reflected in distinct contractual opportunities; those available to the wealthy are more likely to embody incentives supporting efficient outcomes while those available to the wealth poor do not, thereby imposing additional disadvantages on the poor. As a result, those without wealth often are precluded from

undertaking projects that are beneficial from a social efficiency standpoint, or they are constrained to undertake these projects a suboptimal
scale, or engage in contractual arrangements with suboptimal incentive
structures such as residential tenancy, sharecropping, or wage labor.

While other financial markets are involved, the main analytical issues
are best illustrated by the credit market, the subject of this chapter. I
begin with a review of evidence on the extent to which people are credit
constrained. I then introduce the basic problem of incentives arising
from the incompleteness of the contract between borrower and lender
and then explore how the provision of equity or collateral by the borrower or the repetition of the interaction over many periods may attenuate these incentive problems. The next section embeds the borrower-
lender relationship in a model of general competitive equilibrium to
show why prospective borrowers lacking wealth may fail to secure financing (or will be constrained to finance only small projects or to pay
high rates of interest). Like the unemployed prospective workers in the
labor market of chapter 8, wealth-poor individuals will thus be quantity
constrained. As a result, the wealthy will be able to finance (and hence
to implement) projects that are larger and of lower quality than the
projects that wealth-poor are able to finance, and for identical projects
the wealthy will pay a lower interest rate.

An important consequence is that because wealth constraints may
prevent high-quality projects from being implemented, the distribution
of wealth matters for allocative efficiency, contrary to the logic of the
Fundamental Theorem and the Coase theorem. In the penultimate section, I explore the conditions under which an efficient distribution of
property rights will occur through private exchange, and provide an
example in which a redistribution of assets by fiat may generate positive
productivity effects that (unlike the Chilean land transfers) are sustainable in competitive equilibrium.

CREDIT CONSTRAINTS: EVIDENCE

Credit constraints are empirically important. Much of the evidence (surveyed in Jappelli 1990) is based on the cyclical fluctuations of consumption: a consensus of these estimates is that for the United States about a
fifth of families are liquidity constrained. These tend to be younger families with lower levels of wealth. These studies do not observe the borrowing activities of individuals and hence are somewhat indirect. More
direct evidence is based on actual credit histories. Jappelli (1990) found
that 19 percent of U.S. families had their request for credit rejected by a
financial institutions; the assets of these credit-constrained families were

63 percent lower than the unconstrained families. "Discouraged borrowers" (those who did not apply for a loan because they expected to be rejected) had even lower wealth than the rejected applicants. Another study of U.S. families (Gross and Souleles 2002) is based on the fact that credit card borrowing limits are often increased automatically. If borrowing increases in response to these exogenous changes in the borrowing limit, we can conclude that the individual was credit constrained. The authors found "that increases in credit limits generate an immediate and significant rise in debt" (p. 181). Gross and Souleles estimate of the extent of credit limits is as follows:

> It is plausible that many of the one-third of households without bankcards are liquidity constrained. . . . Of the two-thirds with bankcards, the over 56 percent who are borrowing and are paying high interest rates (averaging around 16 percent) might also be considered liquidity-constrained, lacking access to cheaper credit. Combined with the households lacking bankcards, they bring the overall fraction of potentially constrained households to over 2/3. (pp. 152–3)

Other studies are based on the way that exogenous increases in wealth affect economic behavior. Blanchflower and Oswald (1998) found that an inheritance of $10,000 doubles a typical British youth's likelihood of setting up in business. Another British study, Holtz-Eakin, Joulfaian, and Rosen (1994), found an elasticity of self-employment with respect to inherited assets of 0.52, and that inheritance leads the self-employed to increase the scale of their operations considerably. Another study (Black, Meza, and Jeffreys (1996) found that a 10 percent rise in value of collateralizable housing assets in the United Kingdom increased the number of startup businesses by 5 percent. Evans and Jovanovic (1989) found that among white males in the United States, wealth levels are a barrier to becoming entrepreneurs and that credit constraints typically limit those starting new businesses to capitalization of not more than 1.5 times their initial assets: "[M]ost individuals who enter self-employment face a binding liquidity constraint and as a result use a sub-optimal amount of capital to start up their businesses" (p. 810).

A study of Italian households found that those who did not borrow because either they were denied credit or believed they would be refused credit were more likely to be larger poorer families with an unemployed, less well-educated, female, and younger head (Guiso, Jappelli, and Terlizzese 1996). Moreover, by comparison to families unlikely to face credit constraints, poorer, younger, families with more uncertain sources of income (self-employment rather than pensions, for example) tended to avoid holding risky assets, consistent with the view that credit-constrained individuals enjoy lower expected returns of the investments they do make. Asset-poor people in the United States frequently take out short-term "payday loans" against their pay checks. In Illinois, the typical short-term borrower is a low-income women in her mid-thirties ($24,104 annual income), living in rental housing, borrowing between $100 and $200, and paying an average annual rate of interest of 486 percent (Vega 1999).

Several studies have shown that asset-poor producers in developing countries may be entirely shut out of credit markets or out of labor or land rental contracts that elicit high effort. As we have seen in chapter 8, Laffont and Matoussi (1995), for example, show that the financial constraints limit the kinds of contracts that poor Tunisians may engage in, substantially reducing their productivity and hence their incomes. Other studies in low-income countries show that net worth strongly affects farm investment, and low wealth entails lower return to independent agricultural production (Rosenzweig and Binswanger (1993). For example, Rosenzweig and Wolpin (1993) show that poor and middle-income Indian farmers could substantially raise their incomes if they did not confront credit constraints: not only did they underinvest in productive assets generally, but the assets they did hold were biased toward those they could sell in times of need (bullocks) and against highly profitable equipment (irrigation pumps) that had little resale value. Similarly, Rosenzweig and Binswanger (1993) find that a standard deviation reduction in weather risk (the timing of the arrival of rains) would raise average profits by about a third among Indian farmers in the lowest wealth quartile and virtually not at all for the top wealth holders. This evidence suggests that the wealthier farmers pursued riskier strategies with higher expected returns. Thus, lack of insurance and restricted access of the poor to credit not only reduced incomes, it also increased the level of income inequality associated with a given level of wealth inequality.

Consistent with the hypothesis that the poor are credit constrained is the strong inverse relationship between individual incomes and rates of time preference. Hausman (1979) estimated rates of time preference from (U.S.) individual buyers' implicit tradeoffs between initial outlay and subsequent operating costs in a range of models of air conditioners. (By law, operating cost must be listed along with the price.) He found that while high-income buyers exhibited implicit rates of time preference in the neighborhood of the prime rate, buyers below the median income level exhibited rates five times this rate (they bought cheaper but more expensive-to-operate equipment). Green, Myerson, Lichtman, Rosen, and Fry (1996) estimated (hyperbolic) discount rates from high- and low-income respondents in the United States using a questionnaire method. The low-income group's estimated rates were four times those of the high-income group. In both the Green et al. and Hausman studies, the elasticity of the rate of time preference with respect to income was approximately −1.

Thus, there is considerable evidence that those lacking wealth are credit constrained and face unfavorable opportunities in financial markets and other restrictions on the kinds of contracts in which they may engage. The resulting allocative inefficiencies appear to be substantial.

BORROWERS AND LENDERS

The promise to repay a loan is not generally enforceable for two reasons: the borrower may not have the funds sufficient for repayment when the repayment is due, and the borrower's choice of a risk level for a project is not generally subject to enforceable contracts. When an agent who lacks sufficient wealth has a "project" for which the level of risk is chosen by the agent, a standard principal agent problem arises. An example follows, beginning with a case (Robinson Crusoe) in which no coordination failure occurs because the operator of the project is wealthy enough to finance it himself. This is followed by a case in which the same result occurs but for a different reason: complete contracting is assumed. These two cases, like the example in chapter 4 of Robinson Crusoe's labor effort, establish the normative baseline for comparison with the more realistic cases in which the operators of the project are not sufficiently wealthy to finance it themselves and hence must borrow, and in which borrowing contracts are incomplete.

Assume that all actors are risk neutral. A project requires \$1 to complete and will fail with probability f. Imagine that the "project" is a machine, which if it does not "fail" has a one period life (it becomes worthless at the end of the period) and which produces goods in proportion to the "speed" at which it is run. For simplicity, assume the speed is equal to the probability that the machine will break (i.e., fail) or f. The goods produced are available only at the end of the period under the condition that the machine has not failed. (The machine will be worth nothing at the end of the period whether it fails or not, but if it fails it also destroys any goods it has produced.) The project returns μf if it succeeds and 0 otherwise (μ is a positive constant measuring the quality of the project), and the expected returns net of all (noninterest) costs are

$$ r = \mu f(1 - f) $$

While the amount produced (if the machine does not fail) rises in f, the expected returns reach a maximum beyond which the higher output in the success state is offset by the greater likelihood of a failure and zero return. Therefore, the net returns function is an inverted U-shape. The expected returns function abstracts from the opportunity cost of the investment, which is $1 + \rho$ (had the owner not bought the machine but instead had invested the one dollar at the risk-free interest rate ρ, he would have had $1 + \rho$ at the end of the period).

The Robinson Crusoe Case. A single owner of the project (self-financing it) would vary f to maximize expected returns on the project and thus would set $dr/df = \mu(1 - 2f) = 0$, the solution to which is $f^* = \frac{1}{2}$. To be viable, the project must return at least $1 + \rho$, and therefore the quality of the project must be such that $\mu \geq 4(1 + \rho)$. (This is because the expected return on the project when f is optimized is $\mu(\frac{1}{2})(\frac{1}{2})$.)

Fully Contractible Case. Now assume that project is to be operated by an individual without wealth, and that it cannot be sold or otherwise transferred. This individual, called the Agent (A), borrows the funds ($1) from a lender, the principal (P), at interest rate $\delta - 1$. At the end of the period, she repays an amount equal to the "interest factor" δ (the $1 principal plus interest) with probability $(1 - f)$ and 0 otherwise. The assumption that the borrower repays nothing if the project fails is crucial to what follows. It reflects the common institution of *limited liability*; if the project fails, the lender may not take the borrower's house. Therefore the agent's per period expected return is

$$y(f; \delta) = \mu f(1 - f) - \delta(1 - f) = (\mu f - \delta)(1 - f) \qquad (9.1)$$

Assume the agent's next best alternative is to receive zero. If f is known to P and is fully contractible, then P can simply offer A a contract such that $y = 0$, thereby satisfying A's participation constraint as an equality. Using $y = 0$ as a binding participation constraint, A's "supply price of f" (assuming $f > 0$) is just $\delta/\mu = f$, a lower interest rate buying a reduced probability of failure. Note that if this supply price is offered (i.e., if P contracts for f according to $\delta = f\mu$), the agent will be indifferent to any particular level of f, all of them resulting in zero expected gain. The principal then varies f to maximize his expected returns

$$\pi = \delta(1 - f) \qquad (9.2)$$

which, substituting in the "price of f," gives

$$\pi = f\mu(1 - f)$$

When the principal chooses f to maximize this expected profit function, he will set $f^* = \frac{1}{2}$.

Figure 9.1 illustrates this case. The slope of P's iso-return schedule (one of which is shown) is $(1 - f)/\delta$. At P's solution to the above optimizing problem, an iso-return schedule is tangent to A's participation constraint, the slope of which is $1/\mu$. Having determined the optimal failure rate, the principal then uses the supply price of f to determine the

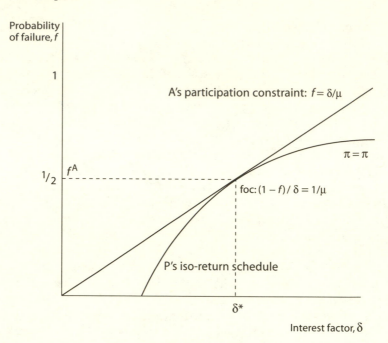

Figure 9.1 Credit market: contractible case

optimal interest rate to offer the agent, namely $\delta^* = \mu/2$. P then offers A the following contract: A agrees to implement $f^* = \frac{1}{2}$ and agrees to pay P an amount $\delta^* = \mu/2$ (which will occur if the machine does not fail with probability $\frac{1}{2}$) satisfying A's participation constraint and giving P an expected gain of $\delta(1 - f)$ or $\mu/4$.

Note that the level of risk implemented is identical to that chosen by Robinson Crusoe. The reason is that the principal's objective function under complete contracting is the same as Robinson Crusoe's.[4] Because the participation constraint was binding, the lender was effectively maximizing subject to a constraint given by the borrower's utility level (her participation constraint) and therefore implementing a Pareto optimum. Complete contracting erases the distinction between principal and agent, and reinstates the world of Crusoe. The results change when we turn to real world credit contracts.

Non-contractible Risk, No Collateral: In this case, f is not subject to contract so the *agent* will choose f to maximize expected returns (which remain as before eq. (9.1)), that is, by setting

---

[4] The same result would have held had we assumed that the promise to repay is enforceable but that f is not subject to contract.

$$\frac{dy}{df} = \mu(1 - 2f) + \delta = 0$$

giving the agent's best response function:

$$f(\delta) = \frac{\delta + \mu}{2\mu} = \frac{1}{2} + \frac{\delta}{2\mu} \tag{9.3}$$

The principal's expected profits are as before eq. (9.2), but f now depends on δ, giving the expected profit function:

$$\pi = \delta(1 - f(\delta)). \tag{9.2'}$$

Varying δ to maximize this function gives us the principal's first order condition:

$$\frac{1-f}{\delta} = f' \tag{9.4}$$

which, using eq. (9.3), gives the solution

$$\delta^* = \frac{\mu}{2} \tag{9.5}$$

and substituting eq. (9.5) back into eq. (9.3) gives $f^* = 3/4$. The agent therefore implements a higher level of risk than in the complete-contracting or Robinson Crusoe cases. Figure 9.2 illustrates the difference. Note the difference between A's participation constraint and A's best-response function (this explains the difference in the level of risk chosen by A). As a result, the borrower's expected income is positive (because the best-response function is above the participation constraint), and thus the borrower is receiving a rent. Returns to P are correspondingly lower: substituting f^* and δ^* into the expression for π gives $\pi = \mu/8$ (rather than the expected profits of $\mu/4$ in the complete contracting case.)

Infinite Horizon with Contingent Renewal: The fact that principal confers a rent on the agent in the one period case raises an interesting question. Could not P profit from this fact by promising to continue lending to A as long as the machine did not fail? Would the incentive problems be attenuated if the lender offered the borrower contingent renewal of a contract over an infinite time horizon (as did the employer and employee in the labor market model)? Suppose the principal uses the failure of the project as a (noisy) signal of the action taken by the borrower. He then offers a loan (for a single period) with a promise to renew the loan if the project does not fail, and not otherwise. If the

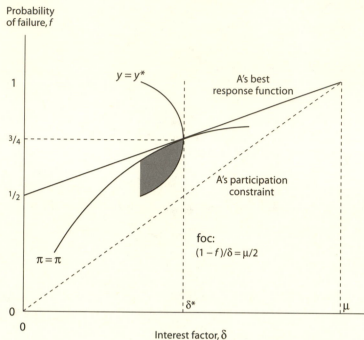

Figure 9.2 Noncontractible risk level. The borrower's iso-expected income locus is $y = y^*$.

present value of the agent's fallback position is z, and rate of time preference is i and treating the interaction as stationary (time invariant), the agents's expected present value, v, is

$$v = \frac{y(\delta, f) + (1 - f)v + fz}{1 + i}$$

which after some rearranging is

$$v = \frac{y - iz}{i + f} + z \qquad (9.6)$$

As in the labor market case, the agent's present value of the transaction is the sum of the fallback and the rent. The best response function for this case is somewhat complicated: to allow a comparison with the above cases I will simplify by assuming $i = 0$ so as to allow a closed form expression (and $z = 0$ as before). Then the expected present value of the transaction v is just the per-period expected income valued as an asset by dividing it by the termination probability, or

$$v = \frac{y}{f} = \frac{\mu f(1-f) - \delta(1-f)}{f}$$

Then the agent's best response is found by varying f to maximize v, giving

$$v_f = \frac{-\mu f^2 + \delta}{f^2} = 0 \qquad (9.7)$$

requiring the borrower to select f such that $f^2 = \delta/\mu$ or

$$f^* = \left(\frac{\delta}{\mu}\right)^{1/2} \qquad (9.8)$$

How does this compare with the nonrepeated case? For $f < 1$, we must have $\delta < \mu$ in which case the agent's best-response function in the infinite horizon case gives lower values of f for all relevant values of δ. That is

$$\left(\frac{\delta}{\mu}\right)^{1/2} < \frac{1}{2} + \frac{\delta}{2\mu}$$

which is easily seen because $2(\delta/\mu)^{1/2} < 1 + \delta/\mu$. The principal's expected profits and first order condition are unaffected, so using eq. (9.4) with the agent's new best response function (9.8) gives the profit maximizing interest factor as $\delta^* = 4\mu/9$ to which the agent's best response is:

$$f^* = \left(\frac{\delta}{\mu}\right)^{1/2} = \frac{2}{3}.$$

These results may be contrasted with the above cases in table 9.1. The per-period expected benefits to the agent in the single-period case 3 are $.0625\mu$, while in the multi-period case 4 they are $.074\mu$. Per-period expected benefits to the principal are $.125\mu$ and $.148\mu$, respectively in these two cases. Thus, the use of a contingent renewal contract in the multi-period case allows a Pareto improvement over case 3. The reason is that the superior incentives allowed by the repetition of the interaction result in a reduction of the risk level chosen by the agent, allowing a larger expected joint surplus than in the single period case (0.22μ as opposed to 0.19μ).

Note the agent's fallback position z equals zero in cases 2 through 4, so in the absence of complete contracting, even in the single-period case,

Table 9.1
Credit market results for the case where the borrower has no wealth

Case	Agent's best response $f^*(\delta; \mu)$	Risk f^*	Interest factor δ^*	Expected payoffs (y, π) per period
1. Robinson Crusoe	na	$\frac{1}{2}$	na	$\frac{\mu}{4}$ (to Crusoe)
2. Contractible risk	$f = \frac{\delta}{\mu}$ (PC)	$\frac{1}{2}$	$\frac{\mu}{4}$	$0, \frac{\mu}{4}$
3. Non-contractible risk: single period	$f = \frac{1}{2} + \frac{\delta}{2\mu}$	$\frac{3}{4}$	$\frac{\mu}{2}$	$\frac{\mu}{16}, \frac{\mu}{8}$
4. Non-contractible risk: multi-period	$f = \left(\frac{\delta}{\mu}\right)^{1/2}$	$\frac{2}{3}$	$\frac{4\mu}{9}$	$\frac{2\mu}{27}, \frac{4\mu}{27}$

the agent receives a rent. However, the reasons why the rent exists in equilibrium differ in cases 3 and 4. In the multi-period case, the prospect of losing the rent should the project fail induces the agent to adopt a lower risk level, and knowing this, the principle offers a larger rent. In the single-period case, by contrast, the agent does not anticipate losing the rent. However, because A responds adversely to higher interest rates, the only way P can implement the profit-maximizing incentives is to offer the agent a transaction superior to her next best alternative. In this case the rent is an unintended byproduct of the principal's limited options in designing a contract for A. Given that a rent will be offered in any case, the principal in the single-period case could raise profits by converting it to a multi-period contract. In the multi-period case the lender has authority over the borrower for the same reason that the employer has authority over the employee: he can threaten to withdraw the borrower's rent, and this threatened sanction induces the borrower to act in ways advantageous to the lender. The excess of the present value of the borrower's transaction over the borrower's next best alternative is thus another example of an enforcement rent.

Wealth Constraints and Credit Market Exclusion

Suppose the agent has two types of income-earning assets. Human capital in the form of skills, schooling, and investments in health is a source of earnings but cannot be used as equity or collateral in a loan contract. By contrast, most forms of material wealth may be used as equity or collateral. I will use the term *wealth* to refer to assets that may be used as collateral or equity. Borrowers generally have some wealth, and if the project yields expected returns in excess of the risk-free interest rate it will be in the borrowers' interest to invest in the project. There are two reasons why investing one's own wealth in a project may be in the interest of the borrower, corresponding to the two sources of incentive problems in principal agent relationships introduced in chapter 7, namely, hidden attributes and hidden actions. First, if, contrary to our assumption, the lender does not know μ, investment of the borrower's own wealth is a credible signal of the borrowers assessment of quality of the project. As we will see presently, in competitive equilibrium those with less wealth will need superior projects to obtain financing, so the borrower has an interest in overstating a project's quality in order to secure a loan. This is the hidden attribute case. The second reason, and the one modeled here, is that the discrepancy between the objectives of the lender and borrower concerning the choice of the level of risk (this is the hidden action) would be attenuated if the borrower invested in the project and thus shared some of the risk of failure with the lender. In what follows I use the terms *wealth* and *level of equity* committed to the project interchangeably: agents devote all their wealth to the project, if they devote any.

   Noncontractible Risk with Borrower's Equity. Suppose the agent has wealth k currently invested in a risk-free asset yielding ρk. Should the agent devote these funds instead to the risky project, she would then borrow only $1 - k$ and the expected returns (including the opportunity cost of the foregone returns on the risk-free asset) would be

$$y(f; \delta) = \mu f(1 - f) - \delta(1 - k)(1 - f) - (1 + \rho)k$$

The agent will then select f so as to maximize y, with the resulting first order condition,

$$f(\delta, k) = \frac{1}{2} + \frac{\delta(1 - k)}{2\mu} \qquad (9.9)$$

which is exactly as before, except for the $(1 - k)$; as the equity share of the agent (k) rises, the chosen risk level falls. As before, a higher interest factor (δ) shifts the best-response function upward, while superior projects (μ) shift it downward. Notice that as $k \to 1$, $f^* \to \frac{1}{2}$, so complete equity financing of the project by the agent reproduces the prudent and socially optimal Robinson Crusoe result, as one would expect. The lender knows the borrower's equity share k. As before, acting as first mover and varying δ to maximize expected profits (9.2') subject to this best-response function (9.9), the lender will select $\delta^* = \mu/2(1 - k)$. The agent, responding according to eq. (9.9) will choose $f^* = 3/4$.

   The outcome, $\{f^*, \delta^*\}$, is an equilibrium for the interaction of the principal and agent in isolation: both actors' first order conditions for

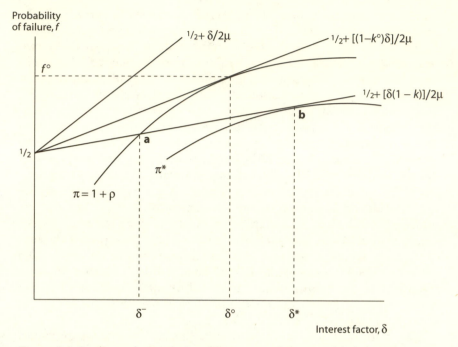

Figure 9.3 Credit market exclusion. The zero profit locus is labeled $\pi = 1 + \rho$. Increased wealth $(k > k° > 0)$ supports a borrower's best response function preferred by lenders.

the relevant maximum problem are fulfilled. Recall that in chapter 8, having analyzed the dyadic principal agent relationship between employer and employee, I then embedded this model in a competitive general equilibrium setting by introducing a zero-profit condition to regulate the level of employment. Here, I treat the credit market analogously.

As there are many lenders in competition, in equilibrium they all receive an expected return equal to the risk free interest rate, ρ. Thus, the end-of-period expected wealth must be the same for those investing in the risk free asset and in the risky project, or

$$\pi = \delta(1 - f) = (1 + \rho) \tag{9.10}$$

This condition expresses the requirement of zero profits in competitive equilibrium. It defines an "iso-expected returns" locus in (f, δ) space, as depicted in figure 9.3. Below this zero-expected profit locus (for lower f or higher δ), the expected rate of return exceeds the competitive risk-free rate, inducing wealth holders to supply more funds to the loan market. Above the zero-profit locus, funds will be withdrawn. Thus, the competitive equilibrium must be along the locus.

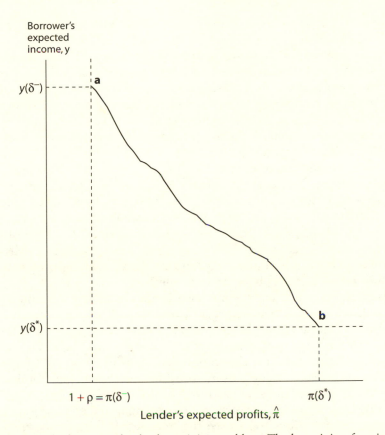

Figure 9.4 The borrower-lender bargaining problem. The bargaining frontier is **ab**. Points **a** and **b** refer to outcomes **a** and **b** in the previous figure.

Now suppose there is some borrower whose wealth, call it k^o, is just enough that her best response function is tangent to this zero-profit condition, with the outcome defined by this tangency designated in the figure by the point (f^o, δ^o). Lesser levels of wealth give a best response function lying wholly above the zero profit locus, and hence there is no offer the lender can make that will generate an expected return to the leader at least equal to ρ. As a result, borrowers with $k < k^o$ are unable to borrow. They are the *credit market excluded*.

What of borrowers with $k > k^o$? A best response function for one such borrower (with wealth k) is depicted in figure 9.3. Before turning to the competitive case, I will first explore the determination of the interest rate and risk level for a noncompetitive bilateral exchange as might take place between an urban pawn shop or "payday lender" and a poor borrower, or a small-town bank or money lender and his clients. If the lender is first mover, he will maximize expected profits subject to the borrower's best-response function, and set $\delta = \delta^*$ as shown in figure 9.3. Note that in this case, both the lender's expected return and the value of δ that maximizes profits vary with the borrower's wealth level. By contrast, if the borrower is first mover (unlikely in the cases just mentioned), she would know that her expected profits vary inversely with the interest rate and so would simply offer to pay $\delta = \delta^-$, the interest rate that (given the borrower's best-response function) would give the lender an expected profit rate just equal to the risk-free rate of return.

Of course any outcome with $\delta \in [\delta^-, \delta^*]$ is possible, depending on the institutions governing the bargain. The borrower-lender bargaining problem is illustrated in figure 9.4, where $y(\rho)$ is the expected income of the borrower if the lender's expected profit rate is equal to the risk-free rate, and $y(\delta^*)$ and $\pi(\delta^*)$ are, respectively, the expected income of the borrower and lender when the lender is first mover. Without specifying more about the institutional structure of the bargaining problem we cannot anything more about the outcome.

Suppose there is competition among lenders such that in competitive equilibrium each lender's expected profit is ρ. Then the equilibrium transaction must be on the zero profit locus, namely, $\delta = \delta^-$, for a borrower with wealth k^o. Because greater wealth shifts the best response function downwards, it is easy to see that δ^- is declining in k for borrowers with wealth $k > k^o$. As a result, the competitive equilibrium interest rate will vary inversely with the wealth of the borrower.

Wealthier borrowers will also be able to finance larger projects and projects of lower quality. To see the first, let the size of the project, initially set at 1, now be $K \geq 1$, so k/K is the borrower's equity share. Now consider two borrowers, one with wealth of just k^o who can finance a project of size 1 at the interest factor δ^o, as above, and the other with wealth $k > k^o$. If the wealthier borrower's project were of size $k/k^o > 1$, then the equity shares and hence the best-response functions of the two borrowers would be identical. Both would then be offered δ^o and as a result would select f^o, thus fulfilling the competitive equilibrium condition. The result is that with identical projects, the wealthier agent transacts at the same interest rate as the less wealthy agent but is able to borrow more to finance a larger project and hence to expect a higher income. The less wealthy in this case are the *credit constrained*, they can borrow but are restricted to smaller amounts than the rich.

So far we have assumed that all projects are of equal quality, that is, that μ did not vary among borrowers. Relaxing this unrealistic assumption will reveal another penalty imposed on the less wealthy. Assume an agent unable to provide equity ($k = 0$) has a project for which $\mu = \mu^o$ and a wealthier ($k > 0$) agent has $\mu^k < \mu^o$ (the poorer agent has a better project). To allow a comparison, suppose both of them are marginal borrowers just able to finance their projects in competitive equilibrium, and hence both pay the same interest rate δ. (In figure 9.3, the best-response function for each is tangent to the zero profit locus.) What do we know about the relative productivity of their projects? Using the best response functions of the two borrowers, we can rewrite the above (zero-profit) equilibrium condition as

$$\pi^k = \delta\left(\frac{1}{2} - \frac{\delta(1-k)}{2\mu^k}\right) = 1 + \rho = \delta\left(\frac{1}{2} - \frac{\delta}{2\mu^o}\right) = \pi^o$$

This may be read to mean that if the two projects are both to be financed in competitive equilibrium, their expected returns must be equal and jointly equal to the risk-free rate $1 + \rho$. This allows us to infer something about the quality of projects offered by a wealthy and a non-wealthy agent that would be observed being funded in competitive equilibrium. To do this we make use of the fact that δ is the same for both borrowers, allowing the following simplification of the above expression.

$$\frac{1-k}{2\mu^k} = \frac{1}{2\mu^o}$$

or, rearranging,

$$\frac{\mu^k}{\mu^o} = 1 - k. \tag{9.11}$$

From eq. (9.11) we conclude that the agent lacking wealth must have a project that is as superior to that of the rich agent as his is wealth inferior. If the wealthy agent can put up half the cost in equity, her project can be half as good as the poor agent's (who can put up none). It is easy to see that had the poorer agent had some wealth available for equity, $k^o < k$, the above relationship would be

$$\frac{\mu^k}{\mu^o} = \frac{(1-k)}{(1-k^o)}.$$

This means that the minimal quality of a project required to secure funding expressed as a ratio among two prospective borrowers, is proportional to the fraction of the project that *cannot* be self financed.

We thus have three results in the competitive equilibrium case: *for borrowers with wealth sufficient to secure lending to finance the minimal sized project (K = 1) but not sufficient to self-finance the entire*

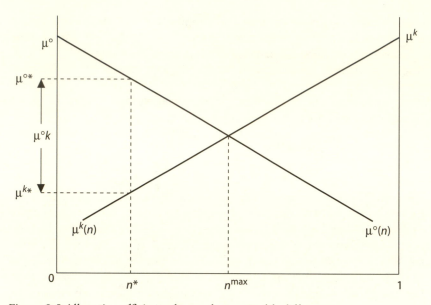

Figure 9.5 Allocative efficiency losses due to wealth differences

project, wealthier borrowers will be able to fund larger projects and projects of lower quality; moreover, for projects of the same size and quality as those of the less wealthy, the wealthier borrowers will pay lower interest rates.

This of course cannot be efficient, as it implies that there will be some poor agents with good projects that will not be attempted, while some rich agents (and rich principals) will either have the wealth or be able to acquire it through borrowing to carry out inferior projects.

To see this, suppose that some given total amount of finance is available, normalized to unity, to be divided among projects (all of the same size, 1) operated by either a wealthy or a wealthless individual, each of whom has a shelf of projects of varying quality. Now rank the projects of each from the best (highest μ) to the worst, and assume that the projects will be financed in order of quality. Assume that the two borrowers have an identical distribution of project qualities. In figure 9.5, the number of projects offered by the poor that are financed is n, with $(1 - n)$ the number of projects offered by the rich that are funded. We can write $\mu^o(n)$ for the quality of the nth project of the poor borrower and $\mu^k(n)$ as the quality of the rich borrower's worst funded project when the poor borrower implements n projects. The social optimum requires that no excluded project of either borrower be of higher quality than any included project. (Were there a large number of small projects this would equate (approximately), the quality of the marginal projects

TABLE 9.2
Efficiency enhancing redistribution

	Joint surplus	Owner's Income	Operator's Income
Before	$3\mu/16 = (1 + \rho)3/2$	$\mu/8 = 1 + \rho$	$\mu/16 = (1 + \rho)/2$
After	$\mu/4 = 2(1 + \rho)$	$\mu/8 = 1 + \rho$	$\mu/8 = 1 + \rho$

Note: the Before line reproduces line 3 from table 9.1, with $\mu = 8(1 + \rho)$. After describes the effect of the asset transfer and tax described in the text.

offered by each.) Suppose this optimum occurs when the poor gain finance for n^{max} projects.

But the competitive equilibrium condition above (9.11) shows that the marginal project of the wealthier borrower will be of lesser quality than the marginal project of the wealthless borrower. Thus, the poor will gain finance for only $n^* < n^{max}$. We can say more: using the fact that for the marginal projects in competitive equilibrium $\mu^k/\mu^o = 1 - k$, we know that $\mu^o - \mu^k$, the difference in the project quality of the marginal projects of the two individuals will be equal to $\mu^o k$. This is a measure of the extent of allocative inefficiency, and it is obviously increasing in k, the wealth difference between the two borrowers. In this model, redistributing wealth from the rich to the poor (assuming its implementation were costless) would increase the social surplus: it would increase n^* and thus improve the average quality of projects.

Could such a redistribution from the wealthy to those without assets followed by a compensation paid to the wealthy accomplish a Pareto improvement? It is commonly thought that a redistribution cannot pass the Pareto test for the simple reason that redistributions create losers as well as winners. To see that this is not necessarily the case, refer back to table 9.1. Suppose $\mu = 8(1 + \rho)$, so in the case of noncontractible risk with a single period model, the lender's expected profits ($\mu/8$) is just equal to one plus the risk-free rate of return, while the wealthless borrower's expected income ($\mu/16$) is $(1 + \rho)/2$. Imagine (for dramatic effect) that at the start of some period the government confiscates the "$1 machine" required by the project from its rich erstwhile owner and gives it to the poor erstwhile borrower, who then operates it as did Robinson Crusoe. (Or the government could tax the rich lender $1 and give that to the poor.) At the same time, the government imposes a tax obligation on the beneficiary of this redistribution, requiring him to pay $1 + \rho$ at the end of the period (if the project fails, he will have to pay the tax from the earnings on his human capital). The beneficiary's expected payoff before paying the tax would be the same as Crusoe's, namely $\mu/4$ or, given the assumed value of μ, $2(1 + \rho)$. If the beneficiary realized this amount, he could pay his tax obligation, which the government would then use to compensate the erstwhile owner, paying the latter his expected return as owner $(1 + \rho)$. The beneficiary of the redistribution would retain an expected amount of $(1 + \rho)$ for himself, and thus be better off as a result. (Recall she made only half this amount as a borrower.) There is nothing special about the numbers; all that is required is that the total surplus is larger in the owner-operator (Crusoe) case. Table 9.2 summarizes these calculations.

If a Pareto improvement is possible, you may wonder why the owners of the machines do not just lease them to the poor in return for a promise to pay the owner a rent of $1 + \rho$ at the end of the period. But this transaction simply replicates the incentive problems encountered in the loan contract, for the promise to pay the rent is unenforceable. The government addressed this problem by extracting the compensation from the beneficiary *irrespective of the fate of the project*, essentially offering an *enforceable* loan contract to the beneficiary at the risk-free interest rate. What the asset transfer plus the tax accomplishes is to make the owner-operator of the project the residual claimant on all of the risk entailed by her choices (rather than being shielded from downside risk by the unenforceability of the promise to repay the loan or to pay the rent). It is this that accounts for the allocational superiority of the Robinson Crusoe case and allows for the seemingly anomalous *Pareto-improving redistribution*.

RISK AVERSION, OWNERSHIP, AND ALLOCATIVE EFFICIENCY

To see why it may be impossible to implement such a redistribution or why such a redistribution, if implemented by fiat, might be welfare-*reducing* even for its purported beneficiaries, we need to make the above model more realistic. We have assumed that all parties are risk neutral. Yet there is good evidence that the poor are risk averse and that risk aversion declines with increases in an individual's income level.[5] Thus, the poor may prefer sharecropping or wage employment because these contracts shield them from risk, even if their expected incomes would be higher as residual claimants. This is the lesson of the Chilean land reform. This section thus addresses two questions. First, under what conditions will the relatively poor prefer to hold productive assets exposed to risk? And second, does there exist a class of redistributions

[5] Binswanger (1980), Saha, Shumway, and Talpaz (1994).

that enhance allocative efficiency, that would not come about through voluntary contracting, and yet are sustainable as competitive equilibria? Answering these questions will require some new tools.[6]

Recall from chapter 3 that if an individual's utility as a function of her income is $U = U(y)$, then the Arrow-Pratt measure of risk aversion is $a = -U''/U'$. If the utility function is less concave at higher levels of income, or $da/dy < 0$, then *decreasing risk aversion* is said to obtain.[7] Recall also that while the concavity of the utility function undoubtedly captures important aspects of behavior in the face of risk, it certainly misses important influences on behavior, such as aversion to uncertainty, ambiguity, fear of the unknown, and so on. I will here introduce a framework that treats the concavity of the utility function as one of many reasons people may wish to avoid risk. The basic idea is to represent expected income as a good and the variance of income as a bad.

Suppose an individual's income, y, varies in response to stochastic shocks according to

$$y = z\sigma + g(\sigma) \qquad (9.12)$$

where $g(\sigma)$ is expected income and z is a random variable with mean zero and unit standard deviation. Thus, σ is the standard deviation of income, a measure of risk. States among which the individual must choose differ in the degree of risk to which the individual is exposed, σ. Then we write the individual's utility function as

$$v = v\{g(\sigma), \sigma\} \qquad \text{with } v_g > 0 \text{ and } v_\sigma \leq 0. \qquad (9.13)$$

This function expresses the individual's positive valuation of higher levels of expected income and negative valuation of more uncertain income without implying that the latter is due to the concavity of the function $U(y)$. Because of the particular way that I have introduced risk, however, this function is also able to capture the logic of the Arrow-Pratt measure.[8] The indifference loci representing an individual with decreasing Arrow-Pratt risk aversion appear in figure 9.6. They are increasing and convex in σ, are flat at the vertical intercept ($\sigma = 0$), become flatter for increasing g when $\sigma > 0$, and become steeper for increasing σ. The slope of an indifference locus, $-v_\sigma/v_g$, $\equiv \eta$ is the margi-

---

[6] This section draws on Bardhan, Bowles, and Gintis (2000).

[7] a is sometimes termed *absolute risk aversion* and distinguished from *relative risk aversion*, which measured by $a_R = -yU''/U' = ya$. Declining relative risk aversion implies that with increasing income, a declines proportionally more than income increases.

[8] The general utility function $U(y)$ can be expressed as a simple two-parameter utility function in this case because the variation in income is generated by what is termed a *linear class of disturbances*. The technical details are in Bardhan, Bowles, and Gintis (2000), drawing on the earlier work of Meyer (1987) and Sinn (1990).

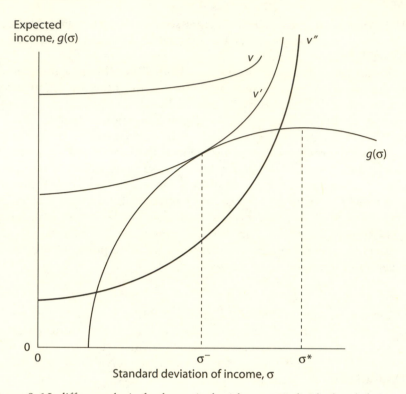

Figure 9.6 Indifference loci of a decreasingly risk averse individual and choice of a risk level. Note σ^* is the risk choice of a risk neutral person.

nal rate of substitution between risk and expected income. Thus $\eta(g, \sigma)$ is a measure of the level of risk aversion experienced by an individual faced with a given level of expected income and risk. It is clear that this measure of risk aversion is increasing in the level of risk exposure. The vertical intercept of each locus is the *certainty equivalent* of the other points making up the locus: it gives the maximum amount the individual would pay for the opportunity to draw an income from a distribution with the mean and dispersion given by each of the other points on the locus.

It is plausible to assume that the so called risk-return schedule, $g(\sigma)$, is an inverted U-shape, first rising and then, after reaching a maximum, falling as shown in figure 9.6. The choice of σ may refer to a technology choice, like the "speed of the machine" in earlier sections or the choice of high-risk high-yield seed varieties over lower-risk lower-expected-return seeds. Or it might refer to a human capital investment or product mix choice such as the degree of specialization, the more specialized education or product mix yielding higher expected returns (over some range) but also incurring greater risks. Risk-return schedules of this type have also been estimated with respect to biodiversity, with greater diversity being a hedge against variations in weather and other environmental influences.

The decision maker faced with this risk-return schedule will vary σ to maximize v subject to $g = g(\sigma)$ and thus will equate

$$g' = -\frac{v_\sigma}{v_g} \tag{9.14}$$

requiring that the marginal rate of transformation of risk into expected income (the left-hand side) be equated to the marginal rate of substitution between risk and expected income. A risk-neutral individual (one for whom $v_\sigma = 0$) simply will set $g' = 0$, maximizing expected income at $\sigma = \sigma^*$. The risk-averse individual (with $-v_\sigma > 0$) will select a level of risk such that $g' > 0$, which implies a lower level of risk (σ), with a correspondingly lower expected return.

We can now answer the first question: under what conditions will an asset-poor agent prefer to be the owner-operator rather than a wage worker on the same project? Assume there is an infinitely lived project generating the income stream described above and requiring capital of amount κ to implement, the per-period opportunity cost of which is just the risk-free interest rate, ρ. If the project is operated by an employee who is not residual claimant, the owner must pay supervision costs m and pay a wage w (equal to the disutility of labor) to the employee, yielding the owner a profit of

$$\pi(\sigma) = \sigma z + g(\sigma) - \rho\kappa - m - w$$

Suppose the employer is risk neutral; he will select $\sigma = \sigma^*$. Assume that competition among many similar employers imposes a zero (expected) profit condition, so that the equilibrium wage w^* is given by (setting $\pi(\sigma^*) = 0$) $w^* = g(\sigma^*) - \rho\kappa - m$.

Would the employee receiving w^* with certainty prefer to be residual claimant on the uncertain income of the project assuming that she could also select the level of risk? Let us first assume (contrary to the previous section) that the capital goods required can be rented for $\rho\kappa$ per period, or that the erstwhile employee can borrow the capital to purchase the capital at the interest rate ρ, which is equivalent. For simplicity, I also assume that as owner-operator, the erstwhile employee expends exactly the same effort as before but without incurring supervision costs. Then the owner operator's income net of opportunity costs is

$$y(\sigma) = \sigma z + g(\sigma) - \rho\kappa$$

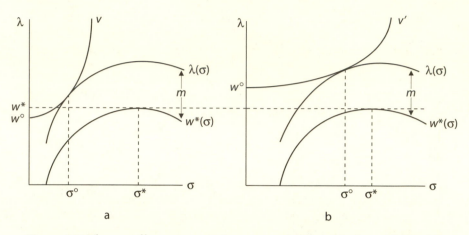

Figure 9.7 The payoff to wage employment and ownership by a highly risk averse (a) and less risk averse (b) individual. Note: the highly risk averse individual prefers wage employment to being an owner-operator.

Writing the owner-operator's expected income as $\lambda = g(\sigma) - \rho\kappa$ gives the owner-operator's utility function $v = v(\lambda(\sigma), \sigma)$. Choosing σ to maximize this function requires that,

$$\lambda' = -\frac{v_\sigma}{v_\lambda}.$$

Let the chosen risk level be σ^o, as shown in figure 9.7, the two panels of which depict two situations that might occur.

In both panels, the risk-return schedule for the owner-operator, $\lambda(\delta)$, is above the wage function, $w^*(\sigma)$, by the amount m because in the former case self-employment obviates the need for supervision costs. But the risk-averse owner-operator selects a level of risk that is less than the expected income-maximizing risk level selected by the employer. In panel **a** the certainty equivalent of the owner operated outcome, w^o, is less than w^*, so the individual would prefer to remain an employee rather than to assume the risk associated with residual claimancy. In panel **b** the individual is less risk averse and the opposite is the case.

If the latter case obtained we would expect to see owner-operated projects rather than wage employment: employees would acquire assets and become owners, implementing a Pareto-improving reassignment of rights of control and residual claimancy. This is exactly Coase's insight: under suitable conditions, voluntary transfers of property rights should implement an efficient allocation, with residual claimancy and control of projects assigned to those who can operate them most productively.

But what makes this possible in our case is the unrealistic assumption that the owner-operator could rent the capital goods or borrow to purchase them at the risk-free interest rate. We know (from the previous section) that under competitive conditions, the rate of interest will vary inversely with the ratio of the borrower's equity, k, to the size of the project κ. Suppose, then, that the interest cost of borrowing to acquire the asset (and the opportunity cost of devoting one's own wealth to equity for the project) is not ρ but rather is r, where

$$r = r\left(\frac{k}{\kappa}\right) \qquad \text{with } r' < 0 \text{ and } r(1) = \rho$$

The expected net income for an owner-operator with wealth k is now

$$\lambda^k = g(\sigma) - r\left(\frac{k}{\kappa}\right)\kappa$$

The situation of figure 9.7b with this new risk-return schedule (labeled λ^k) for an individual with limited wealth is presented in figure 9.8. Note that for the case depicted, the certainty equivalent of the individual's risk return choice is less than w^*. It is clear that the credit-constrained prospective owner-operator will prefer to remain an employee, even if, had she been able to borrow at the rate ρ, she would have preferred ownership. In this case, wage employment would exist in competitive equilibrium if employees had wealth of k or less. (We assume that these nonowners would invest whatever wealth they had in an instrument with a return of ρ.)

However, suppose a redistribution of assets were to take place such that the employee had wealth k^+ greater than κ. Her risk-return schedule (the dashed line in figure 9.8) would now, as in figure 9.7, give her a certainty equivalent greater than w^*. She would then be able to borrow at the rate ρ (or bear an opportunity cost of ρ for the use of her own wealth in the project) and hence would become (and remain) an owner-operator. Thus both the pre-redistribution assignment of residual claimancy and control and the post-redistribution assignment are sustainable as Nash equilibria. It follows that a redistribution of property titles that would not have occurred through private contracting may be implementable by fiat.

Suppose such a redistribution were accomplished by taxing wealth holders who both before and after the redistribution were risk neutral and received a risk-free rate of return on their assets. Such a redistribution (if carried out without administrative or other costs) is total surplus

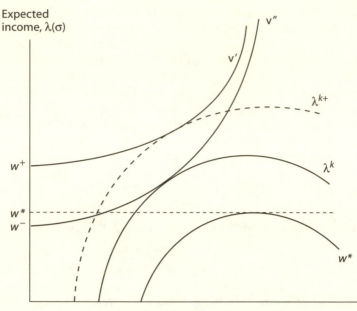

Figure 9.8 Increasing the assets of the employee from k to k^+ lowers the opportunity cost of capital and alters the optimal contract from wage employment to owner-operator

enhancing in the following sense: the opportunity cost of the assets foregone by those bearing the costs (ρ) would fall short of the returns enjoyed by the beneficiaries (we know this because at an interest rate of ρ the employee would have preferred ownership).

The source of the efficiency gain is the elimination of monitoring costs allowed by the substitution of self employment for wage employment. This gain is partially offset by the reassignment of control of the risk choice from the risk-neutral erstwhile owner to a risk-averse owner-operator, coupled with the elimination of the efficient insurance against risk provided by the assignment of full residual claimancy to the risk-neutral owner. Of course, the redistribution is not Pareto improving, as the wealthy would suffer a welfare loss. Moreover, despite the efficiency gains supported by the redistribution, it is difficult to imagine a feasible compensation of the losers, for the redistribution of assets was essential to generating the efficiency gains, and hence compensating the losers would also attenuate the efficiency gains.

I have abstracted from a less obvious effect of the redistribution: the beneficiaries of the asset transfer would as a result be less risk averse, given declining risk aversion. As owner-operators they would therefore choose higher levels of risk, and achieve higher expected incomes. For sufficiently large asset transfers, this reduced risk-aversion effect could induce erstwhile employees to become owners entirely independently of the reduced credit constraints effect above.

The hypothetical redistribution of assets is a vehicle for exploring the interaction of credit constraints, risk aversion, and ownership. It is not a policy design. Design of actual policies of asset distribution would need to address both its administrative aspects as well as general equilibrium and long-term dynamic effects not considered here. For example, whether the once-poor would adopt savings and investment strategies that would preserve or enhance their assets would need to be considered. The above analysis simply shows that they would not prefer to sell the assets should they acquire them at a cost of ρ or less. I return to questions of alternative structures of ownership and control of firms in chapter 10.

The models presented in this chapter predict not only that the asset-poor will pay higher rates when borrowing, or will be entirely excluded from credit markets, but also that the asset poor will also receive lower returns on their wealth. Adam Smith (1937[1776]: 93) had this in mind when he wrote "Money, says the proverb, makes money. When you have got a little it is often easy to get more. The great difficulty is to get that little." There are two reasons for this. First, those excluded from borrowing will have to invest whatever assets they have at the risk free rate, ρ, while among those with sufficient wealth to borrow, all except the marginal borrower can make a higher rate of return (assuming the lending market is competitive). Second, less wealthy and hence risk-averse individuals will select projects with lower expected incomes, as figure 9.6 shows. The prediction finds some empirical support in the United States even for quite wealthy individuals, and restricting the comparison to a given type of asset: corporate stocks held by high income individuals appreciate substantially faster than the stocks held by less wealthy individuals (Yitzhaki 1987).

Conclusion

The models presented here have clear implications for the inheritance of economic status from parents to children. Wealth differences may persist across generations due to the more limited opportunities to borrow and less lucrative investment opportunities of those who do not inherit wealth from their parents. A number of authors have developed these dynamic implications of the noncontractual aspects of financial markets.

Another implication of this chapter is that some distributions of wealth are more efficient than others. Where wealth disparities are sufficiently great that a small reduction in the assets of the rich would not preclude them from engaging in any technically feasible contracts, while granting additional assets to the poor would open up contractual opportunities for them, wealth redistribution can be a means of attenuating the incentive problems that arise in principal agent relationships. This conclusion challenges the efficiency-neutrality asserted by the Fundamental Theorem and the Coase theorem. It also raises doubts about a staple in the folk wisdom of economics, namely, the *efficiency-equality trade-off*. Where the assumptions of the two famous theorems fail to hold, so that the distribution of property rights may have effects on allocative efficiency, the efficiency-equality trade-off asserts that measures that increase equality will reduce efficiency. (This is "folk wisdom" because it is something that "everybody knows" and that still appears in many undergraduate textbooks, but nobody has demonstrated it formally, unlike the Fundamental Theorem. A cogent statement of the idea is Okun (1975).)

The thrust of the above models is not simply that wealth distribution may matter for allocative efficiency. To the extent that it does matter because it attenuates incentive problems arising from contractual incompleteness, it matters asymmetrically. More egalitarian distributions are likely to be more efficient because the asset-poor, not the wealthy, are precluded from engaging in efficient contacts. If a particular asset would be more productive if the relevant rights of control and residual claimancy were in the hands of a wealthy individual, there are few impediments to this coming about through voluntary exchange. In this case, competitive process will tend to assign property rights efficiently. The lack of a corresponding process in cases where an asset-poor individual would be the most efficient owner means that the needed remedy is to enhance the contractual opportunities of the asset-poor.

It is not difficult to think of exceptions to this statement. For example, concentrated wealth may allow the solution of collective action problems in the provision of public goods (Olson 1965). Thus, problems of monitoring corporate managers by owners would be attenuated if a few people were so wealthy that they owned entire firms outright (either because they are risk neutral, or because they have enough wealth to be sole owners without compromising portfolio diversification) (Demsetz and Lehn 1985). While these exceptions are important, there may be that a much more compelling reason to doubt the efficiency effects of egalitarian asset redistribution. The main efficiency gain allowed by concentrated wealth is that it assigns both control and residual claimancy to less risk-averse individuals who then offer contracts providing the less wealthy agents with valuable insurance in the form of fixed wage employment, crop shares, and other contracts that shield these risk-averse agents from income shocks.

The main drawback to this arrangement is that it requires that those performing noncontractible actions (work effort, for example) not be the residual claimants on the consequences of their actions. Incentives to perform the action well are compromised as a result. Wealth redistribution addresses this incentive problem but at a cost of reduced risk-taking. The static model used here fails to capture the long-term impact of the lower risk level; in a more appropriate dynamic setting, it could appear as a reduced level of innovation and as a result a lower level of long-term productivity growth.

Even where risk exposure is not involved, there is little reason to expect that the control of an asset and the residual claimancy on its income stream will be assigned to those who can make best use of the asset. Where the allocation of effort to a task by an agent and the allocation of resources to monitoring effort by a principal are nonoptimal (as in the model in chapter 8), a reallocation of residual claimancy and control to the agent may improve the allocation. But this reassignment of rights is sometimes impeded by the agent's restricted access to credit markets, as in the case of the Chilean land reform. Thus, the effort regulation market failure is not solved due to the credit market failure.

A challenge to economic policy and institutional design is to devise ways of addressing the problem of attenuated incentives to perform noncontractible actions when wealth is concentrated. An example that addresses both the hidden attributes and hidden actions problem are microfinance institutions. Some forms of these make all individuals in a self-selected group of borrowers responsible for the repayment of each member's loans. Another way of enhancing the contractual opportunities of nonwealthy agents is to link the pay of production team members to the observable level of production team output (making team members residual claimants on their efforts). Another challenge is to induce greater risk-taking by nonwealthy owners. A promising approach is enhanced insurance either against publicly observable exogenous shocks affecting the returns to one's productive assets (weather insurance for farmers, for example) or against shocks unrelated to one's ownership of productive assets (health insurance or insurance against local variations in home prices).[9] Pursuing these important issues would take us too far afield.

There is, however, an important implication of the models presented

---

[9] These issues are taken up in more detail in Bardhan, Bowles, and Gintis (2000). On microfinance, see the assessment of Morduch (1999).

here: government mandated transfers of property may implement efficiency improvements that would not have come about by voluntary exchange. The government's unique ability to coerce participants was crucial to the Pareto efficiency gains in the example given in table 9.2. Without the government's ability to extract tax-funded compensation of the erstwhile owner, it would have been impossible to ensure that the beneficiary of the redistribution would be the residual claimant on all of the risk entailed by her decisions. Governmental fiat also played an indispensable efficiency-enhancing role in the asset transfers allowing the technical efficiency gains (better projects, less monitoring) studied in the previous section, for, as we have seen, these transfers would not have come about through voluntary exchange. In chapter 14, I will return to this question, and suggest that governments and markets can play complementary roles in enhancing economic performance.

CHAPTER TEN

The Institutions of a Capitalist Economy

[The labor market] . . is a very Eden of the innate rights of man. There
. . . rule Freedom, Equality, Property. On leaving this sphere [to enter
the factory] we think we can perceive a change in the physiogamy of our
dramatis personae. He, who before was the money owner, now strides in
front as capitalist; the possessor of labor-power follows as his laborer.
            — Karl Marx, *Capital, I* (1867)

Remember that in a perfectly competitive market, it really does not
matter who hires whom; so have labor hire capital.
            — Paul Samuelson, "Wages and Interest" (1957)

IN 1921, a group of loggers, carpenters, and mechanics in Olympia,
Washington, formed the Olympia Veneer plywood cooperative. In return for an investment of $1000, a member gained the right to work in
the plant and to share equally in any profit.[1] Members wishing to leave
were to sell their shares, and prospective members, if approved by the
membership, were required to purchase shares, which by 1923 were
selling for $2550. In 1939, 250 workers in nearby Anacortes invested
$2000 each in a second cooperative plywood mill. Strong wartime de-
mand for plywood boosted the value of their shares to $28,000 in 1951,
and members were paying themselves at rates double the union wage in
nearby conventionally organized plywood mills. Stimulated by the success of Olympia Veneer and Anacortes, between 1949 and 1956 twenty-
one more coops entered the plywood industry in Washington and Ore-
gon, nine of them by buying out existing conventional firms. Some
coops had either transformed themselves into de facto conventional
firms or sold out to conventional firms. For example, by mid-century
the remaining handful of member-owners of Olympia Veneer were employing a thousand workers on conventional wage contracts, remaining
a cooperative in name only. In 1954, they sold their shares to the U.S.
Plywood Corporation; in the sale, twenty-three early members realized
a return averaging $652,000 (in 1954 dollars) on their initial invest-

---

The first epigraph is from Marx (1967:176), the second from Samuelson (1957:894).
[1] The best source on the plywood coops is a series of works by Craig and Pencavel
(Craig and Pencavel 1992, Craig and Pencavel 1995, Pencavel 2002), and on worker
owned cooperatives generally Dow (2002). I draw on these in what follows.

ment. Until the entire industry moved from the Northwest to the Southeast in the 1980s and 1990s, about half of the plywood firms were coops, the rest being conventional firms, some with unionized labor forces and some not. Though the coops and conventional firms used virtually identical machinery, the coops specialized in the more labor-intensive "sanded" plywood because, as one analyst of the coops commented, it "puts a premium on worker effort" (Bellas 1972:30).

The structure of the typical plywood coop was both egalitarian and democratic. With few exceptions, worker-owners received equal pay, and jobs were often rotated. Management was elected by the body of worker-members. Some nonmembers were hired under conventional wage contracts, their numbers making up an average of a quarter of the total workforce. High levels of productivity were maintained through a strong work ethic among members, enforced by peer pressure and mutual monitoring. The resulting saving in supervision costs was substantial: when one conventional firm converted to a coop, the number of supervisors was reduced to a quarter of its previous level. Shares being relinquished by retiring or departing members were advertised in local newspapers. Average share prices ranged from the equivalent of a single year's annual earnings to three times that amount. While considerable, these share values were substantially less than the present value of the difference between earnings in the coops and in the unionized mills: an individual who purchased a share and worked in a coop for a number of years had a much higher present value of income than an individual who put the value of a share in a Portland savings bank and worked at union wages in a conventional firm.

The coexistence of cooperatives and conventional firms producing the same goods using virtually identical technologies over a period of three-quarters of a century provides a remarkable opportunity for comparative institutional analysis. Conventional firms and cooperatives alike were able to attract both labor and capital over this period; but the firms differed markedly in a number of ways. The total factor productivity of the coops was substantially higher—the best estimates, by Craig and Pencavel (1995), ranging from 6 percent higher to 45 percent higher, depending on the method of estimation. Cooperatives also adjusted to insufficient product demand in a very distinctive way: rather than laying off members, they reduced pay of all workers, thereby spreading the impact of negative shocks among the membership. In this particular case, contrary to Samuelson, it mattered very much "who hires whom."

One of the tasks of a theory of economic institutions is to explain such things as the coexistence of coops and conventional firms in the plywood industry and the particular forms taken by conventional firms.

For example, given the superior total factor productivity of the coops, and the higher income returns that their members enjoyed, why did coops not eclipse the conventional firms? Answering questions such as this will typically involve explaining the creation and demise of firms of various kinds along with an analysis of how firms expand, fuse, and divide. Required for this, of course, is an analysis of how suppliers of capital, workers, and customers allocate themselves to firms of various types, in light of their beliefs concerning the expected costs and benefits associated with each.

In this chapter I will use the insights of the models of the credit and labor markets developed in chapters 8 and 9 to study the distribution of contracts in a capitalist economy. By the *distribution of contracts*, I mean the way that rights of control over assets and claims on the residual income of assets are assigned to particular individuals. The conventional and cooperative plywood firms exemplify differing assignments of the relevant rights: in the latter both residual claimancy and control is assigned to the member-owners who supply both labor and capital. In the former, the suppliers of capital and labor are distinct individuals, and residual claimancy and control is assigned to the capital suppliers. I use the terms *residual claimancy* and *control rights* rather than the more general term *ownership* to allow for situations in which control rights (disposition of the use of an asset, including its sale and excluding others from its use) and residual claimancy on the income generated by an asset are assigned to different parties.

The key idea in the chapter may be briefly summarized. Given the benefits of specialization and economies of scale, economic activity is necessarily social rather than individual, and the types of institutional arrangements governing production and exchange reflect the fact that the conflicts of interest among the participants are governed by incomplete contracts. The combined effect of incomplete contracts and conflicts of interest is that the determination of outcomes depends on who exercises power in the transaction. Power is generally exercised by those who hold the residual rights of control, meaning the right to determine what is not specified contractually.[2]

A first task, then, is to understand how these residual control rights are assigned to the various parties to a transaction. In the next section, I consider one possible way to address this question—the assumption of

---

[2] The assignment of control rights is neither sufficient nor necessary for the exercise of power, for the former gives an individual the legitimate authority to take an action, while the latter presumes that the action is effective, something for which legitimate authority is neither required nor adequate. It will be simpler to pursue this point after the concept of power has been introduced more precisely.

efficient design — and explain why it is misguided. While the assignment of control rights appears in all transactions, it is best explored by a study of the firm, to which I turn in the next section. The theories of the firm raise the question: how can power be exercised in competitive exchanges? I provide an answer (along with a definition of power) in the next section. I then explore the way that individual wealth levels determine how individuals come to hold the differing structural positions determined by the available contracts and how this process determines the distribution of contracts in an economy. Three important results will emerge. First, differences in wealth will be reflected in differences in the feasible set of contracts and the individual's choice of contracts from the feasible set. Second, some of these contractual arrangements will include a structure of authority such that participants on one side of the transaction have power (in a well-defined sense) over the others, even when the setting is competitive in the standard sense that there are no barriers to entry and exit. Thus, the fact that participation is voluntary does not prevent power from being exercised. Third, those exercising power will be those with greater wealth. In the penultimate section, I use the above analysis to explore the class structure of a capitalist economy.

Capitalism and Efficient Design

Why are cooperatives, partnerships, and other alternatives to the conventional capitalist firm of such limited importance in modern economies? And what accounts for the extraordinary economic growth of economies whose basic units of production are capitalist firms? It will be instructive to note how the models introduced thus far provide at least partial answers (and doing so will also place in perspective the market failures endemic to a capitalist economy identified in the pages above).

By a *capitalist economy*, I mean one in which the predominant form of economic organization is a firm in which the private owners of capital inputs exercise rights of residual claimancy and control over their assets, hiring other inputs, including labor in return for wages, to produce goods and services for sale with the intention of making a profit. Capitalism is an economic system of recent origin, having its roots in the urban economies of northern Italy, England, and the Low Countries half a millennium ago, and expanding rapidly first in Europe, later in the places where European migrants located, and eventually to most economies in the world. Other aspects of economic life sometimes said to define capitalism — individual gain-seeking in economic matters, market exchange, and the use of money—have been so ubiquitous in human history and have appeared in economic systems so vastly different from one another that a more precise definition of the type offered above seems valuable.

Capitalism inaugurated a new economic era as different from what preceded it as did the emergence of agriculture and the spread of the new institutions associated with it roughly eleven millennia before. The most striking concomitant of the "capitalist revolution" was the rapid increase in the productivity of labor, making possible an extraordinary and prolonged increase in material living standards. This productive accomplishment is not controversial even among the most severe critics of capitalism—Marx and Engels stressed it in the *Communist Manifesto*. The fact that not all capitalist economies have prospered in all centuries, and some other economic systems have also fostered sustained rapid growth in labor productivity (for example, China in the last third of the twentieth century) does not diminish capitalism's record over centuries as a uniquely productive system.

What capitalism accomplished, and what accounts for much of its productive success, is that it allowed some individuals to innovate and take risks on a grand scale with a reasonable expectation of reaping the rewards of a successful project while bearing the costs of a failure. Inequalities in wealth combined with credit and other financial markets (aided by the introduction of limited liability) allowed a single individual or a small group to amass substantial resources under unified direction. Labor markets allowed these material resources to be put to use to employ vast numbers of workers, thereby reaping both technological and organizational increasing returns. The wealth (and the creditworthiness) of those directing these business projects made the risks of innovation tolerable. It also allowed them to offer a modicum of de facto insurance to those whom they employed, in the form of the wage contract. The result was that those with nothing to supply other than their labor could be mobilized into projects the risks of which they would never have been willing to assume personally. For the first time in history, competition among members of the economic elite depended on one's success in introducing unprecedented ways of organizing production and sales, new technologies, and novel products. The success of these arrangements hinged critically on the relative security of possession associated with the rule of law, accomplished in large part by the increasingly powerful national states that grew in symbiosis with capitalist economic institutions.

Capitalism's success did not hinge on contracts being complete. Quite the contrary, capitalism fostered the rapid diffusion of new techniques through a competitive process whereby followers captured much of the increased surplus generated by innovators. This disequilibrium process of innovation and emulation implemented allocations vastly divergent from those implied by the static efficiency conditions characterizing the competitive equilibrium of an idealized Walrasian economy. Capitalism further enhanced productivity by greatly expanding the scope of both labor and financial markets. Both markets were notorious then as they are now for their characteristically incomplete nature of the relevant contracts, not for their conformity to Walrasian tenets. (Similarly, the rapid late-twentieth century growth of the Chinese economy was led by a novel organizational form—the "township and village enterprise"—characterized by incomplete contracts and a poorly defined amalgam of public and private property rights.)

Economists nonetheless often resort to what I term the *assumption of efficient design* as a handy analytical shortcut borrowed from evolutionary biology. Biologists sometimes presume that because living creatures are subject to natural selection, they will over time come to be optimally adapted to their environments. This efficient design assumption shortcuts the need to understand, on a case-by-case basis, the particulars of the process of genetic inheritance, the expression of the genotype in the phenotype, the nature of the selection process, and the like. Economists often invoke similar reasoning. We know from the Fundamental Theorem that if costlessly enforceable contacts regulate all actions that affect the well-being of others, competitive equilibria are Pareto efficient regardless of the distribution of wealth. But even where the complete contracting assumed by the Fundamental Theorem fails, the presumption of efficient design is often retained. The transactions cost economics of Oliver Williamson (1985:22) relies, he explains, "on the efficacy of competition to . . . sort between more and less efficient modes [of organization] and to shift resources in favor of the former." Holmstrom and Tirole (1989:63) describe the conventional view in economics this way: "[C]ontractual designs are created to minimize transactions costs. . . . This follows Coase's original hypothesis that institutions can best be understood as optimal accommodations to contractual constraints." But, they note, "How an efficient arrangement will be found is rarely if ever detailed" (p. 64).

Holmstrom and Tirole's caveat notwithstanding, it is conventional in economics to reason that where property in assets may be readily traded and there are no impediments to efficient bargaining, inefficient assignment of control and residual claimancy rights over assets will be eliminated by voluntary exchange of rights. This Coasean insight motivates the expectation that in competitive market economies with few impediments to private bargaining, assets will be held by those who can use them most effectively, irrespective of their wealth. If a residential tenant could make better use of the home as an owner, the home will be worth more to the tenant than to the owner, and hence one might expect the tenant to buy the asset.

The efficient design assumption thus achieves a dramatic simplification: without knowing in this particular case whether the assignment of property rights is efficient, we may presume either that it is, or that it is approximately so, or is tending in that direction. The presumption of efficiency can then guide us in singling out particular institutional features for analytical attention, while regarding others as ephemeral or exceptional. The widespread (often implicit) use of the efficient design assumption is explained in part by the fact that as an empirical matter it is virtually impossible to determine whether a particular institutional setup *is* efficient. Few attempts to do so exist, and even fewer enjoy the endorsement of a consensus of scholars in the relevant fields.

Reasons why plausible evolutionary processes would fail to support efficient institutions were outlined at the end of chapter 2. I can now explain a further problem with the efficient design assumption. The very informational asymmetries that make some assignments of property rights more efficient than others also systematically impede the Coasean process of productivity-enhancing bargained reassignment of property rights. The flaw in the reasoning underlying transaction economics and similar approaches is that where contracts are incomplete, there is no reason to think that competition (or any other process) will yield outcomes that are optimal (except in the tautological sense that they are the result of individual optimizing). In particular, nonwealthy agents may be credit constrained and hence may not find it possible to acquire those assets for which their exercise of residual claimancy and control rights would allow efficiency gains. Moreover, as we have seen in chapter 5, efficient bargaining is unlikely to obtain under even minimally realistic conditions. Contrary to a common misreading of Coase, in cases such as this the distribution of property rights *does* have effects on allocative efficiency. (The "theorem" is not wrong. The misreading is that the assumption that there are no impediments to efficient bargaining is violated in this case.)

The failure of the assumption of efficient design poses an intriguing challenge: if the structure of contracts and other institutions are not the result of some hidden algorithm that implements efficient solutions to allocational problems, what analytical tools can we deploy to explain empirically observed institutions and their evolution? This question will occupy the rest of the book, beginning with the analysis of the institutions of capitalist economies in this chapter and moving on to the question of the emergence, evolution, and extinction of institutions in the next three chapters, concluding with an analysis of contemporary and novel institutional configurations.

In the framework to be developed, it will matter "who hires whom" because in a world of incomplete contracts, the assignment of control rights gives one or another party the power to determine whatever is not specified contractually. Samuelson's claim is true in the Walrasian model because in that framework the notion of "hiring" simply means "buying." "What does it mean," Oliver Hart (1995:62) asked, "to put someone 'in charge' of an action or decision if all actions can be specified in a contract?" This elementary point also explains why, in Marx's terms, contractual transactions on competitive markets appear to be a free exchange among equals ("a very Eden of the innate rights of man"), while in the workplace the two parties to the employment contract take on a different appearance: the employer is boss, and the employee "his laborer."

FIRMS: WHY CAPITAL HIRES LABOR

As if responding to Samuelson, John Kenneth Galbraith (1967:47) chided economists for not having asked "why power is associated with some factors [of production] and not with others." A useful starting point in providing an answer is what I earlier (chapter 8) termed the Marx-Coase-Simon theory of the employment relationship. Its key feature is that the firm is represented as a group of suppliers of inputs to a common production process whose activities are coordinated by means of an authority structure rather than by market exchanges governed by complete contracts.[3] Modern versions include approaches based on asymmetric (or nonverifiable) information and the resulting contractual incompleteness and misaligned incentives in labor and credit markets analyzed in chapters 8 and 9. Other contributions stress the fact that the parties supplying factors of production to the firm cannot credibly commit not to exploit the reduction in the fallback position of members of a firm who make investments in transaction-specific productive assets. (Transaction-specific investments were introduced as an impediment to efficient bargaining in chapter 5.)

The central analytical problem is to understand how the structure of firms addresses the conflicts and incentive problems arising from the fact that because labor, credit, and other contracts are incomplete, those with decision-making authority in the firm have power over other people's money, other people's assets, and other people's labor. An important question, then, is why is it generally the case that in capitalist economies control rights are not assigned to those who work in the firms but

---

[3] Major contributions are Alchian and Demsetz (1972), Williamson (1985), Milgrom (1988), Grossman and Hart (1986), and Hart (1995). There are differences among these authors, but they share what I have called the Marx-Coase-Simon conception of the firm.

rather to those who supply capital to the firm, or their representatives. Four approaches to answering this question stress (respectively) *wage employment as a form of insurance for risk averse workers*, the *labor-effort monitoring problem*, the *problem of holdup due to transaction-specific assets*, and *credit constraints facing the suppliers of labor*.[4]

The first approach, which may be traced to Frank Knight (1921), explains the structure of the firm by two facts: first, the income flowing from a joint production process varies stochastically, and second, the cost of bearing this risk is greater for the suppliers of labor than for the suppliers of capital. The fixed-wage contract provides insurance against variations in earnings, and this insurance is more valuable to the suppliers of labor than it is costly for the suppliers of capital to provide.[5] The underlying logic of this approach was presented in the penultimate section of chapter 9, where risk aversion explained why labor suppliers might not become residual claimants on the income they generated even if this would allow technical efficiency gains. The fixed-wage contract necessarily makes the suppliers of capital the residual claimants on the income stream of the production process. This being the case, an arrangement in which the capital suppliers also exercise control over the relevant assets reduces the cost of attracting capital to the project. (Being residual claimant on the income stream of an asset that one does not control will be unattractive to investors if, as is generally the case, the manner of use of the asset is not subject to complete contracting.) This approach is readily extended to cases in which labor suppliers bear some risk either as partial residual claimants on the firm's income (profit sharing) or because their pay is based in part on a noisy signal of their own performance. The basic idea is that the structure of the firm is an accommodation to differing levels of risk aversion among the input suppliers.

According to a second approach, that of Armen Alchian and Harold Demsetz (1972), the assignment of control and residual claimancy is explained by the team nature of production and the advantages of having the residual claimant monitor labor effort. If the benefits of specialization and economies of scale preclude individual production, it will be

---

[4] The list is not exhaustive. A fuller treatment is provided in Putterman and Dow (2000).

[5] The fact that the suppliers of labor are risk averse and while capital suppliers are less so does not require that risk aversion be declining in income and that the former be poorer than the latter. The greater risk aversion of the suppliers of labor (as measured, as in chapter 9, by their marginal rate of substitution between expected income and risk) could as well be explained by their greater exposure to risk due to the ability of capital suppliers to reduce the variability of their income by diversified ownership and the impediments workers face in diversifying their sources of earnings.

beneficial to all participants to devise a method of preventing free riding by production team members. Shirking by team members may be curbed by a monitor, but the monitor's effort levels are also variable and not subject to contract: "who will monitor the monitor?" Alchian and Demsetz ask (p. 781). A solution is to pay the team members a fixed wage and let the monitor be residual claimant on the income of the team. To be effective, the monitor must have the authority to revise the contract terms of individual members, including terminating their membership in the team. The assignment of rights that Alchian and Demsetz call "the classical capitalist firm" controlled by an owner-monitor thus solves the shirking problem. Note that the argument does not require that the monitor own the capital supplied to the firm. However, it is a simple matter to show that as long as contracts concerning the care and use of assets are incomplete, a misalignment of incentives will result if the asset owner and the holder of rights of control and residual claimancy are different parties. The problem will be eliminated if the party holding the residual claimancy and control rights is also the owner of the assets.

Two problems with the Alchian and Demsetz firm as an anti-shirking device may be mentioned. First the "classical" firms explained by this approach play a minor role in modern economies, where monitoring of work effort is rarely performed by owners but rather by large numbers of individuals most of whose pay varies little if at all with the performance of those they supervise. Second, as was suggested in chapter 4, mutual monitoring by teammates may be effective if the team is the residual claimant on the income it generates. The experimental evidence from public goods games with punishment (chapter 3) provides support for this alternative model of monitoring, as does the success of the plywood cooperatives mentioned above. The same monitoring problem posed by Alchian and Demsetz might better be solved by making team members residual claimants, letting them hire a manager to whom they could report infractions of work norms by their team mates (if direct methods of social pressure failed), offering a substantial employment rent to the manager who would be retained as long as the (observable) performance of the firm is satisfactory.[6]

The third approach holds that control rights will be assigned to the party for whom protection of the value of transaction-specific investments is the greatest. Recall (from chapter 5) that transaction-specific

[6] Alchian and Demsetz assume that such an arrangement would perform worse than their specialized monitor-owner, but their reasoning — that in large groups of residual claimants there will be strong incentives to shirk — is not supported by either public goods experiments in large groups (Isaac, Walker, and Williams 1994) or the effectiveness of group pay in work teams of substantial size (Hansen 1997, Prendergast 1999).

assets are those whose value in a particular transaction is greater than in their next best alternative. An employee's knowledge of his employer's custom software is an example, as is the investment a firm makes in the recruitment and training of a particular employee, or the location of the firm to take advantage of a particular pool of labor. Transaction-specific investments result in a reduction in the fallback position of the investor compared to the fallback that would have obtained had the investment been general rather than specific. As a result, if a transaction satisfies all relevant participation constraints as equalities ex ante, then the project will generate positive rents ex post, that is, once transaction-specific investments have been made. If the parties cannot commit to a division of these rents ex ante, they will be bargained over ex post. Those making specific investments and experiencing a decline in their fallback position as a result will then be vulnerable to what is termed *hold-up* by the other party, that is, renegotiation of the terms of the transaction in light of the ex post fallbacks. The result (as shown in chapter 5) is that general investments will be favored and there will be a tendency to underinvest in transaction-specific assets.

Now suppose it is the case that for one of the input suppliers, the opportunities for transaction-specific investments are very limited or zero, while specific investments by the other contribute greatly to the joint output of the firm. If the firm is structured so that the input supplier with these specific investment opportunities is granted all the bargaining power, he will capture the entire surplus ex post, irrespective of his investment decision, and hence will have no incentive to under invest in specific assets ex ante. If both suppliers could contribute more to the project by making transaction-specific investments, allocating all of the bargaining power to one will result in zero investment by the other, so the allocation of all control rights to one or the other is not likely to be joint-surplus maximizing. If, as is commonly assumed, the suppliers of capital have the opportunity to make more important transaction-specific investments than the suppliers of labor, then the capital suppliers should have all the bargaining power, and, by implication, control rights in the firm.

This approach thus derives the distribution of control rights in the firm from the extent to which specific investments are capable of enhancing the productive value of labor, capital goods, and inputs supplied by other participants in the firm. This may appear to be a case where technology (as manifested in which inputs are enhanced most by transaction-specific investments) is determining institutional structure (as reflected in the distribution of control rights in the firm). But as Ugo Pagano (1993) pointed out, the causal relation may also operate from institutional structure to technology. Where employees have strong guarantees against job termination, workers will more readily invest in transaction-specific skills and hence firms will have an incentive to adopt technologies using such skills. Pagano shows that many such "technological-institutional equilibria" are possible, some in which capital suppliers have control rights and capital is the more specific factor, and others in which labor is the more transaction-specific factor and workers hold the control rights.

The asset-specificity approach was initially developed to explain the boundaries of the firm and relationships among firms rather than relationships between suppliers of capital and labor in a firm. In many respects it does a better job at illuminating its initial subject matter. One component of the theory is uncontroversial: there is a substantial loss in value associated with the installation of even general purpose machinery—typically, well over half of the initial cost (Asplund 2000). But it is not clear how these investments are vulnerable to hold-up by the firm's employees. Should one or all of them quit, the option for the firm is not to scrap its equipment or sell it on the second hand market but rather to pay the turnover costs to replace the workforce. These, typically, are much smaller than the losses entailed by scrapping the equipment, perhaps of the order of 5 to 10 percent of the employee's first year's pay (Malcomson 1999). A second problem with the asset specificity account is the tension between the assumption that ex ante, the members of the firm cannot commit to an ex post division of rents but they *can* commit to a bargaining framework that ensures the same result.

The final approach to the theory of the firm holds that the assignment of rights of residual claimancy and control to the suppliers of capital results because the cost of capital supplied to a firm controlled by its employees will be higher than the capital costs faced by an otherwise identical firm controlled by its capital suppliers. This follows from the fact that labor suppliers lack wealth, along with the result (from chapter 9) that for a project of given size and quality, the competitively determined interest cost of a loan varies inversely with the wealth of the borrower. The high implicit price of capital to the suppliers of labor is suggested by the undervaluation of the shares of the plywood cooperatives mentioned at the outset. The plywood coops point to a more subtle aspect of the problem. Banks lending to the plywood coops often felt it necessary to conclude agreements with the members of the coop directly rather than simply with the management, given that the individual members could readily terminate the contract of the manager. The added difficulty of these arrangements surely raised the cost of loans (Gintis 1989a). Though management of conventional firms may also be dismissed by the owners, the heterogeneity of interests among the labor suppliers (and hence the scope for sequentially inconsistent decision making) is considerably greater than among capital suppliers. This is true in part because the latter have an arms-length relationship to the project and can readily agree on the objective of maximizing the rate of return on their assets, while labor suppliers' assets are concentrated in the project, and they can only supply labor by being present in the firm.[7]

Separately and (more likely) jointly, these four accounts appear to provide a convincing explanation of the tendency for residual rights of control in firms to be assigned to the suppliers of capital rather than by the suppliers of labor.[8] What has not been explained, however, is why control rights confer power. As an empirical matter, the firm appears to be a political institution in the sense that some members of the firm routinely give commands with the expectation that they will be obeyed, while others are constrained to follow. To say that the manager has the right to decide what the worker will do means only that he has the legitimate authority to do this, not the power to secure compliance. Given that the manager and the monitor are sharply restricted in the kinds of punishment they can inflict, and given that the employee is free to leave, the fact that orders are typically obeyed is a puzzle.

Why, in Coase's initial formulation, is the command of the manager (to move "from department Y to department X") obeyed? Noticing the lack of a good answer, Alchian and Demsitz challenged the Coasean idea that the firm is a mini "command economy," suggesting that the employment contract is no different in this respect from other contracts:

> The firm . . . has no power of fiat, no authority, no disciplinary action any different in the slightest degree from ordinary market contracting between any two people. . . . Wherein then is the relationship between a grocer and his employee different from that between a grocer and his customer? (1972:777)

Hart offers the following response to Alchian and Demsetz:

> [T]he reason that an employee is likely to be more responsive to what his employer wants than a grocer . . . is to what his customer wants is that the employer . . . can deprive the employee of the assets he works with and hire another employee to work with these assets, while the customer can only deprive the grocer of his custom and as long as the customer is small, it is presumably not very difficult for the grocer to find another customer. (1989:1771)

---

[7] The heterogeneous preferences of the labor suppliers may make the exercise of control rights more costly or lead to inconsistency in the decision-making process, providing another reason why control rights are assigned to capital suppliers.

[8] I say "appear to" because these models have been rarely used to explain variations in firm structure empirically, and when they have, the results are mixed (Prendergast 1999).

Hart motivates the difference between the grocer and the employer by the assumption that the employee needs access not just to *a* job (and hence *some* assets) but to *this particular employer's assets*. This might be the case due to a complementarity between the two (the employee may have made an investment in acquiring a transaction-specific skill that is of value only when combined with this particular asset, for example). Other less obvious (and probably more important) examples come to mind. Excluding an employee from access to a particular asset may require the employee to relocate, disrupting family and friendships. The loss of a job may also harm the employee's reputation. While transaction-specific investments of this type undoubtedly explain some authority relationships — in company towns, and for some professional jobs and managers, for example — the explanation seems insufficiently general to provide an adequate explanation of the entire authority structure of the firm, especially in large urban labor markets and for nonprofessional employees. In the next section I develop a complementary explanation based on the fact that the employee excluded from access to *this asset* may not find access to *any asset* even in a competitive economy in which transaction-specific assets are absent. This will require clarity about what we mean by power. Even the author of the most famous definition of power, Robert Dahl, expressed concerns about the vagueness of the term.[9] Yet "power" seems difficult to dispense with and is increasingly widely used, even in economics.

Short-Side Power in Competitive Exchange

Common usage suggests several characteristics that must be present in any plausible representation of power. First, power is *interpersonal*, an aspect of a relationship among people, not a characteristic of a solitary individual. Second, the exercise of power involves the *threat and use of sanctions*.[10] Third the concept of power should be *normatively indeterminate*, allowing for Pareto-improving outcomes (as has been stressed by students of power from Hobbes to Parsons) but also susceptible to arbitrary use to the detriment of others and in violation of ethical principles. Finally, to be relevant to economic analysis, power must be *sus-*

[9] Dahl's definition (1957:202–203): "A has power over B to the extent that he can get B to do something that B would not otherwise do."

[10] Indeed, many political theorists regard sanctions as the defining characteristic of power. Lasswell and Kaplan (1950:75) make the use of "severe sanctions . . . to sustain a policy against opposition" a defining characteristic of a power relationship, and Parsons (1967:308) regards "the presumption of enforcement by negative sanctions in the ease of recalcitrance" a necessary condition for the exercise of power.

tainable as a Nash equilibrium of an appropriately defined game. Power may be exercised in disequilibrium situations, of course, but as an enduring aspect of social structure, it should reflect best response behaviors. The fact that sanctions are essential to the exercise of power makes it distinct from other means of securing advantage, including those such as wealth that may operate even in the complete absence of strategic interaction, as in a Walrasian market setting.

The following sufficient condition for the exercise of power captures these four desiderata: *For B to have power over A, it sufficient that, by imposing or threatening to impose sanctions on A, B is capable of affecting A's actions in ways that advance B's interests, while A lacks this capacity with respect to B* (Bowles and Gintis 1992). The definition clarifies the difference between the employer and the grocer in Hart's response to Alchian and Demsetz: the sanctions imposed on the employee by depriving him of access to the capital good are severe, while those imposed on the grocer by the departing customer are negligible or zero. The reason why the consumer does not impose a sanction on the grocer is that the grocer (in competitive equilibrium) was maximizing profits by selecting a level of sales that equates marginal cost to the exogenously given price, and, this being the case, a small variation in sales has only a second-order effect on profits. Let us check to see that this conception of power applies to the employment relationship in which transaction specificity is absent.

Returning to the model of chapter 8, we know that $e^* > e$: in equilibrium the worker works harder than he would have in the absence of the employer's incentive strategy. Thus, we know that in equilibrium the employee receives a rent ($v^* > z$) and that by working harder than e the employee has allowed the employer a higher profit rate, $\pi^* > \pi(\underline{e}, \underline{w})$. These results together imply that employer has caused the worker to act in the employer's interest by credibly threatening to sanction the worker. The employee lacks this capacity with respect to the employer, for were the employee to threaten the employer with a sanction should he not raise the wage (to damage his machinery or beat him up or simply to work less hard), the threat would not be credible. The employer would simply refuse to respond, knowing that it would not be in the interest of the employee to carry out the threat.

Note that the exercise of power allows a Pareto improvement over a counterfactual condition in which power cannot be exercised, namely, that the worker is hired at his reservation wage w and works at the reservation effort level e. This follows directly as we know from $v^* > v(\underline{e}, \underline{w}) = z$ and $\pi^* > \pi(\underline{e}, \underline{w})$ that both expected worker lifetime utility and firm profits are higher in equilibrium (with power being exercised) than at the (power-absent) reservation position. This is yet another example of a situation in which the exercise of power helps address coordination failures, albeit sometimes with objectionable consequences for the distribution of benefits. An example follows.

Recall the analysis of workplace amenities in chapter 8. Suppose that α refers not to some innocuous workplace amenity such as the quality of the music on the office sound system but to management practices affecting the employee's dignity, such as not being subjected to racial insults, sexual harassment, or other on-the-job indignities. In equilibrium we know that $\pi_\alpha = 0$ and $v_\alpha > 0$. It follows that the employer can inflict first-order costs on the worker (by lowering α a small amount) at second-order cost to himself (the costs are second order because $\pi_\alpha = 0$). Thus, the competitive equilibrium in an employment relationship gives the employer the capacity not only to exercise power to attenuate coordination problems but also to exercise power *arbitrarily*, namely, to inflict costs on another at no cost to himself.

Thus, the strategic interaction between the employer and employee allows the exercise of power in a manner conforming to the four desiderata outlined above: sanctions are credibly threatened (and used) in a strategic interaction describing a Nash equilibrium, and the resulting exercise of power is Pareto improving over a reasonable counterfactual but may also be used arbitrarily.

It is easy to check the that power in the sense defined may be exercised in the contingent renewal model of credit market in chapter 9 as well. The lender offers the borrower terms that are preferred to the fallback position, and as a result the borrower pursues a less risky strategy than would have been the case had the lender not offered a rent or been restricted to a single-period interaction. Where the borrower's participation constraint holds as an equality, power in the sense defined cannot be exercised for the simple reason that the borrower is indifferent between the current transaction and the next best alternative, so the only sanction permitted in a liberal economy — revision or termination of the contract — has no force.

A less obvious case concerns the power of the consumer, sometimes summarized by the term "consumer sovereignty." Recall the principal agent model involving difficult-to-measure product quality (chapter 7). In equilibrium, the buyer pays the seller a price exceeding the seller's next best alternative. The prospect of losing the resulting rent conferred by the buyer on the seller induces the seller to provide higher quality than would have been provided in the absence of the threatened sanction. In this case the buyer has exercised power over the seller.[11]

As the example suggests, the buyer may exercise power over the seller

---

[11] Gintis (1989b) develops this case.

whenever the buyer's threat to switch to an alternative seller is credible and inflicts a cost on the seller. Consider two monopolistically competitive sellers (i.e., firms facing downward-sloping demand functions) and a consumer who is indifferent between purchasing from one or the other. Both sellers have chosen a level of output to maximize profits, setting marginal cost equal to marginal revenue (which is less than the price because the demand curve is downward sloping). For both sellers, price thus exceeds marginal cost ($p > mc$), so the consumer's choice confers a rent on one and deprives the other of the rent. The reader may wonder how the rent can arise if the firm has chosen the output level to maximize profits, each setting $\pi_q = 0$. But the buyer's switch from one to the other seller is not a movement along a demand function (the basis of the firm's output choice) but rather a horizontal shift in the demand function (inward for the firm the consumer left, outward for the firm to which he switched). The result is that the fortunate firm is able to sell one more unit at the going price, capturing the rent, $p - mc$.

Ironically, the idealized Walrasian conditions under which consumer sovereignty is said to hold give the consumer no power in the sense defined here, while deviations from the canonical competitive assumption that price equals marginal cost creates an environment in which the consumer may exercise power. Of course the strategic position of the consumer as one of many principals facing a single agent is quite unlike that of the employer facing many potential employees or the lender facing many potential borrowers. A single consumer will not generally be in a position to command the supplier to improve the product quality and expect the supplier to obey. The power of consumers is thus limited by the limited ability of the many principals to act in a coordinated fashion. I will come back to this point when I consider the term *market power*.

The three cases for which I have analyzed the exercise of power — by the buyer over the seller, the lender over the borrower, and the employer over the employee — are members of a generic class of power relationships that are sustainable in the equilibrium of a system of voluntary competitive exchanges. In all three, those with power are transacting with agents who receive rents and hence are not indifferent between the current transaction and their next best alternative. This being the case, there must exist other identical agents who are quantity constrained, namely, the unemployed, those excluded from the loan market or restricted in the amount they can borrow, and sellers who fail to make a sale. For this situation to characterize an equilibrium it must be that markets do not clear, which, as we have seen, will be the case. Those holding power in these cases are those on the side of the market for which in equilibrium the number of desired transactions is least, or what is termed the *short side of the market*. Note that the short side may be either demand (the employer, the buyer) or supply (the lender). Those on the *long side* of the market will be of two types: those transacting the amount they wish, and those who are quantity constrained (either excluded or transacting less then they wish).

To underline the relationship between nonclearing markets and the exercise of power, Gintis and I refer to the power of the buyer, the lender, and the employer based on the contingent renewal models in the previous chapters as *short side power*. Power as we define it can be exercised in other ways, even when markets clear. A prime example is provided by the case of optimal job fees (chapter 8), in which the fee eliminates the job rent ex ante (so the market clears, the worker being indifferent between taking the job or not), but an ex post rent nonetheless exists, giving the employer the ability to sanction the employee. A job fee of this type is a pure case of an employee's transaction-specific investment, and the basis of the power of the employer in this case is an example of Hart's reasoning, above.

All three of those exercising power in the above examples—buyer, lender, employer—have in common that they contribute money to the transaction—the buyer's purchase price, the lender's loan, the employer's wage offer. In each of the three cases, money is exchanged for a good or service not specified in a complete contract: product quality, the promise to repay, and labor effort, respectively. This may seem an analytical foundation for the familiar adage that "money talks," but the conclusion is misleading. Recall that in the centrally planned Communist economies it was generally the case that consumer durables (and many other consumer goods) sold below market clearing prices. The resulting excess demand was allocated through a process of queuing and by other means (Kornai 1980). In this case the producers (sellers) were on the short side of the market, and those bringing money to the transaction, the buyers, were the longsiders, some of whom failed to make a trade. The notorious inferiority in the quality of consumer goods in centrally planned economies by comparison to capitalist economies may be explained in part by the fact that consumers were longsiders in the former and shortsiders in the latter. Or to put it more graphically, one reason why Fords were better cars than their Cold War–era Russian equivalents is that in Russia customers waited in line to purchase Volgas while in the United States, Ford salesmen lined up to sell customers cars. Another reason is that in the United States workers waited in line to get jobs at Ford.

Other uses of the term *power* are common in economics. *Purchasing power* is just another word for one's budget constraint (or wealth), and it does not concern the exercise of sanctions or indeed any strategic interaction at all.[12] *Market power* arises in thin markets in which an actor can benefit by varying a price. In the standard monopolistic competition case the seller is said to have market power. The seller is less constrained in the sense that he faces a downward-sloping demand rather than horizontal demand function, while the consumer is more constrained in that there may be less choice among suppliers of close substitutes. But we have just seen that in this case, the consumer who switches from one seller to another confers a rent on his favored firm. (This why the Ford sales staff lines up to sell you cars.) Thus if the buyer can credibly threaten to withdraw the rent he may be able to exercise short side power over the seller. It thus is not clear how to reconcile usual notions of power — the use of sanctions to gain advantage — with the statement that the monopolist has power over the consumer.

Finally, there is the vague notion of *bargaining power*, typically meaning the share of the surplus that one gains in a bargain. Reflecting this usage, the exponents used in the "Nash product" to solve the extended Nash bargaining model in chapter 5 are said to refer to the bargaining power of the two. Used this way, bargaining power refers to outcomes — to *how much* advantage one may gain — rather than to any particular *means of attaining it* (for example, by threatening a sanction). If the bargaining problem is embedded in an on-going interaction, then bargaining power and short side power appear not only unrelated but even opposed. In the competitive equilibrium of the standard principal agent model, for example, the employer receives his fallback return (the zero profit condition) while the employee receives a rent ($v^* - z$). Therefore, the bargaining power perspective would say that the employee has all the bargaining power. But the short side power perspective would conclude that far from a sign that the employee is powerful, the rent conferred on the employee as a profit maximizing choice of the employer is the reason why the employer has power over the employee.

I mentioned above Robert Dahl's doubts about the possibility of a single definition of the term power. Here is what he said (Dahl 1957: 201) "[A] Thing to which people attach many labels with subtly or grossly different meanings . . . is probably not a Thing at all but many Things." The contrasting senses of bargaining power, market power, and short side power suggest he may have been right.

---

[12] A weakness of Dahl's definition of power (above, note 9) is that purchasing power is included: if I buy a commodity, there will be a whole series of effects through the economy that entail others doing things they would not otherwise have done. But to say that my purchase of bread is an exercise of power over some unknown wheat farmer with whom I do not interact strategically is to expand the concept of power beyond recognition.

The Distribution of Wealth
and the Distribution of Contracts

Thus far I have simply posited employers and employees, borrowers and lenders, without explaining how particular individuals come to occupy these positions. In the explanation that follows, the key idea is that the assignment of people to these and other economic positions is the result of individual optimization constrained by the available contracts and by one's assets. These assets include not only wealth as conventionally defined but other income-earning attributes such as one's skills and health. But to simplify I will confine attention to wealth.

The analysis I present is an adaptation to a modern capitalist economy of a model by Mukesh Eswaran and Ashok Kotwal (1986). Their work was stimulated by the observation that in agrarian economies, individuals typically allocate their time among various kinds of contracts, tilling their own land while also tilling others' land as a sharecropper or a wage worker, or possibly hiring others to assist them in tilling their own land. (The econometric studies of the effect of distinct contracts on productivity cited in chapters 8 and 9 made use of this fact.) The mix of contracts in which one engages is related to the amount of land one owns, as is suggested by the data in table 10.1, from the same Indian village you have encountered in previous chapters. In Palanpur, those owning more land rarely work for wages ("hires out") and typically hire others to augment their own labor working their own land ("hire in"). None owned large plots; more than half of those surveyed owned less than half an acre (Lanjouw and Stern 1998:46).

The model I present will show that the allocation of time among the available contracts that maximizes the individual's utility depends on the level of the individual's wealth. Individuals will sort themselves into six classes that I define as *pure wage worker, mixed independent producer and wage worker, independent producer, small capitalist, pure capitalist*, and *rentier capitalist*.

On grounds of empirical realism, I assume that contracts are incomplete in two ways. First, if one hires labor, the employee must be supervised, and (borrowing a page from Alchian and Demsetz, above) I assume that only the residual claimant (the employer) can do the supervision (introducing the complication of hired supervisors would add nothing). To distinguish nonsupervisory labor from supervisory labor, I use the term *productive labor* to refer to the labor that appears as an argument of the production function. Second, all individuals may borrow and lend at the same interest rate, r, but the maximum borrowing is determined by one's own total wealth (irrespective of its use). At the

TABLE 10.1
Land ownership and wage labor in Palanpur

Land owned (acres)	Hires in	Hires in and hires out	Hires out only
None	0.25	0.21	0.54
≤0.47	0.30	0.37	0.33
>0.47	0.81	0.15	0.04

The entries are the fraction of the wealth class hiring labor, hiring themselves out, and both hiring in and hiring out.

beginning of each period, an individual may borrow to hire labor or to rent capital goods owned by others, paying the wages and the rent at the beginning of the period and repaying the loan with certainty at the end of the production period. One may also rent one's own factors to others or work for wages (being paid at the beginning of the period).

The relationship between inputs and a single output is described by the linear homogeneous production function $q = f(k, n)$, where n is total productive labor (own and hired), k is the amount of a homogeneous capital good devoted to production, and output, q, is increasing and concave in its arguments. The output price is normalized to unity. To produce at all one must spend a start up cost, K (those who do not engage in production on their own account, hiring out their own labor and any capital owned do not incur the cost K). One may divide one's total time (normalized to unity) into the portion working as self-employed, l, employed by others, t, supervising one's employees, s, or resting, R. The amount of supervision one does varies with the amount of labor hired, L; that is, $s = s(L)$ with $s' > 0$ and $s'' > 0$, $s(0) = 0$ and $s'(0) < 1$. The required level of supervision is just sufficient to induce hired workers to exert as much effort as workers who are residual claimants on their labor effort. Thus total productive labor, $n = l + L$.

The individual's access to credit, B, is constrained by his wealth, measured in units of the capital good owned, $\underline{k}$, so $B = B(\underline{k})$ with $B' > 0$ and $B(0) = 0$ (those without assets cannot borrow, and the borrowing limit increases with assets). Because each individual begins the period with just the asset $\underline{k}$, the choice of contracts is constrained by the borrowing limit. Let w and v be the exogenously determined prices of labor and capital goods. Then if the individual chooses to produce (that is, to pay the start up cost, K, and to devote some labor time to his own project) the borrowing constraint is,

$$B(\underline{k}) \geq w(L - t) + v(k - \underline{k}) + K \qquad (10.1)$$

The first term on the right-hand side is the wage cost of hiring in (net of any hiring out the individual does), while the second term is the rental cost of the use of capital goods additional to those owned by the individual. Of course, these two terms may take either sign.

The (risk-neutral) individual's utility function is additive in income and the utility of rest: $U = Y + u(R)$, with $u' > 0$ and $u'' < 0$. (To ensure that $R > 0$, I also assume that $u'(0)$ is infinite.) If the individual chooses to produce, at the end of the production period his utility will be,

$$\omega_1 = f(k, (l+L)) - (1+r)\{w(L-t) + v(k-\underline{k}) + K\} + u(R) \quad (10.2)$$

where the second term on the right-hand side is end-of-period cost of repaying the loan incurred at the beginning of the production period (production becomes available only at the end of the period, and for convenience I assume that consumption and the enjoyment of rest also occurs at that time). If, instead, the individual hires out as a wage worker and rents out any capital goods owned, the end-of-period utility will be

$$\omega_0 = (1 + r)(wt + v\underline{k}) + u(R) \quad (10.3)$$

where the interest factor appears because wages and rents are paid at the beginning of the period, and hence may earn a return during the production period.

Considering first the case described by eq. (10.2), the individual's utility maximization problem is to select k, R, t, L, and l to maximize eq. (10.2) subject to the borrowing constraint (10.1) and a time-budget constraint. Using the accounting relationship

$$l \equiv 1 - s(L) - t - R \quad (10.4)$$

as a definition of l (not a constraint), we can express the time budget constraint as a non-negativity constraint on self employed labor, l:

$$1 - s(L) - t - R \geq 0 \quad (10.5)$$

as well as the obvious other constraints: $k \geq 0$, $L \geq 0$, and $t \geq 0$.

The individual will thus maximize eq. (10.2) subject to the constraints (10.1) and (10.5). Let μ and λ be the Lagrange multipliers associated with the constraints (10.5) and (10.1), respectively. Using eq. (10.4) to eliminate l (substituting the right-hand side of eq. (10.4) for l in the production function) and defining $\mathcal{L}_i$ as the derivative of the implied Lagrangean expression with respect to variable i, we have the first order conditions

$$\mathcal{L}_k = f_k - (1 + r + \lambda)v = 0 \qquad (10.6)$$

$$\mathcal{L}_L = f_n\{1 - s'(L)\} - (1 + r + \lambda)w - \mu s'(L) \leq 0 \qquad (10.7)$$
(satisfied as an equality if $L > 0$)

$$\mathcal{L}_R = -f_n + u'(R) - \mu = 0 \qquad (10.8)$$

$$\mathcal{L}_t = -f_n + w(1 + r + \lambda) - \mu \leq 0 \qquad (10.9)$$
(satisfied as an equality if $t > 0$)

Eqs. (10.6) and (10.8) are equalities because we assume that $k > 0$ and $0 < R < 1$.

The ordering of individuals into classes will depend on which constraints are binding and which of these equations are instead satisfied as inequalities. But before proceeding with this analysis, consider the economic interpretation of these first order conditions. Eq. (10.6) requires that the marginal product of the capital good be equal to its price times one plus the cost of borrowing, which is the rate of interest plus the shadow price of capital (λ). We can interpret λ in this way because as the Lagrange multiplier for the borrowing constraint, it indicates the marginal increment in utility associated with a marginal relaxation of the borrowing constraint. Note that if one's own labor is devoted to production with one's own capital goods ($l > 0$) the nonnegativity constraint on l is nonbinding, so in this case $\mu = 0$. Then eq. (10.7), which is satisfied as an equality when labor is hired in, requires that the marginal product of labor (net of the supervision costs of hired labor) equal the wage rate multiplied by one plus the cost of borrowing. For the case where $\mu = 0$, eq. (10.8) is the familiar condition that marginal productivity of labor equals marginal utility of leisure. Eq. (10.9) requires that if one is hiring out and at the same time working on one's own account, the marginal product of labor must be equal to the wage rate times one plus the cost of borrowing. (Remember: wages are paid at the beginning of the period, while the marginal product occurs at the end of the period.)

This is a standard Kuhn-Tucker problem; for given values of the exogenous variables v, w, r, and $\underline{k}$, it has a unique solution. This means that by varying the wealth level we can determine the contracts in which the individual engages. There are five distinct regions, each defined by a range of wealth values, as illustrated in figure 10.1.

For asset-poor individuals, the start-up cost of own production may be such that the most profitable use of one's resources is to hire oneself out as a wage worker and rent out any owned capital goods. In other words, the maximum of eq. (10.3) may exceed the maximum of eq. (10.2). These individuals are *pure wage workers*. If K is sufficiently small relative to $\underline{k}$ that production on one's own account is justified, and if $\underline{k}$ is less than a critical value k_1, the individual is a *mixed inde-*

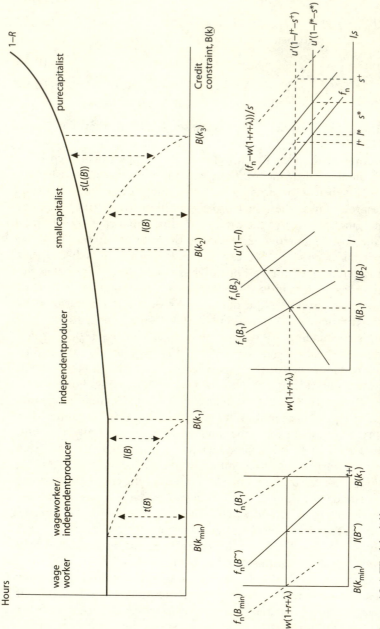

Figure 10.1 Wealth differences account for differing contractual choices. The top panel shows total hours worked, and the distribution of those hours between hiring out, working for oneself, and supervising others, for various levels of wealth. The lower left panel shows how differing wealth levels affect the allocation of time between hiring out (wage work) and working for oneself (independent production). The middle panel shows the independent producer's choice of working hours. The lower right panel shows the capitalist's allocation of time betweenn productive labor and supervision.

TABLE 10.2
The wealth-contracts correspondence

Position	Contracts	Wealth
Pure wage worker	$t > 0, l = k = s(L) = 0, \mu > 0,$ $\lambda = 0$	$[0, k_1]$
Wage worker/independent producer	$t > 0, l > 0, k > 0, s(L) = 0, \mu = 0,$ $\lambda > 0$	$[0, k_1]$
Independent producer	$t = 0, l > 0, k > 0, s(L) = 0, \mu = 0,$ $\lambda > 0$	$(k_1, k_2]$
Petty capitalist	$t = 0, l > 0, k > 0, s(L) > 0, \mu = 0,$ $\lambda > 0$	$(k_2, k_3]$
Pure capitalist	$t = l = 0, k > 0, s(L) = 1 - R,$ $\mu > 0, \lambda > 0$	$(k_3, k_4]$
Rentier capitalist	$t = l = 0, k > 0, s(L) = 1 - R,$ $k < \underline{k}, \mu > 0, \lambda = 0$	$> k_4$

pendent producer and wage worker. Individuals in this class will both hire themselves out and work their own capital goods, the division of time between these two activities being given by the conditions (10.8) and (10.9) with $\mu = 0$. These require one's labor be allocated so that the marginal returns to both types of labor be equated, and also be equal to the marginal utility of rest: $w(1 + r + \lambda) = f_n = u'$.

Note that for values of owned wealth in this region, the fact that the production function is homogeneous and the factor prices are exogenous determines the ratio of capital to productive labor which will be used, irrespective of the wealth level.[13] Thus the greater the individual's wealth, the more time he works with his own capital goods and the less time he devotes to wage labor. So, as k increases to k_1, t falls to zero. The critical value of $\underline{k}$ is defined by $f_n = w(1 + r + \lambda) = u'(R)$, where the marginal product of labor is evaluated at ($t = 0$ and $k = k_1$), namely, it is the value of k such that the marginal product of labor is equal to the wage rate (times one plus the cost of borrowing) when one devotes all of one's work time to self-employment. Higher levels of wealth define a new region. The relevant regions and their boundaries are summarized in table 10.2.

For $k_1 \leq k < k_2$ the individual is *an independent producer*, neither hiring in nor out, with the amount of labor time devoted to production being determined by $f_n = u'$ (because $l > 0$, $\mu = 0$). As $\underline{k}$ rises, the agent works more (the marginal product of labor function is shifting

[13] Homogeneity (a weaker assumption — homotheticity — is sufficient) ensures that the ratio of the marginal products of the two inputs depends only on the capital labor ratio.

outward and u' is therefore also rising as R becomes more scarce). Eventually (at k_2), the higher marginal product of labor is sufficient to justify the supervision costs of hiring labor in. The cost of hiring a unit of labor is $w(1 + r + \lambda) + s'f_n$ (the second term takes account of the fact that hiring labor requires supervision s' which diverts the employer's own time from productive labor, the opportunity cost of which is f_n). So the critical value of $\underline{k}$ is defined by $f_n = w(1 + r + \lambda) + s'(0)f_n$ or $w(1 + r + \lambda) = f_n(1 - s'(0))$. Values of $\underline{k}$ greater that this make the marginal product of hired labor greater than the cost of hiring, so positive hiring is done, introducing a new region.

For $k_2 \leq \underline{k} < k_3$ the agent is a *small capitalist* both performing productive work and hiring in labor, and therefore dividing his day between supervision, self-employment, and rest. The amount of each of s, l, and R are determined by $u' = f_n = w(1 + r + \lambda)/(1 - s')$, where the first inequality determines the optimal level of productive labor and the second inequality determines the optimal level of labor to hire in. Note that the second equality can be rewritten to express the requirement that the opportunity cost of diverting one's own labor from production to supervise a marginal increase in employed labor (namely $s'f_n$) must be equal to the marginal product of labor, minus the cost of hiring.

$$s'f_n = f_n - w(1 + r + \lambda)$$

As $\underline{k}$ increases, the marginal product of labor increases, increasing both sides of this equation. But an increase in f_n has a greater proportional effect on the right hand side of this expression (as shown in by the dashed lines in the lower right panel in figure 10.1). Thus, with larger $\underline{k}$ it is optimal to hire more labor, which (because $s'' > 0$) raises s' and hence must also raise u'. A result of this is that the agent devotes less labor directly to production and more to supervision. At some point (when $\underline{k}$ reaches k_3), $u'(R) = f_n$ for $R = 1 - s$, so the owner has no incentive to perform productive labor. For $\underline{k} \geq k_3$ the agent is a *pure capitalist*, performing only supervisory labor.

There will be some level of owned wealth such that the borrowing constraint will no longer be binding. Additional increases in wealth will then be associated with reduced borrowing and eventually lending. Assume that the wealth levels at which the individual becomes a lender, call it k_4, exceeds k_3. For those with $\underline{k} > k_4$, the individual is a *finance capitalist*, devoting all of his working time to supervising the labor working with (some of) his capital goods while lending the rest. Table 10.2 summarizes the correspondence between wealth and contractual position.

The above analysis, while highly simplified, gives, for every wealth level, the types of contracts in which an individual will choose to engage. The same analysis then gives a correspondence between a distribution of wealth and the distribution of contractual roles in the population. A society with few large wealth holders and many middling wealth holders would support a distribution of contracts with many self-employed, while a distribution with a high concentration of wealth and many individuals with no wealth would be a society of wage workers with a few pure capitalists or finance capitalists. Of course, major shifts in the distribution of wealth (and hence shifts in the demand for participation in particular types of contracts) would alter the wage rate, the rental price of capital goods, and the rate of interest, all assumed to be exogenously given in the above model. People do not sort themselves into contractual positions on the basis of wealth alone. People differ in their degree of risk aversion, level of schooling, rate of time preference, and other traits that influence this process. These are all influenced by one's level of wealth (or the wealth of one's parents) but also vary independently of wealth. Thus, this model is far from complete.

CLASS: UNEQUAL WEALTH, INCOMPLETE CONTRACTS, AND POWER

The distribution of contracts summarized in table 10.2 gives the sorting of individuals into discrete classes resulting from continuous differences in wealth. While historians and other social scientists regularly make use of terms such as "working class" and "white collar worker," economists typically eschew such categorical representations. Discrete groupings often capture less information than continuously measured variables such as income and wealth, an example being the use of the term "middle class" to mean nothing more than middle income. It is partly for this reason that the classical economists' concept of class—which was a staple not only of Marxian economics but also of the economics of Ricardo and Smith—fell into disuse with the rise of the Walrasian paradigm.[14]

The contemporary theory of incomplete contracts presented in chapters 7, 8, and 9 along with the concept of power introduced in this chapter suggest a theory of class structure in which the discrete catego-

---

[14] Knut Wicksell (1851–1926), Walras' contemporary, was the first to show that if the production function is homogeneous of degree one (constant returns) there is no analytical difference in the neoclassical approach between representing the employer as a residual claimant paying the workers their marginal product, or conversely having the workers be residual claimants and pay the suppliers of capital the marginal product of capital. He concluded: "We might equally well have begun by regarding the laborers themselves as entrepreneurs" (Wicksell 1961[1893]:24–25). In this sense, he was the precursor of Samuelson's claim that who hires whom makes no difference.

ries convey information not captured by wealth or other continuous measures. Two aspects of the class structure summarized in table 10.2 provide examples. First, members of a class have more in common than a similar level of wealth: their relationship to other classes is the same. Thus wage workers all interact daily with an employer and receive income in the form of a wage. Independent producers, by contrast, engage with others only in the buying of inputs and selling of outputs, and their income takes the form of sales revenues. Second, an aspect of class relationships is that some have power over others. Thus, being a pure capitalist means being the boss of a group of employees, and being a rentier capitalist may mean having short side power over those to whom one lends (depending on the nature of the contract).

Without the analysis of wealth and contracts above, knowing that an individual had wealth $\underline{k} \in (k_3, k_4)$, for example, would be uninformative about the nature of the social relationships in which that individual would typically engage in the course of making his livelihood. What class adds to the analysis is the social relationships characteristic of particular wealth positions, and particularly the political aspect of these relationships, that is, the asymmetric exercise of power. The analytical importance of these things that members of a class have in common (even if their income and wealth differ) depends on the question one wants to answer. The centrality of the exercise of power in the modern theory of the firm suggests that the concept of class may illuminate not only the usual concerns of historians and sociologists but of economists as well.

The incomplete contracts model of the class structure of a capitalist economy is summarized in figure 10.2, which introduces the market for managers as a distinct kind of contingent renewal contract. In figure 10.2, the shortsiders (B) exercise power ($\rightarrow$) over the longsiders with whom they transact (A) while the excluded longsiders (C) are quantity constrained. The individuals appearing as lenders and successful borrowers in the capital market appear ($\downarrow$) as owners in the manager market, while owners and those who succeed in securing a position in the manager market appear as employers in the labor market. The political dimension of the class structure depicted in the figure is a downward cascade of short side power beginning with wealthy lenders who exercise power over borrowers wealthy enough to secure a transaction. The wealthy and the successful borrowers, then, exercise power over managers (those who secured employment), who in turn, along with owners (in the classical Alchian and Demsetz firm) exercise shortside power over employees.

Of course, employers may exercise power over employees by other means (if the employee is earning a rent associated with a transaction-

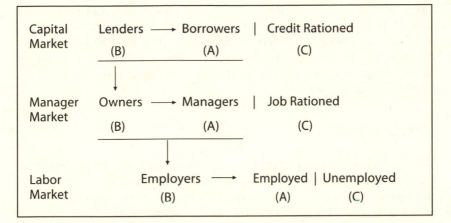

Figure 10.2 The incomplete contracts model of the class structure. The B's are shortside principals exercising power over the A's (the longside agents with whom they transact); the C's are quantity-constrained longsiders.

specific asset, for example). Note that while there is a close correspondence between wealth and the exercise of power, wealth is neither necessary nor sufficient for the exercise of shortside power. Managers need not be wealthy to exercise power over employees. And the independent producers in table 10.2 own significant wealth and yet exercise no power (assuming that goods markets are competitive and clear in equilibrium). Note also that in contrast to the Walrasian model (in chapter 6), the distribution of income is no longer uniquely determined by the distribution of wealth; the employed and the unemployed are identical and yet have very different incomes. The same is true of the successful and the quantity-constrained longsiders in the manager market.

Extending the theory of incomplete contracts to provide a microeconomic foundation for the concept of class thus affirms the sometimes hierarchical nature of competitive exchange relationships alluded to by Marx in the epigraph. The incomplete contracts approach, however, does not simply reproduce older concepts of class. The model developed here contrasts sharply with what may be termed an organic view of classes, according to which people are said to be "born into" classes and to adopt behavioral patterns distinctive of their class (including collective action on behalf of their class interests) without providing an account of why individual class members act in ways that make these statements true. The approach may also be contrasted with Oliver Williamson's markets and hierarchies approach. Rather than seeing firms simply as Robertson did as "islands of conscious power in this ocean of unconscious cooperation," the incomplete contracts approach traces the exercise of power to the structure of markets rather than to the structure of firms. The firm is an important venue in which power is exercised, but as the credit market model makes clear, power may be exercised in the absence of firms or indeed any organizational structure whatsoever. Short side power is exercised *in* markets, not simply outside markets or despite markets.

CONCLUSION

The Walrasian model of general competitive equilibrium presented in chapter 6 was designed to illuminate how exchange among traders with heterogeneous initial endowments might support an equilibrium price vector and final allocation of goods and utilities. The models developed here were designed to illuminate the ways that a competitive economy sorts individuals with heterogeneous initial endowments into differing contracts, and hence into differing class positions, differentiated both by income and by the power they exercise over others. In the competitive equilibrium model, there is but a single complete contract governing the exchange of goods and prices are endogenous. This chapter models the coexistence of many distinct contracts, many of them incomplete, on the assumption that prices are exogenous. Rather than competing models of the same thing, these approaches are better seen as representations of the capitalist economy from distinct vantage points, one stressing market exchange of contractible goods and the other stressing noncontractual social interactions among members of different classes. A major challenge is to model price formation and trade in economies with an array of possible contracts and the endogenous sorting of individuals to contractual positions. Such a model would identify competitive equilibria that simultaneously support a price vector, a political structure of the exchange process, and a distribution of individual well-being.

The seemingly novel idea that the political structure of markets and firms should play a central role in the analysis of the economy is in far from new. The U.S. Supreme Court in *Holden vs. Hardy* (1898) affirmed the logic of what almost a century later would be called the labor discipline model:

> [T]he proprietors of . . . establishments and their operatives do not stand on an equality, . . . their interests are, to a certain extent, conflicting. The former naturally desire to obtain as much labor as possible from their employees, while the latter are often induced by the fear of discharge to conform to the regulations which in their judgement, fairly exercised would pronounce them to be detrimental to their health or strength. In other words, the proprietors lay down the rules and the laborers are practically constrained to obey them.

But many economists consider the exercise of power by employers to be illusory. Joseph Schumpeter took pains to make the point: "What distinguishes directing and directed labor appears at first sight to be very fundamental," he wrote, but in reality the difference "constitutes no essential economic distinction. . . . [T]he conduct of the former is subject to the same rules as that of the latter . . . and to establish this regularity . . . is a fundamental task of economic theory" (Schumpeter 1934:20–21). An important microeconomics text (Alchian and Allen 1969:320) may have surprised some students with the following:

> Calling the employer the boss is a custom derived from the fact that the "boss" specifies the particular task. One could have called the employee the boss because he orders the employer to pay him a specific sum if he wants services performed. But words are words.

I doubt very much that the authors would disagree with the Supreme Court's assessment as an empirical account. Like Samuelson (in the epigraph), they were describing the logic of a model, not an empirical aspect of the economy. In the post-Walrasian approach modeled here, Alchian and Allen's example would look quite different. It is clear that the employer would simply refuse any pay demand by the worker unless it happened to be w^*, namely, the wage that maximized profits. It seems a valuable attribute of the post-Walrasian approaches that they readily accommodate (rather than obscure) what seems such an uncontroversial fact about employment. But the model of power developed here is much too simple to be the basis for more than a cursory understanding of the social relationships making up the workplace or credit market transactions. A key defect is that in attempting to capture the essentially hierarchical nature of relationships between classes—the "downward cascade of power" in figure 10.2—it does not address cases in which power is not asymmetric but rather is exercised bilaterally.

Nonetheless, it does provide a compelling reason to doubt the old adage, "The wealthy are different from everybody else; they have more money." Wealth does indeed determine the position of one's budget constraint and thus commands more goods and services. But those wealthy enough to engage in their own projects or to borrow large amounts at the going rate of interest enjoy more than superior purchasing power. They may command people as well as goods. Their access to capital allows them, but not others, to become employers of labor and as such to occupy positions of short side power in nonclearing markets. Thomas Hobbes had it right "Riches joyned with liberality [generosity] is Power; because it procureth friends, and servants" (1968[1651]:150). Indeed, in Hobbes's day the terms "servant" referred to *any* employee.

PART III

Change: The Coevolution of Institutions and Preferences

CHAPTER ELEVEN

Institutional and Individual Evolution

> Selfish and contentious people will not cohere, and without coherence, nothing can be effected. A tribe possessing . . . a greater number of courageous, sympathetic and faithful members, who were always ready to warn each other of danger, to aid and defend each other . . . would spread and be victorious over other tribes. . . . Thus the social and moral qualities would tend slowly to advance and be diffused throughout the world.
>
> — Charles Darwin, *The Descent of Man* (1873)

> At a certain stage of their development, the material forces of production [technologies] . . . come into conflict with . . . the property relations within which they had been at work before. From forms of development of the forces of production these relations turn into their fetters. Then begins the period of social revolution.
>
> — Karl Marx, "Preface," *Critique of Political Economy* (1859)

IN OCTOBER 1989, the general secretary of the East German Communist Party, Erich Honecker, grandly celebrated the fortieth anniversary of the founding of the German Democratic Republic as a "historical necessity" and a "turning point in the history of the German people." Parades and demonstrations commemorated the event.[1] Anti-regime protesters had mounted a dozen or so demonstrations over the summer months, but they had attracted fewer than 10,000 participants in all. Twelve days after his address, Honecker resigned, as anti-regime demonstrations mounted first in Leipzig and then throughout the country, with a million and a half participating in October and twice that number in November. Within a month, East and West Germans danced on the Berlin Wall, and then dismantled it. Less than a year after Honecker's commemoration of the German Democratic Republic, it passed out of existence, its territory joining the Federal Republic of Germany. As a result, the citizens of the former Communist nation passed from one system of governance to another with an entirely new set of property rights and political processes. Few had anticipated the suddenness

---

The second epigraph is from Marx (1904:11–12), the first from Darwin (1998:134).

[1] This account is based on Lohmann (1994).

and extent of these and the other dramatic changes in institutions that took place throughout most of the formerly Communist world over the same period.

A less heralded but equally dramatic process of institutional change concerns the painful and dangerous practice of female circumcision and other forms of female genital cutting (FGC) in many parts of Africa.[2] Like foot binding, which was once widely practiced in China, FGC is a convention that families adhere to in order to ensure that daughters will be able to marry. The spread of schooling and other modernizing influences on the continent during the twentieth century had left FGC intact; in some regions it was spreading. At the turn of the twenty-first century, it was estimated that two million African girls suffered the practice every year.

But at a meeting in 1997 in the small Bambara village of Malicounda in Senegal, residents pledged they would *all* reject FGC. The about-face in Malicounda had been prompted not by an anti-FGC campaign but rather by a nongovernmental organization that had brought women together to promote literacy and to consider community development and health problems. In nearby Keur Simbara, villagers prudently decided to consult with all of the other villages in the relevant marriage pool; eventually, all thirteen of these villages collectively pledged to abandon the practice. After village-level meetings, representatives of another cluster of eighteen villages of the Fulani ethnic group did the same. Pledge groups spread from village to village. Within a year of the Fulani declaration, the government of Senegal outlawed FGC.

A final example of institutional change comes from the Philippines, where the traditional contract governing the rice harvest is called *hunusan* ("sharing" in Tagalog). According the *hunusan* system, any members of the community may participate in the harvest of a farmer's fields, receiving one-sixth of the amount they personally harvest.[3] The farmer may not rightfully deny anyone this right, and by custom his own family members may not participate, nor may he or they supervise the work. During the 1960s, the one-sixth share provided a return to an hour's harvesting work on a par with wage-earning opportunities in rural areas, constituting a kind of equilibrium between traditional and modern contracts. However, the increased use of high yield varieties of rice during the 1970s and 1980s (the Green Revolution) nearly doubled yields and thus greatly increased the value of the one-sixth of the harvest stipulated by the hunusan system. As a result, by the end of the

---

[2] This account draws on Mackie (1996) and Mackie (2000).
[3] Based on Hayami (1998) and Hayami and Kikuchi (1999).

1970s, harvesting under the *hunusan* system earned a substantial rent above the laborer's next best alternative (wage labor).

Some of the large landowners sought to take advantage of the change by reducing the crop share to one-ninth, but this violation of custom caused much indignation among the harvesters, perhaps explaining the suspicious nighttime burning of unharvested crops. The larger farms subsequently invested heavily in both mechanical threshers and in the supervision of harvest labor. Smaller farms, however, continued to offer the one-sixth share but added to it a traditional obligation that had long been common in some adjacent regions — the restriction of harvest labor to those who had performed unpaid weeding services throughout the prior growing season. In contrast to the strategy adopted by the large owners, the new obligation imposed by the smaller farmers did not violate the reciprocity-based *hunusan* system. Hayami (1998:45) reports that "in the minds of the villagers weeding with no direct payment is considered . . . an expression of gratitude by laborers for the goodwill of the farmer patron who provides them with a guaranteed stable income . . . at a time-honored share." By amalgamating two traditional contracts, the modified *hunusan* system depressed the de facto remuneration of harvest labor to almost exactly the rate for equivalent wage work, thus eliminating the rents introduced by the Green Revolution.

In previous chapters I have sought to illuminate how institutions work: how they provide incentives and constraints accounting both for individual behaviors and for the resulting aggregate consequences, as well as how institutions influence individual preferences and beliefs. In this and the next two chapters, I take up the more difficult questions: how do institutions change? And how do the preferences and beliefs of individuals coevolve with their institutional environments? These questions are among the most important and intellectually challenging in the social and behavioral sciences, and they have occupied some of the greatest minds over the past three centuries — Adam Smith, David Hume, Karl Marx, Karl Menger, Joseph Schumpeter, and Frederich Hayek among them. But since the emergence of the Walrasian paradigm in economics in the late nineteenth century, the processes of institutional change and individual development have occupied a peripheral position in the social sciences, and especially so in economics. Partly as a result, institutional change and individual evolution have not been modeled formally until recent years when the development of new analytical tools made this possible.

In this and the next two chapters, I will make use of these analytical advances to bring some of the evolutionary insights of both Darwin and Marx to bear on the process of institutional change, and in the process identify some of the shortcomings of their perspectives.

Overview of the Issues

Recall that *institutions* refer to the laws, informal rules, and conventions that give a durable structure to social interactions, influencing who meets whom, to do what tasks, with what possible courses of action, and with what consequences of actions jointly taken. For some analytical tasks it makes sense to take the institutional environment as given, often describing the relevant rules by a specific game structure. In the model of the labor market presented in chapter 8, this approach was exemplified by treating the employer as the first mover with a given strategy set (the wage rate, level of monitoring, level of employment), and the employee as the second mover with a different, also given, strategy set. In this case, the game *describes* the relevant institutions.

If we are interested in the process of institutional evolution, however, we need to depict institutions not as exogenously given constraints, but rather as the *outcome* of individual interactions. In other words, we want to go "behind" the game describing the institution to investigate the interaction from which it evolved. To do this, we specify an underlying game that has as it as its possible outcomes a number of different ways that the participants might interact. The *outcomes* of this underlying game are thus institutions; the process of institutional change will then be studied as a change from one to another of these outcomes.

An insightful way to describe the outcomes of the underlying game is to say that they are conventions, that is, Nash equilibria of an n-person game in which individual adherence to the conventional behavior is a best response as long as the individual believes that a sufficient number of others will also adhere to the convention. Institutional change occurs when one convention is displaced by another. Thus, the analysis of institutional innovation and change becomes a problem of *equilibrium selection*, that is, giving reasons why one equilibrium is likely to emerge and persist, when other equilibria are possible.

Consider a specific case. The labor market aspects of South African apartheid were a convention (or a set of conventions) regulating the patterns of racial inequality that had existed throughout most of South Africa's recorded history and had been formalized in the early twentieth century and especially in the aftermath of World War II. For whites, an aspect of the convention might be expressed as: offer only low wages for menial work to blacks. For blacks the convention was: offer one's labor at low wages; do not demand more. These actions represented mutual best responses: as long as (almost) all white employers adhered to their side of the convention, the black workers' best response was to adhere to their aspect of the convention, and conversely. Apartheid can be described as a convention because other nonracial and more egalitarian mutual best responses were in principle feasible.

The power of apartheid labor market conventions is suggested by the fact that real wages of black gold miners did not rise between 1910 and 1970, despite periodic labor shortages on the mines and a many-fold increase in productivity.[4] But a series of strikes beginning in the early 1970s and accelerating after the mid-1980s signaled a rejection of the convention by increasing numbers of black workers. In doing this, of course, workers and others were not conforming to the best responses of the status quo apartheid convention. Their deviation from the convention provoked deviations from business leaders: facing many non-best responding black workers on strike for higher pay, many concluded that the old convention was no longer a best response, leading them to alter their labor relations, raising real wages and promoting black workers. Nonbest-response actions by black workers had altered the employers' best responses; as a result, the convention unraveled. Within a decade, the entire system of apartheid had been abandoned.

The South African case illustrates one of two processes by which institutions change: the emergence *within* a society of a large number of individuals who act in ways that violate the convention, eventually displacing it. This process often takes the form (as in Marx's historical materialism) of conflict among interdependent actors who are differentially benefitted by one or another institutional form. A within-group process of institutional change may be a radical break with the past, as in the case of the demise of East German Communism and FGC in Senegal. But it need not be. Institutional change may also occur through the piecemeal accommodation of institutions to new demands and opportunities (as with the modification of the *hunusan* system in the Philippines). I model a within-group dynamic that induces society to switch from one convention to another chapter 12.

The second process inducing institutional or individual evolution is competition *among groups* governed by differing institutions. According to this view, successful institutions are those that contribute to the survival of nations, firms, bands, and ethnolinguistic units, in competition with other groups. Hayek, for example, uses an argument of this type to explain why the market system — his "extended order" — proliferated throughout the world. Darwin (in the epigraph) thought that competition among groups would diffuse group-beneficial individual traits such as bravery. In chapter 13, I study the evolution of other-regarding preferences as a result of between-group conflicts using a *group selection* (or *multi-level selection*) model. The transformation of

---

[4] This account draws on Karis and Gerhart (1997), Wilson (1972), and Wood (2000).

institutions studied in this chapter — what I call the first property rights revolution — is based on a combined process of between-group competition and within-group tipping from one convention to another.

It is often useful — as a way of disciplining the process of theory making — to have a clear idea of what empirical phenomena one would like to understand. Six facts about institutional change illustrated by the South African, German, Senegalese, and Philippine examples illustrate general characteristics of the process of institutional change, and will figure prominently in the account of institutional innovation offered below.

The first is that many important institutions — those governing relationships among economic classes, for example — are best described by an underlying population game that is asymmetrical in both strategy sets and payoffs, different subpopulations occupying different roles in the game. Examples include institutions governing crop shares, wages and conditions of work of employees, and debt repayment. Because in these cases distributional outcomes vary among conventions, many equilibria will be Pareto optimal. For this reason, subgroups in the population may have *conflicting interests* concerning which convention obtains.

Second, *chance* or *exogenous developments* — literally, events outside the model — play an important role in institutional evolution (for example, the end of the cold war and the unusual leadership of Presidents de Klerk and Mandela in the South African transition). Where exogenous developments represent well-understood secular trends such as technical change (as in the Philippine case), the analytical task is to anticipate the ways that the changes may eliminate the equilibrium representing the status quo convention and to determine which new equilibrium might then be favored. The *locus classicus* of this way of thinking is Marx's idea, expressed in the epigraph, that the advance of technology induces institutional change when the reigning conventions inhibit ("fetter") the realization of technical progress that would be feasible under other institutions. In other cases it is illuminating to introduce such chance elements as "behavioral noise" akin to mutations in the Darwinian framework, except that they are not heritable. I combine exogenous technical change and behavioral noise in modeling the transformation of property rights associated with the rise of agriculture below. In chapter 13, I introduce chance as heritable genetic mutations.

Third, the process of change from one institutional convention to another is often propelled by *collective action* by members of a group disadvantaged under the status quo convention, seeking to displace it in favor of a more beneficial set of institutions. This was the case in the Senegalese, South African, and German examples. Thus nonbest-response play is often deliberate rather than accidental, and is not well modeled as behavioral noise or mutations. The role of collective action will be modeled in chapter 12.

Fourth, even if (as Marx suggests) institutional change can be represented as an accommodation to the process of technical change, we often observe the persistence over very long periods of time of *inefficient conventions* (meaning those like planting late in Palanpur in which nearly everyone is less well-off by comparison to an alternative convention).

The fifth fact, suggested by the South African, Senegalese, and German examples and documented in an impressive number of historical and anthropological studies, is that conventions often exhibit long-term stability followed by a precipitous unraveling, as well as the rapid emergence and then enduring stability of new conventions. The underlying dynamic processes generate what biologists term *punctuated equilibria.* Examples have been given in chapter 2; others include the rapid diffusion of the generalized use of familiar rather than formal personal pronouns in many European languages in the course of a decade (Paulston 1976), and the equally dramatic shift in the long-standing modal tenants' crop share from one-half to three-quarters in West Bengal during the 1980s, described in the Prologue.

A particularly fascinating example was recorded in highland Burma (now Myanmar) by Edmund Leach (1954:198). Two radically distinct social structures succeeded each other over time as systems of governance:

> [T]he *gumsa* conceive of themselves as being ruled by chiefs who are members of a hereditary aristocracy; the *gumlao* repudiate all notions of hereditary class difference. . . . But while the two terms represent . . . two fundamentally opposed modes of organization . . . *gumsa* communities have been converted into *gumlao* communities and vice versa.

Finally, institutional environments affect the distribution of preferences in the population, while the preferences of the actors influence the process of institutional change. For example, the collapse of the institutions of apartheid is in part explained by repugnance and anger provoked by racism, and apartheid's demise also contributed to the proliferation of nonracial preferences and identities in the South African population. An adequate model must thus capture the *coevolutionary processes* by which group level institutions and individual preferences are part of a unified dynamical system.

Formal modeling can, of course, provide only a partial account of the empirical cases I have introduced. I begin with endogenous preferences, providing an interpretation of how economic and other institutions shape the evolution of our motivations. I then introduce a model of the way that preferences change through a process of cultural inheritance to show how the process of institutional change may in turn induce changes in preferences. Finally, I return to the problem of the evolution of property rights introduced in chapter 2, introducing a within-group replicator dynamic model coupled with a between-group selection process. I use this model to account for the emergence and proliferation of possession-based property rights which occurred along with the process of technical change associated with the emergence of agriculture.

The Cultural Evolution of Preferences

We acquire preferences through genetic inheritance and cultural learning. Because both are influenced by economic and other institutions, preferences are endogenous. The models I develop highlight the way that structures of social interaction influence the direction and pace of the evolution of preferences. Preferences may be endogenous in other ways. For example, religious or political indoctrination and advertising are undoubtedly important. But the available empirical studies of preferences for brands of food, soap, movies, and other consumption items for which one would expect an important deliberate inculcation effect, advertising appears to be less important than one's personal contacts and other influences. Preferences are like accents; we can try to acquire them—learning to love Prokofiev and snails, or adopting an "upper-class accent"—but for the most part we are only dimly aware of how we acquired them. For this reason the models below are patterned after studies of language change. On the basis of intensive empirical study of linguistic change in Philadelphia, for example, William Labov concluded that

> linguistic traits are not transmitted across group boundaries simply by exposure in the mass media or in schools. . . . Our basic language system is not acquired from school teachers or from radio announcers, but from friends and competitors: those who we admire, and those who we have to be good enough to beat. (Labov 1983:23)

The inference is not that institutions such as schools and churches are unimportant, but that understanding their evolutionary importance may be enhanced by seeing them—along with markets, firms, families, and governments—as distinct arenas of social interaction affecting the differential replication of behavioral traits.

In cultural inheritance processes, behaviors are learned from parents (vertical transmission), from others of the previous generation (oblique transmission), or from one's own cohort (horizontal transmission). For each type of transmission, learning is represented as copying: adopting the same religion as one's parents or switching to a new religion due to contact with a teacher, for example. Why are some people's behaviors copied and others not? Thus far (chapters 2 and 7), I have modeled payoff-based learning, in which the behaviors of those who are materially successful tend to be copied. But other influences are also important. The cultural replication process may favor the numerous over the rare, independently of their economic success: social pressures for uniformity are among the most convincingly documented human propensities.[5] Following Boyd and Richerson (1985), by *conformist transmission* I mean that the likelihood that an individual will adopt a particular behavior varies with the prevalence of that behavior in the population (independently of other influences on learning, such as relative payoffs). The importance of the population frequency of a behavioral trait could arise if individuals simply sought to adopt what they consider to be the most common behavior. But conformism could arise because social institutions privilege the most common behaviors in the transmission process. This would be the case if the cultural models with the greatest exposure were those adhering to the most common behavioral norms, as occurs in most contemporary school systems in which teachers tend to be drawn from the numerically predominant groups. The simulation model used below to analyze the first property rights revolution introduces conformist transmission in just this way: one's cultural model is disproportionately likely to be drawn from the numerically predominant subpopulation.

The cultural transmission processes just described have *themselves* evolved, presumably under the influence of natural selection, cultural group selection, chance and other evolutionary pressures. Taking account of the endogenous nature of the learning process, a plausible model must posit a transmission process capable of reproducing itself. It is easy to see why copying the successful could be a learning rule that would proliferate. Conformist learning also passes this test, as there are compelling theoretical reasons to believe that, under quite general conditions in which learning is costly, conformist transmission of traits will be contribute to the material and reproductive success of individuals and hence might have evolved under the influence of either genetic or cultural inheritance.[6] The model in the next section clarifies the intuition

---

[5] See Boyd and Richerson (1985:223ff), Ross and Nisbett (1991:30ff), Bowles (1998), and the works cited there.

[6] Feldman, Aoki, and Kumm (1996), Boyd and Richerson (1985), Henrich and Boyd (1998).

behind these results: as long as conformism is not too common, it is an effective way to reduce learning costs.

To illuminate the influence of economic and other institutions on preferences, I will extend the replicator dynamic model presented in chapter 2 to capture both the payoff-based and conformist influences on preference change. Consider a population in which individuals may have one of two learned norms, x and y, with population frequencies p and $1 - p$ with $p \in [0,1]$. Members of the population are randomly paired to interact in a single-period, symmetrical, two-person game, the payoffs of which are denoted $\pi(x,y)$, the payoff to the strategy dictated by the norm x against a partner playing according to the other norm. (I will use "norm" to refer to the strategy dictated by the norm where appropriate.) As in chapter 2, $b_x(p)$ and $b_y(p)$ are the expected payoffs to behaving according to the x and y norms in a population p percent of whom are x-types.

The updating process is formally the same as in the replicator dynamic models of chapters 2 and 7, except that to reduce notational clutter, I assume that every member of the population is in updating mode in every period ($\omega = 1$). However, in place of the payoff-monotonic updating process modeled there, individuals will update in light of *two* pieces of information, their payoffs relative to others' and the frequency of the two traits in the population, the *degree of conformity* measuring the importance of the latter relative to the former. Thus, define the *degree of conformism*, $\lambda \in [0,1)$, as the importance of the conformist aspect of the learning process relative to the payoff-based influences on updating, with $1 - \lambda$ the relative importance of payoffs, and let k be the population frequency of the x-norm for which conformist learning exerts no effect (possibly one-half), while for $p > k$ the prevalence of the x-norm in the population favors it in the updating process, independently of the (also frequency dependent) expected payoffs to the norms.[7] We define the *replication propensity* of a norm, r_x and r_y.

$$r_x = \tfrac{1}{2}[\lambda(p - k) + (1 - \lambda)(b_x - b_y)]$$

$$r_y = \tfrac{1}{2}[\lambda(k - p) + (1 - \lambda)(b_y - b_x)]$$

(11.1)

(As the dynamics depend only on the relative size of the two replication propensities, the $\tfrac{1}{2}$ is an arbitrary convenience that allows a simplification in the expression immediately below.) With probability $\beta(r_y - r_x)$, an x-type will change to a y-type if paired with a y-type and $r_x < r_y$; if

---

[7] The conformist effect need not be linear in p, of course, but nothing would be gained by a more general formulation.

$r_x \geq r_y$, the individual does not switch. Those who are paired with their own type do not switch. The analogous switching process holds for y-types.

Using the derivation of the replicator dynamic in chapter 2, we have

$$\frac{dp}{dt} = p' - p = p(1-p)\beta(r_x - r_y) = p\beta(r_x - \bar{r}) \qquad (11.2)$$

where $\bar{r}$ is the group average replication propensity and, as before, the *adoption coefficient* β is a positive constant reflecting the greater effect on switching of relatively large differences in replication propensities (appropriately scaled so that the probability of switching varies over the unit interval).

From eq. (11.2) it is clear that $dp/dt = 0$ if $r_x - r_y = 0$ which requires

$$\frac{\lambda(p - k)}{1 - \lambda} = b_y(p) - b_x(p) \qquad (11.3)$$

or if p is either 0 or 1 (because when $p = 1$, $r_x = \bar{r}$). When eq. (11.3) is satisfied, p is stationary because the effects of conformist transmission (the left-hand side of eq. (11.3)) just offset the effects of differential payoffs (the right-hand side). Thus, in the presence of conformist transmission, and for $p \in (0,1)$, the equilibrium payoffs to the norm favored by conformism will always be less than the payoffs of the more prevalent norm. Figure 11.1 illustrates such an equilibrium.

For $p \in (0,1)$, dp/dt takes the sign of $r_x - r_y$. An equilibrium is asymptotically stable (self-correcting) if the derivative of eq. (11.2) with respect to p is negative, requiring that

$$\lambda < (1 - \lambda)\left(\frac{db_y}{dp} - \frac{db_x}{dp}\right) \qquad (11.4a)$$

or

$$\frac{\lambda}{1 - \lambda} < \pi(y, x) - \pi(y, y) - \pi(x, x) + \pi(x, y) \qquad (11.4b)$$

which is satisfied if the conformist advantage conferred on x by a small increase in p, namely $\lambda/(1 - \lambda)$, is more than offset by the payoff advantage conferred on y by the same increase in p (the right-hand side). In figure 11.1, p^* represents the solution to eq. (11.3) satisfying eq. (11.4a) and is hence a stable equilibrium distribution of norms.

From eqs. (11.3) and (11.4a) we see that conformism has two effects.

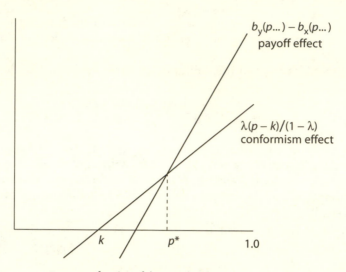

$b_y(p...) - b_x(p...)$
payoff effect

$\lambda(p - k)/(1 - \lambda)$
conformism effect

k p^* 1.0

x-types as a fraction of the population, p

Figure 11.1 Cultural equilibrium. Stationarity of p requires that at $p = p^*$ the conformist pressures favoring the copying of x be offset by payoff advantages of y.

First, eq. (11.3) shows that strategies that yield low payoffs may persist. For example, x is an evolutionarily stable strategy (ESS) in this cultural replication dynamic as long as the expected payoffs for a small number of y-players introduced into a homogeneously x-playing population exceed the x-players payoffs by less than $\lambda(1 - k)/(1 - \lambda)$. This condition is obviously less stringent than the conventional ESS, which requires that the payoffs to the mutant y-players are less than the payoff to the incumbent x-players. Thus, behaviors that are not best responses defined over the game payoffs may persist in the population.

Second, sufficiently high levels of conformism must violate eq. (11.4), making p^* an unstable equilibrium and thus making it the boundary between the basin of attraction of the equilibria at $p = 0$ and $p = 1$. In the absence of conformism, stability requires only that the right-hand side of eq. (11.4b) be positive, obviously a weaker condition. Counterintuitively, conformism thus may help explain both the punctuated equilibria that characterize rapid cultural change, as well as the long-term survival of individually costly norms, whether group-beneficial or not. Conformism is thus added to strategic complementarity (positive feedbacks) of the type encountered in Assurance Games as a reason for the persistence of socially dysfunctional behaviors and conventions.

How might the above model be used to analyze the effect of economic institutions on the evolution of preferences?

ENDOGENOUS PREFERENCES

Changes in the payoff structures or other details of the game individuals are paired to play, or in the degree of conformism, will displace the equilibrium distribution of behavioral norms in a population if p^* is interior and stable. If p^* is unstable, these changes will change the relative size of the basins of attraction of the two extreme equilibria, altering the likelihood of one or the other persisting in a stochastic environment. This observation suggests a way of studying preference endogeneity: use eq. (11.3) to study the displacement of p^* occasioned by institutional changes. In figure 11.1, for example, if a school reform to increase the number of minority group teachers reduced the extent of conformist transmission, it would displace p^* to the left. Similarly, shifts in the parameters reflecting the structure of social interactions in chapter 7—repetition of interactions, nonrandom pairing, and cost of information about one's partner—will displace the equilibrium distribution of norms.

Here is an example of the use of the above model to explore the effect of institutions on a particular preference, one stressed by Joseph Schumpeter in his theory of entrepreneurship, innovation, and economic growth, namely, the disposition to innovate and lead as opposed to imitate and to follow. Consider a changing environment in which members of a population are paired to interact in a symmetrical game with two strategies. Pairing is nonrandom: if the fraction of the population that are x-types is p, then x-types will be paired with their own type on the average not p percent of the time but $\mu_{xx} = s + (1 - s)p > p$ percent of the time. Correspondingly, y-types will be paired with x-types $\mu_{yx} = (1 - s)p < p$ percent of the time. The difference between these two conditional probabilities, s, is the degree of segmentation, introduced in chapter 7.

The *learning* strategy (L) researchs the environment at a cost of 1 and, on the basis of the resulting knowledge, selects an action that yields benefits of 2. The *imitation* strategy (I) costs nothing, yielding benefits of 2 if the imitator is paired with a learner and yielding $2 - \sigma$ if two imitators are paired, where $\sigma > 1$ is a suitably normalized measure of the environmental variability. The payoff structure reflects the fact that the learners always adapt to the current environment (but at a cost), while the imitators only do so if they are paired with a learner and are hence able to free ride on his up-to-date knowledge. When an imitator is paired with another imitator, she copies a behavior that was not updated in light of the current situation. How maladapted her behavior is depends on the extent of change in the environment, σ. Let p

equal the fraction of the population who are "learners." If updating is simply payoff monotonic (ignoring conformism by setting $\lambda = 0$ in eq. (11.1)), the stationarity condition for p is $b_L = b_I$,

$$p^* = \frac{\sigma - 1}{(1 - s)\sigma}$$

We see that $dp^*/d\sigma > 0$, so, as one would expect, an increase in the stochasticity of the environment raises the frequency of learners in the population. It is easily shown that $p^* < p^{max}$, the population frequency that maximizes average payoffs under random pairing. The intuition behind this result is that learners generate social benefits in excess of their private benefits (they convey information to imitators when they are copied). Thus, the equilibrium level of learners is less than the socially optimal level. Likewise $dp^*/ds > 0$, so heightened segmentation increases the equilibrium fraction of learners. Positive assortation (segmentation) deprives the imitators of some of the benefits generated by the learner's up-to-date information, depressing their payoffs and reducing their equilibrium frequency in the population. Like a copyright or patent, positive assortation increases the amount of research. But it also has the same efficiency-reducing effect as copyrighting the information obtained by the learners: it reduces the flow of up-to-date information from learners to imitators. The effect is to reduce average payoffs, because providing the information to the imitators is costless, yet beneficial to the learner.

By contrast to the situation-specific preferences introduced in chapter 3, preferences are endogenous when one's experiences result in durable changes in one's behavior in a given situation. The above models exemplify this, as they show how the behavioral updating process is influenced by individual's interactions with his or her social and material environments. Because preference-change involves a long-term learning process — often occurring during childhood or adolescence — and significant changes in economic institutions are infrequent, compelling empirical studies of the impact of institutions on preferences are rare. Some of the more illuminating studies concern the impact of new economic institutions during a process of economic growth or the impact of institutions from one society on the people of another.

Among the more exotic examples is the following: the penetration of commerce into erstwhile nonmarket societies is frequently accompanied by the proliferation of witchcraft and similar behaviors. This occurred in the Gold Coast (now Ghana) during the expansion of the first cash crop (cocoa). Preexisting communal property rights were no longer adequate as land became very valuable, and so-called witch doctors sprang up to adjudicate disputes on the expanding boundary of the crop. Similar episodes occurred in Bolivia with the advent of tin mining, in Colombia with the spread of sugar cultivation, and in seventeenth-century Salem Village (Massachusetts) with the growth of commerce along the road running north from Boston. Witchcraft, apparently, was at least in part a response to social conflicts and risk-exposure associated with the inadequacy of traditional systems of rights and obligations in coordinating modern market-based economic activity.

Experiments also suggest that preferences are endogenous. Recall (from chapter 3) that in the experiments that my collaborators and I implemented in fifteen simple societies, experimental play appeared to reflect behavioral patterns derived from everyday life, and especially from the mode of livelihood of the group in question. In particular, those who customarily shared substantial amounts of food tended to divide the Ultimatum Game pie equally or even to offer the larger amount to the other. Where voluntary public goods provision was customary (the *harambee* system, among the Orma in Kenya), contributions in the experimental public goods game were patterned after actual contributions in the *harambee* system.

Our experiments revealed large variations in experimental behavior within and across the different cultural groups. We first attempted to explain behavior in the experiments on the basis of information about the individuals' sex, age, relative wealth, and literacy. With the exception of the Orma, none of these measures was systematically related to experimental play. The large between-group differences also presented a puzzle. We wondered if these came about because preferences are affected by group-specific conditions, such as social institutions or fairness norms. The large variance in institutions and norms in our sample allowed us to address this question systematically. We rank-ordered the societies along two aspects of the social interactions involved in making a livelihood, and then sought to use these measures to predict behavior in the Ultimatum Game. The first, *potential payoffs to cooperation*, is a measure of the extent to which the local ecology allows increasing returns to scale of the type that could be productively exploited by cooperative measures. The Lamalera whale hunters were ranked first, and the dispersed Machiguenga forest horticulturalists ranked last. We speculated that in groups with little benefit to cooperative production, there will be few common norms about sharing. By contrast, those whose livelihood depends on large-scale cooperation like the Lamelara must develop ways of sharing the joint surplus. The second dimension, *market integration*, measures what the fraction of a people's livelihood is acquired through market exchange. The rationale for this measure was that the more frequently people experience market transactions, the more they will also experience beneficial sharing of a joint surplus (the gains from trade) with a stranger. Our speculation was that this experience might support abstract sharing principles.

We sought to explain both the group's average Ultimatum Game offer and a measure of the propensity to reject low offers on the basis of these two dimensions of economic structure. Both measures of Ultimatum Game play varied positively (and highly significantly) with our two measures, the two measures explaining half of the variance in both cases. The impact of these measures of economic structure remained large and robust in estimated equations predicting individual (rather than group average) experimental play controlling for the above individual measures.

The fact that even crude ordinal measures of economic structure are such strong predictors of experimental play suggests a significant impact of institutions on preferences.[8] (The objection that the casual relationship runs the other way — fair-minded peoples locate in places in which cooperative activities are beneficial and market integration possible — seems far fetched.) The cultural transmission process modeled above provides an account of how economic structure might impact on preferences. In ecologies offering ample opportunities for cooperative production, fair-minded people would gain higher payoffs than those pursuing purely self-regarding preferences. As a result, the cultural-updating process would favor fairmindedness in such societies more than in places where those excluded from joint ventures suffered no material costs. The updating process is likely to involve socialization institutions, especially methods of child rearing. Thus, we would expect child-rearing practices to vary with economic experiences.

The impact of occupational structure on child-rearing values in advanced industrial societies was mentioned at the end of chapter 8. Here is an example relevant to the process of preference change in the transition from foraging to farming. Herbert Barry, Margaret Child, and Irvin Bacon (1959) categorized seventy-nine mostly nonliterate societies according to the prevalent form of livelihood (animal husbandry, agricultural, hunting and fishing) and the related ease of food storage or other forms of wealth accumulation, the latter being a major correlate of dimensions of social structure such as stratification. Food storage is common in agricultural societies but not among foragers. They also collected evidence on forms of child-rearing, including obedience training, self-reliance, independence, and responsibility. They found large differ-

---

[8] A more complete presentation of the methods, results, and interpretations of these experiments appears in Henrich, Boyd, Bowles, Fehr, and Gintis (2004) and Henrich, Bowles, Boyd, Camerer, Fehr, Gintis, and McElreath (2001).

ences in the recorded child-rearing practices. These covaried significantly with economic structure, controlling for other measures of social structure such as unilinearity of descent, extent of polygyny, levels of participation of women in the predominant subsistence activity, and size of population units. They concluded, "[K]nowledge of the economy alone would enable one to predict with considerable accuracy whether a society's socialization pressures were primarily toward compliance or assertion" (p. 59). The causal relationship is unlikely to run from child-rearing to economic structure, as the latter is dictated primarily by geography in the sample of simple societies under study.

The models and data presented above suggest the following causal logic: the production and distribution of goods and services in any society is organized by a set of rules, that dictate what one must do or be to acquire one's livelihood. They also influence the process of cultural transmission itself. The development of a complex division of labor, for example, was a major impetus to the advent of modern (and compulsory) schooling. Economic institutions thus impose characteristic patterns of interaction on the people who make up a society, affecting who meets whom, on what terms, to perform which tasks, and with what expectation of rewards. These allocation rules and cultural transmission processes influence the way people update their behaviors, affecting personality, habits, tastes, identities, values, and beliefs.

Thus far, I have modeled the way that preferences may evolve in response to institutional differences; but institutions also evolve. The following model and simulation explores this coevolutionary process. For concreteness, I seek to illuminate an important and little understood historical transition: the eclipse of the collectivist social structures typical of foraging bands by agrarian systems based on individual possession-based property rights.

HOBBESIAN AND ROUSSEAUIAN EQUILIBRIA

For most of human history—roughly the 90,000 years before about 11,000 years ago—social interactions were organized without the aid of any institutions even remotely resembling contemporary states or private property. The mobile foraging bands then making up the common form of human social organization apparently did not, however, suffer the chaos of the Hobbesean state of nature. Rather, in all likelihood they were organized in a manner similar to contemporary mobile hunter-gatherers, their lives regulated by social norms (often including monogamy and resource-sharing) enforced by collective punishment of miscreants. Christopher Boehm (1982:421) writes:

In these . . . communities, group sanction emerged as the most powerful instrument for regulation of individually assertive behaviors, particularly those
which obviously disrupted cooperation or disturbed social equilibrium
needed for group stability.

With the development of agriculture about eleven millennia ago, individual claims on property became more extensive, particularly in land,
stored food, and livestock. These new property rights emerged and proliferated without the assistance of states or other centralized enforcement agencies. Eventually (many millennia after the advent of agriculture), centralized forms of punishment and enforcement of property
rights began to emerge as a new form of organization. This is without a
doubt one of the most important cases of institutional evolution on
record.[9] (I will consider the rise of the modern state in chapter 13.)

Suppose the n members of a foraging band are paired randomly to
divide a good whose value is v. They may adopt three strategies: *grabbing*, *sharing*, and *punishing*. An individual's type is not directly observable, and hence is not known before an interaction. When Sharers meet
they divide the good equally. When Grabbers meet Sharers they take the
good; when they meet one another they fight, gaining the good or bearing the costs of defeat, $c > v$, with equal probability.[10] Punishers meeting either Sharers or other Punishers divide the good equally. However,
when a Punisher is paired with a Grabber, all of the Punishers attempt
to punish the Grabber. If they are successful, the good is distributed in
equal shares to all Punishers, while if unsuccessful the Punisher bears
the cost of defeat, c.

The punishment strategy is collective in the sense that other Punishers
assist any Punisher paired with a Grabber, the result being that the
probability of successfully punishing a Grabber depends on the fraction
of Punishers in the population. To simplify the presentation below, I will
assume that the probability of successfully punishing a Grabber is the
population frequency of Punishers, β. In the simulation, I adopt a less
simplified assumption. Thus, given that the Punisher retains $v/\beta n$ if successful, which happens with probability β, the expected payoff to a
Punisher paired with a Grabber is:

$$\pi(p, g) = \frac{v}{n} - (1 - \beta)c$$

[9] See Bowles and Choi (2002) for a more extensive treatment and references to the
relevant empirical studies.

[10] This will be recognized as a modification of the familiar Hawk Dove Game, the
innovation being the punish strategy.

TABLE 11.1
Payoffs in the Punishment Game (row player's payoff)

	Grab	Share	Punish
Grab	$(v - c)/2$	v	$(1 - \beta)v - \beta c$
Share	0	$v/2$	$v/2$
Punish	$v/n - (1 - \beta)c$	$v/2$	$v/2$

(I will consider the distribution of gains from other successful Punishers presently.) Thus, the payoffs are as in table 11.1.

If α is the population frequency of Sharers, the $(\beta n - 1)$ other Punishers successful in an interaction a Grabber will number $(\beta n - 1)(1 - \alpha - \beta)\beta$. Each Punisher will receive $v/\beta n$ from each of these, so Punishers will receive an expected amount

$$(\beta n - 1)(1 - \alpha - \beta)\frac{\beta v}{\beta n} = (1 - \alpha - \beta)v\left(\beta - \frac{1}{n}\right)$$

in redistribution from fellow Punishers.

The expected payoffs to the three strategies are thus,

$$\pi^s = (\alpha + \beta) \tfrac{1}{2} v \tag{11.5}$$

$$\pi^p = (\alpha + \beta) \tfrac{1}{2} v + (1 - \alpha - \beta)(\beta v - (1 - \beta)c) \tag{11.6}$$

$$\pi^g = \alpha v + \beta\{(1 - \beta)v - \beta c\} + (1 - \alpha - \beta) \tfrac{1}{2} (v - c) \tag{11.7}$$

A convenient graphical representation of the state space for this system is the simplex in figure 11.2.

Suppose that the three strategies are cultural traits, learned from others, and that the cultural transmission process based on these payoffs according to a payoff monotonic updating process. Assume that n is sufficiently large that realized payoffs are approximated by expected payoffs. Thus the familiar replicator dynamic representing the updating process is:

$$\frac{d\alpha}{dt} = \alpha(\pi^s - \underline{\pi}) \tag{11.8}$$

$$\frac{d\beta}{dt} = \beta(\pi^p - \underline{\pi}) \tag{11.9}$$

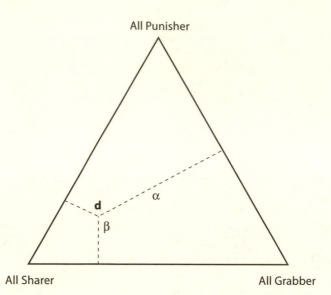

All Punisher

All Sharer

All Grabber

Figure 11.2 The distribution of strategies in a group. At **d** the length of the line segment perpendicular to each edge indicates the frequency of the strategy indicated at the vertex *opposite* the edge. The frequency of Sharers, thus, is α. For **d** and every point in the simplex, these line segments sum to one. Thus at the three vertices, the population is homogeneous.

where the average payoff, $\underline{\pi}$, is

$$\underline{\pi} \equiv \alpha \, \pi^s + \beta \pi^p + (1 - \alpha - \beta)\pi^g.$$

What can we say about the outcomes likely to be generated by this dynamical system? The dynamics implied by the above equations are presented in figure 11.3. The vectors indicate the direction of movement for a population composed by the frequencies given by the point at the base of the arrows. Thus, for example, in region IV α and β are both increasing (the arrows are pointing away from the edge opposite the All Sharer and All Punisher vertices) while γ, the fraction of Grabbers, is decreasing. The figure also gives loci along which each of the population shares is stationary.

Two types of stationary outcome are of substantive interest. In the first, $\beta = 0$, $\alpha = 1 - v/c$ (and $\gamma = v/c$). This outcome, point **b** in figure 11.3, is analogous to the familiar equilibrium of the Hawk Dove Game, and is asymptotically stable. Punishers cannot invade this population. Punishers do no better than Sharers interacting with them, and fare worse than Grabbers when interacting with them (they always fight

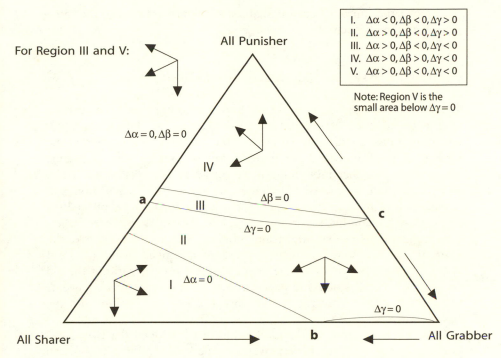

Figure 11.3. Within-group dynamics. The vectors indicate the direction of movement in the regions defined by the loci along which α, β and γ are stationary. To generate this and the next figure we used $v = 2$, $c = 3$.

and almost always lose). I will call this the *Hobbesian equilibrium*, as it is characterized by frequent fighting over property, and as Hobbes concluded in the epigraph to chapter 4, a consequently low level of average payoffs.

The second stationary outcome is the set of outcomes in which $\alpha + \beta = 1$, that is, the left edge of the simplex in figure 11.3. This equilibrium combines the unconditional sharing and collective upholding of social norms admired by Jean-Jacques Rousseau, so, I will call it *Rousseauian*. Of particular interest are the states on the upper portion of this edge, that is, those for which for $\alpha < \alpha^{max}$, the point indicated by **a** in figure 11.3. Each of these points is a Lyapunov (neutrally) stable equilibrium, that is, it is stationary but perturbations are not self-correcting. Every outcome in this set is uninvadeable by Grabbers (or any mixed strategy with grabbing in its support). This is because, for $\alpha < \alpha^{max}$ and $\alpha + \beta = 1$, $\pi^g < \pi^s = \pi^p$. But if nonbest response behavior sometimes occurs, these equilibria are subject to drift downward along the edge of the simplex because Sharers and Punishers receive the same payoffs in the absence of Grabbers.

EQUILIBRIUM SELECTION (HUNTER-GATHERER STYLE)

Which of these equilibria would we expect to obtain? All that can be said in the absence of nonbest-response play is that the outcome depends on initial conditions. To answer the question in a more realistic setting, we need to extend the model to take account of chance events. These could be either mutations (if we considered the behavioral traits to be expressions of genetic inheritance) or some other kind of nonbest-response play, that is, actions undertaken for reasons not accounted for in the model, including experimentation and errors. As the three strategies in this model are cultural traits, nonbest-response actions take the form of switching one's strategy for reasons not given in the model. I will formalize this process in the next chapter, but even without the aid of a model of the stochastic process, it is obvious that chance events may induce a shift from the neighborhood of one equilibrium into the basin of attraction of the other.

Given chance events, in the model thus far developed the Rousseauian equilibrium will not persist over long periods. Suppose $\beta = 1$, so only Punishers are present. Due to nonbest-response play, both Grabbers and Sharers will be introduced into the population. The Grabbers will lose virtually all of their contests with the numerically predominant Punishers and will be eliminated. But in a population composed of just Sharers and Punishers, all will share, and except for the chance occurrence of a Grabber, they will receive the same payoffs. Depending on the rate at which chance events occur, it will take more or less time for sufficiently many Sharers to accumulate so that Grabbers can now invade, the Punishers being too few to impose sufficient punishment on them. In other words, the population will have drifted along the left-hand edge of the simplex in figure 11.3, past point a, that is, into the basin of attraction of the Hobbesian equilibrium.

By contrast to the Rousseauian equilibrium, the Hobbesian equilibrium is asymptotically stable, and thus will not be subject to the chance-induced drift that unravels the former. Of course, the Hobbesian equilibrium will itself be displaced: sooner or later a bunching of chance events will displace the population into the basin of attraction of the Rousseauian equilibrium. But the fact that the Hobbesian equilibrium is not subject to drift means that its displacement will be unlikely in any period and hence will be infrequent. The population would spend most of its time in the neighborhood of the Hobbesian equilibrium. Why then did most of human history witness social arrangements more akin to the Rousseauian equilibrium? What is missing from the model? Three factors might have contributed to its evolutionary success.

First, if groups are subject to periodic encounters with adversity, either environmental or conflicts with other groups, the groups with higher average returns are more likely to survive. Average returns at the Rousseauian equilibrium are $v/2$, and at the Hobbesian equilibrium $v(1 - v/c)/2$, so groups without Grabbers would be favored (and those with Grabbers will be disadvantaged in proportion to the fraction of Grabbers (v/c) in the population). Assuming $v = 2$ and $c = 3$, figure 11.4 gives the expected average payoff of every group composition in the simplex, the contours indicating iso-average-payoff loci. If higher payoff groups expand at the expense of lower payoff groups, the direction of change will be that given by the arrows, namely, not toward the All Punisher state but rather toward the left-hand edge, where Grabbers are absent and average payoffs are maximized.

Second, conformist cultural transmission will work against drift, making the All Punish outcome asymptotically stable. If virtually all members are Punishers, even weak conformism will be enough for Sharers to be eliminated, because the payoffs to Sharing and Punishing are equal in the absence of Grabbers and conformism will favor Punishers.

Finally, *near* the Rousseauian equilibrium, Sharers and Punishers *are* distinguishable because the occasional Grabber who occurs by chance will provide Punishers with an opportunity for collective punishment. The (also rare) Sharer will abstain from the collective punishment, free riding on the civic mindedness of the Punishers. But given human capacities to devise and enforce codes of moral conduct (already practiced by the Punishers against the Grabbers), it is likely that nonpunishing Sharers would also be punished. Once this so-called *second order punishment* is added, the Rouseauian equilibrium will be asymptotically stable even if the cost imposed on free-riding Sharers is small, perhaps nothing but a brief period of shunning or a bit less of a shared food resource. The reason, as in the case of conformism, is that second order punishment need not counteract selection against Punishers; it need only prevent drift.[11]

---

[11] There are other reasons why the Rousseauian equilibrium might persist. It is unrealistic to assume the benefits of the prize are linear rather than concave in the amount acquired. This is particularly so where hunting of large game is concerned, because a single prize—an antelope, say—may represent food enough for the entire membership of the band in a form that is not easily stored. This is the basis of Blurton-Jones' (1987) "toler-

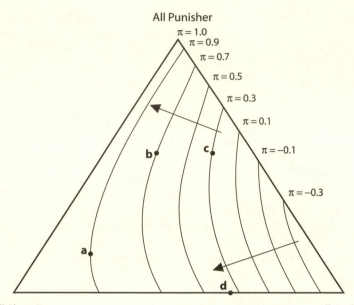

Figure 11.4. Average payoffs and between-group dynamics. The contours indicate distributions of the three strategies in the population for which the group-level average payoff is the same. The arrows indicate the direction of ascent. The highest group average payoff $v/2 = 1$ occurs when Grabbers are absent (the left edge). Thus a group with composition (**a**) (many Sharers, few Grabbers or Punishers) will have higher payoffs than a group (**b**) with many Punishers, few Grabbers and few Sharers. Note (i) that a group with a majority of Punishers such as (**c**) will have lower payoffs than a group at the Grabber-Sharer equilibrium (**d**); (ii) the surface is virtually flat in the neighborhood of the all Sharer distribution. The coordinates of the points indicated are $(1 - \alpha - \beta, \alpha, \beta)$: [**a** = (0.15, 0.70, 0.15), **b** = (0.16, 0.29, 0.55), **c** = (0.33, 0.12, 0.55), **d** = (0.66, 0.34, 0)].

Second order punishment, the shared fates of group members when faced with adversity, and conformist cultural transmission make it plausible that Rouseauian equilibria might have persisted over very long periods of time, even millennia—that is, until the advent of agriculture.

---

ated theft" interpretation of sharing of large food packages in simple societies. Taking account of the concavity of returns would reduce the returns to Grabbing and enhance the returns to dividing the prize (i.e., Sharing or Punishing).

Richerson, Boyd, and Bettinger (2001) show that a dramatic ameliora-
tion of climatic variability about twelve millennia ago transformed the
domestication of plants and animals from a livelihood that was previously "impossible" to one that in the long run became "compulsory."
But the new technology could not readily be deployed in the institutional environment of the typical foraging band. A particular obstacle
was the lack of individual property rights in meat and other large food
resources and land, and the principle of egalitarian division. An example from the recent past of a group of foragers in Malaysia illustrates
the problem:

> The traditional Batek notions that all natural resources are unowned until
> collected and that any food obtained in excess of the needs of the procurer's
> family must be shared with other families seem well suited to a nomadic
> foraging life, but wholly unsuited to . . . peasant farming . . . [G]iving up that
> set of ideas and practices would be psychologically very difficult for them to
> do, as the obligation to share food is one of the fundamental components of
> Batek self-identity and one of the main bonds that link Batek families to-
> gether as a society. (Endicott 1988:126–7)

Endicott reports that some of the Batek planted rice and others (still
foragers) simply harvested it (and, of course, felt obliged to share the
harvest with those foragers who arrived too late) eventually forcing
some of the farming Batek to leave the area.

Because agriculture developed from an intensification of gathering
rather than from hunting, its emergence had impacts on the division of
labor between the sexes. In the American Southwest, groups whose social order remained oriented exclusively toward male activities such as
hunting were displaced by groups that adapted their institutions to better exploit the greater productive potential of what had historically been
"women's work" (Bettinger and Baumhauf 1982).

The Batek case suggests that the development of agriculture depended
on the emergence of rights of possession-based ownership in such things
as crops, stored goods, domesticated animals, and land. Today property
rights are enforced by states, but possession-based ownership emerged
and diffused before the establishment of the centralized enforcement of
claims. How might this have occurred? It seems likely that if the Batek
case were repeated numerous times, a new strategy might emerge and
proliferate: act like a Grabber if one is a possessor, and like a Sharer if
not. This is of course the Bourgeois strategy in the Hawk Dove Game
introduced in chapter 2. Recall that the Bourgeois strategy is evolutionarily stable and can invade the Hobbesian equilibrium, creating a
new asymptotically stable equilibrium (with no Punishers, Grabbers, or

Sharers present) that I will call *Bourgeois*. As long as possession is unambiguous, at this equilibrium no fights occur, so average payoffs are $v/2$. Had something like the Bourgeois strategy not emerged, it seems unlikely that agriculture would have diffused as quickly as it did, if ever.

But if the Bourgeois equilibrium is so good, the reader may wonder, why did it not emerge before the advent of agriculture? A possible answer is that agriculture made possession unambiguous: it is much simpler to determine if this plot of cultivated land or store of nuts is in my possession or not than to know who "possesses" the prey we are stalking but have not yet seen. Ownership of large foraging territory with sparse human population would be equally difficult to define and sustain. We have seen (in chapter 2) that if property rights are sufficiently ambiguous, the Bourgeois strategy may no longer be an ESS. It seems likely that the hunter-gatherer economy militated strongly against the Bourgeois strategy's success, while agriculture created the conditions for its success. Moreover, agriculture favored the Bourgeois equilibrium in two other ways.

First, unlike meat and many gathered foods, grains and other crops could be stored with relatively little loss. This made the relationship between the value of the payoffs and the amount of goods obtained more nearly linear. Not only storage, but also accumulation of stocks became possible. This linearization of benefits reduced the intrinsic advantages of sharing. One could self-insure against adverse future events by storage rather than relying on mutual sharing to smooth out the vagaries of the foraging economy. Second, though initially the productivity advantages of agriculture may have been negligible, subsequent advances in agricultural productivity allowed for those communities adopting it to grow and to survive both environmental and intergroup adversity at a higher rate than the groups that remained foragers.

The resulting diffusion of possession-based property rights gradually eclipsed the social orders of all but a few foraging bands, as the latter came to occupy protected and increasingly confined ecological niches. The greater precision with which possession could be defined in agrarian societies, along with the reduced ability of agrarian community members to simply move to evade punishment, allowed a more effective codification and third-party enforcement of property rights. At the same time, the heightening of inequality among community members (fostered by the ability to accumulate wealth) gave rise to more differentiated economic interests among families and may have made the multilateral forms of norm enforcement more difficult. The resulting growth of centralized enforcement bodies (proto-states) eventually reduced the role of mutual monitoring and peer-based enforcement.

An Agent-Based Model of the First Property Rights Revolution

The account I have just given, while consistent with what is known about the relevant facts, is incomplete in an important respect: I have not shown that the model of the social structure of the foraging band represented by the Rousseian equilibrium could have persisted over the very long run under environmental and other conditions approximating early human existence. Nor have I shown that the causal influences at work would have brought about a revolution in property rights under these empirical conditions. Doing this is a challenging task, not only because of the paucity of data but also because the process is far too complex to be modeled analytically, especially if one takes account of the role of chance events. Even confining our attention to a single group of Sharers, Bourgeois, and Punishers, we can say little more than that there are three equilibria (counting the continuum of Sharers and Punishers as a single equilibrium), one of which is unstable, one is asymptotically stable (the Bourgeois equilibrium), and the other (the Rousseauian) is only neutrally (Lyapunov) stable and hence subject to drift. We would like to be able to answer questions such as: if we observed many such groups over a very long period, what fraction of the time would the population be at or near the Bourgeois equilibrium as opposed to the Rousseauian equilibrium? If a group is at the Rousseauian equilibrium, how long on average will it take for random events to introduce enough Sharers in the population to make it vulnerable to a Bourgeois takeover? Analogously, how long would it take on average for a population at the Bourgeois equilibrium to be displaced to the basin of attraction of the Rousseauian equilibrium? Why, as I suggest actually happened in the early years of our species, would the Rousseauian equilibrium be prevalent over a long period and then be displaced almost everywhere by the Bourgeois equilibrium?

We know that as long as property rights are somewhat ambiguous, the Rousseauian equilibrium will allow higher average payoffs but will be more susceptible to displacement by chance events (drift) than the less efficient but more robust (because it is asymptotically stable) Bourgeois equilibrium. If the groups interact, with the groups with higher average payoffs replacing the weaker groups, how will the group-level selection process affect the distribution of behaviors in the metapopulation? Will the payoff advantages of the Rousseauian equilibrium result in enough victories of Rousseauian groups over Bourgeois groups so that the robustness advantages of the Bourgeois equilibrium are more than offset, and Rousseauian groups predominate? How will migration among groups affect the outcome? And will the perfection of possession-based property rights associated with the rise of agriculture eventually doom the Rousseauian communities?

The mathematical complexity of the underlying model is greatly exacerbated by the fact that both stochastic events and between-group as well as within-group selection processes are at work. In chapter 12, I develop the concept of a stochastically stable state to study evolutionary processes under the influence of stochastic variations in behavior. In chapter 13, I present a clever analytical device — the Price equation (named for the theoretical biologist George Price; it has nothing to do with prices) — for studying the process of multi-level selection. But neither of these analytical tools is entirely adequate. The only practical way to answer the above questions is to simulate an artificial society with characteristics approximating the groups and ecologies of early human history. Simulation gives insights about evolutionary processes that are so complicated that mathematical models do not yield illuminating analytical solutions (or in most cases any solutions at all).

The two main tasks of the simulation are to see if something like the Rousseauian equilibrium could have persisted over many millennia prior to 11,000 years before the present, and to explore the effects of increasing certainty of possession on this social order. For the first task, I study a Sharer-Grabber-Punisher population and then introduce the Bourgeois alternative.

Our artificial society is initially made up of individuals — Sharers, Grabbers, and Punishers — living in groups.[12] Within groups, individuals interact according to the above game (with slight modifications to be described); and they also interact with members of other groups when groups come into conflict over resources or for some other reason. They interact as follows. During each period (a generation), each of the twenty members of a group is randomly paired with another member to play the Grabber-Sharer-Punisher game. Each member plays the game (with a newly selected partner each time) a number of times in a generation (in most simulations, five). If a Punisher and a Grabber meet, the probability that the Punisher will win the fight depends on m, the number of fellow Punishers in the group (who join in punishing the Grabber) and the number of Grabbers, g, with the probability that the Punishers win being $m/(m + g) - \delta$, where $\delta \in [0, \frac{1}{2}]$ is the advantage that the single Grabber has in resisting collective punishment. Note that

---

[12] The simulations are described in Bowles and Choi (2002). The simulation program is available at http://www.santafe.edu/~bowles (go to "artificial histories").

if $\delta = 0$, a single Punisher fighting with a single Grabber would stand an even chance of winning. This and other minor amendments of the theoretical model have been introduced because some of the assumptions adopted above to keep the theoretical model analytically tractable are unrealistic. More plausible assumptions are easily accommodated in the simulation model. As before, if the Punishers win, they share the prize, v.

The agent-based model can accommodate a considerably more detailed account of the process of cultural transmission. We assume the group members live forever, but they occasionally experience a period (call it adolescence) during which they may adopt new behaviors. Once each generation—after all games have been played—each member is paired with a cultural model, possibly a teacher, religious leader, or competitor. This pairing process reflects the way the group socializes its members. If the cultural model and the member are of the same type, the member simply retains his trait. If the two have different traits, then the member compares his total payoffs this period to the model's payoffs, and switches to the model's trait if the model's payoff is higher.

The pairing rule will introduce conformism to the transmission process if each member of the more numerous groups is more likely than others to be drawn to be a cultural model. To allow for this, we let the probability that a Sharer will be drawn as a cultural model be

$$\frac{\alpha^{\eta}}{\alpha^{\eta} + \beta^{\eta} + \gamma^{\eta}}$$

where $\eta > 0$ is a measure of biased cultural transmission. The probability that a Grabber or a Punisher is drawn for the cultural model pool is calculated in similar fashion. Figure 11.5 illustrates the biased assignment of models to members if there are just two types in the population. For $\eta > 1$, the bias is conformist, with larger groups contributing proportionally more to the pool of cultural models. For $\eta = 1$ the pairing of members and cultural models is random. (For $\eta < 1$ the bias is anticonformist, larger groups contributing proportionally fewer to the pool; I do not consider this case.)

Groups were placed on a torus (a donut-shaped graph with no edges, insuring that every group had the same number of neighbors). Each generation, the group engages in a conflict with a randomly chosen neighbor. (Warfare was probably much more common than this; I consider the evidence on the frequency of conflicts in chapter 13.) The group with the higher payoffs wins the conflict with a probability increasing in the payoff difference between the two groups. The payoffs

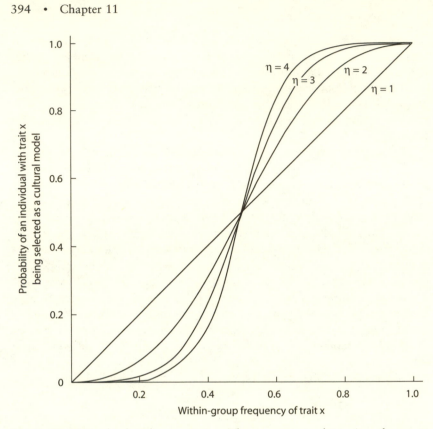

Figure 11.5 Biased cultural transmission. The parameter η determines the extent to which cultural models are drawn disproportionately from the more common types. The figure shows the degree of bias in a group with two types.

to the losers are reduced, and they are assimilated into the winning group.[13] As a result, members of the winning group play a preeminent role in the socialization of the next generation of the losers. I model this as follows. The cultural models for the losing group are all drawn from the winning group according to a pairing rule given by some value of η. Thus, if the winning group is mostly Punishers and the losing group is composed of Grabbers and Sharers, virtually all of the cultural models to which the losers would be exposed will be Punishers, so virtually all of the next generation will not automatically retain their trait but instead will adopt a trait based on a comparison of payoffs. The winners

[13] This model is based on the study of historical assimilation processes as for example took place among the Dinka conquered by the Nuer during the early twentieth century and the assimilation of local European cultures into the nation-states that displaced them between 1500 and 1900. See Weber (1976), Gellner (1983), and Kelly (1985).

Table 11.2

Equilibrium selection: mean distribution of strategies and payoffs

Interaction structure	α	β	γ	π
(a) Group conflict, biased transmission, second order punishment	18.8	72.0	9.2	0.72
(b) None of the above	31.5	8.6	60.0	0.30
(c) Biased transmission and second order punishment	12.9	7.1	79.9	−0.19
(d) Group conflict	39.0	27.6	33.4	0.62
(e) Group conflict and biased transmission	37.7	41.5	20.8	0.74
(f) Group conflict and second order punishment	24.7	57.0	18.3	0.59

The columns headed α, β and γ give the average composition of the total population, that is, the percent Sharers, Punishers, and Grabbers, respectively, in 10 runs totaling 300,000 generations (for each entry). The six interaction structures are the same as in figure 11.6 The average payoff per game is $\underline{\pi}$. The parameter set for these runs is as follows: there are 25 groups with 20 members, the rates of migration and idiosyncratic play are both 0.2 per generation, group conflict occurs every generation, five games are played per generation, with $\eta = 2$, $v = 2$, $c = 3$, $\delta = 0.2$. Following a conflict between Punishers and a Grabber, any Sharers present suffer a second-order punishment of 0.3 while the Punishers bear a cost of carrying out this punishment of 0.15 shared amongst all of them. The post-conflict resource transfer from loser to winner groups is 3 (which when compared to a maximum difference in payoffs per generation of 25 may understate the economic losses in warfare).

of a conflict also seize some of the resources of the losing group, perhaps occupying favored habitats. I model this by a reduction in payoffs to all members of the losing group. The losers thus suffer two effects of their loss, both of which increase the likelihood that they will switch to a trait that was common among the winners: in the generation that they were defeated they are assigned models from the winning group, and their payoffs are reduced.

Jung-Kyoo Choi and I simulated the above dynamic. To explore the viability of the Rousseauian equilibrium, we systematically compared the distribution of types in the total population under the six distinct structures of within- and between-group social interaction listed in table 11.2. Migration takes place among neighboring groups (the so-called stepping stone model of migration) while keeping group size constant at twenty. The parameter set for these runs is as follows: there are twenty-five groups with twenty members, the rates of migration and idiosyncratic play are both 0.2 per generation, group conflict occurs every generation, five games are played per generation, $\eta = 2$, $v = 2$, $c = 3$, $\delta = 0.2$. Following a conflict between Punishers and a Grabber, Sharers in the group suffered a second order punishment of 0.3, while the Pun-

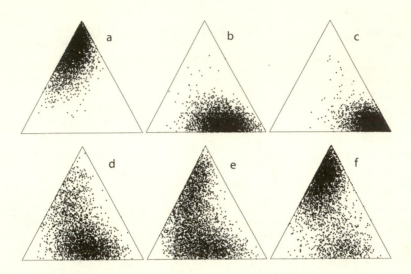

Figure 11.6 Equilibrium selection: simulation results. The simplexes shown here are the same as in figure 11.3: the top vertex in the "all Punisher" outcome, the left vertex is "all Sharer" and the right vertex is "all Grabber": Each simplex represents a distinct structure of within and between group interactions. The dots in each simplex indicate the composition of one group in one generation. The interaction structures represented in each panel are: (a) group conflict, biased cultural transmission, second-order punishment; (b) none of the above; (c) biased cultural transmission and second-order punishment; (d) group conflict; (e) group conflict and biased cultural transmission; and (f) group conflict and second-order punishment. The 5000 observations shown here represent the composition of all 25 groups in 200 consecutive generations selected to correspond closely to the average compositions over the 300,000 generations simulated for each treatment.

ishers share a cost of carrying out this punishment of 0.15 shared among all of them. The post-conflict resource transfer from loser to winner groups is 3 (which, when compared to a maximum between-group difference in payoffs per generation of twenty-five, may understate the economic losses in warfare). We initiated each simulation with a random distribution of types in each of the groups. To be confident that we had captured the long term average behavior of the system, we executed twenty or thirty simulations of 10,000 generations for the results reported, which insured that the initial conditions or occasional long-term lockin to a particular equilibrium did not bias our results.

Figure 11.6 presents a sample of the main results; panels **a** and **b**, respectively, represent specifications for which most groups were in the neighborhood of the Rousseauian and Hobbesian equilibrium.

What accounts for the difference in panels **a** and **b** is that the former is a simulation representing the structure of social interactions that I consider typical of the mobile foraging band: intergroup conflicts, second order punishment, and conformist cultural transmission (i.e., line a of table 11.2). By contrast, the simulation in panel **b** included none of these aspects of hunter-gatherer society (line b). Table 11.2, reporting the average of 300,000 generations for each entry, confirms the visual impression given by the sample of data points in figure 11.6. When all three aspects are present, Punishers constitute almost three-quarters of the population on the average, and when all three are absent, Grabbers make up 60 percent of the population. Average payoffs are more than twice as great under the first condition. Comparison of panels **a** and **b** suggests that these three aspects of social interaction (or some of them in combination) played a central role in the remarkable persistence of the foraging way of life.

To identify the contribution of each, we ran simulations with all the possible combinations. For example, when biased cultural transmission and second order punishment are operative, but there are no group conflicts (panel **c**) an even greater fraction of the population are Grabbers and Sharers are correspondingly fewer. The reason is that conformist transmission favors the Grabbers while second order punishment of Sharers by the few Punishers present reduces the payoffs of both types. When group conflict and second order punishment are combined without conformist transmission (**f**), the population oscillates between the neighborhood of the Rousseauian and Hobbesian equilibria.

Notice that when the population is in the neighborhood of the Rousseauian equilibrium, a substantial number of Sharers are typically present. This is in part the result of drift along the left edge of the simplex, as anticipated. But in addition, group conflict strongly favors groups with many Sharers (recall the group average payoff contours in figure 11.5). A surprising result of this is that group selection per se tends to *de*stabilize the Rousseauian equilibrium by accelerating movement downward along the left edge of the simplex, propelling groups into the basin of attraction of the Hobbesian equilibrium.

By contrast, in simulations in which second order punishment and conformist transmission combined with group conflict, most groups remained close enough to the Rousseauian equilibrium to avoid the unraveling of its social order. The occasional groups near the Hobbesian equilibrium were then readily eliminated by group conflict (recall the substantial difference in payoffs). When group conflict alone is operative, the population is about evenly divided, with a slight preponderance of Sharers, Punishers being the smallest of the three subpopulations (table 11.2). Simulations not shown indicate that if group conflicts are less frequent (once every two or three generations), the Rousseauian equilibrium is sustained most of the time, as long as second order punishment and conformist cultural transmission ($\eta = 2$) are operative. The results are not very sensitive to variations in group size and the rates of non-best response play and migration.

How does the reduction in the ambiguity of property rights associated with the introduction of agriculture and the coincident appearance of Bourgeois players change the picture? As one would suspect, the answer depends on how good the property rights are. As in chapter 2, I assume that property rights may be unambiguous, in which case the possession is never in doubt, so two Bourgeois types, when they meet, never fight. But property rights may be in doubt, in which case some fraction of the time, μ, the intruding Bourgeois believes he is the possessor (or acts that way), resulting in a fight with the possessing Bourgeois. To model this new situation, we eliminate the Grabbers (we know that Bourgeois mimics Grabber when property rights are always mistaken, and will do better than Grabber as long as property rights are *ever* correctly identified, so they would be eliminated by the evolutionary forces we are modeling in any case). But we retain the Sharers, because their role in unraveling the Rousseauian equilibrium is an essential part of the evolutionary process under investigation.

One way to explore the effect of the decline in property rights ambiguity is to simulate the population for the various combinations of structures of between- and within-group interaction, for values of μ from 1 (complete ambiguity) to 0. Figure 11.7 presents these results. Because the Bourgeois strategy is identical to the Grabber under complete property rights ambiguity, the Bourgeois fraction in the simulations with $\mu = 1$ replicates the results for the Grabber column in table 11.2. When group conflict, biased cultural transmission, and second order punishment are all operative, the Bourgeois fraction of the population remains low until μ falls to one-half or less. But with additional improvements in the definition of property rights, the Bourgeois fraction rises steeply. By contrast, when only group conflict is operative, even small reductions in the ambiguity of property rights result in significant increases in the Bourgeois fraction.

What can one conclude from these simulations? We have learned that for the parameter values and model specification implemented, the Rousseauian equilibrium is sustainable against either the Hobbesian or Bourgeois equilibrium if property rights are ambiguous and second order punishment, conformist transmission or group conflict is operative. However, as property rights become more certain, these mechanisms cannot sustain the Rousseauian equilibrium even when all of its supporting mechanisms are operating simultaneously. Both the historical

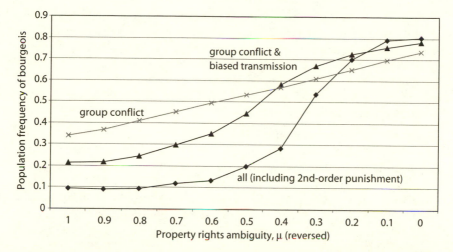

Figure 11.7 A decline in property rights ambiguity favors the Bourgeois strategy. Each point is the average frequency in 20 simulations of 10,000 generations each. Simulations in group conflict and second order punishment were virtually identical to that shown that combine group conflict and biased transmission.

relevance of the hunter-gather social order modeled as the Rousseauian equilibrium and the critical role of the emergence of agriculture and the increasing certainty of possession are strongly suggested by these simulations. Of course, this does not mean that the property rights revolution happened for the reasons given above. All that this or any other simulation can show is that it could have.[14]

The model has stressed the importance of an exogenous technology shock in the emergence of individual property rights. But the commonly held view that a *prior* domestication of animals and plants created the environment in which individual rights could assume greater importance is surely incorrect. As the case of the hapless Batek rice growers suggests, had something like collectivist and egalitarian property rights of the typical foraging band not given way to individual property rights, it is unlikely that agriculture would have proven such a successful alternative to the foraging way of life. The early transformation of the human diet to include more meat provides another example. Winterhalder and Smith (1992:60) write:

[14] Our interpretation will be more persuasive if it proves difficult to model and simulate alternative scenarios that generate the relevant historical transitions for historically plausible parameter sets.

[O]nly with the evolution of reciprocity or exchange-based food transfers did it become economical for individual hunters to target large game. The effective value of a large mammal to a lone forager . . . probably was not great enough to justify the cost of attempting to pursue and capture it. . . . However, once effective systems of reciprocity or exchange augment the effective value of very large packages to the hunter, such prey items would be more likely to enter the optimal diet.

As in the case of domestication, the technological change — targeting big game — apparently does not predate and cause the cultural change; rather it appears that the two developed in tandem. An account of the first property rights revolution recognizing the role of culture in shaping technological evolution, as well as the converse, would identify the climate change as the exogenous shock, with technology (domestication) and culture (new property rights) co-evolving in the newly ameliorated ecological settings.[15]

This model thus may provide the causal underpinnings for the claim that possession-based property rights may be counted among Parsons's list of evolutionary universals (discussed in the next chapter), while vindicating Hayek's suggestion that market institutions may have evolved through cultural group selection.[16] Ironically, the causal mechanism at work in the simulations is Marxian in origin, for Marx was the first to articulate the view that revolutions in social structure are driven by advances in technology (see the epigraph). The same mechanism (albeit with less revolutionary consequences) appears to have been at work in a number of property rights transitions. Examples include the introduction of barbed wire fencing and its impact on property rights in the U.S. Southwest (Anderson and Hill 1975) and the impact of water-driven mills in nineteenth century New England on riparian rights (Horwitz 1977). Oliver (1962) gives a related account of the transformation of the social structure of the U.S. Plains Indians resulting from the introduction of horses. Of course, if this general approach to the evolution of property rights is correct, there is no reason to doubt that future changes in technology may lead to further property rights transformations, suggesting that the teleological implications sometimes read into the work of Parsons, Hayek, and Marx may be misguided.

[15] Richerson and Boyd (2001) advance a similar co-evolutionary interpretation of the evolution of social complexity.

[16] The model may also give a causal basis for the otherwise functionalist explanation of the emergence of individual property rights offered by Alchian and Demsetz (1973) and other seminal works of the property rights paradigm. Many historical and ethnographic studies inspired by the property rights school, however, provide persuasive causal accounts of changes in property rights regimes. Among these not cited elsewhere are Davis and North (1971), Firmin-Sellers (1996), Umbeck (1977), and Libecap (1978).

Conclusion

It seems likely, then, that preferences and institutions *coevolve*, each exerting an influence on the development of the other. The logic of the endogenous preference model earlier in the chapter was to let a given (possibly unconscious) updating rule—copy behaviors that are prevalent and successful—assume the central explanatory role usually assigned to conscious optimization of given preferences. The updating rule, along with the structure of social interactions, influences how preferences evolve. Preferences are thus endogenous, with the exogenous updating rule and a given structure of social interactions performing the analytical work done in the standard model by exogenous preferences.

Institutions are also endogenous. Preferences influence which institutions are feasible and likely to persist. The distribution of behavioral types in a population, as we have seen in chapter 7, influences the equilibrium distribution of contracts. In this chapter, exogenous changes in technology (the rise of agriculture, the feasibility of food storage) have played an important role in promoting change in both institutions and preferences, affirming Marx's view that "the development of the material forces of production" is one of the main dynamic forces in history. Why, as Marx suggests, institutions might be an inertial force periodically disrupted by technical change (rather than the reverse) is something of a puzzle. A possible resolution is that institutions are characterized by high levels of strategic complementarities, so that if just a few members of a population adopt behaviors appropriate to a new institutional convention, they would be unlikely to benefit even if the conventional were payoff dominant with respect to the status quo. The fact that the simulation results cluster around either the Hobbesian or the Rousseauian equilibria (panels **a**, **b**, **c** and **f** of figure 11.6) illustrates this "all or nothing" aspect of institutional evolution. By contrast, new technologies can sometimes be adopted piecemeal, with individual adopters reaping substantial payoff advantages.

In chapter 12, I model this institutional inertia stemming from strategic complementarity. By providing an account of how the inertia may occasionally be overcome, and why some institutions are more robust than others, I address the question of why some institutions are more commonly observed than others.

CHAPTER TWELVE

Chance, Collective Action, and Institutional Innovation

> The central problem of evolution . . . is that of a trial and error mechanism by which the locus of a population may be carried across a saddle from one peak to another and perhaps higher one. This view contrasts with the conception of steady progress under natural selection. . . . Consideration of the means by which the locus of a population may be carried across a saddle may be of interest from this standpoint.
> —Sewall Wright, *Journal of Genetics* (1935)

> Men make history, but they do not make it just as they please; they do not make it under circumstances chosen by themselves but under circumstances . . . given and transmitted from the past. The tradition of all the dead generations weighs like a nightmare on the brain of the living.
> —Karl Marx, *The Eighteenth Brumaire of Louis Bonaparte* (1852)

HERNÁN CORTÉS' long letters to King Charles of Castile describe the exotic and unusual customs he and his armed band encountered as they advanced toward Temixtitan in 1519. But in light of the thirteen or more millennia that had passed since there had been any sustained contact between people of the Old World and the New, what is striking about his account of Mexico is how familiar it all was. Upon reaching Temixtitan (modern day Mexico City), Cortés wrote:

> The city has many squares where trading is done and markets are held continuously. There is one square twice as big as that of Salamanca with arcades all around, where more than sixty thousand people come each day to buy and sell, and every kind of merchandise . . . is found. . . . It seems like the silk market at Granada, except that there is a much greater quantity. . . . Everything is sold by number and size . . . there is in this great square a very large building like a courthouse where ten or twelve persons sit as judges. . . . There are in this square other persons who walk among the people to see

The first epigraph is from Wright (1935:264), the second from Marx (1963:15).

what they are selling and the measures they are using; and they have been seen to break some that are false. (Cortes (1986:103–5)

The Aztec class structure presented no surprises:

> There are many chiefs, all of whom reside in this city, and the country towns contain peasants who are vassals of these lords and each of whom holds his land independently; some have more than others. . . . And there are many poor people who beg from the rich in the streets as the poor do in Spain and in other civilized places. (p. 68)

Cortés continues, describing the "many temples or houses for their idols," and comments that "the orderly manner which, until now, these people have been governed is almost like that of the states of Venice or Genoa or Pisa" (p. 105).

Some types of social arrangements — markets, states, monogamy, private property, worshiping supernatural beings, social ranking, and sharing the necessities of life among non-kin, for example — have been ubiquitous over long periods of human history and have independently emerged and persisted in highly varied environments. Others of passing importance generally occupy limited ecological niches.

Some scholars, like Cortés, are impressed by the similarity of institutions in quite differing environments and have postulated a coherent set of "modern" social arrangements toward which most independent societal trajectories are said to be tending. Talcott Parsons (1964) termed these *evolutionary universals* — those ways of ordering society that crop up with sufficient frequency in a variety of circumstances to suggest their general evolutionary viability. Parsons offered vision as a biological analogy to these evolutionary universals; another example would be sexual reproduction. Both have emerged under a wide variety of circumstances and in a great many species. Parsons identified money, markets, bureaucracy, stratification, and democracy as human social examples. Frederich Hayek (1988) refers to the markets and private property nexus — his "extended order" — in a similar vein. As we saw in chapter 2, many attribute the evolutionary success of these institutions to their societal efficiency. Marx's conception of the historical succession of institutions under the influence of changing technology as illustrated in the epigraph of chapter 11, similarly posits a tendency — albeit a very long-term one — for institutions that advance dynamic efficiency to prevail.

Others have stressed the fundamentally path-dependent evolution of social structure, with distinct societal histories emerging as the result of initially small differences. Chance, not progress, plays the leading role in these accounts, as in the epigraph to this chapter by Sewall Wright. This view stresses not institutional convergence but the long-term coexistence of distinct evolutionarily stable institutions. Mexico provides a telling example of this pattern of institutional divergence as well. Cortés's service to the crown was rewarded with the title of Marqués del Valle de Oaxaca. Modern-day researchers in Oaxaca are puzzled by the juxtaposition of villages with extraordinarily high homicide rates with others in which homicide is virtually unknown. These villages do not differ in any of the commonly ascribed causes of violence such as alcohol use, boundary quarrels, crowding, and political competition. Some of the villagers, however, are distinguished by long-established traditions of "antiviolence" coupled with the absence of social rank and the rotation of village offices (Paddock 1991, 1975, Greenberg 1989). At least one case of a violent convention being displaced by a nonviolent one among the Oaxaca communities is recorded.

These institutional and behavioral differences among the villages in the Valley of Oaxaca along with the familiarity of the institutions that Cortés encountered in Temixtitan pose one of the questions to which this chapter is addressed: what are the general characteristics (if any) of evolutionarily successful institutions? To provide an answer, we will need an understanding of the birth, diffusion, and eclipse of institutions and the process by which one institution supplants another. This will require an account of how characteristics of institutions contribute to their evolutionary success.

As we have seen in chapter 11, the processes bringing about institutional change may involve some combination of between-group competition and within-group dynamics. In this chapter, I confine myself to the within-group processes, returning in chapter 13 to a consideration of between-group processes. Two quite distinct approaches to the within-group processes bringing about institutional innovation may be identified.

The first, similar to Sewall Wright's use of genetic drift to explain a movement from one fitness peak across a fitness valley to another peak, uses stochastic evolutionary game theory, pioneered by Dean Foster and Peyton Young. In this Darwin-inspired approach, change occurs through the chance bunching of individuals' idiosyncratic nonbest response actions. These will occasionally be sufficient to tip the underlying dynamic process from the basin of attraction of one conventional equilibrium to another. Changes in language use, contractual shares, market days, and etiquette have been modeled in this manner.

The second approach, initiated by Marx, stresses asymmetries among the players and explains institutional innovation by the changing power balance among those who benefit from differing conventions. In this framework, revolutionary change in institutions is likely when existing institutions facilitate the collective action of those who would benefit from a change in institutions, and when, because existing institutions are inefficient by comparison to an alternative, there are substantial potential gains to making a switch. This collective action–based approach has been used to model conflicts among classes resulting in a basic transformation of social organization such as the French, Russian, and Cuban revolutions, as well as more gradual changes in institutional arrangements such as the centuries-long erosion of European feudalism.

Do these approaches allow us to say anything about the characteristics of evolutionarily successful institutions? Though the underlying causal mechanisms are different, the Marx-inspired approach shares with Darwin-inspired stochastic evolutionary game theory the prediction that institutional arrangements that are both inefficient and highly unequal will bear an evolutionary disability and will tend to be displaced in the long run by more efficient and more egalitarian institutions.[1] This is quite an arresting claim in light of the long-term historical persistence of social arrangements that would appear to be neither efficient nor egalitarian. I will explore this proposition as a way of both introducing and extending the stochastic evolutionary game theoretic approach.

I begin in the next section with a simple nonstochastic population game in which the stage game exhibits two conventional equilibria. The evolution of institutions is then represented as a problem of equilibrium selection to be studied using a model of institutional persistence and accessibility. To do this, I introduce stochastic evolutionary game theory. Drawing on the work of Young and Kandori, Mailath, and Rob, I show that it yields a rather strong characterization of evolutionary successful institutions akin to Parsons's evolutionary universals.

Stochastic evolutionary game theory makes two major contributions to the study of institutional dynamics. First, it allows us to go beyond the correct but not very illuminating conclusion that "history matters" and to study how evolutionary processes will favor some kinds of institutions over others. Second, it provides a way of taking account of the importance of chance events.

The major shortcomings of stochastic evolutionary game theory as an account of real historical processes of institutional change are two. First, the relevant theorems about the characteristics of robust institutions apply only when the rate of nonbest-response play is arbitrarily small.

Second, it neglects the important part played by collective action in

---

[1] Efficient institutions yield a larger joint surplus, while in a more equal convention, the share of the typical least well-off member is larger.

the process of institutional innovation and transformation. It was not a fortuitous piling up of unlikely accidents that doomed apartheid or Communism, but rather a combination of chance events and the deliberate and coordinated actions taken by reasoning individuals seeking to live under other institutions.

For this reason I augment the stochastic framework by introducing players who intentionally pursue conflicting interests through collective action. Using this extended model, I explore the long-term persistence of equal and efficient conventions when less efficient and less equal conventions are also feasible. The dynamics supported by intentional rather than accidental nonbest-response actions are not the same, and models incorporating intentional action in pursuit of common interests suggest that while more efficient and more equal institutions are indeed favored by this evolutionary process under some conditions, it is also true that inefficient and unequal institutions can persist over very long periods of time.

THE PERSISTENCE AND ACCESSIBILITY OF HISTORICALLY CONTINGENT INSTITUTIONS

Because of their historical importance, I will focus on economic institutions that regulate the size of the social surplus and its distribution. An institution may be represented as one of a number of possible conventional equilibria in which members of a population typically act in ways that are best responses to the actions taken by others and have formed expectations that support continued adherence to these conventional actions. Examples of such distributional conventions include simple principles of division such as "finders keepers" or "first come, first served," as well as more complicated principles of allocation such as the variety of rules that have governed the exchange of goods or the division of the products of one's labor over the course of human evolution. Because a convention is one of many possible mutual best responses defined by the underlying game, institutions are not environmentally determined but rather are of human construction (but not necessarily of deliberate design).

Because nothing of importance concerning the main points below is lost in taking an especially simple case, I confine myself to the analysis of the evolutionary dynamics governing transitions between two conventions in a two-person two-strategy game in a large population of individuals subdivided into two groups, the members of which are randomly paired to interact in a noncooperative game with members of the

TABLE 12.1
Payoffs in the contract game

	B offer Contract 1	B offer Contract 0
A offer Contract 1	$a_{11}\, b_{11}$	0, 0
A offer Contract 0	0, 0	$a_{00},\, b_{00}$

other group. Individuals' best-response play is based on a single-period memory: they maximize their expected payoffs based on the distribution of the population in the previous period.

The two population subgroups, initially assumed to be of equal size, are termed As and Bs, and each when paired with a member of the other group may chose action 1 or 0, with the As' payoffs, a_{ij} representing the payoff to an A-person playing action i against a B-person playing action j, and analogously for the Bs. If the members of the pair choose the same action they get positive benefits, while if they chose different actions they get a lesser payoff. For concreteness, suppose the subgroups are economic classes selecting a contract to regulate their joint production, which will only take place if they agree on a contract. Payoffs are shares of the joint surplus of the project, with the no-production outcome normalized to zero for both. The payoffs, with the As as the row player, and the Bs as column player, are shown in table 12.1.

To capture the conflict of interest between the two groups, let us assume that $b_{00} > b_{11} = a_{11} > a_{00} > 0$ so the Bs strictly prefer the outcome in which both play 0, the As prefer the equal division outcome which results when both play 1.[2] Both of these outcomes are strict Nash equilibria, and thus both represent conventions, which I will denote E_0 and E_1 (or {0, 0} and {1, 1}). Both populations are normalized to unit size, so I refer equivalently to the numbers of players and the fraction of the population, abstracting from integer problems.

The state of this population in any time period t is {α_t, β_t}, where α is the fraction of the As who played 1 in the previous period and β is the fraction of the Bs who played 1. For any state of the population, expected payoffs a_i and b_i, for the As and Bs, respectively playing strategy

---

[2] I refer to {1, 1} as the "equal" convention as a shorthand. The levels of well-being attained by the As and Bs cannot be determined without additional information. If the As are sharecroppers who interact with only one B (a landlord), while Bs interact with many As, the "equal" convention would exhibit unequal incomes of the two groups, for example.

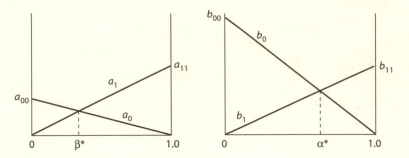

Figure 12.1 Expected payoffs in the contract game. Note: A's payoffs depend on β, the fraction of Bs offering contract 1, while the B's payoffs depend on α, the fraction of As offering contract 1. Because $b_{00} > b_{11} = a_{11} > a_{00}$, the convention E_1 (that is, $\alpha = 1 = \beta$) is preferred by the As while E_0 is preferred by the Bs.

i, depend on the distribution of play among the opposing group in the previous period, or dropping the time subscript,

$$a_1 = \beta a_{11}; \quad a_0 = (1 - \beta)a_{00}; \quad b_1 = \alpha b_{11}; \quad \text{and } b_0 = (1 - \alpha)b_{00}$$

The relationship between the population state and the expected payoffs to each action is illustrated in figure 12.1.

Individuals take a given action — they are 1-players or 0-players — and they continue doing so from period to period until they update their action, at which point they may switch. Suppose that at the beginning of every period some fraction ω of each subpopulation may update their actions. (This might be due to the age structure of the population, with updating taking place only at a given period of life, in which case the "periods" in the model may be understood as "generations." Of course, updating could be much more frequent.)[3] The updating is based on the expected payoffs to the two actions. These expectations are simply the payoffs that would obtain if the previous period's state remained unchanged (the population composition in the previous period being common knowledge in the current period). While this updating process is not very sophisticated, it may realistically reflect individuals' cognitive

---

[3] Giving individuals a longer (than one period) memory, or a less naive updating rule, or a more limited knowledge of the distribution of types in the other subpopulation, would not yield substantially different insights about the questions explored here. The overlapping-generations assumption concerning updating is, however, important as it means that the stochastic shocks due to idiosyncratic play (introduced presently) are persistent as the realized distribution of play in the previous period reflects the shocks experienced over many past periods.

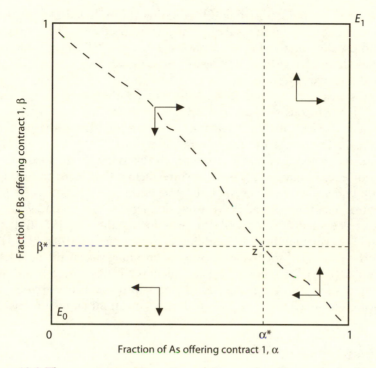

Figure 12.2 The state space. Note: E_1 and E_0 are absorbing states in the non-stochastic dynamic; z is a saddle.

capacities and it ensures that in equilibrium — when the population state is stationary — the beliefs of the actors formed in this naive way are confirmed in practice.

Individuals are represented simply as bearers of the strategies they have adopted, while the distribution of strategies among them varies. I will analyze the single-period change in the population state $(\Delta\alpha, \Delta\beta)$ under the assumption that individual updating of strategies is monotonic in expected payoffs so that $\Delta\alpha$ and $\Delta\beta$ have the signs respectively, of $(a_1 - a_0)$ and $(b_1 - b_0)$. The resulting population dynamics are illustrated in figure 12.2, where the relevant regions are defined by what may be termed the "tipping frequencies":

$$\alpha^* = \frac{b_{00}}{b_{11} + b_{00}}$$

$$\beta^* = \frac{a_{00}}{a_{11} + a_{00}}$$

(12.1)

these two population distributions equating the expected payoffs to the two strategies for the two subpopulations, respectively. These values of α and β define best-response functions: for $\alpha < \alpha^*$ B's best response is to play 0, and for $\alpha \geq \alpha^*$ B's best response is to play 1, with β^* interpreted analogously.

For states $\alpha < \alpha^*$ and $\beta < \beta^*$ (in the southwest region of figure 12.2), it is obvious that $\Delta\alpha$ and $\Delta\beta$ are both negative and the population will move to $\{0, 0\}$. Analogous reasoning holds for the northeast region. In the northwest and southeast regions of the state space, we may define a locus of states from which the system will transit to the interior equilibrium $\{\alpha^*, \beta^*\}$, with states below that locus transiting to $\{0, 0\}$, and above the locus to $\{1, 1\}$. The basin of attraction of $\{0, 0\}$, is the area below the dashed downward-sloping line in figure 12.2; its size will vary with $\{\alpha^*, \beta^*\}$. While the interior equilibrium $\{\alpha^*, \beta^*\}$ is an unstable Nash equilibrium (a saddle), the outcomes $\{0, 0\}$ and $\{1, 1\}$ are absorbing states of the dynamic process, meaning that if the population is ever at either of these states, it will never leave. There being more than one such absorbing state, the dynamic process is *non-ergodic*, that is, its long-run average behavior is dependent on initial conditions.

CHANCE AND CHANGE

How, then, might institutional change occur? Because best-response play renders both conventions absorbing states, it is clear that in order to understand institutional change, some kind of nonbest-response play must be introduced. Suppose there is a probability ε that when individuals are in the process of updating, each may switch their type for idiosyncratic reasons. Thus, $(1 - \varepsilon)$ represents the probability that the individual pursues the best-response updating process described above. The idiosyncratic play accounting for nonbest responses need not be irrational or odd; it simply represents actions whose reasons are not explicitly modeled. Included is experimentation, whim, error, and intentional acts seeking to affect game outcomes but whose motivations are not captured by the above game.

Idiosyncratic play can lead to transitions from one convention to another in the following way: if the status quo convention is $\{0, 0\}$ but a sufficiently large number of As play 1 for some reason not captured by the model, then in the next period, the best response of the Bs, having encountering these 1-playing As will be to play 1 as well. In the next period, the best response of the As who encountered these 1-playing Bs will be to play 1, and so on, possibly leading to the "tipping" of the population from the $\{0, 0\}$ to the $\{1, 1\}$ convention.

For finite populations, the presence of idiosyncratic play transforms the dynamical system described above from a non-ergodic one to an ergodic process with no absorbing states. Ergodicity means that we can specify long-term average behavior independently of the initial conditions, a result of central importance in what follows. The simplest case arises when $\omega = 1$ (everyone updates in every period). Then the Markov process described by the model yields a strictly positive transition matrix, meaning that from any state the system will transit to every other state with positive probability. To see that this is true, suppose all members of both subpopulations are "selected" for idiosyncratic play and note that any distribution of their responses is possible, thus giving positive weight to the probability of moving to any state, irrespective of the originating state.[4] Thus, the population is perpetually in motion, or at least susceptible to movement, and its state is path dependent: where it was in the recent past influences where it will most likely be at any moment. History matters, and it never ends.

The fact that the population state is perpetually changing does not mean, of course, that all states are equally likely: the long-run average behavior of the system can be studied. The basic idea is that conventions that require a large amount of idiosyncratic play to dislodge, while requiring little idiosyncratic play to access, will persist over long periods, and if eclipsed by some other convention will readily reemerge. I call these conventions *robust*. We need to formalize this intuition that robust conventions are "easy to get to, hard to leave."

First, a robust convention is *persistent*: once at or near the convention, it takes a substantial amount of nonbest-response play to dislodge it. By *dislodge*, I mean to create a situation in which no further idiosyncratic play is required to lead the population to abandon the convention. Consider the convention E_0. It can be dislodged in two ways: if more than α^* of the As or more than β^* of the Bs idiosyncratically play 1. The larger are α^* and β^*, the less likely is a dislodging event to take place, so these are measures of persistence of E_0. Likewise, E_1 may be dislodged if more than $(1 - \alpha^*)$ of the As or more than $(1 - \beta^*)$ of the Bs idiosyncratically play 0.

Second, a robust convention is *accessible*: in the 2×2 case, this means the *other* convention is *not* persistent: it does not require much bunching of nonbest-response play at the other convention to displace the population state into the basin of attraction of the robust convention. How accessible is E_0? If more than $(1 - \alpha^*)$ of the As or more

---

[4] Where $\omega < 1$, the above intuition remains correct, because if in every period any distribution of play among the potential innovators is possible, then in a sufficiently long period of time any distribution of play among the entire population is also possible.

than $(1 - \beta^*)$ of the Bs play 0, the population may move from the $\{1, 1\}$ to the $\{0, 0\}$ contract. A bunching of nonbest-response play that tips the population from the basin of attraction of E_1 to the basin of attraction of E_0 is more likely to occur the larger are α^* and β^*, so these are measures of the accessibility of E_0.

Persistence is analogous to evolutionary stability or noninvadeability introduced by Maynard Smith and Price (1973), α^* and β^* representing *the invasion barrier* or the minimum number of mutant 1-players who would proliferate if introduced into a population of 0-players. Accessibility is analogous to the concept of capacity to invade — called *initial viability* by Axelrod and Hamilton (1981).

Note that α^* and β^* thus measure *both* persistence and accessibility of E_0 (with $(1 - \alpha^*)$ and $(1 - \beta^*)$ the persistence and accessibility of E_1). The fact that in the 2×2 coordination game structure the accessibility of a convention is just one minus the persistence of the other will be important below. Thus, if *both* α^* and β^* exceed one-half, E_0 has the "easy to get to, hard to leave" qualities of a robust convention. But what if $\alpha^* > \frac{1}{2} > \beta^*$, or the reverse? Recall that there are two ways to get to a convention and two ways to leave, that is, by the idiosyncratic actions of either As or Bs. We need to take account of both. I will discuss two answers to this question, one proposed by stochastic evolutionary game theory and the other (introduced presently) based on a representation of idiosyncratic play not as accidental but rather as intentional collective action.

Define a *stochastically stable state* as one that occurs with nonnegligible probability when the rate of idiosyncratic play is arbitrarily small. As ε goes to zero, the population will generally spend most of the time at one convention; this is the stochastically stable state. Letting ε go to zero solves the problem above of determining which path the population will take in moving from one convention to another: it is more likely to take the most probable path, and as ε goes to zero, the probability of taking the less probable path is vanishingly small and hence can be ignored. The more likely path is that which requires fewer cases of nonbest-response play.

Following Young (1998), define r_{jk}, the *reduced resistance* on the path from E_j to E_k, as the minimal number of individuals in a population adhering to the convention E_j that, should they idiosyncratically switch their strategy to k, would induce their best-responding partners to switch theirs. Then

$$r_{10} = \min(1 - \alpha^*, 1 - \beta^*)$$
$$r_{01} = \min(\alpha^*, \beta^*). \tag{12.2}$$

The convention *to* which the reduced resistence is least is the stochastically stable state. The reduced resistances to a convention are also the risk factors of the convention (r_{jk} is the risk factor of E_k). So the stochastically stable state is the state with the least risk factor and hence is the risk-dominant equilibria.[5]

Thus, the convention {0, 0} will be stochastically stable if

$$r_{10} = \min(1 - \alpha^*, 1 - \beta^*) < \min(\alpha^*, \beta^*) = r_{01}$$

Using the payoffs $b_{00} > b_{11} = a_{11} > a_{00}$ we have

$$r_{10} = 1 - \alpha^* = 1 - \frac{b_{00}}{b_{11} + b_{00}} = \frac{b_{11}}{b_{11} + b_{00}}$$

$$r_{01} = \beta^* = \frac{a_{00}}{a_{11} + a_{00}}$$

$$(12.3)$$

Thus as ε goes to zero, it is the idiosyncratic actions of the Bs that propel a movement from {0, 0} to {1, 1} while the As' idiosyncratic actions induce the reverse tipping. The convention [0, 0] will be the stochastically stable state if $(1 - \alpha^*) < \beta^*$, or using the above expressions, if

$$a_{00}b_{00} > a_{11}b_{11} \qquad (12.4)$$

Note that the two terms in eq. (12.4) are just the product of the difference between As' and Bs' payoffs and their fallback position (which is zero). Thus, a contract that is closer (in this sense) to the Nash solution for the division game is the stochastically stable state. This should come as no surprise given the result in chapter 5 that the bargain that maximizes the Nash product is the stationary distributional norm in a plausible dynamic with occasional idiosyncratic play.

What does eq. (12.4) tell us about the characteristics of stochastically stable states? Suppose contracts differ in their distributional shares and also in the level of total surplus they yield. Let the total surplus be denominated in units of physical output, and assume that the (von-Neumann-Morgenstern) utility functions of the As and Bs are linear in out-

---

[5] Young (1998), theorem 4.1. In the updating model on which this theorem is based (and the contract theorem below), agents have a memory of m periods, and sample ($s < m$) from their memory to form expectations. (In the model in the text $s = m = 1$.) Young's results concerning stochastic stability generalize beyond the 2×2 coordination games treated here.

TABLE 12.2
Modified payoffs in the contract game

	B offer Contract 1	B offer Contract 0
A offer Contract 1	$a_{11} = 1, b_{11} = 1$	0, 0
A offer Contract 0	0, 0	$a_{00} = \sigma\rho, b_{00} = (1 - \sigma)\rho$

put, so we can retain our assumption that they maximize expected pay-offs. The total surplus varies with distributional shares because some contracts are more efficient than others. This might occur if the use of a particular technology required a distinct set of property rights, which in turn supported a particular equilibrium contract. An example of this technology-contracts mapping was seen in the case of the rise of agriculture and the emergence of individual property rights in the previous chapter. Analysis of the 2×2 contract game will be facilitated if we write $a_{11} = 1$, $b_{11} = 1$, and $a_{00} + b_{00} = \rho$, so $\rho/2$ is a measure of the relative efficiency of the $\{0, 0\}$ convention; when ρ takes the value of 2, the two conventions produce the same the joint surplus. Further, let the A-player's share of joint surplus in the B-favoring $\{0, 0\}$ equilibrium be $\sigma \leq \frac{1}{2}$, with $(1 - \sigma)$ the share of gained by B. These payoffs appear in table 12.2.

To explore the effect of the terms of the contract on the stochastic stability of the state defined by the convention in which that contract is universal, consider the contract space in figure 12.3. The $\{1, 1\}$ contract is defined as the Benchmark contract, with E_1 the associated convention. The contract space depicts a set of Alternative contracts defining convention E_0. Point S' is the Benchmark contract (with $\rho = 2$ and $\sigma = \frac{1}{2}$). Thus, if the two possible contracts are represented by points S' and x, both groups will prefer the Alternative contract because both $\sigma\rho$ and $(1 - \sigma)\rho$ exceed 1 under its terms. Contracts above AS' are Pareto superior to the Benchmark. (Ignore the locus $S'S$ for the moment.)

Conflict of interest between the two groups is confined to the contracts lying below AS' and above BS'. This does not ensure that the S' would be eclipsed by an Alternative contract like x. The reason is that while x is Pareto superior to the S', adherence to S' is a mutual best response and so will only be dislodged by nonbest-response play. Our intuition, however, is that Pareto-inferior conventions must be at a disadvantage in a stochastic environment. Our intuition is correct: Pareto-inefficient conventions are not robust in this evolutionary dynamic, and we can say considerably more.

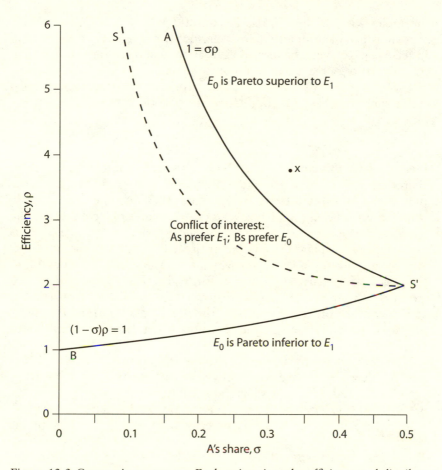

Figure 12.3 Contrasting contracts. Each point gives the efficiency and distributional share of the Alternative contract supporting the equilibrium E_0. Contracts above AS' are Pareto superior to the Benchmark contract with $\rho = 2$ and $\sigma = \frac{1}{2}$. Contracts below BS' are Pareto inferior to the Benchmark contract.

Peyton Young (1998) produced a striking theorem that demonstrates that the institutions supporting stochastically stable states are not only efficient but also egalitarian if we give this term a rather special meaning. For any two contracts call the *relative payoff* π_{ij}, the payoff to members of group i in contract j, *relative to the maximum payoff they get in either of the two contracts.* Under some innocuous restrictions on the updating process, Young's "contract theorem" shows that the stochastically stable state is the one that maximizes the relative payoffs of the group with the lowest relative payoff.[6] Why this is true, and the sense in which the property that stochastically stable states are maximin in relative payoffs can be termed egalitarian, will be clarified by making use of what we already know about these states.

The convention $\{0, 0\}$ will, as we have seen, be the stochastically stable state if $a_{00}b_{00} > a_{11}b_{11}$. Using the payoffs in table 12.2 this requires that

$$\sigma(1 - \sigma)\rho^2 > 1 \qquad (12.5)$$

It is clear from this condition that both relative efficiency and equality of shares contribute to stochastic stability of a convention (the term $\sigma(1 - \sigma)$ is maximized for $\sigma = \frac{1}{2}$). Figure 12.3 illustrates the relationship between efficiency and equality as determinants of stochastic stability: SS' is the locus of combinations of ρ and σ such that $\sigma(1 - \sigma)\rho^2 = 1$ and which thus equate the risk factor of $\{0, 0\}$ to the risk factor of the egalitarian convention $\{1, 1\}$ (for which $\rho = 2$ and $\sigma = \frac{1}{2}$). Thus SS' is the locus of alternative contracts such that both conventions are stochastically stable. Alternative contracts above SS' are stochastically stable when the other convention is the Benchmark contract. For alternative contracts below SS' the Benchmark contract is stochastically stable.

Note that while stochastically stable states are maximin in *relative* payoffs, they are not maximin in payoffs. Alternative contracts lying between SS' and AS' are stochastically stable, but the payoffs of the As are lower in the Alternative contract than in the Benchmark contract. Thus, stochastically stable states are egalitarian only in a rather special sense.

It is easy to see why efficient conventions would be favored in this setup. For at least one group, offering the efficient contract must be risk-dominant in the standard sense that if one believes that the other will offer the two contracts with equal probability, then the best response is to offer the more efficient one. Inefficient conventions are not accessible because it takes a large amount of nonbest-response play to induce best responders to shift from an efficient to an inefficient convention. Note that this is not because best responders anticipate the conse-

---

[6] To see that stochastically stable states are maximin in relative payoffs, it is sufficient to show that the condition $\sigma(1 - \sigma)\rho^2 = 1$, which defines equivalent stochastic stability of the Alternative and Benchmark contracts also equates the minimum relative payoffs of the two contracts. Consider an Alternative contract such that both contracts are stochastically stable. Then we have $\pi_{A0} = \sigma\rho < 1 = \pi_{B0}$ and $\pi_{B1} = \rho(1 - \sigma)^{-1} < 1 = \pi_{A1}$, and the minimum relative payoff in the Alternative and Benchmark contracts, respectively, are $\sigma\rho$ and $\rho(1 - \sigma)^{-1}$. Equating these gives the above condition for the states associated with the two contracts both being stochastically stable.

quences of their switching for the population level dynamics. Rather, their response is purely individual and based on past (not anticipated future) population states; no individual is attempting to implement the more efficient convention. For analogous reasons, inefficient conventions are not persistent.

Less transparent is the result that highly unequal conventions are not good candidates for stochastic stability. This is a consequence of the fact that they are easily unraveled, because as Young (1998:137) puts it: "[I]t does not take many stochastic shocks to create an environment in which members of the dissatisfied group prefer to try something different." Note that in this example, as in the discussion of reduced resistances above, it is the idiosyncratic play of the *privileged* group that unravels the unequal convention, that is, the convention from which they benefit disproportionately. We will return to this anomaly.

To see why the processes of transition between the two conventions depends on the share of the less well-off in the unequal convention, we can use eq. (12.3) and the data in table 12.2 to get the following expressions for the reduced resistances on the paths to the two equilibria.

$$r_{01} = \frac{1}{1 + (1 - \sigma)\rho}$$

$$r_{01} = \frac{\sigma\rho}{1 + \sigma\rho}$$

As σ goes to zero (the poor get nothing in the unequal convention), the resistance on the path to the equal convention (r_{01}) also goes to zero. The reason is that in a population near the $\{0, 0\}$ convention, even if the As (the poor) believed that virtually all of the Bs would play 0, their best response would nonetheless be to play 1. This is because if $\sigma = 0$, they would not benefit from concluding a contract with a 0-playing B, so as long as there was some chance of meeting a 1-playing B, expected payoffs would be maximized by playing 1. Thus, the population will transit to the more equal convention for an arbitrarily small amount of nonbest-response play by the rich. This is the evolutionary game theorist's rendition of Marx's rhetoric about the working class having "nothing to lose but their chains." Thus the unequal convention becomes less persistent as it becomes more unequal.

Figure 12.4 shows that more unequal shares in the $\{0, 0\}$ convention makes both conventions more accessible (i.e., it reduces the resistance to both equilibrium). But the accessibility of the more equal convention is increased relatively more. The reason why $\{0, 0\}$ becomes more accessible is that in the neighborhood of the $\{1, 1\}$ convention, it takes fewer

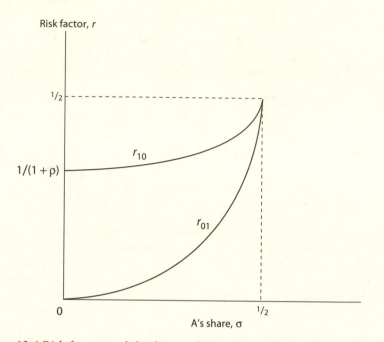

Figure 12.4 Risk factors and the degree of inequality. Note: greater inequality of shares in the unequal convention (lower σ) reduces the risk factors of both conventions, but affects the equal convention more than the unequal one.

nonbest responding As to induce the Bs to take a chance and play 0 (if they happen to meet a 0-playing A, they will do very well). Thus, the resistance on the path to the unequal convention also falls as σ falls. But resistence on this path remains positive even when the Bs get all of the joint surplus in {0, 0} for in this case $r_{10} = 1/(1 + \rho)$.

I have illustrated the insights of stochastic evolutionary game theory using a comparison of just two contracts; but note that *any* two contracts along the SS' locus in figure 12.3 are both stochastically stable states. We may thus interpret SS' as an "iso-stochastic stability" locus, and note that this is just one of a family of such loci. For any two contracts, i and j, along one of these loci it is the case that $a_{ii}b_{ii} = a_{jj}b_{jj}$. Now suppose, given the technologies, preferences, and other relevant data obtaining in some historical period, there is a set of feasible contracts defined in [ρ,σ] space. Two members of the family of iso-stochastic stability loci ($S'S'$ and S'', S'') and the feasible contract set bounded by CC are illustrated in figure 12.5. If only two contracts are considered, points x and y on the same iso-stochastic stability locus, we would expect the population to move between these two conventions in the

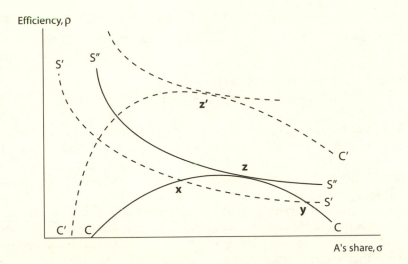

Figure 12.5 Equilibrium selection by chance from a feasible contract set. The shift in the feasible contract set selects a more efficient and more unequal convention.

very long run, spending equal amounts of time at each. But if x were the current convention and z the alternative, then we would expect z to emerge and to persist virtually all of the time.

The advance of technology and the evolution of preferences shifts the feasible contract set. One possible such shift is indicated by the new contract possibility frontier $C'C'$ under which p is maximized under a set of contracts favoring the Bs, by comparison with CC. Stochastic evolutionary game theory would lead us to expect a new contract to emerge, one with a reduced σ, indicated by z' at the tangency of the new contract possibility frontier and a higher iso-stochastic stability locus. A process of this type may have occurred with the introduction of agriculture described in the previous chapter, or the development of capitalism half a millennium ago.

The introduction of idiosyncratic play removes the deterministic dependence of outcomes on initial conditions that characterizes the non-stochastic approach. Rather, the stochastic approach allows predictions of the average population state over a sufficiently long historical period, along with a rather strong characterization of the nature of these stochastically stable states. The approach thus provides one account of how the institutions which Parsons termed "evolutionary universals" might come to be recurrent historically and ubiquitous at any given point in time: institutions supporting stochastically stable states would have been, as Parsons (1964:340) put it, "likely to be 'hit upon' by various systems operating under different conditions" and to persist over long periods.

Intentional Nonbest-response Actions with Subpopulations of Different Size

A quite different and historically more plausible account of institutional persistence and innovation results if nonbest-response play is modeled as intentional collective action by those who have something to gain by displacing the status quo institutions in favor of an alternative. As we will see, once idiosyncratic play is modeled as intentional collective action, it is no longer generally the case that stochastically stable states are egalitarian and efficient. In particular, if the rich are few and the poor many, unequal and inefficient institutions can be very robust. The reason is that when nonbest-response play is intentional, there is just one way (rather than two) that a convention can be overturned (by the actions of those who would benefit more at the other convention), and the larger numbers of the poor militate against a sufficient fraction of them adopting a nonbest response to displace the equilibrium under which they do poorly.

The collective-action approach requires some modifications in the above model. First, the players must be assumed to recognize the possibility of transiting to a new institutional setup, and must have the ability to anticipate the consequences of their actions on the actions of others. Thus, rather than restricting individuals to backward-looking updating, I now introduce a limited capacity to look forward. Second, when the frequency of idiosyncratic play is nonnegligible, the reduced resistances introduced above no longer provide the basis of an account of institutional transformation. The reason is that their relevance is based on nonbest-response play being sufficiently infrequent that the least probable of the two paths from one convention to another can be ignored. Rather than letting ε go to zero, the approach below identifies probable paths from one convention to another by endogenizing the process of idiosyncratic play using of a model of collective action.[7]

---

[7] Young (1998) shows that for a single population 2×2 game the population spends most of the time at the stochastically stable state even when ε is substantial (e.g., 0.05, or even 0.10) as long as the population is large (and hence transitions infrequent even with substantial nonbest response play). Note that in this single population 2×2 case, there is just one way to transit from one convention to the other, so this result is not very surprising. By contrast, in the two-population game, letting ε go to zero selects which of the two paths from one convention to the other is to be the basis of the calculation. It seems likely that for small populations with substantial error rates both paths should be considered

By *collective action*, I mean the intentional joint action toward common ends by members of a large group of people who do not have the capacity to commit to binding agreements before acting (i.e., they act noncooperatively). Examples include strikes, ethnic violence, insurrections, demonstrations, and boycotts. An individual's participation in a collective action may be modeled as an idiosyncratic nonbest response, one that does not take the form of stochastically generated "errors" but instead represents an intentional action motivated by the desire to improve one's well-being and perhaps the well-being of others. For this reason, it is likely that the extent of nonbest-response play will vary among individuals and depend on the payoff structure and other aspects of the pattern of social interaction defining the underlying game.[8]

To clarify the underlying processes, I will first analyze a degenerate case in which individuals participate in a nonbest-response collective action when it is in their individual interest that the action take place. Suppose that everyone updates in each period ($\omega = 1$) and assume that there is a probability $\varepsilon \in (0, 1)$ that each person is "called to a meeting" at which those attending consider undertaking a nonbest-response action. For example, assume the B-favorable convention {0, 0} obtains and some fraction of Bs (resulting from the "call") are considering switching to offer a 1-contract instead. But they cannot benefit from switching because they prefer the status quo convention, and destabilizing it—should sufficiently many of the other possible B-innovators also switch—could propel them to the alternate convention under which they would be worse-off. These potentially idiosyncratic players would thus decline the opportunity to innovate.[9]

By contrast, imagine that the a group of As were randomly called for deliberation of the merits of a switch away from the governing convention {0, 0}, and suppose that should they all adopt a nonbest response, this will be common knowledge. Each then might reason as follows. If

---

(because the least probable path may be followed with substantial likelihood). However, I have not explored this question.

[8] Bergin and Lipman (1996), Young (1998), and van Damme and Weibull (2002) analyze state-dependent mutations. The proviso that play is noncooperative excludes the degenerate case (with which I begin for purposes of illustration) of groups whose structure allows the assignment of obligatory actions to each of its members. While most successful collective actions include a wide range of selective incentives and sanctions to deter free riding, few if any groups have the capacity to simply mandate group-beneficial behaviors by individual members.

[9] Favored groups, like the Bs in convention {0, 0}, may deploy informal or governmental sanctions or to minimize idiosyncratic play of their own members. Examples include the shunning and more severe sanctions imposed on whites offering favorable contracts to nonwhites in racially stratified societies such as apartheid South Africa and the U.S. South before the civil rights movement.

we are sufficiently numerous and if all of us switched, the best response for the Bs would be to switch as well. Knowing this, should they all switch, they would anticipate the Bs' response and so would persist in offering 1-contracts in the next period. As a result, the A-unfavorable convention {0, 0} would be displaced.

Suppose there are n members of the A population (previously normalized to unity). If fewer than $n\alpha^*$ As are called, there could be no benefit to collective action even if it were uniformly successful. Therefore let us analyze the case for which the number called, η, exceeds this critical level, that is, $\eta \geq n\alpha^*$. To lend some concreteness to the case, let us say that switching means to engage with other As in a strike, refusing to accept any outcome less than a_{11} (all this means is to offer a 1-contract, so the strategy set is unchanged). We can explore the long-run behavior of the system by calculating τ_0, the expected waiting time (number of periods) before a strike by the As induces a transition from convention {0, 0} to {1, 1}. This is the inverse of the probability μ_0, that in any period a transition from {0, 0} will be induced or $\tau_0 = 1/\mu_0$. To determine this probability, one may proceed as follows. First, count the subsets of As sufficiently numerous to induce a transition, then determine the probability (given ε) that each subset will be drawn; sum these probabilities to get the probability that any transition inducing event occurs, μ_0. In this degenerate case of ensured collective action when it is beneficial, any subset of As with $n\alpha^*$ or more members will induce a transition. So using $C_{n,m}$ to indicate the number of subsets of m members in a population of n individuals we have

$$\mu_0 = \Sigma C_{n,n\alpha^* + i}\, \varepsilon^{n\alpha^* + i}(1 - \varepsilon)^{n - n\alpha^* - i} \quad \text{for } i = 0 \ldots n(1 - \alpha^*)$$

An example will clarify the calculation. Suppose $\varepsilon = 0.1$, four individuals (W, X, Y, and Z) make up the A subpopulation and $\alpha^* = 3/4$. Then the A-unfavorable convention E_0 will be displaced by idiosyncratic play by any of the following combinations: WXY, XYZ, YZW and $WXYZ$. The first three of each will occur with probability 0.0009 and the last with probability .0001, so, summing these probabilities, $\mu_0 = .0028$ and $\tau_0 = 357$ periods. As we want to know the long-run average behavior of the system, we calculate τ_1 in a manner analogous to τ_0 and express the average time at or near E_0, λ_0 as

$$\lambda_0 \equiv \frac{\tau_0}{\tau_0 + \tau_1}$$

with $\lambda_1 \equiv 1 - \lambda_0$. If there are three Bs and $1 - \beta^*$ (the critical fraction required to displace the B-unfavorable convention E_1) is 2/3, then $\mu_1 = .028$ and $\tau_1 = 35.7$ periods, so $\lambda_0 = 0.90$, meaning that E_0 will obtain most of the time.

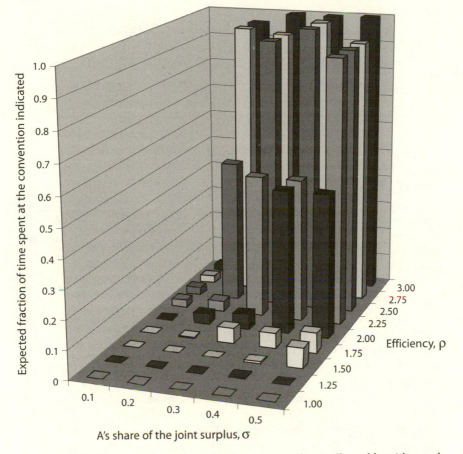

Figure 12.6 Efficient and equal conventions are stochastically stable with equal sub-population sizes. Note: the Benchmark convention is E_1 for which $\rho = 2$ and $\sigma = \frac{1}{2}$. The population spends an equal amount of time at the two conventions if the alternative convention is either $\rho = 2.25$ and $\sigma = .04$ or $\rho = 2.5$ and $\sigma = 0.2$. If the Alternative convention is more efficient or less unequal than these, the population spends vistually all of the time at the Alternative.

Figure 12.6 gives the results of this calculation where the two sub-populations each have twelve members and for various values of σ and ρ. Where E_0 is identical to E_1 ($\rho = 2$ and $\sigma = \frac{1}{2}$, indicated by the dark bar at these coordinates), the population spends half of its time at each convention. One can see a band of conventions (similar to the locus SS' in figure 12.3) that like ($\rho = 2$ and $\sigma = \frac{1}{2}$) generate equal average waiting times (for example, $\rho = 2.5$ and $\sigma = 0.2$ generates this result, as does $\rho = 2.25$ and $\sigma = 0.3$). The population will spend virtually all of the time at conventions more efficient or more equal than these and virtually none of the time at conventions less efficient or less equal.

The reason that more equal conventions are favored in this framework is the following: consider an alternative contract with $\rho = 2$ and $\sigma < \frac{1}{2}$. An increase in the distributional share of the As in the Alternative contract has two effects. First, it lowers α^* and thus requires fewer instances of idiosyncratic play by the As to disrupt the Alternative contract, inducing a movement to the Benchmark (which they prefer). The reason is that when the Alternative is less unequal, it takes fewer idiosyncratic As to induce the Bs to switch to the Benchmark. The second effect of an increase in σ is to raise β^*, thus reducing the minimal fraction of nonbest-responding Bs, $(1 - \beta^*)$, required to induce the As to abandon their preferred Benchmark contract in favor of the Alternative. The two effects of a more equal Alternative contract work in opposite directions, the first leading to a shorter waiting time for a transition from the Benchmark to the Alternative, and the second leading to a shorter waiting time for the reverse transition. But for $\sigma < \frac{1}{2}$, the second effect is larger, so the population will spend more time at the alternative, and the more equal it is.

Note that figure 12.6 confirms that the system will spend most of its time in the stochastically stable states. This may seem remarkable given that the transitions governing the dynamic in the stochastic evolutionary approach are that the Bs' idiosyncratic play disrupts the B-favorable convention and similarly for the As. By contrast, the collective-action approach dismisses these transitions as irrelevant, focusing instead on nonbest-response play motivated by the prospect of increasing one's payoffs by inducing an institutional transition, idiosyncratic play by the As disrupting the B-favorable convention, and conversely.

Why is the long-run average behavior of the system not affected by introducing intentional collective action (instead of eliminating of the least probable path as ε goes to zero)? The reason is that convention E_0 is more vulnerable to intentional collective action (by the As) than E_1 (by the Bs) if $\alpha^* < (1 - \beta^*)$, while abstracting from intentions (i.e., permitting the idiosyncratic play of those benefitting from a convention to displace it), E_1 is the stochastically stable state if $\beta^* < (1 - \alpha^*)$ and the two conditions are equivalent. Thus, the same state is identified as the more robust by the two measures. But this is a special result of the 2×2 game structure and it does not generalize to larger games, or as we will see, to 2×2 games with a more realistic (nondegenerate) process of collective action, and to cases in which the two subpopulations are of different size.

Figure 12.7 shows the effect of assuming subpopulations of different size (retaining the degenerate model of collective action) for an alterna-

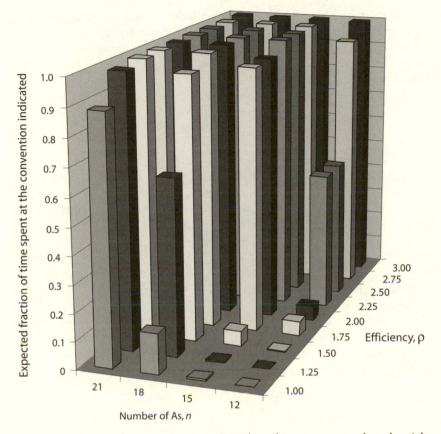

Figure 12.7 Unequal conventions persist when the poor outnumber the rich. Note: total population is 24; the Benchmark convention is E_1 ($\sigma = \frac{1}{2}$, $\rho = 2$). E_0 is characterized by the values of ρ indicated and $\sigma = 0.3$. As the As become more numerous, the population spends most of the time at conventions (even very inefficient ones) that are highly disadvantageous to them.

tive contract with $\sigma = 0.3$ and with the ρ values as shown. By contrast to the equal subpopulation size case depicted in figure 12.6, when population sizes differ, the intentional nature of nonbest-response behavior makes a difference: unequal and quite inefficient conventions may be highly persistent. For example, in the equal population size case a convention with $\sigma = 0.3$ needed a ρ of 2.25 to be equally persistent to E_1; but if the As number 18 and the Bs 6, the two conventions are equally persistent when the unequal convention ($\sigma = 0.3$) is much *less* efficient than the benchmark, that is, $\rho = 1.25$. Where there are 21 As (and 3 Bs), the population will spend most of the time in the unequal convention even if its level of efficiency is half that of the equal convention. Note that the level of inequality measured by the average income of Bs relative to As is $n(1 - \sigma)/\sigma(24 - n)$, each B interacting with more As as their relative share of the population increases. Thus, at the convention E_0 if $\sigma = 0.3$ and the As and Bs are equally numerous, the Bs have an income 2.33 times the As', but when there are 21 As and 3 Bs, the ratio is 16.33. Thus, highly unequal distribution of income may result from unequal subpopulation sizes, and may be persistent because of them.

The evolutionary success of unequal and inefficient conventions that benefit the smaller of the two classes is readily explained. As long as rate of idiosyncratic play is less than the critical fraction of the population required to induce a transition (which I assume), smaller groups will more frequently experience "tipping opportunities" that require that the realized fraction of the population who are "called" by chance exceeds the expected fraction (ε itself). Note that in this case small numbers does not facilitate collective action by making it easier to coordinate the actions of the members and to deter free riding. Rather the advantage of small size arises because (as the theory of sampling error shows) the class whose numbers are smaller will generate more tipping opportunities. To explore the conditions under which these opportunities will result in the displacement of the status quo institutions we need to model the collective action of the group members.

Collective Action

So far I have abstracted from the problem of collective action by assuming that whenever a sufficient fraction of a subpopulation is called, they will adopt a nonbest response if they (and their group) would benefit if all of those called adopted the nonbest response. Extending stochastic evolutionary game theory to more adequately capture the process of collective action can be accomplished by imposing a particular social structure on the process generating nonbest-response play. This structure must explain why actions that are nonbest responses in the contract game may nonetheless be the result of intentional action when the game is amended to include the possibility of collective action. Thus, what is needed is a model of the coordination problem posed by collective action, nested in the larger population game representing institutional evolution. Taking account of both the intentional nature of collective action and the coordination problem peculiar to it will augment the stochastic approach in illuminating ways.

Because collective actions generically take the form of n-person public goods games in which the dominant strategy is nonparticipation if preferences are wholly self-regarding, the extended model must take account of incentives for each to free ride when others act in pursuit of commonly shared objectives. A second desideratum is that the model should reflect the fact that opportunities for collective action often arise by chance, or at least in ways too complex to tractably model, examples being economic depressions, wars, price shocks, booms, and natural disasters. Finally, unlike idiosyncratic play, participation in collective action is not only intentional (rather than accidental) but also conditional on one's beliefs about the likelihood and consequences of a substantial number of one's kind's changing behaviors. For this reason, facts about global rather than simply local payoffs (i.e., payoffs both in the present convention and in the alternative, rather than those in the neighborhood of the current population state alone) may have a bearing on the outcomes.[10] For concreteness, I refer to the nonbest-response collective action as a "strike."

Suppose that striking yields in-process benefits of two types. First, irrespective of the consequences of the action, conformism (or punishment of nonconformists) may impose a cost on those not adopting the most common action. So, let c be the cost of being a sole nonconformist, and the conformism costs to those striking be $(1 - s)c$, where s is the fraction of those called who strike. The costs to the nonstrikers is sc. Second, there are benefits or costs associated with the action that may be independent of the numbers participating, including the time, resources, and possibly risk of harm associated with the collective action as well as the positive value of participating, or what Elisabeth Wood (2003) terms the "pleasure of agency."[11]

It is reasonable to suppose that these subjective benefits depend on the magnitude of the gains to be had if the action is successful, not primarily because these gains are a likely consequence of one's individual participation (which is very unlikely in large groups) but because the magnitude of the gains to be had is plausibly related to the strength of the norms motivating the action. The pleasure of participating in a collective action that if successful would transform the conditions of one's class from squalor to abundance is likely to be greater than the pleasure of striking for a wage increase of a few cents more an hour. So let the net subjective benefits for an A engaging in a collective action to displace convention $\{0, 0\}$ be $\delta(a_{11} - a_{00})$ where δ is a positive constant, reflecting the fact that joining a collective action in pursuit of an institu-

---

[10] This means that individuals are forward looking to the extent that they can anticipate the consequences of successful collective action.

[11] Compelling evidence from the histories of collective action (e.g., Moore 1978) anthropology (Boehm 1993, Knauft 1991), and experimental economics surveyed in earlier chapters suggests that individuals knowingly engage in costly actions to punish violations of norms, even when these actions cannot otherwise benefit the individual.

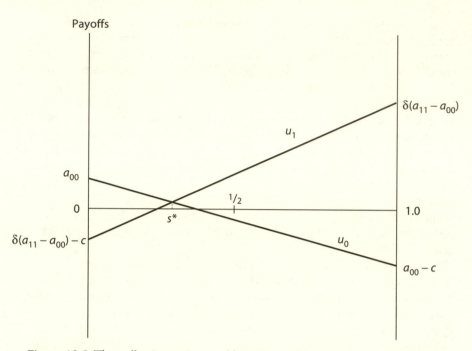

Figure 12.8 The collective action problem. Note if $s^* < \frac{1}{2}$ the risk-dominant equilibrium is universal participation in the "strike."

tional change from which one and one's peers will not benefit confers no benefits.[12]

If the strike fails (because too few participate in it), the status quo convention will persist and all As will get a_{00} in subsequent periods independently of whether they participated in the strike or not. Likewise, if the strike succeeds all As will get a_{11} subsequent periods, irrespective of their actions this period. Thus, the relevant comparison is between the single-period net benefits to striking (insisting on contract 1, refusing contract 0), u_1, and abstaining, u_0, where

$$u_1 = \delta(a_{11} - a_{00}) - (1 - s)c \qquad (12.6)$$

$$u_0 = a_{00} - sc \qquad (12.7)$$

These payoff functions are illustrated in figure 12.8, from which it is clear if those involved believe that at least s^* of their fellows will join

[12] Conventions typically not only allocate gains but also influence the cultural and political conditions relevant to the net costs and benefits of engaging in collective action. But here I abstract from this (the δs are not subscripted to indicate the convention defining the status quo ante).

in, then strikers' expected payoffs will exceed those of nonparticipants, and hence all will elect to strike The critical value, s^*, equates u_0 and u_1.

$$s^* = \frac{1}{2} - \frac{\delta(a_{11} - a_{00}) - a_{00}}{2c} \qquad (12.8)$$

How might the As' beliefs about the numbers likely to participate be formed? The simplest supposition consistent with the above model is that having no information about what the others will do, each believes that the likelihood of each of the others participating is ½, so the expected fraction participating is ½, and all will participate if s^* less than ½.[13]

Thus, unanimous participation (of those called) will occur if striking is the risk-dominant equilibrium of the collective action game, requiring that the numerator of the second term on the right-hand side of eq. (12.8) be positive, or that the "pleasure of agency" outweighs the loss of a single period's income. (Thus while inferior payoffs in the status quo convention ($a_{11} - a_{00} > 0$) is a necessary condition for participation, it is not sufficient as it does not insure that $\delta(a_{11} - a_{00}) - a_{00} > 0$.)

The properties of the dynamical system are substantially altered by modeling idiosyncratic play as intentional collective action. Notice that if $\delta(a_{11} - a_{00}) - a_{00} < 0$, collective action will not take place (irrespective of the numbers of randomly drawn potential innovators), so the A-unfavorable convention {0, 0} is an absorbing state. Thus, the dynamical system with collective action as the form of nonbest-response play is non-ergodic, and institutional lock-ins are possible, with initial conditions determining which of the two conventions will emerge and then persist forever. To see that this must be the case for a finite "pleasure of agency" parameter δ, consider an unequal convention with $a_{11} - a_{00} \equiv \Delta$; letting Δ become arbitrarily small eventually must make $\delta(a_{11} - a_{00}) - a_{00} < 0$, so collective action by the As will not occur, and E_0, should it ever occur, will persist forever. Thus, there must exist a set of conventions, less equal than E_1 and no more efficient, that are absorbing states.

Figure 12.9 reproduces the contract space for the Alternative contract in the case where $\delta = 2$ (the Benchmark, E_1, being {1, 1} and SS' the

[13] The choice of ½ is conventional but arbitrary; individuals may have prior beliefs of the fraction likely to participate based on previous similar situation and the like. If individuals then apply their reasoning to each of the others (each, supposing that half will participate, will also participate), they would then correctly predict that $s = 1$. While this second round of induction may determine whether the individual expects the collective action to be successful in displacing the convention, this belief about the likelihood of success is not relevant to the individual's behavior, as the relative payoffs of participating or not are independent of the success of the action.

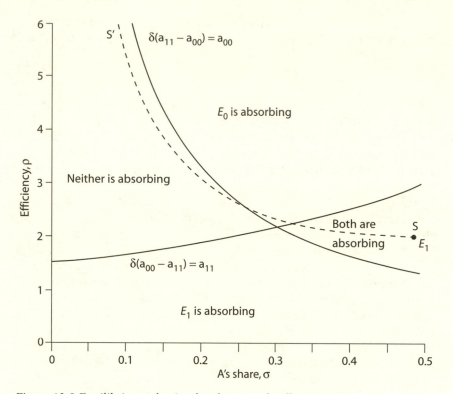

Figure 12.9 Equilibrium selection by chance and collective action.

locus of alternative contracts that are equally stochastically stable to the Benchmark). Very efficient or very equal Alternative contracts are absorbing because they are either Pareto superior to the Benchmark (figure 12.3) or provide those who would prefer the Benchmark payoffs sufficient benefits to preclude their taking collective action. It can be seen that E_0 may be absorbing even if it would not have been stochastically stable in the conventional stochastic evolutionary model. For the region where neither contract is absorbing, the long-term average behavior summarized in figures 12.6 and 12.7 applies.

How are we to interpret the absorbing states? Over relevant time scales, the parameters of the model are likely to shift due to cultural and political changes affecting δ or technical or other changes affecting the payoffs to the relevant contracts. Suppose some unequal Alternative contract defines the status quo convention (E_0), and it represents an absorbing state. If technical change made the {1, 1} contract progressively more efficient by comparison to {0, 0}, then $\delta(a_{11} - a_{00})$ would eventually exceed a_{00}. As a result, the conditions for collective action would obtain, and a transition from E_0 to E_1 would eventually take place. Transitions in the reverse direction would become more unlikely over time as the increase in a_{11} raises the minimum number of nonbest-responding Bs required to unravel E_1. Thus, the institutional demands of new technologies may account for the emergence of new contractual conventions. A cultural change enhancing the pleasure of agency, δ — a role played by liberation theology in some parts of Latin America and by the spread of democratic ideology in South Africa and the former Communist countries — would have the same effect.

This is very roughly Marx's account (in the epigraph of chapter 11), which presents history as a progressive succession of "modes of production," each contributing to "the development of the forces of production" for a period, then becoming a "fetter" on further technological advance and being replaced through the collective action of the class that would benefit by a shift to a new convention more consistent with the new technologies.

Conclusion: The Institutional Ecology of Inequality

The integration of chance and collective action developed here is far from the first proposed marriage of Darwin and Marx. Writing to Engels in 1860, Marx saw parallels between *The Origin of Species* and their own historical materialist analysis of human evolution: "Although it is developed in the crude English style, this is the book which contains the basis in natural history for our viewpoint" (Padover 1979:139). Fourteen years later at Marx's grave side, Engels would say: "Just as Darwin discovered the law of evolution in organic nature, so Marx discovered the law of evolution in human society" (Tucker 1978:681).

Stochastic evolutionary game theory has recently made available powerful analytical tools of Darwinian inspiration, providing an illuminating framework for the study of institutional change and "evolutionary universals." A particularly important contribution is to show that the bunching of nonbest-response play works as an equilibrium selection device and thus provides a causal mechanism — missing from the Parsonian and neo-institutionalist approaches — accounting for the evolutionary success of efficient and egalitarian institutions.

Taking account of differences in group size and the intentional nature of collective action, however, suggests that the standard stochastic evolutionary game theory model may need further development to be relevant to the historical evolution of institutions. The extensions I have introduced are four. First, nonbest-response play is intentional rather than accidental. Second, the rate at which nonbest response takes place is substantial (rather than vanishingly small). Third, nonbest-response play takes the form of collective action rather than uncorrelated deviant individual behaviors. Fourth, population subgroups differ in size, with the less well off typically outnumbering the well off.

I have suggested three reasons why durable institutions may be neither efficient nor egalitarian. First, independent of group size, moderate levels of inequality may deter collective action by the least well-off because the degree of inequality is insufficient to motivate participation. Thus, unequal conventions may persist indefinitely. Second, independent of the problem of motivating collective action, the system will spend most of the time at the unequal shares convention because the Bs, who prefer this convention, are relatively few in number, so that the likelihood that a random draw will yield a number of them sufficient to displace the convention which they do not prefer is greater than for the As. This advantage of small numbers is unrelated to conventional reasoning proposed by Olson (1965) and others as to why collective action in large groups is difficult to sustain. Third, egalitarian conventions are inaccessible from highly unequal Alternative conventions because the number of nonbest responding As required to induce best responding Bs to switch contracts is greater, the more unequal is the Alternative. The conclusion is that societal inequality may be sustained by unequal and inefficient conventions over long periods because moderate levels of inequality may be insufficient to motivate collective action by *any of the poor*, while conventions characterized by extreme levels of inequality can only be displaced through collective actions endorsed by *very large fractions of the poor*.

A concern about the stochastic evolutionary game framework is that it applies only to the very long run. For reasonable updating processes, group sizes, and rates of idiosyncratic play, the average waiting times for transitions from one basin of attraction to another are extraordinarily long, certainly surpassing historically relevant time spans, and for some not unrealistic cases exceeding the time elapsed since the emergence of anatomically modern human life. Figure 12.10 gives the expected number of periods before a transition from an unequal alternative contract to the benchmark when the latter is a stochastically stable state for the case where $\varepsilon = 0.1$. The dynamic assumed is the degenerate case of collective action (whenever there are more than the critical number of As called to the meeting, they refuse the conventional contract and a transition occurs). Note that, as one would expect, the larger is the number of As the longer is the waiting time. Also, when the (unequal) Alternative is as efficient as the Benchmark (the right-hand bars), it is very persistent even when there are as few as 12 As. If there

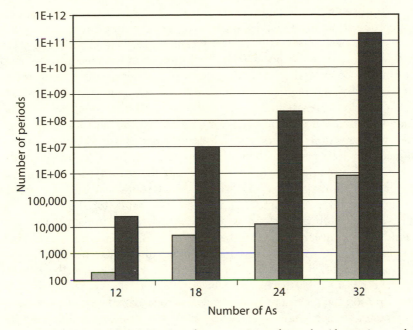

Figure 12.10 Expected waiting time for a transition from the Alternative to the Benchmark convention when the Benchmark is a stochastically stable state. Lefthand bars are for an Alternative with $\sigma = 0.3$ and $\rho = 1$, while the right-hand bars are for $\sigma = 0.3$ and $\rho = 2$.

are 32 *As*, an unequal convention that is only half as efficient as the stochastically stable state persists for an expected one million periods.

While the biological processes underlying the dynamic refered to in this chapter's epigraph by Sewall Wright may work over hundreds of thousands of generations, an analogous approach in the social sciences must be relevant to vastly shorter time scales. If the "period" were very short—say, a day—the long waiting times in the figure would be of little concern, but the appropriate period here is an opportunity for collective action to change a convention, and for this, a year or a decade might be more appropriate. Moreover, many human groups are larger than those illustrated in the figure, with waiting times correspondingly longer. The conclusion is that initial conditions persist over very long periods even if the status quo convention is highly unequal and inefficient by comparison to an alterative convention. Does this mean that the result that the population will spend "most of the time" in the more efficient and more equal alternative is irrelevant to real historical evolution?

I do not think so. A number of plausible modifications in the updating process can dramatically accelerate the dynamic process, yielding transitions over historically relevant time scales. Among these are the following. First, most populations (nations, ethno-linguistic units, and so on) are composed of smaller groups of frequently interacting members. Small group membership increases the relative importance of unlikely random events and hence the likelihood that nonbest-response play will induce transition times among conventions at the group level. Because transitions to stochastically stable states are likely to be sustained over long periods, the entire population is likely to transit to the stochastically stable state (all groups eventually making the switch over a relatively short period). Migration among groups or emulation across groups can induce even more rapid transition times for the population as a whole. Hobsbawm and Rude (1968) describe the spread of late eighteenth- and early nineteenth-century Luddite machine-wrecking in England by a process of propagation in small groups and infection of adjacent groups. Because groups are of quite variable size, the process may be considerably accelerated because the transition times will depend not on the mean group size but on the size of the smallest groups.

Second, chance events affect the payoff structures as well as the behaviors of the members of the population. Recall that the location of the internal unstable equilibrium (the saddle, z) and the boundary between the two basins of attraction in figure 12.2 is determined by the payoff matrix (eq. (12.1)). Variations in environmental effects on payoffs will thus shift the boundary of the basins of attraction, occasionally greatly reducing the size of the basin of attraction of the status quo convention. These effects in conjunction with nonbest-response play (whether intentional or stochastic) will accelerate the process of transition.

Third, there are generally far more than two feasible conventions, and some of them may be adjacent (i.e., the reduced resistances among them are small). Sewall Wright (1935:263), introducing the passage appearing in the chapter epigraph, observed that on a fitness landscape, "[T]here is in general a very large number of separate peaks separated by shallow 'saddles'." A population may rapidly traverse a large portion of the state space by means of a series of transitions among adjacent conventions.

Fourth, conformism will reduce the aggregate amount of idiosyncratic play. But it also gives rise to positively correlated deviant behaviors—each member of the population is more likely to adopt a nonbest response the more others are doing the same. This produces greater bunching of idiosyncratic play and hence, under plausible conditions, accelerates the process of transition.

Fifth, making the process by which collective actions occurs more realistic could drastically reduce waiting times for a transition. Suppose that once "called," individuals remain activated in the next and subsequent periods until they are "deactivated," which happens with some probability in each period. Like clandestine revolutionaries, these latent innovators continue "attending meetings" but do not engage in collective actions unless they are sufficiently numerous to displace the status quo convention. Until this occurs they earn the same payoffs as other members of their subpopulation. Because they suffer no payoff disadvantages as long as they remain latent, their numbers may accumulate from period to period through a drift-like process, thus greatly shortening the waiting time until those "attending the meeting" exceed the critical value.[14]

We do not know, of course, whether these modifications of the dynamic modeled in this chapter can provide a plausible account of historically observed processes of institutional change. This is an empirical question that has yet to be explored systematically. To illuminate such institutional changes as the demise of apartheid or of Communism or female genital cutting in Senegal, or the reduction in the landlords' crop share in West Bengal (described in the Prologue), additional modifications of the model would no doubt be required. Among these would be modeling the role of leadership and organization in coordinating non-best-response play, and the way that governmental repression or reforms alter the payoff matrices and beliefs of the actors.

Moreover, institutions differ in ways not captured by measures of efficiency, distributional shares, and group size, of course. Some institutions may facilitate collective action of the disadvantaged, while others make it more difficult to coordinate. In many situations the effective size of a subpopulation may be greatly reduced if it is composed of smaller groups (families, union locals, corporate bodies) that almost always act in unison. Marx, and many since, have believed that the social conditions of industrial capitalism constituted a schoolhouse of revolution, by contrast with earlier institutions of sharecropping, tax farming in societies of independent peasants, and slavery, for example. Barrington Moore (1966) and others, with perhaps greater accuracy, have

---

[14] This process is analogous to the role of neutral mutations in the emergence of complex features in biological evolution: single mutations may have no phenotypic effect and therefore their bearers suffer no adverse selection pressure and thus may proliferate in a population. But the nonadditive effects of accumulation of many different mutations which singly are neutral may account for the emergence of novel and complex features. (See Stadler, Stadler, Wagner, and Fontana (2001), and Kimura (1968).) Timur Kuran (1995) analyzed the role of *falsified preferences* in a similar vein: those with deviant intentions need not express their true objectives when doing so would be disadvantageous.

seen patron-client relationships in agrarian societies and highly unequal systems of land holding as especially vulnerable to revolutionary overturns.

Rather than pursuing these extensions of models depicting within-group processes of institutional change, we turn now to the manner in which between-group interactions may induce institutional evolution. By contrast to the within-group models, the multi-level selection approach, which combines within- and between-group dynamics, gives rather strong predictions of the evolutionary success of institutions that are both egalitarian and efficient. The reasons why this is so, as we will see, are quite different than those advanced for similar conclusions by the Marxian-Darwin hybrid or the stochastic evolutionary game theory approaches.

CHAPTER THIRTEEN

The Coevolution of Institutions and Preferences

> The Americans . . . are fond of explaining almost all the actions of their
> lives by the principle of self interest rightly understood; . . . In this
> respect I think they frequently fail to do themselves justice; in the United
> States as well as elsewhere people are sometimes seen to give way to
> those disinterested and spontaneous impulses that are natural to man;
> but the Americans seldom admit that they yield to emotions of this kind.
> — Alexis de Tocqueville, *Democracy in America* (1830)

> Whether . . . the extra-group struggle . . . takes the form of actual
> warfare or of still keener competition for trade and food supply, that
> group in which unchecked internal competition has produced a vast
> proletariat with . . . no "stake in the state" will be the first to collapse.
> — Karl Pearson, *Socialism and Natural Selection* (1894)

WHEN FOUR ROWDY young men at the all-night pizzeria in the Italian
beach town of Rimini began throwing food and hurling insults at the
baker, a Senegalese man named Sarr Gaye Diouf intervened, defending
the baker (Meletti 2001). One of the toughs grabbed Diouf by the arms
and the other three stabbed him fifteen times with pizza knives. Diouf
died immediately, and the attackers were arrested. Diouf was working
temporarily as a delivery man, hoping soon to become a taxi driver. He
had not known the baker other than as an occasional customer, and his
attackers, visiting Rimini from Naples, had never seen Diouf before. Yet
Diouf gave his life defending the baker, and the young toughs executed
the stranger — Diouf — undeterred by the certainty of arrest.

The tragedy evokes horror, but not surprise. People routinely make
sacrifices for strangers, and it is not uncommon for people to kill others
with the slightest provocation, especially when the target is an "outsider." These two aspects of human behavior are generally thought to
be antithetical, but as we will see, they may have a common origin:
between-group competition may have favored nations, tribes, bands,
and other groups that fostered preferences promoting generosity toward
some strangers and hostility toward others. Another empirical exam-

---

The first epigraph is from Tocqueville (1945, vol. 2, p. 130). The second is from Pearson (1894:17).

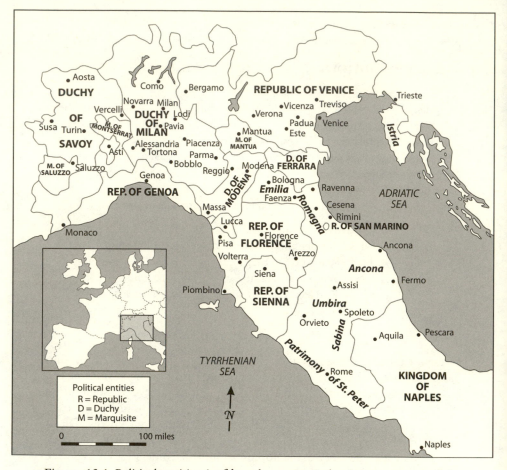

Figure 13.1 Political entities in fifteenth-century Italy. A great many of the smaller sovereign entities (e.g., San Gimignano) are not shown; notice the many once autonomous entities (e.g., Verona, Bergamo, Padua, Vicenza, all absorbed by Venice early in the century). Source: Matthew (1992:212).

ple—the coevolution of modern citizenship and war-making—may suggest some of the underlying processes at work.

Eight centuries ago, the area around Rimini, where Diouf was murdered, was governed by over a dozen sovereign bodies. In what is now Italy, there were two to three hundred distinct city-states. In South Germany a half-millennium ago there were sixty-nine free cities in addition to numerous bishoprics, principalities, duchies, and other state-like entities (Brady 1985). Figure 13.1 illustrates this proliferation of sovereignties in fifteenth-century Italy. The whole of Europe at that time was governed by about five hundred sovereign bodies. But by the First World War, fewer than thirty states remained. This culling of states not only thinned the number of sovereign bodies, it radically reduced the heterogeneity of forms of governance. A single political form—the national state—emerged, where once had ruled, according to Charles Tilly (1990:5), "[e]mpires, city states, federations of cities, networks of landlords, religious orders, leagues of pirates, warrior bands, and many other forms of governance." Unlike the competing forms it eclipsed, the national state exhibited a centralized bureaucratic structure maintaining order over a defined territory, with the capacity to raise substantial amounts revenue in the form of taxation and to deploy permanent armed forces.[1]

What explains the competitive success of this novel form of rule? The simple answer is that when national states warred with other forms of governance, they tended to win. But, Tilly writes, "No monarch could make war without securing the acquiescence of nearly all of his subject population, and the active cooperation of at least a crucial few" (Tilly 1990:75). A system of taxation paid in money, coupled with the capacity to borrow large sums, allowed rulers of national states to make war without resort to more unpopular measures such as the direct seizure of food, weapons, and animals. The establishment of well-defined private property rights and markets facilitated this taxation- and debt-based approach to mobilizing the coercive resources needed to win wars. Market environments favored state formation in a less obvious way, too, by inducing tax compliance. Tilly further comments:

> Participants in markets already do a significant share of the requisite surveillance thorough the recording of prices and transfers. Properly socialized citizens, furthermore, come to attach moral value to the payment of taxes; they monitor themselves and each other, blaming tax evaders as free riders. (p. 89)

European state-making exhibited a distinct concentric spatial pattern, with large but thinly controlled states on the periphery (Muscovy and the Ottoman Empire, for example), a grouping of city-states and federations near the center (the Italian city states, the Swiss cantons), and the eventually triumphant more centralized states such as France and Brandenburg intermediate between the two. Successful national states assimilated the populations they absorbed, and, over the period, they promoted and eventually required a common pattern of childhood socialization through schooling.[2]

---

[1] In addition to Tilly (1990), I draw here on Gellner (1983), Bright and Harding (1984), Tilly (1975), Mack Smith (1959), Anderson (1974), Wallerstein (1974), and Bowles and Gintis (1984).

[2] Weber (1976) describes the assimilation of distinct populations by the French national

In part as a result of its success in Europe, replicas of the European national state were exported (often at gun point) and flourished throughout the world, extinguishing competing forms of organization. Under the auspices of the national state and the emerging capitalist economy, European populations grew rapidly—multiplying 15-fold in Britain in the four centuries after 1500 after having grown hardly at all over the previous four centuries, and eclipsing population growth elsewhere in the world (except, perhaps, for eighteenth-century China). As a result, the global diffusion of the national state was promoted not only by competitive pressures on the states of the European periphery and beyond but also by the substantial emigration of bearers of the European cultural traits and military capacities that had favored state-building in Europe.

In sum, the national state evolved because it won wars with competing organizations, and the ability to win wars depended on its peculiar ability to mobilize soldiers and other military resources. This ability depended on the extent of commerce, the availability of credit, tax compliance, and the willingness to serve rulers in war. These, in turn, were fostered by the diffusion of norms guiding individual behaviors that, while not (at least initially) individually advantageous, contributed to group success in war on the above reasoning. Among these are voluntary tax compliance, willingness to risk danger in war for a ruler or nation, and respect for property rights. The norm of monogamy may have played a similar, if less obvious, role in securing popular cooperation with the projects of the elite.[3] Each of these norms contributes directly or indirectly to the state's war-making capacity but requires the bearer of the norm to forego possible gains and endure losses (including reduced reproductive success).

Of course, national states eventually created legal and cultural environments in which those adhering to the norms that enhanced state war-making capacities suffered little or no material loss by comparison to those rejecting these norms. But the emergence and early diffusion of the national state may have relied critically on group-advantageous but individually costly norms.

---

state. Gellner (1983) develops the connection between the rise of commerce, the national state, and the rise of what he terms "exo-education," that is, childhood socialization by specialists who are not members of one's family or group of close associates.

[3] Herlihy and Klapische-Zuber (1985:157) write: "The great social achievement of the early Middle Ages was the imposition of the same rules of sexual and domestic conduct on both rich and poor." See also MacDonald (1995). While reducing the advantages of the successful and powerful, the norm of monogamy (like the extension of suffrage to male workers much later) may have been instrumental, as Alexander (1979) and others suggest, in allowing the powerful to recruit others to their projects, including war.

Other well-documented empirical cases of between-group contests and assimilation are the conquest the Dinka by the Nuer (Kelly 1985) and the process of cultural evolution in New Guinea (Soltis, Boyd, and Richerson 1995). The meteoric spread of Islam in the century following Mohammed's death—by 750 encompassing a broad swath from beyond the Indus River in the east to the Douro River in Spain in the West is another example. This was possible because (according to Levy 1957:3) the faith in Allah provided "a bond far stronger though more subtle than that of kinship" and facilitated more inclusive systems of taxation and military recruitment and alliance.[4] Thus, the process of group conflict followed by cultural assimilation or physical extinction appears to be quite general.

In this chapter, I explore the role of between-group competition in the evolution of altruistic norms, including the willingness to risk one's life defending a stranger being harassed by young toughs, or to go to war for the glory of the nation.

Reciprocal Altruism and Strong Reciprocity

The models in chapter 7 showed that some structures of social interaction may make cooperative behaviors, such as nice tit-for-tat, a mutual best response, even when individuals have conventional self-interested preferences defined over the outcomes of their actions. Conditional cooperation is a form of what the biologist R. Trivers (1971) termed *reciprocal altruism*, namely, actions that confer a benefit on others at a cost to oneself in cases in which there is an expectation of a subsequent reciprocal benefit sufficient to offset the cost. Reciprocal altruism and *kin altruism*—acts benefitting family members or other close genetic relatives at a cost to oneself—are common explanations of seemingly generous acts among humans and other animals.

Repeated and multifaceted interactions allowing retaliation against anti-social actions undoubtedly contribute to the evolutionary success of seemingly generous acts. But as an explanation of the forms of cooperation and mutual assistance common among humans, reciprocal altruism is not adequate. First, much of the experimental evidence about other-regarding preferences (chapter 3) is from games with nonrepeated interactions, or from the final round of a repeated interaction. It is very unlikely that the subjects are unaware of the one-shot setting in these experiments. The evidence is overwhelming that people readily distin-

---

[4] Another well-documented case of group selection explains the practice of llama sharing among needy non-kin in the Peruvian highlands (Flannery, Marcus, and Reynolds 1989 and Weinstein, Shugart, and Brandt 1983).

guish between repeated and nonrepeated interactions, and adapt their behavior accordingly. The nonexperimental evidence is equally telling: many common behaviors in warfare as in everyday life are not easily explained by the expectation of future reciprocation.

Second, conditions of early humans may have made the repetition-retaliation mechanism an ineffective support for altruistic behaviors. Members of mobile foraging bands could readily escape retaliation by simply departing. And in many situations critical to human evolution, repetition of an interaction was quite unlikely, as when groups faced extinction due to group conflict or an adverse environment.

Third, the celebrated "Folk Theorem" shows that where repeated interactions are sufficiently likely and discount rates sufficiently low, the n-person equivalents of nice tit-for-tat and more complicated strategies may support Nash equilibria with high levels of cooperation (Fudenberg and Maskin 1986). But the Folk Theorem also shows that when the repetition-retaliation mechanism *does* work, it works too well in the sense that it supports a vast number of outcomes — some of them barely more cooperative than mutual defection — while providing no guidance as to why the more cooperative or more efficient equilibria might be favored over the less cooperative outcomes. Some recent models (Fudenberg and Maskin 1990) have been able to considerably restrict the class of equilibria supported by repetition. But they require the actors to be infinitely lived, or (equivalently) to have rates of time preference of zero, or other assumptions inconsistent with facts of human longevity.

Fourth, as Boyd and Lorberbaum (1987), Joshi (1987), and others have pointed out, it is difficult to sustain cooperation through repetition and retaliation where the interaction is not dyadic — as in the market exchanges studied in chapter 7 — but instead involves large numbers. Yet large group interactions are quite common, as in n-person public goods problems such as common defense, risk pooling, group reputation building, and the like. To see the problem, consider a large group of $n + 1$ members playing a public goods game, in which all members will contribute if each of the n others contribute, and will defect otherwise. If members sometimes adopt idiosyncratic (nonbest response) play or if the information concerning others' contributions is subject to error, chance events will led to the unraveling of cooperation, for it will commonly be the case that at least one member will believe that one other member did not contribute.

Exactly the same fragility afflicts strategies that are seemingly more lenient. Consider a strategy of conditional cooperation: cooperate (contribute) if at least $n - m$ others cooperated on the last round where $m < n$. Call this strategy m-Cooperate. The sole other strategy is unconditional Defect. Consider this population at a Nash equilibrium in which $n + 1 - m$ are playing m-Cooperate and $m > 0$ are adopting Defect (there must be m defectors in the Nash equilibrium, for otherwise, switching from m-cooperation to defect would be a best response). Suppose that with some small probability, ε, m-Cooperators switch their strategy (or are perceived to have switched). We have seen above that the population will shift to all defect if a single m-Cooperator defects (or is seen to defect). Thus, this Nash equilibrium will be sustained in a given period only if all $n + 1 - m$ continue playing the m-Cooperate strategy, and this will happen with probability $(1 - \varepsilon)^{n+1-m}$ which becomes very small for large n. Thus, in large groups, cooperative equilibria supported by strategies like m-Cooperate are vulnerable to unraveling due to chance events.

Part of the problem with strategies like m-Cooperate is that in large groups the punishment inflicted on the defectors by the withdrawal of cooperation by other members of the group is poorly targeted. Suppose $m = 0$ so if all $n + 1$ members are m-Cooperators they will continue cooperating if no member defects. If a single member should defect in any period, then all will defect forever. Considered as a form of punishment of the sole defector, the m-Cooperate strategy produces a "public bad": all members—the n m-Cooperators along with the sole defector—bear the subsequent loss of the benefits of cooperation. Note that this problem exists, but in a much attenuated form in the dyadic case with the simple tit for tat strategy: the defector bears half (instead of $1/n$) of the total cost of foregone cooperation. Of course, there are a vast number of possible strategies, and showing that one of them—m-Cooperate—is unlikely to work does not mean that none will. But the problems with the m-Cooperate strategy as a way of harnessing self interest to promote cooperation are quite general, and may afflict most if not all plausible strategies in this setting.

Thus, while self-interested retaliation can induce cooperation in dyadic or other small scale interactions, it is costly to implement and vulnerable to unraveling in large groups. As a result, and also for the reasons reviewed above, the attempt—common in both economics and evolutionary biology—to explain all or most seemingly altruistic behavior as "self-interest with a long time horizon" is unpersuasive. Tocqueville is right. Sometimes an apparently generous act is simply that—a costly behavior that benefits another member of one's group with no likely future reciprocation for the individual altruist.

While such acts of *unconditional altruism* often benefit one's kin, they are frequently directed toward total strangers, as the evidence reviewed at the beginning of chapter 3 shows. As we have seen, *strong reciprocity*—the predisposition to cooperate and to punish or reward others, conditional on their behavior, even in one-shot interactions and in other situations in which there is no prospect of eventual reward — is a also common form of behavior observed in experiments. The "strong" modifier is a reminder that this is an altruistic behavior not to be confused with Trivers' reciprocal altruism, which is not altruistic at all, and might better be called weak reciprocity. In contrast to an unconditional altruist, the behavior of strong altruist depends on his understanding of the intentions or the type of the person with whom he is interacting. In the words of the thirteenth-century Norse epic poem *The Edda* (Clark 1923:55), the strong reciprocator will "be a friend to his friends" and will "meet smiles with smiles, and lies with treachery."

An important form of strong reciprocity is altruistic punishment, that is, at a cost to oneself inflicting costs on those who violate group-beneficial norms. The behavior is altruistic if it induces greater adherence to norms that raise group average benefits. Experimental evidence for altruistic punishment comes from public goods games reviewed in chapter 3, and it was part of the Punisher strategy modeled in chapter 11. Altruistic punishment allows the targeting of violators of norms and does not rely on the expectation of future payoffs, and thus avoids some of the disadvantages of strategies like m-Cooperate in large groups. But like any form of altruism it poses an evolutionary puzzle.

Neither unconditional altruism nor strong reciprocity is readily explained as a best response defined over the material payoffs of a game. But if unconditional altruists and strong reciprocators bear costs to confer benefits on others, they would have been disadvantaged in any evolutionary process which favors behaviors with higher material payoffs. The fact that people commonly exhibit these behaviors needs to be explained: how did we get this way? Part of the answer concerns the effects of competition among groups.

THE COEVOLUTION OF INDIVIDUAL AND GROUP TRAITS

Altruistic *individual* human practices may have arisen and persisted because individuals in groups in which the practices were prevalent enjoyed the group benefits of the practices, even if those engaging in the practices did materially less well than their fellow group members eschewing them. We know that individual behavioral traits may proliferate in a population when individuals copy successful neighbors. So too may distributive norms, linguistic conventions, or individual behaviors underpinning forms of governance or systems of property rights diffuse or disappear through the emulation of the characteristics of successful groups by members of less successful groups. This process often takes place as a result of military, economic, and other forms of competition. Charles Darwin (1873:156), in the epigraph to chapter 11, refers to courage, sympathy, and unselfishness as possible examples, these traits proliferating because "a tribe possessing the above qualities in a high degree would spread and be victorious over other tribes."

Thus, the formally altruistic (individually costly but group-beneficial) traits that may proliferate under the influence of group selection include behaviors that are harmful to members of *other* groups. The processes modeled here might be best described as demonstrating the evolutionary success of *selfish groups* rather than *generous individuals*.[5] Though the conventional definition of altruism refers only to ingroup interactions, individuals in our model interact with outgroup individuals as well; the model works because altruists confer fitness advantages or material benefits on insiders while inflicting fitness costs or material losses on outsiders. Our references to "group-beneficial" or "selfish" behaviors thus refer exclusively to *in*-group effects.

As has been long recognized, in populations composed of groups characterized by a markedly higher level of interaction among members than with outsiders, evolutionary processes may be decomposed into between-group and within-group selection effects. Where the degree of successful replication of a trait depends on the composition of the group, and where between-group differences in composition persist through time, *group selection* (sometimes termed *multi-level selection*) contributes to the pace and direction of evolutionary change. The model of the first property rights revolution in chapter 11 is an example of the process. The classic problem of group selection arises when between-group effects favor the proliferation of a group-beneficial trait such as altruism that is penalized by individual selection within groups. Thus, group selection is a way out of the evolutionary predicament of altruism.

Few students of human populations doubt that institutions, nations, firms, bands, and other groups may be subject to selective pressures operating at the group rather than individual level. But until recently, most of the formal modeling of evolutionary processes was done by biologists, and most concluded that group-level effects cannot offset the effects of individual within-group selection, except where special circumstances heighten and sustain differences between groups relative to differences within the group. The negative assessment of the likely empirical importance of group selection stems primarily from the presumption that the rate of selection within groups is more rapid than between-group selection, which results in part from the fact that differences in group means arise primarily due to drift or random assortment and hence are insignificant relative to within-group differences. Thus group

---

[5] I am paraphrasing Laland, Odling-Smee, and Feldman (2000:224).

selection models were widely judged to have failed in their defining task, namely, to explain the evolutionary success of altruistic behaviors. As a result, while the explanation of group-beneficial behaviors focused on kin-based fitness mechanisms, the impressive levels of non-kin-based altruism in the case of humans was interpreted as reciprocal altruism or remained for the most part unexplained.[6]

But subsequent work (see the suggested readings) suggests that impediments to group selection may be less general than the critics contend. Moreover, group selection may be of considerably greater importance among humans than among other animals. Among the distinctive human characteristics that may enhance the relevance of group selection is our capacity for the suppression of within-group phenotypic differences through resource-sharing, co-insurance, consensus decision making, conformist cultural transmission, forms of social differentiation supporting high levels of assortative interactions, the maintenance of group boundaries, and the frequency of between-group conflict. Other animals do some of these things, but none do all of them on a human scale. Group selection can work on behavioral traits that are transmitted either genetically or culturally. The model of the evolution of property rights in chapter 11 included the effects of group selection on culturally transmitted traits. In this chapter I will model group selection effects on a genetically transmitted trait.

I address two puzzles. First, what accounts for the evolution of individually costly and group-beneficial forms of human sociality towards non-kin? And, second, what accounts for the differential success those common group-level institutional structures that Parsons (1964) termed "evolutionary universals" such as states, resource sharing, and monogamy that have emerged and proliferated repeatedly and in a wide variety of circumstances during the course of human history? The coevolutionary process that I model and simulate are based on the idea that the two puzzles may be more convincingly resolved jointly than singly.

An example of such group-level structural characteristics are leveling institutions, such as monogamy and food sharing among non-kin, namely, those which reduce within-group differences in reproductive fitness or material well-being. By reducing within-group differences in individual success (whether in fitness, material gain, or some other measure), such structures may have attenuated within-group selective pressures operat-

---

[6] These do not exhaust the explanations offered, of course. Simon (1990), Caporael et al. (1989), and others have proposed a mechanism whereby costly but group-beneficial behaviors free ride on the individually beneficial behaviors ("docility," for example) with which they are pleiotropically paired. Gintis, Smith, and Bowles (2002) show that an individually costly group-beneficial behavior may proliferate if it is a truthful signal of one's value as a coalition partner or mate.

ing against individually costly but group-beneficial practices, thus giving the groups adopting them advantages in between-group contests.[7] In this case, the ubiquity of group structural characteristics such as leveling institutions is explained by their contribution to the proliferation of group-beneficial individual traits and the contribution of these traits to group survival.

The idea that the suppression of within-group competition may be a strong influence on evolutionary dynamics has been widely recognized in eusocial insects and other species. In a paper that examines the case of slime mould (*Dictyostelium discoideum*), Steven Frank (1995:520) writes, "Evolutionary theory has not explained how competition among lower level units is suppressed in the formation of higher-level evolutionary units," adding that "mutual policing and enforcement of reproductive fairness are also required for the evolution of increasing social complexity." Christopher Boehm (1999:211) referred to the process of group sanction of anti-social actors modeled in chapter 11 as "a 'political revolution' experienced by Paleolithic humans [that] created the social conditions under which group selection could robustly support genes that were altruistic." Relatedly, Irenaus Eibl-Eibesfeldt (1982:177) pointed to the importance of "indoctrinability to identify with values, to obey authority, and . . . ethical sharing" and thought that "through these bonding patterns, groups become so tightly knit that they could act as units of selection."

In the pages that follow, I will offer a model of the group selection process based on a remarkable simplification of evolutionary processes — the Price equation — interpreted and amended to address the peculiarities of evolution in human populations. Between-group effects are based on periodic between-group "contests" in which "winners" replace "losers," repopulating their sites. Group extinctions thus play an important part in the evolutionary process.

I first explain how an analysis of group conflicts may illuminate the evolution of formally altruistic individual behaviors. I then develop a model of the differential replication of individual traits subject to multi-level selection with group conflicts, extinctions, and births. With minor emendations, this model of group selection effects on genetically transmitted traits can be used to study cultural evolution.[8] I then use an agent-based simulation to determine the conditions under which an individually costly and group-beneficial trait can proliferate in the popula-

---

[7] We model what we term *resource sharing* and note that while it may be motivated by egalitarian, insurance, or other motives, its effects are to attentuate phenotypic differences within a group.

[8] This is done in Bowles (2001).

tion (the key parameter values concern the frequency of group conflict and individual updating, group size, and between-group migration). The simulated population is calibrated to resemble the social and ecological conditions of the 50,000 years prior to the advent of agriculture, a period long enough for the modeled group- and individual-level selection processes to have major effects on gene distributions. The simulations show that in the absence of group-level institutions that protect the altruistic from exploitation by the nonaltruistic, group selection pressures support the evolution of group-beneficial traits only when between-group conflicts are very frequent, groups are small, and migration rates are low. However, when group-level institutions are introduced and subjected to group selection pressures along with individual traits, altruism proliferates for a large parameter set that includes plausible approximations of the environments of our distant ancestors.

The Logic of Multi-Level Selection

Many of the entities central to the study of human society are aggregates of lower-level entities: nations are made up of firms, families, classes, and other groups, which in turn are made up of people, which in turn are aggregates of cells, and so on. One representation of a social structure is simply the distribution of these higher- and lower-level entities and the ways that they interact. The processes of change can then be accounted for by the differential replication of these entities, some diffusing and becoming common, others declining or disappearing altogether, with consequent changes in the interrelationships among the entities. Multi-level selection is the process whereby the evolution of an individual-level characteristic is affected by competitive pressures operating at both the individual level and at higher group levels.

Multi-level selection models sometimes appear as conjuring tricks whereby a group-beneficial but seemingly evolutionarily doomed characteristic may nonetheless proliferate despite experiencing lower rates of replication, violating the fundamentals of evolutionary accounting. It is this that prompted George Williams's memorable judgment of group selection: "A fleet herd (of deer) is a herd of fleet deer" (Williams 1966:16). But, appropriately modeled, group selection is not an alternative to the standard evolutionary practice of accounting for change and stability in the distribution of traits in a population by the differential replication of traits. Rather it is an extension of the standard method that takes account of group effects on replication. There are no rabbits to be pulled from hats: group selection is simply a form of nonrandom pairing already introduced in chapter 7 as social segmentation. Group-

TABLE 13.1
The Altruism Game:
Row's Payoffs

	A	N
A	$b - c$	$-c$
N	b	0

beneficial traits evolve under group-selection pressures because they enjoy a higher probability of interacting with like traits.

Consider a single trait that may be absent or present in each individual in a large population whose members each belong to one of a large number of groups. For concreteness, consider an altruistic behavior (A) — say, bravery in defense of the group in Darwin's example — which costs the individual c and confers a benefit of b on a randomly paired (single) member of the group. Let $p_{ij} = 1$ indicate that individual i in group j has the trait, with $p_{ij} = 0$ otherwise (those without the trait are Ns). Let the benefits and costs of altruism be measured in fitness terms as the number of replicas (in the next period) of the individual bearing the trait, so a member in a group composed entirely of altruists produces $b - c$ more replicas than that of a member a group with no altruists. As we assume $b - c > 0$, altruism is group beneficial. But compared to members of the same group, the fitness of altruists will be lower than that of the nonaltruists, so within-group selection will work against the altruists. Table 13.1 gives the relevant payoff matrix.

Of course, Darwin's point was that if competition between groups also affects fitness, the altruistic trait may nonetheless proliferate. Here is how group selection works. Using a discrete time framework, let p and p' represent the fraction of the population with the trait during a given and the subsequent time period, respectively, and $\Delta p = p' - p$. George Price (1970) showed that Δp can be partitioned into group and individual effects. Define π_{ij} as the number of replicas, next period, of an individual of type i in group j. The process of replication can be cultural copying, genetic inheritance, or any other conforming to the equation below. The model that follows is based on the differential replication of genetically transmitted traits.

Let π_{ij} depend additively on type i's own trait and on the frequency of the trait in the group, $p_j \in [0,1]$, according to:

$$\pi_{ij} = \beta_o + p_j\beta_g + p_{ij}\beta_i \tag{13.1}$$

where β_g and β_i are the partial effects on π_{ij} of the frequency of the trait in the group and the presence of the trait in the individual, respectively (the subscripts refer to group and individual effects), and β_o is baseline fitness. Define $\beta_G \equiv \beta_g + \beta_i$ as the effect on the group average number of replicas of the frequency of the trait in the group (the difference in the number of replicas made by an individual in a group composed entirely of those with the trait and a group entirely without is β_G). Thus, using the definitions above, $\beta_i = -c$, $\beta_g = b$, and $\beta_G = b - c$. Then following Price (1970)

$$\pi \Delta p = \mathrm{var}(p_j)\beta_G + E\{\mathrm{var}(p_{ij})\}\beta_i \qquad (13.2)$$

or

$$\pi \Delta p = \mathrm{var}(p_j)(b - c) - E\{\mathrm{var}(p_{ij})\}c$$

where π is the population-wide average of the number of replicas made (which I normalize to unity) and the expectation operator $E\{\}$ indicates a weighted summation over groups (the weights being relative group size). The first term captures the group-selection effect (which is positive), while the second represents the effect of individual selection (which is negative). (A simple derivation of this decomposition is in Bowles (2001).) Setting aside degenerate cases such as zero variances, it follows that an interior frequency of the trait will be stationary where these two terms are of equal absolute magnitude (assuming that the βs and variances making up these terms are themselves stationary). Because the second term is negative, the frequency of the trait within all surviving groups will fall over time. But as β_G is positive, this tendency will be offset by the higher average fitness of groups with a higher frequency of A's.

Then the stationarity condition for p (eq. 13.2) shows that $\Delta p = 0$ when

$$\frac{c}{b} = \frac{\mathrm{var}(p_j)}{E\{\mathrm{var}(p_{ij})\} + \mathrm{var}(p_j)} \qquad (13.3)$$

with

$$\Delta p > 0 \quad \text{for} \quad \frac{c}{b} < \frac{\mathrm{var}(p_j)}{E\{\mathrm{var}(p_{ij})\} + \mathrm{var}(p_j)}$$

$$\Delta p < 0 \quad \text{for} \quad \frac{c}{b} > \frac{\mathrm{var}(p_j)}{E\{\mathrm{var}(p_{ij})\} + \mathrm{var}(p_j)}$$

The left-hand term is the benefit-to-cost ratio of the altruistic trait. The right-hand term is the ratio of the between group to the within group plus the between-group variance of the trait. It is easily shown (Bowles 2001, and illustrated in an example below) that this ratio measures the difference between the probabilities that an altruist will be paired with an altruist P(A|A) and that a nonaltruist be paired with an altruist P(A|N). Thus

$$\frac{\text{var}(p_j)}{E\{\text{var}(p_{ij})\} + \text{var}(p_j)} = P(A|A) - P(A|N) = r$$

The variance ratio is thus a population-wide measure of the degree of segmentation resulting not because of nonrandom pairing within groups but because the population is group-structured. Eq. (13.3) shows that for an altruistic trait to proliferate in a population, the more costly (relative to the benefits) is the trait, the greater must be the between-group variance (relative to the within-group variance). Eq. (13.3) makes clear the key role of between-group variances. When the variance among group means is zero, the probability of meeting an altruist is independent of one's type. Then group selection is inoperative, so only a costless form of group benefit could proliferate.

Correspondingly, when $\text{var}(p_{ij}) = 0 \; \forall \; j$, all groups are homogeneous, and one meets only one's own type, independently of the composition of the total population. In this case, within-group selection is absent and between-group selection is the only selective force at work. In this (extreme) case, one can say that the group is the sole unit of selection. Thus, the force of group selection will depend on the magnitude of the group benefit relative to the individual cost (b and c in the example) and the degree to which groups differ in the mean frequency of the trait, relative to the degree of within-group variance of the trait.

Those familiar with population biology will recognize eq. (13.3), expressed as $c/b = r$, as a version of Hamilton's rule for the degree of positive assortation, r, permitting an altruistic trait to proliferate when rare. In this respect, multi-level selection is indistinguishable from evolutionary processes based on other forms of assortation (such as kin selection and other forms of within-group segmentation, or clustering).

An example will clarify this process. A population is composed of two groups of equal size with the fractions of altruists in each, $p_1 = \frac{3}{4}$ and $p_2 = \frac{1}{4}$, so $p = \frac{1}{2}$. From the above payoff matrix we know that the payoff to altruists in each group is less than the payoff to nonaltruists. Therefore, altruists will be disadvantaged in the replication process. This can be seen from the payoff functions in figure 13.2: for all values of p, the payoffs to the nonaltruists exceed the payoffs to the altruists. (Ignore the dashed payoff functions for the moment.) But group effects make the payoffs higher for all of those in groups with a high frequency of altruists, so the altruistic trait may not be eliminated. To find the values of b and c such that p will be stationary, we need to equate the average fitness of the two types. Writing p_j for the fraction of group j

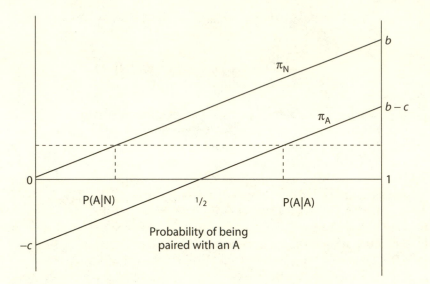

Figure 13.2 The evolution of an altruistic trait. If the population structure is such that the difference in the conditional probabilities of being paired with an A, P(A|A) − P(A|N), is as shown, p is stationary.

that are altruists ($j \in \{1,2\}$), π_{ij} for as the fitness of type i in group j ($i \in \{A,N\}$) and π_i for the average fitness of type i, using eq. (13.1) and noting that $p_1 + p_2 = 1$ and that the groups are of equal size, equal fitness of the two types requires that

$$\pi_A = p_1\pi_{A1} + p_2\,\pi_{A2} = (1 - p_1)\pi_{N1} + (1 - p_2)\pi_{N2} = \pi_N$$

or using the data given above,

$$\pi_A - \beta_o = \frac{3}{4}\left(\frac{3}{4}b - c\right) + \frac{1}{4}\left(\frac{1}{4}b - c\right) = \frac{1}{4}\left(\frac{3}{4}b\right) + \frac{3}{4}\left(\frac{b}{4}\right) = \pi_N - \beta_o$$

Solving, we find the values of b and c for which $\Delta p = 0$, namely, $c/b = \frac{1}{4}$. If we add the further requirement that the size of the total population be constant (so $\pi_A = 1 = \pi_N$) and arbitrarily setting $\beta_o = 0$, we have $b = 8/3$ and $c = 2/3$.

An equivalent method is simply to use eq. (13.2), along with the facts that $\mathrm{var}(p_{ij}) = p_j(1 - p_j) = 3/16$ for $j = 1, 2$ and $\mathrm{var}(p_j) = 1/16$, so, using eq. (13.1), we have

$$\pi\Delta p = \frac{b-c}{16} - \frac{3c}{16}$$

which, for $\pi \neq 0$ gives $c/b = \frac{1}{4}$ as a condition for $\Delta p = 0$, reproducing the above result. Further, reproducing eq. (13.3) and using the empirical values from the example gives us

$$\frac{c}{b} = \frac{\text{var}(p_j)}{E\{\text{var}(p_{ij})\} + \text{var}(p_j)} = \frac{\frac{1}{16}}{\frac{3}{16} + \frac{1}{16}} = \frac{1}{4}$$

as we would expect.

Thus, for values of $b > 4c$, the frequency of the altruistic trait will grow, exceeding one-half in the next period. This occurs because the relative size of the more altruistic group grows, offsetting the decline in the fraction of altruists in each group. The proliferation of the group-beneficial but individually costly trait is explained by the group structure of the population, which accounts for the fact that altruists tend to be paired with other altruists more frequently than the population average (despite random pairing within groups.) Thus, the probability of meeting an altruist conditional on being an altruist is

$$P(A|A) = (p_1)^2 + (p_2)^2 = \frac{5}{8}$$

while nonaltruists meet altruists with probability

$$P(A|N) = (1 - p_1)p_1 + (1 - p_2)p_2 = \frac{3}{8}$$

The difference between these two conditional probabilities — $\frac{1}{4}$ — is the expected advantage enjoyed by the altruistic trait by dint of its favored distribution among groups, giving an equivalent way of representing eq. (13.3)

$$c/b = P(A|A) - P(A|N) = \frac{1}{4}$$

Figure 13.2 shows how the group structure of the population overcomes the disadvantage of bearing the costs of altruistic behaviors. While the payoff to the nonaltruist always exceeds that to an altruist *for a given probability of meeting altruists*, the difference in the probability of meeting an altruist conditional on one's type (i.e., $P(A|A) - P(A|N) = \frac{1}{4}$) offsets this disadvantage.

The example shows how group selection may allow the proliferation of an otherwise unviable trait. But the analysis is incomplete. The Price equation gives a snapshot of an equilibrium rather than a complete dynamical system. It gives the stationarity condition for p, but it does not account for the movement of the variances upon which the movement in p is based. In most biological models, the between-group variance-enhancing mechanisms (mutation, genetic drift) are weak and tend to be swamped by the homogenizing effects of selection itself, along with migration among groups. This is the reason why group-selection pressures among nonhuman animals are thought to be weak. However, among humans, where effective group size is small (e.g., the members of a foraging band) and where groups frequently divide either in response to increased size or to interpersonal tensions within the group, sampling error will increase between-group variance. For any model even minimally faithful to the empirical circumstances of human evolution, the only practical way to determine if these variance-enhancing effects are strong enough to make group selection an important influence on evolution is to simulate a group-structured population under reasonable parameter values.

AN AGENT-BASED MODEL OF MULTI-LEVEL SELECTION

In the absence of the two group-level institutions — resource sharing and within-group segmentation — introduced presently, the selection process within a group is modeled (for group j) by the standard replicator dynamic equation

$$\Delta p_j = p_j(1 - p_j)(\pi_{Aj} - \pi_{Nj}) = p_j(1 - p_j)(-c) \qquad (13.4)$$

Now imagine that the group has adopted the practice, common among foragers and other human groups, of within-group resource sharing. Some fraction of the resources an individual acquires — perhaps specific kinds of food as among the Aché (Kaplan and Hill 1985) — is deposited in a common pot to be shared equally among all group members. This sharing institution may be modeled as a linear tax, $t_j \in [0,1)$, collected from the members payoffs with the proceeds distributed equally to all members of the population. The effect is to reduce payoff differences between As and Ns, that is, $\pi_{Aj} - \pi_{Nj} = -(1 - t_j)c$. Figure 13.3 shows expected payoffs and the effect of resource sharing on the payoff differences of the two types, assuming all groups adopt the same tax rate, t. The difference in the probability of meeting an A (conditional on ones own type) that equalizes expected payoffs is no longer $P(A|A) - P(A|N) = r^*$ as shown in figure 13.2, but is now $P^T(A|A) - P^T(A|N) = r^T$ with $r^T < r^*$. Comparing the two figures, one sees that $r^* = c/b$ while $r^T = c(1 - t)/b$. As a result, were the population structure as in figure 13.3 (r^*) and the sharing institution in place ($t > 0$), then $\pi_A > \pi_N$ and p will increase.

Suppose that in addition to the institution of resource sharing, groups are also segmented, so that in the pairing process *within* groups, As are more likely to interact with As and Ns with Ns than would occur by

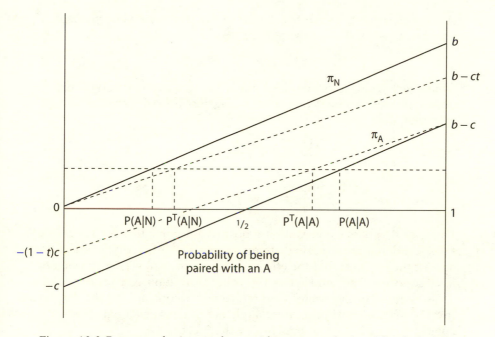

Figure 13.3 Resource sharing weakens within-group selection. The dashed fitness functions indicate the effect of the resource sharing institution: the altruistic trait can proliferate under less stringent conditions than in Figure 13.2.

random matching. Suppose that the probability that an A-member of group j is matched with an A is not p_j but $s_j + (1 - s_j)p_j > p_j$ and the probability that a N-member of group j is matched with an A is $(1 - s_j)p_j < p_j$. Then as in chapter 7, we define $s_j \geq 0$ as the degree of segmentation in group j, or the difference in the conditional probability of an A meeting an A and an N meeting an A in the *within-group* pairing. Then abstracting from the tax ($t_j = 0$): $\pi_{Aj} - \pi_{Nj} = s_j b - c$. Segmentation reduces the expected payoff disadvantage of altruists because within a given group they are disproportionately likely to meet other altruists, while Ns are disproportionately likely to meet other Ns. If $s_j > c/b$, $\forall j$, As will on average do better than Ns within every group and as a result the As will proliferate as a result of both within and between-group selection. Thus, both terms in the Price equation will be positive. To pose the classical group-selection problem, we assume $s < c/b$, so the As will only proliferate if group-selection pressures are strong enough. Like resource sharing, segmentation is a convention and is passed on culturally.

Taking account of both segmentation and resource sharing, the differences in the expected payoffs received by Ns and As within a group will now be $(1 - t_j)(s_j b - c)$ so we have

$$\Delta p_j = p_j (1 - p_j)(1 - t_j)(s_j b - c) \tag{13.5}$$

from which (comparing eqs. 13.4 and 13.5) it is clear that both institutions retard the within-group selection against the As. This can be seen by noting that

$$\frac{\partial \Delta p_j}{\partial t} = -p_j(1 - p_j)(s_j b - c)$$

$$\frac{\partial \Delta p_j}{\partial s} = p_j(1 - p_j)(1 - t_j)b \tag{13.6}$$

For $p_j \in (0,1)$ both expressions are positive, meaning that both segmentation and resource sharing attenuate the rate of negative selection against the As. Note that the effect of each institution is greater when p_j is close to one half, and when the other institution is at a low level. Thus, in terms of their benefits in retarding selection against the As, the institutions are substitutes, not complements: their beneficial effects are enhanced the lesser is the presence of the other.

The structure of the updating process is described in figure 13.4 and its notes. Individual replication is subject to mutations, such that with a small probability, e, offspring may be either A or N with equal probability. The institutions represented by s and t differ among groups and they also evolve. When conflict occurs between groups, the group with the higher total payoff wins. The losing group's members die and the winning group populates the site occupied by the losers with replicas of themselves. The new inhabitants of the site adopt the institutions of the

TABLE 13.2
Key Parameters for the Simulations

	Benchmark Values	Range explored
Mean group size (n/g)	20	7 to 47
Migration Rate (m)	0.2	0.1 to 0.3
Probability of contest (k)	0.25	0.18 to 0.4
Mutation rate (e)	0.001	0.01 to 0.000001

Note: Total population size is n, and there are g groups; m, k, and e are per generation. Other parameters: benefit (b): 2; cost (c): 1; baseline payoffs: 10. We varied group size by varying n. For reasons explained in the text, we restricted s to not exceed ½ while $t \in [0, 1]$ The costs imposed on the group by these institutions are ½ $(s^2 + t^2)$.

winning group from which they descended. Institutions are also subject to stochastic variation, increasing or lowering t and s by chance each period. Both segmentation and resource sharing impose costs on the groups adopting them. More segmented groups may fail to capture the benefits of diversity or of economies of scale, and resource sharing may reduce incentives to acquire the resources to be shared. Neither of these costs are modeled formally, but to capture their impact, group average benefits are reduced by an amount that is rising in convex in both s and t.

Jung-Kyoo Choi, Astrid Hopfensitz, and I simulated an artificial population living in twenty groups. The benchmark values of the parameters in the simulations, and the range of alternative values that we explored appear in table 13.2. The key parameters concern the rate of (random) migration among groups, group size, and the frequency of between-group contests. Because our group contests are lethal for the losers, we have chosen a benchmark rate of just a single war every four generations. The benchmark values were chosen on grounds of empirical plausibility, the evidence for which I review in the penultimate section.

We initiated each simulation with neither altruists nor institutions present at time zero to see if they would proliferate if initially rare (the individual and institutional mutation process will introduce some variability in the population). Baseline fitness (β_o) is 10 and offspring are produced in proportion to the individual's share of the group's total fitness, so in the absence of segmentation and resource sharing, the expected difference in payoffs is $c = 1$ and thus the Ns produce 10 percent more offspring than the As.

A typical simulation appears in figure 13.5 on page 460. The early rise in p is supported by the chance increase in both s and t (between periods 100 and 150). When p reaches high levels (periods 532 to 588, for example) both s and t decline, typically leading to a sharp decline in p. The subsequent rise in s or t occurs by chance.

The pattern emerges for the following reason: when the population is evenly divided between As and Ns, many groups are also approximately evenly divided. As a result (from eq. (13.6)), the beneficial effects of retarded within-group selection gained by higher levels of t or s are maximized in this region. However, when p is well above 0.5, the benefits of the protection of As offered by the institutions is of less value. But the institutions are costly to bear so when p is high, groups with substantial levels of segmentation or resource sharing are likely to lose conflicts with other groups, and the sites they occupied are then peopled by the descendants of winners, who typically bear lower levels of these institutional variables. As a result, when the winner's institutions are imposed on the repopulated site, both s and t fall.

1) Pairing and interacting

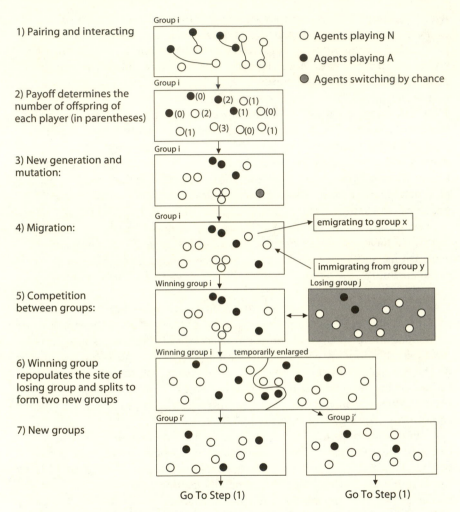

Group i

○ Agents playing N

● Agents playing A

◉ Agents switching by chance

2) Payoff determines the number of offspring of each player (in parentheses)

3) New generation and mutation:

4) Migration:

emigrating to group x

immigrating from group y

5) Competition between groups:

Winning group i

Losing group j

6) Winning group repopulates the site of losing group and splits to form two new groups

Winning group i temporarily enlarged

7) New groups

Group i'

Group j'

Go To Step (1)

Go To Step (1)

Figure 13.4 Individual and group interactions. We assign n individuals to g groups. At $t = 0$ all are N. (1) *Pairing.* In each period, each member of a group is randomly paired to play the game once with another member, with payoffs given in the text (in some runs modified by the resource-sharing rule). With segmentation, the member interacts with a similar type with probability s and is paired randomly with probability $1 - s$. (2) *Reproduction.* Replicas of the current generation constitute the next generation. They are produced by drawing (with replacement) from the current group membership with the probability that any member will be drawn equal to that member's share of the total payoffs of the group. (3) *Mutation.* With probability e, a member of the next generation is not a replica of its parent, but is A or N with equal probability. (4) *Migration.* With probability m each member of the new generation relocates to

Table 13.3
Institutions retard within-group selection
against altruists

Institutions	β_i	t-statistic
None	−0.102	8.5
Resource sharing	−0.080	16.6
Segmentation	−0.063	13.4
Both	−0.055	11.2

Note: Column β_i gives the ordinary least squares estimate of the coefficient of the group mean value of $p_j(1 - p_j)$ as a predictor of Δp_j (the other regressor is the between-group variance, i.e., $var(p_j)$). The last column is the negative of the t-statistic for the estimate.

To explore further the impact of institutions on the updating process we estimated the Price equation econometrically, exploring the effect of each institution separately (i.e., constraining s, t, both, or neither to zero). Using data from four 10,000-generation, simulations we regressed the observed Δp on the previous period's values for $var(p_j)$ and $E\{var(p_{ij})\}$, where the second term is the mean across all groups of the within-group variances. The coefficients of these variables are estimates of β_G and β_i from eq. (13.2). As table 13.3 shows, the combined effect of resource sharing and segmentation is to reduce by half the extent of within-group selection against the altruists. Note that with no institutions, the estimate of β_i (0.102) is very close to the expected value given that the baseline fitness is 10 (so Ns have a 10 percent advantage in fitness). The estimate of the between-group effect, β_G (not shown) varies little in response to which institutions are allowed to evolve, and is in all cases more than four times as large as the within-group effect. The mean within-group variance is correspondingly much larger than the between-group variance.

---

a group randomly selected from the other groups. (5) *Group competition.* With probability k each group is selected, and, among those selected, competition takes place between randomly paired groups. The winning group is that with the highest total payoff (net of the costs of sharing and segmentation, if any). (6) *Repopulation and fission.* The members of the losing group are replaced by replicas of the members of the winning group, and the resulting (temporarily enlarged) winning group splits with members assigned randomly to two new groups. (In simulations with resource sharing or segmentation, the two new groups adopt the institutions of the winning group.)

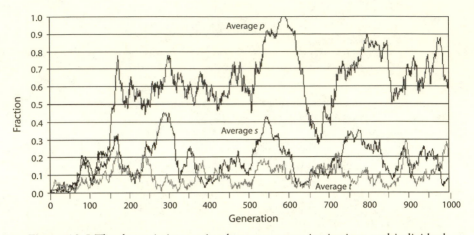

Figure 13.5 The dynamic interaction between group institutions and individual behaviors. The figure presents a 1000 period history of a run using the benchmark parameters from table 13.1. The population average frequency of altruists is p, while t and s give the average across the 20 groups of the level of resource sharing and segmentation. Altruism and both group-level institutions are initially rare. The particular time frame shown was selected because it clearly reveals this dynamic, which is observed over long periods in many runs.

Note that we can rewrite eq. (13.3), the condition for $\Delta p = 0$, as

$$-\frac{\beta_i}{\beta_G} = \frac{\text{var}(p_j)}{E\{\text{var}(p_{ij})\}}$$

with $\Delta p > 0$ if the variance ratio exceeds the ratio of within- to between-group effects, and conversely. Do we observe this in our simulations? Using the econometric estimates of the within and between-group effects described in table 13.3 as well as the mean variance ratios observed in the same simulations, we have the results in table 13.4. With institutions constrained to zero, the ratio of the within-group selection effect to the between-group selection effect, $-\beta_i/\beta_G$, is almost twice the ratio of between to within-group variances. Thus, were the population at these mean and estimated values, Δp would be negative. Thus, it is no surprise to find that in the simulations on which these estimates are based, the mean value of p is 0.06. However, with both institutions unconstrained, the variance ratio is equal to the effects ratio, meaning that the within-group effects operating against the As is exactly offset by the between-group effects supporting their proliferation. In simulation on which these estimates are based, the mean value of p is 0.51.

Between-group conflicts play the key role in supporting both group-

TABLE 13.4
An estimate of the Price equation

Institutions	Effects ratio	Variance ratio	$\underline{p}$
None	0.25	0.13	0.06
Both	0.13	0.13	0.51

Note: The variance ratio is the mean of $var(p_j)/\mathrm{E}\{var(p_{ij})\}$ over the 10,000 generations simulated, while the effects ratio is $-\beta_i/\beta_G$, estimated as described in table 13.2. The average fraction of As in the population is $\underline{p}$.

level institutions and individual-level altruism. In the simulations reported, the expected frequency of conflict was $1/k$, where k is the probability that a group is drawn for a contest in every generation. It seems likely that over long historical periods, the frequency of conflict varied considerably, perhaps in response to the need to migrate in times of climatic variability. To explore the sensitivity of the simulations to the frequency of conflicts, we varied k stochastically using the autoregressive system described in the notes to figure 13.6 on page 462. During periods in which conflict was frequent (e.g., around the 21,000th generation), high levels of altruism were sustained, but periodic outbreaks of relative peace among the groups (around the 25,300th, 27,000th, and 29,600th generations) led to sharp reductions in the fraction of As in the population. The 500-generation period following generation 28,500 illustrates the strong path dependency in the model. The high level of p induced by the sharp rise in the frequency of intergroup conflict around generation 28,500 persists even as the frequency of conflict sharply declines in subsequent generations. But the "lock-in" is not permanent: when k remains below 0.2 for a number of periods, p crashes.

We sought to answer two other questions as well. Could altruism have evolved had group-level institutions not coevolved with individual level altruism? And how sensitive are our simulations to variations in the key parameters? To answer both questions, we varied group size from 7 to 47, and for each size ran ten simulations of 50,000 generations, with the other parameters at their baseline values. We did this with both institutions constrained to not evolve, with each singly constrained to not evolve, and with neither constrained. We performed the same operation for variations in the migration rate from 0.1 to 0.3, and the probability of conflict (k) from 0.18 to 0.51. The results appear in figure 13.7 on page 464.

The top panel shows that with both institutions constrained not to evolve, a group size of 7 supports high levels of altruism, but group

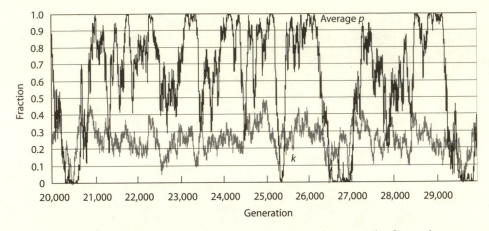

Figure 13.6 High frequencies of group conflict favor altruism. The figure shows a thousand generation period from a run in both institutions evolved endogenously, and in which k, the frequency of between-group conflict varies over time according to $k_t = k_0 + \rho k_{t-1} + \sigma_t$ where $\rho = 0.99$, σ_t is randomly drawn from the uniform distribution $[-0.02, 0.02]$, and k_0 is selected so that the mean of k_t is the same as the baseline k, namely, 0.25.

sizes greater than 8 result in a frequency of altruists of less than 0.3. Taking as a benchmark the group size for which $p > 0.5$, we see that with no institutions the critical size is 8, while with both institutions $p > 0.5$ for group sizes less than 22. The results for the migration rate are similar. In the absence of institutions, sustaining $p > 0.5$ requires a (per-generation) migration rate of 0.13, but with both institutions free to evolve, the critical migration rate is 0.21. The bottom panel shows that institutions also allow the evolution of high levels of altruism with significantly fewer between-group conflicts. A "vertical" reading of the figure is also illuminating: for example, the bottom panel shows that for $k = .3$, p is less than 0.2 without institutions, but is greater than 0.8 with both institutions free to evolve.[9]

[9] Figure 13.7 and table 13.3 suggest that segregation is a more powerful influence than resource sharing: segmentation alone has a larger effect than resource sharing alone both in retarding within-group selection against the As and in broadening the parameter space for which the As constitute large fractions of the population. This is an artifact of our modeling choices. The cost functions for s and t are identical, but s has a greater impact on within-group updating, as can be seen from eq. (13.6). Using these equations to compare the effect of s when $t = 0$ with the effect of t when $s = 0$, we see that the former is b/c times the latter, and $b > c$ because the altruistic act is group-beneficial. (In our simulations, $b = 2$ and $c = 1$, so the s-effect is twice the t-effect.) Also, note that from eq.

Experiments with mutation rates ranging from 10^{-2} to 10^{-5} gave similar results to those shown. Without institutions, p remains low, while with both institutions the average of p in five simulations of 100,000 generations each (for mutation rates of $10^{-2}, 10^{-3}, 10^{-4},$ and 10^{-5}) exceeds one-half. The average p for the five simulations with a mutation rate of 10^{-5} ranged from 0.75 to 0.83; in each case a sharp rise in p occurred between the 17,150th and 25,855th generation, and high levels of p were sustained throughout the rest of the simulation. The waiting time before a take-off depends on the time it takes for a single group to accumulate a significant number of altruists. This waiting time would be shortened considerably where there are more than twenty groups. Because we set $p = 0$ at the initial generation, very low rates of migration (less than 10^{-5}) sustain low levels of p over long periods.

EVOLUTIONARY ENVIRONMENTS

We have described a process whereby institutions such as resource sharing and segmentation provide an environment within which a group-beneficial trait evolves, and in which these institutions proliferate in the population because of their contribution to the evolutionary success of the group-beneficial trait. Does this model illuminate the process by which human group-beneficial behaviors and group-level institutions might have evolved? The answer must depend on whether the parameter space in which this co-evolutionary process occurs in our simulations approximates the relevant environment, namely, the first 50,000 or 100,000 years of modern human existence, prior to the dramatic transformation of social structure accompanying the advent of agriculture around 11,000 years ago.

Little is known about the relevant late Pleistocene environments, and the difficulty in making inferences about the social organization of human groups during this period on the basis of contemporary simple societies is well known (Foley 1987, Kelly 1995). We can say with some confidence, however, that climate was exceptionally variable (Richerson Boyd and Bettinger 2001) and that small mobile foraging bands composed of both kin and non-kin, and lacking complex political organization were a common form of social organization.

Our benchmark value for group size, 20, is based is an approximation of the median of the 235 hunter gather groups recorded in Binford

---

(13.5), if $s = c/b = \frac{1}{2}$, $\Delta p_j = p_j(1 - p_j)(1 - t_j)(s_j b - c) = 0$, but the value of t required to halt within-group selection against the As is 1. (In the quadratic cost function we used, the group-level costs of $t = 1$ are four times the cost of $s = \frac{1}{2}$.)

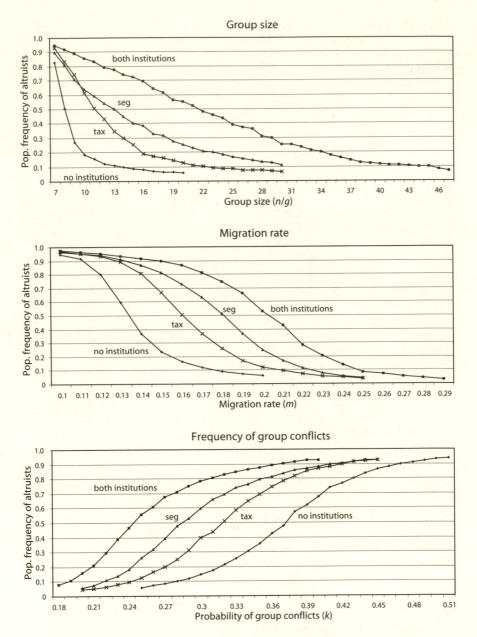

Figure 13.7 Group-level institutions increase the size of the parameter space for which altruistic behaviors are prevalent. Each data point is the average frequency of altruists in the entire population over 10 runs of 50,000 periods each for the parameter value indicated on the horizontal axis. In each panel the other

(2001), namely, 19. Our handling of group size is not entirely realistic, however. Recall that small size contributes to group-selection pressures by increasing the between-group variance arising when successful groups double in size and divide. In reality, group fissioning is not by a random draw but rather appears to be a highly political conflict-resolving process in which kin and coalitions are likely to remain together. Thus, fissioning is likely to contribute to between-group variance in ways which our model does not capture. A study of fissioning among Amazonian peoples (Neves 1995:198) reports:

> The maximum size of a village is constrained by the amount of relatedness or degree of solidarity between individuals [which] springs from three sources: kinship relations, marriage ties, and the influences of political leaders. . . . Village fissioning is thus favored by the loosening of kinship ties provided by population growth; and when it happens it keeps close kin together but separates them from more distant kin. . . . [T]he potential line of cleavage is furnished by the division in patrilineages.[10]

As the bearers of the group-beneficial trait are likely to be numerically and socially dominant in the winning group, they may practice what Hamilton (1975:137) termed *assortative division*, segregating bearers of the "other" trait insofar as recognition of traits or characteristics correlated with traits allows this. Were this the case, much larger group sizes would sustain the evolutionary processes indicated above.

Very little is know about group conflict during early human history. We do know that deaths due to warfare constitute a substantial fraction of all deaths in many of the pre-state societies in the ethnographic and archeological record. The average reported by Keeley (1996) for ethnographic studies of pre-state societies is 0.19, and for pre-state societies studied by archeologists is 0.16. This compares with estimates well

---

parameters are the benchmark values shown in table 13.2 Each run began with p, t, and s set equal to zero. The curve labeled "none" gives the results for runs in which t and s were constrained to zero; the other curves indicate runs in which one or both of the institutions were free to evolve. ("Tax" refers to resource sharing.) The horizontal distance between the curves indicates the enlargement of the parameter space made possible by group level institutions. The vertical distance between the curves shows the impact of institutions on average p.

---

[10] Chagnon (1983:141–3) studied a Yanomamo village that subdivided and found that average genetic relatedness in the prefission village was lower than either of the newly formed units.

below 0.1 for Europe and the United States in the twentieth century, 0.03 for nineteenth-century France, and 0.02 for Western Europe in the seventeeth century. A fifty-year record of 200 wars among the Mae-Enga in New Guinea, for example, took 800 lives from a population of about 5,000, resulting in an annual death rate from warfare (0.0032 deaths per year per head) double that of Germany and Russia in the twentieth century but well below the average of the pre-state societies on record (Keeley 1996:195). Whether these extraordinarily lethal episodes were common during the Late Pleistocene is difficult to say. But some speculations based on what we know about climate change and likely rates of population growth are possible. Christopher Boehm (2000a:19) writes:

> In very rich stable environments it makes sense that prehistoric population densities rose, that increasingly proximate and numerous bands began to compete for resources, and that eventually this would have made for lethal political trouble even if resources originally had been more than adequate. . . . These varying conflict patterns would have periodically increased the force of natural selection operating at the between-group level as some bands were decimated while others flourished and eventually had to fission. [In response to dramatic oscillations in climate in the last Pleistocene interglacial period] foraging bands were obliged to make major adjustments quite frequently, and surely these often included bands adjusting to neighboring bands as well as bands adjusting to changing biomes.

His conclusion is that

> towards the end of the Pleistocene as anatomically modern humans began to emerge, group extinction rates could have risen dramatically as needy bands of well armed hunters, strangers lacking established patterns of political interaction frequently collided, either locally or in the course of long distance migration.

Carol Ember (1978) collected data on the frequency of warfare among 50 foraging groups in the present or recent past. Excluding those who practice some herding or sedentary agriculture, 64 percent of the groups had warfare every two years or more frequently. Even excluding those groups who either had horses or relied on fishing (among whom warfare is more common), warfare is described as "rare" in only 12 percent of the groups.

While movement between ethno-linguistic units was probably uncommon, it seems likely that substantial rates of migration among the bands making up these units occurred. Migration rates for the thirteen societies surveyed by Rogers (1990) averaged 22 percent per generation with the maximum (the !Kung) less than one-half. Because Rogers' data refer to some larger than band-sized groups, these data may understate the rate of migration somewhat.

Notwithstanding the highly speculative nature of these inferences, it seems possible that the social and physical environments of the Late Pleistocene may fall within the parameter space supporting the co-evolutionary trajectories illustrated in figure 13.7. If so, the multi-level selection model with endogenous institutions may provide at least a partial account of this critical period of human evolution.

Conclusion

It thus seems likely that the distinctive human predisposition toward group-beneficial activities could have coevolved with common human institutions implementing resource sharing and social segmentation. If so, this approach may contribute to an understanding of why humans can be so willing to share and to cooperate toward common goals and at the same time to ready to kill and be killed for abstract entities called nations or races. The model also provides some insight into why these behaviors are less common in other animals: most are incapable of creating the facilitating environments constituted by well-defined groups of non-kin with commonly understood behavioral codes that enforce such behaviors as sharing or "us vs them" distinctions. And without these distinctly human structures of interaction, as we have seen, the evolution of group-beneficial individual behaviors is quite unlikely. A further implication, underlined by figure 13.6, is that altruism and war also coevolved. The group-oriented behaviors that make cooperation for mutual benefit possible among humans also make large-scale lethal warfare possible. And frequent warfare, as we have seen, may have been an essential contributor to the evolution of precisely the altruistic traits that facilitate war making. To explore this dynamic, we made the likelihood of a lethal inter-group conflict endogenous; k was assumed to co-vary with the frequency of As in the population. In these simulations (not shown), the population spends virtually all of the time in one of two states: high frequencies of altruism and very frequent wars or few altruists and infrequent wars (Bowles and Choi 2003).

Multi-level selection models similar to the one simulated here have also demonstrated that altruistic punishment of norm violators can proliferate when rare and remain common even in quite large groups. One such model (Boyd, Gintis, Bowles, and Richerson 2003) exploits the fact that the cost of punishing norm violators is quite small when the norm is adhered to by most members of a group. (This is similar to the dynamics of the Punisher-Grabber-Sharer model in the neighborhood of the Rousseauian equilibrium.) In this case, relatively weak group-selection pressures arising from intergroup conflicts (as in the above model) are sufficient to maintain high frequencies of altruistic punishers and to sustain high levels of cooperation. A second model, explicitly about strong reciprocity (Bowles and Gintis 2003), models a form of punishment of norm violators that is common among foraging hunter-gatherers: shunning or ostracism from a group. Group conflict and group extinctions play no role in this model: those punished suffer fitness losses during the spell of time that they are not members of a group. Free riders who adhere to the norm but never punish do not drive out the strong reciprocators because if free riders become common in a group, norm violators proliferate, reducing the average fitness of the groups they are in.

In introducing chapters 10 through 13, I asked how institutions change and how people and the rules governing their lives co-evolve. Three fundamental sources of change have been modeled: accommodation to exogenous secular trends (preeminently, technical change and the physical environment, as in chapter 11), the joint effects of chance and collective action (chapter 12), and the joint effects of chance and between-group contests (this chapter). The models introduced suggest two ways that change may occur endogenously, with collective action and group competition, respectively, producing change from the raw material provided by chance. Taken as a whole the models capture at least some of the desiderata outlined at the beginning of chapter 11, namely, the important parts played by *conflicts of interest, chance,* and *collective action,* the persistence of *inefficient institutions,* and the highly irregular trajectories of change summarized by the term *punctuated equilibria.* The models also provide good reason to expect that inefficient institutions, though capable of persistence over long periods, in the long run will not fare as well as otherwise identical more efficient ones. We have also seen that for two quite distinct reasons (given in chapters 12 and 13), egalitarian institutions may be favored evolutionarily. In models based on stochastic evolutionary game theory, the basin of attraction of egalitarian institutions is larger, and in multi-level selection models, egalitarian institutions retard the within-group selection against the altruists, which enhances the groups' capacity to survive in competition with other groups. We thus were able to provide some of the causal mechanisms accounting not only for institutional and individual evolution, but for Parsons' concept of *evolutionary universals,* namely, institutions that one might expect to be ubiquitous in a variety of environments and on numerous occasions to have emerged and proliferated when initially rare.

The conceptual strategy underlying all of the models presented here has been to extend a number of quite abstract biologically inspired approaches — stochastic evolutionary game theory and the Price equation's decomposition of within- and between-group selection processes — by modeling the distinctive process of human social interaction. Thus, the stochastic evolutionary approach was extended by taking account of the intentional pursuit of conflicting interests through collective action, and the multi-level selection model was amended to take account of both resource sharing and social segmentation within groups, as well as warfare and other forms of conflict between groups.

The results of the simulations suggest the fruitfulness of the approach. The time scale on which history unfolds in the simplest of the stochastic evolutionary models is far too slow to be relevant to human trajectories, but the introduction of local interactions and the correlation of idiosyncratic play through conformist tendencies will greatly quicken the pace of change. Similarly, in the absence of within-group institutions such as resource sharing and segmentation, the conditions for the evolution of individual group-beneficial behavioral traits are quite stringent. But when these two empirically important aspects of human interaction are allowed to coevolve with individual traits, the resulting coevolutionary processes become more recognizable as possible accounts of the human story.

PART IV

Conclusion

CHAPTER FOURTEEN

Economic Governance: Markets, States, and Communities

Which of these systems [*central planning or competition*] is likely to be more efficient depends on the question under which of them can we expect that fuller use will be made of the existing knowledge. And this, in turn, depends on whether we are more likely to succeed in putting at the disposal of a single central authority all the knowledge which ought to be used but which is initially dispersed among many different individuals, or in conveying to the individuals such additional information as they need in order to enable them to fit their plans in with those of others.
— F. A. Hayek, "The Use of Knowledge in Society" (1945)

Lawgivers make the citizen good by inculcating habits in them, and this is the aim of every lawgiver; If he does not succeed in doing that, his legislation is a failure. It is in this that a good constitution differs from a bad one.

— Aristotle, *Nicomachean Ethics* (350 B.C)

The man of systems . . . imagines that he can arrange the different members of a great society with as much ease as the hand arranges the different pieces upon a chess-board; he does not consider . . . that in the great chess-board of human society, every single piece has a principle of motion of its own.

— Adam Smith, *Theory of Moral Sentiments* (1759)

IN SOME Chicago neighborhoods, adults admonish youngsters' skipping school, creating a disturbance, or decorating walls with graffiti. Residents are also willing to intervene in public meetings to maintain neighborhood amenities such as a local firehouse threatened with budget cuts. These are all examples of what Sampson, Raudenbush, and Earls (1997) term *collective efficacy*. Where neighbors express a high level of collective efficacy, violent crime is markedly lower, controlling for a wide range of community and individual characteristics, including past

---

The first epigraph is from Hayek (1945:521), the second from Aristotle (1962:103), the third from Smith (1976:234).

crime rates. In other neighborhoods, residents adopt a more hands-off approach. Sampson, Raudenbush, and Earls found considerable variation in the neighborhood levels of collective efficacy, with examples of rich and poor, and black and white neighborhoods exhibiting both high and low levels. Remarkably, ethnic heterogeneity was considerably less important in predicting low collective efficacy than were measures of economic disadvantage, a low rate of home ownership, and other indicators of residential instability. Chicago's neighborhoods illustrate the informal enforcement of community norms.

The Toyama Bay fishing cooperatives in Japan illustrate another aspect of community problem solving (Platteau and Seki 2001). Faced with variable catches as well as the high level and changing nature of skills required, some fishermen elect to share income, information, and training. One coop, which has been highly successful since its formation in the mid 1960s, consists of the crews and skippers of seven shrimp boats. The boats share income and costs, repair damaged nets in common, and pool information about the changing location and availability of shrimp. Elder members pass on their skills, and the more educated younger members teach others the new electronic methods of locating fish and navigating. The coop's income- and cost-pooling activities allow its boats to fish in much riskier and higher yield locations, and the skill and information sharing raises profits and reduces productivity differences among the boats. Fishing, off-loading the catch, and marketing by individual boats are synchronized to increase the transparency of the sharing process and make opportunistic cheating on the agreement easy to detect.

The success of the Toyama Bay shrimp cooperatives and of collective efficacy in Chicago neighborhoods are examples of *community governance*. The worker-owned plywood coops described in chapter 10 are another example. By community I mean a group of people who interact directly, frequently, and in multi-faceted ways. People who work together are usually communities in this sense, as are some neighborhoods, groups of friends, professional and business networks, gangs, and sports leagues. Connection, not affection, is the defining characteristic of a community. The evolutionary models in chapter 7 showed how the repeated and multi-faceted nature of social interactions in communities, the relatively small numbers of people involved, and, as a result, the availability of information on one's associates may support high levels of what is sometimes referred to as social capital: trust, concern for one's associates, and a willingness to live by the norms of one's community and to punish those who do not.

These other-regarding behaviors were recognized as essential ingredients of good governance among classical thinkers from Aristotle to

Thomas Aquinas, Jean-Jacques Rousseau, and Edmund Burke. Nicolo Machiavelli's *The Prince* (1513) and Thomas Hobbes's *Leviathan* (1651) represented a sharp break with the Aristotelian tradition. These founding works of modern political philosophy took self-interest as a fundamental behavioral assumption and asked how the potentially destructive consequences of the autonomous pursuit of individual gain might be constrained by the authority of a sovereign ruler.

The more radical notion that selfish motives could be harnessed for public good was the key contribution of Bernard Mandeville's *Fable of the Bees*, first published in 1705 (Mandeville 1924). The subtitle of the 1714 edition of the *Fable* announced that the work contained "several discourses to demonstrate that human frailties . . . may be turn'd to the advantage of civil society, and made to supply the place of moral virtues." In place of the Aristotelian view that good laws make good citizens, Mandeville proposed the more modern notion that the right rules of the game governing social interactions might harness selfish motives to promote general well-being. This radical conjecture was given economic content by Adam Smith's invisible hand argument. Thus, most political theorists and constitutional thinkers since the late eighteenth century have taken the self-interested *Homo economicus* as their fundamental assumption about behavior, and partly for this reason, have stressed competitive markets, well-defined property rights, and efficient, well-intentioned states as the critical ingredients of governance. Good rules of the game thus came to displace good citizens as the *sine qua non* of good government.

The contending camps that emerged in the nineteenth and early twentieth centuries advocated laissez faire on the one hand or comprehensive state intervention on the other as *the* ideal form of economic governance.[1] The debate in the 1920s and 1930s on the economic feasibility of centralized planning was emblematic of the truncation of the constitutional menu to state versus laissez faire. Ludwig von Mises and others (Hayek 1935) advanced the view that the rational economic calculation entailed by planning required the knowledge of prices reflecting true scarcity (i.e., measuring social marginal costs and benefits), and that this information could be obtained only by the extensive use of decentralized allocation through markets. Oskar Lange (Lange and Taylor 1938), Enrico Barone (1935), Abba Lerner (1944), and others countered that prices are implicit in any optimizing problem (whether or not markets

---

[1] Outside of academic circles, the menu of options was considerably broader, including the "mixed" economy models pioneered by Nordic social democrats and market socialist models initiated by Oskar Lange. Dahl and Lindblom (1953) is exemplary, but rare, in avoiding the polarization of the planning versus markets debate.

exist). These implicit (or shadow) prices, they claimed, could either be computed directly or extracted from observations of competitive behaviors in an economy using markets to implement the allocations determined by central planners. This being the case, the planner could implement any allocation achieved by decentralized competitive markets but could do better than this in cases in which missing markets or impediments to competition gave rise to allocational inefficiencies.

By the 1940s the debate was all but over. Even the arch-opponent of socialism, Joseph Schumpeter, had conceded: "Can socialism work? Of course it can. . . . There is nothing wrong with the pure theory of socialism" (Schumpeter 1942:167, 172). He was echoing another opponent of socialism, Vilfredo Pareto (1896), who much earlier had affirmed the feasibility of rational economic calculation in what he termed a "collectivist regime." In a section of his famous *Manuel d'Economie Politique* labeled "An argument in favor of collectivist production," Pareto (1909:364) had concluded that "pure economics does not give us a truly decisive criterion for choosing between the organization of society based on private property and a socialist organization."

What then *was* wrong with socialism? And what was wrong with the economic theory that so inadequately captured the economic shortcomings of centralized allocations and vindicated socialist planning in the debate?

A striking feature of the debate had been that both sides deployed the Walrasian model on behalf of their arguments. Hayek soon appreciated the error. His "The Uses of Information in Society" (quoted above) reframed the debate in terms of the costs and limited availability of information, concepts absent from the Walrasian paradigm. The problem with socialism, according to Hayek, was that the information needed by the planner is privately held by millions of economic actors, and they have neither the will nor in many cases even the way to transfer it to a central authority. By contrast, Hayek continued, decentralized markets make effective use of dispersed information, each actor knowing his own preferences and responding to a price vector that under ideal circumstances is both known to the individual actor and reflects the real social scarcities of the goods in question. We now know (chapter 6) that there is no even remotely realistic model of market competition for which these ideal conditions hold, in part because many of the relevant prices simply do not exist, others do not reflect social scarcities, and still others (prices of future goods for example) are unknowable. But by focusing attention on which institutions more effectively utilize the information that *is* available, Hayek's paper, like Mandeville's *Fable*, counts as a landmark work in the theory of economic institutions.

In formalizing a major shortcoming of centralized planning, Hayek also pointed to the deficiencies of the Walrasian paradigm, namely, the assumption of complete information. To Ronald Coase, the debate had revealed an inconsistency, one that was to prompt him to study the theory of the firm. At the beginning of his career, he recalls wondering:

> How did one reconcile the views expressed by economists on the role of the pricing system and the impossibility of successful central economic planning with the existence . . . of these apparently planned societies, firms, operating within our own society. (Coase 1992:715)

Shortly after the fall of Communism, Stiglitz (1994:10) wryly observed that "if the neoclassical model of the economy were correct, market socialism would have been a success [and] centrally planned socialism would have run into far fewer problems." Long before either neoclassical economics or Communism, John Stuart Mill (1976) had provided a critique of the problems of a hypothetical socialist economy — worker motivation, reduced innovation, lack of appropriate property rights — far more searching than any produced within the neoclassical paradigm. Commenting on the role of U.S. economic advisors in the ex-Communist transition economies of the 1990s, Coase remarked: "Without the appropriate institutions no market economy of any significance is possible. If we knew more about our own economy, we would be in a better position to advise them"(Coase 1992:714).

Along with its failure to illuminate the problems of underdevelopment, the inability of Walrasian economics to understand either the economic disabilities of Communism or the appropriate institutions for a transition to a market-based economy is a striking indictment of the approach.

In this chapter, I adopt a post-Walrasian approach to address the contemporary challenges of economic governance. I use results from previous chapters to explore the ways that markets, states, and communities jointly may provide solutions to the coordination problems studied in the previous chapters. (I do not evaluate these solutions from the standpoint of distributive justice but rather focus on their implications for allocative efficiency.) I single out three generic governance structures — communities, states, and markets — for the distinctive ways that they coordinate joint activities and allocate claims on goods and services.[2] Unavoidably, the treatment will be suggestive, not exhaustive. A first task, suggested by the inappropriate use of Walrasian assumptions in the planning versus laissez faire debates, is to pull together the strands

---

[2] The family might be considered a fourth governance structure. Families share many of the characteristics of communities but differ in that roles are assigned by age, sex, and kinship.

of the post-Walrasian perspective. I do this in the next section. I then identify the distinctive capacities and shortcomings of markets, states, and communities. I conclude with a reconsideration of Mandeville's radical conjecture.

ECONOMICS AND EVOLUTIONARY SOCIAL SCIENCE

The Walrasian paradigm provides the only fully worked out, economy-wide model of the way that the actions of large numbers of autonomous actors support aggregate social outcomes. Some of the shortcomings of this model have been identified in the previous pages, and some alternative formulations have been suggested. To synthesize the main features of the Walrasian approach, I will characterize the Walrasian *paradigm* by what its students are *taught* rather than by the impossibly hetero-geneous union of the distinct contributions by scholars representative of this paradigm. This necessarily will involve some discrepancies between the representation of the paradigm and the state-of-the-art knowledge in the field. For an example, consider the uniqueness and stability of general equilibrium: students are regularly taught as if this were true—consider the standard supply and demand diagram—even though (as was pointed out in chapter 6) the assumptions required to demonstrate either uniqueness or stability are exceptionally restrictive. I use the term *evolutionary social science* to refer to the alternatives to the characteristic Walrasian paradigm. There is no unified paradigm of this name, but rather a disjointed set of approaches, many of which are rather rudimentary and most of which have been introduced in the previous pages. Whether in the years to come these approaches will be unified in a coherent replacement for the Walrasian paradigm remains to be seen. (The hunch on which this book is based is that they will.)

Table 14.1 summarizes the contrasting approaches. It would be redundant to comment on each row. But the last line in the table, concerning *reductionism* and *methodological individualism* is worth comment. Reductionism is an approach to science that prefers explanations based on lower-level entities (cells, for example) rather than simply positing the higher-level entities that they make up (multi-cellular organisms, for example). Methodological individualism is an expression of reductionism in social science that insists that explanations of group-level phenomena such as institutions or aggregate output must be built up from the actions of individuals. The approach taken in this book is consistent with methodological individualism in that it has focused on the causal mechanisms connecting what individuals do to aggregate social outcomes. But, as the discussion of endogenous preferences and

Table 14.1
The Walrasian paradigm and some alternative

	Walrasian economics (as taught)	Evolutionary social science (in prospect)
Social interactions	Complete and enforceable claims exchanged on competitive markets	Direct (noncontractual) relationships in noncompetitive settings are common
Technology	Exogenous production functions with non-increasing returns	Generalized increasing returns in both (endogenous) technology and social interactions (positive feedbacks)
Updating	Forward-looking individuals instantaneously update based on knowledge of entire system	Backward-looking (experienced-based) individuals update using local information
Outcomes	A unique stable equilibrium based on stationarity of individual actions	Many equilibria; aggregate outcomes may be long term averages of non-stationary lower level entities
Time	Comparative statics	Explicit dynamics
Chance	Relevant only to risk-taking and insurance	Essential component of evolutionary dynamics
Domain	The economy as a self-contained self-regulating entity: exogenous preferences and institutions	The economy as embedded in a larger social and ecological system: coevolving preferences and institutions
Preferences	Self-regarding preferences, defined over outcomes	Self- and other-regarding preferences, defined over outcomes and processes
Prices and quantities	Prices allocate resources; actors are not quantity constrained	Quantity constraints; wealth-dependent contractual opportunities
Method	Reductionist (methodological individualism)	Non-reductionist; selection on individual and higher order entities

cultural evolution has made clear, the effect of aggregate outcomes on individuals is no less important.

The conventional concept of equilibrium in economics expresses the methodological individualism of the discipline. It is standard practice — and one that has been frequently used in the pages above — to define an equilibrium as a state such that none of the individuals involved has a

reason to alter his behavior. The aggregate properties of the equilibrium—an economy-wide allocation of resources, for example—are then
derived by aggregation of the equilibrium individual behaviors. The aggregate properties are stationary because the individual behaviors are
stationary. But as the model of general equilibrium by Foley (1994),
described in chapter 6, demonstrates, stationarity of aggregate properties does not require stationarity of lower-level entities. Foley's model
shows that for average prices not to change, it is not necessary that
trade cease. The analysis of attendance at his favorite bar in Santa Fe by
Brian Arthur (1994a) conveys a similar message. Nobody wants to go
there when its too crowded, and people estimate how many will attend
based on past experiences. Arthur simulates an adaptive learning process, the result of which is that about sixty people show up at the El
Farol each Thursday. But this does not require that the same people
show up, or that the beliefs of those showing up about how many
others will show up are accurate or stationary.

In this and many other applications, lower-level entities are nonsta-
tionary in ways that average out, producing no change in the aggregate
property. The evolutionary analysis in chapters 11 through 13 adopted
this method. Stochastically stable states (chapter 12) are not stationary
outcomes; rather, they describe long-term average behavior of a system.
The models in chapters 11 and 13 described populations constantly in
motion, propelled by deliberate nonbest-response actions by collectives
of individuals, other idiosyncratic behavior, genetic drift, and institutional innovation. The results of the agent-based simulations were long-
term averages reflecting all of these influences.

Methodological individualism is also evident in a common approach
to the analysis of economic institutions. Schotter (1981:20) provides an
example:

> If economics . . . is going to study the rise and evolution of social institutions,
> a very simple methodological approach is suggested. We should start our
> analysis in a Lockean state of nature in which there are no social institutions
> at all, only agents, their preferences, and the technology they have at their
> disposal. . . . The next step would be to study when, during the evolution of
> this economy, such institutions as money, banks, property rights, competitive
> markets, insurance contracts, and the state would evolve.

There is no question that Schotter's method is interesting, and that it
has proven insightful. But if instead one takes technologies and preferences as endogenous, it would be equally insightful to violate the methodological individualist precepts. One could, for example, posit a set
of institutions and then ask what kind of preferences and technologies
would evolve. The approach adopted here (in chapters 11 through 13,

especially) represents individual preferences and group level institutions as coevolving, *thereby not privileging either the lower- or higher-order entities.*

Whether the group or individual or both (or more) processes need to be modeled depends on the analytical problem at hand and practical considerations of tractability. For most social science applications nothing is lost and much simplicity gained by not modeling the cellular interactions within individuals. But this would be a poor strategy for understanding cancer. Where group characteristics can be taken as given, modeling at the individual level is a reasonable approach. Correspondingly, if we can abstract from within-group variation, the group-level selection process can be the focus of attention, as it is in models of competition among firms. Richard Dawkins (1989b:3), a strong proponent of reductionism in biology, rightly observed that its usually more informative to explain cars in terms of carburetors than quarks.

From this perspective, positing a pristine institution-free environment is a curious way to investigate the historical evolution of real institutions. The reason is that since the advent of biologically modern humans, and even among other primates, social conventions and property rights of various kinds have almost certainly provided an institutional environment for our interactions. Locke, Hobbes, and other philosophers used the state of nature as a hypothetical inquiry into what might *justify* property, the authority of the state, and the like, not as part of an explanation of how these institutions evolved historically. (Recall Hobbes' deliberately fanciful metaphor of the state of nature in the epigraph to chapter 3: people were "sprung out of the earth . . . like mushrooms.")

In the prologue I distinguished the evolutionary method from a social engineering approach to public policy. By the latter I mean the view that social outcomes are determined by the autonomous actions of public-spirited officials, more or less as the chessmen in the Smith epigraph might be moved around the board. Nobody believes this literally (least of all public officials), but many fail to appreciate the extent to which this view misrepresents the process by which outcomes are determined. While I have given no attention to questions of public policy, the models developed here suggest a quite different approach. This is to apply the same behavioral assumptions to state officials as we routinely do to those engaged in private exchange, namely, that their actions are best responses based on their preferences not subject to complete contracting. Adopting an early version of this approach, Jeremy Bentham advocated constitutional arrangements which would structure incentives so that public servants' "duties" would coincide with their "interests." But this objective can rarely be met.

In the evolutionary view, aggregate outcomes are the result of the interactions of the public officials' actions and the best responses of all the individuals involved. This does not suggest that governmental interventions are ineffective, but rather that to be effective in the intended ways requires an understanding of the dynamical system in which one is intervening. For example, the policies required to displace a socially undesirable equilibrium in favor of some other outcome may be entirely different if the system producing the outcomes is characterized by a single equilibrium or if there are many stable equilibria, and the job of public policy is to displace one equilibrium in favor of another. The example of child labor below illustrates this.

A final comment does not concern the contrasting paradigms directly but rather is directed to the normative concerns that are never absent when discussing institutional alternatives. "Utility" is a heavily freighted term: economists commonly use it to refer to motives, behaviors, and well-being. The convenience of collapsing these three distinct usages into a single term is considerable. But it requires the implicit assumption of *substantive rationality*, namely, that people act so as to get what they want, which in turn contributes to their well-being as gauged by some independent evaluation of the relevant outcomes. By contrast, the *formal rationality* explicitly assumed by most economists imposes only consistency requirements (such as transitivity) on behaviors, without any requirements for the individual's hedonistic or other subjective reasons for acting, the reasonableness of the means adopted in pursuit of some outcome, or the consequences for the individual's well being. A consistent masochist is not irrational.

To be of practical or moral relevance, economic reasoning about institutions and policies requires the substantive concept of rationality. If, for example, one believes that third parties should not intervene in transactions voluntarily engaged in by adult economic actors, it is not sufficient to know that they have complete and transitive preferences. We also must have confidence that their choices will not be grossly or irreversibly destructive of their well-being. The same is true of the common interpretation of Pareto efficiency in terms of the "well-being" of individuals. Formal rationality alone does not provide the motivation for preferring Pareto-superior outcomes, except in the minds of extreme libertarians. An allocation preferred by two masochists might not be endorsed by others.

But the assumption of substantive rationality is based on strong empirical claims about why people do what they do, and on the consequences of their actions. These claims are generally false. Extensive empirical evidence suggests that by the standard of well-being, people are bad choosers. We are myopic, fail to predict the preferences we will have when the relevant consequences of our actions take place, do not accumulate accurate information about the hedonic aspects of past experiences, act inconsistently in intertemporal choice situations, and commonly violate the expected utility hypothesis (Kahneman 1994, Camerer 2000). The subjects in experiments and real world settings showing this would find it strange to hear their behaviors termed irrational. They include students at the most selective universities, Harvard professors, and New York City cab drivers.

If preferences are to explain behaviors, they cannot unassisted also do the work of evaluating outcomes. This is true because some common reasons for behavior—weakness of will and addiction, for example—induce behaviors that few would condone. The disjuncture between the reasons for behaviors and the standards by which a liberal and democratic polity should evaluate outcomes raises profound challenges, ones that are sure to pit liberal against utilitarian and paternalistic values. For example, if loss aversion is a powerful subjective reaction among most people, should it be taken into account in evaluating public policies? Doing so would affect a substantial shift in favor of the status quo, as the costs borne by losers would now be at double counted or more. But addressing these questions would take us far afield.

MARKETS AND STATES: A POST-WALRASIAN COMPARISON

Given that the rhetoric of the debate on planning versus laissez faire was highly polarized, a remarkable conclusion was that markets and states are difficult to distinguish from an allocative standpoint. F. M. Taylor's 1928 Presidential Address to the American Economic Association opened with:

> In the case of a socialist state, the proper method of determining what commodities shall be produced would be in outline the same as . . . [u]nder the present economic order of free competitive enterprise. (Taylor 1929:1)

This unexpected similarity in systems of allocations results from the complete information and complete contracting assumptions of most of the participants in the debate. If everyone knew the same things (and what they knew were admissible in court), and if there were no other impediments to contracting, institutional differences would matter less. You have already encountered Samuelson's affirmation (in the epigraph to chapter 10) of the *Walraisan equivalence of worker-run and capitalist-run firms*: if contracting is complete it indeed does not matter who hires whom.[3] This equivalence means that to understand the operational

---

[3] This equivalence was shown formally by Sertel (1982), Fehr (1993), and Dow (1996).

differences between conventional and worker-owned firms like the plywood cooperatives mentioned in chapter 10, one must analyze the differing problems of contractual incompleteness that they encounter, and their differing capacities to surmount them. The same conclusion holds for comparisons of markets and states. As a result, the relevant comparisons are among imperfect institutional configurations. This attention to the relative advantages and shortcomings of flawed institutions is a hallmark of the institutional economics of Ronald Coase and Oliver Williamson (1985) and goes back to Pareto, who, immediately after having shown the equivalence of competitive and collectivist allocations in a highly abstract model, introduced the idea of transactions costs: "A second approximation will take account of the expense of putting the mechanism of free competition in full play, and will compare this expense with that necessary for establishing some other new mechanism society may wish to test" (Pareto 1896:500).

Which combination of market, state, and community is most successful in addressing a given coordination problem depends on the underlying technological and social facts that give rise to interdependence among actors. For example, strong increasing returns in a production process make both solitary production and market competition not only inefficient (because marginal cost pricing is not feasible) but also difficult to sustain (because of the positive feedbacks generated by increasing returns and the resulting winner-take-all aspect of the competitive process). Institutions will affect four aspects of economic interactions. First, institutions influence the distribution of information, the way in which information can be acquired, hidden, shared, and used to enforce contracts. Second, institutions in conjunction with a given distribution of wealth differ in the assignment of decision-making power and residual claimancy status among those participating in an interaction. Third, differing institutions and wealth distributions give rise to distinct patterns of conflict of interest among parties to transactions. Finally, the institutions governing a particular interaction will affect the preferences and beliefs of the participants.

A capsule overview of the argument is the following: institutional differences have important allocative consequences where conflicts of interest exist among actors whose interdependence is not governed by complete contracts. The coordination failures that arise in these situations may be attenuated by institutions that accomplish one or more of the following desiderata. First, they may more closely align rights of control and residual claimancy so that individuals own the results of their actions, reducing the degree of effective interdependence. Second, they may reduce the conflict of interest over noncontractible aspects of a transaction among affected parties. Third, they may reduce the extent or importance of private information, allowing for more complete contracting and more efficient bargaining.

Using these ideas to compare institutions (including communities) will occupy the remainder of the chapter. What are the distinct capacities of markets, governments, and communities that might serve these ends?

Adam Smith's appreciation of the value of competitive markets is distinctively modern: markets make collusion difficult when competition is socially beneficial. "People in the same trade seldom meet together," he wrote, "even for merriment and diversion, but the conversation ends in a conspiracy against the public; or in some contrivance to raise prices" (Smith 1937:128). If such conspiracies are to be effective in a market setting, large numbers of actual and potential participants must cooperate in what is a public goods game. As we saw in chapter 13, sustaining cooperation in these situations through the threat of subsequent retaliation and related strategies becomes exceptionally difficult as the numbers of participants rise. Thus, by increasing the number of "conspirators" necessary to affect prices, competitive markets impede collusion in a situation in which collusion is not socially beneficial.

The first attractive feature of markets is thus a result of the noncooperative interactions that result from large numbers interactions. Market competition is a means of inducing agents to make public the economically relevant private information they hold. It is often said that in markets people vote with their money, which is correct if what is meant is not that markets are democratic but rather that it is costly to express a preference in a competitive market system. Indeed, the only way to register a preference in a market is to make a purchase, and the price at which one is willing to purchase a good conveys what would otherwise be private information, namely, that the good is worth at least as much as the price paid.

Similarly, in a market interaction it is rewarding to reveal a productive capacity and costly to misrepresent the true costs of production. In a competitive market equilibrium with non-increasing returns, profit-maximizing producers will make goods available at their private marginal cost of production, thereby revealing an important and otherwise private piece of information. Those who "misrepresent" their productive capacities by offering goods at prices not equal to the marginal cost will make lower profits than those whose prices convey the true costs. In effect, market competition turns the pricing problem into an n-person prisoner's dilemma in which the n-producers have a common interest in restricting output and "overstating their costs" by setting $p > mc$. But if n is large, each firm has an incentive to defect by undercutting its rivals, thereby revealing its true production conditions.

By contrast to markets, in centralized nonmarket systems, producers typically have an incentive to understate their productive capacities to secure a lower production quota. Consumers similarly have an incentive to overstate their needs hoping to establish a superior claim on goods and services.

Second, where residual claimancy and control rights are closely aligned, market competition provides a decentralized and relatively incorruptible disciplining mechanism that punishes the inept and rewards high performers. Markets are a way of increasing what biologists call selection pressure: they have the effect of reducing the variance of performance and hence (under suitable conditions) increasing average performance. The substantial differences observed between high and low performers (chapter 2) suggest that the process works imperfectly, but also that when it does work, the resulting effects on productivity can be significant.

The disabilities of markets are related to their strengths. Markets, it is said, impose hard budget constraints on the relevant actors, but they do this only when decision makers own the results of their decisions. However, because contractual opportunities are dependent on wealth and for other reasons, residual claimancy and control are often misaligned; as a result, the disciplining process is often poorly targeted. A job well done need not benefit an employee who is paid a fixed wage. A plant closing, to take another example, will eliminate the job rents of hundreds of workers; but it need not punish those responsible for the losses that induced the shut-down. Moreover, even where control over noncontractible actions and residual claimancy over a project's income stream are unified, environmental externalities and other external effects carry the consequences of actions taken by the decision maker far beyond the reach of contracts.

By contrast to markets, states may attenuate coordination failures by their ability to allow and often compel individuals to interact cooperatively in situations where noncooperative interactions are inefficient. The comparative advantage of governments is in the production of rules: states alone have the power to make and enforce universal compliance with the rules of the game that govern the interaction of private agents. Where individuals face prisoners' dilemma–like situations or other coordination problems in which the autonomous pursuit of individual objectives leads to an undesirable outcome, the state may provide or compel the coordination necessary to avert this outcome. Services that governments can perform well that communities and markets often cannot include the definition, assignment, and enforcement of property rights, the provision of public goods, the regulation of environmental and other external or "spillover" effects, the regulation of natural monopolies, the provision of some forms of insurance, and macroeconomic regulation. Less obvious cases include equilibrium selection: where multiple equilibria exist, a one-time state intervention may be able to implement the socially desirable equilibrium. Basu and Van (1998), for example, show that a one time ban on child labor could displace an equilibrium constituting a kind of poverty trap and induce a movement to another equilibrium in which the children and their families would all be better off.

The state addresses prisoners' dilemmas in a manner diametrically opposed to that of markets. Competitive markets hinder the formation of cartels and other forms of collusion by providing incentives for defection, while the state can induce cooperation by impeding defection. Since both defection and cooperation are desirable under different circumstances, markets and states serve complementary roles in solving coordination problems. The state prevents defection by compelling participation in exchanges that would not be voluntarily chosen by economic agents acting singly — for example, cooperating in a prisoner's dilemma situation. This capacity to force compliance can contribute to the solution of coordination problems even where individuals have information that is private and therefore inaccessible to the state.

An example involving the availability of some kinds of insurance illustrates this principle. Before they have learned the capacities, health status, and the special risks they face as individuals, all members of a population might prefer to purchase insurance. But after they have learned their own special position, those with a low probability of collecting on the insurance will not be willing to purchase it since they would be subsidizing those with a high probability of collecting. Thus the low-risk people would drop out of the market and the price of the insurance would be too high for the high-risk people. Since before obtaining specific knowledge of their own risk position, all would have been willing to purchase the insurance, and since it is unavailable on the market, there is a clear market failure. By providing the insurance and compelling all agents to pay for it, the state overcomes this market failure.

Other examples have been provided in the previous chapters. Implementing the social optimum curfew in chapter 6 may require the city planner to set a curfew (and then let the Deadhead and the sleepyhead use their private information to make Pareto improvements over this mandated curfew through Coasean bargaining). In chapter 9 we saw that starting from an assignment of property rights in competitive equilibrium, a redistribution of wealth by governmental fiat could enhance both Pareto-efficiency and technical efficiency. Other, less transparent examples can be given: by conferring the right to collectively bargain on employees, the under-provision of on-the-job amenities and the opportunities for arbitrary use of short side power demonstrated in chapter 10 may be attenuated.

The state, however, has several weaknesses as a governance structure. The first is state officials' lack of access to private information held by producers and consumers. The second is the mirror image of the first: the lack of access by voters and citizens (assuming a democratic polity) to the private information held by state officials. In this case, the agent (the state) is only weakly accountable to the principals (the citizens). The same arguments showing that first-best solutions are generally unattainable in principal-agent relationships in private exchange apply here as well. The third shortcoming of the state as a governance structure is that there exists no ideal system of making decisions that are binding on large numbers of people. Because there is no consistent democratic way to aggregate individual preferences into consistent social choice criteria, the results of majority rule and other voting mechanisms depend critically on who controls the voting agenda. Moreover, unlike markets, voting schemes have difficulty representing the intensity of preferences for different goods or social outcomes. Finally, where government intervention suppresses market outcomes, economic actors privileged by the intervention earn rents — incomes above their next best alternative. Thus groups will engage in rent-seeking behavior, attempting to influence it to intervene on their behalf rather than for another group or the public at large, thereby wasting resources and distorting policy outcomes.

As in the case of markets, these weaknesses derive from the state's unique capacities. To compel while preventing exit requires that the state be universal and unchallenged in some spheres. This universality of the state makes it difficult to render the state accountable by subjecting it to the competitive delivery of its services. Moreover, the inability of voting schemes to aggregate preferences in a consistent manner requires that nonelectoral ways of influencing collective decision making — including interest group activities — must be available as correctives. But it is difficult to regulate the rent-seeking activity directed toward these nonelectoral processes without corrupting democratic procedures. Of course, states can be made more accountable by fostering competition among local governments, other public agencies, and private bodies, by ensuring competition among autonomous parties and civil liberties so as to foster the careful monitoring of the actions of state officials, by subjecting elected and administrative positions within the state to well-designed incentives, and by limiting the state's actions to those that cannot be regulated in a more accountable manner by some other governance structure.

COMMUNITY GOVERNANCE

To Marx and other nineteenth-century modernists, "community" was the antithesis of markets, representing an anachronistic remnant of feudal times, destined to be swept away by the requirements of economic progress or, as Marx and Engels (1978:475) put it, by the "icy water of egotistic calculation." The inertial character of community governance was affirmed by economic historians who, like Marx, pointed to the restrictions placed on individual initiative and the poorly defined property rights associated with the collective decision making required by the open field system of agriculture that prevailed in England and many parts of early modern Europe. Agricultural productivity, according to this view, was held back until the common lands were enclosed and assigned to private owners, as they were in England in the late eighteenth century. But this staple of economic instruction has been overturned by quantitative economic historians during the past generation. A leading contributor to the new literature, Robert Allen (2000:43, 50) writes:

> [T]he open fields were an efficient institution for meeting the needs of small scale, grain growing farmers. These needs included diversification against . . . risk . . . and increasing agricultural productivity . . . Enclosure explains neither the productivity advantage that England enjoyed over other countries c. 1800 nor the rise in efficiency that had occurred since the middle ages.

The communities governing the open field system used local information and peer pressure to foster innovation and solve the allocational problems arising through the unavoidable interdependence of the farmers. In contrast to the farmers in Palanpur whose inability to coordinate an optimal early planting of their crops provided the introduction to chapter 1, in Taston, England, in 1703 "three fieldmen were chosen on the first of each year to establish the dates when [crops] would be planted, when animals would graze and to enforce the maintenance provisions" (Allen 2000:58).

Recent historical research has also demonstrated the importance of community-based governance in handling the incentive problems associated with incomplete credit contracts in nineteenth-century German banking (Banerjee, Besley, and Guinnane 1994). Community-based governance plays a central role in many sectors of the modern economy, from the development and distribution of open source software to the role of ethnic networks in the mobilization and allocation of credit among motel owners in the United States. Thus, far from a vestigial remnant of the past, community governance has survived due to its ability to attenuate the incentive problems arising in contemporary economies.

Communities sometimes solve problems that both states and markets are ill-equipped to address, especially where the nature of the social interactions or the goods and services being transacted preclude complete contracting. An effective community monitors the behavior of its members, thereby making them accountable for their actions. Community governance relies on dispersed private information that is often unavailable to states, employers, banks, and other large formal organizations to apply rewards and punishments to members according to their conformity with or deviation from social norms. In contrast to states and markets, communities effectively foster and utilize the incentives that people have traditionally deployed to regulate their common activity: trust, solidarity, reciprocity, reputation, personal pride, respect, vengeance, and retribution, among others.

Several aspects of communities account for their unique capacities as governance structures. First, in a community, the probability that members who interact today will interact in the future is high, and thus there is a strong incentive to act in socially beneficial ways now to avoid retaliation in the future. Second, the frequency of interaction among community members lowers the cost and raises the benefits associated with discovering more about the characteristics, recent behavior, and likely future actions of other members. The more easily acquired and widely dispersed this information, the more will community members have an incentive to act in ways that result in collectively beneficial outcomes. Third, communities overcome free-rider problems because their members directly punish anti-social behaviors. Monitoring and punishment by peers in work teams, credit associations, partnerships, local commons situations, and residential neighborhoods is often an effective means of attenuating incentive problems that arise where individual actions affecting the well-being of others are not subject to enforceable contracts.

But how might communities enforce such norms in the absence of the state's judicial apparatus? Recall that Alchian and Demsetz (1972) suggest that residual claimancy should be assigned to an individual designated to monitor team members' inputs, thus providing incentives for the (noncontractible) activity of monitoring itself, while addressing the members' incentive to free ride by the threat of dismissal by the monitor. (I explained in chapter 10 the underlying assumptions underlying this argument.) Another well-known solution is provided by Hölmstrom (1982) who models a principal multi-agent relationship in which efficiency or near-efficiency is achieved through contracts that make individual team members residual claimants on the effects of their actions without conferring ownership rights on them. Hölmstrom's solution is infeasible, however, when there are significant stochastic influences on the level of performance of the team, team members have limited wealth, and capital and insurance markets are imperfect.

These explanations have in common that individuals are treated as self-interested. By contrast, many behavioral scientists outside of economics have sought to explain communities by relations of altruism, affection, and other non-self-regarding motives. Many of these approaches, however, have treated the community organically without investigating whether or not the problem-solving capacities claimed for communities are consistent with the fact that individual members are pursuing their own interests (whether self-regarding or not). As a result, some treatments—like Marx's—represent community governance as an anachronism based on collectivist behavioral habits that will be eroded over time and replaced by individual choice. However, we saw in chapters 3 and 4 that motives of reciprocity, shame, generosity, and other social preferences can provide the behavioral foundations of a model of mutual monitoring that avoids these shortcomings. The public goods with punishment experiment and the model presented there indicate that under favorable institutional circumstances and with sufficiently many members motivated by social preferences, high levels of voluntary provision of public goods can be sustained.

Like markets and governments, communities also fail. The personal and durable contacts that characterize communities require them to be of relatively small scale. A preference for dealing with fellow members therefore often limits their capacity to exploit gains from trade on a wider basis. Moreover, the tendency for communities to be relatively homogeneous may make it impossible to reap the benefits of economic diversity associated with strong complementarities among differing skills and other inputs. Neither of these limitations is insurmountable. By sharing information, equipment, and skills, for example, the Japanese fishermen (mentioned above) exploited economies of scale unattainable by less cooperative groups, and reaped substantial benefits from the diversity of talents among the membership. Similarly, cooperation in the local business networks in what is called "the third Italy" along with their associated local governments allow otherwise unviably small firms to benefit from economies of scale in marketing, research, and training, allowing their survival in competition with corporate giants. But compared to bureaucracies and markets, which specialize in dealing with strangers, the limited scope of communities often imposes inescapable costs.

A second community failure is less obvious. Where group membership is the result of individual choices rather than group decisions, the composition of groups is likely to be more culturally and demographically homogeneous than any of the members would like, thereby depriving people of valued forms of diversity. The model of residential segregation in chapter 2 showed that if individuals sort themselves among communities, there will be a strong tendency for communities to end up segregated by race even if this is an outcome that no individual prefers. In cases such as this, integrated communities would make everyone better off, but they will prove unsustainable if individuals are free to move.

When insider-outsider distinctions are made on divisive and morally repugnant bases such as race, religion, nationality, or gender, community governance may contribute more to fostering parochial narrow-mindedness and ethnic hostility than to addressing the failures of markets and states. The problem is endemic. Communities work because they are good at enforcing norms, and whether this is a good thing depends on what the norms are. The recent resistance to racial integration by the white residents of Ruyterwacht (near Cape Town), is as gripping an account of social capital in action as one can imagine (Jung 2001). Even more striking is Dov Cohen's (1998) study of U.S. regional differences in the relationship between violence and community stability. Nisbett and Cohen (1996) described a "culture of honor" that often turns public insults and arguments into deadly confrontations among white males in the U.S. South and West, but not in the North. Cohen's research confirms that in the North, homicides stemming from arguments are less frequent in areas of higher residential stability, measured by the fractions of people living in the same house and the same county over a five-year period. But this relationship is *inverted* in the South and West, residential stability being positively and significantly related to the frequency of these homicides where the culture of honor is strong.

Thus, over some range of governance problems, communities contribute to the desiderata outlined above: aligning control and residual claimancy through the punishment of those inflicting costs on other group members, making information less private by providing incentives to establish reputations through consistent behavior, and reducing the degree of conflict of interest over noncontractible aspects of exchange through the provision of division rules and other norms capable of working even when property rights are not well defined. These reasons may help explain why communities, long dismissed by social scientists as anachronistic remnants of an earlier era, have not been eclipsed by markets and the state.

The ability of communities to address coordination problems depends on the types of property rights in force and their distribution among the population. Where community members are not residual claimants on the results of their actions, there may be little incentive to engage in the forms of sanctioning and reputation building we have stressed. Among the Chicago neighborhoods mentioned at the outset, for example, where most residents are renters rather than home owners collective efficacy was significantly lower. This may be due to the fact that, if some members of a group are vastly more wealthy than others, shared norms may be difficult to maintain, and the punishment of noncooperative actions may lack effectiveness or credibility. For similar reasons, the distinctive capacities of communities are likely to be undermined where the costs of exit are very asymmetrical, for instance when some members have attractive outside options and others do not. In short, the effectiveness of communities depends on the assignment of property rights and on individuals' outside options.

In this respect communities are not unlike markets. The allocational efficiency advantage of the decentralization of control rights (either the extensive use of markets or community-based governance systems) lies in placing decision making in the hands of those who have relevant information that others lack. For this to be beneficial, the holders of private information must be residual claimants on the results of their actions. On efficiency grounds, decentralization to individuals through use of markets is favored over decentralization to communities in cases for which contracts are relatively complete and enforceable at low cost and hence in which interests may conflict without generating coordination failures. Decentralization to communities is favored where complete contracting is precluded but where low levels of conflict of interest within the community and other aspects of community structure facilitate the transmission of private information and mutual monitoring among community members. William Ouchi (1980) suggests that where neither complete contracting nor informal community-based enforcement is possible and where conflicts of interest are significant, bureaucratic organization results, the modern conventional firm being his example. Thomas Schelling (1960:20) put the same point more colorfully:

> [W]hen trust and good faith are lacking and there is no legal recourse for breach of contract . . . we may wish to solicit advice from the underworld, or from ancient despotisms, on how to make agreements work.

Most economic interactions are governed by a heterogeneous set of formal and informal rules reflecting aspects of markets, states and communities. Some combinations work better than others.

INSTITUTIONAL COMPLEMENTARITIES AND CROWDING OUT

For concreteness I will begin with two examples.

The lobster fishermen on the coast of Maine have for decades regulated their catch by limiting access to a defined fishing territory. Only those belonging to a particular so-called harbor gang—those fishing from a particular harbor who have been granted membership—are by local custom allowed to set their traps in the territory (Acheson 1988). Boundary violators are likely to find the buoys cut from their traps, which are then impossible to locate. Intruders have been fired upon. Infringements of environmental regulations or violations of the norms of the gang are also sanctioned by other gang members. In recent years, the State of Maine has formalized the gang system by recognizing the territories of the harbor gangs and setting up democratically elected councils with powers to regulate limits on number of traps and numbers of days fishing. State officials occasionally intervene when conflicts exceed the enforcement capacities of the local communities, as they did during the near collapse of the fishery during the 1920s, or when violence between gangs erupts. But the State employs only six officers to enforce environmental regulations along the entire 4342-mile coastline and to oversee the fishing of 6,800 lobstermen. In recent years, fishing yields have grown and the lobstermen have prospered.

The relationship between the harbor gangs and the state of Maine illustrate *institutional complementarity*. The effectiveness of the state's regulations is greatly enhanced by their informal enforcement by the gangs, while the gang's effectiveness is conditioned on the availability of the state as the enforcer of last resort. Another example of institutional complementarity are the symbiotic effects of trade unions (regulating labor effort) and macroeconomic regulation (reducing volatility of demand for labor) in underpinning the Pareto-improving effort-wage bargains modeled in chapter 8.

The mismanagement of the Himalyan forests of Kamaun and Garhwal districts in Uttar Pradesh, India, provides a sharp contrast to the success of the harbor gangs.[4] Before the twentieth century, large well-defined tracts of forests were considered the exclusive property of each village. Access was regulated by the village *panchayats*; should unauthorized outsiders remove forest products, fighting might break out or fines be levied. To this point forestry management resembled the decentralized regulation by Maine's harbor gangs. But during the First World War, the British colonial administration took over the forestry manage-

---

[4] This account is based on Sethi and Somanathan (1996) and Somanathan (1991).

ment, seeking to meet the demand for railroad ties and other wood products. The colonial intervention disrupted the regulation by the local communities and evoked incendiary protests that destroyed large stands of pine. The government, in retreat, awarded access to the less valuable forests to "all *bona fide* residents of Kumaun" thereby obliterating the traditional boundaries of village forests and making local regulation virtually impossible. For example, in 1932 a group of villagers from Papdev prevented their neighbor, Jeet Lal, from harvesting grass from the forest, because he had not contributed to the construction of fencing for the grass preserve. Jeet Lal took his neighbors to court and *they* were fined, the punishment being upheld on appeal because, according to the new regulations, Jeet Lal had an unconditional right of access.

The government's destruction of the community's capacity to regulate access illustrates the opposite of complementarity, namely, *institutional crowding out*. This occurs when the presence of one institution undermines the functioning of another. Another example of crowding out comes from nearby Palanpur (also in Uttar Pradesh) where the extension of the labor market (and increased geographical mobility) appears to have reduced the costs of exit and hence the value of one's reputation, with the effect that the informal enforcement of lending contracts has been undermined (Lanjouw and Stern 1998:570). The counter-productive imposition of fines to deter tardiness at the daycare centers in Haiffa (chapter 3) is another example of crowding out: using a market mechanism (the fine) seems to have undermined the parents' sense of personal obligation to avoid inconveniencing the teachers.

Experiments confirm that crowding out may be a common problem. To explore the effects of explicit incentives, Fehr and Gaechter (2000a) designed a gift exchange game in which principals (employers) make a wage offer with a stipulated desired level of effort on the part of the agent (worker). The agent may then choose an effort level, with costs to the agent rising in effort. In the "trust" treatment, the interaction ends there, but in the "incentive" treatment, following the agent's choice of an effort level, the employer may fine the worker if the worker's effort level is thought to be inadequate. By contrast with the trust treatment, the incentive treatment links pay to performance and hence represents a more complete contract. In this experiment, the total surplus from the interaction is the principal's profits plus the agent's wage minus the cost of effort (and the fine, where applicable).

In the trust treatment, a self-regarding agent would choose the minimum feasible level of effort irrespective of the principal's wage offer, and, anticipating this, a self-regarding principal would offer the minimum wage. Experimental subjects did not conform to this expectation: employers made very generous offers and workers' effort levels were strongly conditioned on these offers, high wages being reciprocated by high levels of effort. The introduction of explicit incentives had a dramatic effect: average effort levels by agents were substantially *lower*. Only for very low wage offers did the explicit incentives elicit (marginally) higher levels of work. For relatively generous wage offers, the effort performed with explicit incentives was about a third the level performed in their absence.

The experiment was constructed so that had subjects responded optimally on the basis of self-regarding preferences, the surplus would have been more that twice as great under the incentive treatment as under the trust treatment. But the total surplus was higher in the trust treatment, by 20 percent in those cases in which the principal offered a contract such that the expected fine for shirking exceeded the cost of working (so that the no-shirking condition was fulfilled), and by 53 percent where the principal's contract did not meet the no shirking condition.

A striking result of this experiment emerges if we compare the distribution of the surplus under the trust treatment and the incentive treatment. In the incentive treatment (confining our attention to the cases in which the principal's contract fulfilled the no shirking condition), profits are more than double the profits in the trust treatment, while the net payoffs to the agent are less than half. The incentive treatment allowed employers to save enough in wage costs to offset the reductions in work effort. Summarizing this result, Fehr and Gaechter (2000a:17) write, "The incentive opportunities in the incentive treatment allow principals to increase their profits relative to the trust treatment, but . . . this is associated with an efficiency loss."

Similar results occurred in a field experiment in Colombia conducted by Juan Camilo Cardenas (Cardenas, Stranlund, and Willis 2000). The experiment, a variant of the public goods game, captured the logic of a common pool resource extraction problem—degradation of a nearby forest—faced by the rural people who participated. In the absence of explicit incentives the subjects selected extraction levels not far above the social optimum and much less than the Nash equilibrium level based on individual optimization with self-regarding preferences. But when monitoring of the subjects' extraction levels (by the experimenter) and the prospect of a fine for over-extraction were introduced, subjects extracted more rather than less. After a few rounds, their extraction levels approximated the Nash equilibrium level (taking account of the fine). Like the fine imposed on the tardy Haifa parents, the effect of "improving" the incentive structure apparently was to diminish the salience of the other-regarding motives that had been in force in the absence of the incentives.

A final experiment may provide some insight into how crowding out works (Frohlich and Oppenheimer 1992). Subjects played five-person public goods games under two conditions: one group played the standard contribution game and the other played a modified (veil of ignorance) game in which a randomized assignment of payoffs made it optimal to contribute the maximal amount to the public good. Half of the subjects (in each treatment) were allowed to engage in discussion before each play (of course, the discussion should have had no effect on the outcome of the standard game, as the dominant strategy is to contribute nothing). After eight rounds of play, another eight rounds were conducted, this time with the same groups but with all playing the standard game. Among those who had been permitted discussion, those who had experienced the incentive-compatible (veil of ignorance) game contributed significantly less in the final eight rounds, and (in subsequent questionnaires) expressed less concern with questions of fairness.

The authors' explanation is that the incentive-compatible mechanism rewarded those contributing to the public good, thus making self-interest a good guide to action, while those experiencing the standard game gained high payoffs only to the extent that they evoked considerations of fairness as a distinct motive among their group-mates. They conclude:

> The failure of the . . . [incentive-compatible] mechanism to confront subjects with an ethical dilemma appears to lead to little or no learning in ethical behavior in the subsequent period. . . . It is an institution, like other incentive compatible devices, which can generate near optimal outcomes. . . . However from an ethical point of view it is not only unsuccessful as pertains to subsequent behavior; it appears to be actually pernicious. It undermines ethical reasoning and ethically motivated behavior. (Frohlich and Oppenheimer 1992:44)

Fehr and List (2002) offered a different interpretation of counter-productive incentives found in their trust experiments with Costa Rican businessmen. They found that the highest level of trustworthiness was elicited when the principal was *permitted* to fine the agent for untrustworthy behavior, but *declined to use it*, evidently a signal by the principal of trusting behavior that was then reciprocated by the agent. By contrast "explicit threats to penalize shirking backfire by inducing less trustworthy behavior." They conclude that: "the psychological message that is conveyed by incentives—whether they are perceived as kind or hostile—has important behavioral effects."

Experiments by psychologists have demonstrated conditions under which extrinsic rewards (to use their terminology), such as monetary payment for performance of a task, may diminish one's intrinsic motivation to do the task (Deci, Koestner, and Ryan 1999). These crowding-out effects appear for interesting rather than boring tasks and when

498 · Chapter 14

the reward is expected in advance and closely tied to the task performance. One may conclude that performance-based pay in workplaces
may diminish employee's motivation to do tasks that they initially found
intrinsically interesting or challenging. But the evidence is also consistent with an important role for explicit (extrinsic) incentives in motivating individuals to do tasks in which they have little intrinsic interest
(namely, a great many jobs in modern economy).

Conclusion: Mandeville's Mistake

Implementation theory is a branch of economics that studies the ways
in which privacy-preserving contracts and decision rules—in short, constitutions—can lead individuals with self-regarding preferences to implement (as a Nash equilibrium) an outcome not sought by any of the
individual participants but which by some measure is socially valued.
The methods of contemporary implementation theory are new, but the
idea goes back to Mandeville's radical conjecture (in the epigraph to
chapter 2) that interactions could be structured so that "The worst of
all the Multitude Did something for the Common Good." This objective of harnessing indifferent motives to elevated ends has been central
to constitutional thinking ever since. Recall that David Hume (in the
epigraph for chapter 3) recommended the maxim that "in contriving
any system of government . . . every man ought to be supposed to be a
knave and to have no other end, in all his actions, than private interest." But the above examples of institutional complementarity and
crowding out suggest the effectiveness of policies and laws may depend
not solely on their capacity to recruit selfish ends to social purposes but
also on the preferences they induce or evoke. Albert Hirschman
(1985:10) pointed out that economists propose

> to deal with unethical or antisocial behavior by raising the cost of that behav-
> ior rather than proclaiming standards and imposing prohibitions and sanc-
> tions. The reason is probably that they think of citizens as consumers with
> unchanging or arbitrarily changing tastes in matters civic as well as commod-
> ity-related behavior. . . . A principal purpose of publically proclaimed laws
> and regulations is to stigmatize antisocial behavior and thereby to influence
> citizens' values and behavioral codes.

As we have just seen, raising the cost of an anti-social behavior and
other explicit incentive-based devices may actually do harm. There is
thus a norm-related analogue to the second best theorem of welfare
economics: *where contracts are incomplete (and hence norms may be
important in attenuating market failures), more closely approximating*

idealized complete contracting markets may exacerbate the underlying market failure (by undermining socially valuable norms such as trust or reciprocity) and may result in a less efficient equilibrium allocation. A constitution for knaves may produce knaves.

The fact that institutions and preferences coevolve suggests an important (if difficult) extension of implementation theory and a modification of the Humean maxim. In seeking to implement a socially desired outcome, one must check that the preferences necessary to implement the outcome are sustainable under the policies, contracts, or rules used in the implementation. The problem is more difficult than Hume suggested, not only because preferences are endogenous but also because, as we saw in chapter 3, populations are heterogeneous and individuals are versatile. The problem, then, is not to find a way to induce a homogeneous population of self-regarding individuals to implement a socially desirable outcome. Rather, it is to devise rules such that in cases in which cooperation is socially desirable, individuals with other-regarding preferences will have opportunities to express their pro-sociality in ways that induce all or most to cooperate, as in the public goods with punishment experiments discussed in chapter 3. And in situations in which competition rather than cooperation is essential to socially valued outcomes, the task is exactly the opposite.

Providing practical guidance on how this might be done is one of the major challenges to contemporary studies of economic institutions and behavior. Modern microeconomics has demonstrated the important contribution that well-defined property rights can make in meeting this challenge. In his Nobel Prize lecture Ronald Coase expressed this position succinctly:

> It is obviously desirable that these rights should be assigned to those who can use them most productively and with incentives that lead them to do so and that, to discover (and maintain) such a distribution of rights, the costs of their transference should be low, through clarity in the law and by making the legal requirements of such transfers less onerous. (Coase 1992:718)

But modern microeconomics also shows that well-defined and easily transferred property rights are unattainable in important arenas of economic interaction—in labor and credit markets, in neighborhoods, in adherence to socially valuable norms including the rule of law, and in the production and distribution of information, for example. In these cases, the government can contribute to economic performance through the direct assignment of property rights, rather than simply by facilitating their private exchange. Robert Frost's "Good fences make good neighbors" is the epigraph for the chapter entitled "Utopian Capitalism." But the New England poet's point was quite the opposite, namely, that his curmudgeonly neighbor's embrace of well-defined property rights may be unwarranted. Here is some of the rest of the poem:

> He only says, "good fences make good neighbors."
> . . . Why do they make good neighbors? Isn't it
> Where there are cows? . . .
> Before I build a wall I'd ask to know
> What I was walling in or walling out,
> And to whom I was like to give offense.
> Something there is that doesn't love a wall, That wants it down.
> He moves in darkness as it seems to me,
> Not of woods only and the shade of trees.
> And he likes the thought of it so well
> He says again, "Good fences make good neighbors."
>
> (Frost 1915:11–13)

Neighborliness may also be necessary where good fences fail. From Mandeville to Arrow and Debreu, economic thinkers have sought to devise property rights and other rules that would induce self-regarding individuals to implement socially desirable aggregate outcomes. Of particular interest has been the question, under what conditions will the competitive exchange of well-defined property rights among self-regarding individuals result in an outcome that is in some sense optimal. In light of the importance of self-interest in human motivation, the insights produced by this three-century-long tradition are a major contribution to science and to public policy. But as we now know, thanks to the Fundamental Theorem, the invisible hand requires complete contracting and nonincreasing returns, and these do not describe, even approximately, any known economy.

The project that began with the *Fable of the Bees* may be of even less practical relevance in the future. The reason is that the technologies and social interactions of the modern economy increasingly depart from these canonical assumptions. Direct noncontractual interactions with positive feedbacks arise increasingly in modern economies, as information-intensive team production replaces assembly lines and other technologies more readily handled by contract, and as difficult to measure services usurp the preeminent role — as both outputs and inputs — once played by measurable quantitites like kilowats of power and tons of steel. Danny Quah (1996) calls the modern system of production "the weightless economy." The key characteristics of the information-intensive economy are generalized increasing returns, with near zero marginal costs in many cases, along with the fact that most information is either not subject to complete and enforceable contracts, or will be inefficiently allocated if it is. Kenneth Arrow (1999:162, 156) writes that information is a fugitive resource . . . we are just beginning to face the contradictions between the systems of private property and of information acquisition and dissemination. . . . [We may see] an increasing tension between legal relations and fundamental economic determinants.

The information-intensive economy of the future may more closely resemble the economy of the mobile foraging band in human prehistory, rather than the economy of grain and steel that displaced it. Pursuing good ideas with practical applications is a costly and uncertain project, much like hunting large game. Success is rare, but its fruits are immensely valuable. The private appropriation of the prize is both difficult to accomplish and socially wasteful, for the foregone benefits to the those excluded from access to the prize far outweigh the gains to the individual appropriator to be had by excluding others. A new drug or a new software application is not so different in this respect from an antelope. Thus it is not surprising that the system of prestige and norms of sharing in some parts of the modern information-intensive economy — those involved in open source software, for example — in many ways parallel the culture of the foraging band.

The challenges laid out by Arrow are not likely to be addressed simply by greater precision in the definition of private property rights. It appears equally utopian to think that national governments would (or even could) devise centralized solutions to these problems. A complementary configuration of market, states, and community governance may be the best hope for mobilizing the heterogeneous and versatile capacities and motives of people to address these dilemmas, to better harness the potential of expanding knowledge to the objective of human betterment, and thereby to make good what Alfred Marshall a century ago identified as the promise of economic studies.

Problem Sets

[T]he age of chivalry is gone. That of Sophisters, economists, and calculators has succeeded.
— Edmund Burke, *Reflections on the Revolution in France* (1790)

Burke was lamenting the failure of the French aristocracy to avenge an insult to their Queen, but he might have been describing way some students experience microeconomics classes. A large part of mastering economics is learning how to formulate problems in tractable ways and how to solve these problems. The problems below are designed to give you practice in this. (The chapters to which the problems refer are indicated by the symbol § followed by the chapter number.) Be sure that you can provide a verbal account of the economic logic of any results you derive. Devising a figure presenting your results is almost always illuminating.

1 The language of game theory (§1)

1.1 Suppose table A is the payoff matrix for the row player in a two-person symmetrical Hawk Dove, Prisoners' Dilemma, and Assurance Game. Indicate the restrictions on the values of these payoffs which are necessary and sufficient in each case for the game to be properly defined as Hawk Dove, Assurance, and Prisoners' Dilemma Games.

1.2 Using three separate payoff matrices for the three games, circle any Nash equilibria and underline all Pareto optima.

Two farmers consider planting a crop (Plant) or not planting but attempting to steal the other's crop at harvest time (Steal). Consider the noncooperative game described by this payoff matrix, table B.

1.3 Suppose you were the row player and that you assign some probability, p, to the likelihood that the column player will play Plant (you believe they will play Steal with probability $(1-p)$). What is the minimum value of p that would induce you to plant?

1.4 Define *risk-dominant strategy* and *risk-dominant equilibrium*, and say which (if either) of the equilibria is risk dominant.

2 Name the Game (§1)
North and South are selecting environmental policies. The well-being of each is interdependent, in part due to global

The epigraph is from Burke (1955:86).

TABLE A
Symmetrical Hawk Dove, Prisoners'
Dilemma, and Assurance Game (row payoff)

	Cooperate (Dove)	Defect (Hawk)
Cooperate (Dove)	b	d
Defect (Hawk)	a	c

TABLE B
Noncooperative Plant/Steal Game

	Plant	Steal
Plant	1, 1	$-1, \frac{1}{2}$
Steal	$\frac{1}{2}, -1$	0, 0

environmental effects. Each has a choice of two strategies: Emit or Restrict emission. Suppose this is just a two-person game. It may clarify things to let the representative citizen in each region have a reduced form utility function $u^i = u^i(e^i, e^j)$, where e is the level of emissions (0 or 1) and the superscripts i and j refer to North and South. (It is a reduced form because the citizens' well-being is proximately affected not by emissions per se but by the things with which emissions are associated positively (consumption) or negatively (health status).) Some have modeled this problem as a prisoners' dilemma, while others have proposed the Assurance Game or even the Chicken (Hawk Dove) Game (Taylor 1987). Illustrate each of these possibilities with a payoff matrix and explain why it might be a reasonable depiction of the interaction. Suppose North's utility function has the form

$$u^i = \alpha e^i + \beta e^j + \gamma e^j e^i$$

and South's is identical (with appropriate substitution of superscripts). What values of the parameters of these utility functions would make each of these three games the appropriate model of the North-South Emissions Game?

3 Monitoring and Working (§1) Empirical examples of mixed strategies are not very common, but randomizing one's actions—that is, adopting

TABLE C
The Monitor and Work Game

Worker	Employer	
	Monitor	Not Monitor
Not work	0, c	w, −w
Work	w-e, y-w-c	w-e, y-w

a mixed strategy — often makes sense in situations in which one party is monitoring the work effort, legal compliance, emissions reductions, or arms limitations of another. Here is an example. An employer agrees to pay a wage, w, to a worker who may then Work, expending a subjective cost of effort, e, or Not work, the payment of the wage being conditional on whether the worker has been detected Not working (table C). The employer can determine if the worker worked by paying an inspection cost of c. If the worker Works, revenues net of wage and inspection costs are y. Suppose the worker randomizes his actions, choosing the mixed strategy: Not work with probability σ, otherwise Work, and the employer chooses the strategy Monitor with probability μ, otherwise, Not monitor. The mixed strategy Nash equilibrium is a pair (σ^*, μ^*) such that neither employer nor worker could gain higher expected payoffs by adopting a different strategy.

3.1 Show that the mixed strategy Nash equilibrium for this game is $\sigma^* = c/(2c + w)$ and $\mu^* = e/w$

3.2 Explain why the equilibrium level of Not working varies inversely with the wage and the equilibrium level of Monitoring varies with the subjective cost of effort

3.3 Define a strict Nash equilibrium and show that (σ^*, μ^*) cannot be strict. Show that the worker would do equally well by adopting *any* strategy, that is, choosing σ over [0, 1], as long as the employer played the Nash equilibrium strategy, and that the analogous statement is true of the employer.

3.4 Why, nonetheless, might one expect to observe values in the neighborhood of σ^* and μ^*?

4 Fifty-fifty (§1,3,5,12) "A major puzzle unexplained by existing contract theories is the stylized fact of share tenancy that output is almost universally shared between the tenant and the landlord at a 50:50 ratio . . . despite obvious differences in the relative contributions of land and labor to agricultural production among different production environments" (Otsuka, Chuma, and Hayami 1992:1969). There are one hundred and one strict Nash equilibria in the division game in which claims on a dollar must be denominated in pennies. Suppose members of a large population were randomly paired to play a series of one-shot division games, as described in the text. Show that equal division is the only ESS in pure strategies. Does this fact help explain why landlord-sharecropper shares tend to be fifty-fifty? Why or why not? Are there additional pure strategy equilibria in this case, that is, equilibria that make use of the farmer/landlord asymmetry?

5 Residential Segregation (§2) Suppose the housing preferences are as in the text.

5.1 Show that for $\delta = \frac{1}{4}$, the outcome with completely segregated neighborhoods ($f = 1, f = 0$) yields the same level of home values as the completely integrated neighborhoods ($f = \frac{1}{2}$).

5.2 For $\delta < \frac{1}{4}$, show that there exists a value of $\varepsilon > 0$ such that a law permitting house sales only if $f \in [\frac{1}{2} - \varepsilon, \frac{1}{2} + \varepsilon]$ would implement a outcome that is Pareto superior to the competitive equilibrium.

5.3 What accounts for the market failure in this situation?

5.4 Suppose that the greens have the same preferences as in the text, with $\delta = 0.1$ and $p = 1$, but the blues have all converted to the Love Everybody Equally religion and as a consequence are indifferent to the types of their neighbors and simply value all homes at $p_b = 1.1$. Indicate all the equilibria of the resulting housing market and indicate which are stable in the replicator dynamic in the text (i.e., determine the sign of $d\Delta f/df$ for each stationary value of f).

6 Evolutionary stability (§2)

6.1 Must an ESS be a Nash equilibrium? Are all Nash equilibria ESSs?

6.2 For the Prisoners' Dilemma, Hawk Dove, and Assurance Games, indicate which, if any, of the two strategies in each game are ESSs (assuming the only "mutant" strategy is the other one in the payoff matrix). Is Hawk an ESS if $V = C$?

7 Conspiracy of Doves, Bougeois Invasion (§2)

7.1 Show that a stationary interior value of p (the population fraction of Hawks) for the Hawk-Dove Game is not a Pareto optimum, and explain what accounts for this coordination failure.

7.2 Human capacities for collective action often allow us to overrule evolutionary tendencies that predominate in other animals. Imagine that in a human population playing the Hawk-Dove Game, a law was proposed outlawing playing Hawk, its approval being dependent on majority vote (and its cost of implementation assumed to be zero). Assume that player-voters are initially distributed according to the equilibrium frequency of Hawks, V/C, and can change their strategy in response either to the law or (within the limits set by the law) to differential payoffs. Would a majority of the population support the proposed law? Explain why or why not. If passage required unanimity, would the law pass?

7.3 Suppose a yacht with a few Bourgeois types washed up on the shores of Hobbes Island whose (large) population was distributed according to the equilibrium fractions of V/C Hawks and $1 - V/C$ Doves. Can the Bourgeois types invade the mixed population of Hobbes Island?

7.4 Explain why the expected payoff to an invading Hawk in a large population of Contested Bourgeois players is as given in the text, and check that for $\mu = 1$, $\pi(B(\mu), B(\mu)) = \pi(H, H)$, while for $\mu = 0$, $\pi(B(\mu), B(\mu)) = \pi(D, D)$.

8 Solidarity Whenever (§2)

Competition and other forms of social interaction may give rise to convergent or divergent dynamic trajectories. We know a lot about convergence-inducing processes; divergence is less well studied but apparently important empirically. Here is an example: over the past half-century, union density (the fraction of labor force belonging to unions) has risen in those countries in which density was initially high and fallen in those countries in which density was low. Figure A shows the density for the countries on which comparable data are available. (An account of these divergent histories is Western (1997).) Suppose the costs of being a union member are c and the material benefits (e.g., the result of more worker-friendly governmental policies) are b, a public good enjoyed by all workers (whether members or not) in proportion to union density $d \equiv n/N$ and $b = \beta d$, where n is the number of members and N the labor force and $\beta > c > \beta/N > 0$. Feelings of solidarity (or conformism) are strong, however, so being a member among nonmembers is uncomfortable, as is not joining when most have joined. Thus, the utility of a member is $u^m = b - c + \gamma(d - \frac{1}{2})$, while the utility of a nonmember is $u^n = b + \gamma(\frac{1}{2} - d)$, with γ (the strength of conformist feeling) > 0. Assuming that members of the population switch their status (member-nonmember) in response to the utilities associated with each, the following questions concern stationary values of d, that is, d^*.

8.1 Give the parameter values for which union membership is an ESS, and for which nonmembership is an ESS.

8.2 What aspect of the set up of the problem accounts for the possibility of multiple stable equilibria?

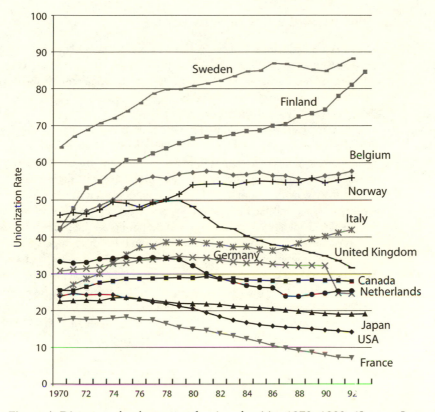

Figure A Divergent development of union densities 1970–1992. (Source: Luxembourg Income Study data set)

9 Inequality Aversion and Reciprocity (§3)

9.1 Consider an individual whose preferences are given by eq. (3.3), with $\alpha = \frac{1}{2}$ and $\delta = \frac{3}{4}$. Were she the respondent in an Ultimatum Game dividing one unit, what is the smallest offer she would accept? If she were the proposer and knew that the respondent had identical preferences to hers, can you say what she would offer?

9.2 Where individuals have social preferences there may be a large number of equilibria even in simple interactions. This is particularly the case if preferences are endogenous or if reciprocity is a strong motive. Here is an example concerning reciprocity. Two individuals are considering contributing effort e_i and e_j, both $\in [0,1]$, to a common project, the output of which, $e_i + e_j$, will be shared equally between the two. The two have preferences as described by eqs. 3.4 and 3.5. Suppose the subjective cost of effort, $c(e)$, is $\frac{3}{4}(e)$ and a and λ are both equal $\frac{1}{2}$ for each person. The belief about the goodwill of the other is simply the amount that each believes other will contribute to the project (so, for example, if i believes j will contribute 1 to the project, then $a_j = 1$). Identify the three pure strategy Nash equilibria of this game, indicate which are stable, and give the critical values of the initial beliefs a_i and a_j, such that the Pareto-superior outcome can be sustained as a Nash equilibrium.

10 Bad Chemistry (§4) Consider the generic coordination problem given by eqs. 4.19.

10.1 For the Nash equilibrium (i.e., a^* and A^*), give conditions under which the external effect is positive or negative and the two strategies a and A are substitutes or complements.

10.2 What is the first order condition for a symmetric Pareto-efficient allocation? Using this first order condition (assuming the second order condition holds) and your expression for the Nash equilibrium above to show that a^* and A^* exceed the Pareto-efficient levels if and only if the external effect is negative. Explain why this is so.

10.3 Assuming that the Nash equilibrium is in pure strategies, show that there will always be a first mover advantage, and that the second mover will do worse (than in the Nash equilibrium) if strategies are substitutes and better if strategies are complements. Explain why this is so.

10.4 Two adjacent farmers (Lower and Upper) choose whether to use a chemical intensive anti-pest strategy or a less chemical-intensive approach that uses natural predators to control the pests which threaten their crops (integrated pest management or IPM). The use of chemicals generates negative external effects (the chemicals kill the natural predators as well), while IPM generates positive external effects (the natural predators do not respect the farmer's property boundaries and prey on the pests throughout the area). Specifically, increased use of chemicals by one raises output of the user and lowers the output and raises the marginal productivity of chemical use in the other farm for any given level of other inputs. Letting a and A be the level of chemical use by the two, give the values of the parameters of the above utility functions that describe this interaction.

10.5 *Conspicuous Consumption.* Suppose individuals differ in some trait that influences hourly wages and that they choose their hours of work (h) to maximize a utility function, the arguments of which are leisure (which we normalize as $1-h$) and what we term effective consumption, c^*, defined as their own consumption level (c) minus a constant v (for Veblen) times the consumption level of some higher income reference group (c^-). The individual's reference group might be the very rich or it might be an intermediate group. The reference group's rank in the income distribution is taken as exogenous, as is the Veblen constant v. It may be convenient to think of each individual as belonging to a homogeneous income class, each member of which takes the next highest income class as its reference group (the richest class have no reference group). Together, the reference group and v measure the nature and intensity of the relevant social comparisons. Individuals do not save, so $c = wh$, where w is the wage rate. Thus for some individual not in the richest group we have

$$u = u(c^*, h) = u((wh - vc^-), h)$$

where u is increasing and concave in its first argument and decreasing and convex in the second. Leisure and consumption are complements so $u_{c^*h} < 0$. (Note: this case differs from the one in the text (eq. (4.19)) in not being symmetric.) Show that the externality from the reference group consumption is negative, and the effect of the reference group's consumption is to increase the hours of work of less well off groups.

11 Tragedy of the Fishers (§4)

11.1 Say how you would determine the maximum Lower would be willing to pay Upper to purchase ownership rights in the lake, assuming that ownership would allow Lower to regulate Upper's access to the lake and that without this assignment of rights the two would fish at the Nash equilibrium.

11.2 Consider the allocations at the (i) Nash equilibrium, (ii) the social welfare optimum as well as the allocations resulting when (iii) both are altruistic with $a \in (0,1)$ and the Nash equilibrium obtains, and when Lower (iv) is first mover and (v) makes a take-it-or-leave-it offer. (These are five distinct outcomes.) Which pairs can you Pareto rank?

11.3 How can being second mover be advantageous (relative to the Nash allocation)? Hint: turn the Fishers Tragedy into a Stag Hunt by assuming $\beta < 0$ (fishing is a group activity and one's catch varies positively with the effort level of the other).

11.4 Assume that the two fishers have utility functions expressing the fact that their concern about the other's well-being is conditional on the other's behavior. So Lower's modified utility function, w, is

$$ w = u + U \frac{a + \lambda(1 - E)}{1 + \lambda} $$

where u and U are given by eqs. (4.6), $\lambda \in [0,1]$, and Upper's modified utility function W is analogous. Derive Lower's best response function and show that there exists no level of λ (in the unit interval) that will result in the social optimum as given by eq (4.11) being implemented if $a = 0$, while $a = 1$ (with $\lambda = 0$) implements the social optimum.

12 Footloose Jobs and Fiscal Competition (§4) Consider two nations, Here and There, whose governments each select a rate of taxation to provide an unconditional income grant to all members of the population of each, choosing the level of the tax which maximizes the grant. Population size is fixed. (Lower case letters refer to Here, while upper case letters refer to There.) The problem facing each government is that capital is mobile between countries and the level of employment depends on the size of the capital stock, which, due to capital mobility, varies inversely with the tax rate. The tax rates in each country, t and T, are levied as a fraction of income produced in each country and vary between 0 and 1. The income produced in each country (y and Y) is the product of the exogenously given level of productivity (q and Q) and the number of people employed (n and N), that is, $Y = QN$ and $y = qn$, so the total payments for the grant in each country are $g = tqn$ and $G = TQN$. The dependence of the level of employment on the tax rates of the two countries is expressed by

$$ n = \underline{n}(1 + m(T - t) - rt) $$

where $\underline{n}$, r, and m are positive constants, the latter reflecting the degree of openness of the economy, and the consequent loss of producers associated with tax rates higher than the other country. (A closed economy is one for which $m = 0$ and a completely open economy is one for which $m = \infty$.) The employment equation for There is analogous.

12.1 Assuming that neither country is either completely closed or open ($0 < m < \infty$), derive the two countries' best-response functions and graph them. Give an explicit expression for the effect on t^* of variations in T, sign this term (if possible), and explain what it means.

12.2 Do you have enough information to determine if an increase in the openness of one economy will increase, leave unchanged, or decrease the responsiveness of its own optimal tax rate to variations in the tax rate of the other country? If you have enough information, derive the appropriate expression and explain what it means. If not, explain why not.

12.3 What is the Nash equilibrium if $m = .75$ and $r = .75$ for both countries?

12.4 Using the first order conditions defining the two best-response functions, show why it must be that at the Nash equilibrium there is some increase in both tax rates that is Pareto improving.

12.5 What would be the (numerical value of the) optimal tax rate if the two nations agreed to adopt a common tax rate (assuming as above $m = r = 0.75$, and ignoring any costs of negotiating the agreement)? Compare your answer to the optimal tax rate for a closed economy and explain why they are similar or different.

12.6 An "imperial" solution. Imagine that Here (a powerful country) dictates tax policy to There, and that There complies because There believes Here's threat to adopt the Nash equilibrium strategy if There does not comply. What optimizing problem would Here solve to determine the tax rate to impose on There and to adopt for itself? Are the two tax rates imposed by Here (i.e., the solution to the above optimizing problem) Pareto optimal? Explain why, why not, or why you cannot say.

12.7 Evaluation. Using whatever graphs, numerical calculations, or other reasoning you have presented above, rank the outcomes resulting from the four solution concepts (Nash, cooperative with identical tax rates, and "imperial") for each country. (For Here indicate which solution gives the highest level of total tax revenues, the next highest, and so on, and then do the same for There.) Where possible, Pareto rank the outcomes.

13 Asymmetric Nash bargaining (§5)

Most bargaining situations are not symmetric: employers and employees have differing strategy sets and outside options. Typically, differences in opportunities to enhance one's bargaining power or differences in preferences due to wealth differences exist.

Endogenous bargaining power. Suppose two individuals engage in a joint production process, both supplying one unit of an input and producing an output (net of costs) of γ. They have agreed on a Nash bargain of the resulting joint surplus. As in the text, the two (Upper and Lower) have fallback positions of Z and z, respectively, and the bargaining power of Lower is given by α. The supply of the input is not verifiable and Lower (but not Upper) discovers that, by spending some fraction μ of her input to enhance bargaining power (employing lawyers, game theorists, etc.) rather than in production, α may be raised. As a result, $\alpha = \alpha(\mu)$ with $\alpha' > 0$ and $\alpha'' < 0$. Of course, diverting resources to a nonproductive use will lower the joint surplus, which we assume is just the sum of the inputs devoted to production or $2 - \mu$.

13.1 Give the first order condition for Lower's choice of μ and explain what it means.

13.2 If $\alpha = \frac{1}{2} + \mu^{1/2}$ for $\mu < 0.7$, give Lower's choice of μ, the level of the joint surplus, and the division of the joint surplus between the two.

Wealth and bargaining power. Consider the Nash bargain between Upper and Lower given by eq. 5.1. Suppose that for relatively poor people the marginal utility of the prize is strongly diminishing in the size of the prize, while for well-off people the utility function is more nearly linear. (Some evidence to this effect is given in chapter 9.) Reflecting this assumption, let Upper be the well-off member of the pair, and let Lower's utility function be the following transformation of Upper's utility function.

$$v(x) = g(V(1 - x)) \text{ with } g' > 0 \text{ and } g'' \leq 0,$$

13.3 Show that Lower will get less than half of the prize in the Nash bargain if $g'' < 0$ and that they will split the prize equally if $g'' = 0$.

14 Bargaining and Transaction Specific Assets (§5) Consider a production process that requires two inputs, labor and a machine. The productivity of each input depends on the extent to which it has been designed specifically for this particular production process (the *transaction specificity* of each). Revenue is

$$Y = \mu(Aa^{\alpha} + Bb^{\beta})$$

where A and B are the number of units of labor and machines, respectively, and a and b are the degrees of transaction specificity, both $\in$ (0,1). That is, $(1 - a)$ and $(1 - b)$ are the ratios of the input's value in the next best use (other than this transaction) to the replacement cost of the input. The exponents α and β are positive constants less than one, and μ is a positive constant when both inputs are present, and zero otherwise (meaning that both inputs are necessary for production). The alternative use of the inputs yields revenue of one for each unit of the input. Making each input more specific is resource using, with costs rising from 0 to c as a or b vary from 0 to 1 (training for the worker whose specificity is b costs bc, and correspondingly for the degree of specificity of the machine).

14.1 *The Robinson Crusoe case.* Suppose a single owner of one unit of both inputs is considering how best (through engineering her machine and training her labor) to design the inputs for the production process. Should production be economically viable, she will vary a and b to maximize revenues minus costs (writing $Y(a, b)$ as the revenue function) or $Y(a, b) - c(a + b)$. Give the first order conditions for this optimization problem and indicate the optimal levels of specificity if $\alpha = \beta = \frac{1}{2}$, $c = 1$, and $\mu = 2$, and show that the parameters have been chosen so that at the resulting optimal allocation the owner of the inputs is indifferent between this allocation and the resources next best use.

14.2 *A Nash bargaining solution.* Now assume that the supplier of labor and the supplier of capital are two different people who will make their design decisions (a and b) independently, then jointly produce, and then bargain over the resulting output. Suppose they have agreed on a Nash bargaining outcome, that is, the division of the surplus which maximizes the Nash product.

  14.2.1 If each owner varies the degree of asset specificity to maximize his or her income, give the relevant first order conditions and, using the numerical values given above, indicate the levels of specificity selected by the two.

  14.2.2 Compare the first order conditions of the bargaining and Robinson Crusoe case and explain why they differ.

  14.2.3 If the two were able to commit to a Nash bargaining solution to divide the output, why can they not also commit to efficient levels of specialization?

14.3 *An alternating offers bargain.* Suppose that following the design of the inputs, the owners engage in alternating offers bargaining over the share of the resulting surplus, that during the bargaining process (until it is concluded) each owner receives the alternative value of their input, that the owner of the capital input is the first mover, and that both owners have a rate of time preference of 10 percent. Anticipating the outcome of the bargaining process in advance, they then design their inputs.

  14.3.1 Give the first order conditions for each owner if each varies the degree of specificity of their factor to maximize the income which will result from their bargain, and using the numerical values given above, indicate the levels of specificity selected by the two.

  14.3.2 Compare this solution to the Nash bargain and Robinson Crusoe cases above and explain why it differs.

14.4 Show that while the transaction in the Robinson Crusoe case is consistent with competitive equilibrium in the sense that there are no ex ante (meaning before the transaction) rents accruing to either of the two inputs, there are ex post rents, and give the value of the ex post rents accruing to both inputs in both the Robinson Crusoe and the two bargaining cases.

15 Deadheads meet Coase (§6) Consider the two neighbors with conflicting late night habits and the utility functions given in the text. Normalize the time over which the curfew may be set so that $x \in [0,1]$ (think of 0 as a 6 P.M. curfew, and 1 as an 6 A.M. curfew) and let a be ¼ and b be ¾ (i.e., 9 P.M. and 3 A.M., respectively). Assume they both care equally about the time of the curfew, so set both α and $\beta = 1$.

15.1 Show that the social planner maximizing the sum of the utilities of the two individuals will set $x^* = ½$, namely, midnight.

Suppose, instead, the curfew is set at 3 A.M. (the deadhead's delight) and B can design a take it or leave it offer to A promising (we'll assume credibly) to voluntarily submit to an earlier curfew in return for a side payment from A (equal to $-y$).

15.2 What offer will B make? Explain why the voluntary curfew is identical to the social optimum.

15.3 Explain why, had the initial curfew been set at ¼ (the nerd's revenge) the selection of x as a result of Coasean bargaining would have been the same as that resulting from the deadhead's delight or the social planners' optimum. This is what Coase meant when he wrote that "all that matters (questions of equity aside) is that the rights of the various parties should be well defined and the results of legal actions easy to forecast."

Assume that A has limited resources and cannot make a payment to B in excess of y^{max}.

15.4 What is the smallest value of y^{max} that will induce B to implement the socially optimal outcome (assuming, as above that he can make a take it or leave it offer to A)?

15.5 Now assume that A rather than B is in a position to make the take-it-or-leave-it offer. (The official curfew is still 3 A.M..) What is the smallest value of y^{max} that will induce A to implement the social optimum? Why are your answers to this and the previous question different?

Suppose that the amount A has available to make a side payment to B is positive, but it is too small to support a bargain between the two resulting in the social optimum curfew.

15.6 Show that there exists some official curfew (earlier than 3 A.M. but later than the social optimum) that, if imposed by the social planner, would allow the social optimum bargained curfew to be implemented under one of the bargaining rules above.

15.7 Why can the social planner plus Coasean bargaining together accomplish what Coasean bargaining alone could not in this case?

16 Optimal Parochialism? (§7) Where contracts are incomplete, exchange is sometimes sustained by trading only with those of known reputation, by trading repeatedly with a limited number of exchange partners, or because social segmentation implements a nonrandom pairing of exchange partners. These may be termed parochial trading practices. In each of the three examples just given, the effect is to limit the selection of exchange partners in some way, and this imposes costs, which may take the form of foregone exchange opportunities, failure to find a partner with whom a mutually beneficial trade can be made, foregone economies of scale, and the like.

Consider a particular case — segmentation, as modeled in the text. Suppose that the more segmented the economy (s), the less is the likelihood (λ) that one will be paired with a person with whom there are beneficial trades to be made (i.e., with probability $1 - \lambda$, the interaction yields zero for both parties). To summarize the relevant tradeoffs, let $\lambda = 1 - s^2$ so that if segmentation is complete, one never makes a trade, and if segmentation is absent, one always makes a trade. Let the payoffs in the "One Shot Exchange Game" in the text be $a = 5, b = 3$, $c = 2, d = 1$, and assume interaction and updating is as described in the text.

16.1 Show that if $s = 0$, $\alpha^* = 0$ (α^* is the equilibrium fraction cooperating).

16.2 What is the minimal value of s such that $\alpha^* > 0$? If $s = .6$ what is α^*? For what value of s is $\alpha^* = 1$?

16.3 Suppose for the moment, as in the text, that $\lambda = 1$ and is exogenous (i.e., it does not depend on s, contrary to the above account). Write an expression for the average payoff in equilibrium (π^*) and show that $d\pi^*/ds > 0$ for those values of s which support an equilibrium value of $\alpha^* \in (0, 1)$.

16.4 Now take account of the endogeneity of the likelihood of a mutually beneficial transaction: $\lambda = \lambda(s)$. Write the expected profits in equilibrium: $\pi^e = \lambda(s)\pi^*(s)$. Is there a level of s that maximizes π^e? If so, say what it is. Give the relevant first order condition and explain what it means.

17 Quality Control (§7) In the principal agent relationship with variable quality in the text (pp. 253ff), suppose the supplier's per period utility varies according to

$$u = p - \frac{\delta}{1-q}$$

Assume the termination probability is $(1 - q)$, the value of the supplier's next best alternative (the fallback position) is zero, and the supplier's rate of time preference is also zero.

17.1 Give the value of the transaction to the supplier, v, show that setting $v_q = 0$ gives the supplier's best response to the buyer's price offer as: $q^*(p) = 1 - 2\delta/p$, and explain why this best-response function requires that the supplier equate the marginal disutility of supplying quality with the marginal effect of higher quality on the probability of retaining the transaction (τ') times the enforcement rent ($v - z$) (see eq. (7.12)).

17.2 Give the buyer's first order condition if he seeks to set p to minimize p/q, knowing the supplier's best-response function. What is the optimal price, p^*, and the resulting equilibrium level of quality supplied, q^*?

17.3 At this equilibrium, give the per period level of utility of the supplier, the expected duration of the transaction (in periods), and the value of the transaction.

17.4 Suppose δ is endogenous so the subjective cost of supplying quality (the disutility of effort, the pride on the quality of one's work) can be altered by actions taken by the buyer. If the buyer could reduce δ for a single period, at a cost, what would be the largest cost the buyer would be willing to pay? Use the equilibrium price of quality to answer this.

18 Sharecropping (§7) A risk-neutral farmer produces goods with the production function $Q = f(L)$, with f increasing and concave in its argument, and L the amount of time the farmer works. The farmer values goods and finds work onerous according to $u = y - v(L)$, where y is the farmer's income and both v' and v'' are positive.

18.1 If the farmer is the residual claimant on his crop, how much labor will he do? Give the first order condition.

18.2 If the farmer is a wage worker whose reservation utility is z and L is contractible, show that the farmer's profit-maximizing employer-landowner will offer a contract implementing the same level of labor as that given in your answer above.

Suppose that contracts in L cannot be written, and that the landowner offers the farmer a share contract, according to which $y = sQ$.

18.3 How much labor will the farmer now do as a function of the share? Give the first order condition.

18.4 What optimum problem will the landlord (as first mover) solve to maximize his net income (assuming the landlord bears no other costs)? Give the first order conditions for the landlord's choice of s.

18.5 Will the Nash equilibrium amount of labor done by the farmer be greater or less than the equilibrium amounts when labor is contractible?

18.6 Is there a Pareto-efficient contract the landlord could offer in this case (assuming as before that no contracts can be written in L)? Say what it is and why it works.

Imagine that the landlord can rent a device which makes information concerning the farmer's labor verifiable

18.7 How much is the most he would be willing to pay to rent this device if the alternative was (i) sharecropping or (ii) the efficient contracting you devised in the last part of your previous answer?

19 Truck and barter (§7) Where the care of a capital good is not verifiable, conventional rental contracts are often unattractive to the owner. This a reason why instead of renting bicycles, some companies sell the bikes to the user and then buy them back at the end of the contracted period, with the price depending on the condition of the bike. Here is another vehicular example: P owns a truck worth \$1 which is to be used by A; it may be run at speed f, resulting in a probability $\varphi \in [0, 1]$ that the truck will be wrecked (in which case its scrap value is zero) with $\varphi'(f) > 0$. If the truck is not wrecked, its value at the end of the period is undiminished. The benefits to the agent are βD, where D is the distance traveled in the period (which, normalizing the hours of work of the agent to 1, is just f). The agent experiences a cost (of effort or anxiety of) cf. The fallback option of the agent is to receive z at the end of the period (if he were not transacting with the principal he would get z). The above information is common knowledge, but it is impossible to write contracts in f. P and A are risk neutral.

P offers the following contract to A: at the beginning of the period, A pays r to P for the use of the truck, and at the end of the period the truck (if it survived) will be sold and A given a share, s, of the proceeds. The opportunity cost to the agent of paying the rent is $r(1 + \rho')$ and the value of the rent (evaluated at the end of the first period) to the principal is $r(1 + \rho)$. Assume that because the wealth levels of the two are different (rich principal, poor agent), the subjective cost of capital or the rate of time preference of the less wealthy person is higher, so $\rho' > \rho$. The principal varies s to maximize expected income while the agent varies f to maximize expected utility.

19.1 What is the first order condition governing As choice of f? Compare this with the f which would be chosen if A owned the truck outright, and show that if $s = 1$ the chosen speed would be the same in the two cases.

19.2 Write down the principal's optimizing problem. Give the first order conditions and show that if $\rho' = \rho$ then s^* (the principal's optimal value of s) is 1 and if $\rho' > \rho$, $s^* < 1$. If you used a Lagrangean expression for the above problem, explain the meaning of the Lagrange multiplier.

20 A Walrasian Labor Market Equilibrium? (§8)

Assume, contrary to the labor discipline problem in chapter 8, that enforceable contracts can be written concerning worker effort. The problem is otherwise the same: the employer varies w and h to maximize profits while the worker varies e to maximize the present value of expected utility.

20.1 What kind of contract would the employer offer?

20.2 Assume the workers' utility function is $U = y - e^2$, where y is the worker's income (either from the wage the employer will offer or from unemployment benefits). Suppose the worker's next best alternative is to be unemployed and that the unemployment benefit is equal to 1, and that, if unemployed, $e = 0$. What wage would the profit maximizing employer offer?

20.3 Show that the resulting wage and effort level are Pareto efficient and the labor market clears in equilibrium.

20.4 The Walrasian equilibrium is a special case of the competitive equilibrium in the contingent renewal model. Exactly what is a Walrasian equilibrium in this model (give the values of e, w, and v), and under what conditions will it obtain assuming that e is not verifiable?

21 Heterogeneous Labor (§8) Suppose that there are two types of workers: Good (low disutility of labor) and Bad (high disutility of labor), and a worker's type is common knowledge. Describe a competitive equilibrium in which both types are hired by a given firm and show that in equilibrium, the fallback position of the good workers must exceed that of the bad workers.

22 No shirking: North/South, Black/White (§8) Suppose the work team members in chapter 8 can either work or not ($e = 0$ or 1), with the cost of working c, and the probability that a shirking worker is detected (and fired) t. The rest of the setup is as in chapter 8.

22.1 Give an expression for the minimal wage (w^*) that must be offered by the employer to deter shirking (this is a variant of the *no shirking condition* of the model of Shapiro and Stiglitz 1984) and show that w^* is increasing in the disutility of labor, the agent's rate of time preference, i, and the worker's reservation position, z, and is decreasing in t.

22.2 A country (South) with a large traditional grain-growing sector protected by tariffs and subsidies shares a border with a country (North) with ideal grain growing conditions and a highly productive agricultural sector. The reservation position for wage workers in the South is to return to working on their family's farm in the traditional agricultural sector. An international trade economist proposes a free trade area for the two countries, removing tariffs and subsidies, showing that substantial gains from trade will result for both countries, and claiming that employees in the South will enjoy higher (real) wages as a result. A worker asks you if the claim is correct. (The question is not entirely hypothetical. At the time of the passage of the North American Free Trade Agreement with Mexico, I was asked exactly this question by Jack Scheinkman, then head of the Amalgamated Clothing and Textile Workers Union. I initially gave him the trade economist's answer but later had second thoughts.) The trade economist is certainly right about the gains from trade, but what about the wage increases? Show that (i) using the no shirking condition as the model of wage determination, the trade economist is wrong, and (ii) assuming that wages and effort are determined by a Nash bargain between employees and employers he could be right, but need not be.

22.3 The apartheid system in South Africa gave nonwhite workers restricted access to the labor market of the modern sector of the economy. According to the infamous pass laws, those working in the urban areas required a pass, which was revoked if their job was terminated, and they were required to return to close to subsistence living in one of the so-called *bantustans*. South African scholars have debated whether this system lowered profits (by restricting the supply of labor) or raised profits (by providing businesses with a favorable labor discipline environment). Use the labor discipline model (the no shirking condition, or the more general model in the text) to develop the latter argument. What additional information would you need to determine which position is more nearly correct?

23 A wage subsidy (§8) Employment subsidies are a widely discussed means of increasing employment in labor surplus economies, or among less skilled workers in the advanced countries. Suppose that n identical firms each hire h hours of identical labor, varying both h and w, the hourly wage, to maximize profits, which depend on total labor effort which is the product of hours hired and effort per hour, e. Consider two types of subsidy paid to owners of each firm: (i) an employment subsidy: the subsidy s is a fixed amount, paid per hour of labor hired, or (ii) a wage subsidy, σ: the subsidy is a fixed fraction of the wages paid. You may assume that the taxes supporting this subsidy have no effects on this problem. Using the zero subsidy case as a benchmark, indicate the effects of the two types of subsidy on the equilibrium wage, effort, and employment levels, assuming (a) that z, the fallback position of each worker, is exogenous, and (b) that z varies with the level of total employment, *nh*

24 The BIG idea (§8) Philippe van Parijs, Robert Van Der Veen, and others have proposed a universal unconditional basic income grant (BIG); this question explores how large a grant could be implemented without reducing workers incentives to supply effort (van Parijs and Van Der Veen 1986, Bowles 1992). Assume all employed work for an hour. A linear tax (meaning a fractional flat rate, τ) is levied on the income of every employed worker, the proceeds being distributed unconditionally to all members of the population (for simplicity, assume that half of those in the population are employed, a quarter are unemployed and a quarter are not in the labor force). Because profits are not taxed and because all workers (including those not working) are identical, we assume this proposal has no effect on the demand for labor so the expected duration of a spell of unemployment is unaffected. You may also abstract from any changes in labor supply. Assume that the implementation of the BIG is accompanied by the elimination of unemployment insurance (define this as b, the replacement income a worker receives if unemployed) and that the net effect of the tax, the BIG, and the elimination of unemployment insurance on the government budget is zero. If the employment relationship is governed by the contingent renewal model in the text, with $w = w^*$, $e = e^*$, and $b = w^*/2$, what is the maximum tax that can be levied without reducing the equilibrium level of effort? What is the resulting per person grant? Check to see that a family composed of two employed workers, one unemployed person and one out of the labor force, experiences no change in income or total effort provided, while those with relatively more nonemployed members gain.

25 Credit contracts(§9) In the model in chapter 9, show that if the promise to repay is enforceable the agent will set $f^* = \frac{1}{2}$, thus duplicating the Robinson Crusoe result, even if f is not contractible. Explain why this is true.

26 Why nobody wants to do business with the poor (§9) The (observable) output of a project depends on the agent's effort because it influences whether a "good" or "bad" state occurs. For example, the crop may fail or it may grow, and this is influenced (but not uniquely determined) by the agent's actions. The agent selects an (onerous and unobservable) effort level $e \in [0, 1]$, which influences whether the good or bad state occurs, the former happening with probability $\pi(e)$ with $\pi' > 0$. Total revenues of the project in the good and bad state respectively are Y and y. The disutility of effort is e^2, and to simplify things by a harmless normalization, let's say that $\pi(e) = e$. Because the agent is risk neutral, she maximizes expected income minus the disutility of effort. (This problem is a variant of the model in Hoff 1996.)

26.1 If the agent were the owner of the output of the project (meaning she owned the revenues y or Y, whichever occurred), how would she select her level of effort? Give the first order conditions and the level of effort she would choose (write e in terms of Y and y, and call this $e^{\max}$). The level of effort $e^{\max}$ maximizes the surplus of the project (in this case, it is just the utility of the agent, but below it will be divided between the principal and the agent).

Suppose the principal owns the project (and hence receives the income Y or y) and seeks to maximize expected profits by devising a payment scheme whereby the agent gets w in the bad state and W in the good state. The agent's fallback utility is zero, but she starts the interaction with wealth z. The wage offered in the bad outcome cannot be less than $-z$ (in the bad outcome, the most the principle can take from the agent is everything the agent has). It may help to think of the agent's wealth as the maximum collateral the agent can put up: by transacting with the principal, the agent stands to receive W and stands to lose some amount not to exceed z. The agent's utility in this period is expected pay minus the disutility of effort plus the consumption of the asset z. In making sense of this problem, you might want to devise a graph in wage-effort space, with (on the horizontal axis) the two wages, one of them possibly negative, and (on the vertical axis) effort. The three things you want to put in this space are: (i) the agent's participation constraint, (ii) the agent's best-response function, and (iii) the principal's iso-expected-profit loci.

26.2 Write down the agent's participation constraint. Hint: start with what you know about the relationship of w to z; using this, eliminate w; and then write the constraint in terms of e and W.

26.3 The agent varies e to maximize utility. What is her best-response function? Knowing this best-response function, the principal varies W to maximize his expected profits:

26.4 Give the relevant first order conditions and indicate what W the principal will choose. Check to see that the resulting pay package (w, W) satisfies the agent's participation constraint.

26.5 If the principal implements his expected-profits-maximizing pay scheme, what level of e, call it e^*, will the agent choose?

26.6 Why does e^* differ from e^{max}, the surplus-maximizing level of effort that occurs when the agent is also residual claimant?

26.7 Suppose an amount of wealth Δz is transferred to the agent. Assuming that Δz is not so large that the agent can undertake the project as an owner-operator rather than as an agent, what effect does this have on e^*, the agent's utility, and the principal's profits?

26.8 Why would the principal prefer to transact with wealthier agents (assuming wealthier agents have the same fallback positions as the less wealthy, namely, zero)?

26.9 Short of simply giving the project to the agent, is there a contract governing the relationship of P to A in this case that would assure the Pareto-efficient level of e, assuming as before that e is not observable? Say what it is and explain why P would not offer this contract.

27 Short Side Power ($\S10$) Do employers have more power over their employees where the employees have a less attractive fallback position? How would you measure the *amount of power* an employer has over an employee? You may assume that all of the terms making up eq. (8.5) are observable (though e is not verifiable). What is the effect of the following on this quantity: a more generous unemployment benefit, an increase in the expected duration of a spell of unemployment, a less "transparent" production process (meaning, a reduction in the absolute value of t_e), and an increase in the probability of an employee's job being terminated due to insufficient demand for the firm's product or other reasons unrelated to the employee's actions? In your response distinguish between three ways of answering this: (i) given these changes, but with no response by the firm, (ii) the new partial equilibrium (employer and employee both implementing their first order conditions), and (iii) a new general equilibrium (ii along with the zero profit condition).

28 Consumer sovereignty ($\S10$) A buyer may exercise short side power over a seller if price exceeds marginal cost. In what ways is this exercise of short side power different from that exercised by an employer over her employees?

29 Domestic labor ($\S10$) Consider the determination of domestic work and the sharing of income by a husband and wife (the amount of domestic work done is not costlessly observable by the other adult, as

much of it is bestowed on the children, and the results of this are only evident in the very long run). Consider only the two adults, one of whom works for pay and other works in their home. Extend the model in chapter 8 to determine the share of the paid worker's income received by the home worker (w) and the amount of domestic work done (e). Contrast this "domestic labor discipline" model with a transactions cost approach to this problem. What are the relevant transaction specific investments? What are the similarities and key differences? In the domestic labor discipline model, does the marriage market clear (zero excess demand for spouses of either sex)? If not, who is on the short side of the market? Can short side power be exercised?

30 Landowning and its Discontents (§10) Institutions are often described as integrated and organic wholes, more or less like a member of a species. Everyone can tell an elephant from a dog, and similarly capitalism, feudalism and socialism are not likely to be mixed up. But when one studies institutions empirically, one is impressed by the diversity of often highly local arrangements. Individual farmers often work under as many as three distinct contracts, working one's own land, hiring out as wage labor, and renting land (possibly under a fixed rent, a crop share, or other distinct contract).This question concerns the mix of contracts which may exist in equilibrium.

Consider a landowner with ten units of land that she does not farm herself. She can offer access to her land under two types of contracts, sharecropping and wage labor. Prospective farmers and the landlord alike have identical utility functions $U = y - e^2$, where y is income (in units of agricultural output), and e effort over a given period. Each farmer, when working full-time, farms exactly one acre of land, and cannot, we will assume, farm more or less. (The farmers can, of course, split their time between wage work and sharecropping.) The production function on each acre of the land is simply $q = e$, where q is the level of output.

There are neighboring landlords identical to this one offering sharecropping contracts, but because these are absentee owners they cannot oversee wage work and hence do not offer wage contracts. If wage labor is used, the monitoring is done by the landlord, who experiences a disutility occasioned by the associated effort. Sufficient monitoring is done to extract $e = .5$ from each worker hired for wages, and the amount of the landlord's effort needed to perform the monitoring to enforce this level of worker effort is $e = 1/8$. (Wages are not used to induce higher levels of effort, so the wage is simply the minimum necessary to secure the supply of labor time, namely, the wage that gives the worker the utility attainable in the neighboring share contracts.)

The landlord is trying to decide how much land to rent to sharecroppers, how much to farm using wage labor, and what contracts to offer each. Local traditions preclude very complex contracts, so she simply wants to know what the landlord's share, s, should be in the sharecropping contracts, what the wage w should be in the wage labor contracts, and how many acres of land should be devoted to cultivation by wage labor, n. (An amount equal to $10 - n$ will be cultivated by sharecroppers.) She asks you for advice. You instruct the landlord to first determine how the tenants' effort levels will be affected by s, the share claimed by the landlord.

30.1 What is the sharecropper's best-response function: $e^* = e^*(s)$? What share will the landlord offer (she sets $s = s^*$ to maximize her utility)?

30.2 Turning now to the possibility of hiring wage labor, and assuming that all landlords in the area are offering s^* contracts, indicate the wage the landlord will offer, w^*.

30.3 Given s*, e*(s*), and w*, determine the landlord's utility maximizing level of n, call this n^*.

30.4 At the equilibrium e^*, s^*, w^*, n^*, what is the equilibrium level of utility of the three types of agents: landlord, worker, and sharecropper? Is the result given by (e^*, s^*, w^*, n^*) Pareto optimal? If you think not, indicate an offer that one or more of the (noncolluding) agents might make which would result in a Pareto improvement and explain why the Pareto improvement was possible. Hint: begin by indicating how much (per period) each would be willing to pay to acquire ownership of an unit of land (or the least amount each would be willing to receive to give up an acre). Then indicate any Pareto-improving offers.

Imagine now that the ten cultivators (sharecroppers and wage workers alike), angry at what they consider to be their exploitation, meet to plan a collective strategy. Before long they have succeeded in securing a binding agreement of all cultivators in the area to refuse any contract with $s > 0.4$. As a result, all sharecropping contracts in the area are now revised so that $s = 0.4$. All other parameters remain unchanged.

30.5 Indicate the resulting new equilibrium values: e', w', and n'. (The value of n' need not be an integer.) Why does the change in s alter the wage rate? Compare the levels of utility gained by the three types of agents in the new equilibrium with their utility levels before the collective action.

One of the ten cultivators suggests that they simply occupy the landlord's land forcibly and farm it themselves as owners on individual plots. The revolutionary cultivator claims that it will be possible to pay the (ex) landlord an amount sufficient so that the landlord's utility is no less after the revolution than under the collective action case with $s = 0.4$, thereby securing the landlord's support or at least attenuating her opposition. The other cultivators are skeptical. They ask for your advice.

30.6 If no compensation were paid to the landlord, what would be the effort levels and resulting utility levels of the cultivators?

30.7 If each of the cultivators paid an equal lump sum tax (per period) to provide the minimal compensation to the landlord necessary to allow her to attain a level of utility not less than in the previous equilibrium (i.e., the collective action case), how much would each pay?

30.8 If the compensation outlined above is possible, why did the cultivators not simply purchase the land?

31 Contrasting Contracts (§10) Each agent has an identical utility function $u(y, e)$, where y is hourly income measured in units of goods (all payments are made in units of goods) and e is work effort per hour and the function is increasing and concave in the first and decreasing and convex in the second argument. Goods (Q) may be produced on an hourly basis according to the production function $Q(E)$, where E is the sum of effort devoted to production of goods (either by a single worker or by the combined members of a team) and $Q' > 0$, $Q'' < 0$. The level of effort not verifiable. Property rights consist of permission to use the production function (there are no inputs other than effort, but use of the production function requires permission from the "owner"). Where property rights are held by someone other than the agent (say an owner), you may assume that the property owner maximizes profits. Suppose that for each agent, the alternative to working is to receive zero utility. Consider the following situations:

a. The agent owns the right to use the production function and works for himself and owns the resulting output.

b. The agent works under a contract where a fraction s of the output is claimed by some other agent (called the "owner") who also determines s.

c. The agent pays a fixed sum, k, per period to the "owner" for permission to use the production function above, and owns the residual income. The owner determines k.

d. The owner offers the agent (who is a member of a team of identical agents) a contingent renewal contract, with wage w.

e. The agent is one of a team of n identical agents who share equally in the product resulting from their efforts.

f. The owner employs a team of workers, offering to pay each worker $Q - x$ per period, where x is some positive constant.

g. The owner offers the agent (one of a team of identical workers) a contingent renewal contract, charging the agent a one time fee equal to B for permission to begin work.

For the above 7 types of contract:

31.1 Describe how the level of effort of each agent will be determined under the above situations. Give the relevant maximizing problem or problems and derive the relevant first order conditions, adding whatever additional information you need to do this.

31.2 Describe how the values of w, s, k, x, and B will be determined in the above situations.

31.3 In each of the above situations, determine if the agent's level of effort and income determined by the relevant first order conditions is or is not a Pareto optimum. Explain why the results differ.

31.4 Consider a population in which every member is very rich, so rich that each is risk neutral and can finance any investment at a subjective cost equal to the economy-wide risk-free interest rate (the rate of return on a riskless asset). To keep things simple, assume that though very rich, each member nonetheless places an undiminished value on gaining additional income. In this population, which of the above contracts, if any, would you expect to observe in a competitive equilibrium? Explain your answer.

32 Conformism and altruism (§11) A major controversy in the social and biological sciences concerns the evolution of formally altruistic behaviors (toward non-kin) in humans and other animals. Conformist (cultural) transmission may have contributed to the evolutionary success of altruism. Suppose individuals are randomly paired to interact, with updating as described in eq. (11.1). Altruists pay a cost c and confer a benefit b on their partner, while nonaltruists confer no benefits and pay no costs. Let k (in eq. (11.1)) be ½. Pairing is random.

32.1 Is there some value of λ, the "degree of conformism," such that both altruism and nonaltruism are ESSs? If so, give the range of values of λ for which this is true. For λ in this range, identify all of the equilibria and say if the interior equilibrium is stable

32.2 Show that an increase in the degree of conformism enlarges the basin of attraction of the all-altruism equilibrium.

33 Learning, imitation and segmentation (§11) For the model of learning and imitation (pp. 377ff.), give the value of p that maximizes average payoffs under random pairing, $p^{\max}$, and give the average payoffs for that value of p. Say what value of s would make $p^{\max}$ stationary in the dynamic given, and give the average payoffs in equilibrium when s has this value. What pairing rule will maximize average payoffs for any $p \in (0, 1)$?

34 Make history (§11,13) A radio announcer in Boston used to end the evening news with "And that's the news. If you don't like it, go out and make your own." Here is a site at which you can access the programs used to generate the simulations in chapters 11 and 13: http://www. santafe.edu/~bowles/ (go to "Artificial Histories").You may use the program to familiarize yourself with agent-based modeling. You may also want to try some parameter combinations not mentioned in the text and write a brief account, giving your interpretations of your results.

35 Evolutionary stable distributional conventions (§12) Landlords and farmers play a Nash Demand Game in which the landlords may claim either ½ or ¾ of the crop, while farmers may claim either ½ or ¼ of the crop. When claims add up to 1 or less, each gets his claim, each getting zero otherwise. Farmers and landlords are randomly paired to play a one-shot game and adopt strategies that are best responses to the previous period's distribution of strategies. (It may clarify things to make a figure of the expected payoffs of the farmers and the landlords.)

35.1 Identify two equilibria that represent plausible outcomes of the interaction described above. There is a third equilibrium of this game. Say what it is and why it is not a plausible outcome of the interaction.

35.2 Suppose that in the (½, ½) equilibrium the total crop to be divided is 1, while in the (¼, ¾) equilibrium it is $1 + \alpha$ where $\alpha \geq -1$. (The value of α may depend on the transactions costs of implementing the various types of contracts, for example.) Which equilibrium is risk dominant if $\alpha = 0$? For what values of α is the (¼, ¾) outcome risk dominant?

36 Multi-level selection (§13) Consider a group-structured population in which groups practice a common level of resource sharing by means of the linear tax described in chapter 13. Rewrite the stationarity condition for p (eq. (13.3)) to take account of the tax and resource sharing and show that the variance ratio that gives a stationary p is declining in the level of resource sharing. Use this result to explain why a reduction in the payoff differences within a group may increase the importance of group selection.

37 The co-evolution of love and hate (§13) Behaviors widely observed in experiments and in natural settings exhibit aspects of both *altruism* — benefiting other group members at a cost to oneself — and *parochialism* — conditioning one's behavior towards others on the degree of similarity in ascriptive characteristics, sometime including a predisposition to kill or otherwise harm "outsiders." Both altruism and parochialism are puzzling from an evolutionary perspective, as both would appear to reduce individual payoffs (fitness or material well-being) by comparison to other members of one's group who eschewed these behaviors. Use results in chapter 13 and the simulation program available at http://www.santafe.edu/~bowles/ (go to "Artificial Histories") to explore the view that altruism and parochialism coevolved, each providing an environment favoring the evolutionary success of the other, and neither being singly capable of proliferation. Begin by making a list of all of the parameters in the model that may be related to parochial practices, e.g., the size of groups.

Additional Readings

These notes provide suggestions for further readings additional to the sources referred to elsewhere in the text.

Prologue

The state of economic theory at the beginning of the new millennium was assayed in a series of papers in the *Quarterly Journal of Economics* in 2000, among which is Bowles and Gintis (2000). Demsetz (1964) gives an early critique of the Walrasian assumption that while goods are scarce, the institutions facilitating their exchange are free. The idea originated with Coase (1937). On the "return of increasing returns," see Arthur (1994b) and Buchanan and Yoon (1994). Divergent growth patterns are studied in Quah (1996). The literature on incomplete contracts is vast and will be extensively referred to below; a good overview by one of its leading contributors is Stiglitz (1987). A review of recent results in behavioral and experimental economics is provided in Fehr and Gaechter (2000b) and Camerer (2003). Readers may wish to consult standard Ph.D.-level texts in microeconomics, among which Mas-Colell, Whinston, and Green (1995) and Kreps (1990a) are exemplary.

Chapter 1: Social Interactions and Institutional Design

Those wanting an introductory text in classical game theory will find it in Rasmusen (1989); and a brief nontechnical introduction to the field is Gibbons (1997). Evolutionary game theory is beautifully exposed in Gintis (2000). Binmore (1993) and (1998) as well as Elster (1989) provide a game theoretic treatment of the structure of social interactions. Kreps's (1990b) assessment of the strengths and shortcomings of game theory (in chapters 3 through 5) is worth thinking about. Cooper and John (1988) analyze macroeconomic coordination failures. Hoff and Stiglitz (2001) and North (1990) advance the view that the wealth and poverty of nations may be explained by institutional differences that give rise to differing success in solving coordination problems. See also Murphy, Schleifer, and Vishny (1989). Other statements of this view, which dates back to Adam Smith, Karl Marx, and other classical economists, are Brenner (1986) and Baran (1957). Taylor (1997), Skyrms (1996), Aoki (2001), and Basu (2000) provide valuable treatments of the relationship between games and institutions.

Chapter 2: Spontaneous Order

Models of wage equalization and productivity growth relevant to the Swedish case mentioned are Moene and Wallerstein (1997) and Agell and Lommerud

(1993). The modeling of segregation and sorting is inspired by the original treatment of neighborhood "tipping" suggested by Thomas Schelling (1971). Young (1998) presents an elegant spatial model of the same process. Skeptical of the behavioral realism of the Walrasian model, Hayek (1945), Alchian (1950), and Becker (1962) pioneered the "as if optimization" approach in economics; but like so many fruitful innovations made at the middle of the last century, this work was for the most part ignored until recently. Useful overviews of evolutionary dynamics in biology are Crow and Kimura (1970), Williams (1992), Hamilton (1996), and Frank (1998). Broader syntheses of evolutionary thinking by masters in the field are Gould (2002) and Mayr (2001). Maynard Smith (1974) and (1982) are a biologist's pioneering attempt to wed game theory with evolutionary modeling. Exemplary treatments of evolutionary game theory are Young (1998), Weibull (1995), and Vega-Redondo (1996), as well as the relevant sections of Gintis (2000). Skyrms (1996), Binmore (1998), and Sugden (1986) use evolutionary game theory to illuminate long-standing philosophical issues such as sharing rules, while Hayek (1988) provides an evolutionary critique of socialism. Sugden's chapters 3 through 5 are a searching treatment of evolutionary explanations of property rights and other division rules. On possession and property among other animals, see Hammerstein and Reichert (1988) and Kummer (1991). An important early work on evolutionary economics is Nelson and Winter (1982). Lewis (1969) is an influential analysis of languages as conventions. The formal modeling of cultural evolution was developed in Cavalli-Sforza and Feldman (1981), Boyd and Richerson (1985), and their subsequent works. An explicitly evolutionary account of economic history is given in Mokyr (1990). A catalogue of failures of evolutionary processes to produce socially optimal results is Edgerton (1992). Additional readings on evolutionary social science are suggested for the material in chapters 9 through 11.

CHAPTER 3: PREFERENCES AND BEHAVIOR

Lucid treatments of decision theory include Kreps (1990a) and the classic Luce and Raiffa (1957). Valuable surveys of experimental and behavioral economics are Camerer (2003) and Fehr and Fischbacher (2001b) and (2003). The hedonic interpretation of utility as well-being is advanced in Kahneman, Diener, and Schwartz (1999). Kahneman and Tversky (2000) provides an excellent overview of *prospect theory*, a reformulation of the standard model of rational choice based on state-dependent utilities and other empirically established behavioral regularities. Elster (1998) is an overview of the role of emotions as causes of behavior. On bounded rationality, see Rubinstein (1998). Fudenberg and Levine (1998) survey how people learn to play games. Ross and Nisbett (1991) provide a review of situation-dependent behaviors. Sen (1977) explains why those conforming to the assumptions of the rational actor model would not make very pleasant company. Useful readings on the ultimatum game include Guth, Schmittberger, and Schwarz (1982), Forsythe, Horowitz, Savin, and Sefton (1994), Camerer and Thaler (1995), and Roth (1995). Gintis, Bowles, Boyd, and Fehr (2004) is a collection of papers on reciprocity. The cross-cultural experiments project—including detailed experimental results and ethnographic evidence—is described in Henrick, Boyd, Bowles, et al (2004). The evolution of other-regarding motives is explored in Sober and Wilson (1998) for humans and in de Waal (1996) for other animals. Bowles (1998), Becker (1996), Lane (1991), and Putterman and Ben-Ner (2000) explore the ways in which economic experience may shape preferences. Rabin and Thaler (2001) critique conventional approaches to risk aversion.

CHAPTER 4: COORDINATION FAILURES AND INSTITUTIONAL RESPONSES

Ostrom (1990) provides a conceptual and empirical overview of commons governance. Taylor (1997) and (1982) models the problem of coordination without governments. On common property problems and public goods problems, see also Taylor (1997), Seabright (1993), and Ostrom and Gardner (1993). Samuelson (1954) is a pioneering study. On Veblen effects and positional goods see Veblen (1934[1899]), Hirsch (1976), Pagano (1998). Maskin (1985) surveys implementation theory. Holmstrom (1982) and Groves (1973) study the problem of incentives in teams. Baland, Bowles, and Bardhan (2004) is a collection of field studies and theoretical models of local commons governance. Hoff and Stiglitz (2001) interpret underdevelopment as a result of failure to solve coordination problems. Durlauf (2002) provides an alternative framework of the study of nonmarket social interactions that may support inefficient outcomes. Models of fiscal competition among states are Sinn (1997) and Bowles (2002). The essays in Bardhan, Bowles, and Wallerstein (2004) discuss the impact of this coordination problem on public policy concerning redistribution to the less well off.

CHAPTER 5: DIVIDING THE GAINS TO COOPERATION

Schelling's essay on bargaining in Schelling (1960) and Johansen (1979) are classics worth reading. On the relationship between the various bargaining models, helpful papers are Harsanyi (1956) and Binmore, Rubinstein, and Wolinski (1986). For a sense of real world bargaining processes, read Juravich and Bronfenbrenner (1999) and Batstone et al. (1978). Useful sources on bargaining are Osborne and Rubinstein (1990), and Elster (1989). Valuable applications to capital-labor bargaining are McDonald and Solow (1981) and Moene, Wallerstein, and Hoel (1993). Akerlof (1984) develops an interesting model of wage determination under the influence of fairness norms. Mueller (1989) and Buchanan, Tollison, and Tullock (1980) provide an analysis of government induced rent seeking, while Wittman (1989) challenges the view that democratic governments induce substantial amounts of unproductive rent seeking. Bargaining experiments are surveyed in Roth (1995). Wars of attrition have been studied by biologists; see for instance Bishop and Cannings (1975).

CHAPTER 6: UTOPIAN CAPITALISM

Good introductions to general equilibrium theory are Arrow and Hahn (1971) and Katzner (2004). Clear statements of the Fundamental Theorem and its relationship to welfare economics are in Arrow (1971), Koopmans (1957), and Bator (1957), while Sunstein (1990) provides an overview of rationales for collective intervention in market transactions. Arrow (1974) gives an overview of the evolution of general equilibrium thinking, including its application to the theory of social choice. A clear modern exposition of this approach is Mas-Colell, Whinston, and Green (1995). Ingrao and Israel (1990) is a survey of the development of general equilibrium theory and the formal obstacles to demonstrating uniqueness and global stability of competitive equilibrium in the Walrasian tradition. See also Kirman (1989) and Ackerman (1997). Non-Walrasian formulations of the way that individual action yields system-wide outcomes are provided in Arthur, Durlauf, and Lane (1997), Anderson, Arrow, and Pines (1988), and Durlauf and Young (2001). These three works present some results of the ongoing research in non-Walrasian economics at the Santa Fe Institute. Related works by Albin and Foley (1992) and Epstein and Axtell (1996) simulate populations of adaptive agents engaging in non-Walrasian trading. Cooter (1987) is a brief summary of the Coase theorem and Farrell (1987) provides an illuminating commentary on both theorems (the model in his paper is the inspiration for the Grateful Dead example in the text). Demsetz (1964) and Alchian and Demsetz (1972) provide valuable overviews of the property rights school, which takes its inspiration from Coase.

CHAPTER 7: EXCHANGE

Classic treatments of markets as institutions are Ben-Porath (1980), Greif (1994), Sahlins (1974), Polanyi (1957), and Polanyi, Arensberg, and Pearson (1957). Geertz, Geertz, and Rosen (1979), and Thompson (1971). Aoki (2001) and Aoki and Hayami (2001) provide a series of models of market transactions and market-community interactions. Klein and Leffler (1981) is a pioneering work on markets with incomplete contracting. Williamson (1985) interprets the institutions of the modern capitalist economy through the lens of transactions costs. A valuable source on transaction costs, network analysis, and ecological approaches to markets is Smelser and Swedberg (1994). Arrow (1986) and Sappington (1991) provide introductions to principal agent models. Arthur (1997) develops a model the social interactions underlying the functioning of a stock market. Rauch and Casella (2001) is a collection of papers on markets as social networks, extending the original ideas of Harrison White (1981); see especially the papers by Kirman, Rauch, and Padgett. See also White (2002).

CHAPTER 8: EMPLOYMENT, UNEMPLOYMENT, AND WAGES

Malcomson (1999) provides a valuable survey of employment contract theory. A useful survey of "efficiency wage" models is Yellen (1984). The theory and historical description of dual (segmented) labor markets is developed in Gordon, Edwards, and Reich (1982). Evidence concerning the relevance of the effort regulation model to actual economies is found in Bowles, Gordon, and Weisskopf (1989) and (1983), Wadhwani and Wall (1991), Weisskopf (1987), and Green and Weisskopf (1990). An unusual survey-based study of wage setting is Bewley (1999). The employment relationship and wage setting in highly unionized economies is modeled in Wallerstein (1999) and Moene and Wallerstein (1995). The theory of social exchange was pioneered by Blau (1964) and applied to the employment relationship by Bowles (1985), Solow (1990) and Akerlof (1984).

CHAPTER 9: CREDIT MARKETS, WEALTH CONSTRAINTS, AND ALLOCATIVE INEFFICIENCY

Stiglitz and Weiss (1981) is an influential model of quantity-constrained borrowers. Hoff, Braverman, and Stiglitz (1993) is a collection of papers using principal agent models to understand labor and credit markets in less developed countries. One of the earliest papers to model the efficiency effects of the wealth inequality is Eaton and White (1991); Hoff (1996) and Bardhan, Bowles, and Gintis (2000) provide surveys. Banerjee, Besley, and Guinnane (1994) model a credit cooperative, with historical examples. Banerjee (1993), Galor and Zeira (1993), and Piketty (1997) address dynamic aspects of wealth accumulation with incomplete credit markets. Bowles and Gintis (2002c) survey evidence on the intergenerational transmission of wealth and other aspects of economic status.

CHAPTER 10: THE INSTITUTIONS OF A CAPITALIST ECONOMY

On employee-run firms, see Dow (2002), and on cooperatives Banerjee, Mookherjee, Munshi, and Ray (2001). On the technological dynamism of capitalist economic institutions see Mokyr (1990), Landes (1998) and (1970), and Brenner (1986). The misuse of the assumption of efficient design in biology is discussed in Lewontin (1987) and Gould and Lewontin (1979). A useful work on nonclearing markets (defining the short side and long side of a market) is Benassy (1982). Aoki (1984) and (1990), Dow (1993), Skillman (1991), Holmstrom and Milgrom (1994), Milgrom (1988), Pagano (1991), and Putterman and Kroszner (1996) are illuminating on the theory of the firm. Marglin (1974), an explanation of the rise of the factory system, is the original statement of the view that organizational structure may determine technology. On power, see Lukes (1974), Hirschleifer (2001), Aghion and Tirole (1997), Rotemberg (1993), Dow (1987), Nozick (1969), Basu (2000), and Parsons (1967). On the political and philosophical implications of shortside power and an argument for subjecting it to democratic accountability, see Dahl (1985) and Bowles and Gintis (1992). Overviews of the institutions of capitalism include Williamson (1985), Lindblom (1977), Lindblom (2000), and Hansmann (1996). Roemer (1982) initiated the modeling of how individuals with different wealth levels sort themselves into distinct classes or types of contracts. Legros and Newman

(1996) model this process for a population of wealth-constrained individuals. Axtell, Epstein, and Young (2001) provides a dynamic agent-based model of this process. Erikson and Goldthorpe (1992) and Wright (1995) provide valuable (and contrasting) sociological overviews and empirical applications of the Marxian notion of class. Influential historical studies of classes are Moore (1966), Aston and Philpin (1985), and Genovese (1965).

CHAPTER 11: INSTITUTIONAL AND INDIVIDUAL EVOLUTION

Good introductions to Marx's and Darwin's approaches to understanding evolutionary change are provided, respectively, in Cohen (1978) and Mayr (1982). Models of the evolution of collective punishment are Greif (1994) and Boyd, Gintis, Bowles, and Richerson (2003). Valuable historical studies of the evolution of property rights and related institutions (not already mentioned in chapters 2 and 11) are McCloskey (1975) and Allen (1992). Boehm (2000b), Binford (2001), and Kelly (1995) provide valuable surveys about the economic and social organization of foraging bands. Bowles (1998) is a survey of the endogenous evolution of preferences drawing on an extensive empirical literature as well as the cultural evolution models of Boyd and Richerson (1985) and Cavalli-Sforza and Feldman (1981). On cultural evolution and the late Pleistocene environment, Boyd and Richerson (2000) is valuable. Pagano (2001) draws parallels between institutional innovation and speciation. See also Richerson and Boyd (2004).

CHAPTER 12: CHANCE, COLLECTIVE ACTION, AND INSTITUTIONAL INNOVATION

The key contributions to stochastic evolutionary game theory are Foster and Young (1990), Young (1993), (1995), and (1998), and Kandori, Mailath, and Rob (1993). Aoki (1998) is a valuable application of this approach to the question of convergence and divergence of institutions. On Marx's theory of historical change, see Marx (1976); for modern expositions see Cohen (1978) and Elster (1985). Historical accounts of institutional change in the Marxian tradition are Soboul (1974), Lefebvre (1947), Trotsky (1932), Brenner (1976), and Genovese (1965). Axtell, Epstein, and Young (2001) is an agent-based model of the emergence of classes. Wright (1986) collects an important biologist's papers including those on equilibrium selection through drift.

CHAPTER 13: THE COEVOLUTION OF INSTITUTIONS AND PREFERENCES

Important contributions on the genetic evolution of altruistic preferences are Hamilton (1964), Hamilton (1975), and Trivers (1971). A collection of recent papers is Hammerstein (2003). Boyd and Richerson (1988) and Boyd and Lorberbaum (1987) give some reasons why game repetition may fail to support cooperation in large groups. Models of multi-level selection are presented in

Lewontin (1965), Price (1970), Crow and Kimura (1970), Boyd, Gintis, Bowles, and Richerson (2004), and Boyd and Richerson (2002). Accounts skeptical of the importance of group selection are Williams (1966), Crow and Kimura (1970), Boorman and Levitt (1973), and Maynard Smith (1976). Boyd and Richerson (1985), Boehm (1996), Boehm (1997), and Wilson and Dugatkin (1997) give reasons why group selection pressures may be considerably stronger for humans than for other animals. A number of prominent sociobiologists have considered group selection an important influence on human genetic evolution: for example, Alexander (1987) and Wilson (1975). Valuable overviews of cooperative behaviors in humans and other animals are found in de Waal (1996), Dugatkin (1997), and Sober and Wilson (1998). Suppression of within-group variance as a contribution to success in between-group competition is a common theme in biology. See Frank (2003), Michod (1997), and Ratnieks (1988). Group selection arguments appear (sometimes implicitly) in Darwin (1873), Alchian (1950), Hayek (1988), Parsons (1964), and Tilly (1990). The simulations reported here are presented in more detail in Bowles, Choi, and Hopfensitz (2003).

CHAPTER 14: ECONOMIC GOVERNANCE

Hayek (1978) provides an account of Mandeville's contribution to the theory of both evolution and spontaneous order. Skinner (1978) and Dumont (1977) are also valuable on the displacement of the Aristotelian perspective. A comparison of "old" and "new" paradigms in economics by Brian Arthur is reported in Collander (2000). The communities, states, and markets framework is similar to the clans, market, and bureaucracies approach of Ouchi (1980). See also Ostrom (1990), Fiske (1991), and Taylor (1996). States and their economic activities have received little attention here. Useful introductions to state-economy relationships are Laffont (2000), Atkinson and Stiglitz (1980), Mueller (1989), and Persson and Tabellini (2000). On the state-market equivalence, see Farrell (1987) and Stiglitz (1994). The tension between using utility to explain behavior and also to evaluate outcomes is expressed in Sen (1977) and (1982), Kahneman, Wakker, and Sarin (1997), and Kahneman and Tversky (2000). The notion of the economy as embedded in a larger social structure was developed by Karl Polanyi; see especially Polanyi, Arensberg, and Pearson (1957), Dalton (1968) and Polanyi (1957). Like Coase, Polanyi asked why some interactions are best coordinated by the price system and others not, but he gave a very different answer. The economic literature on mutual monitoring by self-interested agents includes important contributions by Varian (1990), Stiglitz (1993), Banerjee et al. (1994), and Dong and Dow (1993a) and (1993b). Approaches using social preferences include the treatment of social penalties by Besley and Coate (1995) and of peer pressure by Kandel and Lazear (1992). On mechanism design and implementation theory, see Maskin (1985) and Hurwicz (1974). On institutional crowding out, see Frey (1997) and Bohnet, Frey, and Huck (2001). Milgrom and Roberts (1990a) and Aoki (2001) discuss institutional complementarities.

Works Cited

1898. *Holden v. Hardy*, 169 U.S. 366 (1898). U.S. Supreme Court.

1915. *Coppage v. State of Kansas*, 236 U.S.1 (1915). U.S. Supreme Court.

Acemoglu, Daron, Simon Johnson, and J. A. Robinson. 2002. "Reversal of Fortune: Geography and Institutions in the Making of the Modern World Income Distribution." *Quarterly Journal of Economics*, CXVII:4, pp. 1231–94.

Acheson, James. 1988. *The Lobster Gangs of Maine*. Hanover, NH: University Press of New England.

Ackerman, Frank. 2002. "Still Dead After All These Years: Interpreting the Failure of General Equilibrium Theory." *Journal of Economic Methodology*, 9:2 pp. 119–39.

Agell, Jonas, and Erik Kjell Lommerud. 1993. "Eglaitarianism and Growth." *Scandinavian Journal of Economics*, 95, pp. 559–79.

Aghion, Philippe, and Jean Tirole. 1997. "Formal and Real Authority in Organizations." *Journal of Political Economy*, 105:1, pp. 1–29.

Ainslie, George. 1975. "Specious Reward: A Behavioural Theory of Impulsiveness and Impulse Control." *Psychological Bulletin*, 82, pp. 463–93.

Akerlof, George. 1982. "Labor Contracts as Partial Gift Exchange." *Quarterly Journal of Economics*, 97:4, pp. 543–69.

———. 1984. *An Economic Theorist's Book of Tales*. Cambridge: Cambridge University Press.

Albin, Peter and Duncan Foley. "Decentralized, Dispersed Exchange Without an Auctioneer: a Simulation Study." *Journal of Economic Behavior and Organization*, 18:1, pp. 27–51.

Alchian, Arman. 1950. "Uncertainty, Evolution, and Economic Theory." *Journal of Political Economy*, 58:3, pp. 211–21.

Alchian, Armen A., and William Allen. 1969. *Exchange and Production: Theory in Use*. Belmont: Wadsworth, 1969.

Alchian, Armen A., and Harold Demsetz. 1972. "Production, Information Costs, and Economic Organization." *American Economic Review*, 62:5, pp. 777–95.

Alchian, Armen A., and Harold Demsetz. 1973. "The Property Right Paradigm." *Journal of Economic History*, 33:1, pp. 16–27.

Alesina, Alberto, and Eliana La Ferrara. 2000. "Participation in Heterogeneous Communities." *Quarterly Journal of Economics*, 115:3, pp. 847–904.

Alexander, Richard D. 1979. *Darwinism and Human Affairs*. Seattle: University of Washington Press.

Alexander, Richard D. 1987. *The Biology of Moral Systems*. New York: Adine de Gruyter.

Allais, Maurice. 1953. "Le comportement de l'homme rationnel devant le risque, critique des postulats et axiomes de l'école Américaine." *Econometrica*, 21, pp. 503–46.

Allen, Robert. 1992. *Enclosure and the Yeoman*. Oxford: Clarendon Press.

———. 2000. "Community and Market in England: Open Fields and Enclosures Revisited." Pp. 42–68 in *Communities and Markets in Economic Development*. Masahiko Aoki and Yujiro Hayami, eds. Oxford: Oxford University Press.

———. 2001. "The Great Divergence in European Wages and Prices from the Middle Ages to the First World War." *Explorations in Economic History*, 38, pp. 411–47.

Anderson, Perry. 1974. *Lineages of the Absolutist State*. London: N.L.B.

Anderson, Philip W. P., Kenneth Arrow, and David Pines. 1988. *The Economy as an Evolving Complex System*. Reading, Mass.: Addison-Wesley.

Anderson, Terry, and P.J. Hill. 1975. "The Evolution of Property Rights: A Study of the American West." *Journal of Law and Economics*, 18:1, pp. 163–79.

Andreoni, James, and John Miller. 2002. "Giving according to GARP: An Experimental Test of the Consistency of Preferences for Altrusim." *Econometrica*, 70:2, pp. 737–53.

Angeletos, George-Marois, David Laibson, Andrea Repetto, Jeremy Tobacman and Stephen Weinberg. 2001, "The Hyperbolic Consumption Model: Calibration, Simulation, and Empirical Evaluation." *Journal of Economic Perspectives*, 15:3, pp. 47–68.

Aoki, Masahiko. 1984. *The Co-operative Game Theory of the Firm*. London: Clarendon.

———. 1990. "Toward an Economic Theory of the Japanese Firm." *Journal of Economic Literature*, 28:1, pp. 1–27.

———. 1998. "The Evolution of Organizational Conventions and Gains from Diversity." *Industrial and Corporate Change*, 7:3, pp. 399–431.

———. 2001. *Toward a Comparative Institutional Analysis*. Cambridge: MIT Press.

Aoki, Masahiko, and Yujiro Hayami, eds. 2001. *Communities and Markets*. Oxford: Oxford University Press.

Aristotle. 1962 [c. 350 B.C.]. *Nicomachean Ethics*. Indianapolis: Bobbs-Merrill.

Arrow, Kenneth J. 1971. "Political and Economic Evaluation of Social Effects and Externalities." Pp. 3–23 in *Frontiers of Quantitative Economics*. M. D. Intriligator, ed. Amsterdam: North Holland.

———. 1974. "General Economic Equilibrium: Purpose, Analytic Techniques, Collective Choice." *American Economic Review*, 64:3, pp. 253–72.

———. 1985. "The Economics of Agency." Pp. 37–51 in *Principals and Agents: The Structure of Business*. John W. Pratt and Richard J. Zeckhauser, eds. Cambridge: Harvard Business School Press.

———. 1986. "Agency and the Market." Pp. 37–51 in *Handbook of Mathematical Economics*, volume III. Kenneth Arrow and M. D. Intriligator, eds. Amsterdam: North Holland.

———. 1999. "Technical Information and Industrial Structure." Pp. 156–63 in *Firms, Markets and Hierarchies*. Glenn Carroll and David Teece, eds. Oxford: Oxford University Press.

Arrow, Kenneth J., and Gerard Debreu, 1954. "Existence of an Equilibrium for a Competitive Economy." *Econometrica*, 22:3 pp. 265–90.

Arrow, Kenneth J., and Frank Hahn. 1971. *General Competitive Analysis*. San Francisco: Holden-Day.

Arthur, Brian W. 1994a. "Inductive reasoning and Bounded Rationality." *American Economic Association Papers and Proceedings*, 84:2, pp. 406–11.

Arthur, W. Brian. 1994b. *Increasing Returns and Path Dependency in the Economy*. Ann Arbor: University of Michigan Press.

———. 1997. "Asset Pricing Under Endogenous Expectations in an Artificial Stock Market." Pp. 15–44 in *The Economy as an Evolving Complex System, II*. Brian Arthur, Steven Durlauf, and David Lane, eds. Reading, Mass.: Addison Wesley.

Arthur, W. Brian, Steven N. Durlauf, and David A. Lane, eds. 1997. *The Economy as an Evolving Complex System II*. Reading, Mass.: Addison-Wesley.

Asplund, Marcus. 2000. "What Fraction of a Capital Investment Is Sunk Costs?" *Journal of Industrial Economics*, XLVIII:3, pp. 287–303.

Aston, T. H., and C.H.E. Philpin, eds. 1985. *The Brenner Debate: Agrarian Class Structure and Economic Development in Pre-Industrial Europe*. Cambridge: Cambridge University Press.

Atkinson, Anthony, and Joseph E. Stiglitz. 1980. *Lectures on Public Economics*. New York: McGraw-Hill.

Aumann, R., and S. Sorin. 1989, "Cooperation and Bounded Recall," *Games and Economic Behavior*, 1:1, pp. 5–39.

Axelrod, Robert. 1970. *Conflict of Interest: A Theory of Divergent Goals with Applications to Politics*. Chicago: Markham.

Axelrod, Robert, and William D. Hamilton. 1981. "The Evolution of Cooperation." *Science*, 211, pp. 1390–96.

Axtell, Robert L., Joshua M. Epstein, and H. Peyton Young. 2001. "The Emergence of Classes in a Multi Agent Bargaining Model." Pp. 191–222 in *Social Dynamics*. Steven Durlauf and H. Peyton Young, eds. Cambridge: MIT Press.

Baker, G., and T. Hubbard. 2000. "Contractibility and Asset Ownership: On-Board Computers and Governance in U.S. Trucking." NBER W7634: Cambridge, Mass.

Baker, Wayne E. 1984. "The Social Structure of a National Securities Market." *American Journal of Sociology*, 89:4, pp. 775–811.

Baland, J.M., S. Bowles, and Pranab Bardhan. 2004. *Inequality, Cooperation, and Environmental Sustainability*. New York: Russell Sage Foundation.

Banerjee, Abhijit, and Andrew Newman. 1993. "Occupational Choice and the Process of Development." *Journal of Political Economy*, 101:2, pp. 274–98.

Banerjee, Abhijit, Timothy Besley, and Timothy W. Guinnane. 1994. "Thy Neighbor's Keeper. The Design of a Credit Cooperative with Theory and a Test." *Quarterly Journal of Economics* 109:2, pp. 491–515.

Banerjee, Abhijit, Dilip Mookherjee, Kaivan Munshi and D. Ray. 2001. "Inequality, Control Rights and Rent-Seeking Super Cooperatives in Maharashtra." *Journal of Political Economy*, 109:1, pp. 138–90.

Banerjee, Abhijit, and Lakshmi Iyer. 2002. "History, Institutions and Economic Performance: The Legacy of Colonial Land Tenure Systems in India." MIT working paper 02–27.

Banerjee, Abhijit, Paul J. Gertler, and Maitreesh Ghatak. 2002. "Empowerment and Efficiency: Tenancy Reform in West Bengal." *Journal of Political Economy*, 110:2, pp. 239–80.

Baran, Paul A. 1957. *The Political Economy of Growth*. New York: Monthly Review Press.

Bardhan, Pranab. 1984. *Land, Labor and Rural Poverty: Essays in Development Economics*. New York: Columbia University Press.

Bardhan, Pranab, S. Bowles, and H. Gintis. 2000. "Wealth Inequality, Credit Constraints, and Economic Performance." Pp. 541–603 in *Handbook of Income Distribution*. Anthony Atkinson and Francois Bourguignon, eds. Amsterdam: North-Holland.

Bardhan, Pranab, S. Bowles, and Michael Wallerstein. 2004. *Globalization and Redistribution*. New York: Russell Sage Foundation.

Barone, Enrico. 1935. "The Ministry of Production in the Collectivist State." Pp. 245–90 in *Collectivist Economic Planning*. F. A. von Hayek, ed. London: Routledge.

Barr, Abigail. 2001. "Social Dilemmas, Shame-based Sanctions, and Shamelessness: Experimental Results from Rural Zimbabwe." Centre for the Study of African Economies. Working paper WPS/2001.11.

Barry, Herbert, III, Irvin L. Child, and Margaret K. Bacon. 1959. "Relation of Child Training to Subsistence Economy." *American Anthrolpologist*, 61, pp. 51–63.

Basu, Kaushik. 2000. *Prelude to Political Economy: A Study of the Social and Political Foundations of Economics*. Oxford: Oxford University Press.

Basu, Kaushik, and Pham Hoang Van. 1998. "The Economics of Child Labor." *American Economic Review*, 88:3 pp. 412–27.

Bates, Robert H., Avner Greif, Margaret Levi, Jean-Laurent Rosenthal, and Barry R. Weingast. 1998. *Analytic Naratives*. Princeton: Princeton University Press.

Batstone, Eric, Ian Boraston, Stephen Frenkel et al. 1978. *Social Organization of Strikes*. Oxford: Basil Blackwell.

Ibn Battuta. 1929. *Travels in Asia and Africa: 1325–1354*. London: Routledge and Kegan Paul.

Becker, Gary S. 1962. "Irrational Behavior and Economic Theory." *Journal of Political Economy*, 70:1, pp. 1–13.

———. 1996. *Accounting for Tastes*. Cambridge, MA: Harvard University Press.

Becker, Gary S., and George J. Stigler. 1977. "De Gustibus Non Est Disputandum." *American Economic Review*, 67:2, pp. 76–90.

Bellas, C. 1972. *Industrial Democracy and the Worker-owned Firm; A Study of Twenty-one Plywood Companies in the Pacific Northwest*. New York: Praeger.

Ben-Porath, Yoram. 1980. "The F-Connection: Families, Friends, and Firms and the Organization of Exchange." *Population and Development Review*, 6:1, pp. 1–30.

Benabou, Roland. 1993. "Workings of a City: Location, Education, and Production." *Quarterly Journal of Economics*, 108, pp. 619–52.

Benartzi, S. Shlomo, and Richard Thaler. 1995. "Myopic Loss Aversion and the Equity Premium Puzzle." *Quarterly Journal of Economics*, 110:1, pp. 73–92.

Benassy, Jean-Pascal. 1982. *The Economics of Market Disequilibrium*. Orlando: Acadamic Press.

Bergin, James, and Barton L. Lipman. 1996. "Evolution With State-Dependent Mutations." *Econometrica*, 64:4, pp. 943–56.

Bernstein, Lisa. 1992. "Opting Out of the Legal System: Extralegal Contractual Relations in the Diamond Industry." *Journal of Legal Studies*, 21:1, pp. 115–58.

Besley, Timothy, and Stephen Coate. 1995. "Group Lending, Repayment Incenties and Social Collateral." *Journal of Development Economics*, 46, pp. 1–18.

Bettinger, Robert L., and Martin Baumhauf. 1982. "The Numic Spread: Great Basin Cultures in Competition." *American Antiquity*, 47:3, pp. 485–503.

Bewley, Truman F. 1995. "A Depressed Labor Market as Explained by Participants." *American Economic Review*, 85:2, pp. 250–54.

———. 1999. *Why Wages Don't Fall during a Recession*. Cambridge: Harvard University Press.

Binford, Lewis. 2001. *Constructing Frames of Reference: An Analytical Method for Archeological Theory Using Hunter-gatherer and Environmental Data Sets*. Berkeley: University of California Press.

Binmore, Ken. 1993. *Game Theory and the Social Contract: Playing Fair*. Cambridge: MIT Press.

———. 1998. *Game Theory and the Social Contract: Just Playing*. Cambridge: MIT Press.

Binmore, Ken, John McCarthy, Giovanni Ponti, Larry Samuelson, and Avner Shaked. 2002. "A Backward Induction Experiment." *Journal of Economic Theory*, 104, pp. 48–88.

Binmore, Ken, Ariel Rubinstein, and Asher Wolinski. 1986. "The Nash Bargaining Solution in Economic Modelling." *Rand Journal of Economics*, 17, pp. 176–88.

Binswanger, H. P. 1980. "Attitudes toward Risk: Experimental Measurements in Rural India." *American Journal of Agricultural Economics*, 62 pp. 395–407.

Bishop, D. T., and C. Cannings. 1975. "A Generalized War of Attrition." *Journal of Theoretical Biology*, 70, pp. 85–124.

Black, Jane, David de Meza, and David Jeffreys. 1996. "House Prices, the Supply of Collateral and the Enterprise Economy." *Economic Journal*, 106:434, pp. 60–75.

Blanchflower, David G., and Andrew J. Oswald. 1994. *The Wage Curve*. Cambridge: MIT Press.

———. 1998. "What Makes a Young Entrepreneur?" *Journal of Labor Economics*, 16:1, pp. 26–60.

Blau, Peter. 1964. *Exchange and Power in Social Life*. New York: John Wiley.

Blinder, Alan S., and Don H. Choi. 1990. "A Shred of Evidence on Theories of Wage Stickiness." *Quarterly Journal of Economics*, 105:4, pp. 1003–15.

Blount, Sally. 1995. "When Social Outcomes Aren't Fair: The Effect of Causal Attributions on Preferences." *Organizational Behavior & Human Decision Processes*, 63:2, pp. 131–44.

Blurton-Jones, Nicholas, G. 1987. "Tolerated Theft, Suggestions about the Ecology and Evolution of Sharing, Hoarding, and Scrounging." *Social Science Information*, 26:1, pp. 31–54.

Boehm, Christopher. 1982. "The Evolutionary Development of Morality as an Effect of Dominance Behavior and Conflict Interference." *Journal of Social and Biological Structures*, 5, pp. 413–21.

Boehm, Christopher. 1993. "Egalitarian Behavior and Reverse Dominance Hierarchy." *Current Anthropology*, 34:3, pp. 227–54.

———. 1996. "Emergency Decisions, Cultural-Selection Mechanics, and Group Selection." *Current Anthropology*, 37:5, pp. 763–93.

———. 1997. "Impact of the Human Egalitarian Syndrome on Darwinian Selection Mechanics." *The American Naturalist*, 150, pp. S100–S21.

———. 1999. "The Natural Selection of Altruistic Traits." *Human Nature*, 10:3, pp. 205–52.

———. 2000a. "Group Selection in the Upper Paleolithic." *Journal of Consciousness Studies*, 7:1-2, pp. 211–19.

———. 2000b. *Hierachy in the Forest*. Cambridge: Harvard University Press.

Bohnet, Iris, B. Frey, and Steffen Huck. 2001. "More Order with Less Law: On Contractual Enforcement, Trust, and Crowding." *American Political Science Review*, 95:1, pp. 131–44.

Bolton, Gary E., and A. Ockenfels. 1999. "A Theory of Equity, Reciprocity and Competition." *American Economic Review*, 90:1, pp. 166–94.

Boorman, S., and P. R. Levitt. 1973. "Group Selection on the Boundary of a Stable Population." *Theoretical Population Biology*, 4, pp. 85–128.

Bourguignon, F., and C. Morrison. 2002. "Inequality among World Citizens: 1820–1992." *American Economic Review*, 92:4, pp. 727–44.

Bowles, Samuel. 1985. "The Production Process in a Competitive Economy: Walrasian, Neo-Hobbesian, and Marxian Models." *American Economic Review* 75:1, pp. 16–36.

———. 1989. "Social Institutions and Technical Change." Pp. 67–87 in *Technological and Social Factors in Long Term Fluctuations*. Massimo Di Matteo, Richard M. Goodwin, and Alessandro Vercelli, eds. New York: Springer-Verlag.

———. 1991. "The 'Reserve Army Effect' on the Wage in a Labor Discipline Model." Pp. 385–406 in *Making Economies More Efficient and More Equitable*. T. Mizoguchi, ed. Oxford: Oxford University Press.

———. 1992. "Is Income Security Possible in a Capitalist Economy? An Agency Theoretic Analysis of an Unconditional Income Grant." *European Journal of Political Economy*, 8, pp. 557–78.

———. 1998. "Endogenous Preferences: The Cultural Consequences of Markets and Other Economic Institutions." *Journal of Economic Literature*, 36:1, pp. 75–111.

———. 2001. "Individual Interactions, Group Conflicts, and the Evolution of Preferences." Pp. 155–90 in *Social Dynamics*. Steven Durlauf and Peyton Young, eds. Cambridge: MIT Press.

———. 2002. "Globalization and Redistribution: Feasible Egalitarianism in a Competitive World." Pp. 230–63 in *Inequality around the world*. R. Freeman, ed. London: Palgrave.

Bowles, Samuel, and Jung-Kyoo Choi. 2002. "The First Property Rights Revolution." Santa Fe Institute working paper 02-11-061.

———. 2003. "The Co-evolution of Love and Hate." Santa Fe Institute Working Paper.

Bowles, Samuel, Jung-Kyoo Choi, and Astrid Hopfensitz. 2003. "The Coevolution of Individual Behaviors and Group Level Institutions." *Journal of Theoretical Biology*, 223:2, pp. 135–47.

Bowles, Samuel, and Herbert Gintis. 1984. "State and Class in European Feudalism." Pp. 19–51 in *Statemaking and Social Movements: Essays in History and Theory*. Charles Bright and Susan Harding, ed. Ann Arbor: University of Michigan Press.

———. 1992. "Power and Wealth in a Competitive Capitalist Economy." *Philosophy and Public Affairs*, 21:4, pp. 324–53.

———. 1993. "The Revenge of *Homo Economicus*: Contested Exchange and the Revival of Political Economy." *Journal of Economic Perspectives*, 7:1, pp. 83–102.

———. 2000. "Walrasian Economics in Retrospect." *Quarterly Journal of Economics*, 115:4, pp. 1411–39.

———. 2002a. "Pro-Social Emotions." Santa Fe Institute Working Paper, January. 02-07-028.

———. 2002b. "'Social Capital' and Community Governance." *Economic Journal* 112 (483) F419–F436.

———. 2002c. "The Inheritance of Inequality." *Journal of Economic Perspectives*, 16:3, pp. 3–30.

———. 2003. "The Evolution of Strong Reciprocity: Cooperation in Heterogeneous Populations." *Theoretical Population Biology* (in press).

Bowles, Samuel, D. Gordon, and T. Weisskopf. 1983. "Hearts and Minds: A Social Model of U.S. Productivity Growth." *Brookings Papers on Economic Activity*, 2, pp. 381–450.

———. 1989. "Business Ascendancy and Economic Impasse." *Journal of Economic Perspectives*, 3:1, pp. 107–34.

Bowles, Samuel, David Kendrick, and Peter Dixon. 1980. *Notes and Problems in Microeconomic Theory*, 2nd ed. Amsterdam: North Holland (Advanced Texts in Mathematical Economics).

Bowles, S., and Yong-jin Park. 2001. Emulation, Inequality and Work Hours: Was Thorsten Veblen Right? Sante Fe Institute working paper 01-10-061.

Boyd, Robert, Herbert Gintis, Samuel Bowles, and Peter Richerson. 2003. "The Evolution of Altruistic Punishment." *Proceedings of the National Acadamy of Science* (USA) 100:6, pp. 3531–35.

Boyd, Robert, and J. Lorberbaum. 1987. "No Pure Strategy Is Evolutionarily Stable in the Repeated Prisoner's Dilemma Game." *Nature*, 327, pp. 58–59.

Boyd, Robert, and Peter J. Richerson. 1985. *Culture and the Evolutionary Process*. Chicago: University of Chicago Press.

———. 2000. "The Pleistocene and the Origins of Human Culture: Built for Speed." *Perspectives in Ethology*, 13, pp. 1–45.

Brady, Thomas A. 1985. *Turning Swiss: Cities and Empire, 1450–1550*. Cambridge: Cambridge University Press.

Brenner, R. 1976. "Agrarian Class Structure and Economic Development in Pre-Industrial Europe." *Past and Present*, 70, pp. 30–70.

———. 1986. "The Social Bases of Economic Development." Pp. 23–53 in *Analytical Marxism*. John Roemer, ed. Cambridge: Cambridge University Press.

Bright, Charles, and Susan Friend Harding. 1984. *Statemaking and Social Movements: Essays in History and Theory*. Ann Arbor: University of Michigan Press.

Brown, Martin, Armin Falk, and Ernst Fehr. 2002. "Contractual Incompleteness and the Nature of Market Interactions." CEPR discussion paper no. 3272.

Buchanan, James M., Robert Tollison, and Gordon Tullock. 1980. *Toward a Theory of the Rent-seeking Society*. College Station: Texas A&M University Press.

Buchanan, James M., and Gordon Tullock. 1962. *The Calculus of Consent: Logical Foundations of Constitutional Democracy*. Ann Arbor: University of Michigan Press.

Buchanan, James, and J. Yoon. 1994. *The Return to Increasing Returns*. Ann Arbor: University of Michigan Press.

Bulow, Jeremy I., and Lawrence H. Summers. 1986. "A Theory of Dual Labor Markets with Application to Industrial Policy, Discrimination, and Keynesian Unemployment." *Journal of Labor Economics*, 4:3, pp. 376–414.

Burda, Michael, and Antje Mertens. 2001. "Estimating Wage Losses of Displaced Workers in Germany." *Labour Economics*, 8:1, pp. 15–41.

Burke, Edmund. 1955 [1790]. *Reflections on the Revolution in France*. New York: Bobbs-Merrill.

Burke, Mary, and H. Peyton Young. 2000. "The Terms of Agricultural Contracts: Theory and Evidence." Washington, DC: Brookings Institute.

Camerer, Colin. 2000. "Prospect Theory in the Wild: Evidence from the Field." Pp. 17–43 in *Choices, Values, and Frames*. D. Kahneman and A. Tversky, eds. Cambridge: Cambridge University Press.

———. 2003. *Behavioral Game Theory: Experimental Studies of Strategic Interaction*. Princeton: Princeton University Press.

Camerer, Colin, and Ernst Fehr. 2004. "Measuring Social Norms and Preferences Using Experimental Games: A Guide for Social Scientists." In *Foundations of Human Sociality: Economic Experiments and Ethnographic Evidence from 15 Small-Scale Societies*. Joe Henrich, Samuel Bowles, Robert Boyd, Colin Camerer, Ernst Fehr and Herbert Gintis, eds. Oxford: Oxford University Press.

Camerer, Colin, and Roberto Weber. 2003. "Timing and Virtual Observability in Ultimatum Bargaining and 'Weak Link' Coordination Games." in press *Experimental Economics*.

Camerer, Colin, and George Loewenstein. 1993. "Information, Fairness, and Efficiency in Bargaining." Pp. 155–79 in *Psychological Perspectives on Justice*. Barbara A. Mellers and Jonathan Baron, eds. Cambridge: Cambridge University Press.

Camerer, Colin, and Richard Thaler. 1995. "Ultimatums, Dictators, and Manners." *Journal of Economic Perspectives*, 9:2, pp. 209–19.

Cameron, Lisa. 1998. "Raising the Stakes in the Ultimatum Game: Experimental Evidence from Indonesia." *Economic Inquiry*, 37:1, pp. 47–59.

Caporael, Linnda R., et al. 1989. "Selfishness Examined: Cooperation in the

Absence of Egoistic Incentives." *Behavioral and Brain Sciences*, 12, pp. 683–739.

Card, David. 1990. "Strikes and Bargaining: A Survey of the Recent Empirical Literature." *American Economic Review*, 80:2, pp. 410–15.

Cardenas, Juan Camilo, John K. Stranlund, and Cleve E. Willis. 2000. "Local Environmental Control and Institutional Crowding-out." *World Development*, 28:10, pp. 1719–33.

Carmichael, H. Lorne. 1985. "Can Unemployment Be Involuntary? The Supervision Perspective." *American Economic Review*, 75:5, pp. 1213–14.

Caroll, Lewis. 1982 [1865]. *Alice's Adventures in Wonderland*. New York: Harcourt Brace Jovanovich.

Carter, Michael, Bradford Barham, and Dina Mesbah. 1996. "Agro Export Booms and the Rural Poor in Chile, Guatemala and Paraguay." *Latin American Research Review*, 31:1, pp. 33–66.

Cavalli-Sforza, L. L., and Marcus W. Feldman. 1981. *Cultural Transmission and Evolution: A Quantitative Approach*. Princeton: Princeton University Press.

Chagnon, Napoleon A. 1983. *Yanomamo: The Fierce People*. New York: Holt, Rhinehart and Winston.

Charness, Gary, and Matthew Rabin. 1999. "Social Preferences: Some Simple Tests and a New Model." University of California, Berkeley.

Clark, W.A.V. 1991. "Residential Preferences and Neighborhood Racial Segregation: A Test of the Schelling Segregation Model." *Demography*, 28:1, pp. 1–19.

Clarke, D.E. Martin ed. 1923. *The Hávamál with Selections From Other Poems of the Edda, Illustrating the Wisdom of the North in Heathen Times*. Cambridge: Cambridge University Press pp. 55.

Coase, R. H. 1937. "The Nature of the Firm." *Economica*, 4, pp. 386–405.

———. 1988. *The Firm, the Market, and the Law*. Chicago: University of Chicago Press.

———. 1960. "The Problem of Social Cost." *Journal of Law and Economics*, 3:1, pp. 1–44.

———. 1992. "The Institutional Structure of Production." *American Economic Review*, 82:4, pp. 713–19.

Cohen, Dov. 1998. "Culture, Social Organization, and Patterns of Violence." *Journal of Personality and Social Psychology*, 75:2, pp. 408–19.

Cohen, Gerald Allan. 1978. *Karl Marx's Theory of History: A Defence*. Princeton: Princeton University Press.

Collander, David, ed. 2000. *The Complexity Vision and the Teaching of Economics*. Cheltenham: Edward Elgar.

Cooper, Russell, and Andrew John. 1988. "Coordinating Coordination Failures in Keynesian Models." *Quarterly Journal of Economics*, 103:3, pp. 441–63.

Cooter, Robert. 1987. "The Coase Theorem." Pp. 457–59 in *The New Palgrave A Dictionary of Economics*. J. Eatwell, M. Milgate and P. Newman, eds. London: MacMillan.

Cortes, Hernan. *Letters From Mexico*, translated and edited by Anthony Pagden. 1986. New Haven: Yale University Press.

Craig, Ben, and John Pencavel. 1992. "The Behavior of Worker Cooperatives:

The Plywood Companies of the Pacific Northwest." *American Economic Review*, 82:5, pp. 1083–105.

———. 1995. "Participation and Productivity: A Comparison of Worker Cooperatives and Conventional Firms in the Plywood Industry." *Brookings Papers: Microeconomics*, pp. 121–60.

Crawford, Vincent P. 2002. "Introduction to Experimental Game Theory." *Journal of Economic Theory*, 104:1, pp. 1–15.

Cronon, William. 1991. *Nature's Metropolis: Chicago and the Great West.* New York: W.W. Norton & Company.

Cross, Henry, Charles Halcomb, and William Matter. 1967. "Imprinting or Exposure Learning in Rates Given Early Auditory Stimulation." *Psychonomic Science*, 7:7, pp. 233–34.

Crow, James F., and Motoo Kimura. 1970. *An Introduction to Population Genetic Theory.* New York: Harper & Row.

Dahl, Robert. 1957. "The Concept of Power." *Behavioral Science*, 2, pp. 201–15.

Dahl, Robert A. 1985. *Preface to the Theory of Economic Democracy.* Berkeley: University of California Press.

Dahl, Robert, and Charles Lindblom. 1953. *Politics, Economics and Welfare.* New York: Harper & Row.

Dalai Lama. 1994. *The Path to Enlightenment.* Ithaca, NY: Snow Lion Publications.

Dalton, George, ed. 1968. *Primitive, Archaic, and Modern Economies: Essays of Karl Polanyi.* Garden City: Anchor Books.

Darwin, Charles. 1998 [1873]. *The Descent of Man.* New York: D. Appleton and Company.

Davis, Lance E., and Douglass C. North. 1971. *Institutional Change and American Economic Growth.* Cambridge: Cambridge University Press.

Dawkins, Richard. 1989a. *The Blind Watchmaker.* New York: Norton.

———. 1989b. *The Selfish Gene* (2nd ed.). Oxford: Oxford University Press.

de Waal, Frans B. 1996. *Good Natured: The Origins of Right and Wrong in Humans and Other Animals.* Cambridge: Harvard University Press.

Debreu, Gerard. 1974. "Excess Demand Functions." *Journal of Mathematical Economics*, 1:1, pp. 15–23.

Deci, Edward L., Richard Koestner, and Richard M. Ryan. 1999. "A Meta-Analytic Review of Experiments Examining the Effects of Extrinsic Rewards on Intrinsic Motivation." *Psychological Bulletin*, 125:6, pp. 627–68.

Demsetz, Harold. 1964. "The Exchange and Enforcement of Property Rights." *Journal of Law and Economics*, 7, pp. 11–26.

———. 1966. "Toward a Theory of Property Rights." *American Economic Review*, 57:2, pp. 347–59.

Demsetz, Harold and Kenneth Lehn. 1985. "The Structure of Corporate Control: Causes and Consequences." *Journal of Political Economy*, 93:6, pp. 1155–77.

Dong, Xioa-Yuan, and Gregory Dow. 1993a. "Monitoring Costs in Chinese Agric](lural Teams." *Journal of Political Economy*, 101:3, pp. 539–53.

———. 1993b. "Does Free Exit Reduce Shirking in Production Teams?" *Journal of Comparative Economics*, 17, pp. 472–84.

Dow, Gregory. 1993. "Why Capital Hires Labor: A Bargaining Perspective." *American Economic Review*, 83:1, pp. 118–34.

———. 1996. "Replicating Walrasian Equilibria Using Markets for Membership in Labor Managed Firms." *Economic Design*, 2:2, pp. 147–62.

———. 2002. *Governing the Firm: Workers' Control in Theory and Practice.* Cambridge: Cambridge University Press.

Duesenberry, James S. 1949. *Income, Saving, and the Theory of Consumer Behavior.* Cambridge: Harvard University Press.

Dugatkin, Lee Alan. 1997. *Cooperation among Animals.* New York: Oxford University Press.

Dumont, Louis. 1977. *From Mandeville to Marx: The Genesis and Triumph of Economic Ideology.* Chicago: University of Chicago Press.

Durham, William H. 1991. *Coevolution: Genes, Culture, and Human Diversity.* Stanford: Stanford University Press.

Durkheim, Emile. 1967 [1902]. *De la division du travail social.* Paris: Presses universitaires de France.

Durlauf, Steven. 2002. "A Framework for the Study of Individual Behavior and Social Interactions." In *Sociological Methodology*, pp. 47–87. v.31:1.

Durlauf, Steven, and H. Peyton Young. 2001. *Social Dynamics.* Cambridge: MIT Press.

Eaton, B. Curtis, and William D. White. 1991. "The Distribution of Wealth and the Efficiency of Institutions." *Economic Inquiry*, 39:2, pp. 336–50.

Edgerton, Robert B. 1992. *Sick Societies: Challenging the Myth of Primitive Harmony.* New York: The Free Press.

Edgeworth, Francis Ysidro. 1881. *Mathematical Psychics: An Essay on the Application of Mathematics to the Moral Sciences.* London: C. Kegan Paul and Company.

Eggertsson, Thrainn. 1966. "No Experiments, Monumental Disasters: Why It Took a Thousand Years to Develop a Specialized Fishing Industry in Iceland." *Journal of Economic Behavior and Organization*, 30:1, pp. 1–23.

Eibl-Eibesfeldt, Irenaus. 1982. "Warfare, Man's Indoctrinability and Group Selection." *Journal of Comparative Ethology*, 60:3, pp. 177–98.

Eldredge, Niles, and Stephen J. Gould. 1972. "Punctuated Equilibria: an Alternative to Phyletic Gradualism." Pp. 82–115 in *Models in Paleobiology.* Thomas J.M Schopf. San Francisco: Freeman, Cooper.

Elster, Jon. 1985. *Making Sense of Marx.* Cambridge: Cambridge University Press.

———. 1989. *The Cement of Society.* Cambridge: Cambridge University Press.

———. 1998. "Emotions and Economic Theory." *Journal of Economic Literature*, 36, pp. 47–74.

Ember, Carol. 1978. "Myths About Hunter-Gatherers." *Ethnology*, 17:4, pp. 439–49.

Endicott, Kirk. 1988. "Property, Power and Conflict among the Batek of Malaysias." Pp. 110–27 in *Hunters and Gatherers.* T. Ingold, D. Riches, and J. Woodburn, eds. New York: St. Martin's Press.

Engerman, Stanley, K. Sokoloff, and E. Mariscal. 2002. The Evolution of Schooling Institutions in the Americas, 1800–1925. Unpublished working paper, University of California, Los Angeles.

Ensminger, Jean. 1996. *Making a Market: The Institutional Transformation of an African Society*. Cambridge: Cambridge University Press.

———. 1998. "Experimental Economics in the Bush: Why Institutions Matter." Department of Anthropology, Washington University.

Epstein, Joshua M., and Robert Axtell. 1996. *Growing Artificial Societies: Social Science from the Bottom Up*. Washington DC: The Brookings Institution.

Erikson, Robert, and John H. Goldthorpe. 1992. *The Constant Flux: A Study of Class Mobility in the Industrial Societies*. Oxford: Oxford University Press.

Eswaran, Mukesh, and A. Kotwal. 1986. "Access to Capital and Agrarian Production Organization." *Economic Journal*, 96, pp. 482–98.

Evans, David, and Boyan Jovanovic. 1989. "An Estimated Model of Entrepreneurial Choice under Liquidity Constraints." *Journal of Political Economy*, 97:4, pp. 808–27.

Fafchamps, Marcel. 1992. "Solidarity Networks in Preindustrial Societies: Rational Peasants with a Moral Economy." *Economic Development and Cultural Change*, 41:1, pp. 147–74.

Falk, Armin, Ernst Fehr, and Urs Fischbacher. 2003. "On the Nature of Fair Behavior." *Economic Inquiry*, 41:1 pp. 20–26.

Falk, Armin, and Urs Fischbacher. 1998. "A Theory of Reciprocity." Institute for Empirical Economic Research, University of Zurich: Zurich working paper no. 6, University of Zurich.

Farber, Henry. 2003. "Job Loss in the United States, 1981–2001." Princeton University Industrial Relations Section working paper #471. Princeton University, Industrial Relations Section, May 2003.

Farrell, Joseph. 1987. "Information and the Coase Theorem." *Journal of Economic Perspectives*, 1:2, pp. 112–29.

Fehr, Ernst. 1993. "The Simple Analytics of a Membership Market in a Labor-Managed Economy." Pp. 260–76 in *Democracy and Markets: Participation, Accountability and Efficiency*. Samuel Bowles, Herbert Gintis, and Bo Gustafsson, eds. Cambridge: Cambridge University Press.

Fehr, Ernst, and Urs Fischbacher. 2001a. "Third Party Punishment." Institute for Empirical Research in Economics, University of Zurich (unpublished).

———. 2001b. "Why Social Preferences Matter." Stockholm, Nobel Symposium on Behavioral and Experimetal Economics.

———. 2003. "The Nature of Human Altruism-Proximate Patterns and Evolutionary Origins." University of Zurich Institute for Empirical Research in Economics. Zurich.

Fehr, Ernst, and Simon Gaechter. 2000a. "Do Incentive Contracts Crowd Out Voluntary Cooperation?" CEPR Discussion Paper no. 3017 London, Centre for Economic Policy Research.

———. 2000b. "Fairness and Retaliation: The Economics of Reciprocity." *Journal of Economic Perspectives*, 14:3, pp. 159–81.

———. 2002. "Altruistic Punishment in Humans." *Nature*, 415, pp. 137–40.

Fehr, Ernst, Georg Kirchsteiger, and Arno Riedl. 1998. "Gift Exchange and Reciprocity in Competitive Experimental Markets." *European Economic Review*, 42:1, pp. 1–34.

Fehr, Ernst, and John List. 2002. "The Hidden Costs and Returns of Incentives:

Trust and Trustworthiness among CEOs." Zurich, Institute for Empirical Economic Research working paper no. 134.

Fehr, Ernst, and Klaus M. Schmidt. 1999. "A Theory of Fairness, Competition, and Cooperation." *Quarterly Journal of Economics*, 114:3, pp. 817–68.

Feldman, Marcus W., Kenichi Aoki, and Jochen Kumm. 1996. "Individual Versus Social Learning: Evolutionary Analysis in a Fluctuating Environment." Santa Fe Institute Working Paper 96-05-031.

Firmin-Sellers, Kathryn. 1996. *The Transformation of Porperty Rights in the Gold Coast.* Cambridge: Cambridge University Press.

Fisher, Franklin M. 1972. "On Price Adjustment without an Auctioneer." *Review of Economic Studies*, 39:1, pp. 1–15.

Fisher, Ronald A. 1930. *The Genetical Theory of Natural Selection.* Oxford: Clarendon Press.

Fiske, Alan Page. 1991. *Structures of Social Life: The Four Elementary Forms of Human Relations.* New York: The Free Press.

Flannery, Kent, Joyce Marcus, and Robert Reynolds. 1989. *The Flocks of the Wamani: A Study of Llama Herders on the Puntas of Ayacucho, Peru.* San Diego: Academic Press.

Fogel, Robert, and S. Engerman. 1974. *Time on the Cross; the Economics of American Negro Slavery.* Boston: Little, Brown.

Foley, Duncan. 1994. "A Statistical Equilibrium Theory of Markets." *Journal of Ecomonic Theory*, 62:2, pp. 321–45.

Foley, Robert. 1987. *Another Unique Species: Patterns in Human Evolutionary Ecology.* New York: John Wiley & Sons.

Fong, Christina. 2001. "Social Preferences, Self-Interest and the Demand for Redistribution." *Journal of Public Economics*, 82:2, pp. 225–46.

Forsythe, Robert, Joel Horowitz, N. E. Savin, and Martin Sefton. 1994. "Replicability, Fairness and Pay in Experiments with Simple Bargaining Games." *Games and Economic Behavior*, 6:3, pp. 347–69.

Foster, Andrew, and Mark Rosenzweig. 1994. "A Test for Moral Hazard in the Labor Market: Contractual Arrangements, Effort, and Health." *Review of Economics and Statisitcs*, LXXVI:2, pp. 213–27.

Foster, Dean, and H. Peyton Young. 1990. "Stochastic Evolutionary Game Dynamics." *Theoretical Population Biology*, 38, pp. 219–32.

Frank, Robert. 1997. "The Frame of Referance as a Public Good." *The Economic Journal*, 107:445, pp. 1832–47.

Frank, Steven. 1995. "Mutual Policing and Repression of Competition in the Evolution of Cooperative Groups." *Nature*, 377, pp. 520–22.

———. 1998. *Foundations of Social Evolution.* Princeton: Princeton University Press.

———. 2003. "Perspective Repression of Competition and the Evolution of Cooperation." *Evolution*, 57:4 pp. 693–705.

Frey, Bruno S. 1997. "A Constitution for Knaves Crowds Out Civic Virtues." *Economic Journal*, 107:443, pp. 1043–53.

Frey, Bruno S. and Iris Bohnet. 1995. "Institutions Affect Fairness: Experimental Investigations." *Journal of Institutional Theoretical Economics*, 151:2, pp. 286–303.

———. 1996. "Cooperation, Communication and Communitarianism." *Journal of Political Philosophy*, 4:4, pp. 322–36.

Frohlich, Norman, and Joe A. Oppenheimer. 1992. *Choosing Justice: An Experimental Approach to Ethical Theory*. Berkeley: University of California Press.

Frost, Robert. 1915. *North of Boston*. New York: Henry Holt.

Fudenberg, Drew, and David Levine. 1998. *The Theory of Learning in Games*. Cambridge: MIT Press.

Fudenberg, Drew, and Eric Maskin. 1986. "The Folk Theorem in Repeated Games with Discounting or with Incomplete Information." *Econometrica*, 54:3, pp. 533–54.

———. 1990. "Evolution and Cooperation in Noisy Repeated Games." *American Economic Review*, 80:2, pp. 275–79.

Galbraith, John Kenneth. 1967. *The New Industrial State*. Boston: Houghton Mifflin.

Galor, Oded, and Joseph Zeira. 1993. "Income Distribution and Macroeconomics." *Review of Economic Studies*, 60:1, pp. 35–52.

Garcia-Barrios, Raul, and Luis Garcia-Barrios. 1990. "Environmental and Technological Degradation in Peasant Agriculture: A Consequence of Development in Mexico." *World Development*, 18:11, pp. 1569–85.

Gauthier, David. 1986. *Morals by Agreement*. Oxford: Clarendon Press.

Geertz, Clifford, Hildred Geertz, and Lawrence Rosen. 1979. *Meaning and Order in Moroccan Society: Three Essays in Cultural Analysis*. Cambridge: Cambridge University Press.

Gellner, Ernest. 1983. *Nations and Nationalism*. Ithaca: Cornell University Press.

Genovese, Eugene. 1965. *The Political Economy of Slavery; Studies in the Economy and Society of the Slave South*. New York: Pantheon.

Gibbons, Robert. 1997. "An Introduction to Applicable Game Theory." *Journal of Economic Perspectives*, 11:1, pp. 127–47.

Gilens, Martin. 1999. *Why Americans Hate Welfare*: University of Chicago Press.

Gintis, Herbert. 1989a. "Financial Markets and the Political Structure of the Enterprise." *Journal of Economic Behavior and Organization*, 11:3, pp. 311–22.

———. 1989b. "The Power to Switch: On the Political Economy of Consumer Sovereignty." Pp. 65–80 in *Unconventional Wisdom: Essays in Honor of John Kenneth Galbraith*. S. Bowles, Richard Edwards and William G. Shepherd, eds. New York: Houghton-Mifflin.

———. 2000. *Game Theory Evolving*. Princeton: Princeton University Press.

Gintis, Herbert, Eric A. Smith, and S. Bowles. 2002. "Costly Signaling and Cooperation." *Journal of Theoretical Biology*, 213:1, pp. 103–19.

Gintis, Herbert, Samuel Bowles, Robert Boyd, and Ernst Fehr, eds. 2004. *Moral Sentiments and Material Interests: The Foundations of Cooperation in Economic Life*. Cambridge, MIT Press.

Giri, J. 1983. *Le Sahel Demain*. Paris: Editions Karthala.

Glaeser, Edward L., David Laibson, Jose A. Scheinkman, and Christine L. Soutter. 2000. "Measuring Trust." *Quarterly Journal of Economics*, 65, pp. 811–46.

Glaeser, Edward, and Denise DiPasquale. 1999. "Incentives and Social Capital:

Are Homeowners Better Citizens?" *Journal of Urban Economics*, 45:2, pp. 354–84.

Gneezy, Uri, and Aldo Rustichini. 2000. "A Fine is a Price." *Journal of Legal Studies*, 29:1, pp. 1–17.

Gordon, David M., Richard Edwards, and Michael Reich. 1982. *Segmented Work, Divided Workers: The Historical Transformation of Labor in the United States*. Cambridge: Cambridge University Press.

Gould, S. J., and R. C. Lewontin. 1979. "The Spandrels of San Marco and the Panglossian Paradigm: a Critique of the Adaptationist Programme" *Proceedings of the Royal Society of London, B Biological Sciences*, 205, pp. 581–98.

Gould, Stephen J. 2002. *The Structure of Evolutionary Theory*. Cambridge: Belknap Press of Harvard.

Grafen, Alan. 1979. "The Hawk-Dove Game Played between Relatives." *Animal Behavior*, 27:3, pp. 905–7.

Green, Francis, and T. Weisskopf. 1990. "The Worker Discipline Effect: A Disaggregative Analysis." *Review of Economics and Statistics*, 72:2, pp. 241–49.

Green, Leonard, and Joel Myerson. 1996. "Exponential versus Hyperbolic Discounting of Delayed Outcomes: Risk and Waiting Time." *American Zoology*, 36, pp. 496–505.

Green, Leonard, Joel Myerson, David Lichtman, Suzanne Rosen, and Astrid Fry. 1996. "Temporal Discounting in Choice Between Delayed Rewards: The Role of Age and Income." *Psychology and Aging*, 11:1, pp. 79–84.

Greenberg, James B. 1989. *Blood Ties: Life and Violence in Rural Mexico*. Tucson: University of Arizona Press.

Greif, Avner. 1994. "Cultural Beliefs and the Organization of Society: An Historical and Theoretical Reflection on Collectivist and Individualist Societies." *Journal of Political Economy*, 102:5, pp. 912–50.

———. 2002. "Institutions & Impersonal Exchange: From Communal to Individual Responsibility." *Journal of Institutional and Theoretical Economics* 158:1 pp. 168–204.

Gross, David, and Nicholas Souleles. 2002. "Do Liquidity Constraints and Interest Rates Matter for Consumer Behavior? Evidence From Credit Card Data." *Quarterly Journal of Economics*, 117:1, pp. 149–85.

Grossman, Sanford, and Oliver Hart. 1986. "The Costs and Benefits of Ownership: A Theory of Vertical and Lateral Integration." *Journal of Political Economy*, 94:4, pp. 691–719.

Groves, Theodore. 1973. "Incentives in Teams." *Econometrica*, 41:4, pp. 617–41.

Guiso, Luigi, T. Jappelli, and D. Terlizzese. 1996. "Income Risk, Borrowing Constraints, and Portfolio Choice." *American Economic Review*, 86:1, pp. 158–72.

Guth, Werner, R. Schmittberger, and B. Schwarz. 1982. "An Experimental Analysis of Ultimatum Bargaining." *Journal of Economic Behavior and Organization*, 3:4, pp. 367–88.

Hall, Robert, and Charles Jones. 1999. "Why Do Some Countries Produce so Much More Output per Worker than Others?" *Quarterly Journal of Economics*, 114:1, pp. 83–116.

Hallward-Driemeier, Mary, Giuseppe Iorossi, and K. Sokoloff. 2001. *Manufac-*

turing Productivity in East Asia: Market Depth and Aiming for Exports;
World Bank.

Hamilton, W. D. 1964. "The Genetical Evolution of Social Behavior." *Journal of Theoretical Biology*, 37, pp. 1–52.

———. 1975. "Innate Social Aptitudes of Man: an Approach from Evolutionary Genetics." Pp. 115–32 in *Biosocial Anthropology*. Robin Fox, ed. New York: John Wiley and Sons.

———. 1996. *Narrow Roads of Gene Land: The Collected Papers of William D. Hamilton*. New York: W.H. Freeman and Company.

Hammerstein, Peter, ed. 2003. *Genetic and Cultural Evolution of Cooperation*. Cambridge: MIT Press.

Hammerstein, Peter, and Susan Reichert. 1988. "Payoffs and Strategies in Spider Territorial Contests: ESS Analysis of Two Ecotypes." *Evolutionary Ecology*, 2, pp. 115–38.

Hansen, Daniel G. 1997. "Individual Responses to a Group Incentive." *Industrial and Labor Relations Review*, 51:1, pp. 37–49.

Hansmann, Henry. 1996. *The Ownership of Enterprise*. Cambridge: Harvard University Press.

Hardin, Garrett. 1968. "The Tragedy of the Commons." *Science*, 162, pp. 1243–48.

Harsanyi, John. 1956. "Approaches to the Bargaining Problem Before and After the Theory of Games: A Critical Discussion of Zeuthen's, Hicks' and Nash's Theories." *Econometrica*, 24:144–47.

Hart, Oliver. 1995. *Firms, Contracts, and Financial Structure*. Oxford: Clarendon Press.

Hausman, Jerry. 1979. "Individual Discount Rates and the Purchase and Utilization of Energy-using Durables." *Bell Journal of Economics*, 10:1, pp. 33–54.

Hayami, Yujiro. 1998. "Norms and Rationality in the Evolution of Economic Systems: A View From Asian Villages." *The Japanese Economic Review*, 49:1, pp. 36–53.

Hayami, Yujiro, and Masao Kikuchi. 1999. "Technology, Market, and Community in Contract Choice: Rice Harvesting in the Phillipines." *Economic Development and Cultural Change*, 47:2, pp. 371–86.

Hayek, F. A. 1935. *Collectivist Economic Planning: Critical Studies on the Possibilities of Socialism*. London: George Routledge.

———. 1945. "The Use of Knowledge in Society." *American Economic Review*, 35:4, pp. 519–30.

———. 1978. *New Studies in Philosophy, Politics, Economics and the History of Ideas*. Chicago: University of Chicago Press.

———. 1988. *The Fatal Conceit: The Errors of Socialism*. Chicago: University of Chicago Press.

Henrich, Joe. 2000. "Does Culture Matter in Economic Behavior? Ultimatum Game Bargaining among the Machiguenga of the Peruvian Amazon." *American Economic Review*, 90:4, pp. 973–80.

———. 2002. "Demography and Cultural Evolution: Why adaptive cultural processes produced maladaptive losses in Tasmania." Unpublished paper, Department of Anthropology, Emory University.

Henrich, Joe, S. Bowles, Robert Boyd, Colin F. Camerer, Ernst Fehr, Herbert Gintis, and Richard McElreath. 2001. "In Search of *Homo Economicus*: Behavioral Experiments in 15 Small-Scale Socieites." *American Economic Review*, 91:2, pp. 73–78.

Henrich, Joe, Robert Boyd, Samuel Bowles, Ernst Fehr, and Herbert Gintis. 2004. *Foundations of Human Sociality: Economic Experiments and Ethnographic Evidence in 15 Small-Scale Societies*. Oxford: Oxford University Press.

Henrich, Joseph, and Robert Boyd. 1998. "The Evolution of Conformist Transmission and the Emergence of Between-group Differences." *Evolution and Human Behavior*, 19, pp. 215–42.

Herlihy, D., and C. Klapische-Zuber. 1985. *Tuscans and Their Families*. New Haven: Yale University Press.

Herodotus. 1998. *The Histories*. New York: Oxford University Press.

Hibbs Jr., Douglas A. 2000. "Wage Dispersion and Productive Efficiency: Evidence for Sweden." *Journal of Labor Economics*, 18:4, pp. 755–82.

Hirsch, Fred. 1976. *Social Limits to Growth*. Cambridge: Harvard University Press.

Hirsch, Morris W., and Stephen Smale. 1974. *Differential Equations, Dynamical Systems, and Linear Systems*. San Diego: Academic Press.

Hirshleifer, Jack. 1991. "The Technology of Conflict as an Economic Activity." *American Economic Review*, 81:2, pp. 130–34.

———. 1994. "The Dark Side of the Force: Western Economic Association International 1993 Presidential Address." *Economic Inquiry*, 32, pp. 1–10.

Hirshleifer, Jack. 2001. *The Dark Side of the Force: Economic Foundations of Conflict Theory*. Cambridge: Cambridge University Press.

Hirschman, Albert O. 1985. "Against Parsimony: Three Ways of Complicating Some Categories of Economic Discourse." *Economics and Philosophy*, 1:1, pp. 7–21.

Hobbes, Thomas. 1968 [1651]. *Leviathan*. New York: Penguin.

———. 1949 [1651]. *De Cive or The Citizen*. New York: Appleton-Century-Crofts.

Hobsbawm, Eric, and George Rude. 1968. *Captain Swing*. New York: Pantheon.

Hoff, K. 1996. "Market Failures and the Distribution of Wealth: A Perspective from the Economics of Information." *Politics & Society*, 24:4, pp. 411–32.

Hoff, K., A. Braverman, and J. E. Stiglitz, eds. 1993. *The Economics of Rural Organization: Theory, Practice and Policy*. New York: Oxford University Press.

Hoff, K., and Arijit Sen. 2002. Home-ownership, Community Interactions and Segregation unpublished.

Hoff, K., and J. E. Stiglitz. 2001. "Modern Economic Theory and Development." Pp. 389–459 in *The Future of Development Economics in Perspective*. Gerald Meier and J. E. Stiglitz, eds. Oxford: Oxford University Press.

———. 2002. "After the Big Bang: Obstacles to the Emergence of the Rule of Law in Post-Communist societies." NBER working paper no. 9282.

Hoffman, Elizabeth, Kevin McCabe, Keith Shachat, and Vernon L. Smith. 1994.

"Preferences, Property Rights, and Anonymity in Bargaining Games." *Games and Economic Behavior*, 7:3, pp. 346–80.

Hoffman, Elizabeth, Kevin McCabe, and Vernon L. Smith. 1996. "On Expectations and Monetary Stakes in Ultimatum Games." *International Journal of Game Theory*, 25:3, pp. 289–301.

Hoffman, Richard C. 1975. "Medieval Origins of the Common Fields." Pp. 23–71 in *European Peasants and Their Markets*. William Parker and Eric Jones, eds. Princeton: Princeton University Press.

Holmstrom, Bengt. 1982. "Moral Hazard in Teams." *Bell Journal of Economics*, 13:2, pp. 324–40.

Holmstrom, Bengt, and Paul Milgrom. 1994. "The Firm as an Incentive System." *American Economic Review*, 84:4, pp. 972–91.

Holmstrom, Bengt, and Jean Tirole. 1989. "The Theory of the Firm." Pp. 61–133 in *Handbook of Industrial Organization*, volume I. R. Schmalensee and R. Willig, eds. Amsterdam: North-Holland.

Holtz-Eakin, Douglas, David Joulfaian, and Harvey S. Rosen. 1994. "Sticking it Out: Entrepreneurial Survival and Liquidity Constraints." *Journal of Political Economy*, 102:1, pp. 53–75.

Horwitz, Morton. 1977. *The Transformation of American Law*. Cambridge: Harvard University Press.

Hume, David. 1964. *David Hume, The Philosophical Works*. Darmstadt: Scientia Verlag Aalen.

———. 1967 [1739]. *A Treatise of Human Nature*. Oxford: Clarendon Press.

Hurwicz, Leonid. 1974. "The Design of Mechanisms for Resource Allocation." Pp. 3–42 in *Frontiers of Quantitative Economics, II*. M. D. Intriligator and David Kenrick, eds. Amsterdam: North Holland.

Ingrao, Bruna, and Giorgio Israel. 1990. *The Invisible Hand: Economic Equilibrium in the History of Science*. Cambridge: MIT Press.

Isaac, R. Mark, James M. Walker, and Arlington W. Williams. 1994. "Group Size and Voluntary Provision of Public Goods: Experimental Evidence Utilizing Large Groups." *Journal of Public Economics*, 54:1, pp. 1–36.

Japelli, Tullio, 1990, "Who is Credit Constained in the U.S. Economy?" *Quarterly Journal of Economics*, 105:1 pp. 219–34.

Jarvis, Lovell. 1989. "The Unraveling of Chile's Agrarian Reform, 1973–1986." Pp. 240–65 in *Searching for Agrarian Reform in Latin America*. William Thiesenhusen, ed. Boston: Unwin-Hyman.

Jensen, Michael C., and William H. Meckling. 1979. "Rights and Production Functions: An Application to Labor-Managed Firms and Codetermination." *Journal of Business*, 52:4, pp. 469–506.

Johansen, Leif. 1979. "The Bargaining Society and the Inefficiency of Bargaining." *Kyklos*, 32:3, pp. 497–522.

Jones, A.H.M, ed. 1968. *A History of Rome through the Fifth Century. Volume I: The Republic*. New York: Harper & Row.

Joshi, N. V. 1987. "Evolution of Cooperation by Reciprocation within Structured Demes." *Journal of Genetics*, 66:1, pp. 69–84.

Jung, Courtney. 2001. "Collective Action and Trust Revisited: Evidence from a Small Case." New School University, Department of Political Science.

Juravich, Tom, and Kate Bronfenbrenner. 1999. *Ravenswood: The Steelworkers' Victory and the Revival of American Labor*. Ithaca: Cornell University Press.

Kahneman, Daniel. 1994. "New Challenges to the Rationality Assumption." *Journal of Institutional and Theoretical Economics*, 150:1, pp. 18–36.

Kahneman, Daniel, Ed Diener, and Norbert Schwartz, eds. 1999. *Well-being: The Foundations of Hedonic Psychology*. New York: Russell Sage Foundation.

Kahneman, Daniel, and Amos Tversky. 2000. *Choices, Values and Frames*. Princeton: Princeton University Press.

Kahneman, Daniel, Peter Wakker, and Rakesh Sarin. 1997. "Back to Bentham: Explorations of Experienced Utility." *Quarterly Journal of Economics*, CXII:2, pp. 375–405.

Kalai, Ehud, and M. Smorodinsky. 1975. "Other Solutions to Nash's Bargaining Problem." *Econometrica*, 45, pp. 513–18.

Kandel, Eugene, and Edward P. Lazear, 1992. "Peer Pressure and Partnerships." *Journal of Political Economy*, 100:4, pp. 801–17.

Kandori, M. G., G. Mailath, and R. Rob. 1993. "Learning, Mutation, and Long Run Equilibria in Games." *Econometrica*, 61:1, pp. 29–56.

Kaplan, Hillard, and Kim Hill. 1985. "Food Sharing among Ache Foragers: Tests of Explanatory Hypotheses." *Current Anthropology*, 26:2, pp. 223–46.

Karis, Thomas, and Gail Gerhart. 1997. *From Protest to Challenge: A documentary history of African politics in South Africa, 1882–1990*. Stanford: Hoover Institution Press.

Katzner, Donald. 2003. *Walrasian Microeconomics*. Unpublished manuscript.

Keeley, Lawrence. 1996. *War Before Civilization*. New York: Oxford University Press.

Kelly, Raymond C. 1985. *The Nuer Conquest: The Structure and Development of an Expansionist System*. Ann Arbor: University of Michigan Press.

Kelly, Robert L. 1995. *The Foraging Spectrum: Diversity in Hunter-Gatherer Lifeways*. Washington, DC: Smithsonian Institution Press.

Kennan, John, and Robert Wilson. 1993. "Bargaining With Private Information." *Journal of Economic Literature*, 31:1, pp. 45–104.

Kimura, M. 1968. "Evolutionary Rate at the Molecular Level." *Nature*, 217, pp. 624–26.

Kirman, Alan. 1989. "The Intrinsic Limits of Modern Economic Theory: The Emperor Has No Clothes." *Economic Journal*, 99, pp. 126–39.

Kirman, Alan, and K.J. Koch, 1986. "Market Excess Demand in Exchange Economies with Identical Preferences and Collinear Endowments." *Review of Economic Studies*, 53:3, pp. 457–63.

Klein, Benjamin and Keith Leffler. 1981. "The Role of Market Forces in Assuring Contractual Performance." *Journal of Political Economy*, 89, pp. 615–41.

Knauft, Bruce M. 1991. "Violence and Sociality in Human Evolution." *Current Anthropology*, 32:4, pp. 391–428.

Knez, Marc, and Duncan Simester. 2001. "Firm-wide Incentives and Mutual Monitoring at Continental Airlines." *Journal of Labor Economics*, 19:4, pp. 743–72.

Knight, Frank. 1921. *Risk, Uncertainty and Profit*. New York: Houghton Mifflin.

Kohn, Melvin. 1969. *Class and Conformity*. Homewood, Ill: Dorsey Press.

Kohn, Melvin L. 1990. "Unresolved Issues in the Relationship Between Work and Personality," in *The Nature of Work: Sociological Perspectives*. Kai Erikson and Steven Peter Vallas eds. New Haven: Yale University Press, pp. 36–68.

Kohn, Melvin, Atsushi Naoi, Carrie Schoenbach, Carmi Schooler, and Kazimierz Slomczynski. 1990. "Position in the Class Structure and Psychological Functioning in the U.S., Japan, and Poland." *American Journal of Sociology*, 95:4, pp. 964–1008.

Kohn, Melvin L., Carmi Schooler, et al. 1983. *Work and Personality: An Inquiry into the Impact of Social Stratification*. Norwood, N.J.: Ablex.

Kollock, Peter. 1992. "The Social Construction of Exchange." *Advances in Group Processes*, 9, pp. 89–112.

Kollock, Peter. 1998. "Transforming Social Dilemmas: Group Identity and Cooperation." Pp. 186–210 in *Modeling Rational and Moral Agents*. Peter Danielson, ed. Oxford: Oxford University Press.

Koopmans, Tjalling. 1957. "Allocation of Resources and the Price System." Pp. 4–95 in *Three Essays on the State of Economic Science*. New York: McGraw-Hill.

Kornai, Janos. 1980. *Economics of Shortage*. Amsterdam: North-Holland.

Kreps, David M. 1990a. "Corporate Culture and Economic Theory." Pp. 90–143 in *Perspectives on Positive Political Economy*. James Alt and Kenneth Shepsle, eds. Cambridge: Cambridge University Press.

———. 1990b. *A Course in Microeconomic Theory*. Princeton: Princeton University Press.

———. 1990c. *Game Theory and Economic Modelling*. Oxford: Clarendon Press.

Kummer, Hans. 1991. "Evolutionary Transformations of Possessive Behavior." *Journal of Social Behavior and Personality*, 6:6, pp. 75–83.

Kupperman, Karen Ordahl. 1993. *Providence Island, 1630–1641: The Other Puritan Colony*. New York: Cambridge University Press.

Kuran, Timur, 1995. *Private Truths, Public Lives: The Social Consequences of Preference Falsification*. Cambridge: Harvard University Press.

Labov, William. 1983. "De Facto Segregation of Black and White Vernaculars." University of Pennsylvania, Linguistics Laboratory.

Laffont, Jean Jacques. 2000. *Public Economics*. Cambridge: MIT Press.

Laffont, Jean Jacques, and Mohamed Salah Matoussi. 1995. "Moral Hazard, Financial Constraints, and Share Cropping in El Oulja." *Review of Economic Studies*, 62:3, pp. 381–99.

Laland, Kevin N., F. J. Odling-Smee, and Marcus Feldman. 2000. "Group Selection: A Niche Construction Perspective." *Journal of Conciousness Studies*, 7:1/2, pp. 221–24.

Landes, David. 1970. *The Unbound Prometheus: Technological Change and Industrial Development in Western Europe from 1750 to the Present*. London: Cambridge University Press.

———. 1998. *The Wealth and Poverty of Nations: Why Some Are So Rich and Some So Poor*. New York: W.W. Norton.

Lane, Robert E. 1991. *The Market Experience*. Cambridge: Cambridge University Press.

Lange, Oskar, and F. M. Taylor. 1938. *On the Economic Theory of Socialism.* Minneapolis: University of Minnesota Press.

Lanjouw, Peter, and Nicholas Stern, eds. 1998. *Economic Development in Palanpur Over Five Decades.* Delhi: Oxford University Press.

Lasswell, Harold, and Abraham Kaplan. 1950. *Power and Society: A Framework for Political Enquiry.* New Haven: Yale University Press.

Lazear, Edward. 1996. "Performance Pay and Productivity." NBER Working Paper w5672.

Leach, Edmund Ronald. 1954. *Political Systems of Highland Burma; A Study of Kachin Social Structure.* Cambridge: Harvard University Press.

Ledyard, J. O. 1995. "Public Goods: A Survey of Experimental Research." Pp. 111–94 in *The Handbook of Experimental Economics.* A. E. Roth and J. Kagel, eds. Princeton, NJ: Princeton University Press.

Lefebvre, Georges. 1947. *The Coming of the French Revolution.* Princeton: Princeton University Press.

Legros, Patrick, and Andrew Newman. 1996. "Wealth Effects, Distribution, and the Theory of Organization." *Journal of Economic Theory,* 70:2, pp. 312–41.

Leibenstein, Harvey. 1950. "Bandwagon, Snob, and Veblen Effects in the Theory of Consumers' Demand." *Quarterly Journal of Economics,* 64, pp. 183–207.

———. 1957. *Economic Backwardness and Economic Growth.* New York: Wiley.

Lerner, Abba. 1944. *The Economics of Control; Principles of Welfare Economics.* New York: Macmillan.

———. 1972. "The Economics and Politics of Consumer Sovereignty." *American Economic Review,* 62:2, pp. 258–66.

Levine, David K. 1998. "Modeling Altruism and Spitefulness in Experiments." *Review of Economic Dynamics,* 1:3, pp. 593–622.

Levy, Reuben. 1957. *The Social Structure of Islam.* Cambridge: Cambridge University Press.

Lewis, David K. 1969. *Convention: A Philisophical Study.* Cambridge: Harvard University Press.

Lewontin, R. C. 1965. "Selection in and of Populations." Pp. 299–311 in *Ideas in Modern Biology.* John Moore, ed. New York: The Natural History Press.

———. 1987. "The Shape of Optimality." Pp. 151–59 in *The Latest on the Best: Essays on Evolution and Optimality.* John Dupre, ed. Cambridge: MIT Press.

Libecap, Gary D. 1978. "Economic Variables and the Development of the Law: The Case of Western Mineral Rights." *Journal of Economic History,* 38:2. pp. 338–62.

Lindblom, Charles E. 1977. *Politics and Markets: The World's Political-Economic Systems.* New York: Basic Books.

———. 2000. *The Market System.* New Haven: Yale University Press.

Lipsey, R., and K. Lancaster, 1956–1957. "The General Theory of the Second Best." *Review of Economic Studies,* 24:1, pp. 11–32.

Livy (Titus Livius). 1960 [27 B.C.] *The History of Rome from Its Foundation.* London: Penguin.

Lizot, Jacques. 1971. "Aspects économique et sociaux du changement cultural chez les Yanomami." *L'Homme*, XI:1, pp. 32–5.

Loewenstein, George. 1999. "Experimental Economics from the Vantage Point of Behavioural Economics." *Economic Journal*, 109:453, pp. F23–F34.

Loewenstein, George F., Leigh Thompson, and Max H. Bazerman. 1989. "Social Utility and Decision Making in Interpersonal Contexts." *Journal of Personality and Social Psychology*, 57:3, pp. 426–41.

Loewenstein, George, and Drazen Prelec. 2000. "Anomalies in Intertemporal Choice: Evidence and an Interpretation." Pp. 579–97 in *Choices, Values and Frames*. D. Kahneman and A. Tversky, eds. Princeton: Princeton University Press.

Lohmann, Susanne. 1994. "Dynamics of Informational Cascades: The Monday Demonstrations in Leipzig." *World Politics*, 47:1, pp. 42–101.

Luce, R. Duncan, and Howard Raiffa. 1957. *Games and Decisions*. New York: John Wiley.

Lukes, Stephen. 1974. *Power: A Radical View*. London: Macmillan.

Lundberg, Shelly, and Robert Pollak. 1993. "Separate Spheres Bargaining and the Marriage Market." *Journal of Political Economy*, 101:6, pp. 988–1011.

Luria, Daniel. 1996. "Why Markets Tolerate Mediocre Manufacturing." *Challenge*, 39:4, pp. 11–16.

MacDonald, Kevin. 1995. "The Establishment and Maintenance of Socially Imposed Monogamy in Western Europe." *Politics and the Life Sciences*, 14:1, pp. 3–23.

Mack Smith, Denis. 1959. *Italy: A Modern History*. Ann Arbor: University of Michigan Press.

Mackie, Gerry. 1996. "Ending Footbinding and Infibulation: A Convention Account." *American Sociological Review*, 61, pp. 999–1017.

Mackie, Gerry. 2000. "Female Genital Cutting: The Beginning of the End." Pp. 253–281. In *Female Circumcision in Africa: Culture, Controversy, and Change*, eds. Bettina Shell-Duncan and Ylva Hernlund. Boulder Lynne Rienner Publishers.

Malcomson, James. 1999. "Individual Employment Contracts." Pp. 2293–372 in *Handbook of Labor Economics*. Orley Ashenfelter and David Card, eds. Amsterdam: North-Holland.

Malinowski, Bronislaw. 1926. *Crime and Custom in Savage Society*. London: Routledge & Kegan Paul.

Mandeville, Bernard. 1924 [1705]. *The Fable of the Bees, or Private Vices, Publick Benefits*. Oxford: Clarendon Press.

Mantel, R. 1974. "On the Characterization of Aggregate Excess Demand." *Journal of Economic Theory*, 7:3, pp. 348–53.

Mare, Robert, and Elizabeth Bruch. 2001. "Spatial Inequality, Neighborhood Mobility, and Residential Segregation." Working Paper, California Center for Population Research, University of California at Los Angeles.

Marglin, Stephen. 1974. "What Do Bosses Do?" *Review of Radical Political Economics*, 6:2, pp. 60–112.

Marshall, Alfred. 1930 [1890]. *Principles of Economics*, 8th ed. London: MacMillan.

Marx, Karl. 1904 [1859]. *A Contribution to the Critique of Political Economy.* New York, London: K. Paul, Trench, Truber & Co..

———. 1963 [1851]. *The Eighteeenth Brumaire of Louis Bonaparte.* New York: International Publishers.

———. 1967 [1867]. *Capital: A critique of political economy, I. The process of capitalist production.* New York: International Publishers.

———. 1973. *Grundrisse: Foundations of the Critique of Political Economy.* New York: Vintage.

Marx, Karl, and Friedrich Engels. 1978 [1848]. "The Communist Manifesto." Pp. 469–500 in *The Marx-Engels Reader*, 2nd ed. Robert Tucker, ed. New York: W.W. Norton.

Masclet, David, Charles Noussair, Steven Tucker, and Marie-Claire Villeval. 2003. "Monetary and Non-monetary Punishment in the Voluntary Contributions Mechanism." *American Economic Review* 93:1, pp. 366–88.

Mas-Colell, Andreu, Michael D. Whinston, and Jerry R. Green. 1995. *Microeconomic Theory.* New York: Oxford University Press.

Maskin, Eric. 1985. "The Theory of Implementation in Nash Equilibrium: A Survey." Pp. 173–341 in *Social Goals and Social Organization; Essays in Memory of Elisha Pazner.* Leonid Hurwicz, David Schmeidler, and Hugo Sonnenschein, eds. Cambridge: Cambridge University Press.

Matthew, Donald, 1992. *Atlas of Medieval Europe.* Oxford: Andromeda, Ltd.

Maynard Smith, John. 1974. "The Theory of Games and the Evolution of Animal Conflicts." *Journal of Theoretical Biology*, 47, pp. 209–21.

———. 1976. "Group Selection." *Quarterly Review of Biology*, 51, pp. 277–83.

———. 1982. *Evolution and the Theory of Games.* Cambridge: Cambridge University Press.

———. 1998. *Evolutionary Genetics.* New York: Oxford University Press.

Maynard Smith, John, and G. R. Price. 1973. "The Logic of Animal Conflict." *Nature*, 246, pp. 15–18.

Mayr, Ernst. 1982. *The Growth of Biological Thought: Diversity, Evolution, and Inheritance.* Cambridge: Harvard University Press.

———. 2001. *What Evolution Is.* New York: Basic Books.

McCloskey, Donald. 1975. "The Persistence of English Common Fields," in *European Peasants and Their Markets: Essays in Agrarian Economic History.* William Nelson Parker and E. L. Jones, eds. Princeton: Princeton University Press, pp. 73–119.

McDonald, I. M., and Robert Solow. 1981. "Wage Bargaining and Employment." *American Economic Review*, 71, pp. 896–908.

Mehra, R., and E. C. Prescott. 1988. "The Equity Risk Premium Puzzle: A Solution?" *Journal of Monetary Economics*, 21:1, pp. 133–36.

Meletti, Jenner. 2001. "Difende un fornaio, assassinato." *La Republica* (June 28), p. 13.

Mencken, H. L. 1949. *A Mencken Chrestomathy.* New York: Alfred A. Knopf.

Meyer, Jack. 1987. "Two-Moment Decision Models and Expected Utility." *American Economic Review*, 77:3, pp. 421–30.

Michod, Richard E. 1997. "Cooperation and Conflict in the Evolution of Individuality. 1. The Multilevel Selection of the Organism." *American Naturalist*, 149:4, pp. 607–45.

Milbank, Dana, and Joan E. Rigdon. 1991. "Replacement Scholarships." *Wall Street Journal*: (January 29), p. 1.

Milgrom, Paul. 1988. "Employment Contracts, Influence Activities, and Efficient Organization Design." *Journal of Political Economy*, 96:1, pp. 42–60.

Milgrom, Paul, and John Roberts. 1990a. "Rationalizability, Learning, and Equilibriium in Games with Strategic Complementarities." *Econometrica*, 59, pp. 1255–77.

———. 1990b. "Bargainng Costs, Influence Costs, and the Organization of Economic Activity." Pp. 57–89 in *Perspectives on Postive Political Economy*. James E. Alt and Kenneth A. Shepsle, eds. Cambridge: Cambridge University Press.

Mill, John Stuart. 1965. [1848] *Principles of Political Economy*. New York: Kelley.

———. 1976. *On Socialism*. Buffalo: Prometheus.

———. 1998 [1861]. *Utilitarianism*. New York: Oxford University Press.

Moene, Karl Ove, and Michael Wallerstein. 1995. "How Social Democracy Worked: Labor-market Institutions." *Politics and Society*, 23, pp. 185–212.

———. 1997. "Pay Inequality." *Journal of Labor Economics*, 15, pp. 403–30.

Moene, Karl Ove, Michael Wallerstein, and M. Hoel. 1993. "Bargaining Structure and Economic Performance." Pp. 63–131 in *Trade Union Behaviour, Pay-Bargaining, and Economic Performance*. Karl Ove Moene, Michael Wallerstein and Robert J. Flanagan, eds. Oxford: Clarendon Press.

Mokyr, Joel. 1990. *The Lever of Riches: Technological Creativity and Economic Progress*. New York: Oxford University Press.

Moore, Barrington, Jr. 1966. *Social Origins of Dictatorship and Democracy, Lord and Peasant in the Making of the Modern World* Boston: Beacon Press.

———. 1978. *Injustice: The Social Bases of Obedience and Revolt*. White Plains, N.Y.: M.E. Sharpe.

Morduch, Jonathan. 1999. "The Microfinance Promise." *Journal of Economic Literature*, XXXVII:(December), pp. 1569–614.

de Moraes Farias, P. F. 1979. "Silent Trade: Myth and Historical Evidence." *History in Africa*, 1, pp. 9–24.

Mueller, Dennis C. 1989. *Public Choice II*. Cambridge: Cambridge University Press.

Murphy, Kevin, Andrei Schleifer, and Robert W. Vishny. 1989. "Industrialization and the Big Push." *Journal of Political Economy*, 97:3, pp. 1003–26.

Myrdal, Gunnar. 1956. *Development and Underdevelopment: A Note on the Mechanism of National and International Economic Inequality*. Cairo: National Bank of Egypt.

Nash, John F. 1950a. "Equilibrium Points in *n*-Person Games." *Proceedings of the National Academy of Sciences*, 36, pp. 48–49.

———. 1950b. "Non-cooperative games." Princeton University (doctoral dissertation).

Nelson, Richard, and Sidney Winter. 1982. *An Evolutionary Theory of Economic Change*. Cambridge: Harvard University Press.

Neumann, John Von, and Oskar Morgenstern. 1944. *Theory of Games and Economic Behavior*. Princeton: Princeton University Press.

Neves, Eduardo Goes. 1995. "Village Fissioning in Amazonia." *Rev. do Museo de Arqueologica e Ethnologia* (*S. Paulo*), 5, pp. 195–209.

Nisbett, Richard E., and Dov Cohen. 1996. *Culture of Honor: The Psychology of Violence in the South.* Boulder: Westview Press.

Nisbett, Richard E., and T. D. Wilson. 1977. "Telling More than We Can Know: Verbal Reports on Mental Processses." *Psychological Review*, 84:3, pp. 231–59.

North, Douglass C. 1981. *Structure and Change in Economic History.* New York: W.W. Norton & Co.

———. 1990. *Institutions, Institutional Change and Economic Performance.* Cambridge: Cambridge University Press.

Nowak, Martin A., and Karl Sigmund. 1998. "Evolution of Indirect Reciprocity by Image Scoring." *Nature*, 393, pp. 573–77.

Nowell-Smith, Patrick Horace. 1954. *Ethics.* London: Penguin Books.

Nozick, Robert. 1969. "Coercion." Pp. 440–72 in *Philosophy, Science and Method.* Ernest Nagel, ed. New York: St. Martins.

Okun, Arthur. 1975. *Equality and Efficiency: The Big Trade-Off.* Washington, DC: Brookings Institution Press.

———. 1981. *Prices and Quantities: A Macroeconomic Analysis.* Washington, DC: The Brookings Institution.

Oliver, Symmes C. 1962. *Ecology and Cultural Continuity as Contributing Factors in the Social Organization of the Plains Indians.* Berkeley: University of California Press.

Olson, Mancur. 1965. *The Logic of Collective Action: Public Goods and the Theory of Groups.* Cambridge: Harvard University Press.

Osborne, Martin J., and Ariel Rubinstein. 1990. *Bargaining and Markets.* New York: Academic Press.

Ostrom, Elinor. 1990. *Governing the Commons: The Evolution of Institutions for Collective Action.* Cambridge: Cambridge University Press.

———. 1999. "Coping with Tragedies of the Commons." *Annual Review of Political Science*, 2, pp. 493–535.

Ostrom, Elinor, and Roy Gardner. 1993. "Coping with Asymmetries in the Commons: Self-Governing Irrigation Systems Can Work." *Journal of Economic Perspectives*, 7:4, pp. 93–112.

Ostrom, Elinor, Joanna Burger, Christopher Field, Ricahrd Norgaard, and David Policansky. 1999. "Revisiting the Commons: Local Lessons, Global Challenges." *Science*, 284, pp. 278–82.

Ostrom, Elinor, Roy Gardner, and James Walker. 1994. *Rules, Games, and Common-Pool Resources.* Ann Arbor: University of Michigan Press.

Otsuka, Keijiro, Hirouki Chuma, and Yujira Hayami. 1992. "Land and Labor Contracts in Agrarian Economies: Theories and Facts." *Journal of Economic Literature*, XXX:December pp. 1965–2018.

Ouchi, William. 1980. "Markets, Bureaucracies and Clans." *Administrative Science Quarterly*, 25, pp. 129–41.

Paddock, John. 1975. "Studies on Anti-Violent and 'Normal' Communities." *Aggressive Behavior*, 1, pp. 217–33.

———. 1991. "Violence and Sociality in Human Evolution." *Current Anthropology*, 32:4, pp. 391–428.

Padgett, John. 2002. "Economic and Social Exchange in Renaissance Florence." Santa Fe Institute Working Paper no. 02-07-032: Santa Fe.

Padover, Saul, ed. 1979. *The Letters of Karl Marx*. Englewood Cliffs, N.J.: Prentice-Hall.

Pagano, Ugo. 1991. "Property Rights, Asset Specificity, and the Division of Labour under Alternative Capitalist Relations." *Cambridge Journal of Economics*, 15:3, pp. 315–42.

———. 1993. "Organizational Equilibria and Institutional Stability." Pp. 86–116 in *Markets and Democracy: Participation, Accountability and Efficiency*. S. Bowles, H. Gintis and B. Gustafsson, eds. Cambridge: Cambridge University Press.

———. 1998. "Positional Goods." Pp. 63–84 in *The Politics and Ecnomics of Power*. S. Bowles, M. Franzini and Ugo Pagano, eds. London: Routledge.

———. 2001. "The Origin of Organizational Species." Pp. 21–47. in *The Evolution of Economic Diversity*. Ugo Pagano and Antonio Nicita, eds. London: Routledge.

Pareto, V. 1896. "The New Theories of Economics." *Journal of Political Economy*, 5:4, pp. 485–502.

———. 1909. *Manuel d'Economie Politique*. Paris: Giard et Briere (First Italian edition published 1905).

———. 1971. *Manual of Political Economy*. New York: Augustus Kelly.

van Parijs, Philippe, and Robert Van Der Veen. 1986. "A Capitalist Road to Communism." *Theory and Society*, 15, pp. 635–55.

Parsons, Talcott. 1964. "Evolutionary Universals in Society." *American Sociological Review*, 29:3, pp. 339–57.

———. 1967. "On the Concept of Political Power." Pp. 297–354 in *Sociological Theory and Modern Society*. Talcott Parsons, ed. New York: Free Press.

Pearson, Karl. 1894. "Socialism and Natural Selection." *Fortnightly Review*, LVI, N.S:July 1, pp. 1–21.

Pencavel, John. 2002. *Worker Participation: Lessons from the Worker Co-ops of the Pacific North-West*. New York: Russell Sage Foundation.

Persson, Torsten, and Guido Tabellini. 2000. *Political Economics: Explaining Economic Policy*. Cambrige: MIT Press.

Petersen, Trond. 1992. "Payment Systems and the Structure of Inequality." *American Journal of Sociology*, 98:1, pp. 67–104.

Phillips, Peter, and Martin Brown. 1986. "The Historical Origin of Job Ladders oin the U.S. Canning Industry and Their Effects on the Gender Division of Labour." *Cambridge Journal of Economics*, 10, pp. 129–45.

Piketty, Thomas. 1997. "The Dynamics of the Wealth Distribution and the Interest Rate with Credit Rationing." *Review of Economic Studies*, 64:2, pp. 173–89.

Platteau, J. P. 1995. "A Framework for the Analysis of Evolving Patron-Client Ties in Agrarian Economies." *World Development*, 23:5, pp. 767–86.

Platteau, Jean-Philippe, and Erika Seki. 2001. "Community Arrangements to Overcome Market Failures: Pooling Groups in Japanese Fisheries." Pp. 344–402 in *Communities and Markets in Economic Development*. Masahiko Aoki and Yujiro Hayami, eds. Oxford: Clarendon, pp. 344–402.

Polanyi, Karl. 1957. *The Great Transformation: The Political and Economic Origins of Our Time*. Beacon Hill: Beacon Press.

Polanyi, Karl, Conrad M. Arensberg, and Harry W Pearson. 1957. *Trade and Market in the Early Empires: Economies in History and Theory*. Glencoe: The Free Press.

Posel, Dorrit. 2001. "Women Wait, Men Migrate: Gender Inequality and Migration Decisions in South Africa." Pp. 91–118 in *Women Farmers, Enhancing Rights, Recognition and Productivity*. Patrick Webb and Katinka Weinberger, eds. Frankfurt: Peter Lang.

Prendergast, Canice. 1999. "The Provision of Incentives in Firms." *Journal of Economic Literature*, 37:1, pp. 7–63.

Price, G. R. 1970. "Selection and Covariance." *Nature*, 227, pp. 520–21.

Price, George R. 1972. "Fisher's 'Fundamental Theorem' Made Clear." *Annals of Human Genetics*, 36:129, pp. 129–40.

Price, John A. 1980. "On Silent Trade." *Research in Economic Anthropology*, 3, pp. 75–96.

Przeworski, A, Michael E. Alvarez, Jose Antonio Cheibub, and Fernando Limongi. 2000. *Democracy and Development: Political Institutions and Well-being in the World, 1950–1990*. Cambridge: Cambridge University Press.

Putterman, Louis, and Avner Ben-Ner. 2000. *Economics, Values and Organization*. Cambridge: Cambridge University Press.

Putterman, Louis G., and Randall Kroszner. 1996. *The Economic Nature of the Firm: A Reader*. Cambridge: Cambridge University Press.

Putterman, Louis, and Gregory Dow. 2000. "Why Capital Suppliers (usually) Hire Workers: What We Need to Know." *Journal of Economic Behavior and Organization*, 43:3, pp. 319–36.

Quah, D. 1996. *The Invisible Hand and the Weightless Economy*. London School of Economics Centre for Economic Performance Occasional Paper no. 12.

Rabin, Matthew. 1993. "Incorporating Fairness into Game Theory and Economics." *American Economic Review*, 83:5, pp. 1281–302.

———. 2000. "Risk Aversion and Expected Utility Theory: A Calibration Theorem." *Econometrica*. 68:5, pp. 1281–92.

Rabin, Matthew, and Richard Thaler. 2001. "Risk Aversion." *Journal of Economic Perspectives*, 15:1, pp. 219–32.

Raff, Daniel M. G. 1988. "Wage Determination Theory and the Five-Dollar Day at Ford." *The Journal of Economic History*, 48:2, pp. 387–99.

Ransom, Roger L., and Richard Sutch. 1977. *One Kind of Freedom: The Economic Consequences of Emancipation*. Cambridge: Cambridge University Press.

Rapoport, Amnon. 1997. "Order of Play in Strategically Equivalent Games in Extensive Form." *International Journal of Game Theory*, 26, pp. 113–36.

Rapoport, Anatol, and Albert Chammah. 1965. *Prisoner's Dilemma*. Ann Arbor: University of Michigan Press.

Rasmusen, Eric. 1989. *Games and Information: An Introduction to Game Theory*. Cambridge: Blackwell Scientific.

Ratnieks, Francis. 1988. "Reproductive Harmony via Mutual Policing by Workers in Eusocial Hymenoptera." *American Naturalist*, 132:2, pp. 217–36.

Rauch, James E., and Alessandra Casella, eds. 2001. *Networks and Markets.* New York: Russell Sage Foundation.

Richards, Jerry B., Suzanne H. Mitchell, Harriet de Wit, and Lewis S. Seiden. 1997. "Determination of Discount Functions in Rats With an Adjusting-Amount Procedure." *Journal of the Experimental Analysis of Behavior,* 67:3, pp. 353–66.

Richerson, Peter, Robert Boyd, and Robert L. Bettinger. 2001. "Was Agriculture Impossible During the Pleistocene but Mandatory During the Holocene? A Climate Change Hypothesis." *American Antiquity,* 66:3, pp. 387–411.

Richerson, Peter, and Robert Boyd. 2004. *The Nature of Cultures.* Chicago: University of Chicago Press.

Robbins, Lionel. 1935. *An Essay on the Nature and Significance of Economic Science.* London: Macmillan.

Roemer, John. 1982. *A General Theory of Exploitation and Class.* Cambridge: Harvard University Press.

———. 1988. *Free to Lose: An Introduction to Marxist Economic Philosophy.* London: Radius.

Rogers, Alan R. 1990. "Group Selection by Selective Emigration: The Effects of Migration and Kin Structure." *American Naturalist,* 135:3, pp. 398–413.

Rosenthal, Jean-Laurent. 1998. "The Political Economy of Absolutism Reconsidered," in *Analytic Narratives.* Robert H. Bates, Avner Greif, Margaret Levi, Jean-Laurent Rosenthal, and Barry R. Weingast, eds. Princeton: Princeton Univesity Press, pp. 64–108.

Rosenzweig, Mark, and Hans P. Binswanger. 1993. "Wealth, Weather Risk and the Composition and Profitability of Agricultural Investments." *Economic Journal,* 103:416, pp. 56–78.

Rosenzweig, Mark, and Kenneth I. Wolpin. 1993. "Credit Market Constraints, Consumption Smoothing, and the Accumulation of Durable Production Assets in Low-Income Countries: Investment in Bullocks in India." *Journal of Political Economy,* 101:2, pp. 223–44.

Ross, Lee, and Richard E. Nisbett. 1991. *The Person and the Situation: Perspectives of Social Psychology.* Philadelphia: Temple University Press.

Rotemberg, Julio J. 1993. "Power in Profit Maximizing Organizations." *Journal of Economic & Management Strategy,* 2:2, pp. 165–98.

Roth, Alvin. 1995. "Bargaining Experiments." Pp. 253–342 in *The Handbook of Experimental Economics.* John Kagel and Alvin Roth, eds. Princeton: Princeton University Press.

Rousseau, Jean-Jacques. 1987 [1755]. "Discourse on the Origin and Foundations of Inequality Among Men." in Pp. 25–109 *Basic Political Writings.* Donald A. Cress, ed. Indianapolis: Hackett.

Rubinstein, Ariel. 1982. "Perfect Equilibrium in a Bargaining Model." *Econometrica,* 50:1, pp. 97–109.

———. 1998. *Modeling Bounded Rationality.* Cambridge: MIT Press.

Saha, Atanu, Richard C. Shumway, and Hovav Talpaz. 1994. "Joint Estimation of Risk Preference Structure and Technology Using Expo-Power Utility." *American Journal of Agricultural Economics,* 76:2, pp. 173–84.

Sahlins, Marshall. 1974. *Stone Age Economics.* Chicago: Aldine.

Sally, David. 1995. "Conversation and Cooperation in Social Dilemmas." *Rationality and Society*, 7:1, pp. 58–92.

Salop, Steven C., and Lawrence J. White. 1988. "Private Antitrust Litigation: An Introduction and Framework." Pp. 3–60 in *Private Antitrust Litigation*. Lawrence J. White, ed. Cambridge: MIT Press.

Sampson, Robert J., Stephen W. Raudenbush, and Felton Earls. 1997. "Neighborhoods and Violent Crime: A Multilevel Study of Collective Efficacy." *Science*, 277, pp. 918–24.

Samuelson, Paul. 1954. "The Pure Theory of Public Expenditure." *Review of Economics and Statisitcs*, XXXVI:4, pp. 387–89.

———. 1963. "Risk and Uncertainty: A Fallacy of Large Numbers." *Scientia*, 98, pp. 108–13.

Sappington, David. 1991. "Incentives in Principal-Agent Relationships." *Journal of Economic Perspectives*, 5:2 (Spring), pp. 45–66.

Sato, Yuzuru, Eizo Akiyama, and J. Doyne Farmer. 2002. "Chaos in Learning a Simple Two Person Game." *Proceedings of the National Acadamy of Science*, 99:7, pp. 4748–51.

Savage, Howard. 1995. "Who Could Afford to Buy a House in 1995?" Washington, DC: U.S. Census Bureau: 1–6.

Scarf, H. 1960. "Some Examples of Global Instability of Competitive Equilibrium". *International Economic Review*, 1:3, pp. 157–72.

Schelling, Thomas. 1960. *The Strategy of Conflict*. Cambrdige: Harvard University Press.

———. 1971. "Dynamic Models of Segregation." *Journal of Mathematical Sociology*, 1, pp. 143–86.

Schor, Juliet B. 1988. "Does Work Intensity Respond to Macroeconomic Variables? Evidence from British Manufacturing, 1970–1986." Harvard Institute of Economic Research Working Paper.

———. 1998. *The Overspent American: Upscaling, Downshifting, and the New Consumer*. New York: Basic Books.

Schotter, Andrew. 1981. *Economic Theory of Social Institutions*. New York: Cambridge University Press.

Schumpeter, Joseph. 1934. *The Theory of Economic Development: An Inquiry into Profits, Capital, Credit, Interest and the Business Cycle*. Oxford: Oxford University Press.

———. 1942. *Capitalism, Socialism, and Democracy*. New York: Harper & Row.

Seabright, Paul. 1993. "Managing Local Commons: Theoretical Issues in Incentive Design." *Journal of Economic Perspectives*, 7:4, pp. 113–34.

Sen, Amartya K. 1977. "Rational Fools: A Critique of the Behavioral Foundations of Economic Theory." *Philosophy and Public Affairs*, 6:4, pp. 317–44.

———. 1982. *Choice, Welfare and Measurement*. Cambridge: MIT Press.

———. 1985. "The Moral Standing of the Market" Pp. 1–19 in *Ethics and Economics*. Ellen Frankel Paul Jr., Jeffrey Paul, and Fred D. Miller, eds. London: Basil Blackwell.

Sertel, Murat R. 1982. *Workers and Incentives*. New York: North-Holland.

Sethi, Rajiv, and E. Somanathan. 1996. "The Evolution of Social Norms in

Common Property Resource Use." *American Economic Review*, 86:4, pp. 766–88.

Shafir, Eldar, Itamar Simonson, and A. Tversky. 2000. "Reason-Based Choice." Pp. 597–619, in *Choices, Values and Frames*. D. Kahneman and A. Tversky, eds. Princeton: Princeton University Press.

Shaked, Avner and John Sutton. 1984. "Involuntary Unemployment as a Perfect Equilibrium in a Bargaining Model." *Econometrica*, 52:6, pp. 1351–64.

Shapiro, Carl. 1983. "Premiums for High Quality Products as Returns to Reputations." *Quarterly Journal of Economics*, 98:4, pp. 659–79.

Shapiro, Carl, and Joseph Stiglitz. 1984. "Unemployment as a Worker Discipline Device." *American Economic Review*, 74:3, pp. 433–44.

Shearer, B. 2001. "Piece Rates, fixed Wages, and Incentives: Evidence From a Field Experiment." Quebec: Universite Laval.

Siamwalla, Ammar. 1978. "Farmers and Middlemen: Aspects of Agricultural Marketing in Thailand." *Economic Bulletin for Asia and the Pacific*, 39:1, pp. 38–50.

Sigg, H., and J. Falett. 1985. "Experiments on Respect of Possession in Hamadryas Baboons (*Papio hamadryas*)." *Animal Behavior*, 33, pp. 978–84.

Simon, Herbert. 1951. "A Formal Theory of the Employment Relation." *Econometrica*, 19:3, pp. 293–305.

———. 1955. "A Behavioral Model of Rational Choice." *Quarterly Journal of Economics*, 69, pp. 99–118.

———. 1990. "A Mechanism for Social Selection and Successful Altruism." *Science*, 250, pp. 1665–67.

———. 1991. "Organizations and Markets." *Journal of Economic Perspectives*, 5:2, pp. 25–44.

Singleton, Sara. 2004. "Managing Pacific Salmon: the role of distributional conflicts in Coastal Salish Fisheries." in *Inequality, Cooperation, and Environmental Sustainability*. J. M. Baland, Pranab Bardhan, and Samuel Bowles, eds. New York: Russell Sage Foundation.

Sinn, H. W. 1990. "Expected Utility, mu-sigma Preferences, and Linear Distribution Classes: A Further Result." *Journal of Risk and Uncertainty*, 3, pp. 277–81.

———. 1997. "The Selection Principle and Market Failure in Systems Competition." *Journal of Public Economics*, 66, pp. 247–74.

Skillman, Gilbert L. 1991. "Efficiency vs. Control: A Strategic Bargaining Analysis of Capitalist Production." *Review of Radical Political Economics*, 23:1&2, pp. 12–21.

Skinner, Quentin. 1978. *The Foundations of Modern Poltical Thought*, volumes I and II. New York: Cambridge University Press.

Skyrms, Brian. 1996. *Evolution and the Social Contract*. Cambridge: Cambridge University Press.

Smale, Stephen. 1976. "Exchange Processes with Price Adjustment." *Journal of Mathematical Economics*, 3, pp. 211–26.

Smelser, Neil J., and Richard Swedberg, eds. 1994. *The Handbook of Economic Sociology*. Princeton: Princeton University Press.

Smith, Adam. 1937 [1776]. *The Wealth of Nations*. New York: Modern Library.

————. 1976 [1759]. *Theory of Moral Sentiments*. Oxford: Clarendon Press.

Smith, Vernon, and Arlington W. Williams. 1992. "Experimental Market Economics." *Scientific American*, 267:6, pp. 116–21.

Sober, Elliot, and David Sloan Wilson. 1998. *Unto Others: The Evolution and Psychology of Unselfish Behavior*. Cambridge: Harvard University Press.

Soboul, Albert. 1974. *The French Revolution*. London: NLB.

Sokoloff, K., and S. Engerman. 2000. "Institutions, Factor Endowments, and Paths of Development in the New World." *Journal of Economic Perspectives*, 14:3, pp. 217–32.

Solow, Robert. 1990. *The Labor Market as a Social Institution*. Cambridge: Basil Blackwell.

Soltis, Joseph, Robert Boyd, and Peter J. Richerson. 1995. "Can Group-Functional Behaviors Evolve by Cultural Group Selection: An Empirical Test." *Current Anthropology*, 36:3, pp. 473–83.

Somanathan, E. 1991. "Deforestation, Property Rights and Incentives in Central Himalaya." *Economic and Political Weekly*: 37–46, v. XXVI:4.

Sonnenschein, Hugo. 1973a. "Do Walras' Identity and Continuity Characterize the Class of Community Excess Demand Functions?" *Journal of Ecomonic Theory*, 6, pp. 345–54.

————. 1973b. "The Utility Hypothesis and Market Demand Theory." *Western Economic Journal*, 11, pp. 404–10.

Stadler, Barbel M.R., Peter F. Stadler, Gunter P. Wagner, and Walter Fontana. 2001. "The Topology of the Possible: Formal Spaces Underlying Patterns of Evolutionary Change." *Journal of Theoretical Biology*, 213, pp. 241–74.

Stahl, Ingolf. 1971. *Bargaining Theory*. Stockholm School of Economics.

Stiglitz, Joseph. 1974. "Incentives and Risk Sharing in Sharecropping." *Review of Economic Studies*, 41:2, pp. 219–55.

————. 1987. "The Causes and Consequences of the Dependence of Quality on Price." *Journal of Economic Literature*, 25:1, pp. 1–48.

————. 1993. "Peer Monitoring and Credit Markets." in *The Economies of Rural Organization: Theory, Practice, and Policy*. Karla Hoff, Avishay Braverman, and Joseph Stiglitz, eds. New York: Oxford University Press, pp. 70–85.

————. 1994. *Wither Socialism?* Cambridge: MIT Press.

————. 2002. "Information and the Change in the Paradigm in Economics." *American Economic Review*, 92:3, pp. 460–501.

Stiglitz, Joseph, and Andrew Weiss. 1981. "Credit Rationing in Markets with Imperfect Information." *American Economic Review*, 71:3, pp. 393– 411.

Sugden, Robert. 1986. *The Economics of Rights, Co-operation and Welfare*. Oxford: Basil Blackwell.

————. 1989. "Spontaneous Order." *Journal of Economic Perspectives*, 3:4, pp. 85–97.

Sunstein, Cass R. 1990. "The Functions of Regulatory Statutes." in Pp. 47–73 *After the Rights Revolution: Reconceiving the Regulatory State*. Cass Sunstein, ed. Cambridge: Harvard University Press.

Taylor, F. M. 1929. "The Guidance of Production in a Socialist State." *American Economic Review*, XIX:March, pp. 1–8.

Taylor, Michael. 1982. *Community, Anarchy, and Liberty*. Cambridge: Cambridge University Press.

———. 1987. *The Possibility of Cooperation*. New York: Cambridge University Press.

———. 1996. "Good Government: On Hierarchy, Social Capital, and the Limitations of Rational Choice Theory." *Journal of Political Philosophy*, 4:1, pp. 1–28.

———. 1997 [1976]. *The Possibility of Cooperation*. Cambridge: Cambridge University Press.

Thaler, Richard. 2001. "Anomalies." *Journal of Economic Perspectives*, 15:1, pp. 219.

Thompson, E. P. 1971. "The Moral Economy of the English Crowd in the Eighteenth Century." *Past and Present*, 50, pp. 76–136.

Tierney, John. 2000. "A Tale of Two Fisheries." *New York Times Sunday Magazine*, August 27, pp. 38–43.

Tilly, Charles. 1975. *The Formation of National States in Western Europe*. Princeton: Princeton University Press.

———. 1990. *Coercion, Capital, and European States, AD 990–1990*. Cambridge: Basil Blackwell.

Tocqueville, Alexis de. 1945 [1830]. *Democracy in America*, vol. II. New York NY: Vintage.

Tocqueville, Alexis de. 1958 [1833–1935]. *Journeys to England and Ireland*. London: Faber and Faber.

Townsend, Joseph. 1971 [1786]. *A Dissertation on the Poor Laws*. Berkeley: University of California Press.

Trivers, R. L. 1971. "The Evolution of Reciprocal Altruism." *Quarterly Review of Biology*, 46, pp. 35–57.

Trotsky, Leon. 1932. *The History of the Russian Revolution*. London: V. Gollancz.

Tucker, Robert C. 1978. *The Marx-Engels Reader*. New York: W.W. Norton.

Udry, Christopher, John Hoddinott, Harold Alderman, and Lawrence Haddad. 1995. "Gender Differentials in Farm Productivity: Implications for Household Efficiency and Agricultural Policy." *Food Policy*, 20:5, pp. 407–23.

Umbeck, John. 1977. "The California Gold Rush: A Study of Emerging Property Rights." *Explorations in Economic History*, 14, pp. 197–226.

van Damme, Eric, and Jorgen W. Weibull. 2002. "Evoution in games with endogenous mistake probabilities." *Journal of Economic Theory*, 106:2, pp. 296–315.

Van Huyck, John, R. Battalio, and Richard Beil. 1990. "Tacit Coordination Games, Strategic Uncertainty, and Coordination Failure." *American Economic Review*, 80:1, pp. 234–48.

Varian, Hal R. 1990. "Monitoring Agents with Other Agents." *Journal of Institutional and Theoretical Economics*, 46:1, pp. 153–74.

Veblen, Thorsten. 1934 [1899]. *The Theory of the Leisure Class*. New York: Modern Library.

Vega, Sara. 1999. "Short-Term Lending Final Report." Illinois Department of Financial Institutions.

Vega-Redondo, F. 1996. *Evolution, Games, and Economic Behavior*. Oxford: Oxford University Press.

Verba, Sidney, Kay Lehman Schlozman, and Henry Brady. 1995. *Voice and Equality: Civic Voluntarism in American Politics*. Cambridge: Harvard University Press.

Wadhwani, S. B., and M. Wall. 1991. "A Direct Test of the Efficiency Wage Model Using UK Micro-data." *Oxford Economic Papers*, 43, pp. 529–48.

Wallerstein, Immanuel. 1974. *The Modern World-System: Capitalist Agriculture and the Origins of the European World-Economy in the Sixteenth Century*. New York: Academic Press.

Wallerstein, Michael. 1999. "Wage-setting Institutions and Pay Inequality in Advanced Industrial Societies." *American Journal of Political Science*, 43, pp. 649–80.

Walras, Leon. 1954 [1874]. *Elements of Pure Economics*. London: George Allen and Unwin.

Weber, Eugen. 1976. *Peasants into Frenchmen: The Modernization of Rural France, 1870–1914*. Stanford: Stanford University Press.

Weibull, Jorgen W. 1995. *Evolutionary Game Theory*. Cambridge: MIT Press.

Weinstein, D. A., H. H. Shugart, and C. C. Brandt. 1983. "Energy Flow and the Persistence of a Human Population: A Simulation Analysis." *Human Ecology*, 11:2, pp. 201–23.

Weisskopf, T. 1987. "The Effect of Unemployment on Labor Productivity: An International Comparative Analysis." *International Review of Applied Economics*, 1:2, pp. 127–51.

Western, Bruce. 1997. *Between Class and Market: Postwar Unionization in the Capitalist Democracies*. Princeton: Princeton University Press.

White, Harrison C. 1981. "Where Do Markets Come From?" *American Journal of Sociology*, 87, pp. 517–47.

White, Harrison C. 2002. *Markets From Networks: Socioeconomic Models of Production*. Princeton: Princeton University Press.

Wicksell, Knut. 1961 [1893]. *Lectures on Political Economy*. London: Routledge & Kegan Paul Ltd.

Williams, G. C. 1966. *Adaptation and Natural Selection: A Critique of Some Current Evolutionary Thought*. Princeton: Princeton University Press.

Williams, George C. 1992. *Natural Selection: Domains, Levels, and Challenges*. New York: Oxford University Press.

Williamson, Oliver E. 1985. *The Economic Institutions of Capitalism*. New York: Free Press.

Wilson, David Sloan, and Lee A. Dugatkin. 1997. "Group Selection and Assortative Interactions." *American Naturalist*, 149:2, pp. 336–51.

Wilson, Edward O. 1975. *Sociobiology: The New Synthesis*. Cambridge: Harvard University Press.

Wilson, Francis. 1972. *Labour in South African Goldmines*. Cambridge: Cambridge University Press.

Winkelmann, Liliana, and Rainier Winkelmann. 1998. "Why Are the Unemployed So Unhappy? Evidence From Panel Data." *Economica*, 65:257, pp. 1–15.

Winterhalder, Bruce, and Eric Alden Smith, eds. 1992. *Evolutionary Ecology and Human Behavior*. New York: Aldine de Gruyter.

Wittman, Donald. 1989. "Why Democracies Produce Efficient Results." *Journal of Political Economy*, 97:6, pp. 1395–424.

Wood, Elisabeth Jean. 2000. *Forging Democracy From Below: Insurgent Transitions in South Africa and El Salvador*. Cambridge: Cambridge University Press.

Wood, Elisabeth. 2003. *Insurgent Collective Action and Civil War In El Salvador*. Cambridge: Cambridge University Press.

Wood, Elisabeth. 2004. "Forging an End to Civil War: Distributional Aspects of Robust Settlements." Unpublished paper. Santa Fe Institute.

Wright, Erik Olin. 1995. *Class Counts: Comparative Studies in Class Analysis*. Cambridge: Cambridge University Press.

Wright, Sewall. 1935. "Evolution in Populations in Approximate Equilibrium." *Journal of Genetics*, 30, pp. 257–66.

———. 1986. *Evolution: Selected Papers*. Chicago: University of Chicago Press.

Yellen, Janet. 1984. "Efficiency Wage Models of Unemployment." *American Economic Review*, 74:2, pp. 200–05.

Yitzhaki, Shlomo, 1987. "On the Relation Between Return and Income." *Quarterly Journal of Economics*, 102:1, pp. 77–95.

Young, H. Peyton. 1993. "An Evolutionary Model of Bargaining." *Journal of Economic Theory*, 59:1, pp. 145–68.

———. 1995. "Economics of Conventions." *Journal of Economic Perspectives*, 10:2, pp. 105–22.

———. 1998. *Individual Strategy and Social Structure: An Evolutionary Theory of Institutions*. Princeton: Princeton University Press.

Young, H. Peyton, and Mary Burke. 2001. "Competition and Custom in Economic Contracts: A Case Study of Illinois Agriculture." *American Economic Review*, 91:3, pp. 559–73.

Yule, Henry. 1886. *Cathay and the Way Thither: Being a Collection of Medieval Notices of China*. London: The Haklyut Society.

Zajonc, Robert B. 1968. "Attitudinal Effects of Mere Exposure." *Journal of Personality and Social Psychology Monograph Supplement*, 9:2, Part 2, pp. 1–27.

Zeuthen, F. 1930. *Problems of Monopoly and Economic Welfare*. London: George Routledge and Sons.

Index